AUDITING

THEORY AND PRACTICE

Arun Kumar

Rachana Sharma

ATLANTIC PUBLISHERS & DISTRIBUTORS

Published by

ATLANTIC PUBLISHERS AND DISTRIBUTORS

B-2, Vishal Enclave, New Delhi-110 027

Phones : 5413460, 5429987

Sales Office :

4346/4C, Ansari Road, Darya Ganj,

New Delhi-110 002

Phones: 3273880, 3285873, 3280451

Fax: 91-11-3285873

Typeset at :

Shiva Graphics

B-45, Chanakya Place, Delhi

Printed in India at :

Mehra Offset Press, Delhi

PREFACE

This book covers syllabi on Auditing, as prescribed by Indian Universities and Institutes of Commerce and Management. The authors have tried their best to cover every single topic, leaving none but at the same time avoiding unnecessary details. While the subject matter of the book has been gathered from authentic text books, reports and journals, it has been explained through examples drawn from the actual business world. Cases with Court decisions have been cited wherever necessary. Regulations and Laws have been authentically reproduced from original sources. Language of narration has been kept as much free from technical jargon as possible. Thus the authors have tried their best to present an ideal textbook for the students and a reference book for all those who are concerned with auditing, the teachers, the company secretary, the chartered accountant and last but not the least, the entrepreneur himself.

Comments and suggestions are most cordially invited from the readers for future improvement of this work.

Arun Kumar
Rachana Sharma

CONTENTS

1

Introductory

The word 'audit' is derived from the Latin word, *audire* which means 'to hear'. Originally, it was customary for persons responsible for maintenance of accounts to go to some impartial and experienced persons, ordinarily judges, known as 'auditors' who used to hear these accounts and express their opinion about their correctness or otherwise. Thus, the term 'auditor' literally means 'hearer', *i.e.,* 'one who hears.' The term is used in this sense ever since the days when public accounts were accepted and approved on the basis of hearing the accounts read.

ORIGIN OF AUDITING

The methods of maintaining accounts were very crude in the early stages of civilization. The size of business-houses, the amount of capital and the number of transactions to be recorded were so small that each individual maintained his accounts and checked all his transactions himself. Therefore, it was a sheer waste of time and money to get the accounts checked by some-one from outside.

The origin of auditing may be traced back to the 18th century when as a result of Industrial Revolution the practice of large-scale production was developed. As early as the days of the ancient Egyptians, the Greeks and the Romans, some systems of checks and counter checks were applied for the purpose of maintaining public accounts, rather accounts of public institutions.

Italian Renaissance

A great impetus was given to trade and commerce by the Renaissance in Italy in the last decade of the 15th century. In 1494 the principles of double-entry book-keeping were evolved and published by *Luca Paciolo* at Venice in Italy. This system of accounts could record all kinds of mercantile transactions. Luca Paciolo defined and described the duties and responsibilities of an auditor. Since then, there have been far reaching changes in the scope and definition of audit. The duties and responsibilities of an auditor have enormously increased.

Industrial Revolution in England

In the history of trade and commerce the Industrial Revolution in England led to a great increase in the volume of trading operations necessitating the use of more capital. As the average trader was compelled to combine in partnership with others, big enterprises in the form of partnership firms and joint stock companies were formed. Before and after the Revolution the growth of business enterprises was accompanied by improved accounting system. The separation of ownership from management in British Companies made stock-holders realise that their interests could be well-protected by an independent and impartial audit. These developments had a direct effect on the evolution of the practice of auditing. The audit of business accounts, however, could not be common until the 19th century. The enormous increase in the trade, commerce and industrial activities necessitated the use of proper devices of checking the accounts of big business-houses. The commercial public became aware of the advantages of the services of auditors. The importance of audit increased to such an extent that unless audited the accounts were thought to be misleading and incorrect.

On May 11, 1880 the Institute of Chartered Accountants in England and Wales was incorporated by Royal Charter with the sole purpose of preparing auditors. This Institute usually prepared auditors in India. The British Association of Accountants and Auditors was established in January 1923. After passing his examination from this Association a person was fully competent to work as professional auditor in India.

HISTORY OF AUDITING IN INDIA

1. *From 1914 to 1932.* The history of auditing in India dates back to April 1, 1914 when the Indian Companies Act, 1913 came into force resulting in the growth of the accountancy profession in this country. This Act, made it obligatory on the part of every company registered under it to have the accounts audited at least once every year. The Act prescribed the qualifications for an auditor.

Initially, the provincial governments were charged with the responsibility of conducting the examinations. The Government of Bombay was the first to arrange for conducting the courses of study. By passing the examination of the Government Diploma in Accountancy (G.D.A.) conducted by the Bombay Government, the qualification of being an auditor was obtained.

2. *From 1932 to 1949.* Till 1932, it was the concern of the Provincial Governments to prepare qualified auditors. Thereafter under the Auditors' Certificate Rules, 1932 the Central Government established an Indian Accountancy Board. Under its rules, Registered Accountants (R.A.) could work as qualified auditors. With the new developments and with the growth of the accountancy profession, there emerged a growing demand for autonomy of auditors in India.

3. *From 1949 to 1956.* Passed in 1949 The Chartered Accountants Act came into force on July 1, 1949. This Act granted autonomy to the accountancy profession and the regulation, control and management of the profession passed from the Central Government to the Indian Institute of Chartered Accountants formed under the provisions of this Act. Now, in order to obtain his certificate of Chartered Accountant (C.A.) a person has to follow the rules and regulations of this Institute and has to pass the examinations conducted by it.

The Institute also maintains a register of two types of members :

(i) *Associates of the Institute of Chartered Accountants (A.C.A.).* Associates are ordinary members of the Institute whose names appear in the register kept by for the purpose by the Institute. These members may write the abbreviation, 'A.C.A.' after their names.

(ii) *Fellows of the Institute of Chartered Accountants (F.C.A.).* Associates become fellows after they have fulfilled certain prescribed conditions, such as, at least 5 years' practice, payment of the prescribed fee, etc. These members can now write the abbreviation, 'F.C.A.' after their names.

4. *From 1956 onwards.* In 1960, some important amendments were made in the Companies Act, 1956. The Companies (Amendment) Act, 1960 came into force on December 28, 1960. Further amendments, made in 1965 and 1966, brought about changes in the duties of an auditor. The Companies (Amendment) Act, 1965 inserted a new section (233B) under which the Central Government was empowered to order audit of cost accounts in certain cases by a person possessing the prescribed qualifications.

5. *Amendments Act 1974.* Amendments of far reaching importance were introduced by the Companies (Amendment) Act, 1974 (Act 41 of 1974) into the law relating to companies in order to protect the interests of the public and the shareholders. The Amendment Accountant Act, 1974 introduced new regulations and also some serious changes in the system of company jurisprudence. The power of confirming alterations in the Memorandum was now vested in the Company Law Board. Administrative controls were strengthened in other respects also.

Section 224-A of the Amendment Act, 1974, was introduced to specify the cases in which an auditor may be appointed only by a special resolution. For the purpose of restricting the number of companies in which a person can be appointed as an auditor two new sub-sections were added to section 224. A proviso added to section 224 (1) requires that while appointing or re-appointing an auditor every company should obtain certificate from the auditor that the appointment is within specified limits.

6. *Amendment Act 1976.* Under the powers conferred on the Central Government as per provisions of section 64(i) of the Companies (Amendment) Act, 1976, the Form VI of the Act which relates to the Form of Balance Sheet has now been changed since December 23, 1978. Now the Balance Sheet shall be in horizontal form or in vertical form.

7. *Scope of Audit and Duties of Auditors.* Various changes were made in the scope of audit, the duties of auditors and reports to be submitted by them. The Government of India is keen to bring about desirable reforms in the procedure and technique of auditing. One of such examples is the Manufacturing and other Companies (Auditor's Report) Order, 1975 which came into force on January 1,1976. The auditors of companies engaged in manufacturing, mining or processing, supplying and rendering services, trading and the business of financing, investment, Chit Fund, *nidhi* or mutual benefit societies, must include such matters in their reports as specified in this order. The Company Law Board made a new order, namely — The Manufacturing and other Companies (Auditor's Report) Order, 1988 (G.S.R. No. 909 (E) dated 7-9-88) replacing the previous order of 1975. Some important changes and improvements were brought about by the Manufacturing (Auditor's Report) order, 1988. Similarly, Indian President promulgated an Ordinance on March 1, 1976 under which the Comptroller and Auditor-General of India was relieved of the responsibility of compiling the entire accounts of the Union Government either at once or by stages.

8. *Amendment Act 1977.* The Companies (Amendment) Act, 1977 has dealt mainly with the acceptance of deposits by companies. The Act has amended section 58-A, 220, 293, 620 and 634-A of the Companies Act, 1956. The auditor's responsibility in regard to companies accounts has been further increased by the amendments to the Act made in 1978, 1979 and 1980. The Companies (Amendment) Act, 1988 has now made comprehensive changes in regard to appointment of a company auditor, redemptions of irredeemable preference shares, issue of share certificates, repayment of public deposits accepted by companies and remuneration of directors.

9. *Chartered Accountants Act and Regulations.* Besides the Chartered Accountants Act 1949, Chartered Accountants Regulations were first formed in 1949 and later amended in 1964.

10. *Cost and Work Accountant Act 1959.* After 10 years of the introduction of the Chartered Accountants Act, 1949, another professional institute in the name of the Institute of the Cost and Works Accountants of India came into existence with the passing of Cost and Works Accountants Act, 1959.

AUDITING PRINCIPLES

Meaning of Auditing Principles

The *Webster's New International Dictionary,* defined the word 'principle' as 'a fundamental truth; a primary or basic law or doctrine; a settled rule of action'. Applied to auditing, 'principle' is the fundamental truth necessary for the effective accomplishment of the auditing objectives.

Though the principles of auditing are not as finely developed as the principles of accounting the following fundamental principles of auditing have evolved over the years :

1. Principle of Independence. Independence is a basic veracity of auditing. Without it objectives of auditing cannot be obtained with all fairness.

2. Principle of Objectivity. Auditing must be conducted objectively. The auditor must be free from bias, emotions and whims while auditing. It demands verification of the transactions and the use of reasonable skill and diligence.

3. Principle of Full Disclosure. The client should provide to the auditor all possible evidence, explanations and records. The principle implies that the auditor should make full disclosure of his findings.

4. Principle of Materiality. This principle indicates that more attention must be paid to those items which are materially important, and in the areas where the risk of error and/or fraud is relatively more. The fact of materiality has to be determined in accordance with the situation.

AUDIT STANDARDS

The term "standards" means an acceptable level of quality which must be maintained in ten basic different areas, as set forth initially by the AICPA.

1. General Standards

(i) *Training the Proficiency.* The examination is to be conducted by a person or persons having adequate technical training and proficiency as an auditor.

(ii) *Independent attitude.* In all matters relating to the assignment an independence in mental attitude is to be maintained by the auditor/auditors.

(iii) *Professional care.* Due professional care is to be exercised in the performance of the examination and preparation of the report.

2. Standards of Field Work

(i) *Planning and Supervision.* The work is to be adequately planned and assistants, if any, are to be properly supervised.

(ii) *Study and Evaluation.* There must be a proper study and evaluation of the existing internal control as a basis for reliance thereon and for the determination of the resultant extent of the tests to which auditing procedures are to be restricted.

(iii) *Competent evidence.* Sufficient competent evidential matter should be obtained through inspection, observation, inquiries and confirmations to provide a reasonable basis for an opinion regarding the financial statements under examination.

3. Standards of Reporting

(i) *According to Principles.* The report shall state whether the financial statements are presented in accordance with the generally accepted principles of accounting.

(ii) *Observation in current period.* The report shall state whether such principles have been consistently observed in the current period in relation to the preceding period.

(iii) *Informative disclosures.* Informative disclosures in the financial statements are to be regarded as reasonably adequate unless otherwise stated in the report.

4. Opinion

The report shall either contain an expression of opinion regarding the financial statements taken as a whole or an assertion to the effect that an opinion cannot be expressed. Reasons should be stated when an overall opinion cannot be expressed. According to Auditing Standards Executive Committee, American Institute of Certified Public Accountants, Statement on Auditing Standards No. 1, Codification of Auditing Standards and Procedures (1973) in all cases where the auditor's name is associated with financial statements, the report should contain a clear-cut indication of the character of the auditor's examination, if any, and the degree of responsibility he is taking.

Questions concerning standards

The above standards involve questions of degree, evaluation, and judgement:

(i) Is the auditors technical training adequate ?

(ii) Has due professional care been exercised ?

(iii) Has internal control been properly evaluated as a basis for determining the extent of the tests to be made ?

(iv) Has sufficient and competent evidential matter been obtained?

(v) Are the informative disclosures adequate ?

Audit Procedures

1. Examination. Examination of the nature, extent and efficacy of the system of internal checks and controls.

2. Ascertaining. Ascertaining the arithmetical accuracy of the books of accounts by checking postings, castings, cross-castings, carry-forwards, opening and closing balances, etc.

3. Ensuring. Ensuring that the entries have been made and the Profit and Loss Account and Balance Sheet prepared in accordance with well recognised accounting principles and practices, e.g. the distinction between capital and revenue, accrual system of accounting, valuation principles, etc.

4. Evidence. Examining the documentary evidence (internal or external) in support of the transaction, e.g. vouching third party confirmations, etc.

5. Validity. Checking the validity of the transactions with reference to:

(i) provisions affecting the accounts and audit in an Act of Rules;

(ii) rules and regulations governing the constitution and management of the organization, e.g. the memorandum and articles of association in the case of a firm; and the trust deed in the case of a trust;

(iii) minute books for appropriate sanctions of the transactions by a competent authority;

(iv) other legal documents such as the prospectus; returns submitted to legal authorities; contracts and agreements, lease agreement, selling agency agreements, e.g. vendors' agreement, technical collaboration agreement, etc., if any.

6. Disclosures. To see that there is adequate disclosure of information and particulars in the annual accounts in such a manner as to convey the real picture of the net worth and earning capacity of the undertaking. The auditor must conform to the prescribed legal requirements, about the form of accounts. He should have due regard to the best current accounting practice.

7. Tests, Checks and Methods. Application of various types of overall tests; checks and counter-checks, reconciliation methods, etc. in order to test the integrity of the accounting records.

8. Verification. Verification of existence, title and value of the assets and determination of the extent and nature of the liabilities.

STANDARDS V/S PROCEDURES

1. Activity v/s Quality. Procedures refer to what is done, whereas standards refer to the quality of permanence, involving among other things, decisions about how much evidence is necessary and how and when the required evidence is to be obtained. For instance, generally accepted auditing standards require that accounts receivable be confirmed by correspondence with the debtors. The actual process of confirming the accounts is an auditing procedure, but the requirement that this procedure must be used is a generally accepted auditing standard. If an independent auditor issues an opinion when confirmation procedures have not been employed, he assumes the burden of justifying the opinion in the absence of the required confirmation procedure.

2. Relationship. Generally accepted auditing standards also extend to the matter of how any necessary procedure is performed. The question of sufficient and competent evidence in relation to the confirmation procedure encompasses such questions as whether to confirm all the accounts or only a few on a test basis, which accounts to select if only a part of it is to be confirmed, whether to confirm, at the balance sheet date or some other date, what will constitute an adequate percentage of returns from such a request, how differences are to be investigated and disposed of, and many such points. These problems or questions must be resolved in terms of what a majority of auditors would do if faced with an identical situation.

Investigation and Auditing

Investigation is an enquiry into the state of affairs of a business for a special purpose. It is an examination of the accounts and records of a business to know its actual earning capacity and its real financial position. It may be made on behalf of the owners, prospective investors and the Central Government.

INVESTIGATION V/S AUDITING

1. Scope. The scope of investigation is wider than that of auditing. Auditing involves checking the accuracy of the accounts with the help of documentary evidence and through the methods of vouching verification and valuation. On the other hand, investigation involves critical examination of accounts, verification and exhaustive enquiry of specific records of the business concern.

2. Nature. Whereas the process of auditing is normally carried out on the basis of test checking the investigation is carried out on the basis of thorough checking of accounts. Investigation has no place for test checking.

3. Objectives. Accounts are audited for :

(i) Verification of their accuracy, and

(ii) Disclosure of true and fair view of business concern.

The investigation is a type of special audit being carried out for some particular purpose of (a) Ascertaining value of goodwill and

(b) Inquiring about suspected frauds or mismanagement.

4. Appointment. While an auditor is appointed by shareholders or Directors or Government as the case may be, investigator is not necessarily appointed by any of these but by an outsider who may be interested to know the functioning of the business concern as prospective buyer of the business or taxation authorities etc.

5. Coverage. Whereas the process of auditing covers the whole of accounting records of the business, investigation may cover only specific portion of accounts and records depending upon the specific purpose of investigation.

6. Period. While the period of audit is normally one particular financial year of the business the period of investigation may be more than one financial year.

7. Compulsion. While the Joint Stock Companies are under compulsion to get their accounts audited it is not so in case of investigation for any purpose. While auditing is legally compulsory investigation is voluntary.

8. Report. Whereas the audit report is prepared according to the provisions of the Companies Act and is submitted to the shareholders of the company the report of investigation is prepared according to the purpose and is submitted to the employers who may not be the owners of the business concern.

9. Qualification. Whereas to audit the accounts of a company, the auditor must be a qualified Chartered Accountant he need not be this to investigate.

10. Use. Whereas the audit report is widely used by the shareholders, investors etc. the report of investigation is used by the employers since it was carried out for a specific purpose.

11. Process of Work. Whereas the process of audit is carried on according to a standard set programme, there cannot be such programme for investigation. It depends upon the specific purpose and the availability of different records and evidences.

FACTORS INFLUENCING EVOLUTION OF AUDITING

1. *Industrial Revolution.* Industrial Revolution brought about tremendous changes in the system of production and distribution. With that the organisational set-up of the business enterprises also advanced and changed tremendously. It increased the size of enterprises enormously. It brought about the change in the technique of auditing as thorough and detailed checking of all the accounting records is rather impossible. It changed the objects of auditing. It helped in the emergence of auditing as an independent profession.

2. *Divorce of Ownership from Management.* As the size of the business enterprises grew, there has been a tendency for the divorce of ownership from the management which necessitated a thorough checking of the records by independent auditor so that the owners may be able to get a clear picture of the working of the concern, managed by others.

3. *Regulation by the State.* The Governments of all the countries started regulating the concerns to protect the interest of large number of investors. In India, the Companies Act, 1956, The Industries (Development and Regulations) Act, 1951, Capital Issues Control Act, 1947 and various labour and mercantile laws of the country have been passed affecting the auditing of the accounts.

4. *Pronouncements by Court of Law.* Judiciary has considerably influenced and helped the evolution of auditing. Important judgements have been passed by the Court of Law demanding a change in the attitude of the auditors. They have made it easier for the aggrieved party to sue an auditor and make him responsible for negligence. Through their judicial pronouncements, they have started demanding the establishment of "generally accepted accounting principles and auditing standards". Thus they are playing a very important role in bringing about necessary changes in the practices and standards adopted by the auditors.

5. *Mechanised Accounting.* With the growing use of mechanisation, specially, computers, for recording the transactions, one finds a growing change in the techniques and practices of auditing, necessitating considerable change and rethinking on the part of auditors. They cannot depend upon the traditional tools and techniques of auditing.

6. *Regulation by Profession.* Today accounting profession is duly regulated in almost all countries of the World. In India, the Institute of Chartered Accountants is making considerable efforts "to evolve its own standards of education, training, professional expertise, ethics and discipline". This has made a marked influence on the growth of auditing.

7. *Establishment of International Accounting Standards.* Today, efforts are being made to evolve international accounting standards. This would bring about uniformity in practices followed by the auditors in various countries of the World. International Accounting Standards Committee was constituted for this purpose. In India The Institute of Chartered Accountants and the Institute of Cost and Works Accountants are associate members of this Committee. The standards laid down by the Committee are applicable to all the member bodies of various countries, including the above Indian Institutes.

8. *Social Responsibility.* Today, business concern is not only responsible to its proprietor, but owes its responsibility to the society also. This has been an important factor in the enlargement of the duty of the auditor today much more is demanded from the auditor than mere routine audit.

9. *Emphasis upon efficiency audit.* Today, more and more emphasis is being laid upon efficiency or propriety audit rather than the regularity audit. Large number of Government undertakings have been set up in the country. There is a growing emphasis upon use of efficiency audit so that they may fulfil the social responsibility more faithfully.

10. *Compulsory audit of certain firms and professions.* In the Budget of 1984 the Government of India introduced the compulsory audit of accounts of firms whose annual turnover exceeds Rs. 20 lakhs and of professions whose annual gross receipts exceed Rs. 10 lakhs. This has enlarged the scope of auditing considerably.

DEFINITION OF AUDITING

In olden days, a person was appointed to check the accounts of the parties responsible for financial transactions. He used to call them and hear the explanations needed. The person, who *heard* the accounts, came to be known as an auditor. The word 'audit' has been derived from the Latin word *audire* which means 'to hear'.

Originally, the audit included only the ascertainment of the fact whether the accounting party has properly recorded the receipts and payments of cash on behalf of his principal. It was merely a cash audit. But today the scope of audit has much widened. It is to ascertain whether the Balance Sheet and the Profit and Loss or Revenue Accounts exhibit a true and fair view of financial state of affairs of a concern. It has become the most important part of the auditor's duties to form and disseminate opinion as to the state of soundness of financial situation of the concern.

Following are some of the definitions of audit given by well known authors on the subject :

1. *Spicer and Pegler.* An audit is "such as examination of the books, accounts and vouchers of a business, as will enable the auditor to satisfy himself that the Balance Sheet is properly drawn up, so as to give a true and fair view of the state of the affairs of the business, and whether the Profit and Loss Account gives a true and fair view of the profit or loss for the financial period, according to the best of his information and the explanations given to him and as shown by the books; and if not, in what respect he is not satisfied".[1] In this definition, emphasis has been laid on the comparison of Balance Sheet and Accounts with the books "in order to see that they agree therewith". The auditor has to satisfy himself in this respect. Thus the main objective of an audit is to ascertain the truth and fairness of the state of affairs of the business concerned.

2. *F.R.M. de Paula.* Audit "denotes something much wider, namely, the examination of a balance sheet and profit and loss account prepared by others. As a result of his examination of the books, accounts, vouchers etc., and of his inquiries, the auditor must satisfy himself that such balance sheet and profit and loss account are properly drawn up so as to exhibit true and fair view of the state of the affairs and of the earnings of a particular concern."[2] This definition adds an important point that the accounts are to be prepared by an accountant and not an auditor.

3. *L.R. Dicksee.* "An audit is an examination of accounting records undertaken with a view to establishing whether they correctly and completely

1. Spicer and Pegler, *Practical Auditing,* p.3.
2. F.R.M. de Paula, *The Principles of Auditing,* p.3

reflect the transaction to which they purport to relate. In some instance it may be necessary to ascertain whether the transactions themselves are supported by proper authority."[3] This definition lays greater emphasis on the technique of auditing, though it does not state the objective clearly. It lays stress on also checking the authority behind the transactions.

4. *Ronald A. Irish.* "Auditing in its modern concept, is a scientific and systematic examination of books, vouchers and other financial and legal records in order to verify and report upon the facts regarding the financial condition disclosed by the Balance Sheet and the net income revealed by the Profit and Loss Account." This definition lays stress on the fact that audit is a scientific and systematic examination which should not be carried on haphazardly. A report has to be submitted after the examination of accounts is complete.

5. *Taylor and Perry.* "An audit is an investigation by an auditor, into the evidence from which the final revenue accounts and Balance Sheet, or other statement, of an organisation have been prepared, in order to ascertain that they present a true and fair view of the summarised transactions for the period under review and of the financial state of the organisation at the end date, so enabling the auditor to report thereon".[4] This definition describes the object of the auditing in simple clear words.

6. *Montgomery.* "Auditing is a systematic examination of the books and records of a business or other organisation, in order to ascertain or verify, and to report upon, the facts regarding its financial operations and the results thereof." Besides the business concern, this definition extends the application of the audit to other organisations also. It points out that audit should be carried on scientifically and systematically and a report has to be submitted in the end disclosing facts.

7. *Eric L. Kohler.* An audit is "an exploratory, critical review by a public accountant of the underlying internal controls and accounting records of a business enterprise or other economic unit, precedent to the expression by him of an opinion of the propriety of its financial statements."[5] This definition includes the examination of internal controls by the auditor. It includes the audit of economic units and not business enterprises alone. Kohler further says, "The words of the above definition require no special technical interpretation; they have fairly specific and commonly understood meanings among persons familiar with business operations".

8. *R.K. Mautz.* Auditing is "concerned with the verification of accounting data, with determining the accuracy and reliability of accounting statements and reports."[6]

---

3. L.R. Dicksee, *Auditing,* p.1.
4. Taylor and Perry, *Principles of Auditing,* p.3.
5. Eric L. Kohler, *Auditing,* p.10.
6. Mautz, R.K., *Fundamentals of Auditing,* 2nd ed., p.1.

9. *Robert E. Schlosser.* Auditing is a "systematic examination of financial statements, records and related operations to determine adherence to generally accepted accounting principles, management policies or stated requirements."[7] This definition lays emphasis on the point that auditing does not simply involve examination of financial statements and records but also 'related operations.' It reflects the modern trend of auditing and points out that its scope has enlarged considerably.

The above definitions reveal that auditing of books of accounts of a concern is carried on *in a scientific and systematic manner.* The technique of auditing is based on scientific principles. It is conducted by persons who are technically qualified and fully experienced in the job of examining the books of account of various types of concerns. It contemplates verification of accounting records with certain pre-determined objectives, testing their reliability and competency, and finding out adequacy of evidences for those records. It involves *critical assessment of whole affairs of a concern.* It involves retrospective and analytical examination. The audit is *carried on regularly or periodically* half-yearly or annually. Big concerns may even get it done throughout the year.

The auditor has *to satisfy himself about the truth and fairness* of the statement of financial affairs of the business. He has to give his report honestly to the owner of the concern. His integrity, honesty and independence are essential otherwise the very purpose of audit may be defeated. He examines the books of accounts and checks their arithmetical accuracy. He ascertains the various policies about the operation and control of concern and how far they have been carried out by the management and to what extent the accounts reflect them. He has *to form opinion about* the ability of financial statements to convey clearly the meaning of what they purport to stand for. He carries on audit *as thoroughly as possible.*

CHARACTERISTICS OF AUDITING

1. It is a thorough, systematic and analytical examination of the accounting records of the client;

2. The accounts are prepared by the accountant and not by auditor;

3. The examination of accounting records is made throughout the year or periodically;

4. The auditing is to be carried on by independent but duly qualified person;

---

7. Robert E. Schlosser, Field of Auditing, in J.A. Cashin (Ed.) *Handbook for Auditors*, 1971, p.4.

5. The auditor examines the accounting records with the help of relevant records, vouchers, documents information and explanation etc. following accepted tools and techniques of auditing;

6. The auditor has to report with regard to the truth and fairness of the profit or loss of the period and financial position of the concern, as reflected in its Balance Sheet;

7. Besides the business concerns the scope of audit may be duly extended to non-commercial concerns; and

8. Today, auditing is more concerned with the latest developments in the business world and its changing requirement. There is a growing emphasis upon the efficiency audit, social audit and systems audit etc.

FUNCTIONS OF AUDITING

1. Examination. A critical review of the system of book-keeping, accounting and internal control and its design and operations in a business enterprise to ascertain its adequacy and appropriateness to the enterprise.

2. Comparison. A comparison of Profit and Loss Account and Balance Sheet with the underlying records to ensure that they are in agreement therewith.

3. Verification. Verification of results shown by Profit and Loss Account and the state of affairs disclosed by the Balance Sheet.

4. Confirmation. Confirmation as to compliance with the statutory requirements relevant to joint-stock companies.

5. Opinion. Finally, expression of opinion by the auditor by way of report to the clients stating whether in his opinion the accounts present a true and fair view or not.

PHILOSOPHY OF AUDITING

According to Mautz and Sharaf, the philosophy of auditing is based on the following primary concepts ;

1. Evidence.
2. Due Audit Care.
3. Fair Presentation.
4. Independence.
5. Ethical Conduct.

1. Evidence. It "includes all influences on the mind of an auditor which effect his judgement about the truthfulness of propositions submitted to him for review". Though the auditor is not required to get at the absolute proof which may be difficult to find in a large number of cases, yet the proof admitted

by him should be such that would lead any reasonably competent person to conclude that the representations made in the financial statements are true and fair.

2. Due Audit Care. The concept of "duc audit care" is concerned with the determination of *adequacy* of evidence in support of the representations made in the financial statements. The auditor has often to be satisfied with the second best alternative of sufficient proof since there may be no such thing as absolute proof. Regarding a sufficient proof the auditor's judgement will be based on his own sense of judgement.

3. Fair Presentation. Presentation of financial statements is deemed to be fair when it conforms to the following three requirements :

(i) *Accounting Propriety.* Accounting propriety mean a faithful compliance with the generally accepted accounting principles concerning accounting methods and presentation of financial statements. In the words of Mautz and Sharaf, "acceptable accounting methods are those which realistically recognise enterprise transactions and their effects as they occur and which through the use of the accrual system, relate efforts (costs) and accomplishment (revenues) on the basis of their pertinence to one another within time period." Consistent compliance with acceptable accounting methods is essential to provide reliable financial data.

(ii) *Adequate Disclosure.* Adequate disclosure is a duty of the auditor *vis-a-vis* third parties. He must satisfy himself that the financial statements provide adequate information for investment decisions by the interested third parties. He must express his professional opinion as regards reliability of that information. Finally, to the best of his professional ability he must use the best of his professional ability to protect the interests of investors.

(iii) *Audit Obligation.* The report of an auditor is a valuable document for all those who read it and rely upon it to make investment and other decisions. Hence, the auditor is under an obligation to prepare his report in such a way that any one reading it is not misled about the extent of examination or the nature of his opinion.

4. Independence. An auditor has to report on the financial statements prepared by his client. His report lends credibility to these statements which are relied upon by various sections of the public such as owners, creditors, labour unions, governmental agencies and others having legitimate interest in the business of the client. Thus, though he is an appointee of his client, his primary responsibility is towards the public. However, in other review matters he is only responsible to his client.

In order to fulfil his extensive responsibilities to third parties, the auditor must be independent of his client. He should not be influenced by any person connected with the enterprise under audit. He should be free from bias and prejudice. Otherwise, his opinion will fail to lend credibility to the financial accounts thus defeating the very purpose of auditing. Several provisions in the Companies Act and also rules framed by the Institute of Chartered Accountants, ensure the auditor's independence *vis-a-vis* his client. However, as observed by Howard Stettler, "Independence is also an attitude of mind, and independent thought and action are equally as important as the independent relationship between the accountant and his client."

5. Ethical conduct. The auditor belongs to a valued profession. It imposes on him several legal, ethical and moral responsibilities. The public has faith in his competence and relies on his integrity. It is commonly believed that he can be trusted with any private and important matter, and that he will always work to protect the public interest and to benefit the public.

NATURE OF AUDITING

An audit is a systematic examination of books, accounts, documents and vouchers of a business with a view to determine the accuracy and reliability of accounting statements. It is to see the arithmetical accuracy of the books of accounts. It finds out whether the transaction entered in the books of original entry are correct or not. The purpose of auditing lies in ascertaining whether the working results and financial position as shown by the Profit and Loss Account and the Balance Sheet for a particular period are truely determined and presented by those responsible for their compilation. Auditing does not mean the preparation of accounts. It is the verification of accounts by an independent person who examines and checks them and makes best use of the information supplied to him. The auditor is required to prove and establish the authenticity of the transactions by vouching all the relevant documentary evidence at his disposal. Thus auditing primarily involves testing the reliability, competency and adequacy of evidence in support of monetary transaction of an organisation.

OBJECTIVES OF AUDIT

Opinion of L.R. Dicksee

As enumerated by L.R. Dicksee, originally the function of audit was simply to detect errors and frauds. Accordingly to him the objects of audit were the following :

1. Detection of frauds;
2. Detection of technical errors; and
3. Detection of errors of principle.

To achieve these objectives an auditor had to do detailed checking of transactions. Dicksee has also mentioned the concept of "internal check". He was of the view that a detailed audit was not necessary where a good system of internal check existed.

Detailed audit of transactions became difficult with the passage of time, growth and development of large scale industries and improved systems of internal control. Hence the objectives of the audit function have changed considerably.

Main objective of Audit

Today the main objective of audit is to find out that the Balance Sheet and the Profit and Loss Account of a company show a true and fair view of its financial position and earnings. Certain frauds and errors may be detected in the process of this ascertainment. However, the detection of errors, frauds and irregularities is incidental to the main objective. It is a subsidiary advantage or benefit flowing from the audit. Owners or directors of the company are responsible for the prevention of errors and frauds. The primary concern of the auditor is to examine the system of internal checks and controls within the business and to determine the extent to which this responsibility has been exercised. He must satisfy himself that no fraud or error has been committed by the directors, partners, managers or employees. He is expected to apply reasonable skill and care while checking the accounts.

Modern Objectives of Auditing

Thus the objectives of audit today can be classified into the following:

1. Primary Objectives. Confirmation of truth and fairness of financial statements (i.e. Balance Sheet and Profit and Loss Account). This aims to establish the degree of reliability of the annual statement of accounts and to report whether the same has been prepared properly and in accordance to the Companies Act and they portray true and fair state of affairs.

2. Secondary or Subsidiary Objectives

(i) Detection and prevention of errors.

(ii) Detection and prevention of frauds.

(i) *Detection and Prevention of Errors.* Errors may be of two kinds (a) clerical errors and (b) errors of principle. Errors of principle may make an important difference in the accounts, whereas the effect of clerical errors probably will be very small.

(a) *Clerical errors.* Clerical errors may be either errors of commission or that of omission. Errors of commission include incorrect postings, additions or calculations. Errors of omission may include omission to enter invoices in the purchase day book, omission of sales from the sale-day book, or the non-provision for interest, rent, salaries and other such outstanding amounts. Made intentionally, errors of omission may affect the results shown by the accounts considerably, thus constituting a fraudulent falsification of accounts.

(b) *Errors of principle.* Errors of principle include errors such as incorrect allocation of expenditure as between capital and revenue, valuation of assets upon incorrect basis, and inadequate provision for depreciation and bad debts. These are committed on purpose or by accident. These considerably affect the accounts. If intentional that may amount to falsification of accounts. However, they may also arise inadvertently, due to the lack of proper knowledge of the principles of accounting. Hence, an auditor must have a wide knowledge of the generally accepted principles of accounting. He should make a thorough investigation to detect such errors.

No amount of routine checking will disclose errors of principle. These can only be detected by intelligent enquiries and investigation.

(ii) *Detection and Prevention of Frauds.* Frauds may take the form of (a) misappropriation of cash or goods, or (b) falsification of accounts unaccompanied by misappropriation.

(a) *Misappropriation of cash.* This may be committed either by omitting to enter receipts, or by entering fictitious payments. In order to detect the first, the auditor must check the receipts shown in the cash book with the original records, such as bill books, salesmen's diaries and desk books, counterfoil receipt books, agents' returns, etc. Fictitious payments should be discovered by a careful examination of vouchers, invoices, wages sheets and other direct evidence of this nature.

Misappropriation of goods is even more difficult to detect, unless accurate stock records are kept. It is almost impossible to discover small misappropriations of this nature. Without such records sometimes the losses already incurred may be discovered by checking the percentage of profit to sales but this will not locate the fraud itself.

(b) *Falsification of accounts.* It is generally perpetrated by the people at the top such as (a) the directors or the managers who wish to boost the image of the concern by showing fictitious profits in order to :

1. Declare higher rates of dividend,
2. Obtain additional credit,
3. Increase commission/remuneration due to their sales,
4. Dispose of their shareholdings in the company at inflated prices,
5. Avoid or minimise the amount of texture.

SUBSIDIARY OBJECTIVES OF AUDIT

Audit seeks to verify the accounts and to report whether the Balance Sheet and the Profit and Loss Account have been drawn properly according to the Companies Act and whether they exhibit a true and fair view of the state of affairs of the concern. Verification of accounts and reporting to

management are vital factors for promoting efficiency and accuracy in the maintenance of accounts so that the owners of a business may get accurate information about the financial condition of their business. Accounts are verified to see if they are correct, complete and in conformity with the law. Thus the subsidiary objects of audit are:

(i) The detection of errors and fraud, and

(ii) The prevention of the recurrence of those errors and fraud.

If the auditor is in a position to discover errors and fraud, he cannot certify the account as correct. It will be a great mistake on his part if he does so.

ERRORS

While fraud involves some intention to gain out of manipulating records, errors generally arise out of the innocence or carelessness on the part of those responsible for the preparation of accounts.

Kinds of Errors. The following are the various kinds of errors.

1. Errors of Omission,
2. Errors of Commission,
3. Compensating Errors,
4. Errors of Principles.

1. Errors of Omission

Errors of omission arise due to clerical mistake. If a transaction has not been entered in the books of accounts, wholly or partially, it is an example of error of omission. There are items like purchase or sales which ought to have been recorded in the books of accounts. Due to oversight or carelessness they have been wholly committed from being recorded.

Secondly, there are cases where items remain partially recorded, *e.g.,* (i) the rent or interest may have been paid for 10 or 11 months and the remaining part of it which is unpaid or outstanding has not been recorded in the journal. Such a mistake can be detected by careful audit but this is a clear case of omission. (ii) Secondly, error of omission may arise if an item has been recorded in the journal but has not been posted in the ledger. This is an example of omission in ledger-posting in which a transaction has been recorded but not posted to the relevant accounts in the ledger.

The errors which produce some effect on the agreement of Trial Balance are easily detectable. The errors which arise due to non-recording of certain items will not affect the Trial Balance and, as such, the omission can be detected by careful scrutiny. But if one aspect of an item, such as purchases or sales, has been entered in the books, such an omission will affect the Trial Balance and, hence, will be easily detected.

2. Errors of Commission

Errors of commission are those which arise through negligence in the matter of recording some business transactions in the books of accounts. They occur due to a sort of wrong doing on the part of clerks. If an item is incorrectly recorded in the journal or posted in the ledger, it is an error of commission.

Types of Errors of Commission

(i) *Wholly or Partially Incorrect Recording.* Error of commission is said to arise when a transaction, though recorded in the journal, has been wrongly entered in the books of original entry, e.g., a sale of Rs. 1000 is entered in the sales book as Rs. 100. Such an error does not affect the Trial Balance.

(ii) *Posting an Item to a Wrong Account.* It is possible that a transaction may be entered correctly in the journal, but when posted in the ledger, a wrong amount may be entered, e.g., sale of Rs. 1000 may be written as Rs. 100 to the debit of the Customer's account, thus debiting Rs. 900 less than the real figure. The effect of this erroneous posting on the Trial Balance woul be that the debit side would be short by Rs. 900 and it would show a diff-ence.

(iii) *Incorrect Posting.* A wrong account may be debited instead of another when there is nothing wrong on the credit side. When an amount of Rs. 1000 is posted to the debit of Bharat's account instead of Laxman's account to whom goods are actually sold, error of commission may creep up by posting an item to a wrong account. Such an error will not affect the agreement of the Trial Balance.

(iv) *Errors in Totalling and Balancing.* Sometimes errors of commission arise in the books through incorrect castings and calculations. Such errors will affect the Trial Balance. The error in the total on the debit side would lead to the error on debit side of the Trial Balance and so on.

(v) *Errors in Carrying Forward Totals to Trial Balance.* Errors of commission may creep into the books when balances of different accounts are carried forward to the Trial Balance. The balance of accounts may be carried forward less or more than the real figure of double of it and sometimes also to the other side of the Trial Balance. For example, the balance of Rs. 1250 on the debit of an account may be carried forward to the Debit column of the Trial Balance as Rs. 1150 or Rs. 1350 or Rs. 2500 and even Rs. 1250 may be written to the credit column of the Trial Balance, thus entering the correct figure against this account but in the wrong column.

(vi) *Wrong postings as debit and credit.* When an amount pertaining to the debit side is posted to the credit side of a ledger account and another different amount of credit side posted to the debit side, error of commission arises and such an error will affect the trial balance.

(vii) *Errors of duplication.* Error of commission is said to arise when an entry in a book of original entry has been made twice and is also posted twice. Some writers call it an error of duplication. It is also a case of error of commission. Such an error will not affect the trial balance.

(viii) *Posting to one side only.* When an item is posted to only one side of a ledger account, it is a case of error of commission. Such a mistake will affect the trial balance.

(ix) *Error of commission.* It may arise when a wrong figure is entered in a particular account. This error has its effect on the trial balance.

3. Compensating Errors

When an error is counter-balanced or compensated by any other error or errors so that the adverse effect of one on debit or credit side is neutralised by that of another on credit or debit side it is called compensating error. For example, A's account which was to be debited for Rs. 2000 was credited for Rs. 2000 and similarly, B's account which was to be credited for Rs. 2000 was debited for Rs. 2000. If Rs. 1200 is posted to the debit of the wages account in place of Rs. 1000 and similarly to the credit of rent account Rs. 1200 posted in place of Rs. 1000 it is an example of compensating error. Such errors also creep up when an undercasting of an account is counterbalanced by the overcasting of another account to the same extent and on the same side. These errors will not affect the trial balance and, as such, will not be detected easily. Their detection requires a complete and exhaustive preparation on the part of an auditor.

4. Errors of Principle

Errors of principle arise out of a disregard for the principles of accountancy. These are sometimes committed intentionally to falsify and manipulate accounts with an objective of showing more or less profits than their actual figures. The following are some of the examples of such types of errors:

(i) *Incorrect Allocation of Expenditure between Capital and Revenue.* Error of principle occurs when revenue expenditure is treated as capital expenditure and profits are inflated thereby. For example, it would be an error of this nature if repairs to machinery are treated as an addition to it in the machinery account. The result would be an increase in the cost of machinery without any charge on the Profit and Los Account. As such, the Balance Sheet would not exhibit a true and correct position of the business.

(ii) *Posting Revenue Items to the wrong class of Revenue Account.* Sometimes an item of wages is posted to general expenses account and similarly, an amount of salary account is posted to Advertisement Account. Such errors will not affect the ultimate profit and hence, are said to be minor errors of principle. But accounts of a concern are falsified and become incorrect due to these errors.

(iii) *Posting an Item of Revenue or Expenditure to a Personal Account.* If rent paid to landlord is posted to the debit of his personal account, it is an example of error of principle, due to which profits would be inflated and the Balance Sheet would be wrong.

(iv) *Valuation of Assets against Fundamental Principles of Accountancy.* Such errors arise when different types of assets are not valued in accordance with the principles of accountancy, these directly affect the profit and ultimately the Balance Sheet.

Thus, errors of principles are serious types of errors. They can be detected only if the auditor makes a searching and exhaustive scrutiny. However, errors of principles do not affect the trial balance.

(v) *Other examples of Errors of Principle.*

(i) Provision for inadequate or excess depreciation;

(ii) Non-provision of depreciation;

(iii) Wrong provision for outstanding expenses and income accrued;

(iv) Wrong adjustment of prepaid expenses;

(v) Wrong provision for bad and doubtful debts; and

(vi) Undervaluation and overvaluation of stock.

DETECTION OF ERRORS

The auditor uses the following devices to locate an error:

(i) Errors can be located with an exhaustive scrutiny of the books of accounts, if the books are maintained on the self-balancing system.

(ii) The trial balance should be thoroughly checked and the castings of ledger accounts should be tallied with those given in the trial balance, if the books are not maintained on the self-balancing system.

(iii) Books of original entry may be checked and postings into the ledger verified, if necessary.

(iv) The names of the accounts in the ledger should be compared with the names of accounts recorded in the trial balance. There are possibilities that some balances may not have been carried forward to the trial balance.

(v) The lists of debtors and creditors should be totalled and properly compared with the trial balance.

(vi) If the various items given in the trial balance of the current year are tallied with those given in the trial balance pertaining to the previous year, errors can be located.

(vii) The figures which appear to be doubtful and are struck off for some fraudulent purpose should be carefully checked.

(viii) Costs and carry-forward should be examined and wrong totalling, if any, should be corrected. To check difference involving round figures, as 10,000 or 1,000. The difference in rupees and paise should be traced through checking of postings and balancing of accounts.

(ix) If the difference is divisible by two, it may be due to wrong posting or posting to the wrong side of an account in particular, e.g., a difference of Rs. 500 in the trial balance may be due to the posting of Rs. 250 to the debit side in place of the credit side of an account.

(x) Sometimes, errors culminate due to misplacement or transposition of figures. Putting 450 for 540, 180 for 810, 270 for 720 etc., are some of such examples. If such a difference is divisible by 9, it should be noted that the reason for this difference is misplacement of figures.

To sum up, the following table will reveal the error and its probable cause:

ERROR	PROBABLE CAUSE
1. Round sum, *e.g.,* Re. 1,000	Error in additions
2. Multiple of *e.g., Rs. 63*	Misplaced or transposed figures, *e.g.,* Rs. 20 or 72.
3. Odd amount, *e.g., Rs.* 17.89. (a) If there is an excess of debits over credits in the Trial Balance	(i) Item not posted in Purchases Journal; debit side of Cash Book; Return inward book; Bills Receivable Book. (ii) Balance omitted from creditors journal. (iii) Credit balance omitted from Impersonal ledger. (iv) Old balance in (ii) and/ or (iii) not brought forward at the beginning of the period. (v) An amount equal to half the difference wrongly posted from any of the books in (i) to the debit instead of the credit or a credit balance equal to half the difference extracted as a debit balance.

(b) If there is an excess of credit over debits in the Trial Balance	(i) Item not posted in Sales Journal; credit side of Cash Book; Returns Outward Book; Bills Payable Book. (ii) Balance omitted from Debtors Ledger. (iii) Debit Balance omitted from Impersonal Ledger. (iv) Old balance in (ii) and\or (iii) not brought forward at the beginning of the books in the credit instead of the debit or a debit balance equal to half the difference extracted as a credit balance.

FRAUD

Fraud is really a false representation or entry which is made always intentionally with some mischievous objectives.

Fraud may be mainly of two types:

1. Misappropriation of (a) Cash (b) Goods
2. Manipulation of accounts

MISAPPROPRIATION

1. Misappropriation of Cash

Cash is misappropriated as follows:

(i) The theft of cash receipts and petty cash.

(ii) The theft of cheques and other negotiable instruments.

(iii) Payments made to fictitious creditors or workmen.

Misappropriation of cash is a rather easy affair. Anybody with a little skill in his part can misappropriate money, particularly in a big business house where the contacts between the proprietor and the persons handling cash are not so close as in the case of small proprietary business. A transaction relating to the receipt of cash may either go totally unrecorded or recorded at a figure less than the actual one in the Cash Book. Thus a part or the total of the cash may be pocketed by the cashier. Again, it is possible to record false payment of money and to enter cash payment at more than the actual figure. There may be concealment of money by the cashier. Thus, strict control should be exercised over the receipt and payment of cash in a big business so that there may be a system of checking the work of one clerk automatically by another. Technically, such a system is known in auditing as a system of internal check.

Some of the examples of misappropriation of cash are the following :

(i) *Omission of Sales record.* Sales and pocketing money received from customers;

(ii) *Teeming and lading.* This is concealing money received from first customer and, entering in his account the cash received from second one. When cash is received from the third customer it is not recorded in the Cash Book but is entered to the credit of the second customer. This process continues till the fraud is discovered. Thus, misappropriation of cash is concealed by a false entry relating to a later transaction.

(iii) *Making fictitious entries.* There may be discount, returns, bad debts, etc., in the customers' accounts.

(iv) *Omission of cash.* Omitting to enter cash received from sale.

(v) *Misappropriation of sale or return cash.* Misappropriating money received from the sale of goods on 'sale or return' basis or per V.P.P. by showing such goods as returned in the books.

(iv) *Misappropriation of purchases*

Fictitious purchases. Recording fictitious purchases and thus, misappropriating the cash involved;

Suppression of credit notes. Suppressing credit notes received from creditors for purchase returns and discount.

(vii) *Misappropriation of Receipt of Cash*

Concealment. Concealing cash received on miscellaneous or extraordinary account e.g., from sale of some rejected stock or from a debtor declared previously as bad debt, etc.,

Omission of cash record. Omitting to record cash received by a cashier as a donation and removing the counterfoil of the receipt from the receipt book,

(viii) *Misappropriation in payment.* Misappropriating money shown as wages in the wages sheet by entering dummy names of workers therein.

2. Misappropriation of Goods.

Sometimes the proprietors of business houses do not bother so much for the misappropriation of goods as for the defalcation of money. The defalcation of goods is easy in those business houses which produce or deal with goods which are less bulky and are of higher value.

Thus, goods can be misappropriated by:

(i) The actual theft of stock, and/or

(ii) The issuing of fictitious credit notes to customers where there is collusion of the employee with the customer.

MANIPULATION OF ACCOUNTS

The accounts of a business may be falsified by making false entries in respect of fictitious sales or purchases not necessarily resulting in the same type of misappropriation. Whenever such a class of fraud occurs, it involves usually very large amounts. As it is committed by high officials of a business, viz, Directors, Managers or other responsible persons it may be detected with a great difficulty by the auditor.

Objectives of Manipulation

There are normally two objects behind:

(a) Showing more profits than the actual ones

(i) to earn more commission on profits if they get it on profit basis;

(ii) to win the confidence of shareholders by claiming that higher profits are a result of their efficiency;

(iii) to fetch high price for their shares as high profits will lead to the declaration of more dividends;

(iv) to enjoy better reputation to get credit in the market by showing more sound financial position than what it actually is;

(v) to attract more persons to subscribe more for the shares.

2. Showing less profits than the actual ones

(i) to mislead Income-tax authorities and to reduce or avoid the liabilities for income tax;

(ii) to deceive competitors by creating wrong impressions in their minds about the success of the business.

Devices of falsification

1. Wrong Depreciation. Providing less or more of not providing for depreciation on various assets;

2. Variation. Overvaluation or undervaluation of assets and liabilities;

3. Changing capital expenditure to revenue account or *vice versa;* or

4. Inflating profits by omitting to record some items of expenditure or showing less profits by entering fictitious expenditure;

5. Utilizing secret reserves without making the fact known to the shareholders during a period when there is no profit or less profit;

6. False income entries showing income of the next year to the current year's Profit and Loss Account, or not recording the accrued income in the Profit and Loss Account with the object of manipulating the accounts thereby;

7. Window dressing. This involves showing outwardly a more prosperous position than what it actually is. It is a process by which the Balance Sheet is made to show a state of affairs that is far better than the normal position of the business. Just to improve the working capital position of the business; if an overdraft is extinguished before the date of Balance Sheet out of the proceeds of a loan from a subsidiary company, it would not be justifiable.

8. Inflation Deflating. This may be in case of :

(a) purchases and expenses;

(b) sales and other items of income;

(c) the value of closing stock;

(d) Outstanding liabilities or prepaid expenses and/or profits.

Thus, the falsification of accounts may be of the following types:

(i) Inflation of the values of assets;

(ii) Omission or undervaluation of liabilities;

(iii) Inflation of profits to enhance commission payable to officials or to affect share values;

(iv) Window dressing.

Subsidiary Objectives of Auditing

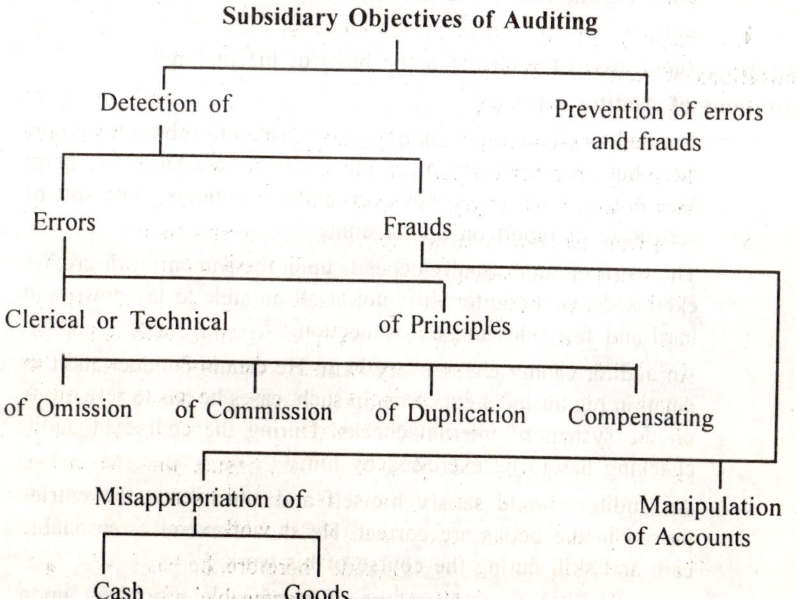

SCOPE OF AUDIT

The scope and dimensions of auditing greatly increased in the seventies. The evolution of new concepts such as Tax Audit, Management Audit and Operations Audit further laid emphasis on its adoption on a wider scale. The primary audit objective of detection of fraud now shifted to the determination of the fairness and authenticity of reported financial position together with the detection and prevention of errors and fraud. This vastly enhanced the scope of auditing. Exhaustive rules and regulations were framed in all the countries of the world for conduct of independent and professional audits.

An auditor certifies the correctness of the books of accounts and detects errors committed by the clerks and accountants in the preparation of financial records. If this verification is not conducted in a proper and satisfactory manner, the results would be wholly unreliable. There may be various ways and reasons due to which the financial books may be incorrect and inaccurate. The auditor should bring them to light and report them to the owners of the business.

The scope of Audit is clear from the following duties of an auditor:

1. Checking the arithmetical accuracy of the accounts;
2. Checking the books of accounts with the help of all the relevant vouchers, invoices, correspondence, minute books etc.;
3. Verifying the assets and liabilities shown in the Balance Sheet; and
4. Reporting to the client on the basis of his findings.

Limitations of Auditor's Duties

1. The auditor of a limited company is expected to submit his report on annual accounts which are placed before an Annual General Meeting. In other cases, however, auditors submits some sort of certificate or report on the accounts.
2. The work of audit usually depends upon the amount of discretion exercised by an auditor. It is not at all possible to lay down and hard and fast rules in this connection.
3. An auditor cannot check every item. He cannot conduct audit in detail in big business concerns. In such, cases he has to rely much on the system of internal checks. During the course of audit, checking has to be exercised by him.
4. An auditor should satisfy himself and ensure that the entries passed in the books are correct. He should exercise reasonable care and skill during the course of his work.
5. An auditor is not a technical man. Therefore, he has to rely upon the statements and explanation of responsible officials.

6. An auditor should investigate such matters properly and thoroughly which arouse suspicion and doubt.

Thus, the duties of an auditor provide a guideline towards the scope and subject-matter of auditing. The scope of auditing is what an auditor does. It depends mainly upon the extent of the work done by the auditor. It includes the bringing of inaccuracies in the books of account to light.

BOOK-KEEPING, ACCOUNTANCY AND AUDITING

Three aspects of Accountancy.

Some of the writers believe that Book-keeping, Accountancy and Auditing are the three aspects of the term 'Accountancy'. These are as follows:

(i) The aspect of recording transactions, *i.e.,* the practical part (known as 'Book-keeping').

(ii) The constructive aspect, *i.e.*, the theoretical part (commonly known as 'Accountancy Proper'); and

(iii) The critical aspect, *i.e.,* the analytical part (known as 'Auditing').

Functions of these aspects

There was a time when no proper demarcation could be made between the duties of a book-keeper and an accountant. In the present industrial age, however Book-keeping and Accountancy have become separate functions. The following description makes this distinction clear:

1. **Book-keeping.** Book-keeping is the art of recording the daily transactions in a set of financial books. The book-keeper is mainly concerned with journalizing, posting, totalling and balancing the various accounts in the ledger. The work is more or less mechanical for which it is not necessary to be familiar with the accounting principles.

Following are the activities of Book-keeping

(i) Journalizing,

(ii) Posting into Ledger,

(iii) Totalling of different accounts in the Ledger, and

(iv) Balancing,

2. **Accountancy** "Accountancy begins where Book-keeping ends." An Accountant comes into the picture only when the book-keeper has done his job, as he has to go behind the work of a book-keeper and satisfy himself that the transactions have been properly recorded and posted in the books of accounts. His makes the Trial Balance agree. He prepares the Profit and Loss Account and the Balance Sheet after making the necessary adjustments and the rectification of errors. He prepares summary in the form of Trial Balance. He makes analysis after preparing the Balance Sheet and Profit and Loss

Account. He is expected to be an expert in the accounting procedures as he has to examine analytically the final accounts.

Following are the activities of accountancy:

(i) Checking the work of the Book-keeper,

(ii) Preparation of Trial Balance,

(iii) Preparation of Trading and Profit and Loss Account,

(iv) Preparation of Balance Sheet, and

(v) Passing entries for rectification of errors and making adjustments.

3. Auditing. "Where accountancy ends, auditing begins." Auditing involves verification of the entries passed by the accountant and the final accounts prepared by him It is the scrutiny of the accounts of a business with the help of vouchers, documents and the information given to him and also the explanations submitted to him. Unlike an accountant, the auditor has to satisfy himself after due verification and thorough scrutiny of accounts as to whether the transactions entered into the books are *bona fide.* An auditor is required to submit his report to the effect whether or not the Balance Sheet is a true and fair representation of the existing state of affairs of a business concern.

Thus an auditor must be well-versed in accounting. He should be a Chartered Accountant. He has to express his impartial opinion in his report after satisfying himself with proper recording of transactions. No auditor can certify a Balance Sheet as true and fair by simply acting as an accountant. Thus while auditing is based on accountancy, accountancy is not-based on auditing. An auditor must be familiar with the principles and practical aspects of accountancy. On the other hand, it is not necessary for an accountant to be an expert in the audit work.

An auditor is requested to write up the books of accounts of his client from the records and documents produced to him. He has nothing to do with the preparation of accounts. An accountant is to put his signature as a token of his having drafted the Balance Sheet and Profit and Loss Account. An auditor has to certify that they are correct, properly drawn up and that they reveal true and fair view of the state of affairs of the concern.

ACCOUNTANCY V/S AUDITING

The following points draw a line of demarcation between accountancy and auditing.

1. While Accountancy is mainly concerned with the preparation of summary and analysis of the records prepared by the book-keeper, auditing is the examination of the completed records.
2. While accountant ascertains the trading results of a business during

a financial year, auditor certifies as correct the financial statements prepared by the accountant.

3. While an accountant is an employee of the business, an auditor is an independent outsider.

4. As an employee of the business, the accountant draws his monthly salary regularly from the business itself. An auditor, on the other hand, is paid a remuneration agree upon between him and his client.

5. While an accountant is not expected to have a knowledge of auditing it is very essential for an auditor to possess a thorough knowledge of accountancy.

6. While an accountant is usually a permanent employee of the business, an auditor can be changed from year to year.

7. While an accountant does not submit his report on the financial statements prepared by him, an auditor has to submit his report to his client that the Balance Sheet and Profit and Loss Account give a true and fair view of the state of affairs of the business and are correct to the best of his knowledge and information supplied to him.

Is auditing a luxury?

The following points have been given to prove that auditing is a luxury:

(i) The remuneration paid to the auditor is a charge on the profits of a concern and a sheer wastage of a funds;

(ii) An average businessman finds it difficult to observe formalities necessary for the purpose of auditing;

(iii) Auditing involves a lot of obstructions in the daily routine of work of the office staff and hence it is an unnecessary waste of time; and

(iv) As auditing cannot detect and prevent all the errors and fraud it is of no use.

The following remarks prove that the above arguments are not sound and are based on illusory grounds. If accounting is a necessity, auditing is still more important. Auditing may not be necessity and legally compulsory in the case of small business-houses where only small amounts of capital are invested and accounts are maintained in a very crude form. But, for big business, auditing has a great practical utility. Every firm must maintain proper accounts and get them audited by some independent and qualified auditor. Hence, it is wrong to say that "auditing is a luxury, while accounting is a necessity."

ADVANTAGE OF AUDITING

Firms now get their accounts audited by a qualified auditor so that they may be sure of the smooth running of their business and profitability of the investment that they have made therein. Irrespective of the fact whether it was opted compulsorily or statutorily or voluntarily, the advantages of audit are numerous to every type of business concern. Its advantages are grouped as follows :

(A) Advantages to the Business

1. Care and System. Employees in charge of maintenance of books of accounts and other records remain regular, careful and systematic in their work.

2. Moral Check. Errors and frauds, if any, committed by employees of the business are promptly detected. In any case, knowledge of an impending audit exercises a moral check on the employees who may otherwise be tempted to commit defalcations and embezzlements.

3. Loans and Credit. Loans and credit may be obtained on the basis of audited accounts which are regarded as reliable index to the state of affairs of the enterprise.

4. Determination of liability. Liability of the enterprise as to income-tax, wealth-tax, sales-tax, etc., can easily be determined on the basis of audited accounts as these are readily believed by the tax authorities. The Income-tax Act contains a provision for holding tax audit.

5. Determination of Sale price. In case a running business is proposed to be sold, purchase considerations can easily be determined on the basis of audited accounts.

6. Settlement of higher wages and bonus. Audited statements of account provide a mutually satisfactory basis for the resolution of disputes about higher wages and bonus payments of workers.

7. Determination of claims. In Case of loss or damage to business property, audited accounts facilitate the determination of claims against the insurers.

8. Detection of weaknesses of control. Weaknesses of the existing system of internal check and internal control may be detected so that remedial steps may soon be initiated.

9. Ascertaining maintenance of accounts. Audit is an easy means to ascertain whether the undertaking is in fact maintaining the registers and books of account as required under the law.

10. Suggestions of Improvements. The enterprise can benefit from the professional competence and experience of the auditor who is always at hand to appraise the efficacy of various control measures, and to suggest improvements therein.

(B) Advantages to the owners

1. Sole Ownership. If the business is owned by a sole trader, he can rely well on the audited accounts and on his accounts clerks who are responsible for the maintenance of accounts.

2. Partnership Firm. If the business is organised as a partnership firm its partners can utilise the audited accounts to settle their disputes in regard to adjustment of capital and valuation of goodwill at the time of admission, retirement and death of a partner.

3. Joint Stock Company. If the business is constituted as a joint stock company, its shareholders who reside at places distant from the head office of the company rely on the audited accounts and can be sure of their investment being sage with the company.

4. Trusts and Cooperative. In case of trusts, cooperative societies etc., auditing serves as an evidence for the beneficiaries, members etc. that their interests a are being properly and efficiently looked after.

(C) Advantages to Management

1. Comparison of accounts. Audit enables comparison of accounts of different departments from one period to another and the fluctuation if any, may be analysed in detail.

2. Help in Decision making. Audited accounts are relied upon for the purposes of decision making by the management.

(D) Advantages to Others

1. Banks. In case of banks, audited statements of a business serve as a reliable guide to make decisions about loans to that business.

2. Insurance of companies. Insurance companies also rely on audited accounts to settle claims in respect of damage of loss of business assets.

3. Tax authorities. For determination of liability under income tax, sales tax, wealth tax etc., tax authorities unquestioningly accept the audited statements.

4. Purchaser. The purchaser of a business can easily calculate the amount of purchase consideration on the basis of audited final accounts.

5. Court. The audited accounts of a business are readily accepted as evidence before the court.

LIMITATIONS OF AUDITING

1. Conceptual Restriction. Conceptually, auditing is confined to the techniques of checking, vouching, verification, totalling etc. In a modern business, there are several vital aspects such as finances, managerial efficiency and effectiveness, business ethics etc., which are not covered by the auditing. Hence, auditing cannot serve its objects.

2. Post-mortem Techniques. Auditing begins when accountancy ends. The auditor may be nowhere around when the accounts are being finalised. The auditor may not be able to discover systematic manipulations in the books of accounts at the preparatory stage.

3. Dependence on Inside Information. An auditor has to depend on various personnel of the enterprise to seek additional information clarifications and explanations. If the personnel providing it have themselves been a party to the manipulation of books of account, these informations etc., may not be reliable.

4. Faulty Techniques. Where there is use of faulty techniques which are inconsistent with nature of business type of business transactions, methods of book-keeping and accountancy, audited accounts do not show real condition and fair view.

5. Inadequate or Faulty External Evidence. External evidences may not always be wholly reliable. For example, a debtor of the business may not provide correct information about the debt owed by him; a valuer may go wrong in valuing the asset. In these circumstances, even audited accounts may not be authentic.

6. Faulty Judgements of Auditor. The auditor's judgements about the correctness and fairness of the propositions in the books of account may not be based on an objective evaluation and critical review. Some times, auditor's assessment is not supported by relevant material evidence. Any faulty value judgement of the auditor will affect the true and fair view of the financial statements.

Utility and need of auditing can be summed up in the words of Arthur W. Homes, "Through the auditor, the businessman receives date, ideas and reactions that otherwise would be lost to him for the more efficient and most profitable operation of his business." Auditing is a must for every business concern. It should be done by an expert and open-minded auditor. Indian Companies Act, 1956 has provided for compulsory auditing for every company by an independent and an qualified auditor.

QUESTIONS FOR EXERCISE

1. Trace the origin of auditing. Explain history of its development with particular reference to India.
2. Explain in detail the auditing principles, standards and procedures. Distinguish between standards and procedures.

3. Explain the meaning of investigation and distinguish it from auditing.
4. What is the broad philosophy of Auditing?
5. Discuss the nature and scope of auditing.
6. Give the main classes of errors and fraud. Give illustrations. Can the auditor prevent such errors and fraud?
7. Describe briefly the main classes of errors and fraud. Is the auditor expected to detect all errors and fraud ?
8. "Fraud does not necessarily involve misappropriation of cash or goods.''. Discuss giving illustrations.
9. ''Among the principal objects of an audit is the detection of (i) technical errors, and (ii) errors or principle". Discuss and illustrate your answer with examples.
10. Distinguish between accounting errors and commercial fraud in the books of a business concern and give illustrations of each. How can errors and fraud be prevented ?
11. Explain clearly the concepts of Book-keeping, accounting and auditing. How do they differ from each other?
12. "Accountancy is a necessity while auditing is a luxury." Discuss.
13. Distinguish between book keeping, Accountancy and Auditing .
14. "Auditing begins where accountancy ends." Explain. How does accountancy differ from auditing?
15. Discuss in brief the advantages and limitations of auditing.
16. Enumerate and explain the advantages of audit to (a) business (b) owners of business and (c) others.
17. Make out a case that audit is essential whether it is a sole trader business or partnership or a limited company or a Government Corporation.

2

Classification of Audits

R. Roberts Coomber has classified audits on the following four bases:

A. Audits on the basis of authority:

1. Audit under statute,
2. Audit under private instructions of private institutions,
3. Internal audit.

B. Audits on the basis of scope:

1. Complete audit,
2. Partial audit.

C. Audits on the basis of time:

1. Continuous audit,
2. Periodical or final audit,
3. Interim audit.

D. Audits on the basis of objective:

1. Special audit,
2. Cost audit,
3. Management audit.

A. Audit on the basis of Authority

1. Audit under Statute. Statutory audit is compulsory under an statute or law. It can be conducted only by a qualified chartered accountant whose rights, duties and liabilities are determined by the concerned statute. The duties and rights may be extended by an agreement between the auditor and the concerned institution. Audits are compulsory under statute in the following cases:

(a) *Companies.* The Companies Act, 1913 made audit of companies registered under the Act compulsory for the first time in India. The Companies Act, 1956, as amended up-to-date has made significant changes in the rights, duties, powers, etc. of an auditor. Qualifications of an auditor have been laid down in Section 226 of the Act.

(b) *Other Institutions.* Audit is compulsory in the case of the following institutions:

(i) Banking companies governed by the Banking Companies (Regulation) Act, 1949.

(ii) Insurance companies governed by the respective Insurance Acts.

(iii) Cooperative societies registered under the Cooperative Societies Act.

(iv) Public and charitable trusts registered under various concerned Acts.

(v) Local authorities, government undertakings and departments.

(vi) All business organisations having annual sales over Rs. 40 lakhs.

Essential Characteristics of a Statutory Audit

(i) *Mandatory.* It is mandatory by nature.

(ii) *Qualified Auditor.* The auditor must be a qualified chartered accountant or a costs & works accountant (for permitted audits only).

(iii) *Not disqualified Auditor.* The auditor must not suffer from any prescribed disqualifications during the course of his audit work.

(iv) *Appointment according to rules.* Appointment of the auditor is made according to set rules/norms of the relevant Acts.

(v) *Not partial.* Statutory audit can never be partial audit. It always has to be a complete audit.

(vi) *Full and correct-report.* This kind of audit enables the appointing authority (shareholders, members and the government) to obtain full and fair disclosure of all material facts. They are able to secure the correct reporting about the affairs of the concern.

2. Audit under private Instructions of private institutions. In the case of private institutions an auditor is appointed by an agreement which states in detail the rights and duties of the auditor.

In the case of audit of the private institutions the auditor is governed by the contract and the customary/natural law of the land and no other statute regulates their contract except the Contract Act.

Types of Audit under Private Institutions

Audit under private institutions may be applicable to the following: (a) Partnership firms (b) Proprietary concerns (c) Private industries.

(a) *Audit of Partnership Firms.* In the case of audit of a partnership firm, the auditor must work according to instructions and provisions of the partnership deed. He must ensure that the provisions enumerated in the Partnership Act, 1932, are observed.

The audit of partnership offers the following advantages:

(i) *Avoid Disputes.* It helps in settling accounts between the partners themselves and thereby avoids the possibility of future disputes.

(ii) *Facilitates settlement of accounts.* It facilitates the settlement of accounts required on the retirement or death of a partner. Adjustments arising on the admission of a partner are also facilitated.

(iii) *Helps in raising loans.* It helps to a great extent in raising loans from the financial institutions who trust only audited accounts.

(iv) *True reporting.* Sleeping partners can expect true reporting about the financial state of affairs.

(v) *Reasonable purchase.* In case of an eventuality resulting in the sale of business as a going concern, audited accounts help in arriving at reasonable purchase consideration.

(b) *Audit of Proprietary Concerns.* Audit of proprietary concerns is not compulsory. In case the owner does not have direct control over transactions, the accounts must be audited. The owner gains many advantages, e.g.

(i) checking of frauds and errors is possible,

(ii) raising of loans becomes easy,

(iii) such audited accounts may be accepted by concerned authorities for income tax, sales tax assessments.

(c) *Audit of Accounts of Private individuals.* Sometimes even private individuals having considerable incomes, derived from a number of sources and whose expenditure is heavy do get their accounts audited. This gives following advantages:

(i) the incomes and expenditures are a properly accounted for,

(ii) the incomes tax and gift tax returns, etc. can be filed accurately,

(iii) after their death, no difficulty is faced in calculating estate duty. (Note that the Finance Act, 1985 has done away with the Estate Duty Act.)

3. Internal Audit. According to L.R. Howard, Internal audit may be defined as "a review of operations and records, sometimes continuous, undertaken within a business by specially assigned staff". It is done by the employees of the business undertaking who are not necessarily qualified chartered accountants. Undertakings prefer to adopt this system so that routine errors and frauds can be minimised. On such audits, the auditor is not necessarily required to submit his report to management.

B. Audit on the Basis of Scope

1. Complete Audit. In complete audit the auditor is supposed to check all the documents such as financial transactions relating to a particular financial year. Nothing is unchecked. It is convenient for small business houses. In large businesses, however, it is rarely practicable, as the time required to do it is considerable, and it may delay the presentation of audited accounts beyond a reasonable period.

2. Partial Audit. Partial audit is the audit of accounts relating either to a part of the year or a part of the documents or transactions. For example, a client may appoint an auditor to audit only the payment side of Cash Book because he himself receives cash and cheques on behalf of his business, and there are no chances of misappropriation of cash. Audit of this type is not permitted in the case of joint stock companies.

C. Audit on the Basis of Time

1. Continuous Audit. Continuous audit is suitable only for big business houses and not for small ones where accounts can be audited at the end of the financial year when they are ready. In continuous audit the auditor's staff is occupied continuously with the audit of accounts throughout the year, or the auditor attends at intervals fixed or otherwise, during the continuation of the financial year and completes the audit work in parts. The auditor is constantly engaged in checking the accuracy of the accounts during the whole accounting period.

2. Periodical or Final Audit. According to De Paula, periodical audit is one where the auditor does not attend until the completion and closure of financial accounts by the undertaking or client. The auditor takes the audit task as a whole and the checking is done at one go. Thus final audit is performed only after the completion of the financial year and the preparation of final accounts. It is the most satisfactory form of audit from the auditor's point of view. It is usually adopted in the case of small concerns. In large organisations, it is not practicable, as the time involved by audit after the completion of final accounts delays the presentation of the audited accounts beyond a reasonable period.

D. Audit on the Basis of Objective

(1) Special Audit. In India Section 233(A) of Companies Act, 1956 empowers the Central Government to direct special audit in the following circumstances:

(i) Unsound management. Where the affairs of a company are not being managed in accordance with sound business principles or prudent commercial practices.

(ii) Injurious management. Where any company is being managed in a manner likely to cause serious injury or damage to the interests of trade, industry or business to which it pertains.

(iii) Danger to solvency. Where the financial position of any company is such as to endanger its solvency.

Indian government specifies the period of such an audit. The auditor appointed is known a special auditor with powers and duties governed by Companies Act, 1956. He reports to the Central Government. His fees are fixed by the Central Government though paid by the company. On the basis of the report of the auditor, the Central Government may take any action it may deem fit. Where no action is taken within four months, the Central Government may send the report to the concerned company for onward circulation to the members, or for the circulation in the forthcoming annual general meeting of the shareholders.

2. Cost Audit. Under Sec.233(B) of the Companies Amendment Act, 1965, the Government of India is empowered to issue directions for the conduct of cost audit of companies engaged in production, processing, manufacturing or mining activities. It may require such companies to include particulars relating to material or labour utilisation or to other items of cost as may be prescribed. It is conducted by the cost accountant within the scope of the Costs and Works Accountant Act, 1959, with same powers and duties which an auditor of a joint-stock company has under Section 277(1). The company must give all facilities and assistance for performing the cost audit work to the cost auditor. He is to report to the Central Government in such form and within such time as may be specified. He also forwards a copy of the cost-audit report to the company.

3. Management Audit. It is the audit conducted to examine all aspects of management in business. It is a tool of management control. It includes the examination of plans, objectives, means of working, utilisation of physical resources, organisational pattern, coordination of various activities at all levels and control of the entire business. Thus it concerns every activity of the business. It covers all the areas of management, i.e., plans, organisation, co-ordination, and control etc.

VARIOUS CLASSES OF AUDIT

1. From the point of coverage. Audit may be complete or partial. A *Complete audit* is one in which all the transactions recorded in the books of accounts are audited thoroughly. A *Partial audit* is one in which only particular type of transactions is audited.

2. From the point of legality. Audit may be voluntary or compulsory. A *Voluntary audit* is one which is carried on at the sweet will of the proprietor of the concern. He may or may not get his accounts audited. Whereas, the *compulsory audit* is one which has been made compulsory under specific statute and the proprietors of the concern must get their accounts audited compulsorily. For instance, it is compulsory for all the companies to get their accounts duly audited under the Indian Companies Act, 1956.

3. From the point of nature of organisation. Audit may be private or Government audit. *Private audit* is one which is undertaken by the private organisations such as sole traders, partnership firms or joint stock companies. *Government audit* is applicable to the Government departments and departmental undertakings.

4. From practical point of view. It may be broadly classified as *Final, Continuous*, and *Interim* audit.

5. From the point of specific objectives. The audit may be *Cash audit, Special audit, Cost audit, Joint audit, Systems audit, or Proprietary audit.*

6. From the point of degree of independence. Audit may be *Independent or Statutory audit* and *Internal audit.* Independent audit or Statutory audit refers to the audit undertaken in case of various business or other organisations independently by duly qualified auditors, mainly in accordance with the statutory provisions under certain Acts. Whereas, the Internal audit is undertaken by the employee of the concern, specially large in size. The internal audit is neither a compulsory nor undertaken by the duly qualified auditor under certain statutory provisions.

CLASSIFICATION OF AUDIT

1. From the point of average	(a)	complete
	(b)	Partial
2. From the point of legality	(a)	Voluntary
	(b)	Compulsory
3. From the point of nature of organisation	(a)	Private
	(b)	Government
4. From practical point of view	(a)	Final
	(b)	Continuous
	(c)	Interim
5. From the point of specific objective	(a)	Cash audit
	(b)	Special audit
	(c)	Cost audit.
	(d)	Joint audit
	(e)	Systems audit
	(f)	Propriety audit
6. From the point of degree of Independence	(a)	Independent or Statutory audit
	(b)	Internal audit

FINAL AUDIT

Meaning

A final audit begins after the close of the period of accounts and is carried on until it is completed. In it complete and detailed checking is done at stretch. It is also known as Completed audit, Periodical audit or a Balance Sheet audit. Sometimes, a differentiation is made between the Balance Sheet audit and the Final audit. The Balance Sheet audit is one which relates to examination of items of Balance Sheet alone. But, the audit of items of the Balance Sheet cannot be carried on in isolation. The final audit is the most satisfactory from the point of the auditor as the full facts relating to the year under review are in his possession and he can carry on the audit at a stretch until the whole work is over. It is used in most of the concerns and organisations. It is more suited to relatively smaller concerns than the giant concerns where transactions may be numerous. In such huge concerns it will be impossible to finish the audit of their accounts within the limited time.

Advantages of Final Audit

1. At one stretch. Audit work can be completed easily at a stretch. Thus the auditor does not lose the thread of his work and maintains continuity.

2. No dislocation of work. It does not cause any dislocation of work of the client as the audit is undertaken at the end of year when accounting records related to that period duly over.

3. Thorough. Audit work can be undertaken thoroughly and it does not become dull, monotonous or mechanical.

4. Convenient. It is convenient for the auditor also as he need not maintain a larger organisation and can easily allocate his work of audit among his staff.

5. Less Expensive. It is less expensive as compared to the continuous audit.

6. Easy. The audit can be completed easily and within reasonable time, as the final audit may be undertaken methodically at a stretch.

7. Checks collusion. It helps in minimising the collusion among the employees of the client and there is no question of alteration of the figures when the audit work is over, as it happens in case of continuous audit.

Limitations of Final Audit

1. Incomplete. Thorough and complete checking of all the accounting records is not possible in case of final audit, as it can be in case of continuous audit.

2. Unsuitable for large concerns. It is not suitable for the organisations of the large size, where the transactions are numerous.

3. Possibility of Errors. As the auditor depends much upon test checking, errors and frauds can exist even after accounts have been audited.

4. Time Consuming. It takes time to finalise the report in case of final audit, therefore, it is not suitable for organisations which require report soon.

5. No moral check. It is not much effective in imposing moral check over the clients staff.

INTERIM AUDIT

Meaning

It means carrying out of audit work at any time during the financial year in order to ascertain the interim profit or loss or state of financial affairs of the concern. If the directors of a company may desire to declare interim dividends or bonus only when first half-year is over. It would require the interim audit to be carried out to ascertain true profits of the concern for the period. Audit of final accounts may become necessary in the case of firm in the middle of the year in the event of admission, retirement or death of a partner. This would, save time in the final audit. It may enable the auditor to gather some important points with regard to the concern which may be helpful while conducting the final audit.

Continuous V/s Interim Audit

1. Interim audit is undertaken with a specific object of finding and checking the profit or loss for a given period. The object of continuous audit is not to find out the profit or loss of the concern for a given period.

2. In interim audit, accounting records are checked up to a certain date only. Under the continuous audit, the accounting records of one accounting or financial year are examined thoroughly.

3. In Interim audit the trial balance must be prepared and checked at the time of such audit. In continuous audit, the trial balance is not prepared at intervals.

4. Whereas in continuous audit, the verification of assets, and liabilities is undertaken at the close of the financial period, in interim audit, it is undertaken at the time of such audit.

5. In continuous audit, the auditor's report is submitted at the end of financial year, but in interim audit, it is submitted at the time of audit.

CASH AUDIT

The cash audit is undertaken with the purpose of examining the cash receipts and payments. It does not involve thorough checking of all the records. The auditor has to be very careful in auditing Cash Book as it may contain manipulations. In order to satisfy himself that all the cash receipts and payments have been duly recorded, he must refer to all the relevant vouchers and documents, while reporting he should mention that he undertook only cash audit.

SPECIAL AUDIT

Besides the general audit, there are two other kinds of audit related to the joint stock companies in India. They are Special Audit and Cost Audit.

The Companies (Amendment) Act, 1960 has empowered the Central Government to order special audit of the companies in certain cases. Under section 233A it can direct special audit of company accounts when it is of the opinion:

1. that the affairs of any company are not being managed in accordance with sound business principles or prudent commercial policies; or
2. that any company is being managed in a manner likely to cause serious injury or damage to the interest of the trade, industry or business to which it pertains; or
3. that the financial position of any company is such as to endanger its solvency.

Due to inefficient management of financial position of the company, special audit is quite necessary in the interest of the growth of trade or industry so that the national interest may not be subservient to the interest of a few individuals.

The Central Government may pass an order for conducting special audit of the accounts of any company for such period or periods as may be specified in the order. By the same or a different order, it may appoint either a chartered accountant or the company's auditors himself to conduct such special audit. The auditors, so appointed, is known as special auditor and his powers and duties are provided under section 227.

The special auditor has to prepare a report addressed and submitted to the Central Government. On receipt of his report, the Government may direct such action as it considers necessary in accordance with the provisions of the Companies (Amendment) Act, 1960 or any other law for the time being in force. If the Government does not take any action on the report within four months from the date of its receipt, a copy of the report of relevant extracts from it with comments thereon will be sent to the company by the Government. It may require the company either to circulate the report (or its extracts) to the members or to have it (them) read at its next general meeting. The expenses of, and incidental to, any special audit including the remuneration of the special auditor shall be determined by the Central Government and are final. These shall be paid by the company. In case of default of such payment these shall be recoverable from the company as an arrear of land revenue.

COST AUDIT[1]

Meaning

The cost audit implies thorough examination of cost accounting records of a company. It has been defined as "the verification of the correctness of cost accounts and of the adherence of the cost accounting plan." It involves the examination of cost account and whether the plan prepared in this connection has been duly executed.

Procedure

Under section 233B, the Central Government may direct for the cost audit of a company engaged in production, processing, manufacturing or mining activities. In these cases, proper books of account would include "such particulars relating to utilisation of materials or labour as may be prescribed, if such company is required by the Central Government to include such particulars in the books of accounts." The Government may also direct that the audit of cost accounts of a company shall be conducted in such a manner as to obtain a true and fair view of the state of affairs of the company.

Duties and powers of cost auditor are the same as prescribed in the case of auditor in general under section 221(1) of the Act. He will submit his report to the Company Law Board in such form and within such time as may be prescribed and shall also, at the same time, forward a copy of the report to the Company.

JOINT AUDIT

Meaning

A joint audit means when two or more persons or firms of Chartered Accountants are jointly appointed to conduct the audit of a company. This is done by large-sized companies, specially the Government Companies, which want the pooling of the resources of two or more auditors so that the audit work may be undertaken effectively, expeditiously and quickly. Today, most of the large-sized companies do not appoint single auditor but the joint auditors. These joint auditors stand on equal footing so far as the professional work is concerned. The Companies Act, 1956 has not yet recognised this development statutorily.

Problems

There may be some difficulty in division of work and coordination. There may also be difference of opinion between auditors. These problems can be solved by mutual discussion, consultation and agreement.

---

1. Walter W. Bigg, *Cost Accounts*, seventh edition, p. 319.

Liability

The joint auditor has an individual responsibility only. As Section 227 of the Act does not contemplate any division of work of audit between two or more persons, there is no question of joint liability. It would not be proper to hold an auditor responsible for the work not done by him but by another auditor. If there are two auditors and both of them are held responsible jointly, that would create many practical problems.

The Institute of Chartered Accountants of India has issued a *Statement on the Responsibility of Joint Auditors*. It would not be correct to hold an auditor responsible for the specifically allotted work of another. Each joint auditor will be responsible only for the work allotted to him. If the work can be easily and clearly divided on the basis of identifiable operating units or specified areas of work, the responsibility to perform the work assigned to one of the joint auditors with reasonable care and skill will be his alone. The extent of work to be carried out is a matter of professional judgement. It may differ from auditor to auditor as no two firms or individuals will exercise this judgement in an identical manner. Thus, one cannot hold auditor responsible for the work done by another auditor who is equally qualified and competent to undertake the audit work. Where the work cannot be clearly divided, the responsibility will be joint between them.

PROPRIETY AUDIT

History

Prof. W.A. Robson had made a strong plea for the adoption of efficiency-cum-propriety audit in 1937 in his book *Public Enterprise*. He had advocated for the appointment of Efficiency Audit Commission for the purpose of carrying on detailed checking specially for the nationalised industries of U.K. In July 1967, he made a strong case for such audit for the nationalised industries. Thus, it is only very recently that the efforts are being made in this direction. Indians have yet to evolve such audit in its fullness.

Definition

1. *Eric L. Kohler*. The term 'propriety' may be defined as "that which meets the tests of public interest, commonly accepted customs and standards of conduct."[2] Thus, the propriety audit implies verification of accounting records in such a way as to find out whether the actions and decisions have been taken in the "public interest" and in accordance with the "commonly accepted customs and standards of conduct". Mere comparison of accounting records with the related evidences is not enough and the auditors would have to take pains to see whether the transaction was "justified" or not.

---

2. E.L. Kohler, *A Dictionary for Accounts*, 1970, p. 349.

2. Kamal Gupta, "Propriety audit refers to an audit in which the various actions and decisions are examined to find out whether they are in public interest and whether they meet the standards of conduct."[3] Thus, the propriety audit is the one undertaken for verifying that there has not been any leakage of revenue, misappropriation of assets, or wastage of funds, due to a transactions or a group of transactions having, been entered into either inadvertently or deliberately in disregard of any legal requirement or an economic or financial consideration. It is a special investigation carried out for ascertaining that contracts, except relating to routine transactions entered into with third parities, are in the best interest of the concern and that there is a system which ensures adequately the safety of the assets of the concern.

Distinction from Performance Audit

The propriety audit has to be distinguished from the *performance audit*. The performance audit is a procedure for "(i) analysing the profits and losses of different economic activities in which the concern is engaged; (ii) determining the relationship between production and sales; (iii) determining whether the sales pattern has deviated from the one considered ideal; (iv) for maximising profits; and (v) determining the imbalance, if any, in the inventory."

Functions of the Auditor

The propriety audit is undertaken in some way or the other in the various Government departments. It is the prime concern of the Comptroller and Auditor-General of India. In case of the Government audit, its importance has been duly recognised, though not enforced with sincerity. According to Ashok Chanda, the past Comptroller and Auditor-General of India, "Audit is not an inquisition and its mission is not one of fault finding. Its purpose is to bring to the notice of the administration lacunae in the rules and regulations, and to suggest, wherever possible, ways and means for the execution of plants and projects with greater expedition, efficiency and economy."[4] This brings in its ambit the idea of propriety audit. It implies that mere testing the accuracy of accounting and estimating is not enough but it is more important that the expenses should be incurred wisely and economically and extravagance and wastes are duly avoided. Auditor's functions are not merely to ensure that the expenditure conforms to rules, but also to satisfy himself as to its wisdom, faithfulness and economy. The audit has to be directed towards discovering waste and matters beyond accounting, which though *intra vires*, are apparently unwise or extravagant.[5]

3. Kamal Gupta, *Contemporary Auditing*, 1977, p. 334.
4. Ashok Chanda, *Aspects of Audit Control*, 1960, p. 26.
5. Ashok Chanda, *Indian Administration*, 1958, p. 247.

In *An Introduction to Indian Government Accounts & Audit*, published by the Government of India, certain principles have been mentioned which have long been recognised as standards of financial propriety. The auditor has to see that those general principles have been duly adhered to.

Scope

While explaining propriety auditing, Laxmi Narain[6] points out that "it extends beyond the formality of expenditure to its wisdom, faithfulness and economy. The general principle applied there is that every public officer should exercise the same vigilance in respect of expenditure incurred from public money on a person of ordinary prudence would exercise in respect of expenditure of his own money. The audit investigates the necessity for the expenditure incurred and asks whether individual items are in furtherance of the scheme for which the budget provided; whether the same result could have been obtained otherwise with greater economy and whether the rate and scale of expenditure were justified in the circumstances." The audit claims to ask here every question that an intelligent taxpayer, bent on getting the best value for his money, could ask. It involves enquiry against the propriety of expenses and not merely that expenses have been incurred and vouchers are present.

Statutory Provisions

1. Sub-section (1A) added to section 227 of the Companies (Amendment) Act, 1965. It has become obligatory for an auditor to enquire into the propriety aspect of certain types of transactions entered into by a company. If his enquiries show that some of the transactions entered into by the company are not in the best interest of the shareholders, it is his duty to report the fact to them. The additional reporting requirements prescribed under Section 227(4A) of the Companies Act also contain the matters when propriety aspects require due consideration on the part of an auditor.

2. *Section 227(1A).* It requires a company auditor to enquire whether or not the loans and advances made by the company on certain terms are not prejudicial to the interest of the company or its members. It also requires an auditor to enquire whether transactions of the company which are represented merely by book entries are not prejudicial to the interests of the company or whether the personal expenses have been charged to revenue account. Thus, it has extended the duty of an auditor to look into the propriety aspects also while auditing the accounts of a company.

3. *Section 227(4A).* Under it Central Government has extended the duty of a company auditor to look into some propriety aspects of certain transactions. The Government accordingly may direct that the auditor's

---

6. Laxmi Narain, *Efficiency Audit of Public Enterprises*, 1972. p. 2.

report shall also include a statement on such matters as may be specified therein.

4. *Provisions of Sections 233(B) of the Companies Act, 1956.* These are related to the Cost Audit also require the auditor to include in his report certain aspects related to the propriety of the transactions. Section 619 (3) of the Act which deals with the audit of Government Companies also provides for propriety audit of such companies on several vital issues.

SYSTEMS AUDIT

History

Systems Audit technique has been developed very recently in Canada and U.S.A. It is gaining considerable popularity as an aid to the Balance Sheet auditing due to with the growth in size, very rapid growth of automation, use of computer and other sophisticated techniques to maintain records, and substantial improvement in the designs of internal control. These developments have relieved the auditor from various onerous work of verification of evidences and other records thoroughly.

Meaning

The systems audit is a detailed enquiry about the various systems of accounting and controls prevailing in the enterprises. It finds out whether they are working efficiently or not to formulate the opinion about the financial statements. According to Skinner and Anderson the system audit is an attempt "to explore inside the system and discover exactly how it produce results. If the mechanics of the system were analysed intensively and the detailed survey showed it to be designed with appropriate controls, checks and balances to forestall errors, then this would be a good indication that the results produced by system were accurate." They further point out that with this background the auditor attempts to "make inferences about the whole of the accounting results from a knowledge of the detailed system which produced them."[7]

Advantages

A systems audit, may also be termed *analytical auditing.* It does not totally replace the independent balance sheet auditing. It is an aid to the latter, as it helps the auditor in finding out whether the control systems are effective and reliable or not. It saves the time, botheration and cost of the independent auditing. In traditional auditing efforts are made to make a thorough checking of the accounting records with the related evidences. In the systems audit as the control systems, as operative in the enterprise, are

7. Skinner, R.M. and Anderson R.L., *An Outline of Flow Chart Approach to Audits*, 1966.

quite effective and reliable, the auditor need not check the data and in the above fashion. He can, fairly rely upon the accounting data and devote more time formulating his opinion as to the truth and fairness of the financial statements.

Precautions

Systems audit is highly technical. It requires full technical knowledge of the enterprise and various systems which may be adopted. Mere knowledge of methods of keeping accounts would not do. The auditor would have to be conversant with the various systems and their analysis. The technique of flow charting and the procedural tests are very much helpful in finding out the effectiveness and reliability of the systems.

Steps in Systems Audit

(1) Review the systems thoroughly;

(2) Test the systems with some representative samples and see their effectiveness;

(3) Prepare the flow charts thoroughly and analyse the same;

(4) With thorough examination, find out the weakness and strength of the system;

(5) Plan the audit on the basis of degree of reliability of the systems;

(6) Make detailed verificatory checks of transactions wherever the weaknesses exist in the system;

(7) Suggest for the improvement of the systems, if necessary.

Limitations

In a country like India where most of the enterprises do not have a well-designed system and the mechanised accounting, specially use of computer, is not used in practice. The systems audit is of very limited use. A systems audit presupposes a well-designed system. In its absence, there is no question of adopting this technique of auditing. With the adoption of automation and latest techniques in data recording and processing it will become more popular.

AUDITING IN DEPTH

Meaning

According to Leslie R. Horward, "By auditing in depth is implied the examination of the system applied within a business entailing the tracing of certain transactions from their origin to the conclusion, investigating at each stage the records created and their appropriate authorisation."[8] Such

8. Leslie R. Howard, *Taylor and Perry's Principles of Auditing*, 19th ed. 1978, p.43.

an examination would enable the auditor "satisfy himself as to the efficacy or otherwise of the system of internal control being operated". "A moderately large number of purchase requisitions may be examined as to proper authorisation and then tested with purchase orders; a rather less number of these may be examined as to adherence with the rules governing orders to suppliers; a number of these may be then tested with the goods inwards books, and subsequently with the invoices received and their proper recording." This would entail breaking down the entire system into sections and testing each of them on the 'pyramid basis'. This implies testing greater number first and then lesser number at each stage.

Duties of the Auditor

It has been stated by Leslie R.Howard[9], that in order to carry out such searching examination, the auditor must fully acquaint himself with the prevailing systems. He should make himself conversant with the following main aspects: (i) the nature of business and its activities; (ii) the accounting system in operation; (iii) The duties and responsibilities of the staff; (iv) the internal check system; and (v) the internal audit system.

The auditor may have to make efforts to gather necessary information in this respect. He may have to examine the nature of the business itself. If the control in the business is efficiently operated, he may get due information from the office manual, written staff instructions or flow charts if they exist. In case, efficient control system is not in operation, he would have to gather necessary information from the management and staff and prepare the necessary records himself.

Thus, an auditor may be required to undertake detailed examination of certain transactions from origin to the conclusion and then satisfy himself with regard to its reliability. More use of auditing in depth would bring about greater accuracy and reliability of the accounting records.

INTERNAL AUDIT

Definition

1. H. Washerbrook, "In its narrow sense, such an audit is one that is carried out by the specialist staff of the organisation being audited, and concern itself mainly with the routine checking of (usually) accounting transactions on a daily basis, with the object of quickly locating irregularities, thus making it more difficult to perpetrate a fraud, because of the constant nature of the checking."[10] This definition is quite comprehensive. It brings out the various features and objects of internal audit clearly.

---

9. *Ibid.*, p.43.

10. Washerbook H., *The Board and Management Auditing*, Business Books, 1978, p.3.

2. *The Institute of Internal Auditors, U.S.A.* Internal auditing is "an independent appraisal activity within an organisation for the review of accounting, financial and other operations as a basis for service to management. It is a managerial control, which functions by measuring and evaluating the effectiveness of other controls."[11] This definition laid emphasis upon "independent appraisal" of the related individuals in the organisation and is not concerned mainly with the routine checking. It requires the internal auditor to go beyond the records in the books and review and report the performance in the area of finance, accounting and other related operations.

Fundamental Operations

According to R.S. Waldron, there are twelve fundamental operations of internal audit : "(1) A service to management; (2) Provides assurance of an effective system of internal control that is *not excessive;* (3) Ensures a reliable basis for production of accounts and statements of trading; (4) Policies the operation of established procedures and policies and sees that they are adequate, not wasteful and are observed; (5) Highlights departures from established procedures; (6) Draws attention to deficiencies (in the system, control, practice etc.); (7) Finds inefficiencies; (8) Suggests remedies and *improvements;* (9) Is able to do specially assigned work and report; (10) Needs status and independence; (11) Staff need training, objective judgement and experience; (12) Looks beyond mere *accounting* functions."[12]

Functions of Internal Auditor

The internal auditor ensures the effective application of established policies, rules, procedure, and internal check. He makes constant review of internal control procedure and suggest necessary changes for the same. He sees that the absolute procedures are scrapped, loopholes are plugged and prompt corrective measures have been taken, wherever necessary. He encourages accurate and careful work by the other employees of the concern. He assists the independent auditor in final auditing. He makes various special checkings or investigations of the business. He makes constant efforts to find out weaknesses and defects in the procedures and methods followed and in the organisation of the concern and suggests improvements. He ensures that the procedures and policies laid down by the management are carried out properly. He keeps a watch over the income and expenditure of the concern and conserves its resources as far as possible. He verifies the accounts. He examines all the records made in the account books to ensure that they are accurate and reliable. Thus, he performs the

---

11. *Statement of the Responsibilities of the Internal Auditor*, The Institute of Internal Auditors, U.S.A., New York.

12. R.S. Waldron, *Bigg and Davies' Internal Auditing*, 5th ed. 1980, p.4.

functions relating to evaluation, compliance, conservation, verification and a host of other activities.

Internal Auditing V/S Statutory Auditing

1. *Objective.* The main objective of internal audit is to fulfil the needs of the management whereas in independent audit the objective is to fulfil the needs of proprietors as well as third parties for reliable financial data.

2. *Means.* The internal audit may be carried out by a firm of practising accountants or by own staff but statutory audit can be entrusted in India only to a Chartered Accountant or a firm of Chartered Accountants, engaged in public practice, or to a Restricted State Auditor.

3. *Approach.* The internal auditor's approach is to ensure that accounting system is efficient, so that the accounting information presented to the management throughout the period is accurate and discloses all the information that the management desires or requires. The approach of statutory auditor is, governed by his duty to satisfy himself that the accounts to be presented to the shareholders exhibit a true and fair view of the profit or loss and of the concern's financial state of affairs.

4. *Remuneration.* The remuneration of internal auditor is fixed by management, while that of independent auditor is fixed by shareholder.

5. *Freedom.* The internal auditor is dependent of the management but the independent auditor is independent of the management, both in fact and in mental attitude.

6. *Duties.* The duties of an internal auditor may be reduced as desired by the management but it cannot be done in case of independent auditor.

7. *Periodically.* Internal audit is carried on continuously throughout the year but independent audit is carried on periodically and usually once a year.

8. *Techniques.* In internal audit the examination work is quite detailed but in case of independent audit the testing techniques on the basis of random samples are utilised to a large extent.

9. *Responsibility.* An independent auditor has to submit a report to the shareholders after the audit work is over, but as internal auditor is not required to do so. The report, if any has to be submitted to the management.

10. *Termination.* The services of an internal auditor can be easily terminated by the management but in case of an independent auditor only shareholders can remove him.

Degree of Reliance

Internal audit is of great help to the statutory auditor but it is not substitute for the final audit. The extent of its reliance would differ from case to case. It is, however, a question of discretion which the statutory auditor, must exercise carefully, as he cannot plead that he had relied upon the work done by the internal auditor. The statutory auditor cannot, divest himself of the responsibilities laid on him by the statute. If he curtails the extent of his checking, putting reliance on the work of internal auditor, the responsibility for any deficiency in the financial statements, will be that of statutory auditor.

The degree of reliance of the internal audit, depends on the following facts:

1. *Efficiency.* He should ascertain the efficiency of the internal audit. In order to assess its efficiency, he should examine the audit programme, working papers and reports etc. thoroughly. He should also make a test check of the work done by the internal auditor.

2. *Experience and Qualification.* He should find out the experience and qualifications of the internal auditor and his staff. He should also examine the character of his reports to the management and the action taken by the management on the same.

3. *Authority of Internal Auditor.* He should find out the authority vested in the internal auditor and the level of management to which he is directly responsible.

4. *Degree of Dependence.* He should see whether the Internal Audit Department does only internal audit of the transactions or performs some other jobs also. He should ascertain the degree to which the Internal Audit Department is independent of Operating Departments. Its dependence on other Departments would very much reduce its value to the statutory auditor.

Examining the usefulness of the work done by the internal auditor, from his own point of view, the statutory auditor should apply his own discretion regarding the degree to which he may depend upon the internal audit. However, there should be co-operation between internal and external auditors.

Internal and External Audit

R.S. Waldron has stated that "the purpose of internal audit are substantially different from those of external audit, though an internal auditor will in the course of his work do a certain amount of purely financial auditing, and also test the checking of the operation for system in the same way as external auditors." He further states that "there are substantial overlapping areas where both auditors are involved in checking the same book entries and testing the operation of the same system, where the external auditor can use the work performed by the internal as a form of reliance, which can save his work. There is, however, less available benefit to be obtained by internal auditors from the external audit functions." However, the wide experience of the independent auditor may be of assistance to the internal auditor. On the other hand, the latter's intimate acquaintance with the business concerned might be of help to the independent auditor.

According to Leslie R. Howard, the *cooperation between the internal and external auditors* may be had in the following matters:

1. The independent auditor may be able to rely to large extent on the internal auditor regarding the continuous operation of the internal check system and in the reliability he may place on the accounting records.

2. Agreement as to various aspects of the work being carried out only by the internal auditor or together with the independent auditor, such as cash counts and visits to branches.

3. Where the internal auditor so cooperates independent auditor may accept work done in respect of such matters as the confirmation of customers' accounts, the verification of assets and the audit working schedules prepared by the internal auditor.

According to the *statements on Auditing*, "The internal auditor's responsibility is to the management and he is in no sense a servant of the independent auditor. It follows therefore that the extent to which the internal auditor can so arrange his work as to be of specific assistance to the independent auditor will depend upon decisions of the management on the scope of the internal audit and the number of staff employed thereon. Consultation between the two auditors, and where necessary with the management, should however ensure that so far as is practicable the fullest possible assistance is available to the independent auditor."

Discussing about the report on a survey held in Germany, Andrew D. Chambers concludes that "There is an increasingly close relationship between internal and external audit." He sums up that "co-ordination exits in the majority of cases *where this implies simply that the external auditor adapts his work in of what the internal auditor is doing;* co-ordination is less common, though increasing, where this implies that the external auditor *participates in the determination of what the internal auditor shall audit."*

M.G. Crabtree has very rightly pointed out that "extended reliance by external audit on the internal auditors certainly reduces the external audit fee.'' In near future, the internal auditor will play an increasing part in the annual audit process. There is increasing trend of reduction in time and scope of external audit's activities due to a greater use of internally generated reports and working papers which were formerly prepared by the external auditor. The external auditors are finding it more useful to release more and more of their work to the internal auditors. According to Chambers, it is happening "at a time when internal audit's emphasis has also been adapting to embrace operational audit areas outside accounting and finance which are not of primary significance in the statutory audit."

New Provisions

The importance of the internal audit has increased tremendously with the passing of Manufacturing and Other Companies (Auditors' Report) Order, 1975. It came into effect from January 1, 1976 and requires that the Auditors report shall include a statement in relation to companies, the paid up capital of which at the financial year concerned exceeds Rs. 25 lakhs, whether the company has an internal audit system, commensurate with the size and nature of its business. Thus, for *such companies, the internal audit has been made compulsory.*

The Order has covered about 5,686 companies of the country. India has the third largest membership of internal auditors with about 908 members already enrolled. The U.S.A. and U.K. rank first and second with membership of 15,000 and 8,000 respectively.

Internal Audit and Management

Today, internal audit is being used by the management "to bridge the gap by serving as an independent check on the accounting and other operations of the organisation." The internal audit can assist management in controlling the operations of the organisation in the following ways : "(a) ensuring compliance with the manual of operations; (b) recommending improved systems especially, to cover areas where control is lacking or objectives are not being achieved; (c) simplifying over-complicated or over-costly controls or recommending their abandonment where their value is not equal to their cost; (d) protecting the company's assets and recommending improvements in such safeguard; (e) ensuring economic use of resources within a business; (f) improving the form, content and reliability of information; (g) eliminating and controlling waste."[13]

Resent Trend

Some important trends in Internal audit are as following :

1. Serving whole Organisation. There is an increasing emphasis that the internal audit should serve the organisation as a whole and not merely the management of the organisation. The old theory that the internal auditing is the 'arm of management' is changing fast.

2. Expansion of scope. It is evolving "to embrace the audit (whether compliance, efficiency or effectiveness auditing) of all operations and not merely accounting and financial matters." It is not simply concerned with

---

13. R.S. Waldron in Bigg and Davies, *Internal Auditing, op. cit.*, pp. 52-53.

audit of compliance with internal and external procedures and regulations but, in fact, it is more concerned with the appraisal of efficiency and effectiveness.

3. Risk Management. Today the internal audit is giving due emphasis to the risk management and more audit effort is being extended at the *pre-event* stage.

4. Concern with Corporate Attitudes. Internal auditors are now more concerned and think over reviewing the corporate attitudes (to innovation, work, risk, resource stewardship, staff development etc.) It is quite important as success or failure of the organisation depends upon them also.

5. Participative Auditing. The internal auditors are now required to undertake participative auditing and have to adopt the team-work approach for the purpose. This has become necessary because of growing emphasis upon the efficiency and effectiveness auditing.

6. Freedom. Being an employee of the organisation, internal auditor is supposed to lack independence in his working. However, today there is a growing realisation that within the given framework, he should be given the desired independence to work. It does not imply independence from management, but it means independence from the management of a particular audit area.

7. Professionalisation. The trend towards professionalisation of internal auditing is very strong and efforts are being made to develop a full-fledged professional body in various countries of the world.

SOCIAL AUDIT

What is Social Audit ?

Social audit aims at the protection of the interests of all those who are affected by the decisions of the company. It is a sophisticated and scientific technique of testing the truth of the social performance of a company with reference to its means and motives by an independent authority to detect and prevent abuse of power. Its concept emanates from the basic democratic principle that those entrusted with authority must account for the use of it so that every one knows as to what is going on in the business and other centres of authority.

Advantages of Social Audit

Social audit is good for public reporting as well as for internal management. It attempts to assess the contribution of an enterprise to the society or the social performance of an enterprise.

In it the social auditor tries to ascertain whether:

(i) the acts of the business are in public interest;

(ii) they meet the generally accepted standards of conduct;

(iii) the decisions taken have been prudent and have been implemented with wisdom; and

(iv) the business meets the tests of public interest and commonly accepted customs and standards of conduct.

Scope of Social Audit

1. Pollution control
2. Reducing environmental hazards
3. Reclamation of new lands and proper harnessing of natural resources
4. Energy conservation
5. Material conservation
6. Education and training of employees
7. Health, safety and welfare of the workers
8. Workers' participation in management and profits
9. Improving the quality of products
10. Reducing the cost of production
11. Encouraging arts, sports, community living, advancement in efficiency, productivity, research and development
12. Maintaining good employee and employer relations
13. Policies regarding wages, prices and profits and
14. Fair trade practices, etc.

Auditor's Report Order, 1975

Modern consumers' movement has enhanced the role of social audit which has assumed a special significance, in view of the widespread illiteracy, ignorance of people and corrupt business practices. Under manufacturing and other Companies (Auditor's Report) Order, 1975, the auditor is required to report on recording and physical verification of fixed assets, on revaluation of assets, verification and valuation of items of closing stock, loans from companies under the same management, internal control regarding purchase of assets, reasonableness of the prices of purchases made from companies in which the directors are interested in various positions, adequacy of provisions for unserviceable or damaged stock, compliance regarding rules for public deposits, recording of the sale of scrap and by-products, adequacy of the internal audit system, regularity regarding deposit of provident fund, etc.

The auditor must include in his report the various matters specified in the order.

Auditors report order applies to joint-stock companies including government companies engaged in one or more of the following activities.

1. Trading
2. Manufacturing, mixing and processing
3. Supplying and rendering services
4. *Nidhi* or mutual benefit schemes
5. The business of financing, investment and chit funds.

To achieve the objectives of social audit, some non-profit-earning organisations such as the Social Audit Limited have been set up in west to ensure corporate responsiveness to public for social interests. In India Tisco made a pioneering effort in this direction by publishing their social audit report in July, 1980 which enumerates the company's contribution to the local community in the form of provisions for housing roads, schools, hospitals, markets, playgrounds, clubs, etc.

OPERATIONAL AUDIT

In the words of Frederic E. Mints an operational audit should aim at making "an appraisal of the way in which a particular operation or activity is administered ; whether its objectives have been clearly defined in conformance with sound business principles and communicated to all concerned ; whether the policies under which it operates conform to the established objectives; whether those policies are implemented by specific procedures and whether the procedures are followed as intended : whether necessary administrative information is accumulated by orderly methods; and whether management is provided with adequate, timely and accurate reports containing information on matters of primary concern."

Operational auditing is the same as internal auditing. Its scope extends to operational (administrative) areas. According to Lawrence Sawyer operational auditing is not a distinct and separate type of auditing which is characterised by special programmes or techniques. It is rather a manner by which the internal auditor approaches his assignment, analyses the subject of his review and regards the results. It is essentially a frame of mind, and a method of approach with which the auditor views his work.

Distinction from Financial Audit

While financial auditing is primarily concerned with the verification of financial statements, establishing the reasonableness of accounts, and interpreting the historical financial data, operational auditing deals, with operating (administrative) controls and is equally at home in financial and non-financial areas. It no doubt uses and analyses historical data, but only with a view to finding ways of improving future business operations.

CONTINUOUS AUDIT

What is Continuous Audit ?

1. R.C. Williams. Continuous audit is "one where the auditor or his staff attends at regular or irregular intervals during the period."

2. Spicer and Peglar. "A continuous audit is one where the auditor's staff is occupied continuously on the accounts the whole year round or where the auditor attends at intervals, fixed or otherwise, during the currency of the financial year, and performs an interim audit; such audits are adopted where the work involved is considerable, and have many points in their favour, although they are subject to certain disadvantages."

Scope of Continuous Audit

The accounts in continuous audit are audited as and when they are prepared. The auditor pays visits at regular or irregular intervals during the year round and examines the accounts. It is necessary only for big business houses and not for small ones where accounts can be audited at the close of the financial year when they are ready.

Continuous audit is applicable in the following cases :

(i) Where it is necessary to prepare final accounts just at the closure of financial year e.g., railways, banks etc.

(ii) Where the transactions are many in number and it is considered necessary to assess them at regular intervals.

(iii) Where the scope of business is wide.

(iv) Where the system of internal check is not satisfactory.

(v) Where the management requires the review of financial position of their concern monthly or quarterly.

Advantages of Continuous Audit

1. Early discovery of errors and frauds. As the auditor visits his clients at regular intervals, he checks the accounts in details discovering errors and frauds easily and quickly. If the accounts were checked at the end of the year, it is not easy to locate an error and the clerks get more opportunities to defraud accounts.

2. Close and Extensive Checking. As the auditor visits the client's office at regular intervals, a detailed, close and exhaustive checking can be possible.

3. Quick Presentation of Accounts. As the accounts are checked throughout the year it becomes possible to present the final audited accounts to the shareholders soon after the close of the financial year.

4. Enforced regularity at client's end. The regular visits performed by the auditor keeps the clerks alert to maintain the accounts up-to-date and accurate as the auditor may land-up in the office any time.

5. Moral Check. As the auditor pays surprise visits to the business it has a considerable moral check on them.

6. Familiarity with technical details. As the auditor comes more and more in touch with the business affairs and its technical details, he can give valuable suggestions to his clients for improving the working of the business and the system of maintaining accounts.

7. Relief to the auditor. The several visits paid by the auditor to the client's office enable his work to proceed easily and smoothly. It increases his confidence in his capacity to do his work efficiently and effectively.

8. Ease in declaring Interim Dividend. Continuous audit helps in preparing interim accounts without much delay, where the directors of a company desire to declare an interim dividend. They will have properly audited accounts to get an idea about the profits actually earned till the date of the declaration.

Disadvantages of Continuous Audit

1. Tampering with figures. In continuous audit, records and figures in the books of accounts which have already been checked by the auditors, may be altered after the audit it over.

2. Interruption of client's work. As the auditor visits the client's office at regular intervals to check the accounts and records, these frequent visits may dislocate the work of his client.

3. Loss of link in work. As the auditor comes at regular intervals to check the accounts the link between the past and present work cannot be maintained.

4. Chances of collusion between client's staff and auditor's staff. Frequent visits of the auditor may establish some unhealthy relationship between client's staff and auditor's staff. Thus there are chances of mitigating moral check upon them and there may be collusion between them.

5. Expensive. A continuous audit is an expensive form of audit, as the more frequent visits by the auditor mean higher fees.

6. Spoon feeding. Frequent visits by the auditor may induce the client's staff to depend upon him even for minor things.

Safeguards against Disadvantages

1. Rules against alteration. There should be strict rules against alteration of figures after they have been checked by the staff of the auditor. If any alteration is necessary the permission to alter the transaction must be obtained from the auditor.

2. Checking in one sitting. The auditor should try to check the accounts of the similar nature in one and continuous sitting as far as possible and note important totals and balances.

3. No loose ends. During the course of each visit, the work should be completed to a particular stage so as to avoid any loose ends as far as possible.

4. Explanations. The explanations of important questions which he finds unsatisfactory should be noted down in his note book.

5. Glance on past. The auditor should glance over the past work done or any alteration before he begins his work.

6. Impersonal accounts in the end. As it is relatively easy to perpetrate fraud in personal accounts by passing corresponding fictitious entries in the impersonal accounts, the auditor should leave the examination of impersonal accounts till the time of final audit. He may confine his work for the present to the vouching of cash transactions, subsidiary books etc.

7. Sensible allocation of work. By a just and sensible allocation of work among its staff, the auditor can prevent the work becoming tedious or boring.

8. Work Rotation. To prevent collusion between audit staff and client's staff the auditor may rotate work among them in such a way that no audit clerk is allowed to check an account from beginning to end.

CONTINUOUS AUDIT AND INTERNAL AUDIT

1. Interval. While continuous audit involves a detailed examination of all the transactions attending at regular intervals, Interim audit implies carrying out of audit work any time during the year or in the middle of financial year in order to find out the interim profit or loss or state of financial affairs of the concern.

2. Objective. While the object of continuous audit is not to ascertain the profit or loss of the undertaking for a given period, the object of Interim Audit is to ascertain and check the profit and loss for a given period.

3. Period of Audit. While in continuous audit the accounting records of one accounting or financial year is examined, in Interim audit accounting records upto a certain date only are checked and examined.

4. Scope of the Audit. While in continuous audit detailed and extensive checking of books of accounts is done, in Interim audit a detailed and extensive checking of books of accounts is not done.

5. Trial Balance. While in continuous audit the Trial Balance is not prepared at intervals, in interim audit the Trial Balance must be prepared and checked at the time of such audit.

6. Administration. While continuous audit is an independent administrative work, internal audit is an integral part of extensive administration system of the concern.

7. Status. While continuous audit is done by an independent and professional auditor, internal audit is done by the internal auditor who is an employee of the concern itself.

8. Auditor's Qualification. While in continuous audit, the auditor must be a Chartered Accountant, in internal audit, the auditor need not possess professional qualification.

9. Auditor's Responsibility. While in continuous audit, the auditor is responsible to shareholders, in internal audit, the auditor is responsible to managers.

10. Report. While in continuous audit the auditor's report is submitted at the end of the financial year, in interim audit there is no question of submitting the report.

11. Verification. While in continuous audit the verification of assets and liabilities are undertaken at the close of financial year, in Interim audit the verification of assets and liabilities are undertaken at the time of such audit.

Continuous Audit and Balance Sheet Audit

1. Period. While in continuous audit the auditor or his staff is constantly engaged in checking the accounts during the whole period, in Balance Sheet audit, the auditor attends only at the end of the financial year.

2. Nature of Audit. While in case of continuous audit detailed and extensive checking of accounts is done, in Balance Sheet audit the work is not done in such details.

3. Suitability. While continuous audit work is suited to very big business concerns, Balance Sheet audit is recommended for small business concerns.

4. Cost. While Continuous audit is expensive, Balance Sheet audit is comparatively cheap.

5. Moral Check. While Continuous audit exerts more moral check upon the staff the moral check upon the client's staff in Balance Sheet audit is comparatively less.

6. Popularity. While Continuous audit is more popular in England, Balance Sheet audit is more popular in America.

AUDIT OF PUBLIC V/S PRIVATE COMPANY

1. Compulsion. The audit of public company has been made compulsory by Indian Companies Act, 1956. The audit of a partnership firm is not compulsory. It depends on the will of the partners.

2. Appointment. In the audit of a Public Limited Company the appointment of auditor is made by the shareholders in their general meeting according to the provisions of the Companies Act. In the case of the audit of a partnership firm the appointment of auditor is made by the agreement between the partners.

3. Scope of audit. In audit of a Public Limited Company the rights and duties of a Company auditor cannot be limited by the Articles of Association of the Company or through any resolution passed in the general meeting. The scope of the audit of a partnership firm may be limited by the partners and in that case the auditor should get clear instructions in writing.

4. Operation. In Public Limited Company audit, the audit work is carried on according to the provisions of Companies Act and according to the decisions of the Court. In case of partnership audit, the audit work is carried on according to the instructions of employer and partnership deed.

5. Qualifications of the Auditor. In Public Limited Company audit, the auditor must be a Chartered Accountant, in case of partnership audit, the auditor need not possess any professional qualifications.

6. Inspection of Papers. In the audit of a Public Limited Company it is necessary to give full knowledge about the memorandum and Articles of the Company to the auditor. In case of the audit of a partnership firm it is not necessary to present the partnership deed before the auditor.

7. Report. In the audit of a Public Company, the auditor has to report to the members of the company. In case of the audit of a partnership firm the auditor has to report to the partners of the firm.

8. Liability. In public limited company audit, the liability of the auditor becomes double-one under common law and the other under Companies Act. The auditor of a partnership firm is liable only for negligence and not for mispeasance.

BALANCE SHEET AUDIT

As compared to other types of audits Balance Sheet Audit is of recent origin. It is more popular in U.S.A. Balance Sheet Audit will be more widely used in future due to the development of industries and consequently the establishment of larger economic units. The term "balance sheet audit" means verification of the values of assets, liabilities, the balances of reserves and provisions and the amount of profit earned, or loss suffered by a firm during the year.

According Prof. Howard F. Stettler the audit which concentrates on the balance sheet must include some review of operations. For example, repairs and maintenance expense accounts should be reviewed to ascertain whether any expenditures of a capital nature have been improperly expensed. However, the item Profit and Loss Account does appear in the balance sheet. The auditor who conducts balance sheet audit does review the transactions which appear in the profit and loss account.

According to Prof. Stettler the "balance sheet audit" and its lengthier counterpart are now being replaced by the more accurate and descriptive term "examination of financial statements", because the balance sheet alone is not considered to be an adequate basis for making credit for the credit granter. Examination of financial statement is a brief form of audit. It avoids cursory review of the income statement. The opinion of the auditor is expressed both on the balance sheet and the profit and loss account.

Balance Sheet Audit v/s Post and Vouch Audit

While in Balance Sheet Audit procedural tests are applied, in the case of Vouch and Post Audit, the auditor takes the most important items which have a great bearing on the balance sheet and the routine audit is reduced to a great extent. Thus in the Balance Sheet Audit the items which have no bearing on the final accounts do not come under the review of the auditor.

Procedure

1. Examination of Minute Book. The auditor should examine the minute book of the concern, especially those items which have a bearing on the accounts.

2. Examination of Profit and Loss Account. The auditor should examine and compare the profit and loss account with that of the previous year to see whether there is any material difference between the two.

3. Comparison of Expenses. The auditor should compare the increase or decrease in the expenses between the two periods with turnover, making necessary adjustment regarding allowances, sales tax or any other variations during the period under reviews.

4. Investigation of Variation. The auditor should investigate into the causes of any variation in the gross profit and pay attention to the valuation of closing stock.

5. Examination of Depreciation. The auditor should see whether there has been any change in the rate of depreciation charged during the current year and if so, what is its effect on the revenue account.

6. Examination of Non-recurring items. The auditor should investigate into the items of non-recurring nature, e.g., profit made or loss suffered on the sale of a fixed asset.

7. Valuation of Assets. The auditor should pay attention to any substantial change in the fixed assets as compared to the previous year especially regarding the valuation of assets.

8. Enquiry into Variation of Assets. The auditor should inquire into any variation in the current assets as compared to previous year.

9. Examination of Pre-payment and Accruals. If there is any material alteration in the pre-payments and the accruals, the auditor should pay attention to such a variation.

10. Examination of other items. The auditor should pay attention to other items of the balance sheet for any substantial change from the normal figure.

11. Verification of Assets and Liabilities. The author should verify the assets held and liabilities owing.

12. Commitment and Losses. The auditor should ascertain whether any capital commitment exists and whether there is any item on which a subsequent loss may arise and whether any provision has been made thereof.

Role of Auditor

As the auditor checks only the items appearing on the balance sheet he does not check all the transactions taking place. However, Section 227(3) of the Chartered Accountants Act requires him to state in his report *inter alia,* "whether the balance sheet and the profit and loss account dealt with by the report are in agreement with the books of account and returns". He performs his duty dishonestly when he signs such financial statements without checking. Though the law does not prescribe any procedure or lays down any method by which the audit of a firm is to be conducted, however, the auditor may do so if he is satisfied that he has discharged his duties and responsibilities by conducting the balance sheet audit.

Under Balance Sheet audit, the audit is commenced from the balance sheet working back to the books of original entry and the relative documents, etc. The conventional method of vouching and costing, posting, etc., are dispensed with.

Limitations

"Balance Sheet Audit" is an American term having the following two limitations :

1. Limited audit. It is a limited audit in which all the balance sheet accounts are verified and tests imposed only on those profit and loss items which are directly related to the assets such as repairs and maintenance, depreciation or bad debts. These accounts are analysed, but otherwise no detailed audit is conducted.

2. Tests for specific period. The balance sheet audit tests are imposed on internal control but generally for a specific period. The transactions for the closing months of the year are closely scrutinised. Further tests include scrutiny of records, comparison of income and expenses, investigation of material fluctuations and analysis of appropriation accounts.

Suggestions for Improvements

Balance Sheet Audit may prove to be more efficient in a good system of internal check or control in operation. It can prove to be more efficient in following situation:

(i) in big business concerns where the volume of transactions is very large,

(ii) where there is a good and efficient system of internal check and control,

(iii) where qualified accountants are employed, and

(iv) where mechanised accounting system is in operation.

The audit work like vouching and costing which is considered necessary under the normal audit, is dispensed with in Balance Sheet Audit.

AUDITING IN DEPTH

According to Taylor and Perry, "Auditing in depth implies the examination of the system applied within a business, entailing the tracing of certain transactions from their origin to their conclusion, investigating at each stage the records created and their appropriate authorisation". It is a method according to which a few selected transactions are subjected to a thorough scrutiny in forming an opinion as regards the accuracy of the date so scrutinised. In it the auditor has to examine a few transactions in detail, i.e., from the origin of the transactions to their conclusion. These transactions are traced through various stages from the beginning to their end. Every record maintained relating to a them is scrutinised, to see whether a very efficient internal check and control system is in operation.

The auditor should make the following enquiries in "audit in depth".

1. Demand for purchase. The auditor should inquire whether there was a demand from the storekeeper or the godown keeper to the administrative officer or the purchase department that such and such goods having reached the minimum or the ordering level should be purchased.

2. Tenders. The auditor should enquire whether the tenders were invited for the purchase of the goods.

3. Order by Authority. The auditor should check whether the order was placed by an authorised person.

4. Delivery note. The auditor should examine the delivery note.

5. Inspection Report. The auditor should examine the inspection report of the technical supervisor that the goods are according to the order placed and the invoice from the suppliers of the goods.

6. Invoice. The auditor should examine the invoice.

7. Registration. The auditor should see whether the goods were entered in the stock register and the bin cards (if in use) by the storekeeper or the godown keeper.

8. Entries. The auditor should examine the necessary entries regarding the purchase in the purchase journals, ledger and the relative vouchers.

9. Payments. The auditor should see whether the account of the supplier had been credited with the correct amount according to the invoice.

The technique "auditing in depth" may be followed in large firms but it is not suitable for the small firms as in them the internal system is not in existence and all the entries in the books of account have to be checked by the auditor. The auditor should resort to depth auditing only when he is satisfied with the efficacy of the internal check system which enables the auditor to decide how far he should apply the technique of auditing in depth. Therefore, he should select only those transactions which are material in relation to the affairs of the company as a whole. However, he should also select a number of entries and the nature of the business.

This system will enable the auditor to satisfy himself as to the efficiency or otherwise of the system of internal checks in operation. He will also know whether the procedure for the receipt and payment of cash, purchase and sale of goods, etc. as prescribed has been properly followed or not. He will be able to find out the weak points of the existing procedures for making entries in the books of account. Therefore, he may suggest to the management a better procedure for recording the transactions to avoid any loopholes for committing frauds.

VOUCH AND POST AUDIT

In vouch and post audit the auditor checks each and every transaction right from its origin in the books of prime entries till they are posted. It is not used in the case of large firms where the numbers of transactions run into millions and where a good internal check system is prevalent or where the mechanised system of accounting has been introduced. The auditor relies on the examination of some of the transactions scientifically selected at random.

Procedure

The following procedure may be adopted in Vouch and Post Audit.

For additions, postings, ledger balances, carry forwards, etc., distinctive ticks of different colours should be adopted. Their significance should not be made known to the clerks of the client. The same kind of 'tick' should not be used for every firm and for the same kind of transactions or for all the visits. The work of checking of one book should be completed at one sitting as far as possible otherwise some fraudulent alterations may be made by the clerks after the audit clerk has left the office for the day. On the next visit, the auditor should check that there has been no alteration by rubber or by scratching of the work he had already checked on the previous visit. If it has been done, the auditor should get an explanation and check the whole of the work again. No alteration of a figure should be allowed. If any adjustment is found to be necessary, it should be made by a journal entry. Special ticks should be used for figures which had already been erased. The auditor should write the correct figure with his own ink just close to the erased one and tick his own figure or he may put a circle around the erased figure with a coloured pencil. If the clients have put the total figures with pencil, the auditor should refuse to start his work until these figures are inked. If the audit clerk is asked to check the books, he will be acting in the capacity of an accountant rather than an auditor. Sometime, the auditor is asked to begin the audit work even before, the balancing of books, in order to compete the audit in a short time. In this procedure there is danger of the errors being overlooked because there has been so clerical test like the preparation of the trial balance. An auditor must not certify what he does not believe to be true. Hence no report about transaction should be passed unless he understands it.

The auditor should not discuss anything about the meaning of different 'ticks' etc., lest the client's-staff should know about it. It should be carried out by two clerks, the senior examining the voucher and calling out the amount and the junior comparing the amount and placing a special tick against the item in the Cash Book. The audit clerk must be very clear in speaking out the figures, otherwise mistakes may crop in. Work done by each clerk should be recorded in the Audit Note Book which is known by different names such as Working Papers, Audit Notes, Memoranda, etc.

QUESTIONS FOR EXERCISE

1. Classify Audit according to different bases.
2. What are the different kinds of audit? Give the merits and demerits of each.
3. What is social audit ? Discuss its importance.
4. What is cost audit ? For whom is it statutory ?
5. Write short note on Operational Audit.
6. What is meant by continuous audit and to what class of business is it especially applicable ? State briefly the advantages and disadvantages of such an audit.

7. What do you understand by 'continuous audit' ? State the advantages of, and objections to, an audit of this nature. Suggest ways to guard against its shortcomings.
8. Distinguish between:
   (a) Continuous Audit and Interim Audit.
   (b) Continuous Audit and Internal Audit.
   (c) Continuous Audit and Balance Sheet Audit or Final Audit.
9. How would you compare Continuous Audit with Internal Audit? What are the points of similarity and dissimilarity between them?
10. In what respects do the position and duties of an auditor of a public company differ from those of an auditor of a private firm.
11. Write short-note on Distinction between Interim Audit and Internal Audit.
12. What is meant by Balance Sheet Audit ? Give a programme to be followed in such an audit ?
13. Distinguish between Balance Sheet Audit and Post and Vouch Audit. What is the role of Auditor in a Balance Sheet Audit ?
14. Write short note on -
    (a) Auditor in Depth,
    (b) Vouch and Post Audit.

3

The Auditor: Qualities, Qualifications, Appointment and Rights

An auditor must possess certain professional and personal qualities which help in performing his duties efficiently and honestly.

Professional Qualities

1. *Expertness in accounts and their interpretation.* The auditor must possess thorough knowledge of all the systems of Accountancy in use. He should be able to read the various scripts in which the accounts may be kept, e.g, English, Hindi, Muria, or Marwari. He is supposed to know how to record facts in accounts, and to understand the significance of the facts in their relation to the past, present and future of the business. He acts both as a reporter and an analyst. He has to deal with the various systems of Accountancy in different businesses. He must be capable of understanding their methods of preparation.

2. *Knowledge of Organisation and Method.* The auditor must have considerable knowledge about the organisation and operational methods of various types of business concerns. He should be able to grasp various technical details though he is not expected to have as intimate knowledge of business as the client whom he serves.

3. *Mastery of various techniques of auditing.* Mere knowledge of accountancy, though essential, would not help the auditor as the art of auditing is quite different from accountancy. He must not think that if the trial balance and the Balance Sheet agrees, everything else is all right. Agreement of trial balance may show only arithmetical accuracy. His duty is not to check arithmetical accuracy alone.[1] At the same time he must avoid thinking and talking as a book-keeper. He must keep himself in touch with the advancements in the techniques of auditing.

1. *Deputy Secretary to the Government of India,* Ministry of Finance v. S.N. Das Gupta (1955).

4. *Knowledge of Principles and Practices of Business laws.* The auditor must be familiar with the principles and practice of various business laws that may affect his profession. Though he is not expected to have sufficient legal training, he must possess thorough knowledge of various common and statutory laws relating to contracts, sales, agency, negotiable instruments, partnership, company or bankruptcy etc. He must also have knowledge of economic and financial matters.

Personal Qualities

1. *Integrity and Moral Courage.* An auditor must be a man of integrity and moral courage capable of solving intricate problems patiently. His duty is not to his client alone but to the public and other parties also. He must carry on his duties faithfully without being led or influenced by others. Sometimes, he may find himself in a position when his own interests clash with those of his client. Under such circumstances, he must act tactfully and honestly without thinking of his own loss. In making decisions regarding the client's affairs, which may or may not be in accordance with his wishes, he must try to be absolutely impartial, unbiased and independent.

2. *No Complexes.* An auditor must never adopt an attitude of suspicion nor should he go about his work with an air of superiority or conceit.[2] He should not be hasty to criticise. He should give full weight to assertions and opinions of the client's staff. He must try to develop a spirit of mutual trust and goodwill between himself and the members of his client's staff. He should instruct his own staff to create a cordial atmosphere, though, friendliness should not be carried to the point of familiarity as it might involve loss of independence.

3. *Honesty.* The auditor must work honestly. He must not issue a report containing statements which he has reason to believe to be untrue or misleading. Lord Justice Lindley said "An auditor must be honest—that is he must not certify what he dose not believe to be true and he must take reasonable care and skill before he believes that what he certifies is true."[3]

4. *Confidential.* The auditor must understand that the nature of his work is confidential. He must not, therefore, divulge to others what he has learnt about his client during the course of auditing.[4] He will commit breach of moral duty if he does so.

---

2. In *re Kingston Cotton Mills* (1896), Lord Justice Lopse said, "An auditor is not bound to be a detective or, as was said to approach his work with suspicion, or with the foregone conclusion that there is something wrong."
3. In *re London and General Bank,* 1895.
4. Chartered Accountants Act, 1949, Second Schedule, Part I (I).

5. *Care, Firmness and Patience.* The auditor must exercise constant care, firmness and patience, he should never do his work mechanically.[5] He must possess an inquiring mind. He should never display false pride of being an expert just because his ignorance may be exposed. He should always seek clarity and elucidation on technical matters which he does not follow by discussions with those who know them. He must not pass any transaction unless he finds it to be true and in order.

6. *Sincerity.* The auditor must be sincere in his profession. He must follow the professional ethics, customs and regulations properly. He should do nothing which may turn out to be a blot on his profession. He should keep the professional standards in his mind and must follow them.

7. *Practical.* The auditor must be practical in his approach while giving advice to his clients as and when desired by the latter. He must appreciate the practical needs and circumstances of the business. He should give such advice as may fit in the particular situation. While doing so he may ignore such concepts which may be theoretically correct but may not be suitable in the particular circumstances. It is not part of his duty to give advice but if his advice is sought he should willingly give it without insisting that it must be implemented.

8. *Sound common sense.* "The auditor should have a full share of that most valuable commodity—common sense.[6] A thorough training in all the branches of theory may be of little use to him when he will be called upon to apply his common sense. He must have ability to discriminate between the essentials and non-essentials.

Importance of Independence

Unless the auditor is independent of management or his client, his opinion is no more acceptable than the statements of accounts prepared by the management. As the auditor is not an employee of the business, this situation alone creates considerable independence, but independence is also an attitude of mind. That is why his report becomes the charter of business confidence and his findings are held in high esteem. Independent thought and action are as important as independent relationship between the auditor and his client.[7] Independence implies that "the judgement of a person is not subordinate to the wishes or directions of another person who might have engaged him or to his own self-interest." The reports submitted by the

5. In re *The City Equitable Fire Insurance Co. Ltd.*, 1924, Justice Romer said, "If an auditor has even in one instance, fallen short of the strict duty of an auditor, he cannot, I apprehend, be excused merely because in general he has displayed the highest degree of care and skill."
6. Spicer and Pegler, *Practical Auditing,* p. 32
7. H.A. Settler, *Auditing Principles.* p. 18.

auditor may continue to have some value only so long as he enjoys the reputation of being independent. His impartiality is the cornerstone of the trust placed in his findings, but he can remain unbiased or impartial only when he is independent to act. His difficulty in being independent arises because of the fact that he has to serve two masters. He must please his client as well as all others who are interested in the client's business or financial statements under such circumstances he will have to act very carefully. Much tact and prudence is required of him. There is always a natural desire to please a client, but this might result in giving a misleading report. If loss of independence to a certain extent does not come in the way of his duties, legal as well as contractual, he may remain dependent to that extent. However, he must try to remain independent as far as desirable for fulfilling his duties otherwise the very purpose of his appointment will be jeopardised. It is necessary specially in case of a joint stock company where the management may put some pressure on him in self-interest. But he must remember that he has to serve his real master, *i.e.* the shareholders.

Programming Independence

Hussain A. Sharaf and R.K. Mautz[8] have suggested the following guidelines under each of the dimensions or components of independence of an auditor:

1. Freedom from managerial interference or friction intended to eliminate, specify, or modify any portion of the audit.
2. Freedom from interference with or an uncooperative attitude respecting the application of selected procedures.
3. Freedom from any outside attempts to subject the audit work to review other than that provided for in the audit process.

Investigating Independence

1. Direct and free access to all company books, records, officers and employees, and other sources of information with respect to business activities, obligations, and resources.
2. Active co-operation from managerial personnel during the course of the auditor's examination.
3. Freedom from any managerial attempt to assign or specify the activities to be examined or to establish the acceptability of evidential matter.
4. Freedom from personal interest or relationship leading to exclusion of limitation of the examination of any activity, record, or person that otherwise would have been included in the audit.

---

8. J.C. Ray, *An Operational Concept of Independence in Independent Auditing Standards,* p. 75.

Reporting Independence

1. Freedom from any of loyalty or obligation to modify the impact of reported facts on any party.
2. Avoidance of the practice of excluding significant matters from the formal report in favour of their inclusion in an informal report of any kind.
3. Avoidance of internal or unintentional use of ambiguities of language in the statement of facts, opinion, and recommendations and in their interpretations.
4. Freedom from any attempt to over-rule the auditor's judgement as to appropriate content of the audit report, either factual matter or his opinion.

STATUTORY PROVISIONS

Provisions have been made in the Companies Act, 1956, Chartered Accountants Act, 1949, and the Cost Accountant Act, 1959 for ensuring independence of an auditor.

1. The Companies Act, 1956. (a) It has laid down specific conditions which may make a person disqualified to act as auditor of a company; (b) the right to appoint an auditor has been given to the shareholders; (c) an auditor can be removed before the expiry of his term only with the previous approval of the Central Government; (d) a retiring auditor, who is not being reappointed, or who is being removed before the expiry of the term, has the right to make written representations to the members of the company and he can be heard orally at the general meeting.

2. Chartered Accountant Act, 1949. It prohibits auditors the acceptance of contingent fees. An auditor may be held guilt for professional misconduct, if he expresses his opinion on financial statements of any business or any enterprise in which he, his firm or a partner in his firm has a "substantial interest", unless he discloses the interest also in his report. The Council of Institute of Chartered Accountants of India has also, by a notification, specified that a member of the Institute shall be deemed to be guilty of professional misconduct, if he expresses an opinion on financial statements of any business or enterprise in which one or more persons who are the "relatives", within the meaning of section 6 of the Companies Act, have either by themselves or in conjunction with such a member who has a substantial interest; unless he discloses the interest also. The auditors should also try to avoid the situations when there are some conflicts between them.

AUDITOR OF A SOLE TRADER

From 1984 Audit of business concerns, whose annual turnover exceeds Rs. 20 lacks has been made compulsory. In case of professions also, it has been made compulsory, if its annual gross receipts exceed Rs. 10 lacks.

1. Appointment. In case of sole trader an auditor is appointed under a contract with the trader. Their mutual agreement specifies the terms and conditions of his appointment. This agreement may be in writing or oral. But it is advisable to have it in writing as emphasised in *Apfe*l v. *Annan Dexter & Co.* (1926).

The auditor should make it clear whether his appointment is for auditing only or also for writing the books of account. If he is appointed simply to maintain accounts and not to audit them, he must be cautious that his signature at the footnote of the Balance Sheet may not be utilized by his client for obtaining loans or for securing a partner or for affecting the sale of the business or even for holding him responsible as an 'auditor' for any inaccuracy in accounts. In such a case the auditor must not simply sign as chartered accountant but qualify his signature with the words "Prepared from the books without verification" so that he may not be held responsible as to the accuracy of the Balance Sheet prepared by him.

2. Remuneration. The auditors remuneration depends upon the conditions of the agreement entered into with the client. There are no legal provisions for this. His remuneration should not depend upon the results of his work but upon the basis of extent of work undertaken by him. For example, it should not be fixed on the condition that he will be paid only if he could detect certain suspected fraud.

3. Rights and Duties. In a sole trading concern, the auditor's duties are not statutory but customary and moral. He has to exercise reasonable care and skill in the performance of his duties. He should carry on his audit work intelligently, honestly and with due care. He should take pains in verifying the incomes and expenditures etc. He should examine the books of account thoroughly as the transactions in most of the cases would not be numerous. He should satisfy himself as to the correctness of the accounts. He should obtain all the necessary informations and seek explanations, wherever necessary. After he has carefully audited the accounts of the concern, he must submit a report duly signed by him.

AUDITOR OF A PARTNERSHIP FIRM

From 1984, Audit of a firm's accounts has been made legally compulsory for those firms whose annual turnover exceeds Rs. 20 lacks.

1. Appointment and Remuneration. The appointment and remuneration of an auditor depends upon the agreement with the client. There are no statutory requirements for it. In case of the sole trader he must see all those points mentioned earlier.

2. Rights. The rights and duties of an auditor of a firm are customary and moral. He has a right to see the Partnership Deed of the firm which contains the various terms and conditions regulating the functioning of the partnership firm. He has a right to see the books of account of the firm. He has a right to seek explanations and secure informations if he feels necessary. He has a right to receive his remuneration for the audit work done by him.

3. Duties. The auditor must perform his work with reasonable care, honesty and intelligence. He must satisfy himself with regard to the correctness of the accounts. He must see that the rules and regulations laid down in the Partnership Deed or, in the absence of such Deed, as given in the Indian Partnership Act, 1932, have been duly observed, otherwise he must bring the facts to the notice of the partners in clear words.

After the examination of the books of account is over, he must submit his report bringing the correct situation of the financial affairs of the firm to the knowledge of the partners. Finally, he should render necessary advice if he is called upon by the client to do so.

AUDITOR OF A LIMITED COMPANY

In India, the company audit has been made compulsory by the Indian Companies Act, 1956. It contains provisions with regard to company audit and the auditor. It provides for the appointment, remuneration, removal, duties and qualifications etc. of a company auditor. Sections 224 to 233 of the Act cover various provisions related to the company auditor. It is the law and not the contract which governs the auditor of a company unlike the auditor of the sole traders or partnerships. These provisions are necessary to ensure the independence of the company auditors so that they may be able to serve the interest of shareholders of the company and arouse their confidence in general in company form of business enterprises.

QUALIFICATIONS OF AN AUDITOR

Provisions of the Chartered Accountant Act, 1949

1. Section 226. It lays down qualifications with the object of ensuring that a person possesses adequate educational qualifications needed for a serious profession like auditing and that he is independent of all influences, controls, and personal interests in the company. It states, a person shall not be qualified for appointment as auditor of a company unless he is a Chartered Accountant within the meaning of Chartered Accountants Act, 1949. The Central Government has the power to recognise foreign qualifications to enable a person to become the member of the Institute.

2. Section 25. No company whether incorporated in India or elsewhere shall practise as chartered accountants. Only a chartered accountant holding a certificate of practice granted by the Institute of Chartered Accountants of India can practise and be engaged in the public practice of accountancy.

3. Section 226(i). It provides that a firm whereof all the partners practising in India are qualified for appointment as auditor may be appointed by its firm's name to be the auditor of the company in which case any partner so practising may act in the name of the firm. However, if a chartered accountant is practising as a sole proprietor, he can be appointed as an auditor only as an individual and not in the name of his 'firm'. This means that a practising chartered accountant, a firm of practising chartered accountants or a restricted state auditor can be appointed as the auditor of a company subject to the conditions:

(a) that he does not suffer from any of the five disqualifications stated in Secs. 226(3) and 226(4),

(b) the audit so given does not exceed the limits specified in Sec. 224(1B).

The Restricted Auditors

Under Sec.226(2) a person who holds a certificate under the Restricted Auditors Certificate (Part B States) Rules, 1951, is also qualified to act as an auditor of a company no matter registered anywhere in India. However, the Central Government may, by notification in the Official Gazette, make rules providing for the grant, renewal, suspension or cancellation of such certificates to persons and may prescribe conditions and restrictions for such purposes [Sec. 226(2)(b)].

Certified Auditors

A person who holds a certificate under the Certified Auditors' Rules, 1961, can act as an auditor anywhere in India.

Disqualifications of a Company Auditor

1. Section 226(3). It provides that none of the following persons shall be qualified for appointment as auditor of a company:

1. a body corporate,
2. an officer or an employee of the company,
3. a person who is a partner, or how is in the employment as an officer or employee of the company, and
4. a person who is indebted to the company for an amount exceeding one thousand rupees, or who has given any guarantee or provided any security in connection with the indebtedness of any third person to the company for an amount exceeding one thousand rupees.

A person who, for one of the above reasons, cannot be appointed as auditor of the company's holding or subsidiary companies or co-subsidiary companies cannot be so appointed as an auditor for the company.

2. Section 226(4). It states that a person shall also not be qualified for appointment as auditor of a company if he is, by virtue of sub-section (3) disqualified for appointment as auditor of any other body corporate which is that company's subsidiary holding company, or would be so disqualified if the body corporate were a company.

An auditor, who after his appointment becomes subject to any of the above disqualification, shall be deemed to have vacated his office as an auditor thereby causing a casual vacancy.

The guiding objectives of Sec. 226 are to ensure that (i) an auditor has the adequate educational qualifications for the accountancy profession, (ii) he is independent of all influences, controls and personal interests in the company. For that reason the list of disqualification stated in Sec.226(3) can be and has been enlarged from time to time.

Who Disqualify under Sec. 226(3) and (4)

1. Company undertaking Accounting/auditing — Sec. 226. It exclusively aims at ensuring that the auditor is completely independent of the companies he audits and shall be fully responsible for any act of negligence on their part. Every body corporate has a distinct status than that of its members and a company undertaking public accounting/auditing work will have limited liability independent of its members and hence cannot be appointed as an auditor.

2. Officer or Employee. An officer or an employee of the company will naturally feel more concerned about his salaries/allowances and obviously should not be allowed to act as an auditor in the interest of a company and of auditor's independence and its preservation.

3. Relatives of director or partner. There seems to be no bar on a director's relative or partner of such relative to be appointed as auditor though there exist conflicting views on this count. One group of experts believe that Sec. 297(i) does not apply for such an appointment. The Company Law Committee of the Institute of Chartered Accountants of India opines that Sec. 297(i) does apply. It can, however, be deducted by operation of other sections that while a partner or an employee of a director of a company cannot be appointed as auditor of the company, a relative of a director can be so appointed if the annual remuneration does not exceed Rs.6,000. Where it does exceed Rs. 6000 per annum, a relative of the director can be appointed as auditor of the company only by a special resolution, and in appropriate cases the Central Government's prior permission as required under Sec.314.

4. Indebted person. The disqualification coming under the Rs. 1,000 indebtedness clause needs explanations. If in accordance with a resolution passed in the shareholders general meeting the auditor receives his fees on a progressive basis, he cannot be held as indebted to the company at any stage (as per opinion of Research Committee of ICAI). If an auditor purchases goods over the same credit and other conditions allowed normally to other customers, the auditor is deemed to be indebted to the company and hence stands disqualified. If the firm of which the auditor is a partner, stands indebted to the company in excess of Rs. 1,000, the partner is disqualified from appointment as an auditor. In case the partner is indebted in excess of the prescribed limit the firm will stand disqualified.

5. Professional misconduct. According to the Second Schedule Clause II of the Chartered Accountants' Act, a chartered accountant in practice shall be deemed to be guilty of professional misconduct, if he expresses his opinion on the financial statements of any enterprise, in which he, his firm or a partner in his firm or any of his firm or any of his relatives have a substantial interest unless he discloses the interest also in his report. In this connection the term relatives is to be constructed with reference to Sec. 6 of the Companies Act and substantial interest corresponds to the earning as given thereto under Explanation 3 to Sec. 13 of the Income Tax Act, 1961. This by itself is not a disqualification but does refer to a serious disability if not reported.

6. Employer-employee relationship. Sec 226(e) does not disqualify an auditor to act as an adviser to the same company under audit in the matters of finance, taxation, management, and allied areas simultaneously, provided he does not become an employee of the company. If he does enter into some sort of employer-employee relationship he *ipso facto* becomes disqualified and must vacate his office. However, he can be appointed as an auditor if his employee acts as a director, secretary or otherwise an officer of the company. For example, a registrar is not an officer of the company if his contract with the company is 'for service' and 'not of service'. Similarly, a financial adviser or consultant is not a servant of the company unless the company has the right to control his services.

7. Listed disqualifications. An auditor should be deemed to have vacated his office, the moment he becomes subject to any of the listed disqualifications after his appointment.

8. Sec. 8. A chartered accountant is also subject to the disabilities contained in Sec. 8 of the Chartered Accountant Act, 1949.

APPOINTMENT OF A COMPANY AUDITOR

Appointment of a company auditor is significant because he is the only 'on the spot' spokesman of the shareholders—the real owner of the company. The law zealously guards the shareholders' right to appoint the auditor. It provides to the Board limited powers and those too arising only in certain circumstances. For example, in order to let the company work, the first auditors may be appointed by the Directors. If shareholders do not appoint an auditor or fail to appoint an auditor thereto, the central government may do so. Besides there may special auditors or cost-audit be specially ordered.

Shareholders' Special Privileges to Appoint Auditors

Except in the case of appointment of the first auditors and auditors to fill the casual vacancy, the shareholders have the exclusive right to appoint the auditor because he holds a position of trust *vis-a-vis* the shareholders. The Central Government acts only in special circumstances and not in all cases. An auditor can perform his duties well as a trustee only when he is independent of the management. It should be ensured that the management does not have any hand in his appointment. However, all this seems to be a purely abstract imagination because the shareholders themselves are dependent on management.

First Auditors of a Company

Being an artificial body created by law with a clear-cut separation between the owners and the management a company requires some sort of a check machinery right from its inception, generally exercised through the auditors. A company and an auditor go hand-in-hand. The first auditor are those auditors who are appointed to do the first audit of the company. Section 224(5) lays down all about appointments of first auditors. The main aspect in terms of this section are as follows:

1. The first auditors are generally to be appointed by the Board of Directors by means of a resolution.
2. The Board must exercise this power within one month of the date of registration of the company.
3. The auditors shall hold office until the conclusion of the first annual general meeting.
4. If the Board of Directors fail to appoint the first auditors, the company at a general meeting may do so.
5. The auditors so appointed by the Board of Directors may be removed by the company at a general meeting which may appoint any other auditor provided, (i) a nomination for appointment of new auditors has been made by any member of the company; (ii) the said nomination notice has been given to the members not less than fourteen days before the date of the meeting; and (ii) a copy of the nomination has been sent to the existing auditor who is given a statutory right to (a) make a written representation to the company, (b) to have such representation sent to the members, (c) to have it read at the meeting; (d) to be heard on the nomination resolution at the meeting.

6. An auditor cannot be appointed as first auditor if his name has been stated in the Articles of Association as it will be a defective appointment. However, such an appointment is valid if decided by a resolution either of the directors or that of the shareholders in general meeting.
7. Legally, the first auditor should not be intimated by the company of their appointment as first auditors.
8. The first auditors are themselves not require to inform the Registrar of Companies about their acceptance or refusal of such an appointment.
9. It should be merely a general meeting and not necessarily an annual general meeting in which such a removal/appointment is made.

Subsequent Auditors

Sec.224(1) of Chartered Accountant Act, 1949 spells out the mode of appointment of subsequent auditors of a company as follows:

1. It should be appointed by the company and not, in any case, by the Board of Directors at each annual general meeting.
2. They will hold office from the conclusion of that meeting until the conclusion of the next annual general meeting.
3. Within seven days of such an appointment the company shall give information thereof to every auditor so appointed.
4. According to Sub-sec. (I-A) within thirty days of the receipt from the company of the intimation of his appointment every auditor so appointed shall inform the Registrar in writing that he has accepted or refused to accept the appointment.
5. The auditor so appointed must give the notice to the Registrar in Form No. 23-B prescribed under the Companies Act, for which no filling fee is to be charged by the Registrar.

Statutory Limits on the Number of Audits

Appointment of an auditor under Sec. 224(1) is subject to a written certificate submitted by him to the company stating that his appointment or reappointment, if made, will be in accordance with the limits specified in Sub-sec. (1B). As a result of the Companies Amendment Act, 1974, on and from 1st February 1975, a person or firm cannot be an auditor of more than twenty companies at a time. He can have ten large companies, i.e. having paid up share capital of Rs.25 lacks or more, and ten small companies or less than large companies and the balance in small companies. This ceiling was imposed in order to have rotation and fair distribution of audits among a larger number of auditors instead of these being concentrated in a few hands.

Computation of Specified Ceiling

Statutory Limits on the specified number of 20 companies is subject to following provisions:

1. In the case of a firm of auditors. The ceiling here is applicable per partner. Accordingly, two partner-auditors in a firm not holding any audits in their personal capacity or as partners of other firms not the total audits with them can be 40, each partner being entitled to audit 20 companies of which not more than ten should be large companies.

2. Where any partner of a firm is also a partner of any other firm. Here the ceiling will be determined by taking into account the number of the firms, i.e. the total number of audits held by him individually and by different firms on his account, must be considered in determining whether or not he is holding more than the specified number of audits. If one of the partners is also a partner in some other firm of auditors and have 5 small companies to his name, he cannot have 20 audits in the first firm of auditors, as all the firms in which he is partner or proprietor will be together entitled to 20 company audits on his account, subject to the sub-ceiling of 10 large company audits.

3. Where any partner of a firm is also holding office in his individual capacity. Here the ceiling would apply to him in the aggregate.

4. Joint Auditors. In case a company appoints joint auditors, each part audit would be counted as one audit, i.e. both the firms shall count separately the joint audit assignment as one company audit.

5. All types. The specified number shall include all types of companies including non-profit companies and the companies limited by guarantee.

6. The exclusions or the non-applicability. These are as follows:

(i) The specified number shall not include branch audits. An auditor doing audit work of one company and its 19 branches has actually one company audit. He can go for 19 other company audits. Sections 228 does not equate branch auditors and company auditors and Circular no. 21 of 1975 issued by the Department of Company Affairs clarifies that branch audits should be excluded.

(ii) 'Non-Company audits' or 'to jobs rendering other services'.

(iii) Special audits, investigation and audit of corporations set up under a separate Act.

(iv) Audits of the accounts of foreign companies.

APPOINTMENT BY CENTRAL GOVERNMENT

Under Sec.224(3) the Central Government gets power of the Chartered Accountant Act, 1949 to appoint the auditor of a company where auditors are not appointed or re-appointed at an annual general meeting in terms of

Sections 225, 190 or 188. Similarly, where a company is required to appoint an auditor at an annual general meeting by a special resolution, but omits or fails to pass such a resolution due to any reasons, it shall be deemed that no auditor has been appointed by the company and the central government will become eligible to appoint an auditor. The company shall within seven days of the central government's power [under Sub-sec.(3)] becoming exercisable, gives notice of that fact to the government. If a company fails to give such notice the company and every officer of the company who is in default, shall be punishable with a fine that may extend upto Rs. 500.

In all such matters the power of the central government has been delegated to the regional directors to whom an application must be made as and when the appointment by the central government becomes necessary. Accordingly, the company must notify to the Regional Director within one week of the power becoming exercisable. There is no prescribed form of application, though it must mention the circumstances in which the company failed to appoint an auditor in its annual general meeting. From a panel of names suggested by the applicant company and after ascertaining the antecedents of the auditors concerned from the records of Department of Company Affairs the central government will appoint for the company. It has separate powers for appointing Special Auditors for the government companies.

COMPULSORY RE-APPOINTMENT OF RETIRING AUDITOR

The shareholders enjoy an exclusive right about appointment of the auditors. This fact indicates many essentials of proper auditing in general, and independence of the auditor, in particular. An auditor may have some doubts or disagreement regarding the true and fair state of affairs as transmitted by the accounts so prepared by the management. The law ensures that the fact that the auditors disagree with the management should not be a justification for their displacement. They can be displaced only when shareholders no longer have confidence in the judgment, competence or conduct of the auditors as their representatives. A resolution must be passed to re-appoint even a retiring auditor.

Section 224(2) stipulates that subject to the provision of Sub-sec. (1-B) and Sec.224-A at annual general meeting, a retiring auditor, by whatsoever authority appointed, shall be reappointed except in the following cases:

1. If he is not qualified for reappointment;
2. If he has given a notice in writing of his unwillingness to be re-appointed;
3. A resolution (of which special notice, the 14 days' notice has already been given) is passed to the effect that he shall not be reappointed or that somebody else be appointed in his place; and

4. Where notice has been given of an intended resolution to appoint someone else in place of the retiring auditor and the resolution cannot be proceeded with, on account of death, incapacity or disqualification of the proposed auditor.

Thus, the law tries to ensure that the auditor enjoys an effective degree of independence because, except for the above reasons he cannot be replaced. Their disagreement with the management is not valid defence for their removal or displacement. However, in exceptional cases where no general meeting has been held and no auditor appointed for two years, the retiring auditor is deemed to be re-appointed without any resolution being passed provided he is qualified and he has not given the company, a written notice of his unwillingness to act.

APPOINTMENT UNDER CASUAL VACANCY

Section 224(6)(a) states 'The Board may fill any casual vacancy in the office of an auditor, but while any such vacancy continues, the remaining auditor or auditors, if any, may act; provided that where such vacancy is caused by the resignation of an auditor, the vacancy shall only be filled by the company in the general meeting.'

Section 224(6)(b) states that any auditor appointed in a casual vacancy shall hold office until the conclusion of the next annual general meeting.

An accidental or irregular vacancy is a casual vacancy. A casual vacancy in the office of a company auditor is caused by any of the following circumstances:

1. Death or Disability. When the existing auditor dies or becomes completely disabled to perform his duties, e.g. he becomes totally blind.

2. Disqualification. When the existing auditor becomes disqualified, e.g. when his name is removed from the Register of Members of the Institute of Chartered Accountants of India on account of misconduct.

3. Debt. When the existing auditor becomes disqualified for any other reason, e.g. when he becomes a debtor of the company for an amount exceeding Rs. 1,000 or when he becomes an employee of an officer of the company.

4. Resignation. A casual vacancy may be caused by the resignation of the auditor. Differentiating this cause from other causes of a casual vacancy the law does not empower the Board of Directors to fill such a casual vacancy. It can be filled by the company only in the general meeting. This is done to ensure the auditor's independence and integrity. The shareholders in the general meeting may request the auditor to reconsider his decision and take steps to cure the managerial problems, ill-will or evils, if any. Section 224(6)(a) stipulates that in case there are more than one auditor, the remaining auditor or auditors, may act while a general casual vacancy continues.

5. Omission or failure. Any vacancy, however, is not a casual vacancy if the company fails or omits to appoint or reappoint auditor at an annual general meeting. Such a vacancy cannot be filled by the Board. The Government assumes power to appoint an auditor to fill the vacancy. The company shall give notice to the central government within seven days of such power becoming exercisable and in case of default the company shall be punishable with a fine which may extend to Rs. 500.

AUDITOR'S REFUSAL TO ACCEPT APPOINTMENT

A peculiar situation might arise when the auditor does not accept his appointment as resolved in the general meeting of the shareholders. Following are the recommendations of the Research Committee of ICAI in this connection:

1. Non-Acceptance. In terms of normal law of contract, an appointment becomes complete and effective only when accepted by the appointed person. If he does not accept, it amounts to a situation as if no appointment has been made.

2. No vacancy. It shall be noticed, however, that it is neither a vacancy caused by the resignation nor a casual vacancy arising out of other reasons. As a matter of fact, in all cases of refusal there is no post from which the auditor resigns, nor is there any accident or abnormality to imply a casual vacancy.

3. Appointment by shareholders. A number of company law expert hold the view that the Companies' Act, obliges the shareholders to treat appointment of auditor as their fundamental right and privilege and as such any attempt to get this authority to the Board of Directors should not be cherished. The auditor should be appointed only by the shareholders in order to look into and protect their interests in the organisation.

In view of these considerations the Board of Directors has no option but to call a new general meeting to appoint a new auditor.

Auditor's Refusal to Accept Nomination

If the auditor refuses to accept-nomination no auditor had been appointed at the annual general meeting. Accordingly, the central government would be eligible to appoint the auditor.

PROVISION ABOUT TENURE OF AN APPOINTED AUDITOR

1. Particular period. The Companies Act does not bind the appointed auditor to a fixed period though it does specify that he is appointed for a particular period.

2. Period between two meeting. Section 224(1) provides that the term of the auditor will start from the conclusion of one annual general meeting (the meeting in which he is so appointed) until the conclusion of the next annual general meeting.

3. No fixed time. This implies that a fixed time of 12 months or more or less is neither prescribed nor relevant to the appointment of an auditor. The Department of Company Affairs *vide* circular No. 19/73, 1977 states that an auditor is not appointed with reference to the accounts of a particular year and if a meeting is not held, it does not cause a casual vacancy or vacancy of any other type.

4. Till next meetings. In case the general meeting is not held within the period prescribed by Sec. 166, the auditor will continue in office till the conclusion of the adjourned meeting.

5. Till conclusion of adjourned meeting. In case the annual general meeting is adjourned, the auditor will continue to hold office till the conclusion of the adjourned meeting.

6. Term Basis. Provision under Sec. 227(2) wherein an auditor is required to report on every Balance Sheet and Profit and Loss Account which is laid before the company in the general meeting during the tenure of his office indicates that an auditor holds his office on a term basis. His duty is continuous and not confined to auditing the account for one particular year only.

If, in a particular annual general meeting the audited accounts and the report cannot be placed before the shareholders for approval, as the auditors could not finish the same due to certain reasons and a new auditor is appointed, this auditor will finish the job of the earlier auditor as well as that for which he is so appointed.

7. Bypassing. Section 224(1) read with Sec. 227(2) also indicates a possible manipulation by the Board of Directors to bypass an 'inconvenient auditor' without following the procedure of his removal. Section 227(2), however, bestows a power as well as duty on such auditors to report on the affairs of the company even if no Balance Sheet and Profit and Loss Account are prepared.

APPOINTMENT OF AUDITORS BY SPECIAL RESOLUTION

An auditor may be appointed or reappointed by a special resolution at annual general meeting in case of certain companies or under certain circumstances.

Appointment by certain Companies

Section 224-A of the Act provides that in case of a company in which not less than 25% of the subscribed capital (equity and preference) is held, whether singly or in any combination by:

1. a public financial institution or a government company or central government or any state government,
2. any financial or other institution established by any provincial or state Act in which a state government holds not less than 51% of the subscribed share capital.
3. a nationalised bank or an insurance company carrying on general insurance business.

The appointment or reappointment, at each annual general meeting of an auditor shall be made by special resolution, in all such cases.

It is further provided that if, as required by Sec.224(A)(1) the auditors are not appointed by special resolution it shall be deemed that no auditors have been by the company and, therefore, under Sec. 224(3), the central government may appoint a person to fill the vacancy.

Explanation of this Position

1. According to Sec. 4A of the Act the following financial institutions are public financial institutions:
   (i) The Industrial Credit and Investment Corporation of India.
   (ii) The Industrial Finance Corporation of India.
   (iii) The Industrial Development Bank of India.
   (iv) The Life Insurance Corporation of India.
   (v) The Unit Trust of India.
   (vi) Any other financial institution declared as a public financial institution by the central government under a notification in the Official Gazette, provided that no institution shall be specified unless
      (a) it has been established or constituted by or under any Central Act, or
      (b) not less than 51% of the paid-up share capital of such institution is held or controlled by the central government.
2. According to the clarifications of the Deptt. of Company Affairs, the material date on which 25% of the subscribed capital must be held by the specified institutions to seek the appointment by special resolution under Sec. 224A, is the date of the annual general meeting at which the special resolution is required to be passed.
3. This provision seems to ensure an effective say by such financial institution in the appointment/reappointment of auditors.
4. In calculation of 25% limit, even if a nationalised bank holds shares in its name as security for loans advanced by it, such shares will be taken into account.

5. The subscribed capital includes preference share capital also.
6. In case the financial institution shareholding which was less than 25% at the time of issuing notice for the annual general meeting, is found to be 25% on the date of the annual general meeting, the called meeting should be adjourned, and another notice to the members for appointment of auditors by special resolution must be sent for a decision at the adjourned meeting.

Circumstances of Appointment

1. Under Sec. 314, where a relative of a director of the company is appointed auditor on a remuneration exceeding Rs. 6,000 per annum.

2. In the case of companies with paid-up capital of Rs. one crore or more, no relative of a director or firm in which such relative is a partner or any other partner of such firm can be appointed auditor without the previous approval of the central government.

Appointment by Government Companies

Notwithstanding anything contained in Secs. 224 to 233, Sec. 619 makes special provision for appointment and reappointment of auditors in the case of government companies. In the procedure stipulated in Sec. 619, the central government depends exclusively on the Comptroller and Auditor General of India, who not only advises about the auditor to be appointed but also determines the extent and manner of the audit work which is further subject to his own test and additional information.

Role of Comptroller and Auditor General of India

The Comptroller and Auditor General of India has the power to direct the manner in which a company's accounts shall be audited and to give instructions to the auditor in regard to any matter relating to the performance of his functions as such. He may also conduct a supplementary or test-audit of such company's accounts by persons authorised by him on this behalf. He has the power to require information or additional information to be furnished to the persons so authorised, for the purposes of such audit, on such matters and in such form, as he may direct. The auditor must submit a copy of his audit report to the Comptroller and Auditor General of India who has the right to comment upon or supplement the report in such a manner as he may think fit and the same should be placed before the annual general meeting at the same time and in the same manner as the usual audit report is put.

Appointment of Government-owned or Controlled Companies

In certain companies more than 51% shares of the company are held by public financial corporations either by themselves or along with the government or government companies. As distinguished from government companies such companies are known as government owned or controlled companies.

The Companies Amendment Act, 1974 has introduced Sec. 619-B according to which the provisions of Sec. 619 of the Act shall also apply to a company in which the central government or any state government or any government company or any corporation hold either singly or jointly not less than 51% of the paid-up share capital as if it were a government company, namely:

- the central government and one or more government companies;
- any state government, or governments and one or more government companies;
- the central government, one or more state governments and one or more government companies;
- the central government and one or more corporations owned or controlled by the central government;
- the central government, one or more state governments and one or more corporations owned or controlled by the central government;
- one or more corporations owned or controlled by the central government or state government;
- more than one government company.

The government *vide* notification issued on 10th September, 1976, has clarified that the following are the government owned and controlled companies falling within the meaning of Sec. 619B.

1. Nationalised banks
2. General Insurance Company of India
3. Life Insurance Corporation of India
4. Industrial Development Bank of India
5. Industrial Finance Corporation

It excludes Industrial Credit and Investments Corporation of India and the Unit Trust of India and as such their accounts are not subject to audit by the Comptroller and Auditor General of India.

Conflict Between Sec. 224 and Sec. 619-B

While accepting an appointment, no auditor can ignore the provisions of Sec. 619-B. However, a problem arises when an auditor has already been appointed under Sec. 224 and later on it is discovered that he should have been appointed under Sec. 619-B only. In clarification of a decision in such a situation, the Company Law Board, has stated in its circular, "the onus of complying with the provisions of section 619-B lies with the concerned companies. All the same it would be necessary on the part of auditors appointed/reappointed under Sec. 224 of the Act, to ensure, before accepting the appointment/reappointment that the company is in fact outside the ambit of Sec. 619-B of the Act, any appointment/reappointment of auditors is likely to be *abinitio void*".

The clarification, however, confuses matters more than it simplifies. For one thing Sec. 619-B is itself dependent on Sec. 619 according to which an appointment under Sec. 224 is valid till the central government exercises its power under Sec. 619. The ICAI has accordingly recommended that instead of making detailed enquiries, they may procure and rely upon a certificate from the management in this regard. It shall also be noted that the provisions of Sec. 224(IB) and (IC) in regard to the limit on quantum of audits apply to the appointment under Sec. 619-B as well.

REMOVAL OF AN AUDITOR

1. Removal before Expiry of Term. It may pertain either to removing the first auditor or subsequent auditors.

2. Removing the First Auditor. No prior permission of the central government is required in such a case. Though the directors appoint the first auditors they do not have any power to remove them. Though the first auditor of a company appointed by the directors holds office until the conclusion of the first general meeting, but the company can remove him, at a general meeting and appoint in his place any other person who has been nominated for appointment by a member of the company and whose nomination notice has been given to the members, at least 14 days before the date of the meeting.

3. Removal in Other Circumstances. Section 224(7) provides that an auditor appointed under Sec. 224 (except the first auditors) can be removed before the expiry of his term, after obtaining prior approval of the central government (Company Law Board), only at a general meeting. A copy of the proposed resolution to remove the auditor must be sent to him by the company. The auditor has a statutory right to make written representations to the company, to have such representations sent to the members and to have them read at the meeting and also the right to be heard on resolution at the meeting.

4. Removal after the Expiry. After the expiry of his term, an auditor can be removed by merely passing an ordinary resolution. Sec. 225, however, lays down following procedural aspects which must be observed before appointing a new auditor in place of a retiring auditor.

(i) Section 225(1) specifies that for appointing a person other than the retiring auditor or for proposing that the retiring auditor shall not be reappointed, a special notice of 14 days before the meeting is required for a resolution to be moved at the annual general meeting.

(ii) Sub-sec. 2 of Sec. 225 specifies that on receipt of the notice, the company shall send a copy thereof to the retiring auditor forthwith.

(iii) The company shall also notify the fact of having received such a notice of nomination to all the members, not less than seven days before the date of the meeting.

(iv) According to Sec. 225 (3) the retiring auditor makes any representation in writing to the company, not exceeding a reasonable length and requests for its notification to the members, the company must so notify unless it is received by it too late for it to do so.

(v) If the retiring auditor's representation is not notified he has a right to have this read at the meeting.

(vi) He also has the right to be heard at the meeting.

(vii) The retiring auditor may lose his rights if a competent Court is satisfied that the right is being misused or abused to secure the needless publicity for defamatory matters.

The above mentioned procedure is equally applicable to a resolution to remove the first auditors or any of them appointed by the directors under Sec. 224(5), and removal of any auditors before the expiry of their term under Sec. 224(7) and to the resolution that a person other than the retiring auditor shall be appointed under Sec. 224(2).

5. Unjustified Removal and ICAI Committee (1980). The ICAI formed a committee in 1980 to consider cases of unjustified removal of auditors, thereby providing an additional moral safeguard without jeopardising the legal framework, to ensure the independence of auditors of companies.

AUDITOR'S REMUNERATION

Sec. 224(8) of the Companies Act provides that the remuneration of an auditor of a company may be fixed by the authority so appointing him. Accordingly, the Board of Directors may fix the remuneration in case of the first auditors or auditors appointed by them to fill a casual vacancy. When the auditor is appointed by the company at its general meeting, the remuneration shall be fixed by the company at its general meeting. When the central government appoints an auditor his remuneration may be fixed by it. This is subject to following explanation :

1. Section 224(8)(c) provides that any sum paid by the company in respect of the auditor's expenses shall be deemed to be included in the expression remuneration.
2. One basic assumption of this is that where a fixed sum is approved as remuneration of the auditor, it includes his expenses.
3. The law, however, does not make it necessary either to specify the amount of remuneration in its general meeting or to fix the remuneration in the same meeting in which the auditor is appointed. However, the manner in which the remuneration is to be fixed must be laid down in the general meeting.

4. In case of reappointment of an auditor, the existing remuneration will be deemed to be fixed unless a new amount is fixed.
5. Under Schedule VI Part II clause 4-B, the Profit and Loss Account shall further contain or give by way of note, detailed information in regard to the amounts paid to the auditor, whether as fees, expenses or otherwise for services rendered,
   (i) an auditor,
   (ii) as adviser, or in any other capacity, in respect of (a) taxation matters, (b) company law matters, and (c) manage ment services, and
   (iii) in any other manner.
6. In case the exact remuneration cannot be determined at the date of completion of accounts the ICAEW recommends that "an estimated amount should be included in the accounts and any subsequent adjustment, if material in respect of the estimated amount previously disclosed should be shown in the accounts of the following period". In the usual cases where auditors charge an inclusive fee for auditing the company's books and other work, the fee should be apportioned, the remuneration for the auditor's duties under the Act being separately specified.
7. The Council of the Institute of Chartered Accountants of India, regards the Schedule VI categorisation as a narrow one and expects, as per Statement of Payments to Auditors for Other Services (No. 472117) that the precise and adequate disclosure should be made in the following manner for :
   (i) tax representation,
   (ii) company law matters,
   (iii) management services,
   (iv) internal auditing, and
   (v) other services.

STATUS OF A COMPANY AUDITOR

A company auditor is a central figure in the overall scheme of work. Different people may view him differently. The shareholders may regard a company auditor as their trustee or agent. The general public may think of him as an officer of the company. To many he may mean a mere employee of the company. His status should be viewed from the standard of responsibilities taking into consideration his appointing authorities, his accountability and his role as an auditor in the day to day affairs of the company.

1. As an Officer of the Company. In London and General Bank (1895) Lindley said, "It seems impossible to deny that for some purposes, and to some extent, an auditor is an officer of the company. He is appointed by the company and his position is described in the section as that of an officer of the company. He is not a servant of the directors. On the contrary, he is appointed by the company to check the directors and for some purposes and to some extent, it seems to be quite impossible to say that he is not an officer of the company."

Lord Lindley said in the famous *Kingston Cotton Mills Co. Ltd.* case, it was held that 'auditors are officers of the company'.

In *Connell* v. *Himalaya Bank*, it was held that auditors, if appointed at a general meeting of the company and if also paid by the company were officers of he company. However, a casual auditor may fail to qualify as an officer of the company. Lord Lindley specified in the case of the Western Countries Steam Bakeries and Milling Company Ltd. "If all persons who did auditor's work of a company were officers of the company, the case would be easy but noodecision has yet gone into this length. An auditor need not be an officer of a company. So may anybody else, e.g. a banker or a solicitor. *Prima facie* such persons are not officers. To be an officer there must be an office and office imparts a recognised position with rights and duties annexed to it, and it would be abuse of words to call a person an officer who fills no position either *de jure* or *de facto,* but who happens to do some of the work which he would have to do if he were officer in the proper sense of the word."

Thus casual auditors appointed by a company to do a particular accounting work are not officers. In *Lindley* v. *Waddell* it was held that an accountant to whom books have been handed over to prepare a balance sheet is not an officer. The case *Hudson* v. *Official Liquidating Dehradun Mussoorie Electric Tramway Company* 1989, held that auditors were not officers except for the purpose of sections mentioned therein.

According to Sec. 2(30) of the Indian Companies Act the definition of the term 'Officer includes an auditor for the purposes of Secs. 477, 487, 539, 543, 621, 625 and 633.

(i) **Section 477** refers to Court's power in winding up, to summon persons suspected of having property or books or papers of the company.

(ii) **Section 478** deals with Court's power to order public examinations of the promoters, directors or persons guilty of frauds, etc.

(iii) **Section 539** stipulates penalties for the falsification of accounts and other books.

(iv) **Section 543** deals with the power of the Court, in the course of winding up, to assess damages against delinquent officers.

(v) **Section 545** deals with the prosecution of delinquent officers and members of the company.

(vi) **Section 621** takes cognisance of offenses under the Act.

(vii) **Section 625** makes provisions for payment of compensation in cases of frivolous or vexatious prosecutions.

(viii) **Section 633** empowers the Court to grant relief in certain cases, i.e. in proceedings for negligence, default, breach of duty, misfeasance, etc.

Thus except for the above quoted provisions a company auditor is not one of the officers.

2. As Agent of the Shareholders. A company auditor works for and on behalf of the shareholders. Thus it is but natural that he is treated as the agent of shareholders. Barring first auditors the shareholders have the exclusive right to appoint auditors. It is only when they fail to do so under special but specified reasons, that the central government intervenes and appoints them. An auditor has to safeguard the interests of the shareholders. Accordingly, he must be considered as an agent of the shareholders.

In *Spockman* v.*Evans* said Lord Cranworth, "the auditors may be agents of the shareholders so far as it relates to the audit of the accounts. For the purposes of audit the auditors will bind the shareholders".

In the same case Lord Chemsford clarified the extent of the agency though agreeing that the auditor is the agent of the shareholders. He opined that although auditors may be the agents of the shareholders, the latter could not be deemed to be precluded from objecting to any actions of the directors or others merely on the grounds that the auditors were aware of such actions. The mutuality between principal and agent as applied to shareholders and the auditor works only when the auditor informs them through the Report. In *Nicls* case re. *Royal British* Bank Turner L.J. said, "These were auditors of the company appointed by the shareholders. These auditors were within the scope of their duty, at least as much the agent of the shareholders as the directors were, and the false and fraudulent representations were discoverable by them".

For the purposes of Sec. 240 dealing with powers of inspectors in an investigation of the affairs of a company an auditor is an agent of the company. He may be examined on oath by an inspector. He owes a duty of care to the company. But he owes no duty to third persons with whom he is not in contractual relationship. The decisions in *Candler* v. *Crane Christmas & Co. and De Savary* v.*Holden Howard & Company* have confirmed this position. However, the decision in *Headley Byrne Co. Ltd.* v. *Heller &Partners Ltd.* makes the auditor liable to third parties in certain circumstances.

Sec. 201 stipulates that the articles cannot exempt the auditor from liability for negligence, breach of duty or breach of trust, but may provide for indemnity when he has successfully defended proceedings brought against him. He performs the duties of agent as well as that of an officer of the company and his actual position is to be viewed from the merits of each case.

Thus, for the purposes of the audit the auditor is the agent of the shareholders, on whose behalf he is given access to books of accounts, records and vouchers of the company and can require such information and explanation as he considers necessary for audit purposes and for which he is required by law to report.

The dictum that knowledge of the agent is the knowledge of the principal is not valid *per se* about an auditor. He is not deemed to be the agent of the shareholders as regards knowledge acquired by him in the course of the audit. The shareholders are not bound thereby, unless he has communicated the same to them. Any communication by the auditor to the directors is not a communication or information to shareholders on the plea that directors are basically shareholders first and they themselves act as agent of the shareholders. If the auditor has to convey some information to the shareholders, he must inform them through the report only and definitely not by informing the directors alone.

STATUTORY RIGHTS AND POWERS OF A COMPANY AUDITOR

As compared to a non-company auditor, a company auditor is altogether a different personality. Within the overall orbit of professional conduct and general duties, a non-company auditor is free to determine his rights and duties with the organisation he agrees to audit. A company auditor cannot have this flexibility. The law binds him with certain duties. It bestows certain rights and powers on him so that such duties could be honestly and justifiably performed. Sec. 227 of the Companies Act, 1956 relates to the powers and duties of a company auditor. Rights are linked with the duties cast upon him by the statute. These rights are statutory ones. These cannot be avoided or curtailed in any way by any resolution or even under a provision in the Articles of Association. If any limitation or abridgement was to be permitted the very independence and professional conduct of an auditor will be lost. Auditors may agree to do as required by the management just to increase their clientage or remuneration. The judgement in *Newton* v. *Birmingham Small Arms Co. Ltd* stated that any regulations which preclude the auditors from availing themselves of all the information to which, under the Companies Act they are entitled, are inconsistent with the Act.

1. Right of Access to Books and Vouchers. Section 227(1) provides that "every auditor of a company shall have a right of access at all times to the books and accounts and vouchers of the company, whether kept at the head office of the company or else where...." This is subject to following explanations:

(i) *Absolute Right.* It is an absolute, an all-time and a wherever right. It gives sweeping powers to an auditor to examine any book, accounts and vouchers anywhere and at anytime as long as he is the auditor of the company.

(ii) *Times.* As 'all times' is confined to normal business hours, it does not denote after office hours or late nights.

(iii) *Books and Papers.* Under Sec. 298 of the Act 'books and papers' and books or papers include accounts deeds, vouchers, writings and documents.

(iv) *Books and Accounts.* Books of Accounts remain undefined though books include the financial, statutory and statistical books. Sec. 209 deals with the books to kept by the company. It includes cost records maintained under Sec. 20(1)(d).

(v) *Voucher.* The term 'voucher' includes all documents, correspondence, agreement, etc. which support any of the transactions or data disclosed in the financial statement, directly or indirectly.

(vi) *Surprise checks.* In the scheme envisaged, an auditor need not wait for the closing of the accounts for conducting the audit. He can also make surprise checks during business hours. He is not supposed to notify his visit, though as a matter of convenience most of the auditors do fix up with the directors the date on which the audit is to be commenced and the timings for personal visits subsequently, if necessary.

(vii) *Branch records.* In terms of Sec. 228(2) the right also extends to branch records, if the auditor considers it necessary to have access thereto.

2. Right to Obtain Information and Explanation. Under Sec. 227(3)(a) wherein the auditor is duty-bound to state in his report whether he has obtained all the informations and explanations which to the best of his knowledge and belief were necessary for the performance of the audit. Section 227(1) of the Act empowers a company auditor "to require from the officer of the company such information and explanation as the auditor may think necessary for the performance of his duties." This right is subject to following explanation:

1. *Wide Discretion.* This is a discretionary right. Its range of discretion is very wide. The auditor is the best judge of what explanation or information he considers necessary and no officer can dispute his discretion.

2. *Guarded.* This right is jealously guarded; Sec. 221 makes it obligatory for the officers of a company to furnish without delay information to the auditor, whether or not such information is available from the accounts of the company.

3. Report of Non-Compliance. In case information or explanation is refused to him on the plea that directors consider it as unnecessary for the performance of auditor's duties, he must report this fact to the members.

4. Right to Attend General Meetings. Section 231 states, "and the auditor shall be entitled to attend any general meeting and to be heard at general meeting which he attends or any part of the business which concerns him as auditor". This is subject to following explanation:

(i) The auditor has a right to attend any general meeting: though he is not obliged to do so. He may or may not attend the meeting. It is a permissive right extending to meeting of the members and not the meeting of the directors.

(ii) The auditor is not expected to indulge in a question-answer session with the members present. He may make any statement or explanation with regard to the accounts as he may desire.

(iii) If the auditor made certain observations in the general meeting it does not absolve him from making a clear and unambiguous report in the usual manner as required under Sec. 227(2).

(iv) In the following circumstances : an auditor must attend the general meeting :

(a) If he has reasons to believe that the directors may deliberately attempt to conceal a serious state of affairs from the shareholders;

(b) If his audit contains significant qualifications directly affecting the management, so that his remarks may not be misinterpreted or misunderstood;

(c) If he receives a notice from the company showing that someone else is going to be proposed for appointment in his place;

(d) If he has been specially asked by the management to be present;

(e) If any 'material' matter has come to his knowledge subsequent to his signing the report and would have made him report differently if he has known it before signing the report; and

(f) If the accounts have been altered after the report was appended to the account.

5. Rights to visit Branch Offices and Access to Branch Accounts. Section 224 puts an obligatory right on the auditor to audit the accounts of the various branches of the company. Under Sec. 226, a company has the option of getting the branch accounts audited by some other local auditor subject to the statutory rights of the main auditor. Section 228(2) of the Act gives specific rights to the company auditor even where the accounts of any branch are audited by another person. Thus, the company auditor is entitled to visit the branch office, if he deems it necessary to do so for the performance of his duties as auditor. He has a right of access at all times to the books and vouchers of the company maintained at the branch office. In the case of a banking company having a branch office outside India, it is sufficient, if the auditor is allowed access to such copies of, and extracts from, the books and accounts of the branch as have been transmitted to the principal office of the company in India. The following explanation may be noted in this connection:

(i) The auditor is not entitled to visit the foreign branch of a banking company.

(ii) He has a right to visit and of access to books and vouchers of the branch office in case of branches of all non-banking companies.

(iii) The auditor of a holding company has no right of access to the books of accounts of a subsidiary company unless he has been especially authorised by a resolution of the holding company. This is so because: (a) every holding company has to attach a copy of the subsidiary companies' balance sheet, profit and loss account, directors report and auditor's report to its accounts, and (b) under Sec. 214(1) of the Act, a holding company can, by passing a resolution, authorise any person to inspect the books of any subsidiary company.

Certain rights come to an auditor not through the Companies Act but by application of Common Law.

6. Right to Correct Wrong Statement. As auditor not only acts as an agent of the shareholder or an officer of the company for limited purposes but also as an observer for law. The law assigns him a specific duty and power to report on the observance of the various legalities involved. He has the right to advise the directors to amend their faulty system of accounts and, to report the inadequacy of the method of accounting by specifying that the proper books of accounts have not been kept by the company. He may also comment on and correct the wrong statements, if any, made by the directors.

7. Right to Report and Sign the Audit Report. The auditor is legally obliged to sign the audit report and verify other documents constituting audited accounts to be submitted at company's general meeting. Sec. 209 stipulates that only a person appointed as company auditor can sign the audit report.

8. Right to Seek Legal and Technical Advice. The auditor has a right to seek legal and technical advice or opinion from experts though he must report his own opinion only (London and General Bank).

9. Right to be Indemnified or Granted Relief. According to Sec. 633, an auditor has a right to be indemnified against any civil or criminal proceeding by the company, provided it is proved to the satisfaction of the Court that he has acted honestly.

10. Right of Lien. (i) *Auditor's Lien.* A lien is the right of one person to satisfy a claim against another by holding the other's property as security or by seizing and converting the property under the procedures provided by law. Because of his peculiar position, an auditor does not enjoy an undisputed right of lien as his actual 'property' or 'construction' concerning the 'auditing services' may be insignificant and pose certain conflict with other laws. Section 209 makes it mandatory for every company to keep all books of accounts at its registered office or at such other place in India as the directors think fit, and that these books of accounts shall be open to inspection by any director during business hours. It is believed that silence about the auditor's lien can be positively interpreted as entitling the auditor to have lien without prejudicing the director's right of inspection.

(ii) *Auditor's Lien v. Accountant's Lien.* While an accountant prepares the accounts and as such he alone must enjoy the lien over books prepared by him, an auditor merely audits the books and cannot claim lien unless he has acted as an accountant also.

(iii) *Lien on Working Papers.* Working paper means those documents which the auditor or his staff prepares in connection with audit. An auditor's working papers are his own property. A client has no claim over these. The auditor actually owns the following working papers, namely, (a) working papers and schedules relating to the audit, (b) draft accounts of the company, a copy of the final accounts and notes and calculation relating to the accounts made by the auditor, and (c) the draft tax computations prepared by the auditor or his staff.

(iv) *Lien on Communication Documents.* An auditor may communicate with third parties either as an agent of the company or as an auditor to discharge his professional duties. Such communication documents are naturally the property of the company and an auditor has no such lien in all such cases. When he acts as a professional auditor to carry out his professional duties, all such communication documents will be the property of the auditor. Communication received by the auditor from his client and copies of he auditor's letter to the client are property of the auditor.

(v) *Lien on Client's Money.* An auditor has no lien on client's money. If at all he possesses some money, it is in trust with him. Any misuse of that will amount to a breach of trust for which he is liable to be criminally punished.

(vi) *General or Particular Lien.* An auditor's lien is a particular lien only on those documents that can be retained and which are related to the work for which he remains unpaid and on which lien is available otherwise. These documents must have come into the possession of the auditor in the legal manner and through proper means.

DUTIES OF THE COMPANY AUDITOR

1. Auditor's Report. The first and foremost duty of an auditor is making a report to the members on the accounts of the company. This duty cannot be performed unless he examines and enquires about the various aspects of accounts as well as the mode of keeping these. His legal duties should be within his power and justify his profession.

2. Duties Concerning his Work. Section 227(IA) stipulates the following duties of the auditor:

(i) *Loans and Advances.* The auditor should see that whether loans and advances made by the company on the basis of security are properly secured and the terms on which they have been made are not prejudicial to the interest of the company or its members.

(ii) *Transactions.* The auditor should see that transactions of the company which are represented merely by book entries are not prejudicial to the interests of the company.

(iii) *Sale of Assets.* In case of a company which is not an investment company within the meaning of Sec. 372 or a banking company, the auditor should see that so much of the assets of the company as consist of shares, debentures and other securities have been sold at a price less than that at which they were purchased by the company.

(iv) *Deposits.* The auditor should enquire, whether loans and advances made by the company have been shown as deposits.

(v) *Personal expenses.* The auditor should enquire whether personal expenses have been charged to revenue accounts.

(vi) *Shares.* Where it is stated in the books and papers of the company that shares have been allotted for cash the auditor should enquire whether cash has actually been received in respect of such allotment, or if no cash has actually been so received, whether the position is stated in the account books and the Balance Sheet is correct, regular and not misleading.

3. Duty to Report Directly to Members. Section 227(2) binds an auditor with a duty to report. Section 227(3) explains the minimum contents of such a reporting. The auditor has to make a report to the members of the company on the accounts examined by him and on Balance Sheet and Profit and Loss Accounts of the company and every other document purported to be the part of or annexed to the Balance Sheet and the Profit and Loss Account and which are laid before the company in its general meeting during his tenure of office.

Auditor report shall state that in his opinion and to the best of his information and according to the explanations given to him, the said accounts give a true and fair views:

(i) in the case of the balance Sheet of the state of the company's affairs as at the end of the financial year, and

(ii) in the case of the Profit and Loss Account, of the profit or loss for its financial year.

This duty of the auditor is subject to the following explanations:

(i) The auditor dose not certify the financial statements but merely reports on them.

(ii) The report may be on anything concerning accounts through the auditor reports on the accounts, the Profit and Loss Account and the Balance Sheet including any documents annexed thereto.

(iii) The report is not confined to the financial statements of one particular period but for such accounts as are laid before the company at a general meetings during the auditors tenures of office irrespective of accounting years.

(iv) The auditor has to sign his report and the Balance Sheet and send it to the secretary for the company. It is not his duty to see that his report has been sent or put before the shareholders. The meaning of the following phrases used in the Act, may be noted as given below :

(a) *According to the best of his information and the explanations given to him.* This phase offers limited protection to an auditor to escape liability if he has acted *bona fide* to believe the information supplied and explanation given and had exercised reasonable skill and care in testing the same even though it turns out to be untrue or incorrect.

(b) *True and fair view.* This phase means everything and nothing at the same time though it is for the auditor to determine whether the Balance Sheet shows a true and fair view of the state of the company affairs and Profit and Loss Account shows a true and fair view of the working results of the company.

4. Duty to report certain aspects of his working. Section 227(3) makes it mandatory for an auditor to state certain aspects of his working in his report. It is the duty of the auditor to see that his audit report states the following:

(i) Whether he has obtained all the information and explanation which to the best of his knowledge and belief were necessary for the purposes of his audit. He must be fully satisfied about the scope of work carried out by him. He must also affirm that he has maintained professional standards of diligence and care in the discharge of his duties. He may express his inability to give an opinion on the truth and fairness of the financial statements. He may qualify his opinion if he faces a situation where the required information hasn't been supplied.

However, he does not guarantee that his Balance Sheet is accurate, according to the books of the company. He can rely upon responsible and trusted officers of the company provided he takes reasonable care to ensure that the information supplied is true and that no circumstance exists which should arouse his suspicion.

(ii) Whether in his opinion, proper books of account as required by law have been kept by the company and proper returns adequate for the purposes of his audit have been received from the branches not visited by him. Section 209(3) states, "Proper books of account shall not be deemed to be kept with respect to the matters specified therein, if there are not kept such books as are necessary to give a true, and fair view of the state of affairs of the company or branch office, as the case may be, and to explain its transactions."

Proper books of account are required to be kept with respect to the following:

(a) all sums of money received and expended by the company and the matters in respect of which the receipt and expenditure take place;
(b) all sales and purchases of goods by the company;
(c) the assets and liabilities of the company; and
(d) cost records as prescribed under Sec. 209(1)(d).

Sec. 54(2) provides that a company that is being wound up shall be deemed not to have maintained proper books of accounts if it has not kept:

(a) Such books of accounts as are necessary to exhibit and explain the transactions and financial position of the business of the company including books containing entries made from day to day in sufficient detail of all cash received and all cash paid; and
(b) Where the business of the company has dealings involving goods, statements of the annual stock-takings and (except in the case of goods sold by way of ordinary retail trade) of all goods sold and purchased, showing the goods and the buyers and sellers thereof in sufficient detail to enable those goods and those buyers and sellers to be identified.

A company cannot keep its accounts on cash or receipt basis.

(iii) Whether the report on the accounts of any branch office audited under Sec. 228 by a person other than the company's auditor, has been forwarded to him as required by clause (c) of Sub-sec.(3) of that section and how he has dealt with the same in preparing the auditor's report.

ICAI has opined that a mere statement that the auditor has dealt with the branch audit report as he considered necessary will not suffice, he must make disclosure of anything in regard to the branch which he thinks is not order and which has come to his notice.

(iv) Whether the company's Balance Sheet and Profit and Loss Account dealt with by the report are in agreement with the books of accounts and returns.

It is a specific duty. The work of an auditor culminates in the verification of statements of accounts.

5. Duty of Statement in Prospectus. According to the Companies Act there are three circumstances which oblige a chartered accountant to report on the statements of accounts, operating results and assets and liabilities of a going company which issues a prospectus. These are as follow:

(i) when it issues more capital for public subscription.

(ii) if the proceeds of the issue of the shares or debentures are to be applied directly or indirectly,

(a) in the purchase of a business, or

(b) in the purchase of an interest in any business which would make it a holder of more than 50% interest, and

(c) if the proceeds of the issue of shares or debentures are to be applied for purchasing shares in a company, making the investing company the majority shareholder.

In reference to first case the report is to be made by the auditor of the company. In remaining cases report may be made by any chartered accountant.

Under Sec. 56(i) the prospectus issued by an existing company shall contain a report by the auditor of the company regarding the profits or losses and assets and liabilities of the company and its subsidiaries. It shall also include the rates of dividends paid by the company for each of the five financial years proceeding the issue of the prospectus, giving particulars of each class of shares on which such dividends have been paid and particulars of the cases in which no dividends have been paid in respect of any class of shares for any of these years. This statement may also indicate the nature of provisions made or to be made.

6. Duty to Certify Statutory Report. Every public company limited by shares and every company limited by guarantee and having share capital must certify a statutory report for being placed before the shareholders in accordance with Section 165. A deemed public company will not be required to hold statutory meetings or issue statutory report if a period of 6 months has expired after incorporation at the time, it is so deemed. Under Sec. 165(4) the statutory report shall be certified as correct by not less than two directors of the company, one of whom shall be a managing director, where there is one. After the statutory report has been certified as laid down, the company auditor must certify as correct that part of the same as relates to (i) the shares allotted by the company, (ii) the cash received in respect of such shares,

(iii) an abstract of the receipts and payments of the company upto a date within seven days of the date of the report.

7. Duty Regarding Public Deposits by the Company. Under Sec. 58(A) and rules made thereunder and under the directives of the Reserve Bank of India Act non-banking company the auditor is obliged to enquire whether the company has furnished the necessary statement regarding public deposits.

8. Duty to Produce Documents and Evidence. Under Sec. 240 it is the duty of a company auditor to preserve and produce to an inspector or any other person authorised by him in this behalf with the previous approval of the central government, all books and papers of, or relating to, the company or, as the case may be, of or relating to the other body corporate which are in their custody or power and otherwise to give to the person all assistance in connection with the investigation which they are reasonably able to give.

9. Duty to Report on Accounts on Voluntary Winding Up. Under Sec. 488(1) where it is proposed to wind up a company voluntarily, the directors of the company have to make a declaration of solvency which includes:

(a) a Profit and Loss Account for the period beginning from the end of the last financial year and ending with a practicable date before the making of the declaration;

(b) a Balance Sheet as on the last mentioned date; and

(c) a statement of the company's assets and liabilities.

The auditor of the company is required to make a report on such Balance Sheet and Profit and Loss Account.

10. Duty to comply with the directives of he central government and that of the Institute of Chartered Accountant of India. This relates to the power of the government to amplify the scope of audit, Sec. 227(4)(a). If the company auditor does not comply with directions given by such bodies, he shall be guilty of professional misconduct.

11. Duties of Assistance. The auditor should carry out the following duties of assistance:

(i) To assist the Inspector appointed by the central government either on the application of the members or on a report by the Registrar of Companies, under Sec. 235 of the Act, in the investigation of the affairs of the company. This duty extends to all persons who were employed as auditors whether as statutory or as internal auditors [Sec. 240(1)(b)].

(ii) To assist government in the prosecution of directors, etc. provided the auditor is not himself involved, in pursuance of the Inspector's report under Sec. 241 of the Act [Sec. 242(1)].

(iii) Under Sec. 545(7) give such reasonable assistance as is necessary in cases where prosecution has been instituted against delinquent officers and members of the company in the capacity of an officer of the company.

(iv) Under Sec. 33(2) to makes declaration that all the requirements of the Act have been complied with.

12. Duty to Acquaint Himself with His Duties. In performance of his duties a company auditor is not expected to ignore any law, particularly the provisions of the Companies Act. In the *Bolivia Exploration Syndicate* case it was held that auditors are obliged to acquaint themselves with their duties. In the *Leeds Estate Building Investment Co.* v. *Shapherd,* it was decided that ignorance of the Articles of the company under audit and the exceptional duties, if any, imposed by it on the auditor would not provide a defence to him for not observing these.

13. Duty of Care. An auditor must be honest and not casual or negligent. He must exercise reasonable skill and care in performance of his duties otherwise he may be sued for damages. In the *Kingston Cotton Mills* case Justic Lopes remarked, "It is the duty of an auditor to bring to bear on the work he has to perform that remarked skill, care and caution which a reasonable competent, careful and cautions auditor would use. What is reasonable skill, care and caution must depend on the particular circumstances of each case. If there is anything calculated to excite his suspicion he would probe it to the bottom but in the absence of anything of that kind he is only bound to be reasonably cautious and careful. He is not an insurer. He does not guarantee that the books do correctly show the true position of the company's affairs. He must be honest."

In *London and the General Bank* case, Justice Lindley remarked. "An auditor, however, is not bound to do more than exercise reasonable care and skill in making inquiries and investigations. He must be honest, i.e. he must not certify what he does not believe to be true and must take reasonable care and skill before he believes that what he certifies it true." In *International Laboratories Ltd.* v. *Dewar,* Donovan J. held that though the auditor may only be a watchdog, "he will not have performed the functions of his office, if, after one howl, he retreats under the barn or if he confines his protests to fellow-watchdog."

14. Duty Regarding his own appointment. The auditor should see that his own appointment as auditor is proper and conforms to the general law in this regard. In B.N. Mohan v. K.C.I. Satyawati, it was held that an auditor should correspond in writing with the previous auditor. He should see that for his appointment, the Articles of Association have been complied with.

WORK AND RESPONSIBILITY OF JOINT AUDITORS

Sec. 227 of the Act does not contemplate division of work and responsibility among joint auditors. However, there can be joint auditors if the company so desires though it cannot be compelled to have joint auditors. In many cases, where the company is so large that it may be virtually impossible for one auditor to do audit effectively, two or more than two persons or firms of chartered accountants may be appointed as joint auditors of a company. Specific provisions regarding joint audits can be had from the Statement on the Responsibility of Joint Auditors issued as Members' Handbook by the Institute of Chartered Accountants of India. Work and responsibility of joint auditors has been classified according to possibility of division of work.

1. When Division of Work is Possible. The joint auditors divide the work between themselves in a clear cut manner preferably on the basis of identifiable operating units or specified areas of work. It is a good practice to communicate the actual division of work to the clients so that they may deal only with some auditor with reference to the matters relating to a particular unit. Even where the work cannot be divided into specific operating units, division of the work should be made on the basis of time periods or classifications of assets/liabilities or income from the branches may be divided among the joint auditors. Each auditor is entitled to adopt his own criteria regarding the selection of items, the extent of test checks, the extent of auditing, and the materiality of the items involved. If auditors arrive at a mutual agreement it brings uniformity in the approach. Each of the joint auditors is individually responsible for the manner and application of audit tests in particular area of work allotted to him. In case the work is divided on the basis of divisions, in a large scale concern, each auditor will have the specific responsibility of reviewing the returns of the divisions allocated to him and to incorporate them in the accounts of the division. Each auditor should collect suitable information and explanations from the management regarding the affairs of the division/unit/branch returns assigned to him. After the work has been divided among the auditors each auditor must prepare a separate report for his area. All these reports may then be compiled into the final report. "But where the joint auditors are in disagreement with regard to report, each one of them would be justified in expressing his opinion through a separate report. Even when more than two joint auditors are appointed each auditor is entitled to express his view or opinion and in fact it is his duty to do so."

2. Work and Responsibility when the Work is Indivisible. If the work cannot be divided, the joint auditors have to carry out the work jointly. To achieve effective coordination on such an occasion joint auditors preferably bring a matter to the notice of their colleagues, in writing. To quote the opinion of the Council of the Institute of Chartered Accountants of India,

"It would not be correct to hold an auditor responsible for the work of another and each joint auditor will be responsible only for the work allocated to him." There cannot be a joint responsibility for clearly assigned work because the extent of the work to be carried out is a matter of professional judgement and that no two firms, whatever be their standing and competence, will necessarily exercise their judgement in an identical manner so as to perform the same volume of work in the same manner." In case the work cannot be divided all the joint auditors will be responsible. The performance of mutually allocated work is the individual responsibility of the joint auditors. Each of the joint auditors is expected to carry out the work assigned to him in accordance with the generally accepted principles and standards of auditing. A joint auditor, then may not review the work of the co-auditor. The company auditors will not be responsible for the work entrusted to the branch auditors appointed under Sec. 228(3) of the Act. The Board of Directors may be authorised to appoint branch auditors in consultation with the company auditors. The provision does not imply "that the statutory auditors have accepted the responsibility for the work done by branch auditors merely by concurring with the decision to the Board."

The branch auditor is responsible for the proper performance of the audit of branch accounts.

BRANCH OFFICE

According to Sec.2(9), the term 'branch office' in relation to a company means :

1. any establishment described as a branch by the company; or
2. any establishment carrying on the same or substantially the same activity as that carried on by the head-office of the company; or
3. any establishment engaged in any production, processing or manufacture.

However, under Sec. 8, the central government has the power to declare that any establishment included in (2) and (3) above shall not be treated as a branch office of any company.

Audit of Branch Office

The audit of branch office of a company is governed by Sec.228 which provides as follows:

1. Persons Authorised to Audit. The accounts of a branch office shall be audited in the following manner:

(i) Where the branch office is in India. Accounts will be audited by the company's auditor or by a person qualified to act as a company's auditor, i.e. a chartered accountant or a restricted state auditor.

(ii) Where the branch office is in a country outside India. Audits will be audited by the company's auditor or by a person qualified as aforesaid or by an accountant duly qualified to act as a company auditor according to the law of that country.

2. Appointment of Auditor. When in general meeting a company decides to have the accounts of a branch office audited by a person other than the company's auditor for the audit of those accounts, or authorise its Board of Directors to appoint such an auditor in consultation with the company's auditor.

3. Remuneration of the Auditor. The Auditor's remuneration is fixed by the company or the Board appointing him. He has the same powers and duties in respect of the audit of branch accounts as the company's auditor has in respect of the same.

4. Auditors' Visits to Board

(i) The company's auditor shall be entitled to visit the branch office except the foreign branch of the company, if he considers it necessary to do so, and

(ii) The auditor shall have a right of access at all times to the books and accounts and vouchers of the company kept at the branch office.

5. Report. After preparing a report on the accounts of the branch office examined by him the branch auditor shall forward the same to the company's auditor who shall deal with the same in such manner as he considers necessary in preparing his audit report. According to Sec. 227(3)(bb), the company's auditor is required to state in his audit report whether the report on the accounts of any branch office has been forwarded to him and how has he dealt with it. He has to do the following:

(a) Evaluation. By merely incorporating the branch auditor's comments in his own report the company auditor does not discharge his duty. He has to consider the branch auditor's report on the basis of his own judgement, the transactions of the company as a whole and any other information in his possession. He has to ascertain whether the branch accounts disclose any defects or irregularities not noticed or commented upon by the branch auditor. He will then be able to decide the extent to which the branch auditor's comments should be included in his own report. It is not always necessary that all the comments of the branch auditor should be included in the company's auditor's report. If the branch accounts are in order, the company auditor includes in his audit report the following clause:

"The reports on the account of (specified) branch offices of the company audited by other auditors have been considered in preparing my report."

(b) Qualification. The company auditor considers carefully any qualifications contained in branch auditor's report. He decides which of them are to be incorporated in his own report. In the following circumstances he may drop a qualification found in the branch auditor's report:

(i) If the branch auditor has been unable to verify a particular transaction for want of relevant records or information which are available at the head office.

(ii) If certain provisions (e.g. those for bonus, depreciation, taxation etc.) relating to the branch accounts have been made at the head office.

(iii) If a policy decision (e.g. regarding a principle of accounting) has been taken at the head office and the branch auditor was not aware of it.

(iv) If subsequent events affecting the branch accounts (e.g. the settlement of a legal dispute) come to the notice of the company auditor.

6. Exemptions. As the provisions relating to the compulsory audit of branch accounts might cause some hardship, particularly to companies whose branches are spread all over the country such as banking companies or where the branch concerned is a small one, Sec. 228(4) authorises the central government to make rules for exempting any branch office from the requirements of compulsory branch audit. The Companies (Branch Audit Exemption) Rules, 1961 made by the central government provides as follows:

(a) Rule 3. Exemption based on quantum of activity. The expression 'quantum of activity means the aggregate value of goods produced or sold or of services rendered or the amount of expenditure (capital or revenue) incurred by a branch office during a financial year. In case of a company carrying on any manufacturing, processing or trading activity has a branch office, whose average of the quantum of activity during the relevant financial year does not exceed Rs. 2 lacks or two per cent of the total turnover of the company including all its branches and other offices and the earnings from services and from any other source during the same period, whichever is higher, the branch office shall be exempt from compulsory audit. The average quantum of activity shall be the average for the three financial years immediately proceeding the relevant financial year.

(b) Rule 4. Grant of exemption in other Cases. On application made to it in this behalf the central government may after making such inquiry as it thinks fit, by a written order, exempt the branch office of a company from compulsory audit on any of the following grounds under Rule 4:

(i) That a company, not engaged in trading, manufacturing or processing has made satisfactory arrangements for the scrutiny and check at regular intervals, of the accounts of branch offices by a person who is competent to do so.

(ii) That a company has made arrangements for the audit of the accounts of the branch office by a person qualified for appointment as branch auditor, even though such person is an employee of the company.

(iii) That having regard to the nature and quantum of activity carried on at the branch office or for any other reason, a branch auditor is not likely to be available at a reasonable cost.

(iv) That, for any reason, central government is satisfied that exemption may be granted.

7. Internal Audit. If company seeks exemption from compulsory branch audit on that ground the following are the legal requirements of an internal audit system :

(i) The internal audits of branch accounts should be carried out by a person qualified for appointment as a company auditor.

(ii) The internal auditor should be given access at all times to the books of accounts and vouchers maintained at the branch office and he is furnished with such information and explanations as he may require.

(iii) During the period when the exemption is in force, the internal auditor shall, prepare in respect of each financial year a report of the accounts of the branch office examined by him and forward the same to the company's auditor.

(iv) There shall be attached to the Balance Sheet of the company for each financial year, a certificate that no material change has taken place in the internal audit arrangements made for the audit of branch accounts. This certificate is to be signed by the same persons who sign the Balance Sheet.

(v) The company auditor shall expressly state in his audit report that an exemption from compulsory branch audit has been granted by the central government. An application on the ground mentioned here must be accompanied by:

(a) a certificate signed by the managing director or manager of the company that there are satisfactory internal audit arrangements for the audit of branch accounts, and

(b) a written statement from the auditor of the company that in his opinion, the internal audit arrangement are adequate and the branch accounts are properly kept.

8. Revocation of Exemption. After giving the company reasonable opportunity to make its objections, the Central Government may revoke an exemption granted under these rules, under the following conditions:

1. That there has been a contravention of any of terms and conditions subject to which the exemption was granted.
2. That there has been a material alteration in the circumstances relating to the security, check or audit of the accounts of the branch office on the basis of which the exemption was granted.
3. The central government is satisfied that exemption is no longer necessary or justified.

Relationship between Branch Auditors and Company Auditors

1. No responsibility of Company Auditor. According to ICAI Expert Advisory Committee, 1982, the statutory auditors would not be responsible in respect of the works entrusted to the branch auditors appointed under Sec. 228(3). The statutory auditors are not supposed to have accepted responsibility for the work done by the branch auditor merely by concurring with the decision of the Board which in terms of the section is authorised to appoint the auditor in consolation with the statutory auditor.

2. Right of Inspection. A company auditor may rely on a branch auditor but legally is authorised to visit the branch if he finds it necessary to do so.

3. Proper account. The branch auditor prepares financial statements and records in such a way as to let the company auditor meet the requirements of disclosure and presentation and also helping him in forming his opinion to be expressed in the audit-report.

4. Right to enquire and communicate. The company auditor has a right to communicate with and enquire from the branch auditor to ensure proper liaison.

5. Duty bound consideration. The company auditor is duty bound to consider the branch auditor's report carefully to judge its impact and relevance for the concerned issues. He has to state in his report how he has dealt with branch auditor's report.

6. The company auditor is not bound to reproduce branch audit report.

SPECIAL AUDITOR— AUDIT UNDER SEC. 233A

The provisions of Sec. 233(A) relating to special audits of companies are as follows:

1. Where the Central Government is of the opinion:

(i) that the affairs of the company are not being managed in accordance with sound business principles or prudent commercial practices; or

(ii) that the company is being managed in a manner likely to cause serious injury or damage to the interest of the trade, industry or business to which it pertains; or

(iii) that its financial position is such as to endanger its solvency. The central government may at any time order a special audit of the company's account for such period or periods as may be specified.

2. The central government shall appoint either a chartered accountant (whether he is in practice or not) or the company's auditor himself to conduct the special audit, and the auditor so appointed is referred to as special auditor.

3. The special auditor shall have the same powers and duties in relation to the special audit as an auditor of a company has under Sec. 227 though he shall make his report to the central government instead of, to the members of the company.

4. The auditor's report shall include all the matters required to be included in the report of a company auditor, but it shall also include a statement on any other matters, if any, referred to him by the central government.

5. The central government may order any person to furnish to the special auditor within the specified time such additional information as may be required by him in connection with the special audit. On failure to comply with such order, such person shall be punishable with fine upto Rs. 500.

QUESTIONS FOR EXERCISE

1. Who can be and who cannot be appointed auditor of a company? Who can dismiss an auditor and how?
2. Give the provisions of the Companies Act in regard to the auditor of Branch Accounts of a company.
3. On being appointed an auditor of a limited company, what steps should be taken by him to ascertain that his appointment is in order and what documents would be inspected before commencing his audit?
4. Explain provision of appointment of a company auditor.
5. What are the provisions of the Companies Act, regarding the appointment of an auditor in the following cases:
   (i) When no auditor has been appointed at the annual general meeting.
   (ii) When no general meeting has been held and no auditor appointed for two years.
   (iii) When it is desired to appoint an auditor other than the retiring auditor.
   (iv) On the resignation of existing auditor.
6. Explain the provisions about compulsory reappointment of retiring auditor and appointment under casual vacancy.

7. What are the conditions of auditor's refusal to accept appointment or nomination ? Give provisions concerning tenure of an appointed auditor.
8. By which companies and under what circumstances an auditor is appointed by resolution?
9. Explain rules concerning removal of an auditor.
10. In What manner does the Companies Act, 1956, afford protection to an auditor whom the directors seek to remove from office?
11. Discuss fully the duties of a Company Auditor under the Indian Companies Act.
12. Discuss the principal objects of an auditor and indicate the difference between the auditor of the accounts of partnership and those of a company.
13. What are the provisions of the Companies Act, 1956 regarding the appointment, remuneration and termination of the services of auditors of limited liability companies?
14. Explain rules concerning auditor's remuneration. What is the status of a company auditor?
15. Discuss the rights and powers of the auditor of a company.
16. Discuss the position of an auditor with reference to the Companies Act, 1956, regarding his (i) Rights, (ii) Duties, and (iii) Responsibilities.
17. Explain the work and responsibility of Joint Auditors.
18. What is a branch office? Explain the procedure of audit of branch offices and the relationship between Branch Auditor and Company Auditor.
19. Write short note on Special Auditor under Sec. 233A.

4

Planning the Audit: Preparation and Procedure

The audit of accounts of a concern involves sound planning, conduct and judgment. The auditor has to face several problems in the course of audit. He has to determine the future course of action, frame his policies, lay down programmes and procedures and divide carefully the whole work amongst the staff. Much of his efficiency and success would depend upon how well he has been able to plan his work.

Agreement with the Client

An Auditor should first consult the client about certain aspects of audit of the concern before finalising any agreement. He should have prior agreement about the nature of audit, period by which the audit report is to be delivered and remuneration etc. He should consult about the extent of his duties. He should also discuss limitations as regards internal controls etc. as they affect his work. He should enquire about the nature of audit and also whether it would be annual, continuous or interim audit. So far as the auditor's report is concerned client needs should be discussed. The date on which the report has to be submitted is an important point as it limits the period of audit. He should reach an agreement for remuneration whether it would be on a flat-fee basis, a per diem basis plus travelling expenses, if any, or a per diem basis plus expenses with a minimum total fee. Auditor's generally prefer a per diem basis so that if any unforeseen event arises that may be fully explored without any monetary loss to him.

Audit Memorandum

Now, the auditor should try to gain familiarity with the nature and various other aspects of the client's concern. He should prepare a memorandum containing all useful information regarding the business of the client, all the conditions relating to audit. The object of preparation of the memorandum is to record relevant general information about the concern which may be of practical use to him while conducting the audit. These include facts about the organisation, its personnel, its methods of operation, its policies about sales, advertisement, investments depreciations or reserves etc. A first audit will have to be prepared thoroughly so as to cover various aspects about the concern. If audit has been carried on earlier, only changes, in the various items should be noted. Sometimes the auditor just talks to the officers of the concern and collects all these informations and does not commit such records to writing. However it is always advisable to prepare such a memorandum.

According to Eric L. Kohlar[1], an audit memorandum should contain the following points :-

1. Ownership and control ; reorganisations in recent years.
2. A brief history of the net-worth accounts.
3. Principal kinds of products.
4. Nature of the market in which the products are sold.
5. Price conditions and trend of sales.
6. Advertising methods.
7. Location of plants and offices.
8. Character and adequacy of manufacturing facilities.
9. Sources of raw materials and trends in prices.
10. Names and inter-relation of principal officers.
11. Responsibility of controller.
12. Books of account, nature of and where kept.
13. Who gets controller's monthly reports and how they are used.
14. How this year differed from last year ; new products, new equipment, changes in cost, financial problems.
15. How next year will differ from this year; changes in production, plan, costs, management.
16. Purposes of investments.
17. Purposes of contingency and similar reserves.
18. Subsidiary companies and how they are operated and controlled.
19. Special problems raised by the management : opinions of internal controls, accounting policies, costing methods, promptness and accuracy of internal reporting.
20. Tax returns : preparation or review.
21. Preparation of government reports.

---

1. *Auditing,* p. 89.

CONSIDERATIONS IN A NEW AUDIT

Before beginning the audit work, an auditor must review the various arrangements with his client to decide his future course of action. Usually, the following points must be considered in this connection.

1. The Client. An auditor must know about his appointee well in advance.

(i) Whom to report ? and (ii) Who will pay his fees ?

Sometimes the client may be a dissatisfied shareholder, member or a banker or the government or some other person and not the person whose accounts he is auditing.

2. Scope of Duties. The auditor should ascertain the scope of his duties and responsibilities from statutes, or from the instructions received from those employing his services. If he is appointed under any statute, his duties and responsibilities are enumerated under it and cannot be contracted. However they may be increased by an agreement between the client and the auditor. The auditor's duties and responsibilities are determined by reference to terms of agreement entered into between him and his client, who may be partners in a firm or a sole trader. He has no statutory obligation to comply with. He has only to carry out the instructions he receives from his clients. The dividing line between accountancy and audit work is sometimes so uncertain, that it is always proper for the auditor to ascertain what exactly his client requires. He should check that this is formulated in writing especially where accountancy work is also involved. The scope of auditor's duties is also affected by the purpose for which the audit is to be made.

3. Period to be covered. The auditor should ascertain the period to be covered in the audit. Usually the period is one year, but the period may be more or less than one year if conducted for a specific purposes.

4. Use of clients' staff. The auditor may have his own staff or may take the assistance of his client's staff where some clerical work is also to be performed. He should know whether he can use the client's staff as per agreement.

5. Place of Audit Work. Thc auditor should know the place of his work. This place is where he will open his office with his staff and conduct his enquiries. Regarding working conditions proper arrangement must be made with the client as it is in the interest of effective conduct of his audit work.

6. Review of Business. This includes the review of the following:

(i) *Nature of Business.* The auditor should know the precise nature of his client's business, its technicalities, etc. In the case of the audit of accounts of a manufacturing concern he should go around the factory, as it would help him see and appreciate the nature of transactions that are recorded in the books, and he will have a rough idea about the process, the nature of machinery, materials and men involved, etc. This acquaintance will enable him to acquire grasp of affairs and appreciate the essentials.

(ii) *Organisation of Business.* The auditor should know the organisation of the business, human as well physical, with the help of organisation charts, work flow charts, the chart of accounts, the list of officials, the authority and responsibility of the persons with whom he has to deal during the conduct of audit.

In order to have a clear idea of the physical organisation, the auditor should go around the plant and other physical conditions. Knowledge of the physical conditions, such as the location of the purchase department, the sale department, the material handling store, etc. help the auditor in establishing his audit procedures and methods.

(iii) *Basic Documents of the Business.* The auditor should study the legal documents governing the concern, such as the partnership deed in the case of a partnership, the memorandum and articles of association in the case of a company, any contracts with vendors and other special acts in the case of government capital, the will or settlement in the case of a trust. The auditor should note the clauses that are likely to affect the accounts.

(iv) *Accounting Frameworks.* A study of the opening trial balance previous year's accounts and financial statements, trends of rates, and the accounting policy will assist the auditor in determining the scope of his examination if the audit is a repeat engagement. For this purpose the auditor should study the following :

(a) *Previous Accounting Records and Balance Sheets.* In case the accounts of the business have been audited previously, the auditor will get a good background of financial history of the organisation by studying the accounts and balance sheet for previous years. He should note the comments and suggestions of the previous auditors on the accounting system. He may study some of the items of trial balance to ascertain whether the accounting principles have been followed to value stock-in-trade from year to year, so that costs of sales figures are comparable.

(b) *Additional Accounting Work.* If the client has done some additional accounting work the auditor should go through it. For example he should know if the client has calculated accounting ratios and trends etc., as this will help him in planning his audit work. The comparison of ratios and trends may indicate some variations or unusual fluctuations on which the auditor should focus his attention.

(c) *Basic Accounting Policies.* Though there are well established principles in accountancy the accountants sometimes apply varying postulates according to their own judgement. These affect the audit work, hence the auditor should know the accounting policies of his client.

(d) *Various Control Systems.* After review of accounting from works the auditor should thoroughly investigate the entire system of book keeping and internal control in force in the organisation. The details involved are enormous even in a medium-sized business. The auditor should consider carefully the whole system in order to decide what ground his audit should cover and to what extent he may rely on internal control. In the words of Paula and Paula, "If this investigation is to be done effectively it must be done systematically, and best modern practice is to complete an internal control questionnaire. This document contains a series of questions that the auditor should ask, the replies being sufficiently detailed to give a comprehensive record of the accounting system, showing the effectiveness of the internal checks. When completing the questionnaire the auditor must not accept casual explanations. He must make detailed inquiries, inspect records, and wherever possible, observe the procedures in operation. During subsequent audit work he must satisfy himself that checks are in fact carried out, and make any revisions necessary to the questionnaire to keep it continually up-to-date."

7. Clarification. The auditor should clear the following points with the client :

(i) the confirmation of receivables;

(ii) the time of starting the examination;

(iii) fees to be charged;

(iv) the preparation of tax returns;

(v) whether or not the client's records are to be closed prior to the start of the examination.

Note that if the audit is a repeat engagement, work papers and correspondence of prior years should be reviewed.

CLIENT'S PREPARATION FOR THE AUDITOR

If the client prepares certain data and schedules prior to the audit work it saves money and time, both of the auditor and the client. Preparation of the following items is an internal audit function.

1. Trial balances

(i) General,

(ii) Accounts receivable and accounts payable.

2. Cash

(i) Returned bank cheques and bank statements,

(ii) Bank reconciliations,

(iii) Schedules of cash items in transit,

(iv) Confirmation request to be mailed by the auditor.

3. Receivables

(i) Statements to customers, to be verified and mailed by the auditor,

(ii) Again schedules for receivables,

(iii) Notes receivables and schedules of the notes.

4. Investments

Schedules, by types, including current-year purchases and sales, and interest received and interest accrued.

5. Inventories

(i) Original inventory-count data,

(ii) Inventory price schedules and total summaries,

(iii) Sales price schedules.

6. Prepaid expenses and outstanding expenses

(i) Schedules of all prepaid items,

(ii) Schedules of all outstanding expenses.

7. Fixed assets

(i) Schedule showing agreement of control and subsidiary records,

(ii) Schedules of additions to and deductions from fixed assets, and all supporting documents,

(iii) Analysis of depreciation accumulations, showing charges and credits,

(iv) Analysis of repair and maintenance accounts.

8. Current liabilities

(i) Statements from creditors,

(ii) Schedules of notes and any collateral security given,

(iii) Copies of all current-year tax returns prepared by the client.

9. Long-term liabilities

(i) Copies of bond indentures,

(ii) List of bond owners, if there is no trustee,

(iii) Schedules of interest payments and accruals,

(iv) Cancelled bonds retired during the current period.

10. Corporate capital

(i) Schedules of ownership of capital stock, by name and number of shares, if there is no transfer agent,

(ii) Analysis of charges and credits made to each non-capital stock proprietorship account during the year.

11. Profit and Loss

(i) Labour summaries and overhead distribution summaries,

(ii) Schedules of actual manufacturing expenses,

(iii) Analysis of expenses and revenues, as indicated by the auditor.

12. Miscellaneous

Copies of contracts, leases and so on.

What is Audit Programme ?

1. Montgomery. "An audit programme is a list generally in detail of steps to be performed in the course of an examination. It controls the nature and extent of examinations, aids in arranging, timing and distributing the work; guards against possible omissions and duplications and provides part of evidence of work done."

2. Prof. Melgs. "An audit programme is a detailed plan of auditing work to be prepared specifying the procedures to be followed in verification of each item and the financial statements and giving the estimated time."

3. Howard Stettler. "The programme is an outline of all procedures to be followed in order to arrive at an opinion concerning a client's financial statement."

Contents of Audit Programme

1. Name of the undertaking/client/business place,
2. Objects of the undertaking,
3. Date of commencement of audit,
4. Approximate duration of audit (say one month or so),
5. System of accounting adopted by the client,
6. System of internal check and its effectiveness,
7. Reports of the previous auditors and remarks, if any,
8. Examination of the various books (date-wise schedule):

(i) Cash book including petty-cash book,

(ii) Purchase and purchases returns books,

(iii) Sales and sales returns books,

(iv) Bills receivable and bills payable books,

(v) Journal proper,

(vi) Various ledger accounts and other books,

(vii) Statutory books and registers being maintained by the company under the requirements of the law.

Objects of Audit Programme

An audit is generally conducted with some definite objects in view, which should be constantly kept in mind in the initial stages of the audit.

1. Validity of appointment. The auditor should see that in case of a joint-stock company his appointment is in accordance with the provisions of the Companies Act. If he has been appointed in place of another auditor, he should enquire the reasons for the changes from the retiring auditor.

2. Determination of nature and scope of work. The auditor should obtain definite instructions from his clients about the nature and scope of his work and duties. He should know whether he is to do the accountancy work or audit work or both; by which date the work is to be completed; his honorarium, time by which the report is required, etc. To avoid any dispute later on, it will be better if the auditor sends a letter of confirmation embodying the terms of contract, scope of work, time when the work is to be done, audit fee payable and so on. In the case of audit of accounts of a joint-stock company the auditors duties, rights, powers, liabilities, etc., are all laid down by the Companies Act itself.

3. Examination of system of Accounting. He should examine the system of accounting employed by his client. He must study weak points and make recommendations to remove them.

4. Procurement of list of Books. The auditor should procure a list of all the books maintained in the office, together with the names of the keepers of such books and their specimen signatures, duly signed by a responsible official of the company. In case of joint stock companies, he is required by the Companies Act to state in his report that proper books have been kept by the company. He is also required to state that the balance sheet and the profit and loss account are in agreement with the books of account and returns. Thus, he runs a great risk 'if he omits to examine any of the books which has a bearing on the accounts.

5. Examination of internal check system. If internal check system is in operation the auditor should get a written statement to that effect and examine that system.

6. Particular life of officials. The auditor should procure list of the officers of the company containing particulars about their duties, powers and their specimen signatures.

7. Technical Knowledge. If the business is of a technical nature, auditor should visit the works and acquire technical knowledge before actually commencing the work.

8. Preparation for Audit. The auditor should ask the clients to balance the books, prepare the final accounts and the balance sheet, file the vouchers in order of occurrence of the transactions, prepare the schedules of the debtors-good, doubtful and bad debts, creditors, important legal papers, contracts, list of securities, etc. before starting his work of audit. He should never begin his work until the books have been balanced.

9. Checking of previous audit The auditor should obtain the previous year's audited balance sheet, if any. He should see that the accounts during the current year have been opened with those balances which appeared in the previous balance.

10. The auditor should get the report of the auditor relating to the accounts of the previous year for information about the state of the affairs of the company during that year.

11. The auditor must read those clauses of the Memorandum of Association and the Articles of Association of the company which have a bearing on the accounts of the firm whose accounts are being audited.

12. If it is the first audit of a company, the auditor should also go through the prospectus, contracts with the vendors, promoters etc.

Senior and Junior Audit Clerks

The chief auditor has simply to supervise and give a finishing touch to the work already done by his assistants.

He should allot the audit work to one of his senior audit clerks assisted by a few junior clerks. These junior clerks get instructions from their senior audit clerk who is directly responsible for their work. The work assigned to the juniors is of a routine nature. It requires less skill and technical knowledge. Examples of such work are checking of original records with documentary evidence such as vouchers, casting of subsidiary books, posting of such books to the ledger, checking of stock and wages sheets, etc. Usually the senior audit clerk comes on the vouching of the receipts and payments, verification of the cash balance, verification of the journal entries, adjustments, apportionment of the capital and revenue items, etc. In case of doubt or difficulty, the juniors refer the matter to their senior audit clerk who gets a clarification from the client.

Factors like experience, fact, skill, etc., must be borne in mind in selecting the senior and junior audit clerks for the work. One should not be led by the age of the clerk or the length of his service. The juniors should try to understand the transactions and take lively interest in their work. They may suggest ways of improvement to the senior audit clerk under whom they are working and work in full co-operation with the senior. They should not pass entry which they do not understand. The senior audit clerk should supervise the work of juniors under him in contact with the client or with the management. In consultation with the auditor, the senior should chalk out the programme, assign duties to different juniors and decide the work to be done by himself. Having done so, he should submit the final accounts to the auditor together with his notes who in his turn certifies the balance sheet, and prepares the report to be submitted to the shareholders of the company. He is responsible for the whole work and he signs the balance sheet.

A Specimen of Audit Programme

1. Cash Book Balanced.
2. Bank Balance Checked.
3. Cash Book Vouched.
4. Petty Cash Book Vouched.
5. Cash Book Postings Checked, Dr. Side.
6. Cash Book Postings Checked, Cr. Side.
7. Bought Ledger Vouchers.
8. Bought Ledger Cash Postings.
9. Sales Book—Additions and Postings.
10. Returns Book—Additions and Postings.
11. Journal Entries Examined and Postings.
12. Stock Account.
13. Bought Ledger Balances Checked.
14. Sales Ledger Balances Checked.
15. Trial Balances Checked.
16. General Ledger Balances Checked.
17. Profit and Loss Account Checked.
18. Balance Sheet Checked.
19. Remarks.

Advantages of Audit Programme

1. All necessary work ensured. It ensures that all necessary work has been done and nothing has been omitted.

2. Knowledge of progress. The auditor is in a position to know about the progress of the work done by his assistants.

3. Uniformity of work. A uniformity of the work can be attained as the same programme will be followed at subsequent audits.

4. Division of work. Audit can be divided amongst the different juniors responsible for their work. If a clerk goes on leave, his work may be resumed by another clerk who should know what work has already been done.

5. It simplifies the allocation of work to various grades of article and audit clerks.

6. Self-defence. If some negligence is levelled against the auditor he may defend himself that the work had been done by him or his assistant who had duly signed the audit programme.

7. Guidance. Audit programme is a kind of guidance to the audit clerk for the work he has to perform and an assurance to the auditor that the junior will not overlook essential points while checking the accounts.

8. Assurance. The audit programme junior will not overlook essential points while checking the accounts.

9. Fixing responsibility of negligence. In case of fraud or error the responsibility for negligence may be fixed on the clerk who had performed that work because initials are put on the audit programme.

10. Final review. The audit programme facilitates the final review before the report is signed.

11. Guide to new clerk. The audit programme is a guide to his duty for a new clerk.

12. Planning. Audit programme is a useful basis for planning the programme for the subsequent year.

Disadvantages of Audit Programme

1. Loss of initiative. Due to audit programme efficient clerk loses his initiative as he adheres to the programme fixed for him. He cannot make any suggestion.

2. Incomplete. The audit programme is incomplete even if it is well drawn up; as it may not cover everything that might come up during the course of audit.

3. Mechanical. Though some changes in the routine of internal check might have been introduced by the client the audit programme may be followed mechanically year after year. Each new audit programme should be an improvement over the previous year according to experience.

4. Rigidity. Each business may have a separate problem of its own, a rigid programme cannot be laid down for each type of business.

5. Unnecessary. An audit programme may be necessary for a small concern.

6. Maximum. Due to the audit programme, the audit clerk may regard the work entrusted to him as the maximum work to be done by him.

In order to eliminate these disadvantages the audit clerk should be told that the audit programme is only a guidance and he may use his initiative and intelligence during the course of audit. He should be encouraged to make suggestions, from time to time and made up-to-date according to experience and changes made in the business

AUDIT NOTE BOOK

An Audit Note Book is a book maintained by the audit clerk. A clerk comes across several difficulties or new points during the course of audit which he has to discuss with his senior or the auditor. His inquiries have not been satisfactorily answered. In order to remember all these points, he notes down these in a book which is called Audit Note Book or Audit Memoranda. It is a written record of queries made, replies received thereto and correspondence entered into, etc. It may be of great help to the auditor preparing his Audit Report from such a record. A separate Audit Note Book is maintained for each concern.

Contents of an Audit Note Book

1. A list of books of account maintained by the client;
2. The names of the principal officers, their powers, duties; and responsibilities;
3. The technical terms used in the business;
4. The points which require further explanation and clarification;
5. The particulars of the missing voucher;
6. The mistakes and errors discovered;
7. Totals or balances of certain books of accounts, Bank reconciliation statements etc.
8. Notes and queries required at a subsequent audit;
9. The points to be incorporated in the Audit report;
10. Matters requiring discussion with the senior or with the auditor;
11. Accounting method followed in the business;
12. Dates of commencement and completion of the audit;
13. Provisions in the Articles and Memorandum of Association affecting the accounts and audit.

Advantages of an Audit Note Book

If notes have been properly made in the Audit Note Book, it may prove of great value to the auditor particularly when a suit is filed against him for negligence, Audit Note Book is a documentary evidence in favour of the auditor even after several years when the auditor might have forgotten everything about that particular audit. Lord (then Mr.) Justice Vaughan Williams emphasised the importance of such a Note Book in the *London and General Bank* Case.

In order to secure the above advantages the audit note book should be clear, concise and complete so that it may be a guide quite intelligible to the clerk who audits the accounts of the same concern next year.

AUDIT FILES

The auditor should take care to preserve all working papers so that he may make best use of these when required. Files maintaining such record or working papers are called audit files.

Audit files may be of two types :

A. Permanent Audit Files.

B. Current Audit Files.

A. *Permanent Audit Files.* A permanent audit file provides useful information regarding the financial history, nature of business operations and recurring items calling for review. It includes those working papers which are useful in conducting the audit examination year after year. Information content in it is useful in the future audits also.

Following are items of a permanent audit file:

1. Client. Clients name, address and telephone numbers.

2. Business. Brief description of the business and its operations.

3. Office. A plan of the client's office layout.

4. Memorandum. Copies or excerpts of the Memorandum and Articles of Association of a company, and Partnership Deed of a Partnership firm.

5. Administration. Management instructions about administrative and other procedures which are relevant to the work of audit.

6. Organisation. Organisation and authority-responsibility structure, preferably in chart form, along with informal relationship among members of client's staff.

7. Authorities. List of persons authorised to sign cheques, contracts, and other major documents.

8. Accounts. List of accounts, books, records and procedure manuals covering all phases of operations.

9. Finance. Special financial arrangements and other significant contracts.

10. Operation. Details of operations, such as plant facilities; location of plant, warehouses, offices; proposed capital expenditure, products and by products; production of items and their demand; purchases, their mode and volume; etc.

11. Permanent Accounts. Auditor's analysis of accounts which have little or no changes such as land, buildings, plant, machinery and so on.

12. Others. Other relevant information.

B. *Current Audit File.* It contains papers and information obtained during the current audit. Items of continuing interest are transferred to the permanent audit file at the end of the audit.

The contents of the current file should be indexed either on the cover or on the first page. These will vary according to the type of business under audit. These comprise the following :

1. Engagement letter and correspondence,
2. List of items to be reviewed before releasing the report or filing the working papers,
3. Internal control questionnaire,
4. Audit programme,
5. Risk areas or loopholes in the operation of internal control,
6. A copy of the annual accounts under review and different schedules relating to the items of Balance Sheet,
7. Minutes of meetings of directors, shareholders, board of trustees,
8. A list of missing vouchers,
9. Tax, bonus and gratuity computation sheets,
10. Bank and branch reconciliation statements,
11. Correspondence with clients,
12. Correspondence with tax officials.

AUDITING WORKING PAPERS

Auditing Working papers are competent records of pertinent information about the material under audit. Skill and care in their preparation is evident from the various purposes which they serve. These are as follows :

1. Assistance in the conduct of the audit,
2. Provision of historical record of all the work that has been done,
3. Basis for the auditor's opinion,
4. Information to be used for preparation of audit report,
5. Basis for audit decisions,
6. Record of the audit conclusions,
7. Aid to partners, managers and other responsible officials in reviewing and evaluating the work of those under their supervision,
8. Showing reliance of the systems of internal control and internal audit as indicated by the comments concerning internal control and internal audit appearing on the various working papers,
9. Assisting auditor in the solution of problems arising from various

taxing units and government regulatory bodies,

10. Serving a guide for subsequent audits of the same client,
11. Proving valuable in record reconstruction, if the records of a client are stolen, lost, burnt or altered.

In the event of legal action, they serve for the auditor as a proof of defense of position in cases involving negligence and fraud.

Principles for work papers

The above purposes show that skill and experience is necessary in the preparation of adequate work papers. The work papers are an excellent preparation. From the work papers prepared by one auditor, another auditor can prepare an audit report. Following are the principles for preparation of work papers:

1. Data. (i) Irrelevant (non-material) data should not be included.

(ii) Data supporting any item in the report should be included.

(iii) Data which might (even remotely) be used in the future should be included.

2. Neat and Accurate. All work papers should be neatly prepared and must be mathematically accurate.

3. Final. The work must be so prepared that it is ready to be filed on "sign-off" day.

4. Dates and initials. All work papers must be dated and initialled.

5. Statement. Each work papers should contain a concise statement of the work performed in connection with the preparation of that paper.

6. Suggestions. The suggestions for next year should be better than those for last year.

7. Responsibility. Responsibility for the preparation of each work paper must be allocated to each person engaged in the audit. In order to identify responsibility for preparation of individual work paper, it must be completed, signed and dated by the person preparing it.

Filing of Working Papers

1. Annual audit files contain the papers covering a specific engagement in the following arrangement :

(i) Point sheet or agenda or work to be done, listing questions that have arisen in the course of the examination or as a result of the review of the working papers, and the comments providing the answers to the questions or the disposition of points that have been raised,

(ii) Audit programme,

(iii) Internal control questionnaire,

(iv) List of adjusting and reclassification entries,

(v) The auditor's trial balance or working balance sheet and income statement,

(vi) Lead schedules or grouping sheets,

(vii) The detailed working papers and supporting schedules pertaining to each lead schedule.

2. Permanent. The permanent files contain information which will be of value to each audit in future. For example, it may include audit data concerning the corporate charter (or partnership agreement), long-term leases, bond provisions, accounting procedures and data showing bad-debt, experience or changes in the accounts for accumulated depreciation.

Control of Working Papers

Due to the following reasons the auditor should have a close control over the working papers :

1. The staff of the client may try to alter information in the work papers to mislead the auditor or conceal some of their own misdeeds.
2. The papers may contain some information which should not be leaked out to the client's staff.
3. The client may be hiding the amount of salaries of certain officials from other employees although he has told the auditor who has noted it in his work papers.

Ownership of Working Papers

The working papers accumulated during the course of an independent audit are the property of the auditor. This has been established by the court cases of *Sockockinsky* v. *Bright Graham and Co.* (1938) and *Chantrey Martin and Co.* v. *Martin* (1953). The auditor may give a copy of any work paper to a client, however, a client cannot demand and receive all work papers as these may be offered by an auditor as evidence to establish the fairness of his opinion and the propriety of his audit in a court. They may also be offered in evidence by a plaintiff to support his allegations. A court order can force an auditor to divulge the contents of his work papers. Several jurisdictions have statutory laws specifically vesting ownership of work papers in the accountant.

TICK MARKS

An auditor uses many symbols or tick marks of various shapes, sizes and colours, while examining the records of the client and in the personal working papers, for recording, posting, totalling, balancing and costing.

Holmes and Overmyer have here given following examples of tick marks.

√ Use in records of original entry to indicate comparison with an invoice or any other appropriate document.

√ Place under vertical totals to indicate footing.

√ Place opposite amounts in ledger accounts to indicate the tracing of postings from records of original entry.

— Place under an amount in a record to indicate the last current-period item examined.

● In the check record, place beside each outstanding check amount to be listed in the bank reconciliation.

⊙ In the check record, place beside each amount for which the paid check was compared.

S Use in the trial balance to indicate that a schedule is to be prepared.

$ When the above schedule is completed, place a slant line through the S.

^ When a comment has been investigated and accepted, or adjusted and accepted, use this inverted check mark.

There are many additional codes for ticks. Frequently, more than one tick is used in one place, for example v and √.

Precautions in the Use of Tick Marks

1. The meaning of each tick should be made clear.
2. The same type of tick marks should not be used for the same transactions in all the firms.
3. The system of tick marks adopted should not be explained to the client's staff.
4. The audit work should be completed up to a specific point on a specific day leaving loose ends.
5. All important totals and materials must be noted in the audit note book.
6. Before the auditor starts the actual audit, all the totals in the books should be in ink and not done with pencil.

ROUTINE CHECKING

Routine checking means checking of arithmetical accuracy of books of original entry and ledgers in order to detect clerical errors of principle or clever frauds. In order to discover these the auditor has to go behind the actual books of accounts and examine original records and make intelligent inquiries. Routine checking is common to all types of business organizations. It is a type of simple checking though a significant part of the auditor's duty. It is done in a routine way revealing the clerical errors and frauds of a very ordinary nature. It can verify the arithmetical accuracy of the entries made in the books of accounts. It can ensure that no alterations are made in the figures after they have been checked and ticked accordingly. It normally involves four types of checking as the following :

(i) Casts, subcasts, carry-forwards and other calculations in the books of original entry;
(ii) Postings into the ledgers;
(iii) Casts and balances of various accounts in the ledger; and
(iv) Transfer of balances from the ledger on to the trial balance.

Advantages of Routine Checking

(i) The books of original entry may be thoroughly checked.
(ii) The errors and frauds can be easily detected.
(iii) Postings can be checked.
(iv) It helps in the checking of final accounts ultimately.
(v) It helps in the verification of the arithmetical accuracy of the entries.
(vi) It is the simplest device for audit work which can be done easily by a person with an ordinary knowledge of accounts.

Disadvantages of Routine Checking

(i) As it is a mechanical process it can cause monotony to those who are entrusted with this task.
(ii) Major items of fraud cannot be brought to light.
(iii) There is a lot of difficulty in tracing out compensating errors and errors of principle.
(iv) It is not always considered important where self-balancing system is used.

Due to the above mentioned disadvantages the work involved in routine checking is very important and must, therefore, be carried on very intelligently and carefully.

TEST CHECKING (OR SELECTIVE VERIFICATION)

In test checking the auditor does not check all the records made into the books of accounts but selects a few items through a process of sampling and if they are found correct, he presumes that the remaining entries would also be correct likewise. Thus, test checking is based on a simple principle that "if a representative number of transactions, so selected at random by the auditor for test checking, is found to be correct, the remaining ones would also be correct."

Universe and Sampling

Test checking implies selecting and checking only a few selected transactions so as the enable the auditor to form his final judgement as to the whole set of transaction which is called universe of population. The portion of the universe of population to be examines is known as sampling. Thus universe is composed of all items of one type. Test check is *'selective verification'* or *'sampling process'*. Thus, part of cash sales, cash purchases, cash receipts, cash payments, credit sales or credit purchases etc., constitute sampling for respective items although taken separately they are universe, i.e. all items of similar nature.

In applying 'test check', the selection of transactions is made by the auditor at random and no specific principles are followed in it. The choice for adoption of testing methods is fully dependent on the discretion and judgement of auditor who depends on the situation of individual cases. If the system of internal check is satisfactory, test checking can be of immense help to the auditor. It can reduce the volume of work involved in audit It should be applied and carried out intelligently and carefully as it may lead to dangerous consequences. But much depends on the test system of internal check and the intelligence of the auditor.

Safeguards for the Application of Test Checking

(i) Representative or sample transactions should be selected from every book or ledger covering the whole of the period under audit.

(ii) The selection of transactions should be distributed in such a way that the work of almost all the clerks of the client is checked.

(iii) The selection of items should be made at random.

(iv) The entries pertaining to the first and the last months of a year should be thoroughly checked as fraudulent manipulations are usually made during these months.

(v) Selection of entries and accounts for applying test checks, should be made in different portions of the work at each audit. For example, if accounts pertaining to June and November were selected for test checking in 1986, accounts pertaining to March and October may be selected in 1987 for the purpose.

(vi) Cash Book and Pass Book should be thoroughly checked.

(vii) While selection of transactions for test checking is made by the auditor no consultation should be made with the staff of the client.

There are no universally accepted percentage tables or rules for selection of audit sample which are applicable to each type of test. However, statistical sampling is always preferable in the conduct of an audit to arbitrary sampling.

Advantages of Test Checking

(i) It saves time and energy.

(ii) It is useful and purposive if the selection of transactions is done intelligently.

(iii) The auditor can undertake different audits easily and simultaneously, reducing volume of work.

(iv) The auditor may arrive at a definite conclusion about the true and fair view of the state of affairs of the concern.

(v) It reduces the cost of audit.

Disadvantages of Test Checking

(i) As it is based on the selection of representative transactions, all the errors and frauds may not be detected.

(ii) Knowing that their work will not be checked in detail the clerks in the staff of the client may become careless.

(iii) The auditor's responsibility increases. Suspicion and doubt will remain in his mind although the whole of the work is checked by him through test checking.

(iv) It is of no use if proper and effective systems of checks and controls are not being adopted in business.

(v) It is unsuitable for small business houses.

(vi) In test checking an auditor can easily cover up his negligence.

DIFFERENCE IN BALANCE BOOKS

Locating difference in balance books is a question to be decided ultimately by the auditor. This involves the following points:

1. If the ledgers are maintained on the self-balancing method, the auditor should locate the ledger in which the difference lies.
2. Differences existing in the impersonal and private ledger should not be allowed to remain undiscovered.
3. If the ledgers are not kept upon the self-balancing system, following steps should be taken:

   (i) Check the balance of various ledger accounts on to the trial balance and the list of debtors and creditors.

   (ii) Check up the castings of the trial balance and the list of debtors and creditors.

(iii) The castings and carry forwards should be carefully checked while checking the ledger accounts and their balance.

(iv) The books of original entry should be checked and compared with the ledger accounts as there might be mistakes in postings.

(v) Any cancellation or alteration in figures should be thoroughly enquired into.

(vi) If there is a difference of some round figures as Rs. 10 or Rs. 100, it may be the result of wrong totalling or error in carrying forward.

(vi) If the difference is divisible by 2, it may be the result of wrong postings on the wrong side of a ledger account, e.g., if there is an excess of debits over credits in the trial balance by Rs. 20.50, and by dividing it by 2, it comes to Rs. 10.25, it is possible that an amount of Rs. 10.25 has been wrongly posted to the debit of an account and not to its credit. Hence books of accounts should be thoroughly examined for such a difference.

(viii) Sometimes, mistakes creep up due to some misplacement of a figure, e.g., 18 instead of 81 or 19 in place of 91, etc. In such a case, the difference should be divided by 9 and if it is fully divisible by 9, then the mistake may be on account of misplacement of a figure.

(ix) If the difference is due to mistake committed in entering a wrong amount, e.g., Rs. 10.90 in place of Rs. 90.10, it will not be very easy to locate it. The auditor will have to put in a lot of hard work and only then, he will be in a position to trace it out.

QUESTIONS FOR EXERCISE

1. What are the considerations to be kept in mind before an auditor starts a new audit ? How for do they change in a repeat engagement ? Discuss in details.
2. What preparation does a client have to make before the start of the audit?
3. What is an audit memorandum and an audit programme? What are the contents of audit programme ?
4. What are the objects of an Audit programme and how should it be kept?
5. What is an Audit programme ? What are the advantages and disadvantages of conducting audits in accordance with a fixed audit programme?

6. How does the maintenance of an Audit Note Book help an auditor ?
7. What do you understand by "Audit Files" ? What type of information the auditor should maintain in the audit file of a particular client?
8. What are auditing working papers? What purposes they serve for an audit? Discuss the question of ownership of using papers.
9. "The working papers are in fact a record of work done." Explain the statement in the light of object and importance of working papers.
10. Write short note on :
    (i) Tick Marks
    (ii) Routine checking
    (iii) Test Checking
    (iv) Difference in Balancing Books.

5

The Internal Control, Internal Check and Internal Auditing

Montgomery has rightly stated that "Internal control has long been recognised as fundamental and indispensable to modern auditing. The recognition emerged gradually in the early days of the profession as auditors sought to explain the practical discovery that, for most purposes, an examination of every transaction was seldom necessary. In recent years, understanding of internal control and its relationship to auditing has deepened, in part as a result of the advances in cybernetics and in the technology of control made by management scientists and computer specialists."

In the earlier days, the *internal control* was simply viewed as one involving certain checks and procedures to prevent direct financial fraud or misappropriation of property. Today, the concept has assumed greater significance, though it does not imply that the old concept of control, as an aspect of administration, has now been completely rejected. However, the major issues in relation to control are fast developing. It involves keeping the administrator posted with the up-to-date information which reflects the result of policy and which would also provide a sound basis for ascertaining the future course of action. In brief, *it involves various methods and procedures, adopted in an organisation in order to safeguard its assets, to ensure that the accounting and statistical data produced are reliable and accurate; to promote greater efficiency in operation; and to carry out effectively general policies as laid down by the management.*

Definitions of the Internal Control

1. *W.W. Bigg.* Internal control "is best regarded as indicating the whole system of controls, financial and otherwise, established by the management in the conduct of a business, including internal check, internal audit and other forms of control." Thus, the internal control is a broader term which includes financial and other forms of control and includes internal check and internal audit.

2. *The American Institute of C.P.As.* "Internal control comprises the plan of organization and all of the co-ordinate methods and measures adopted within a business to safeguard its assets check the accuracy and reliability of its accounting data, promote operational efficiency and encourage adherence to prescribed managerial policies."[1] Thus, the internal control includes all the systems of control adopted in the business organisation.

3. *Council of the Institute of Chartered Accountants in England and Wales.* Internal control is "the whole system of controls, financial and otherwise, established by the management in order to carry on the business of the company in an orderly manner, safeguard its assets and secure as far as possible the accuracy and reliability to its records."[2] The scope of internal control, according to this definition, extends beyond accounting controls and includes all operational controls like quality control, work standards, budgetary control periodic reporting, internal checks, internal audit, policy appraisals, quantitative control etc.

ADMINISTRATIVE CONTROL V/S ACCOUNTING CONTROL

Accounting Control

An accounting control involves adopting measures so that all the transactions may be duly recorded, as authorised and executed by the management of the concern. It also involves adoption of generally accepted accounting practices. It should ensure that the accounting records are such that they can be duly relied upon. It would involve proper maintenance of the assets of the concern. The accounting controls are concerned mainly with the "plan of organisation and the procedures and records that are concerned with the safeguarding of assets and the reliability of financial records."

Administrative Control

On the other hand, the administrative control refers to the system which is related to the decision-making processes which lead to the authorisation of the transactions of the concern. Such controls do not have direct relation with the accounting controls and the financial records. The "distinction between accounting controls and administrative controls is significant. An auditor has to primarily undertake a detailed review of the accounting controls since these have a direct and significant bearing on the reliability of financial statements. Administrative controls, on the other hand, have only a remote relationship with financial records and the auditor may evaluate only those administrative controls which have a bearing on the reliability of financial records."

---

1. *Statement on Auditing Statements,* issued by the Committee on Auditing Procedure of the American Institute of Certified Public Accountants, New York, p. 15.
2. *Internal Control,* Statement No. U.4, Members' Handbook. The Institute of Chartered Accountants in England and Wales, London, 1964.

S.A.P. No. 54 (SAS No. 1, paragraph 320.27 and 320.28) revised and expanded the definitions of administrative control and accounting control as follows :

"27. *Administrative Control* includes, but is not limited to, the plan of organisation and the procedures and records that are concerned with the decision processes leading to management's authorisation of transactions. Such authorisation is a management function directly associated with the responsibility for achieving the objectives of the organisation and is the starting point for establishing accounting control of transactions.

28. *Accounting Control* comprises the plan of organisation and the procedures and records that are concerned with the safeguarding of assets and the reliability of financial records and consequently are designed to provide reasonable assurance that,

(a) Transactions are examined in accordance with the management's general or specific authorisation.

(b) Transactions are recorded as necessary (1) to permit preparation of financial statements in conformity with generally accepted accounting principles or any other criteria applicable to such statements and (2) to maintain accountability for assets.

(c) Access to assets is permitted only in accordance with management's authorisation.

(d) The recorded accountability for assets is compared with the existing assets at reasonable intervals and appropriate action is taken with respect to any differences."

Accounting controls cover many aspects, as mentioned earlier, but from the auditor's point of view, it mainly comprises of the internal check and internal audit.

INTERNAL CONTROL

Characteristics of Internal Control

1. Plan of Organisation. There should be an appropriate plan and structure of the organisation for internal control. Organisational structure provides for the proper assignment of authority and responsibility among departments, individual officers and employers to furnish the necessary segregation of duties. The plan of organisation is a system of checks and balances under which persons charged with responsibility for custody of assets and for operations have a part in keeping the accounts and those having responsibility for keeping of accounts have no part in the custody of assets or the conduct of operations. The duties of various individuals should be divided to provide a reasonable guard against irregularities and falsification of accounts by any one individual.

2. Authorisation, Record and Control Procedures. The system of internal control ensures reasonable accounting control over assets, liabilities, revenues and expenses. It involves devising of suitable producers for proper review and authorisation of transactions before they are entered in the books of accounts. Documents pertaining to each transaction should bear signatures or initials of the persons connected to make for effective accountability. An accounting manual should lay down the authority and responsibility of persons connected with the accounting work.

3. Sound Practices. Sound practices should be followed in performance of duties and functions of each of the organisational departments, in the form of an effective system of internal check laying down that no single person should alone handle a transaction completely from beginning to end.

4. Quality of Personnel. Personnel of necessary competence make internal control system effective as only by them the prescribed procedures are carried out in efficient manner. This requires proper selection and training of the personnel backed by effective direction, supervision and control.

Advantages of Internal Control

1. Reduction in quantum of work. To help the auditors in reducing the quantum of work and allow him to concentrate on selected weaker areas.

2. Efficiency. To help in the orderly and efficient conduct of the business.

3. Optimum use. To aim at optimum use of the resources of the business.

4. Check on errors. Ensuring prevention and detection of errors of business.

5. Maintenance of Accounts. To facilitate maintenance of complete, up-to-date, accurate and reliable accounts and records of business.

6. Testing. To determine the nature and extent of audit tests.

7. Policy. To ensure the adherence to managerial policies and protection of business assets.

Kinds of Internal Controls

1. Accounting Control.
2. Administrative Control.

1. Accounting Control. It comprises the plan of organization and the procedures and records that are concerned with the safeguarding of assets and the reliability of financial records and consequently are designed to provide reasonable assurance for the following :

(i) Transactions are executed in accordance with management's general or specific authorisation.

(ii) Transactions are recorded as necessary (a) to permit preparation of financial statements in conformity with generally accepted accounting principles or any other criteria applicable to such statements, and (b) to maintain accountability for assets.

(iii) Access to assets is permitted in accordance with management's authorization.

(iv) The recorded accountability for assets is compared with the existing assets at reasonable intervals and appropriate action is taken with respect to any difference.

2. Administrative Control. It includes the plan of organisation and the procedures and records that are concerned with the decision processes leading to management's authorisation of transactions. This is a management function directly associated with the responsibility for achieving the objectives of the organisation and is the starting point for establishing accounting control of transactions.

Thus internal control means a number of checks and controls exercised in a business to ensure its efficient and economic working. It involves a sort of vigilance and direction over important matters like budget and finance, purchases and sales and internal administration by the management. It provides a measure for the management to obtain information, protection and control which are quite important for the successful working of a business organisation. Therefore, every business enterprise develops a properly developed system of internal control which may include accounts control, standard of cost control, budgetary control, and an internal audit staff and other activities such as time and motion studies and quality controls through inspection.

Divisions of Internal Control

The main divisions of an overall internal control system cover: (i) general financial control; (ii) cash control; (iii) employees remuneration; (iv) trading transaction; (v) stock maintenance; (vi) fixed assets; and (vii) investments.

(i) *General Financial Control.* It includes a proper efficient system of accounting, adequate supervision, recording and duplicating systems, good efficient staff and maintenance of staff relationships. An adequate system of flow of information to the management should be developed through returns and statements submitted by the supervising staff. Healthy staff relations should be maintained to ensure more efficient and effective working. As staff turnover is injurious from the viewpoint of general financial control therefore adequate stress should be laid on their proper maintenance.

(ii) *Cash Control.* It includes certain important aspects of control for receipts, payments and balances held. There may be internal audit staff responsible to exercise checks at regular and irregular intervals. Due safeguards should be exercised to avoid misappropriation of cash. In this regard specific instructions should be given to all the staff in writing. The system of payment by cheques is the best at all times and at all levels of business. There should be proper allocation of duties.

(iii) *Employee Remuneration.* Internal control system must cover all sections of employees' remuneration and maintenance of records for remuneration. Their preparation and their methods of payment should be brought under tight control. This requires issue of specific instructions in writing to the staff engaged in the various processes of work connected with the employees' remuneration.

(iv) *Trading Transactions.* These pertain to the purchases, sales, etc. In purchases, effective procedures should be laid down for acquisition and handling of goods and for accounting technique adopted for such goods. A good system of procedures should be devised for authorization, recording, handling and accounting of goods sold. The entire system of control should be kept strictly under regular review and constant check.

(v) *Stock Maintenance.* Stock of raw materials, work-in-progress and finished goods should be properly maintained and accounted for. The flow of goods from outside to the store and *vice versa* should be made under and efficient control and supervision. Regular stock-taking procedures are means of independent checks and reconciliation of records.

(vi) *Fixed Assets.* Capital expenditure on fixed assets should be kept under strict check and supervision. Right from sanctioning of capital expenditure to its use the authority should be clearly defined so that any sort of misappropriation by officials of the organisation can be reduced to the minimum. Proper safeguards should be exercised at all stages.

(vii) *Investments.* These cover such measures as authorization, recording of all transactions including the maintenance of records of investments held and safeguarding of documents of title. This requires written instructions issued to enforce rigidly the procedure of internal control.

Internal Control and Auditor

The management has to introduce a well-developed system of internal control. The auditor can simply guide and help if he is required to do so. He must possess an expert's knowledge of such procedures. In the second standard of field work set out by the AICPA, it is made clear that "there is to be a proper study and evaluation of the existing internal control as a basis for reliance thereon and for the determination of the resultant extent of the tests to which auditing procedures are to be restricted." The auditor should establish a basis for reliance on the system of this control so as to enable him to assess the extent to which he should apply tests during the course of audit. If there is a good system of internal control, the work of an auditor becomes quite easy. The following points would be helpful in screening the internal control system :

1. Study of accounting routine, its weaknesses and sources from which they would arise;
2. Financial powers vested in the various officials and the circumstances in which they are to be used;
3. Study of limits of inspection over financial and other accounting duties;
4. Whether some mechanical appliances are used to prevent any defalcation of cash, etc.; and
5. Whether any device of checks and balances is used to measure the success of accounting methods of techniques.

The auditor can perform audit efficiently if there is a good and effective internal control system in use. However, he cannot shirk his duties. There is nothing to protect him if he does his work carelessly and with negligence. The audit should impose the most rigorous possible examination on the systems of internal control. It should cover every aspect of the administration from the purchasing procedure to the control of sales invoices and despatch of goods. It should be arranged in such a way that the system is checked at the same time when the books and records are verified.

Basic Principles of Internal Control

1. The physical handling of an asset should be separated from the accounting work which should be done by a separate hand. The collusion between a person handling an asset and another performing accounting work should be avoided.
2. The work should be so divided between persons that the work done by one is checked by another.

Thus, the result expected from the work done and the check thereof is the basis for the reliability of records and reports maintained in the business. This practice ensures that what one does can be compared well with the results obtained by another.

Evaluation of Internal Control

If the internal control is devised and installed by the management to carry on business of the company in an orderly manner, safeguard its assets and secure as far as possible the accuracy and reliability of its records relying upon the internal control system. An auditor should make the evaluation of the system and find out its deficiencies and strong points. If internal control is effective he may confine his examination and audit procedures to a representative number of transactions such as the following :

1. Business. The auditors should understand and review internal control to make preliminary evaluation. He should ascertain the characteristics of the client's business audit activities, the system of book-keeping and accounts, the nature and extent of delegation of authorities and responsibilities, the system of internal check and internal audit.

2. Procedure. The auditor should study and examine the procedural manuals, job descriptions and flow charts etc. to acquaint himself thoroughly with the related controls. He may make necessary queries from the persons responsible for exercising these controls.

3. Audit in depth. The auditor may conduct auditing-in-depth with regard to a few representative transactions to acquaint himself of the actual controls and their effectiveness. He may test check the proper compliance of internal controls by asking following questions :

(i) Were the prescribed procedures followed ?

(ii) If so, how were they undergone ? and

(iii) By whom were they undergone ?

4. Break down. Break down of the control procedures should be enquired into. The controls should be consistently followed, throughout the period of audit.

5. Changes. The auditor should take note of all changes in the nature and size of the business. He should mention material deficiencies distinct from the minor ones.

Thus, the auditor should ascertain the truth and fairness of the financial statements and also the weaknesses in the running of the business. He will be able to perform his duties effectively only after a proper evaluation and assessment of the system of internal control. Now he can plan the nature, extent and timings of the audit tests that he must undertake and suggest improvements in the techniques of management.

Methods of Reviewing the System of Internal Control

1. Narrative Record
2. Check List
3. Questionnaire
4. Flow Charts.

1. Narrative Record. It includes a complete written description of the internal control system of the enterprise under audit. The type and extent of narrative record will vary according to the requirements and individual judgement of each auditor. The compilation of a narrative record of internal control is usually a very lengthy process.

2. Check List. Check list contains a set of instructions to be followed by the auditor or questions to which he must find answers. After an instruction has been followed, he puts his initials in the space provided opposite it. The check list is submitted to the chief accounting executive of the enterprise with a request to write "Yes", "No" or "Not applicable" in answer to each of the questions. After completing the check list for all individuals/departments, the auditor makes his own tests and inquiries to ascertain that the procedures and practices being actually followed are in conformity with the answers. He himself fills in the answers after interrogating the persons involved with accounting operations.

3. Questionnaire. In order to assess the effectiveness of the controls involved therein for each functional area, the questions should be simple, logical and to the point; well thought out, brief, compact and without any ambiguity. The answers should be brief and to the point. The questionnaire should be filled in during their leisure time.

The preparation of a questionnaire is an exercise easier than the narrative form. It may be prepared section-wise rotating from one official to another for independent filling. It is more effective and easier to understand and convenient. The required information can be pin-pointed and the chances of omission of any important information are eliminated.

4. Flow Charts. Flow chart is intended to provide the auditor with a coherent understanding of the system he is receiving. It provides a foundation for his subsequent evaluation of controls. It enables to pin-point quickly and accurately the weaknesses in internal method of a business. It is an effective exercise for the auditor in concentrating his own attention on these weak points. If the charts are not drawn properly, they may confuse the whole situation. The entire diagramme may become unwieldy for comprehension.

INTERNAL CHECK

What is internal check?

1. American Institute of Public Accountants Committee. "Internal check is a system under which accounting methods and details of an establishment are so laid out that the accounts and procedures are not under the absolute and independent control of any person —that on the contrary the work of one employee is complementary to that of another— and that a continuous audit of the business is made by the employees."

2. Davar. "Internal check is a system or method introduced with defined instructions given to staff as to their sphere of work with a view to control and verification of work and also maintenance of accurate records as the ultimate aim."

3. Ronald A. Irish. "Internal check refers to the organisation of office duties in such a way as to prevent or disclose both errors and frauds."

4. Spicer and Pegler. "A system, of internal check is an arrangement of staff duties whereby no one person is allowed to carry through and to record every aspect of the transaction, so that without collusion between two or more persons, frauds prevented and at the same time the possibilities of errors are reduced to the minimum."[3]

5. Montgomery. "Internal check comprises those accounting procedures or physical, statistical or other controls designed to safeguard assets against defalcations or other similar irregularities or against loss from other causes."[4]

6. F.R.M. De Paula. "An internal check means practically continuous internal audit carried on by the staff itself, by means of which the work of each individual is independently checked by the other members of the staff."[5]

7. Dicksee. "Internal check may be defined as such an arrangement of the accounting routine that errors and fraud are automatically prevented or discovered by the very operation of book keeping it sees."[6]

Functions of Internal Check

It is evident from the above definitions that an efficient system of internal check provides for an independent and automatic scrutiny along with the work assignment. It involves the following four things:

(i) That the work is properly divided in such a way that all the duties are assigned to different clerks.

(ii) That the clerks get the work-load according to their capacities and qualifications.

(iii) That one person does not perform any single task from the beginning to the end.

(iv) That the work done by one clerk is checked independently and automatically by another.

Thus, persons are made responsible separately for doing the job connected with such of the three functions in regard to wage payment. This may be done in two ways:

(i) Either one-third of the work connected with all the three portions of work relating to wages may be performed by two persons; or

3. Spicer and Pegler, *Practical Auditing,* p. 33

4. *Op. Cit.,* p. 58.

5. F.R.M. De Paula, *The Principles of Auditing* p. 10.

6. L.R. Dicksee, *Auditing,* p. 48.

(ii) Two persons may be made responsible, for every portion of this work, i.e., maintenance of wage record, preparation of Wage Sheet and the payment of wages.

Thus while two clerks maintain records, another set of two clerks should prepare Wage Sheet and the remaining two clerks should arrange for the payment of wages.

Out of these two arrangements the first one is defective as it provides scope of collusion between two persons when they have to perform one-third of the work from the beginning to the end. The second device is more reliable and efficient as in this case the whole of the work is suitably and rationally divided and there is no possibility for fraud as the work involved in each portion can be checked by the clerks. The work and its checking are carried on independently. This division of work is known as a system of internal check.

This internal check is an arrangement of duties in a business in such a way that all the duties connected with the accounting work are properly allocated so that one person may not be in a position to pursue a single job from the beginning to the end and along with this, the work of one person may be checked automatically and independently by another.

Objects of Internal Check

1. To allocate duties and responsibilities of every clerk so that he may be held responsible for a particular error or fraud;
2. To minimize the possibilities of errors, frauds or irregularities;
3. To detect errors or frauds.
4. To enhance the efficiency of clerks as the assignment of duties is based on the principle of division of labour;
5. To distribute work in such a way that no business transaction is left from recording;
6. To prepare final accounts with ease and efficiency as an efficient system of internal check makes accounts regular and reliable;
7. To exercise moral pressure over staff.

FUNDAMENTAL PRINCIPLES OF INTERNAL CHECK

(a) General Principles

1. The work of the business should be so allocated amongst various clerks that their duties, rights and responsibilities may be clearly and judiciously divided and there may not be left any room for interference.
2. The distribution of work should be done in such a way that no single person is allowed to do a job solely by himself from the beginning to the end.

3. In order to ensure for efficiency and specialization, one person should be entrusted with all the similar nature of work.
4. No clerk should be engaged on a particular job. Change in duties would for long absolutely depend upon the circumstances prevailing before a business. Such a change in duties should be made without making it known to those concerned.
5. An efficient system of internal check should provide for an automatic checking of the work of an assistant by another.
6. The division of work should not be expensive.
7. No clerk of the business should be relied upon too much.
8. Self-balancing system should be used for making the system of internal check efficient and successful.
9. Labour-saving devices should be used such as cash register, calculating machine, time recording clocks, etc.
10. There should be a proper system of filing vouchers, correspondence, etc.
11. A responsible official should be entrusted with receiving important letters, registered envelopes and moneyorders which should be entered in a proper register and then passed on to the clerks concerned.
12. All the cash received should be sent daily to the bank.
13. Persons dealing with cash, securities, cheques, etc., should be compelled to take annual holidays in unbroken periods.
14. Purchase, receipt and issue of books should always be done under strict supervision and control.
15. Jobs relating to bad debts, allowances, returns, etc. should be performed under strict control.
16. Some responsible person should be assigned the task of dealing and corresponding with the debtors and creditors of the business.
17. Important work like payment of wages, valuation of stock, sales, etc., should be done under strict supervision and control.

Advantages of Internal Check

1. Proper Distribution of Work. Internal check entails a proper and rational distribution of work between the members of the staff of a business. It determines their duties precisely.

2. Accountability. Internal check determines the responsibilities of employees for particular acts, defaults or omissions. Every member of the staff may be held responsible for any irregularity carried on by him.

3. Moral Check on Employees. The whole system of internal check is based on principles of division of labour and specialisation. It exercises a moral check on the clerks of a business. This leads towards more efficient and economic operation.

4. Preparation of Final Accounts. By the efficient work which results from efficient operation of internal check the staff is enabled to prepare the final accounts with ease and quickness.

5. Accuracy of Records. Internal check results into correct and complete records of all the transactions on each balancing of the books of accounts. It ensures accuracy of the fact and entries, physical or financial by the maintenance of records.

6. Smooth flow of Work. Internal check facilitates divisional accounting. It fixes working quotas for the members of the staff. Break up of the accounting procedures in various segments is made to avoid bottlenecks and to establish a very smooth flow of work.

7. Prevention and detection of Errors and Frauds. Internal check maintains an accurate record of all the business transactions by reducing the possibilities of errors and frauds remaining undetected for a long time.

8. Convenience to Auditors. If the system of internal check is operating, the external auditor may conveniently avoid detailed checking of the transactions, books and accounts. He is to select certain representative transactions or documents for detailed checking.

Disadvantages or Limitations of Internal Check

1. Costly. The system of internal check is more expensive and time consuming. It involves additional costs which a small business may not afford.

2. Sacrifice of Quality. In internal check system quality of work tends to decline because employees perform their work quickly and do not care for the quality of work which tend to slacken their efforts.

3. Difficulty in the Introduction. An effective system of internal check is difficult to introduce if the size of the business is very small. It cannot work effectively without a large number of employees. It cannot be introduced in a business where supervisors and managers are not prepared to divide authority between the employees.

4. Risky for an Auditor. While an auditor relies on the books and accounts of and enterprise which has adopted effective internal check system, he should apply tests and procedures of his own to ascertain the soundness of the system, otherwise he may be held liable for negligence.

ESSENTIALS OF INTERNAL CHECK SYSTEM

1. Fixed Responsibility. Responsibility of each individual should be properly defined and fixed. Detailed records of the accounting procedures should be laid down. There should be a schedule of duties of every employees in all the departments. An organisation chart should be prepared.

2. Standard Forms. Internal check system should have standard ruling and arrangement of forms and accounting records with numbering etc.

3. Separation of Accounting and Control. No person should be able to establish accountability over his operations.

4. Rotation of Employees. If the employees are in a large number there should be a rotation of the various employees so that they may not develop some alienation with the staff of the concerned department. There should be internal transfers of the employees from one job to another or from one department to another from time to time.

5. Use of Mechanised Method. Keeping in view the requirements of the undertaking the mechanised system of accounting should be adopted so that eraser or overwriting can be avoided.

6. Safeguards. Adequate safeguards should be prescribed to keep un-used receipts, cheque books, files, bills etc. so that their misuse may be avoided.

7. Strict Supervision. Strict supervision should be observed to ensure that the prescribed internal checks and procedures are fully operative.

8. Proper use of Assets. Proper use of assets should be ensured. Unauthorised use of assets should be prevented.

9. Division of Work. According to the fundamental principle of division of labour there should be segregation of responsibilities for carrying on the transactions and recording the same. Hence, there should be a proper division of the responsibilities of the members of the staff.

10. Personal Care. The senior and responsible official should take a personal care regarding receipts and payments of cash, issue of goods, valuation of stocks etc.

11. Use of Self-Balancing Method. Accounts department should use self-balancing method so that the employees may not get any information about the combined ledgers. The accounts should be under the control of a responsible official of a company.

12. Flexible. The system of internal check should be flexible. It may be changed according to the changing requirements of the concern.

Position of Auditor in Internal Check System

1. Duties. An auditor's duties are confined only the examination of the system in force in the concern. He should do the following work in order to examine the effectiveness of internal check system:

(i) Receive a written statement from the concern regarding the system of internal check.

(ii) Study carefully the system in force in the organisation applying a few test checks.

(iii) Find out the defects and weak points of the internal check system which may result into errors or frauds.

2. Dependence. The extent to which an auditor may rely upon the system of internal check depends upon the effectiveness of the operation of the system. The work of an auditor becomes easy in an efficient and effective system of internal check. He is relieved of the detailed checking of the transactions automatically taken care of by internal check. He need not go by a detailed checking of the transactions. He can thus devote his attention to the more important section of his audit work.

3. Suggestions. If the system in force is not efficient *i.e.,* there are certain weaknesses the auditor should make suggestions to avoid the defects and weak points. He should also suggest changes necessary to strengthen the system of internal checks.

4. Liability. An efficient system of internal check helps and auditor in reducing the detailed checking of the transactions but does not reduce his legal liability. In the event of any mistake or fraud being discovered subsequently in the areas of account which the auditor has accepted to be correct, he may be guilty of negligence regardless of the fact that he relied upon the internal checking.

KINDS OF INTERNAL CHECK SYSTEM

Internal Check on Cash Receipts and Payments. Checking of all cash transactions is important because misappropriation of cash has become quite common now a days. Employees prone to commit a fraud, find the temptation difficult to resist and may not record receipts in cash book. Record of cash received may be understated by preparing duplicated receipts for amounts less that the original parts of the amounts received with the objective of lapping them with subsequent receipts. Amount of a cheque may be increased after it has been signed. A cheque may be made payable to a wrong payee. Cash sales may be treated as credit sales charging the amounts fictitious debtors. To check these frauds there must be a proper system of internal checks.

Following points must be considered in this connection:

(a) Check on Cash Receipts

1. Some responsible person must handle inward mail and correspondence.
2. All cheques and postal orders should be cancelled on receipt by a stamp with a crossing "Not Negotiable— Account Payee Only."

3. Cash for disbursement purposes should not be withdrawn from cash receipts.
4. All cash remittances should be entered in a diary be a specified clerk.
5. Serially numbered receipt books with counterfoils should be used for the receipt of cash.
6. Unused receipt books should be kept under lock and key.
7. Cashier should not be allowed to make entries in the ledgers. Accounts staff should not be allowed to make entries in the cash book.
8. A responsible officer who must be other than cashier must reconcile pass book and cash book from time to time.
9. All cash sales like sale at the counter, sales by travelling agents postal sales etc. must be subject to sound system of recording and checking.
10. An independent daily control of cash receipts should be such as checking of the first list of cash receipts with summary of receipts issued or posted to the payers and entries in the respective ledger accounts.

(b) Check on Cash Payments

1. Beyond a certain amount all payments must be made by crossed cheques against relevant supporting documents.
2. Persons authorised to sign cheques should not be allowed to prepare credit list or cheques. Two persons must sign the cheques.
3. Blank cheques should be held under lock and key with some responsible person.
4. Receipts duly signed and stamped should be obtained for each payment.
5. These should be properly arranged and maintained through proper filing in cash book.
6. To ensure the availability of discounts, all monthly accounts should be paid on the fixed date.
7. Before they are passed for payment, there should be proper checking of statements with initialed invoices.

Internal Check on Cash Sales. Cash sales in a big retail business consists of the following:

(i) Sales at the Counter
(ii) Sales by Travelling Agents
(iii) Postal Sales

(i) *Sales at the Counter.* Following steps should be taken for effective and efficient internal check system:

1. Separate chief salesmen should be appointed for each section, department or counter, to look after their respective positions.
2. Each salesman should be provided with Counter Book and carbon copy.
3. Salesmen should be forbidden to receive cash. Instead there should be a central counter to handle cash.
4. Salesman should only write a sales note, when sale is make.
5. Another salesmen or chief salesman should check sales note which along with its carbon copy should be taken by the customer to cash deck for payment.
6. After receiving the payment the sales note should be handed back to the customer. The cashier should retain the carbon copy which is used as voucher for the receipt of payment against books sold by the salesman.
7. All cash receipts should be deposited in a bank daily.
8. From the carbon copies of sales note, a summary of sales for each salesman is prepared.
9. Everyday a responsible official should verify cash received with
   (i) Cashier's summary;
   (ii) Salesman's summary.

(ii) *Sales by Travelling Agents.* In a big retail business, travelling agents are appointed to sell consumable items directly to the consumers at their doorsteps. There travelling agents go from door to door, book the orders of different consumers and make arrangements to supply the required goods at their doors through the big retail business concern. As such travellers agents are not allowed to collect cash, adequate arrangements should be made for payments to be made to head office directly. Sometimes in order to enforce terms of credit, it is desirable to authorise travellers to collect cash. The following steps must be taken under such circumstances:

1. The travelling agents should not be allowed to directly collect the sales amounts from the customer.
2. The travelling agents should not be allowed to meet out any expenditure in connection with the sales out of sales amounts collected by them.
3. If allowed to collect the amount of the sales from the customers the travelling agents should have clear instructions to deposit in the local bank or to remit it intact to the central office in the name of the firm.

4. The office should be kept informed about the balances which are over due.
5. Reminders to the customers should be sent by the office.
6. The office should carry on correspondence to find out whether the balance indicated therein is correct or not.
7. The office should prepare a statement about the debtors.
8. The office should correspond with those old customers from whom no orders have been received for a long time.
9. The area of every travelling agent should be changed from time to time.
10. Some senior person should properly check the periodical statement submitted by the travelling agents.

(iii) *Postal Sales* : Following points should be considered about postal sales:

1. A separate V.P.P. Register should be maintained with the following particulars recorded in it : (i) Customer, (ii) Quality of goods, (iii) Price, (iv) Date of despatch, and (v) Amount received.
2. Proper record should be maintained about the goods returned by the customers and received through post office.
3. The amount received from postal sales in a day should be recorded in cash book.
4. The amount received in advance from the customer should be entered into V.P.P. Register.
5. Some responsible official should check the V. P. P. Register frequently and compare it with cash book.

(C) Internal Check on Wages and Salaries Payments. Remuneration to employees and labour of the organisation sometimes constitutes 25 to 30 per cent of the total business expenditure. In the preparation of the wage sheets and the subsequent payment of wages, call for a carefully planned system of internal check, as a large number of defalcations have their origin in the payment of wages.

1. System of Internal Check. The system of internal check regarding wages is by the circumstances of a business. In designing and enforcing a system of internal check as regards wages the basic points worth considering are given below:

(i) The management should be duly authorised for the engagements and rates of pay.

(ii) Proper record should be maintained about the employment of each workman, his trade, department, date of joining and leaving and intermediate changes.

(iii) Accurate records should be maintained about the employee's attendance from day to day and the actual time spent on each job so as to constitute the basis for ascertainment of wages.

(iv) In case the payment is made on piece-work system, it should be accurately compared with the viewer's certificate and the authorised piece work.

(v) A responsible official must be authorised for all overtime and working at exceptional hours.

(vi) Having been computed accurately wages must be made up accurately and paid out to the correct persons.

(vii) To prevent collusion, separate clerks and officials should be engaged in the preparation and checking of the wage sheets and the payment of wages.

2. Record of Wages. In case the wages are to be paid according to time spent, the time keeper should be provided with either a time board on which each workman can hang a brass check bearing his number or a mechanical clock work device in which the workman punch card at the time of entering the factory premises and while leaving it. The time keeper should be present to ensure that no workman hangs the check number or punch the time of an absentee worker or a worker coming late.

In case of time workers, every worker must be provided a time card showing the time of departure and arrival or the job on which he is engaged, along with the department in which he works. Each entry in the card must be initialled by the foreman. In the case of piece-workers every worker must be supplied a 'piece-work return' form or job card specifying job undertaken. He should hand over the form or card to the authorised person as soon as work is completed who initials it after inspection of the work done.

3. Compilation of wage sheets. For proper compilation of payrolls the following steps are necessary:

(i) Records prepared by various departments should be tallied with the records written by the workmen to claim wages and any variances be removed.

(ii) The payrolls should comprise details about each workman's number, time worked, nature of work done, rate, amount of wages, bonus, gross amount payable, deductions (if any) and the net amount payable.

(iii) The above details should be filled up by a set of clerks engaged to enter it from the job cards and piece-work cards. Now all the necessary details should be checked by some other clerks.

(iv) The net amount of wages due to each worker should be worked out and the wage sheets be cast by another set of clerks.

(v) The job cards and piece-work cards should be sent to the casting department so that the wages chargeable to each job or process may be ascertained.

(vi) Every person concerned with the preparation of wage sheets should put up his initials thereon. These should be countersigned as a whole by the works manager or some other responsible officer.

3. Payment of Wages. The management or owner must ensure the following about payment of wages:

(i) The persons preparing the wage sheet should not be associated with the payment of wages and salaries in order to eliminate any chance of collusion.

(ii) All workers receiving wages should be present at the time of payment.

(iii) The foreman or concerned officer of each department should be present at the time of payment to prevent any sort of impersonation for workers who are absent.

(iv) The signature of the recipient should be obtained on the pay sheet wherever possible. If the number of workers is large and obtaining individual signatures is not feasible, the payment should be made by the officers present, e.g. the foreman, the works manager and cashier.

(v) In the case of casual labour, a separate list of such workers should be prepared and the payment should be made in the presence of a responsible officer. In order to avoid fraud, the officer employing casual labour should not be connected with the payment of wages.

(vi) Proper arrangements should be made with regard to unclaimed wages.

(vii) In case the wages and salaries are paid by cheque:

(a) the persons preparing those signing and bank transfer lists should independent of those responsible for preparing pay sheets,

(b) a separate bank account of wages and salaries should be maintained and the net amount payable transferred on the due date. A regular reconciliation should be done by some officer independent of those responsible for maintaining pay records.

8. In connection with deductions, appropriate arrangements should be made for dealing with statutory and other authorised deductions from the pay.

Internal Check on Trading Transaction

1. Purchases and Creditors. In framing the internal check system regarding purchase, following points are important:

1. Purchase procedures including the requisition, authorisation and placing of purchase order must be laid down in detail.
2. If tenders are invited for purchases, the person who can invite and open tenders must be specified clearly.
3. If the firms are stated for purchase, the procedure must specify the order placing authority. Order forms should be kept under lock and key.
4. Proper arrangements should exist for examining quantity, quality and condition of goods received.
5. The proper allocation of duties must cover the following in the field of accounting:
   - (i) checking of invoices received
   - (ii) maintaining of a day book to make proper records of purchases and purchase returns.
   - (iii) the writing up of the ledger accounts and checking of suppliers' statements.
   - (iv) the following must; be ensured before making payment for goods bought:
     - (a) goods have actually been received, the price is as agreed, and a proper invoice is there;
     - (b) advantage has been taken of any discount availability
     - (c) payment has been duly authorised by the specified official;
     - (d) as far as possible, payment is made through account payee cheques only; and
     - (e) if the goods have been bought from companies under the same group or from employees, the price is not more than the market price.
   - (v) the suppliers' accounts should be checked periodically by either direct verification from them or from the statements received from them.

2. Purchase Returns. Following must be ensured about purchase returns:

(i) Goods returned to suppliers are entered in the purchase returns book/goods, outward book at once; and

(ii) A debit note is obtained at the earliest for making a claim or getting the amount adjusted where payment has yet to be made.

3. Sales. The following measures must ensure about the system of internal check regarding sales:

(i) Immediately on receipt of an order, it should be numbered and entered in the Register of Orders received, where full details are given about the date of the invoice number.

(ii) Either the original order or a copy thereof should be then handed over to the despatch department with necessary particulars and instructions as to packing, mode of transport, etc.

(iii) After the goods ordered are got ready for delivery, they should be checked with the original order before being packed.

(iv) After the order is executed by the despatch of goods, the original order or the copy thereof should be returned by the despatch department to the counting house for the purpose of an outward invoice being made out in the name of the customer.

(v) Some responsible person should check that the rates charged to the customer are proper.

(vi) After the outward invoice is made out with a carbon duplicate copy, the particulars stated therein such as the quantity, quality and rates of goods charged should be compared with the original order, and the invoice initialled accordingly by the person who did the checking.

(vii) Some other clerk should check the calculations and extensions. He should also initial the invoice to indicate the work done by him.

(viii) The invoice should then be passed on to the invoice clerk to be entered in the Sales Day Book. One copy of the invoice with perforations is torn off and sent to the customer, while the other remains in a bound form in the Outward Invoice Book.

(ix) After being executed, the original orders are numbered consecutively and properly filed. Each outward invoice is marked with its corresponding order number, while the number of the invoice is marked on the original order.

(x) The gate-keeper should maintain a book called the 'Goods Outwards Book' in which he should enter particulars of all goods going out of the premises. The entries in this book should be checked with the outward invoices by some responsible person from time to time.

(xi) If a large number of orders are executed every day involving numerous entries in the Day Book, two sets of Sales Day Books should be maintained, to be issued on alternate days, so that the postings into the customers' ledgers may be done uninterruptedly without inconvenience to anyone.

(xii) As a prompt execution of orders always impresses the customers most favourably, great attention should be paid to the timely despatch of goods.

(xiii) All sale contracts and orders executed against these should be entered in a special book from time to time.

(xiv) If sales are effected by travelling salesmen, each salesman is supplied with a triplicate Sale Note Book, in which he enters particulars of each sale. One copy of this entry be delivered to the customer, another should be despatched to the head office for execution of the order and the third be kept in book for reference.

4. Sales Returns

(i) When returned by customers, the particulars in sales returns should be entered by the Gate Office in a special book called Goods Inwards Book, a carbon copy of which should be sent daily to the counting house.

(ii) After such goods are duly checked with the debit note received from the customer, a credit note should be made out in duplicate in respect of the same.

(iii) Some responsible person should check and initial each credit note before despatch.

(iv) Entries should be made in the Returns Inwards Book.

(v) Each credit note should be numbered consecutively. This number must be indicated against the corresponding entry in the Returns Inwards Books.

5. Stock Controls.

Stock control procedure ensure that stocks held are adequately protected against loss or misappropriation. Checks are properly applied in the operations of the business and are duly accounted for. According to the nature of the business, separate arrangements are necessary for different categories of stocks, e.g. raw materials, components, work-in-progress finished goods and consumable stores. The following must be ensured about stock control:

(i) On receipt of stocks, a Goods Received Note is prepared in triplicate, one for the purchase department, second for the accounts department and third for the stores department.

(ii) Stocks should be kept safe under the custody of some responsible persons, so that these are protected against theft, misuse and deterioration.

(iii) Maximum and minimum stock limits should be determined in advance. Purchase requisitions should be automatic on stock item hitting the minimum level.

(iv) Procedure should be clearly laid down for movement of stock out of store.

(v) The stock should be frequently counted and checked by a responsible official who should compare the bin card's with the stores ledger.

(vi) Arrangements should be made for dealing and maintaining accounting control over company stocks held by others such as goods in warehouse, on consignment, or in course of processing and goods belonging to others held by the company such as how withdrawals are to be authorised and evidenced, and how goods belonging to others are to be distinguished from own goods.

(vii) Method of valuation of stocks should be followed on a consistent basis. Such valuations must be checked by an independent person.

(viii) Adequate control should be instituted over scrap and wastage. Periodical reports should be prepared comparing actual wastages with wastage normally allowed. Receipts from disposal of scrap and wastage should be properly accounted for.

6. Fixed assets. Fixed assets are the assets of a permanent nature in any business. Fixed assets are not held for resale but for the purpose of running the business. The expenditure incurred on fixed assets is known as capital expenditure. A strict control and vigilance over fixed assets is necessary due to huge expenditure in acquiring these. The following control procedure may be utilised about fixed assets:

(i) Only top management personnel are authorised to purchase these assets and proper records evidencing such authorisation maintained.

(ii) The authority for sale, exchange or disposal of such assets vest with responsible official of the organisation. No single person may handle all the aspects mentioned above.

(iii) Proper accumulated records such as plant registers should be maintained so that proper information may be available regarding all fixed assets. Arrangements should be made for physical verification as frequently as possible.

(iv) If such assets are transferred to sites, branches or within a group, proper recording should be ensured and records must be verified from time to time at least once a year.

(v) Fixed assets shouid be properly maintained and applied in the service by the business unit. This may be done by periodical physical inspection their location, position and condition.

(vi) a responsible official should be authorised to fix the rates of depreciation, to be applied to different types of fixed assets within the legal framework applicable. A separate team of persons should be responsible for carrying out and checking the necessary calculations.

7. Investments. The control on investment checks the possibility of misappropriation, especially by staff in higher paid grades. The important checks in investments may be the following :

(i) The persons authorised to buy and sell investments should be specified clearly.

(ii) The documents and the titles of investments should be kept under lock and key in the personal custody of responsible persons.

(iii) A register of investments must be maintained. Some responsible person should tally it periodically with the actual investments and physically verify the documents of title.

(iv) In order to ensure that charges are correctly recorded, arrangements should exist for checking the brokers notes relating to the purchase and sale of investments.

(v) Arrangement should exist to ensure that interest, vouchers, repayments, dividends and other claims or rights are received and properly accounted for.

INTERNAL AUDITING

Definition

1. Professor Walter B. Meigs. "....internal auditing consists of a continuous, critical review of financial and operating activities by a staff of auditors functioning as full-time salaried employees."

2. The Institute of Internal Auditors, Inc., New York. "Internal audit is an independent appraisal activity within an organisation for the review of accounting, financial and other operations as a basis for service to the management."

Objective of Internal Auditing

The objective of internal auditing is to assist all members of management in the effective discharge of their responsibilities, by furnishing them with analyses, appraisals, recommendations and pertinent comments concerning the activities reviewed. The internal auditor may check the accounting and financial records to obtain a full understanding of the operations under review.

Scope of Internal Auditing

1. To review and appraise the soundness, adequacy, and application of accounting, financial and other operating controls, and promote effective control at reasonable cost;
2. To ascertain the extent of compliance with established policies, plans and procedures;
3. To ascertain the extent to which company assets are accounted for and safeguard them from losses of all kinds;

4. To ascertain the reliability of management data developed within the organisation;
5. To appraise the quality of performance in carrying out assigned responsibilities; and
6. To recommend operating improvements.

INTERNAL AUDIT VIS-A-VIS INDEPENDENT AUDIT

Relationship

Today many large organisations have an internal audit department, the standard and scope of which varies considerably from organisation to organisation. However, even if an efficient internal audit system exists, the need for an independent audit by external professional auditor exists, who must make careful inquiries before determining the extent to which he can rely on the internal audit in drawing his own programmes. Before taking any decision the independent auditor must be sure about :

1. The competence of internal audit staff;
2. The extent and nature of the work undertaken by the internal audit department;
3. The extent and effectiveness with which the internal audit programme is carried out;
4. The internal audit reports;
5. The way in which points raised in the internal audit reports have been dealt with; and
6. The authority given to the head of the internal audit department and the level of management to which he is directly responsible.

There is a close similarity between the internal auditor's work and that of an independent auditor. On accounting matters the internal auditor and the independent auditor operate largely in the same field. They have a common interest in certain areas of operations, about :

(i) Ensuring that there is an effective system of internal check to prevent or detect errors and fraud and that it is operating satisfactorily;

(ii) Ensuring that there is an adequate accounting system to provide the information necessary for preparing true and fair financial statements; and

(iii) Verification of assets and liabilities.

Distinctions

1. Scope of work. Since internal auditor is appointed by the management, his scope of work is determined by the management only. He primarily serves the management. External/independent auditor is normally appointed under sone statute which places certain responsibilities on him which cannot be altered. He serves the needs of third parties.

2. Approval. Internal auditor has to review the operations and internal control primarily to make improvements and induce compliance with established policies and procedures, not limited to financial matters. He is directly concerned with detection of errors and frauds. Independent auditor has to review the operation and internal control primarily to determine the scope of examination and reliability of financial data. He is only incidentally concerned with the detection of errors and frauds.

3. Responsibilities. Internal auditor should be independent of management particularly the chief accountant, yet ready to respond to the needs and desires of all elements of management. He is neither obliged nor required to report to auditors. Review of company activities is his crucial contribution. External Auditor is always independent of management factually and in mental attitude. He examines the supporting data with financial statements periodically usually once a year. He is forced by the statute to report to shareholders of the company in the Annual General Meeting.

INTERNAL CONTROL AND INTERNAL AUDIT

1. While internal control is an arrangement of duties allocated in such a way that the work of one employee is automatically checked by another, internal audit is an independent review of operations and records undertaken by the staff specially appointed for the purpose.
2. While there is no separate staff engaged to carry out the system of internal control, a separate staff is engaged specially for carrying out internal audit.
3. While internal control the work is allocated to different employees in such a way that the work of one is independently checked by another, in internal audit, the work of a clerk is checked by an internal auditor after the former has completed his work.
4. While system of internal control is devised in such way that the possibilities of errors, frauds and irregularities are minimised, in internal audit, errors and frauds already committed can be discovered.
5. While the system of internal control is a device for doing work, internal audit checks the work done in the light of policies and procedures laid down by the people at the helm of affairs.

INTERNAL AUDIT V/S STATUTORY AUDIT

Following are the points of distinction between the Internal Audit and Statutory Audit:

1. Appointments

(i) While Internal auditor is appointed by the management, the statutory auditor is appointed by the shareholders except in certain cases when he is appointed by the directors of the company or the Government.

(ii) While the appointment of internal auditor is optional that of the statutory auditor is obligatory.

(iii) While the appointment of internal auditor is according to the decision of the management, that of the statutory auditor is according to the Companies Act.

2. Qualifications. While the Internal auditor need not possess the qualifications as are laid down under Section 226 of the Companies Act, a statutory auditor must have those qualifications.

3. Status. While the Internal auditor is an employee of the company statutory auditor is an independent person.

4. Conduct of Audit. While the internal audit is a kind of continuous audit, a statutory audit is generally conducted after the preparation of the final accounts.

5. Scope of Work. While the scope of the work by the internal auditor is determined by the management, the scope of the work and the responsibilities of the statutory auditor are determined by law.

6. Objective. While an internal auditor has the primary duty to find out whether any error or fraud has been committed, the statutory auditor has to report whether the balance sheet and the profit and loss account of a company has been drawn up in conformity with law and whether they show true and fair view of the state of affairs of the company. Detention of errors and frauds are incidental duties of a statutory auditor.

7. Determination of Duty. While the scope and duties of an internal auditor can be reduced, it is not so in the case of a statutory auditor.

8. Suggestion. While the internal auditor has to make suggestions to the management as to how to run the business efficiently and to avoid wastages, a statutory auditor need not do so unless he is specifically asked.

9. Checks. While the internal auditor has to check all the transactions, the statutory auditor may apply test checks.

10. Report. While the internal auditor has not to submit any report to the shareholders, a statutory auditor has to do so.

11. Application of Chartered Accountants Act. While the internal auditor cannot be prosecuted for professional misconduct unless he is a Chartered Accountant, a statutory auditor can be prosecuted.

12. Removal. While the internal auditor can be removed by the management or the directors, a statutory auditor can be removed only by the shareholders and not by the management or the directors.

13. Watching While the internal auditor acts as a watch-dog for the directors, the statutory auditor has to act as a watch-dog for the shareholders.

14. Satisfaction. While the internal audit is carried out for the satisfaction of the management of the concern, the statutory audit is carried out for the satisfaction of the shareholders and third parties for the financial data.

15. Remuneration. While the remunerations of the internal auditors are fixed by the management, for the statutory auditors they are fixed by the shareholders.

16. Attendance at Meetings. While the internal auditor has no right to attend a meeting of the shareholders, a statutory auditor has such a right.

17. Duration. While the activities of the internal auditor are continuous, those of the statutory auditor are periodic, usually for a year.

INTERNAL CHECK ON STOCK OR STORES

Particularly vulnerable to misappropriation, these stores may also at times be used to cover payments other than those relating to purchase of stores. The following points deserve to be considered in respect of the internal check system in relation to stores:

1. Responsibility about safeguarding and maintenance of stores should be clearly determined.
2. Persons engaged in maintenance of stock record should have nothing to do with stores.
3. There should be a separate place for each category of stores.
4. For proper stores control, a system of code number should be established for each item and the place where it is kept. The use of code numbers prevents unauthorised purchases or purchases by unauthorised persons.
5. Bin cards containing particulars as to receipt, issues and balance of stores should be used for maintenance of stores.
6. There should be an independent checking of stores by a responsible person who is not involved in any way with purchase, issue or maintenance of stores.
7. Procedure should be clearly specified with regard to stores held outside the business, or goods held on behalf of others. Goods kept at outside warehouses should be strictly controlled and inspected.
8. Stock-taking should be done at regular and even at times irregular intervals.

9. Stores records should also be compared with those of corresponding periods of the previous years in order to discover possibilities of material omission and/or inclusions.
10. Responsibility for the issue of stores should be fixed on an individual/department. The stores should be issued only on the authority of a requisition or demand note duly sanctioned by a responsible person.
11. The system of requisitioning stores should be very carefully gone into to ensure against wastage or losses.
12. A gate pass should be given to those authorised persons who will take out the goods from the store.
13. A Material Returned note should be prepared and entry should be made in the Bin Card when materials are returned from the job.

INTERNAL CHECK V/S INTERNAL AUDIT

1. Meaning. While internal check is the organisation of staff for checking the work of one by the other, internal audit is continuous audit of accounts by the employees of the business concern.

2. Object. While Internal check aims at preventing errors and frauds, Internal audit aims to detect errors and frauds which have already been committed.

3. Nature. While Internal check consists of a set of rules of procedure which are a part of accounting system, internal audit involves thorough examination of the accounting transactions and system of accounting. While in internal check, recording and checking of entries is simultaneously done, in internal audit, only checking is done.

4. Scope. While the scope of internal check is limited, the scope of internal audit is comparatively broad.

5. Appointment. While no new member is employed in the case of internal check as duties are so assigned that these involve cross checking in internal audit, the process of auditing is carried by special staff appointed for this purpose.

6. Procedure. While in internal check entries are passed in such a way that the work of one clerk is checked by the other at the time of the making of the entries in internal audit, the work of a clerk is checked automatically by another after the former has finished the work.

7. Detection of frauds and errors. While in the case of internal check any error or fraud is detected at the time of inter-checking in internal audit, any error or fraud is detected at the end of audit work.

EXTERNAL AUDIT V/S INTERNAL AUDIT

In accounting matters, there is not much difference between internal and external audit. Both the internal and the external auditor have a common interest in ascertaining that there is :

(i) an efficient and effective system of internal check to prevent or detect errors and fraud.

(ii) an adequate accounting system to provide the data necessary for preparing true and correct financial statements.

(iii) verification of assets and liabilities.

Distinctions

1. Objectives. External auditors are engaged to give an unbiased and impartial report to the shareholders and outsiders on financial position of the company. They are more concerned with the legality and validity of transactions. Internal auditors are the tools of management who help in taking suitable administrative and policy decisions. The internal auditing more managerial than the accounting.

2. Appointment. While the internal auditor is appointed by the management, independent auditor is either appointed by the shareholders or by the Government. While the appointment of an internal auditor is not compulsory that of an independent auditor is compulsory by law.

3. Qualification. While professional qualifications are not necessary for the internal auditor an independent auditor must have professional qualifications as laid down in the Companies Act.

4. Procedure. The internal auditor carries on his work continuously. He performs detailed checking and examination of all the account books and other related records and documents. The independent auditor, on the other hand, carries his work periodically, near the financial year, not devoting his time on the detailed checking he adheres to test checking.

5. Status of Auditor. While the external auditor is altogether independent of the enterprise hiring him for his services, the internal auditor is an employee of the enterprise, appointed for the purpose of conducting internal audit.

6. Scope. In case it is legally compulsory, the scope of external audit is determined by the law applicable to the enterprise under audit. It cannot be curtailed in any manner. In case of non-statutory external audit, the scope is determined by the agreement between the client and the auditor. On the other hand, the scope of internal audit is determined by the management. It may be enlarged or curtailed at any time.

7. Approach. The external auditor's approach is determined by the duties and liabilities cast on him by the relevant law in case of statutory audit, by the agreement under which he has been appointed in case of non-statuary audit. In either case, it is his duty to give opinion on the truth and fairness of the assertions under his review. On the contrary, the internal auditor's approach is governed by his duty to ensure that the accounting system is adequate and effective so the information presented to the management round the year is true and based on material facts.

8. Responsibility. The external auditor's responsibility is primarily to the owners who have appointed him. In certain cases it may extend to interested third parties who have acted on the faith of his opinion upon the financial statements examined by him. The internal auditor is primarily responsible to the management. The independent status of an external auditor is unthinkable in the case of internal auditor.

Limitations of Internal Audit

1. If the staff employed is not very efficient and does not undertake adequate examination of the records, internal audit may prove ineffective.
2. If the records or the operations are not checked immediately after they are completed or there is time lag between two audits internal audit may become ineffective.
3. If the auditor involves himself in the performance of executive functions internal audit will not serve any purpose.

Objectives of Internal Auditor

1. To review and appraise the soundness, adequacy and application of accounting, financial and other operating controls and to promote effective controls at reasonable costs.
2. To ascertain the extent of compliance with established policies and plans as well as procedures.
3. To ascertain the extent to which company assets are accounted for and safeguarded from losses of all kinds.
4. To ascertain the reliability of management date developed within the organisation.
5. To appraise the quality of performance in carrying out assigned responsibilities.
6. To recommend operational improvements.

Responsibilities of Internal Auditor

In order to ascertain the adequacy and efficiency of the system of internal audit of a business, an auditor must remember the following points:

1. He must ascertain the number of members of the staff of the internal audit department, their qualifications and experience.

2. He should determine the adequacy and efficiency of the staff of the internal audit department in relation to the nature and size of the business of his client, complexities of its operations, decentralisation of authority, internal control of the assets etc.
3. He should ascertain the areas covered by internal audit and the frequency of the reports submitted by the internal auditors to the top management. The internal audit should be carried out with regard to each type of the work and of all the branches and departments.
4. With the help of internal audit reports the auditor must evaluate the functioning of the internal audit system and determine its effectiveness. He should see that all possible technical assistance is made available to the internal auditor by the management of the business to ensure the effectiveness of internal audit. He should go through the audit programme and the working papers of the internal auditors to assess the extent and the quality of the work done by them.
5. Without a proper follow up action internal audit is useless. Its practical utility and significance depends upon the follow up action taken by the management. The auditor must ascertain the extent to which the management has shown respect to the reports of the internal auditor and has implemented the communications contained therein.

Common Interest of Internal and external Auditors

In spite of fundamental differences in the scope, approach, emphases and responsibilities of internal auditor and statutory auditor, there is strong relationship between these. Both have common interests and the common field of operations. In recent years, while qualified accountants are being appointed as internal auditors, it is widely accepted that their functions can be integrated. Following are the common interests of internal and external auditors:

(i) Examination of the system of internal check to test its soundness.
(ii) Examination and checking of accounting records.
(iii) Verification of assets and liabilities.
(iv) Observation, enquiry and comparison of financial results with statistical records and such other measures.

Due to similarities in their means, methods and objectives, there is need for active co-operation between the internal and external auditor to avoid unnecessary duplication of work. While wide experience of the independent statutory auditor may be of immense assistance to the internal auditor, the intimate knowledge of the internal auditor with the various activities of the business concerned is helpful to the external auditor.therefore, they should complement rather than compete with each other.

Coordination

Coordination between the two may be achieved in the following ways:

1. In ascertaining whether the system of internal check is operating satisfactorily and also in assessing the general reliability of the accounting records the statutory auditor may rely on the internal auditors. The statutory auditor may fix-up the extent and depth of his work after studying the work of the internal auditor.
2. The programme of the internal auditor should include work which may give direct help to the statutory auditors by participation in the matters such as the counting of cash and visits to the branches made either by the internal auditor alone or jointly by the statutory auditor.
3. The internal auditor should arrange his programme at the end of the accounting period so that the assistance is given to the statutory auditor in connection with matters such as the confirmation of customer's accounts, verification of assets etc.
4. Internal auditors should obtain necessary guidance from the statutory auditor regarding accounting propriety.
5. Both of them should make their individual experience available to each other in the discharge of their duties.
6. Both should organise and review the systems of accounts and business management policies.

However, the co-operation of internal and external auditor has to be limited due to the division of their responsibilities to the management in one case and to the shareholders in the other. Consistent with his statutory responsibilities, the statutory auditor has to decide the extent, he can rely on the work of internal auditor. His decision should be based on his judgement of each individual case and on the following facts:

1. Examination of the organisation, extent and effectiveness of the internal audit department.
2. Strength of the internal audit staff.
3. Experience and the qualifications of the Chief Internal Auditor.
4. Examination of the procedures regarding internal audit.
5. The authority vested in the Chief Internal Auditor and the level of management to which he is directly responsible.

QUESTIONS FOR EXERCISE

1. How would an auditor evaluate the system of internal controls prevailing in a business? What are the various methods of internal control?
2. What do you understand by the term "Internal Check" ? What are its main objects and principles?
3. Distinguish between internal check and internal control. What are the advantages and disadvantages of internal check?
4. What are the essential characteristics of a good system of internal check? What is the position of Auditor in it ?
5. What should be a good system of internal check concerning receipts of cash payments?
6. Suggest a suitable system of internal check about cash sales in a big retail business.
7. Describe a good system of internal check as regards cash sales, cash collected by travellers and postal sales.
8. Suggest a suitable system of internal check as regard wage payments.
9. You are informed by the management of a factory that they suspect the existence of 'ghost' workers. How can payment to such 'ghost' workers be avoided?
10. Explain internal check on trading transactions.
11. What is internal auditing? Discuss its nature and scope.
12. Distinguish between internal Audit and Independent Audit.
13. Distinguish between - (i) Internal control and Internal Audit,

    (ii) Internal Audit and Statutory Audit.
14. Write short note on internal check on stock or stores.
15. Distinguish between:

    (a) Internal check and Internal audit.

    (b) External audit and Internal audit.
16. Point out the limitations of internal audit. What are the objectives and responsibilities of an internal auditor?
17. What are the common interests of internal and external auditors? How can a statutory auditor coordinate his work with that of the internal auditor?
18. What is the relationship between the statutory and the internal audit ? To what extent and for what purpose can a statutory auditor rely on the work of an Internal auditor?

6

Routine Checking, Vouching and Materiality

Routine checking is the checking of common records and books. It is carried on by the auditor as a matter of routine. It can verify the arithmetical accuracy of the entries made in the books of accounts. It is carried on regardless of the nature and size of a business undertaking and the volume of its transactions. It is checking of certain books and records, such as books of original entry, ledgers and trial balances. Thus, routine checking involves checking of the following:

1. Castings, sub-castings, carry forwards and other calculations in the books of original entry;
2. Postings into the ledgers;
3. Casting and balances in the ledger; and
4. Transfer of balances from the ledgers to the trial balance.

Objects of Routine Checking

1. To check the clerical errors, frauds and arithmetical in accuracies of original entries made in the books of accounts.
2. To verify the entries posted into the ledgers.
3. To confirm the accurate balance of the accounts.
4. To use special types of ticks for checking so that figures duly checked are not erased or changed after the routine checking is over.

Advantages of Routine Checking

1. It helps in checking the arithmetical accuracy of original entries.
2. It helps to detect clerical errors or frauds of simple nature.
3. It ensures that after it is over the figures have not been erased or altered as special types of ticks are used for checking.
4. It forms the basis for final and thorough checking of books of accounts.

5. It ensures reliability of final accounts and statements to some extent.

6. It is helpful in finding out whether all postings have been made from Journal to Ledger and other subsidiary books.

Limitations of Routine Checking

1. Mechanical. The checking of castings and postings etc. is more or less of a mechanical nature. It may be monotonous for those who are entrusted with this work.

2. Errors of principles and well-designed frauds are not revealed. Routine checking does not reveal errors of principles and frauds. It reveals only clerical errors or frauds of a simple nature only.

3. Neglect. If the job of routine checking is given to the junior clerks. They are likely to attach less importance to it. Hence a proper care should be taken that routine checking is carried on with efficiency.

TEST CHECKING

In big concerns where the number of transactions to be checked is very large and time at disposal of the auditor is limited, a few transactions may be checked at random. This checking is called test check. Test checking is a substitute for detailed checking. In the words of Prof. Meig, "Testing and test checking means to select and examine a representative sample from a large number of similar items." It is based on the simple theme that if a representative number of transactions, selected at random by the auditor for test checking, is found to be correct, the remaining would be correct. For example if while vouching credit sales transactions of week for a month the transactions so checked are all correct and there is no suspicion of any error or fraud, the auditor may presume that all the other transactions may be correct. Test checking has become popular. With the increase of business transactions, it minimises the work of the auditor. As the auditor is held liable for any negligence in detecting errors and frauds, he should apply test checks if he has to be fully satisfied that the internal check system is quite efficient.

Methods of Selection of Sample

1. Block Method. In this method, the whole population or universe is divided into different blocks. These may be chronologically arranged and thus selection of sample may be from different periods of time. It may be alphabetically arranged and the selection of sample may be from the different accounts from A to Z. This method is simplest to apply but this does not give all items an equal chance of being selected.

2. Random Selection Method. In this method, each item or business transaction is numbered and then a table of Random Numbers is used to select the items to be included for test checking. Though cumbersome and time consuming, this method ensures an equal chance to every item of being selected.

3. Internal Selection Method. In this method, the sample is selected systematically after every specific interval. In order to select a sample of 100 items from a population of 1000 sales transactions, every tenth transaction may be selected.

4. Stratified Sampling Method. In this method, the auditor determines a breaking point. All items of transactions having larger amount than the breaking point are thoroughly verified while those less than this breaking point are subject to test checking.

Precautions for Test Checking

1. Representative transactions should be selected from every book or ledger covering the whole of the period under audit.
2. The selection of transactions should be distributed is such a way that the work of all the clerks of the client is checked.
3. The selection of items should be made at random.
4. Care should be taken to check the different portions of the work at each audit.
5. Transactions of the first and last months of a year should be thoroughly checked.
6. Selection of transactions should be done with perfect secrecy and without consultation with the staff of the client.

Advantages of Test Checking

1. Economy. As the auditor is not to check each and every transaction, test checking offers economy in time and energy.

2. Useful and purposive. It saves a lot of time as the auditor is left free to check important matters and sensitive transactions more cautiously.

3. Accuracy. Test checking enables to keep accurate books of accounts. It critically assesses internal check, internal audit and internal control system and thereby helps to improve these.

Disadvantages of Test Checking

1. Failure to detect errors and frauds. Based on the selection of representative transactions, test checking may not detect all the errors and frauds.

2. Unreliable Reports. As the auditor checks only items included in the sample, his report cannot be said to be reliable.

3. Liability for lapse. The auditor remains liable for any lapse or negligence in fulfilling his duties to check the accounts thoroughly.

Precautions before applying Test Checking

1. *Review.* The auditor must review the system of internal check, internal audit or internal control thoroughly. If he finds that the internal control system is either defective or ineffective, he should not apply test checking.

2. *Homogeneity.* The Auditor should apply test checking if he finds that the transactions to be checked are homogenous in nature. He should not, in general, adopt test checking if the transactions are dissimilar in nature.

3. *Sample of Records.* The sample of records, selected for test checking, should be taken on random basis and should be, as far as possible, representative in character.

4. *Bias.* There should be no element of bias or arbitrariness in the selection of sample.

5. *Large Number of Transactions.* In case the auditor finds that there is a change in the personnel or documents-flow, the sample selected for the test checking should include fairly large number of transactions of the period, both before and after the change.

6. *Review of Results.* The auditor must always review the results of test checking with a view to find whether there is any further scope of checking records, not checked so far. The nature of errors detected throughout test checks may reveal this, if they are probed carefully.

Transactions not suitable for Test Checking

1. Opening and closing entries.
2. Bank reconciliation statement.
3. Matters involving estimation as well as computation, e.g., depreciation, royalty etc.
4. Presentation and disclosure of information in the profit and loss account and the balance sheet.
5. Items which are material or which have material effect on disclosure in a financial statement.
6. Transaction which may be small in number but may be important.
7. Transactions which are recognised by law to be looked into by the auditor carefully, e.g., managerial remuneration and purchase transactions etc.
8. In case of seasonal industry, the auditor should not resort to test checking on annual basis.
9. Transaction of non-recurring nature or exceptional transactions need not be test checked.

Audit Procedure

For conducting the audit of various concerns, each auditor follows his own method according to his skill and experience, nature of the concern and the way in which accounts are maintained and checked internally. He must be guided by the exigencies of the situation which he comes across. He has to combine thorough knowledge of principles and procedures, sound judgement and an open mind. There is a common procedure with regard to the use of ticks, calling backs etc.

Code of Ticks

An auditor should devise a code of distinctive ticks for different types of transactions. There should be ticks of different colours for posting, additions, vouching, carry forwards, controls, cancellations etc. Different colours of pencils or ink should be used for each period of audit and for different concerns. Special ticks should be used for figures erased out and cancelled. The code of ticks should be kept secret and should not be disclosed to the client's clerks. If the system of ticking is used logically, it may be of great help to the auditor.

Principle of Simultaneity

The Audit should adopt the *principle of simultaneity* and efforts should be made to check all the related transactions at one time while the books are under his control. He should see that checking of the work of each section is completed before the books and vouchers are returned.

No erasure should be allowed and all the wrong or bad figures should be scored out and correct figures entered in their place. If any adjustment is necessary, it should be made through passing entries in the Journal. He should not accept pencil figures. If he finds alteration in the figures on his subsequent visit he should investigate the matter thoroughly and carefully. If he is asked to audit the books before the accounts are balanced, he should not accept it as a rule. It is not his duty to balance the books.[1]

The clerks engaged in calling back the figures should speak very clearly and avoid slovenly or excessively fast calling out the figures. The calling back carelessly may cause trouble and arouse confusion. Figures like ninety or nineteen should be clearly and carefully called back.

Notes of Material Figures

The auditor should try to make notes of materials figures or erased or altered figures in his Audit Note Books. It will be of great use to him in future when any confusion or dispute arises. He should exercise his own discretion as to what he should note down and what not.

---

1. Spicer and Pegler, *op. cit.*, p. 25.

Surprise Check

The auditor should undertake *surprise checks* during the course of his audit. It has been recommended by the Council of Institute of Chartered Accountants of India, in November 1925, that surprise checks should be made "by a desirable part of each audit." Such checks should be undertaken specially to verify cash investment, statutory books, stores etc. The frequency of such checks would depend upon the circumstances prevailing in each case. However, it should be "at least once in the course of an audit." The auditor must realise its importance fully. He must not simply rule it out as an outmoded technique, not necessary today. It would help him in finding out weaknesses, if any, imposing moral check on the staff. It would definitely improve the effectiveness of audit, on the whole.

VOUCHING

Meaning

Vouching is a potent tool in the hands of auditors to ascertain the accuracy of various transactions entered in the books of account. It is the essence of auditing. *It means the examination of the transactions with sufficient underlying evidences to satisfy an auditor about the validity, accuracy, authority and authenticity of the records entered in the books of account.* To substantiate an entry in the book, the auditor has to examine the supporting documentary evidences such as vouchers, receipts, invoices, minutes, contracts, correspondence etc.

Definitions

1. *Toylor and Perry.* Vouching "may be defined as the examination of the evidence offered in substantiation of the entries in the books, including such examination the proof, so far as possible, that no entries have been omitted from the books."[2]

2. *F.R.M. de Paula,* "Vouching dose note mean merely the inspection of receipts with the cash book, but includes the examination of receipts with the transactions of a business, together with documentary and other evidence of sufficient validity to satisfy an auditor that such transactions are in order; have been properly authorised and are correctly recorded in the books." This definition, suggests that an auditor has to satisfy himself, with the help of sufficiently valid evidences, with regard to the records of the transactions in the concern.

3. *Joseph Lancaster,* "It is often thought that vouching consists of the mere examination of the vouchers or documentary evidence with the book entries. This, however, is quite wrong, for vouching comprises such an

---

2. *Principles of Auditing,* p.86

examination of the ledger entries as will satisfy the auditor not only that the entry is supported by documentary evidence but it has been properly made upon the books." Lancaster has very rightly summed up the distinction between the technical and commonly understood meaning of the vouching. He has made the concept and object of vouching quite clear.

Characteristics

1. It involves collection of vouchers and related evidences;
2. It involves evaluating the collected evidences and vouchers;
3. It refers to examination of the vouchers or evidence in such a manner that the auditor may satisfy himself with regard to the correctness and authenticity of the records of transactions;
4. It implies finding out whether entries have been properly made in the books of account or not.
5. It involves finding out that there is no omission of any records;
6. It also refers to checking the entries with a view to find out that transactions which are not related to the concern have not been recorded in books of account; and
7. It forms the basis for final conclusion to be drawn by the auditor.

Steps in Vouching

Mautz and Sharaf have listed following five steps in this connection :[3]

1. Recognition of the proposition to be proved.
2. Evaluation of the proposition in terms of materiality or significance.
3. Collection of evidence within the given limits of time and cost.
4. Evaluation of the evidence obtained as valid or not valid.
5. Formulation of judgement as to the proposition at issue.

Importance of Vouching

According to De Paula vouching is the very essence of auditing. He says "The whole success of an audit depends upon the intelligence and thoroughness with which the part of the work is done." In the opinion of Joseph Lancaster "The very nature of vouching renders it a practically indispensable phase of every audit and that where curtailment of the auditor's duties in this direction is contemplated, the risk that may be incurred should not be over-looked." Thus vouching is a sort of preliminary work which forms an important part of audit work. The accounts of a business begin with the passing of entries. It becomes a basis for further scrutiny to be made at a later

---

3. Mautz, R.K. and Hussein, A. Sharaf, *op. cit.*, p. 103

stage. The purpose of checking entries by reference to appropriate documentary evidence is to ensure that the transactions relating to a particular period have been recorded and there is no voucher left unrecorded in the financial books. After satisfying himself with regard to the authority and authenticity of transaction the auditors can say categorically that the books of accounts are correct and the balance-sheet and profit and loss account exhibit the true and correct state of the financial affairs of a business. If vouching is done with care and caution by the auditor, he can proceed well further in his work.

The success of an audit depends upon the intelligence and thoroughness with which vouching is done. Vouching is not only the inspection of receipts with the cash book, it includes the examination of the transactions of a business, together with documentary and other evidence of sufficient validity to satisfy an auditor that such transactions are in order, have been properly authorised and are correctly recorded in the books. Thus the auditor goes behind the books of account and traces the entries to their source. It is in this way alonc that he can ascertain the full meaning and circumstances of the various transactions. If he confines himself to the entries as they appear in the books of account, his information will be incomplete, and he may pass matters of the utmost importance which affect the accounts very materially. The entries in the books show only such information as the book-keeper chooses to disclose. This information may be purposely or unintentionally contrary to the true facts. An auditor can ascertain the real state of affairs only by examining external evidence. Clever frauds can only be discovered by vouching. Therefore it is essential that this part of an audit should be conducted with great care and intelligence. This importance of proper vouching was emphasised in the case of *Armitage V. Brewer & Knott,* where the auditors were found guilty of negligence because of their failure to detect defalcations perpetrated by manipulations of wage records and petty cash vouchers. In the course of his judgement the learned judge stated. "It was clear that a good may documents were suspicious on their face and called for enquiry." The auditor has to apply his experience, knowledge of accountancy, critical faculty, keen observation and common sense to get the best result out of vouching. Vouching has been rightly called the backbone of auditing.

Routine Checking and Vouching

Broadly speaking, vouching includes routine checking. However, in routine checking, it is the arithmetical accuracy of entries that is verified whereas in vouching, entries are to be checked with the help of documentary evidences. Thus, in vouching, checking goes beyond arithmetical accuracy. It concerns itself with the authenticity and completeness of the transactions.

Routine checking includes checking of castings, postings, carry-forwards etc. The auditor uses distinct tick marks in routine checking. He tries to establish genuineness of records, e.g. that the casts are correct, postings are correctly made and no alterations have been made. Thus both vouching and routine checking are important in their own way.

Objectives of Vouching

1. Primary Objectives. The process of vouching involves examination of the documentary evidence necessary to authenticate and support the recorded transactions which are said to have taken place during the period under review. Such examination primarily establishes (i) the correctness of the monetary amount at which the transaction is recorded, cost in the case of purchases, and proceeds in the case of sales, and (ii) that the transaction was properly authorised in the first place. 'Authority' means a good deal more than signature on a petty cash voucher. Appropriate to the transaction in question, authority is necessary at all levels. It is obvious that the auditor should be on familiar terms with the authority required for each of these.

The signature of the responsible officer will suffice at the lowest level. However, when larger expenditures are involved, rules may be laid down requiring, say, two signatures on the cheque issued in payment. At the next level, the sanction of a director or possibly of the full board may be needed. Beyond Board level, authority must reside in a company's own Articles and Memorandum of Association and beyond that the law itself. Neither company nor its officers can execute transactions specifically prohibited by company law.

2. Subsidiary objectives

1. Ascertaining that the transaction took place within the period under review;
2. Ascertaining that goods and services acquired (or, in the case of sales, provided) are compatible with the company's normal trading activities, i.e. in the context of the ordinary course of business;
3. Ensuring that all calculations of costs (proceeds), extensions, discounts, etc. are arithmetically accurate;
4. Establishing that the expenditure (income) has been correctly allocated, so that effect has been given to the distinction between capital, revenue and deferred revenue, i.e. the correct determination of "write-offs", as opposed to "carry forwards",
5. Checking that there is an evidence (e.g. rubber stamp, initials or signature) that the document in question has been authorised and checked internally as part of the company's own control procedures.

CONCEPT OF MATERIALITY

Importance

The principle of materiality is fundamental to the whole process of accounting. An auditor has to be concerned with regard to the concept of materiality. He has to analyse and take decisions regarding various items whether they are material or not during the course of an audit. This would require thorough knowledge, competence and experience. If he finds that an item is quite material in nature, he would have to give careful consideration to its checking and would call for more evidences in support. He would have to undertake an 'audit in depth' to satisfy himself regarding such material item.

Meaning

It is not very easy to define the term 'material' as its meaning would differ in different circumstances. The dictionary meaning of the term is "of serious importance, especially of legal importance".[4] It implies that any item or transactions is material, if it is serious importance under a given condition or auditing situation. An auditor should apply his own discretion to decide whether an item is of serious importance or not in the circumstance of a particular case. If the circumstances change, he would have to think afresh.

Accounting Sense

In an accounting sense, an item may be taken to be material if its non-disclosure, mis-statement or omission would be likely to distort the view given by the accounts or other statements under consideration. Arithmetical accuracy, although fundamental important in accounting, is not itself sufficient to satisfy the legal requirements. Hence the widest possible appreciation must be made and the consideration of materiality must be kept in view.

Thus, every auditor must decide about the items to the material in the given situation and must include those items in his audit programme carefully so that they may be examined properly and in detail. If he is not careful about them, he may be held liable for the same.

Statutory Provisions

1. Companies Act, 1956. The world 'material' has been used on several occasions. The Schedule VI attached to the Act requires that the financial statements should disclose all 'material items' so as to give true and fair view of the financial state of affairs of the company. Part II of Schedule VI requires that the profit and loss account should disclose every 'material feature'. What is material, however, has been left to the discretion of the accountant and auditor. Any criteria to be adopted for the decision about the materiality, however, should be firmly based upon a real understanding of the full significance of the words 'true and fair' as introduced for the first time in the Companies Act, 1956 in place of words 'true and correct.'

4. Chamber's Twentieth Century Dictionary, 1964.

2. *The Second Schedule to the Chartered Accountants Act, 1949.* Clauses 5 , 6, 7, 8 and 9 of Part I of this Schedule refers to 'material fact', material mis-statement', 'material exceptions', and 'material departure from the generally accepted procedure of audit' etc.

3. *Statement on Auditing Practice issued by the Institute of Chartered Accountants of India.* It has been stated in it that the recommendations contained in it would "apply primarily to items which are material and significant in relation to the affairs of a company. Items of little or no significance may be dealt with as may be found expedient, as it neither desirable nor necessary that members should devote their time and energies in the pursuit of matters of a trival nature. However, freedom to deal expediently with non-material items should not extend to a group of items whose cumulative effect on the accounts may be material and significant."

CRITERIA FOR JUDGING MATERIALITY

1. The question of materiality can arise in relation to (i) disclosure, including manner of disclosure; (ii) correction of errors or omission; (iii) methods of computation etc.

2. Materiality has to be seen and judged only in relative context, and not in absolute term. For instance, Rs. 1,000 may be a material amount in case of a smaller concern whereas it may not be so in case of a large concern. In the latter case, even Rs. 10,000 may not be material.

3. Items of small amount are not necessarily insignificant, especially where they might have been expected to be larger. Even a small amount may become material if its disclosure is essential statutorily. For instance, payment to the directors as sitting fee has to be disclosed precisely and separately.

4. Several individually insignificant items might represent a material amount in total. That is why, it is necessary to see as to what is the impact of an item on the total of the category of items to which it belongs. For instance, amount received as dividend would be material if it affects total amount of income from investment considerably.

5. Case should be exercised before offsetting item of opposite effect where each on its own might have been referred as material, e.g., a non-recurring loss against a profit arising from a change in the basis of accounting.

6. The impact of the item concerned on the profit and loss account and the balance sheet also should be duly taken into account while judging the materiality. If the item is such that it would affect profit or loss significantly that should be taken to be material. Similarly, if an item affects the financial position of the concern significantly that should also be taken to be a material one.

7. Sometimes, the percentage comparisons may be made to judge the materiality of an item. The Companies Act, 1956 itself has indicated it as an indicator of materiality. For instance, Part II of Schedule VI to the Act requires that any item exceeding 1 percent of the total revenue of the company or Rs. 5,000, whichever is higher, shall be shown as a separate and distinct item under an appropriate account head in the profit and loss account and shall not be combined with any other item to be shown under miscellaneous expenses.

8. Comparison with the corresponding figure in the previous years may also serve to be useful indicator of materiality. For instance, if the amount of an item is not significant this year but it was quite significant in the previous year, then that item would become material this year.

9. While judging the materiality, it would also be seen whether the items are capable of precise and accurate determination or no. If it so, even a small error in the same would become material. But if the amount of a particular item is to be complied on the basis of estimation, a small error would not be material. For instance, depreciation cannot be calculated correctly or precisely but can be simply estimated. Therefore, an excess provision of the depreciation by Rs.100 or 200 would not be material.

CUT OFF

The term "cut off" refers to the procedure adopted by the management to ensure the separation of transactions as at the end of one accounting year from those at the commencement of the following year. It becomes quite necessary for those items which normally overlap. Examples of such items are purchase, sale, stock etc. The basic principle of accounting is that transaction related to a particular year alone should be recorded.

Importance of cut off

Cut off is important in auditing as the auditor has to ensure that transactions related to a particular year alone should be recorded in the books of account. In this connection, the auditor should pay special attention to the following aspects:

1. The goods purchased during the year under audit have been duly included in the closing stock.

2. The goods purchased during the year under audit for which the ownership has been transferred to the client have been duly included in the inventories and related liability has been taken for the sales in the accounts.

3. All the goods sold during the year under audit have been excluded from the inventories and due credit has been taken for the sales in the accounts.

4. All sales invoices for which the goods have yet to pass to the purchasers have been duly excluded from the sales of the year under audit.

5. It has to be seen that receipts and payments of cash related to the previous year or next year have not been included in the accounts. Similarly, receipts and payments of the current year should not be included in the following year's accounts.

QUESTIONS FOR EXERCISE

1. What do you understand by the term 'routine checking' ? Discuss its objects, advantages and limitations.
2. What is test checking? What precautions should be taken before applying test checking ?
3. Define test checking and describe the transactions which are not suitable for test checking.
4. What is test checking? Discuss its advantages and limitations.
5. Define Vouching. What precautions should be taken by the auditor while examining the vouchers?
6. Write short note on Materiality.
7. What do you mean by routine checking? Discuss its objects, advantages and limitations.
8. What is test checking? What precautions should be taken before applying test checking ? Also describe the transaction which are not suitable for checking and advantages and disadvantages of test checking.

7

Vouching of Cash Transactions

Cash transactions daily take place in every business concern. There may be receipts of cash from various sources such as from debtors, sales or investments etc., Payments of cash have to be made to creditors or for purchases or establishment expenses etc. Such receipts and payment may be made either in cash or by cheque whose records are found in Cash Book and Bank Pass Book. As it is the cash which prompts anybody to be dishonest, the auditor who has to vouch the Cash Book, Petty Cash Book and the Bank Cash Book.

1. Joseph Lancaster. "A voucher may be defined as any documentary evidence by which the accuracy of book entries may be substantiated."

2. Ronald A. Irish. "A voucher may be a receipt, invoice, an agreement, a written requisition slip or in short any suitable written evidence which confirms a written transaction."

3. J.R. Batliboi. "A voucher may be defined as a documentary evidence in support of an entry appearing in books of accounts."

4. Arthur W. Halmes. "A voucher is any documentary evidence in support of a transaction."

Characteristics of Voucher

On analysing the above definitions we find the following characteristics of a voucher:

1. Voucher is documentary evidence.
2. It is an evidence in black and white.
3. It is a documentary evidence in support of an entry in the books of accounts.
4. Voucher may be a simple receipt.
5. Voucher presents the full description of a transaction.
6. It helps in substantiating the accuracy of book entries.

Types of Voucher

1. Primary Voucher. An original written evidence of supporting a transaction, e.g. invoice for a purchase.

2. Collateral Voucher. When some original evidence is lost or destroyed, duplicate copies thereof are produced in support as subsidiary evidence to remove suspicions from the mind of the auditor.

Schedule of Vouchers

The following schedule shows the nature of transaction and various vouchers with regard to them.

(i) *Cash receipts.* Counterfoils of receipts issued, carbon copies of receipts, contracts, minutes, correspondence and letters from the debtors confirming the balances of their accounts.

(ii) *Cash payments.* Original receipts from payee, invoices, bills, demand notes, salary books, payroll records, wage sheets, contracts and confirmation of balances by creditors.

(iii) *Purchases.* Invoice, copies of orders, goods inward book, correspondence, purchase return book and credit notes, etc.

(iv) *Sales.* Orders records, copies of invoices/bills and goods, outward books and correspondences, sales return books/credit notes etc.

(v) *Miscellaneous vouchers.* Opening Journal entries, bills payable and bills receivable books, closing balance sheet of last year, etc., partnership deed in the case of partnership firm, memorandum and articles of association in the case of company, pass book, salesman's abstracts, cashier's summaries, agreements, divided warrants, share certificates, debentures certificates, lease deeds, auctioneer's note books, brokers sold note, title lease deed, job cards, various resolutions and the minute books of shareholders and director's meetings, insurance policy requisition slips, etc.

To conclude vouchers are correspondence, contracts, documents, receipts, invoices, bills, minute books maintained for recording resolutions of directors or shareholders and any other similar documentary evidences.

EXAMINATION OF VOUCHERS

Considerations. The auditor should have following two main considerations in mind while examining the vouchers.

(i) How much evidence should be obtained in support of a transaction ?

(ii) To what extent should he rely upon the available evidence ?

The quantity of evidence to be secured by the auditor will depend upon the degree of internal control applicable in the client's organisation, the materiality of the relative size of figures and the relative risks involved in particular items. The auditor should realise the need for examining additional evidence in case of items subjected to more than normal risk.

Reliability of the Vouchers

1. Most reliable. Vouchers which have been prepared by a third party and sent directly to the auditor are ordinarily the most reliable.

2. Sometimes reliable. Vouchers which have been prepared by a third party but are in the possession of the client have a lower degree of reliability. These may be fictitious or altered by the client's staff, but they are not valueless as evidence.

3. Least Reliable. Vouchers which originate within the client's organisation are the least reliable. There are chances of falsifying these vouchers deliberately to conceal any fraud or manipulation. The employees may get a chance to prepare a voucher giving false evidence. If good internal control exists about the preparation and use of documents the degree of such vouchers increases.

General Consideration while Checking Vouchers

1. Numbered and Filed. The auditor should see that all the vouchers are consecutively numbered and filed serial-wise and in order of entries in the books. If it is not done so, then the auditor should ask the client to do so. Otherwise the auditor would lose a lot of time in finding cut a particular voucher.

2. Cancelled. The auditor should see to it that to avoid any possibility of their being produced again in support of any other transaction all the inspected vouchers are cancelled by a stamp or mark.

3. Personal. The auditors check those vouchers, which are in the personal name of the partners, directors or officers of the company. These may not be related to the transaction pertaining to the interests of the business. For example, if the voucher is related to purchase the goods inward book should be examined to ensure that goods have actually been received in the business. The client should be asked not to adopt this practice in future.

4. Special Scrutiny. Where a voucher requires some special scrutiny the auditor should proceed cautiously and use special tick marks for its checking.

5. Payment. The payment made must relate to the nature of business carried on by the client. In case of doubt the matter should be thoroughly investigated.

6. Separate vouchers of capital and revenue. The auditor should see that vouchers relating to capital expenditures are posted separately and no capital expenditure is assumed as revenue expenditure.

7. Authority. The auditor should see that every voucher is passed on in order by an authoritative officer whose signature should be noted.

8. Independent Checking. While checking the entries and the vouchers no help from the members of the staff of client should be sought.

9. Pre-receipted invoice. The auditor should not accept pre-receipted invoice as voucher because there is danger of the payment being made twice, once as a credit purchase and again as a cash transaction against the pre-receipted invoice.

10. In one sitting. The work relating to a particular period or a set of books should be completed in one sitting or as a continuous process as far as possible.

11. Test checking. The auditor should resist from test checking of voucher only when he is fully satisfied about the system of internal check in operation. It must be ascertained that only printed and not hand-written forms are used as vouchers.

12. Reconciliation with minutes. The auditor should reconcile minutes of the Board of Directors with the accounting entries arising therefrom, in accordance with the vouchers.

Specific Considerations regarding Vouchers

1. Compare. The auditor should compare the date, name and amount of each voucher with the corresponding date appearing in the original to accounting record. This will ensure that no voucher which is unrelated business has been entered in the books.

2. Related to business. The auditor should see that the voucher is related to business either for purchase of goods, fixed assets or revenue expenses.

3. Period. The auditor should ensure that every voucher relates to the period under audit.

4. Tally in works and figure. The auditor should see that the amount of the voucher in words would tally with the figure amount and every voucher with a receipt for cash payment over Rs. 20, bears a revenue stamp of 20 paise.

5. Signed. The auditor should see that every voucher has been signed by a responsible official on behalf of the payee.

6. Alteration Installed. Wherever any alteration is made in a voucher, the auditor should see that it is initialled by the invoice clerk.

7. Duplication. The auditor should investigate duplicate vouchers in order to determine that duplicate accounting entries are not made.

8. Complete. The auditor should see that voucher is complete in all respects. It should comprise all the relevant documents which could be expected to have been received or brought into existence on the transaction having been entered into.

9. Genuine. The auditor should see that in general the voucher appcars to be genuine on the face of it.

10. No persuasion. The auditor should never allow himself to be persuaded to pass any transaction which is not properly supported by some voucher or other satisfactory evidence under the promise of future explanation, for fear of losing the client's goodwill or patronage.

MISSING VOUCHERS

Auditor's Duties

During the course of the audit an auditor may find certain missing vouchers. He must prepare a list of all the missing vouchers and make the following inquiries about them :

1. Voucher not available. Do they relate to such items or transactions for which usually a voucher is not available such as taxi charges, open-market purchase of controlled goods, etc. ?

2. Amount. Whether the amount involved is material? This will decide the scope of checking.

3. Record. Are the materials purchased under missing vouchers entered in the stress records? If those materials have been consumed, does the production date corroborate their consumption or else do they exist as closing stock.

4 Voucher Available. Does any missing voucher relate to such matter for which a regular voucher should be available? For example, purchase of goods from recognised suppliers.

5. Duplicate. It should be inquired if the duplicate copy of the missing vouchers has to be obtained. If possible, the same should be called for and verified. However, care should be taken to see that the original document thereof has not been separately entered.

6. Certificate. The auditor should obtain a certificate from a competent official covering all the missing vouchers that the expenses where actually incurred for the company and the benefit of the expenses has been received by the company. In case of a company, the Board of Directors should approve the missing vouchers.

VOUCHING OF CASH BOOK

Objectives

Vouching of the Cash Book is done to ensure the following objectives:

1. That all receipts and payments are duly accounted for.

2. That all such receipts and payments are entered under their appropriate heads of accounts.
3. That no unauthorised or fraudulent payment is made;
4. That the closing cash and bank balances are correctly arrived at.

Vouching Cash Receipts—General Considerations

Before starting the audit of cash receipts, the auditor should examine the internal check in operation and draw the attention of the management to any weakness therein, as well as to the possible consequence that might follow if it is not removed. Failing to do so, he may be held responsible at some later date for not having detected a defalcation or misappropriation in cash, the cause of which was the absence or inadequacy of the internal check.

Cash receipts are usually checked with counterfoils of the receipts issued. However, the issue of receipts with counterfoils in respect of amounts collected by itself does not ensure that all the amounts collected have been fully accounted for, or have been correctly adjusted. For example, a receipt might be issued for a larger amount than entered on its counterfoil. Only one receipt may have been issued for two or more amounts collected from a party while the counterfoils may show that separate receipts have been issued in respect of each amount collected and the one or more receipt forms, thus saved, may have been used for issuing receipt in respect of another amount collected which has been misappropriated. Therefore, the auditor should satisfy himself that there exists an efficient system of internal check which would prevent any receipt from being misappropriated, before accepting counterfoils of receipts as an evidence of the correctness of the amount. The following enquiries should be made for this purpose.

1. Who opens letters, what record is kept, and whether all cheques and postal orders are immediately endorsed to bankers and marked, 'Account Payee only' ?
2. Who is responsible to enter cash, cheques and other forms of remittance in the 'Pay-in-slip' book and who deposits it in the bank ?
3. Are all receipts banked daily ?
4. Who prepares receipts and who countersigns them before these are issued to the parties from whom the amounts have been received ?
5. Whether printed receipts with counterfoils numbered serially by a machine are used? Who maintains the stock of unused receipts ?
6. Are the receipt books kept in safe custody ? Are they issued only when the current receipt book has been used up ?

7. What internal check is being exercised over the collection of cash sale and miscellaneous income ?
8. Are travelling salesman allow to collect any advances against orders booked and what control exists over such collections ?
9. How often do the bank prepare and despatch monthly statements of account to customers ?
10. Who controls the preparation and despatch of monthly statements of account to customers ?
11. Are ledgers posted by the cashier or some other person ?

Certain firms insist upon a receipt being furnished to them on their own forms. This fact should be noted on the counterfoil of the receipt which has been issued and the unused receipt form cancelled, as an additional precaution. Balances should be got confirmed periodically in such customers' accounts.

Steps in Reconciliation of Bank Balance

1. All items on both the sides of the Cash Book should be checked in detail with the Bank Pass Book.
2. Adjustments of contra entries in respect of cheques returned or bills receivable dishonoured, should be carefully seen.
3. Items of interest debited or credited by the bank, bank charges and expenses of noting dishonoured bills should also be verified.
4. The Bank Reconciliation Account should be verified and the Bank Pass Book balance tallied with the bank balance as per the Cash Book.

Checking of Receipt Side of the Cash Book

While checking the receipt side of the Cash Book it should be remembered that a loose system of acknowledging money received always leaves scope for fraud. It is impossible to eradicate entirely all chances of fraud. However, the possibilities may be reduced. For this purpose, a special form of Counterfoil Receipt Book should be used, the receipts being printed with consecutive numbers. For every single item of cash received a receipt should be given from this book. The number of such a receipt should be entered in the Cash Book against each entry, in a special column provided for the purpose. This method facilitates reference and makes the auditor's work easy.

Some firms follow the practice of sending out along with the cheques specially printed receipt forms for acknowledgment and return by the payees. In such a case the firm receiving the remittance should also send its own official receipt preferably from a Counterfoil Receipt Book and marked "Confirmatory Receipt", giving reference to the cheque. This will prevent the receiving firm omitting to account for any of such receipts.

Precautions about Counterfoil Receipt Books

The auditor should ensure the following, where counterfoil receipt books are used for acknowledging all cash receipts :

1. All unused books should be kept under lock and key, and the issuing of new books should be controlled by some responsible official.
2. The dates, amounts and names on the counterfoils should agree with the entries in the Cash Book.
3. Spoils receipt forms should not be destroyed, but attached to the respective counterfoils, and initialled as cancelled by someone in authority.
4. Number must be checked before using, no number should be missing;
5. The discounts allowed should be in tune with the usual terms of credit of the firm.

Precautions in Various Types of Vouching

1. Vouching Cash Receipts. While vouching cash receipts, it should be checked that the date of each receipt as is entered in the cash memo or the counterfoil of the receipt thereof corresponds with the date on which it is entered in the Cash Book. If there is a time lag between them, it is possible that the person who had collected the amount had failed to deposit it with the cashier immediately thereafter, the cause of this discrepancy should be ascertained.

2. Vouching Cash Sales

(i) *Verification of Internal check system.* First of all, the system of internal check should be checked to find out loopholes therein, if any, whereby cash sales could be misappropriated.

(ii) *Check on Cash Memos.* Further, the practice followed in the matter of issuing cash memos should be ascertained, for, if cash memos are issued not only for cash sales but also for credit sales, the amount thereof collected long after, there would be no guarantee that all the amount of cash sales has been collected before the close of year or that some of the amounts collected have not been misappropriated. Cash sales, usually, are verified with carbon copies of cash memos.

(iii) *Check on Summary Book.* If sales are large and a Cash Sales Summary Book is maintained, the cash memos should be traced into it, the totals of the Summary Book should be verified and the daily totals of Summary Book should be traced into the Cash Book. The dates on the cash memos should tally with those on which cash collected in respect thereof has been entered in the Cash Book.

(iv) *Calculations of cash sales.* The computations of cash sales should be test checked to verify that cash price of goods sold has been calculated correctly.

(v) *Sanction of trade discount.* Where a trade discount has been allowed, the sanction thereof should be ascertained.

(vi) *Check on cancelled cash memos.* If a cash memo has been cancelled, its original copy should be inspected, to check if the amount thereof, has been misappropriated.

3. Vouching Postal Sales. For postal sales the auditor should vouch the V.P.P. register. It is the most important documentary evidence which shows the goods sold, goods returned, any advance received, etc. The register should be checked by a responsible official. The auditor should thoroughly examine the amount receivable on account of postal sales.

4. Sale and Collection by Salesman. Where the sales are made by salesmen and they are also authorised to make collections, the auditor should verify that the travelling salesmen are not allowed to deduct their commission from collected sales amounts. They should send their total sales collections.

5. Receipts from Debtors. The following checks should be made in this connection :

(i) The auditor should examine the system of internal check in operation regarding the receipts from customers.

(ii) While checking the sales ledgers, the auditor may not specifically verify receipts on account of credit sales, particularly where it is not the custom of the business to issue printed counterfoil receipts to its customers.

(iii) In case counterfoils receipts are issued, the auditor should consider the regulations in force regarding them and vouch a certain numbers of counterfoils with the cash book. In a large business the auditor cannot check each and every counterfoil. Therefore, an appropriate sample should be selected for checking based on the efficacy of internal check system for sales as a whole.

(iv) The auditor should see that the dates on the counterfoils correspond with those in the cash book.

(v) The daily list of receipts should be verified with the cash book, where there is no custom to issue printed receipts.

(vi) The auditor should check the regulations in force in the organisation in this respect, where the travellers are authorised to collect money from debtors.

(vii) The auditor should vouch the travellers' returns with the counter foils of receipts and cash book.

(viii) The auditor should test a certain number of the entries to know whether the discount is in order, where discount is allowed to debtors. He should check the discount column of the cash book with the discount payable account in the impersonal ledger.

(ix) While attending the amount shown as bad debts written off, the auditor should ascertain as to who is responsible for writing off debts as bad since cash can be misappropriated by writing off the whole or part of the debit balance as bad. With the permission of the client the auditor should establish direct contracts with the debtors by sending them the statements or verification slips and asking them to send their confirmation directly to him.

TEAMING AND LADING — A METHOD OF FRAUD

"Teaming and Lading" is one of the most common devices of misappropriating cash collections from customers. According to Prof. Meigs, "Teaming and Lading" or "lapping" is "the concealment of a shortage by delaying the recording of cash receipts." This type of fraud may be understood with the following example:

No entry is made in the cash book by the cashier. The cashier simply pockets the money. Later, when cash is received from 'Q' the amount is credited to the account of 'P' and when the amount is received from 'R' it is credited to 'Q' and so on.

Since the cashier is able to make good the amounts misappropriated before the cash balance is checked, such a fraud, usually remains undetected for long time. Though, chances of amounts being misappropriated are lesser in this type of fraud, yet the practice should be checked as (a) there is the loss of interest for the period the money is misappropriated and (b) the cashier may be tempted to commit such a fraud of bigger amount and may not be able to replace the same. (c) Sometimes the cashier who has committed such a fraud may cover up the amounts misappropriated by raising fictitious debits in the expense account.

How to detect such a fraud ?

1. The auditor should scrutinise the debtors accounts which show part-payments from time to time although such debtors have been making full payments in setting the accounts in the past.
2. The auditor should compare the amount deposited in the bank with the entries made in the counterfoil of the paying-in-slip to see whether full amount had been deposited in the bank or whether some money had been misappropriated.
3. The auditor should compare the carbon copies of the receipts or the counterfoils of the receipt book with the entries in the Cash

Book. He should pay special attention to the amount and the date of the receipt of the money and the date on which the amount was deposited in the bank.

4. The auditor should get the balance of the customers confirmed by them. The statement of accounts sent to the debtors for confirmation should be prepared under the supervision of a responsible officer. The customer should be requested to send direct to the auditor the correctness or otherwise of the statement.
5. Before he commences the checking auditor should find out the system of internal check regarding the receipt of cash from customers and deposits into the bank and the preparation of Bank Reconciliation Statements from time to time.

STEPS IN VOUCHING BILLS RECEIVABLES

1. Examination of the internal check system regarding cash receipts against bills receivables and note loopholes, if any, to be cautious regarding those.
2. Examination of the B/R book to ascertain the due dates of various bills.
3. Vouching of the cash collected in respect of bills receivable with reference to Bills Receivable Book.
4. In the case of bills purchased (in the case of banks), provision for the amount of the discount, not earned till the close of the year, is made in the books of account.
5. (i) Proceeds of the bills discounted before the due date is received prior to maturity and vouched with reference to the Bill Book, Bill discounted book and the rate of discount charged, and

   (ii) Special inquiries are to be made about bills which may have matured but the amount in respect thereof has not been received. Such bills might have been dishonoured or returned. But there is also a possibility that their proceeds might have been misappropriated by the cashier.
6. The contingent liability in respect of the discounted bill is disclosed on the Balance Sheet, if the bills have been discounted. The bills which have been paid off are shown, separately.
7. Enquiry is made from the client regarding the position of a bill or bills receivable dishonoured, and if it is suspected that the amount due on a bill may not be recovered, a provision therefor made in the books.

STEPS FOR VOUCHING RENT RECOVERABLE

1. Particulars are obtained of total accommodations available for being let out, in different buildings belonging to the client;
2. The counterparts of leases and agreements are checked noting the rent payable, and the provision as to repairs and allowances (e.g. house tax, water tax, electricity consumed etc.);
3. It is ascertained that all rents that should have been received and also vouch deductions made by the tenants;
4. Enquiry is made about the genuineness of arrears of rent outstanding for a long time;
5. Precautions are taken of the point similar to (4) in respect of properties which are shown as inlet;
6. The counterfoils of rent receipts are checked with reference to entries in the cash book;
7. The accounts of agents are checked where the rents are collected by agents;
8. The Rental Register, if the client is maintaining it, is scrutinised to find out amounts of rents which have not been recovered and are considered bad and irrecoverable for deciding whether these should be written off or provision against the same should be made.

STEPS FOR VOUCHING INTEREST RECEIPTS

1. Interest receipts are checked with the counterparts of the interest and dividend warrants or the letters covering the cheques.
2. The bearer bonds are inspected along with the torn-off coupons to note as to what interest should have been received.
3. Where the banker is authorised to collect interest or dividends, the entries in the bank pass book or statement are checked along with the bank pass-book for interest on fixed deposits.
4. The necessary agreement between the borrower and the business is checked to note the rate of interest, date of payment, etc.
5. It is ensured that all the dividends or interest in respect of investment, deposits or lending have been received and accounted for.

VOUCHING DUTIES OF AUDITOR

(I) Sale Proceeds of Goods Sent out on Consignment

1. The auditor should carry out a thorough examination of account sales received from the consignees.
2. The auditor should see that the consignees have strictly complied with the agreed terms and conditions as to the duration of credit, selling price, discount, expenses to be incurred.

3. The auditor should see that stock in the hands of consignees has been properly valued.
4. The auditor should see that the stock is correct with reference to goods sent, sold and returned.

(II) Dividend Receipts

1. The auditor should check dividends received with reference to dividend warrants or "Tops";
2. The auditor should see that no credit has been taken for dividend yet to be declared;
3. The auditor should see that all dividends collected have been received;
4. The auditor should check the rate of dividends, amounts of gross and net dividends and tax deducted at the source;
5. The auditor should check actual receipt with reference to Cash Book or Bank Pass-Book;
6. The auditor should check the reports of all the companies of which the shares have been held;
7. The auditor should see that the amount of dividends has been shown separately under (i) income from trade investment, and (ii) other investment.

(III) Sale of Investment

1. The auditor should see that investments are usually sold through brokers. He should examine the 'Broker's Sold Note' to note the date of sale, the amount received and the commission charged.
2. If the sale has been effected through bank, the auditor should examine the bank advice.
3. The auditor should note as to whether the sale has been cum-dividend or ex-dividend. In case of ex-dividend sale, he should see that the ex-dividend or dividend has been received if declared. In case of cum-dividend sale, the auditor should note that the sale proceeds have been properly apportioned between capital and revenue.

(IV) Sale of Assets

1. In this case too, as in the case of sales or investments the auditor should check the authority for sale.
2. The auditor should check the basis of sale, whether it was by auction or by negotiation. Thus for determining that the asset was sold at the maximum price that could be obtained for it and that the sale proceeds of the asset have been fully accounted for, the auditor should further confirm that the sale proceeds have been credited to an appropriate head of account and the amount of profits, if any, and

accordingly appropriate accounts are credited, where there is a loss, the same should be written off.

(V) Vouching Payments

In case of vouching payment an auditor does not merely seek proof that money has really been paid but also satisfies himself about the following :

1. The payment has been actually made for the business itself.
2. The payment relates to the period under audit.
3. The payment has been made to the right person.
4. The payment is properly sanctioned.
5. The payment is properly recorded.
6. The payment is supported by a proper voucher.
7. The particulars given in the voucher tally with those of the cash book. The auditor should pay special attention to the following points while vouching payments:
   (i) He should check internal check system regarding payments.
   (ii) All vouchers should be collected, properly filed, serially numbered and arranged date wise. Duplicates of lost vouchers must be obtained.
   (iii) He should vouch all vouchers pertaining to a particular period. He should cancel vouchers by marking with a rubber stamp and initial so that they may not be presented again.
   (iv) (a) The auditor should see that all vouchers have been made out in the name of his client's business, (b) that they pertain to the business, and (c) they are properly authorised.
   (v) The auditor should see that the date of the voucher tallies with the date of entry in the cash book and it belongs to the period under the audit.
   (vi) The auditor should see that transactions are in conformity with the nature of clients' business.
   (vii) Missing vouchers should be carefully noted and brought to the knowledge of the owner of the business.
   (viii) The auditor should get explanations and information regarding any vouchers at the earliest.
   (ix) The auditor should see that the receipt over Rs. 20 bears a proper revenue stamp.
   (x) The auditor should see that the vouchers have been correctly posted to the appropriate accounts and distinction has thoroughly been observed between capital and revenue expenditure.

(xi) The auditor should see that vouchers have been checked and passed for payment by some responsible official.

(xii) The auditor should note the payments which cover a period beyond the period under audit.

(xiii) Payments on accounts of wages, postage etc. should be checked with reference to subsidiary registers containing a detailed record of all such payments.

(xiv) If the payment of more than Rs. 10,000 has been made in cash instead of cheque, the auditor should see the circumstances under which such payment has been made.

(xv) The auditor should see that no payment have been made contrary to the terms and conditions of the agreements, and that benefits of cash discounts have been availed of wherever available, and the same have been properly adjusted in the accounts.

VOUCHING OF CAPITAL EXPENDITURES

Payments are made for two types of expenditures : (a) Capital expenditure, and (b) Revenue expenditure. To quote Spicer and Pegler "Capital Expenditure is all expenditure incurred for the purpose of acquiring, extending or improving assets of a permanent nature, by meants of which the business may be carried on, or for the purpose of increasing the earning capacity of the business."

To ensure that payments are in order, are duly authorised and proper capital charges including incidental expenses in respect of the fixed assets acquired, all capital expenditure should be vouched most carefully and cautiously in view of the fact that any erroneous accounting treatment may affect the profit and financial position. The question as to what documents will be required for auditor's examination will vary with the nature of the transaction as illustrated about different types of capital expenditures.

Types of Capital Expenditure

1. Land and Building. The auditor should do the following while vouching the purchase of land and buildings:

(i) He should examine the documents of title of the property;

(ii) He should ascertain whether the land or buildings are purchased on freehold or leasehold basis. Where the land/building is purchased on leasehold basis, he should ascertain the terms of lease, i.e. the rent of lease, etc.;

(iii) He should see the account submitted by the auctioneer when the property has been purchased in auction;

(iv) He should examine brokers' note in case the property has been purchased through a broker;

(v) He should examine the correspondence, where the property has been bought direct from the seller;

(vi) He should examine the receipts issued by the contractor, where the property was erected through the contractor;

(vii) He should vouch the expenditure on building material purchased, cartage paid, wages paid to the workers, where the building has been constructed by engaging direct labour; and

(viii) He should check that auctioneers' commission, brokerage, architects' fees, registration fees and legal charges, etc. have been capitalised. He should also vouch all such payments with reference to receipts obtained.

2. Plant and Machinery. The auditor should take the following steps while vouching payments in connection with the plant and machinery:

(i) He should examine the invoices from the vendors and also the receipts for payments towards the cost of assets;

(ii) He should make proper enquiries to ascertain that the items included under this head are *bona fide* capital charges including the cost of carriage and erection;

(iii) He should inspect the auctioneer's statement of account where it has been bought on auction;

(iv) He should examine the agreement and the relevant vouchers when the plant and machinery has been purchased under hire-purchase agreement, and also see that proper apportionment is made of the instalment paid between capital and revenue;

(v) He should see that no repairs and expenses of maintenance are capitalised; and

(vi) He should see that the loss on sale of any obsolete plant etc. has been treated as revenue loss.

3. Investments. The auditor should adopt the following procedure while vouching investment:

(i) He should vouch payments for the purchase of investments with reference to the Broker's Sold Note, in case they were purchased through a stockbroker.

(ii) The allotment letter and banker's receipt for the instalments paid should be inspected in the case of a new issue, for which application has been made if the share certificates have not yet been received. In case share certificates or debentures have been received they should be examined.

(iii) The auditor should examine the actual investment.

(iv) In case of cum-dividend purchase, the auditor should see that the expenditure has been properly apportioned between capital and revenue.

(v) Where investments have been made in the shares of companies under the same management and the investments exceed the limits as laid down under Sec. 372 of the Companies Act, 1956, the auditor should see that the approval of the central government as required under the Act should have been obtained.

(vii) In the case of new issue the auditor should examine letters of allotment, share certificates, etc. The purchase of investments should be properly authorised. The certificate from the bank should be obtained, if the investments consist of inscribed stocks.

4. Patents and Copyrights

(i) The auditor should get a list of Patent held by the assessee in the business and examine it with reference to registration number, date, name of the seller, consideration paid etc.;

(ii) The auditor should check thoroughly the existence of patents, registration certificates, certificates of grant of patent, documents of assignment, copyright agreements and receipts for the renewal fees;

(iii) The auditor should check the agents' receipted accounts, where patents have been bought through some agent to (i) ascertain the agent's fees, and (ii) verify the amounts so included in the assessed account;

(iv) The auditor should see that the patent renewal fees has not been charged to the patent account as it represents revenue expenditure;

(v) The auditor should see that the lapsed patents have been written off from the books of accounts; and

(vi) The auditor should see that the patents have been valued properly and the method of valuation is the same from year to year.

5. Loans. The auditor should do the following to vouch the figure of loan:

(i) He should inspect the loan agreement and the security held (if any);

(ii) He should check that the loan has been properly authorised; e.g minutes of the Board meetings; and

(iii) He should see that where loans have been given to officers of the company (e.g. directors, managing director or any other official), the necessary approval of the central government under Sec. 295 of the Companies Act, 1956 has been obtained.

6. Furniture, Fixture and Fittings. Considerations similar to those in the case of plant and machinery should apply and the same vouching procedure should be adopted in case of vouching of furniture, fixture, and fittings.

VOUCHING OF REVENUE EXPENDITURES

Expenses incurred under revenue expenditures relate to the day-to-day expenses incidental to the conduct or administration of the business. These may include selling and distribution expenses, general and administration expenses and financial expenses. These are incurred to keep the concern going. These are consumed during the period to which they relate. The benefit of such expenses is derived in the period in which they are incurred. Thus reverse expenditures include salaries, wages, rent, sales taxes, insurance, travelling expenses, agents' and travellers' commission, discounts, freight brokerage and customs duties, bank charges, etc. The auditor should vouch these expenses with reference to the acceptable original evidence. He should check the posting to the appropriate revenue accounts in the general or impersonal ledger from the cash book.

He should make sure that they are charged against revenue earned in the year concerned. Otherwise, the operating results shown by the revenue account and the position show by the balance sheet will be misleading.

Types of Expenditures : Auditors Duties

1. Wages. While vouching 'wages' the auditor should do the following:

(i) He should see the internal check system in force for wages;

(ii) He should check a proportion of addition and alteration;

(iii) He should check some of the calculations at random;

(iv) He should check the system of preparation of wage sheet and the payment of wages;

(v) He should see that the wage sheets have been signed by the preparer and a responsible official;

(vi) He should see that only exact amount of wages to be paid has been withdrawn from the bank;

(vii) He should test check the totals and other calculations;

(viii) He should try to pay a surprise visit in person at the time of payment of wages;

(ix) He should check the system of calculating overtime wages who authorises overtime and within what limits;

(x) He should see that overtime does not exceed any statutory limit;

(xi) He should check overtime payment with reference to work records and acknowledgment receipts;

(xii) He should see that there is not much variation from month to month in overtime wages;

(xiii) He should check the system by calling out the time records, piecework cards, production control records, income tax deduction cards and insurance cards to ensure against the inclusion of dummy names on the pay roll;

(xiv) He should ensure suitable arrangements for the preparation of and payment of pay roll for casual labour; and

(xv) He should see that unclaimed wages are held by the Cashier and are banked if not claimed within a definite period, usually a month. Payments of unclaimed wages should be made only against authorisation signed by a responsible official.

2. Salaries. While vouching the salaries, the auditor should do the following:

(i) He should check the system of internal check especially with reference to the maintenance of the record of attendance of the employees, preparation of monthly salary bills and their disbursement;

(ii) He should see that the payment has not been made without the sanction of the responsible officer;

(iii) He should check the accuracy of the salary bill with reference to original records, earlier months' records in case of old employees and appointment letters in case of new employees;

(iv) He should see that the whole salary bill is drawn by one cheque and the disbursement is made before a responsible official;

(v) He should see that all payments above Rs. 20 bear a 20 paise revenue stamp; and

(vi) He should check any abnormal increases/decreases in total salary bills from month to month.

3. Petty Cash. The auditor should do the following to vouch petty cash:

(i) He should examine system of internal check existing for petty cash and find out its weakness, if any;

(ii) He should tally the cheques drawn for petty cash with the credit side of the cash book and debit side of the petty cash book;

(iii) He should see that the Imprest system of petty cash has been followed in the organisation;

(iv) He should see that all the vouchers have been numbered consecutively and are in order;

(v) He should check who approves vouchers and replenishes the imprest;

(vi) He should give surprise checks to petty cash balance;

(vii) He should see that no credit to employees is given out of petty cash;

(viii) He should check casts, cross casts and posting of this book;

(ix) He should examine thoroughly all vouchers over a certain amount;

(x) He should inspect postage books with reference to their regular balancing, and reasonableness of expenditure and stock in hand; and

(xi) He should to check the petty cash balance by personally visiting on the date of the balance sheet, i.e. the last day of the accounting year. Where it is not possible he should instruct the client to get the balance deposited in the bank.

4. Travelling Expenses. In case of travelling expenses paid to the employees for official work, the auditor should, while vouching take the following steps:

(i) Seeing that the rules and conditions for granting travelling allowance are followed and ensuring that payment is passed under an order by a responsible official;

(ii) Seeing that these expenses are in connection with the business alone and have not been paid in excess;

(iii) Seeing that the directors have not been allowed travelling allowance unless authorised by the Articles of Association;

(iv) Tallying the cheque drawn with reference to the cash book and the travellers' receipts;

(v) Tests checking the figures a in some of the travellers' accounts with the vouchers submitted by them; and

(vi) Legally directors are not entitled to get travelling expenses to attend meetings of the board unless these are expressly granted by Articles of Association or by a resolution of the company. However, there is no bar for the directors to get travelling expenses in connection with the business of the company. The auditor should scrutinise the payment vouchers submitted by the directors. He should examine the details to see that they are reasonable . If he feels that the expenses so paid are not reasonable and that they virtually amount to additional remuneration to directors, he should refer the matter in his report.

5. Commissions. The auditor should check the following in case of vouching of commission:

(i) The commission book with reference to cash book and the receipts from commission agents;

(ii) The calculations;

(iii) The basis of calculation with reference to related agreement, i.e. whether commission is some percentage of sale or profit; and

(iv) That all unpaid commissions have been brought into account at the termination of the financial period.

6. Insurance Premium. Following steps may be taken in this connection:

(i) The auditor should examine the premium notice, the insurance company's receipts and the insurance policies.

(ii) Details about the amount of premium payable, mode of payment and the date of maturity of the policy should be verified from the insurance policy.

(iii) In case of new policies the auditor should inspect the cover note or the receipt from the insurance company.

(iv) The renewal receipt should be examined in case of renewals.

(v) If the number of policies is large, the auditor should require the preparation of a schedule of insurance containing information about the number of the policy, the amount, the date of maturity, the amount of premium payable, etc. After carefully examining these particulars if he finds that some policy has lapsed, he should check as to under whose authority it has been allowed to lapse.

7. Postage. The auditor should take the following steps in this connection:

(i) He should examine the system of internal check on postage expenditure;

(ii) He should check the postage book with reference to amount drawn from petty cash and also count the postage stamp in hand. Where franking machines are in use the auditor should also check the following :

(a) As to how the machine is controlled;

(b) The automatic counting register of the machine with the available records and the receipts of Post Office showing the amount paid in this connection; and

(c) That the postage includes only the postage expenses connected with the business and not private account.

8. Bank Charges. To vouch bank charges such as commission, interest on overdraft and loan, etc. the auditor should examine the Bank Pass Book. He should check the calculation of interest and see the bank's advice note.

9. Director's fees. Though the directors of a company are not entitled to get any monthly salary, they can claim fees for attending meetings if the articles of the company provide for it. The auditor should examine the following while vouching director's fees:

(i) The Articles of Association to know whether directors can be paid fees for attending a Board meeting or not and also the amount of fees payable to the directors for attending the Board meeting;

(ii) The director's minute book and the attendance register to ascertain the number of meetings attended by them and the total fees payable to them;

(iii) The receipts obtained from directors for this payment; and

(iv) The resolution of the shareholders to calculate the amount payable as director's fee and compare the figure with the amount actually paid.

10. Cash Purchases. The auditor should adopt the following procedure in vouching the items of cash purchases:

(i) He should test the entries in the book by reference to cash memo or receipted invoices issued by the suppliers;

(ii) He should see that the goods paid for have actually been received by checking the entries in Goods Inward Book or Purchases Book or Stock Ledger;

(iii) He should see that a proper distinction has been made between a payment for goods and an advance against supplies to be made in future , the latter should be classified as advance recoverable in cash or in kind or for value to be received;

(iv) As the amount shown as paid in advance against goods may only a camouflage for an assistance to a party, it is very necessary for an auditor to confirm that the advance was made pursuant to a normal trade practice and supplies were later on received within a reasonable period of payment of the advance; and

(v) The auditor should see that only net amount (i.e. purchases minus trade discount) has been shown in the books of account.

VOUCHING OF CREDIT SIDE OF CASH-BOOK

1. Vouching Payment to Creditors. The following vouching procedure should be adopted for payment to creditors:

(i) Check payments made against credit purchases with reference to receipts issued by suppliers and the credit to their accounts on the basis of invoices entered in the Purchases Day Book.

(ii) See the evidence of the goods having been received an entry in the Goods Inward Book or Stock Ledger.

(iii) Certain concerns issue invoices in duplicate. In such a case, there can be a possibility of an invoice being paid twice, first by its being entered in the Purchase Book and the account of the supplier being credited and the second time by the duplicate copy of the invoice being paid as a cash purchase. Hence on noticing a receipted invoice, the auditor should verify that neither the original nor the duplicate thereof has already been entered in the Purchase Day Book.

(iv) In the case of goods purchased at the end of the year, verify that even though not received or entered in stock before the close of the year, they have been included in the closing stock.

(v) Confirm that all the goods, payment for which have been made, during one week preceding the close of the year should be traced into the Goods Received Book maintained by the storekeeper, also it should be verified that every purchase invoice is stamped with the date of receipt of goods in stock and ledger folio at which invoice has been entered.

2. Vouching Bills Payable. The auditor should take the following steps in this connection:

(i) He should examine the duly cancelled returned bills as an evidence of the amount having been paid;

(ii) He should inspect Bills Payable Books at the same time; and

(iii) In case the payments on certain bills have been made through the bank, the auditor should see the Bank Pass Book and the banker's advice.

3. Vouching Freight and Carriage. The auditor should make reasonable considerations in case of freight and carriage. He should examine the receipts for the amount paid with the statement of accounts, rebates received, if any, and the same should be properly accounted for.

4. Vouching Tax and Other Taxes. About vouching taxes the auditor with reference to the assessment order, notices of demand, and the receipted challans, etc. where taxes have been deducted from the salary of the employees or collected from the customers, the same must have been paid from time to time to the concerned government. He should check the amount deposited with reference to the returns submitted by his client, receipted challan, etc.

5. Vouching Customs and Excise Duties. The following points should be noted in this connection:

(i) Customs duty is usually paid through clearing agents. Their bills duly supported by receipted bills of entry should, therefore, be available for verification.

(ii) The bill of entry relevant thereto, together with the receipt should be checked, if a payment has been made directly.

(iii) In the event of a dispute, where a provisional payment has been made, the amount determined as payable finally should be ascertained. Any additional duty payable or refund of the amount paid in excess which is recoverable should be brought into account.

(iv) Drawback of customs duty is allowed if goods imported or containing imported materials are exported. The auditor should see that the refund of the duty has been claimed on export.

(v) (a) Excise duty is payable before the issue of the excisable goods from the factory. Therefore the amount is deposited with the State Bank of the credit of the Controller of Excise and the duplicate copy of the challan is forwarded to him for obtaining the permit. In order to vouch such payments, the amount of duty paid must be checked with quantity of goods in respect of which the issue permits for the goods have been received. If a triplicate copy of the challan is available in the file in respect of each payment, it serves as an additional evidence of the duty having been paid.

(b) Some concerns maintain a current account with the excise authorities. In such cases, permits are issued in advance and duty is paid according to the quantity of excisable goods, issued during each month or a shorter period.

6. Vouching Partner's Drawings

(i) He should inspect that in vouching drawing by the partners, the auditor should do the following partnership deed so as to note :

(a) the maximum amount permissible as drawings;

(b) the maximum time for which a partner can draw money; and

(c) whether drawings by partner's are to be subject to any interest.

(ii) He should check the amount of drawings as shown in the Cash Book with reference to the partner's Drawing Book or Account.

(iii) He should see that each and every drawing has been duly signed by the concerned partner.

(iv) If payments are made to third parties on behalf of partners, the auditor should see that payments are vouched with direct reference to the partner concerned.

7. Miscellaneous Expenses. In the case of miscellaneous expenses such as rent, rebates, taxes, lighting, etc. the auditor should :

(i) Examine whatever documentary evidence is available;

(ii) Carefully note that the expenditure has been properly appropriated between the periods, where necessary.

8. Research and Development Expenditure. According to International Accounting Standard No.9 research and development cost include the following items.

The amount of research and development costs in these items should be charged to the profit and loss account for the period in which they are incurred :

(i) Salaries, wages and other related costs of personnel engaged in research and development activities;

(ii) Costs of materials and services consumed in research and development activities;

(iii) Depreciation of equipment and facilities to the extent that they are used for research and development activities;

(iv) Overhead costs related to research and development activities; and

(v) Other costs related to research and development activities such as the amortisation of patents and licences.

Expenses which satisfy the following criteria are however deferred for payment :

(i) The product or process is clearly defined. The costs attributable to the product or process may be separately identified.

(ii) The technical feasibility of the product or process has been demonstrated.

(iii) The management of the enterprise indicates its intention to product and market, or use, the product or process.

(iv) There is a clear indication of a future market for the product or process.

(v) If it is to be used internally rather than sold, its usefulness to the enterprise may be demonstrated.

(vi) Adequate resources exist or are reasonably expected to be available, to complete the project and market the product or process.

The auditor should see that the following principles are observed in this connection:

(i) The deferral of development costs of a project should be limited to the amount that can reasonably be expected to be recovered from related future revenues. Thcsc include further development costs, related production costs and selling and administrative costs directly incurred in marketing the product.

(ii) The accounting policy of deferral of development costs should be applied to all development projects that meet the above criteria.

(iii) Deferred development costs of a project should be allocated on a systematic basis to future accounting periods by reference either to the sale or use of the product or process or to the time period over which the product or process is expected to be sold or used.

(iv) The deferred development costs of a project should be reviewed at the end of each accounting period. If the criteria which previously justified the deferral of the costs, no longer apply the unamortised balance should be charged as an expense immediately. If the criteria for deferral continue to be met but the amount of deferred development costs is exceeded by the unamortised balance of such costs, the excess should be charged as an expense immediately.

(v) Development costs once written off should not be reinstated even though the uncertainties which had led to their being written off no longer exist.

The auditor should adopt the following procedure while vouching Development Expenditure :

(i) He should ascertain the nature of research and development work, i.e. the benefit will arise in one year or in many years to follow.

(ii) He should see that the research activity has been properly authorised by the proper authority and has relevance with the objective of the company.

(iii) He should see that they are written off in the Profit and Loss Account of the same year.

(iv) Generally, research expenses for developing products or for inventing a new product may be treated as deferred revenue expenditure to be written off over a period of three to five years, if successful. The entire expenses incurred should be written off to the Profit and Loss Account if it is found that the research effort is not going to succeed.

(v) When some machinery and equipment have been purchased especially for the research activity, the cost thereof, less the residual value, should be debited to the Research and Development Account over the years of research. In case such machinery or equipment is utilised in the company after the research effort is over, the asset should be transferred to the general plant and machinery account at the written down value.

(vi) The auditor should see that tax benefit arising out of research and development expenses has been taken into account in creating tax provision.

(vii) He should see that no expense unrelated to the research and development programme are allowed to be debited to Research and Development Account.

(viii) He should see that the development costs once written off are not re-instated even when the uncertainties are leading to their being written off no longer exist.

(ix) He should see that the total of research and development costs, including amortisation of deferred development costs, charged as expenses has been fully disclosed in the books of accounts.

9. Payment of Political Party. Section 293A of the Companies Act specifically prohibits a company from making any contribution to a political party or for a political purpose due to the various interpretations of the expression by various authorities.

The Institute of Chartered Accountants of India issued a guidance note in 1976 which directs as follows:

(i) *Monetary Contributions.* Cash contribution to a political party is specifically prohibited though this does not mean that no monetary payment can be made against adequate consideration.

(ii) *Advertisement in Souvenirs, etc.* About such payments the auditor should check that :

(a) There was a genuine *quid pro quo* for the payment;

(b) The advertisement was duly authorised by the Authorised official of the company;

(c) The souvenir was in fact published and the advertisement was carried in that. This can be checked from a copy of the souvenir received by the company;

(d) The payment is *prime facie* not grossly: (i) unreasonable having regard to the space booked, the possible advertisement effect and the commercial rates for booking advertisement, (ii) rate charged is same as had been quoted in the request for advertisement letter issued by the political party and (iii) the transaction of advertisement is supported by an adequate bill and a receipt.

QUESTIONS FOR EXERCISE

1. What is a voucher ? What are the types of voucher ? Give a schedule of available vouchers.
2. "Reliability of the vouchers available to an auditor depends upon the sources of documents." Discuss.
3. Enumerate and explain the general and specific considerations which the auditor should keep in mind while checking vouchers.
4. "In vouching payments, the auditor does not merely seek proof that money has been paid away." Discuss the statement in detail.
5. Discuss in details the duties of the auditor with regard to missing vouchers.
6. What is the need of vouching Cash Book ? Enumerate and explain the general considerations that the auditor should keep in mind while vouching cash receipts.

7. How will you vouch the following cash receipts?

   (i) Cash sales, (ii) Receipts from debtors, (iii) Receipts against bills receivable, (iv) Rent, (v) Interest, (vi) Proceeds of sale of sundry assets, (vii) Dividend receipts, (viii) Sale of investments.

8. Explain in detail 'Teaming and Lading' as a method of fraud in connection with receipts from debtors.

9. Describe steps in the Vouching of Bills receivables (i) Rent recoverable and (ii) Interest receipts.

10. What are the duties of the auditor with reference to the vouching of (i) Sale proceeds of goods sent out on consignment (ii) Dividend receipts (iii) Sale of investments (iv) Sale of assets (v) Payments.

11. What are capital expenditures ? How will you vouch them ?

12. How will you vouch the following ?

    (i) Land and building; (ii) Plant and machinery (iii) Investments, (iv) Patents and copyrights, (v) Loans, (vi) Furniture and fixtures.

13. What is revenue expenditure ? How will you vouch the following ?

    (i) Wages, (ii) Salaries, (iii) Petty cash expenses, (iv) Travelling expenses, (v) Director's travelling expenses, (vi) Commission, (vii) Insurance premium, (viii) Postage, (ix) Director's fees, (x) Cash purchases.

14. How would you verify the correctness of the wages paid in a Cotton Textile Mill ? Explain the extent of the internal check which you would expect to come across in the case of a well-managed mill.

15. "In vouching payments, the auditor does not merely seek proof that money has been paid away." Discuss fully this statement.

16. How would you vouch the payment *i.e.* credit side of cash book ? Discuss.

8

Vouching of Trading Transactions

Trading transactions include purchases and sales. The following procedures are adopted by the auditor in checking vouching of trading transaction:

A. Purchases. In case of vouching of purchases the auditor must first satisfy himself about the effectiveness of internal check and control system relating to purchases. Subsequently he should proceed in the following way:

1. Invoices. He should check the invoices and compare them with entries in the day book. According to Spicer and Pegler the following are the most important considerations vouching invoices:

(i) The auditor should see that the invoices are initialled by the clerk whose business it is to check them.

(ii) Each invoice relating to goods should have attached to it a docket signed by the gate-keeper acknowledging receipt of the goods, or bear a reference to a Goods Inwards Book, to which the auditor should refer to see that the goods stated in the invoice have actually been received.

(iii) Care should be taken to see that the invoices are made out in the name of the firm and appear to be of a nature relating to the business carried on.

(iv) It should be seen that each item is extended into its proper subsidiary column in the Bought Day Book or Cash Payments Book, and if any column is provided for capital expenditure, such as plant and machinery, the items contained therein should be checked to see that they are strictly of a capital nature.

(v) All such items should be passed and initialed by some competent official.

(vi) The details relating to discounts and sales tax and the various calculations and extensions should be examined.

(vii) It should be seen that the date of the invoice falls within the accounting period under review.

2. Inflation of profit. The figures of purchases are shown lower than the actual ones, thereby inflating the amount of profit. In such cases the auditor should compare the Goods Inward Book and the stock sheets with the Purchases Book, particularly for the goods received during the last few weeks. He should inspect the invoice file for a few weeks of the beginning of the next financial year to see if any of these has been charged to the period under audit.

3. Checking from the supplier. The auditor should ask his client to send notice to each and every supplier who has an account in the purchase ledger requesting him to furnish a statements showing the balance due on the Balance Sheet date. These statement should be examined and compared with the ledger accounts. If they agree it will provide a sufficient proof that invoices with regard to these accounts have not been omitted.

4. Checking fraud. De Paula and De Paula mention a simple but significant fraud which may be perpetrated in connection with purchases. The invoices may be entered twice in the Day Book in each case the creditor's account being credited. To quote De Paula, "In due course and at different dates, two cheques are drawn, one being set to the creditor and the other misappropriated". Both cheques are debited to the Creditor's Account the balance upon which will agree with creditor's periodical statements. In order to provide a receipt in support of the second and fraudulent payment, the *bona fide* receipt may be produced twice. If the auditor takes no precaution in marking vouchers, the invoice might be receipted fraudulently, for a duplicate receipt on the pretext that the original had been lost. Unless the invoices are carefully checked with the Day Book of the creditor such a fraud cannot be discovered.

This fraud cannot be committed if check, and the day book, ledger and cash book are under separate control.

5. Checking in the absence of Bought-Day Book and Ledger. The absence of a Bought Day Book increases the risk of omissions. If a firm has dispensed with a Bought Day Book and Bought Ledger, the invoices in the 'unpaid' accounts files should represent the outstanding liabilities at the Balance Sheet date. The auditor should call for the list of such invoices, prepared at the close of the financial period. He should vouch therefrom the adjustments made on the relevant impersonal ledger accounts and the closing balances on these accounts. Each item on the list, or a representative number thereof, must be vouched by a reference to the appropriate invoices, which will probably have been paid before the audit is completed. The auditor should take the normal precautions to ensure that the list of outstanding liabilities is complete.

6. Agreement for forward purchases. In such a case if there is any exceptional forward commitment the outcome of which may be a big loss affecting the financial position of the company, the auditor should see that a suitable disclosure is made about this fact in the Balance Sheet.

7. Test checking. The auditor should test-check totals, sub-totals, carry-forwards and calculations in the Purchases Book along with postings from the Purchases Book to the ledger accounts.

The auditor should examine the system of internal check in operation so as to ensure that full credit is obtained for all goods returned. He should adopt the following approach in this connection :

1. He should compare the notes sent by creditors and the entries in the Purchases Returns Books.
2. He should see that the proper adjustments (regarding goods returned) have been made before making payments to the creditors.
3. He should ensure that full credit has been received subsequently where payment has already been made.
4. He should check castings and postings of the Purchases Returns Book and also their posting to the ledger accounts.

B. Sales. Sales vouching may be of two types: vouching of cash sales and vouching of credit sales— Vouching of cash sales is the same as "vouching of cash receipts". While vouching credit sales the auditor should adopt the following procedure:

1. He should check the system of internal check and control with regard to credit sales. He should check the system of receiving orders, preparing invoices, delivery of the goods, etc.
2. Subsequently, he should proceed in the following way:

(i) *Sales Day Book.* If the organisation maintains Sales Day Book, he should test-check (a) the entries therein with the carbon copies of the sales invoices; (b) posting to the sales ledgers and (c) the casts of the book and the total transferred to the sales account.

(ii) *Carbon Copies of Sales Invoices.* If the organisation does not maintain Sales Day Book but the system followed is that the carbon copies of the sales invoices are listed and added by machine the auditor should test-check the machine lists with the relevant copies of the invoices and the totals to the sales account.

(iii) *Sales of Asset.* He should check that no sale of an asset has been entered in the Sales Day Book because they, when received, will be the capital receipts. Only profit or loss on sale of asset should be credited or debited to the Profit and Loss Account.

(iv) *Sale on approval or return basis.* If the concern gives goods to the customers on approval or on sale or return basis, the auditor should see that: (a) such sales are not included in the sales unless confirmed by letter of acceptance etc., (b) the goods in hand with the customers have been included in the closing stock shown in the Balance Sheet, (c) the provision for damages to these goods, if any, have been made.

(v) *Goods sent on consignment.* The auditor should do the following:

(a) Goods still unsold with the consignee are treated as stock with him and are valued at cost plus proportionate expenses incurred till the goods reach the consignee or at his own godown. Where market price of such goods has fallen goods are valued at market price;

(b) Where the number of consignments is large, a consignment ledger having account of each individual consignment is maintained;

(c) Each individual consignment has been debited with the cost of the goods and expenses incurred by the consignor;

(d) Entries tally with the consignment note, account sale, vouchers for the expenses and cash books;

(e) The entries for sales proceeds, expenses incurred by the consignee, his commission, etc. are in agreement with the account sale sent by the consignee;

(f) Where *del-credere* commission is paid the bad debts are met by the consignee and not by his client;

(g) The proper unloading has been done when the goods are invoiced at sale price.

(vi) *Sales under instalment system.* Under the instalment payment system, ownership or title in the goods passes immediately at the time of the contract and on the payment of the first instalment.

(vii) *Sale on hire-purchase basis.* Under sale on hire-purchase basis, title of the goods does not pass until the last instalment has been paid. Thus, under the hire-purchase system goods can be recovered if any instalment is not paid.

In practice, however, there are two methods adopted to credit the sale proceeds. One is to debit the total cash price in the year of sale and to treat the buyer as debtor for the instalment not yet due. The other is to take credit only for that amount which has become due. If the first method is followed, provision should be made at the date of the Balance Sheet for an amount equal to the unrealised profits included in the instalments remaining unpaid. However, the second method is better. In it the profit on the sale is equitably distributed over the whole period during which these instalments are payable. In it profit which has not yet been realised is not taken into account. In this method the auditor should ensure that the amount of unpaid instalment is shown as stock out on hire.

(viii) *Goods subjected to sales tax.* The auditor should see that the sales tax has been segregated from the sale price of the goods. The amount of sales tax should be entered in the Sales Day Book in a separate column or listed separately on machine lists.

(ix) *Check on inflation of profits.* Number of sales invoices should be checked with the Goods Outwards Records. This is to ensure that sales actually belonging to the next financial period have not been treated as sales for the current period, thus inflating the profits.

(x) *Sales Returns.* The auditor should do the following about the sales returns :

1. He should inquire into the internal control with regard to sales returns. It is quite possible that misappropriations of cash received from debtors may be covered up through inflating the figure of sales-returns. Hence all credits should be authorised by a responsible official and the credit note should be initialled and duplicated by means of carbons.
2. He should carefully scrutinise large credits, and test them with documents, such as credit notes, correspondence with the purchasers, Goods Inwards Books, etc.
3. He should note the large entries in this respect immediately after the close of the financial year, as sometimes, to elevate the figure of profits, such returns may be held back until after the date of the Balance Sheet.

TRANSACTIONS RECORDED IN JOURNAL

According to Spicer and Pegler, "The use of the Journal is principally confined to recording adjusting entries and all entries of a special nature for which no subsidiary book or record is kept".

Thus, the following transactions are generally recorded in the journal :

1. Opening entries.
2. Entries for the issue and allotment of shares and debentures.
3. Closing entries.
4. Entries for the forfeiture of shares and the reissue of forfeited shares.
5. Various adjusting entries, e.g., provision for bad debts and doubtful debts, outstanding depreciation, interest on capital, prepaid expenses, etc.
6. Entries for the acquisition of the various assets taken over from the vendors.
7. Entries for the acquisition of the different liabilities taken from the vendors.

8. Entries relating to consignment and dishonour of bills, etc.
9. Entries for making calls.

Vouching of Journal Transactions

The following procedure may be adopted for vouching journal transactions :

1. Opening entries. Opening entries should be vouched with reference to last year's audited Balances Sheet. In case of new business, the same are examined with reference to purchase agreement, correspondence, receipts issued by the payee, documents of title, minutes of the Board meetings, etc. The auditor should pay special attention to the narration of each journal entry.

2. Closing entries. Closing entries are passed when the accounts are balanced at the end of the accounting period. The auditor should ensure that all the accounts are properly balanced.

3. Adjusting entries. The auditor should check the necessary evidence available for adjusting entries. For example in case of "provision for bad and doubtful debts", he may inspect the accounts contained in the Sales Ledgers. Provision for depreciation may be vouched by discussion with the management.

4. Share transactions. Entries for the issue allotment, forfeiture, reissue, of shares, etc. are vouched with the copies of allotment letters, shareholders' registers and minutes books. Entries in respect of the transactions related to other activities are vouched with original records, minutes book of the Board meetings, and member's meetings.

5. Bought ledger. It consists of individual creditors' accounts. It is posted from the books of original entry when goods are purchased, payments are made, goods are returned and bills are accepted, etc. The auditor should proceed in the following way to vouch the Bought Ledger:

(i) Open balances in the Bought Ledger with reference to last year's audited Balance Sheet. Check postings from the various subsidiary books like Purchase Book, Purchase Returns Book, Cash Book, Bills Receivable Book, Bills Payable Book, Journal, etc.

(ii) Obtain a list or schedule of creditors and compare the same with the balances shown by the ledger accounts.

(iii) If self-balancing system of ledgers is in operation, see that the total of the creditors agrees with the balances shown by the Bought Ledger Adjustments Accounts in the General Ledger.

(iv) Obtain confirmatory statement direct from the creditors with the consent of his client. If there is any discrepancy, inquire into it.

(v) Insist upon a provision for the amount under dispute. Advise the client to increase the amount of provision if it already exists but is inadequate.

(vi) It is usual to find debit balance in some of the accounts due to advance against orders or return of goods after the payment has been made. Ascertain that they are not fictitious and in fact represent items which are recoverable.

6. Sales Ledger. It contains the accounts relating to debtors. The auditor should proceed in the following way, while vouching the Sales Ledger :

(i) He should check the opening balances with the audited Balance Sheet of the previous year.

(ii) He should examine supporting books like Bills Receivable Book, Cash-Book, Goods Outward Book, Sales Returns Book, etc.

(iii) Where the books are maintained on the Self-Balancing system, the total of the balance should be checked as per the Schedule of Debtors Ledger Adjustment Account.

(iv) The auditor should test check the postings to the Sales Ledger, keeping in mind the efficacy of the internal control system. Special attention should be paid to the credit postings, since any attempt to conceal defalcations will more usually take the form of fictitious credit entries.

(v) The auditor should confirm the balances with the debtors, and examine if any claim is disputed.

(vi) The auditor should ascertain the composition of each balance while examining the accounts. He should note whether it represents specific items of goods, or is an accumulated balance. He should ensure that accumulated balance does not represent doubtful or bad debt.

BAD AND DOUBTFUL DEBTS

From the evidence at this disposal the auditor should ascertain whether any of the individual balances represent debts which are irrecoverable, or of such a doubtful nature that some provision for possible loss should be made.

Spicer and Pegler have suggested the following considerations in determining whether a debt should be considered doubtful or bad:

1. The term of credit allowed by the business.
2. The age of the debt.
3. Whether the account is regularly settled within the term of credit, and an advantage of any cash discount offered.
4. Whether payments are being made on account, and if so, whether the balance has tended to increase.
5. Whether an old balance is being carried forward to be paid off by instalments, new goods being supplied for cash.

6. Whether any bills of exchange have been dishonoured or retired.
7. Whether any cheques have been dishonoured.
8. Whether any notes have been made on the ledger account relating to suspension of payment, deeds of arrangement, bankruptcy, liquidation, receivership or of the placing of account in the hands of solicitors or debt collectors.

Vouching of Bad and Doubtful Debts

1. Schedule. Before commencing his examination of the ledger balances, the auditor should ask that a schedule of bad and doubtful debts be prepared and presented to him. It should be certified by the manager, secretary or other responsible official, as representing, in his opinion, a complete list of all doubtful debts for which provision should be made. Now, the auditor, will be in a position to know whether all those debts which appear to him to be bad or doubtful are included therein. It will be necessary for him to make further enquiries in respect of any other debts which in his view should have been included in the schedule. He should mark these on the schedule of ledger balances and discuss with the appropriate official. If no certified list of bad and doubtful debts is presented to him, he should mark on the schedule of ledger balances all those against which he considers that provision should be made.

2. Bills. If bills have been dishonoured or renewed it is an evidence of weakness. If a provision is considered necessary, and any bills are outstanding on the account, they will form part of the balances of the Bills Receivable Account unless discounted. Hence provision should be made against them accordingly. Where such bills have been discounted, a provision should be made in respect of the contingent liability.

3. Cheques. Return of cheques may be due to reasons other than sufficiency of funds. However, if a cheque is returned for lack of funds, the account may be considered doubtful.

4. Bad debts. Bad debts should not be written off without the sanction of some responsible official. Bad debts written off during the period should be passed through the journal, the entries being initialled by the authorising official, in order to prevent the possibility of misappropriations being concealed by the creation of fictitious bad debts.

QUESTIONS FOR EXERCISE

1. Explain vouching of trading transaction. How will you vouch credit sales ?
2. What transactions are recorded in a Journal ? Explain the procedure of recording internal transaction.
3. A company maintains all the necessary subsidiary books of accounts. What types of transactions would be entered in its Journal proper ? State briefly the technique of vouching any three such entries.
4. How will you determine bad and doubtful debt ? Explain its vouching procedure ?

9

Vouching of Personal and Impersonal Ledgers

Posting from various subsidiary books is made in the respective accounts in the Ledger Book which may be sub-divided as personal and impersonal.

1. Personal Accounts. *Personal* accounts are usually related to those persons from whom the goods are purchased or to whom the goods are sold in a trading concern. Accounts of the former, known as creditors, are maintained in Purchases Ledger. Accounts of the latter, known as debtors, are recorded in Sales Ledger. Personal accounts may also be related to accounts of the proprietor or partners such as Partner's Capital and Current Accounts etc., these accounts are, however, maintained in Impersonal Ledger.

Impersonal Accounts. *Impersonal* accounts, as the name suggests, are related to the accounts affecting the business and not persons. These accounts are of two types — nominal and real.

1. *Nominal accounts.* These are related to the items of profit or loss, income or expenditure, *e.g.* rent, salaries, commission, accounts etc.

2. *Real Accounts.* These are concerned with the assets such as building, plant and machinery or furniture accounts etc.

PERSONAL LEDGER

After vouching the various subsidiary books *viz.,* Purchases Book, Cash Book, Purchases Returns Book, Bills Payable Book and the Journal Proper the auditor should vouch Purchases and Sales Ledgers carefully. He should check the cash and the balances of the Ledger accounts. He should examine the Ledger accounts to see whether he has already vouched every item including the balances brought forward at the commencement of the period. If the Ledger is maintained on the Self-Balancing system, the total of the list of the creditors and debtors should agree with the total of the shown in the Creditors' and Debtors' Ledger respectively.

Kinds of Personal Ledger

(1) Purchases Ledger. It contains the accounts of various creditors, from whom the goods are purchased on credit, are maintained.

The auditor should compare the statement received from the creditors with the balances of the Purchases Ledger. If statement of the creditors is not available he should ask for it from the client or correspond directly with the credits ascertaining the balances on the date of the Balance Sheet. If the two disagree, it should be inquired into and the proper explanation must be sought. A possible explanation may be that goods may have been despatched by the creditors on or before the date of the Balance Sheet but actually the goods may not have been received by the client by that date.

If certain accounts of creditors are disputed or claims have been made by them and a law suit is pending, it results into disagreement of creditor's statement and Purchases Ledgers. For such contingent liability adequate provision should be made and shown in the Balance Sheet by way of a note to that effect. If adequate or no provisions have been made for such claims and the fact has not been mentioned in the Balance Sheet, it must be stated in his audit report.

The auditor must very carefully enquire if the debit balance appear in the Purchases Ledger, which may be on account of payment made in advance, returns or allowances etc. If payments have been made in advance and the goods have not been received but property or ownership in the goods has passed to the client, 'Goods in transit Account' should be opened and the balance closed. If the property has not passed to him, the debit balance should be allowed to remain. The auditor should enquire whether the debit balances are *bona fide* or not and show them in the Balance Sheet with the sundry debtors rather than as deducted from the sundry creditors.

(2) Sales Ledger

After checking the posting from various books of original entry into the Sales Ledger, the auditor should proceed with the casting of the Sales Ledger and examination of the balances with the help of the List of Debtors. He should be ensured that the trade discounts, goods sent on approval or on consignment have not been included in the balances. The opening debit balances should also be checked with the help of the previous audited Balance Sheet. If the ledgers are maintained on the self-balancing system, the auditor should see that the total of List of Debtors agrees with the balance of the particular Debtors' Ledger Adjustment Account in the General Ledger. Errors should be located and rectified if there is disagreement between the two.

By cautious examination the auditor should ensure that no fraud has been committed by passing fictitious entries on the credit side of the Sales Ledger by way of allowances or bad debts etc. A statement of account should be sent to each debtor to confirm the balances. The auditor should instruct that the replies should be sent to him directly. He should insured that the balance shown in the client's Ledger agree with those confirmed by the debtors. Proper explanation must be sought for if there is any disagreement.

If the credit balances appear in the Sales Ledger, the auditor should ascertain that they are *bona fide.* He should ensure that they appear in the Balance Sheet along with the sundry creditors rather than as deducted from the sundry debtors. He should then ascertain the amount of bad and doubtful debts.

Debtors' Ledgers

Having checked the accuracy of the balances in the Sales Ledgers the auditor should examine whether all the debts are recorded or not. In case of debts whose recovery may be doubtful or which may be irrecoverable at all, the auditor should obtain a duly certified schedule from the client scrutinizing it he should carefully note the following points:

(i) The conditions and the period of the credit allowed by the client.

(ii) The age of each debt.

(iii) The regularity of cash payment for such debts and fulfilment of conditions of credit.

(iv) Whether payments are made on account and the balance tends to increase without any trade done.

(v) Whether new goods are being supplied whereas old accounts stand and are being paid in instalments.

(vi) Whether cheques or bills drawn for payment have been dishonoured.

(vii) Whether the notes appear on accounts such as "account stopped," "suspension of payment," "in insolvency," "in liquidation," "suit filed against," "disappeared" and "address unknown" etc.

The auditor should see that the schedule contains all the bad and doubtful debts. He should examine the Cash Book of the next period. If any debtor has paid in full it should be cancelled from the schedule. The position of other debts may also be confirmed by looking into the age and regularity of payments etc. However, merely, the age of the credit cannot determine whether a debt is good or not. The length of credit varies in different businesses. It also depends upon the class and status of the customer and the ease with which the client can keep touch with them. The auditor see whether certain doubtful debts have been included in the schedule or not. He should discuss each debt with the client or a responsible official. He could hear explanations regarding the debts marked by him as doubtful, in order to form an idea of the proportion thereof which may subsequently be recovered. While forming any opinion he should not ignore the special circumstances obtaining in the particular business.

The auditor should see that so long as there is slightest hope of its recovery any bad debt is not written off. If it is written off and subsequently the money is realised in part or full, that may be misappropriated since no debit appears in the ledger therefor. It should be properly recorded. If there is no hope of its recovery, it may be written off with proper sanction of some responsible official.

The auditor should examine the provision or reserve for bad and doubtful debts. He should ensure that all the bad debts have been fully provided for and the doubtful debts have been provided to the extent estimated to be irrecoverable. If insufficient provision has been made, he should persuade the client to make additional provision. If the client does not yield to his persuasion he should refer the matter in his report. He should obtain a certificate from a responsible official to the effect that the provision made in this connection is sufficient in his opinion.

The auditor must consider with due attention the whole question of bad and doubtful debt.[1] As such debts affect the profit or loss and financial picture of concern, any carelessness on his part may hold him liable. The Trading and Profit and Loss Account and the Balance Sheet will not show the correct financial picture of the concern if correct estimates of such debts are not made. The debtors represent the credit sales that have been credited to Trading Account but which have not been paid for. If part or full payment is not received the sales would not represent loss but would show earnings, and profits will be inflated to that extent. Similarly, the debtors will be shown as overstated in the Balance Sheet. It is difficult to estimate the amount of loss and no hard and fast rule can be laid down for its estimation. The auditor should, therefore, be careful in estimating the amount of bad and doubtful debts.

IMPERSONAL LEDGER

Also known as General Ledger or Nominal Ledger, Impersonal Ledger contains nominal and real accounts which affect the Trading and Profit and Loss Account and Balance Sheet of a concern substantially. The auditor must vouch them intelligently and carefully. He should satisfy himself with regard to the truth and fairness of the net results or the accounting period and the financial state of affairs on the date of the Balance Sheet. He should check in detail the entries in the Impersonal Ledger and examine it exhaustively since the entries in it are numerous, except in case of some very large business undertakings. This is necessary because it also ascertains the accuracy of Personal Ledgers. In practice, manipulation in the personal accounts is concealed through passing fictitious entries in the impersonal accounts. Such frauds may be detected if the auditor examines it thoroughly.

1. Refer to *re London and General Bank* (1895) and *A. E. Green & Co.* v. *The Central Advance and Discount Corporation Ltd.* (1920).

Posting in the Impersonal Ledger will be mainly from the various subsidiary books, Cash Book and the Journal proper. While vouching them, the auditor would have already consulted the vouchers in connection with the various items whose accounts are found in the Impersonal Ledger. For example, when he vouches the Cash Book, he vouches the receipts from commission, rents, dividends etc. whose account will be there in the Impersonal Ledger.

General Consideration

Following are the general considerations which the auditor should keep in mind while vouching the impersonal ledger:

1. (i) Checking the posting of cash transactions to the Impersonal Ledger.

   (ii) Vouching the journal so as to ensure that each entry is supported by sufficient evidence.

   (iii) Checking their posting to the Impersonal Ledger.

2. Checking the totals of the various books of prime entry with the accounts in the Impersonal Ledger.
3. Testing the posting from the Cash Book to the Impersonal Ledger to ensure that the entries have been posted to the correct accounts.
4. If direct entries are passed from one account to another in the Impersonal Ledger, the auditor must proceed in the same manner as if they had been passed through the journal.
5. Checking the adjustments which are usually done at the end of the year when the final accounts are prepared. These relate to outstanding assets and liabilities, depreciation, etc. Their posting in the Impersonal Ledger should be checked, as these adjustments pass through the journal, special attention should be paid to them as they ultimately affect the position shown by the final accounts.
6. Checking the balance of the various accounts in it and comparing with the balance shown in the trial balance.
7. Checking the balances of the various accounts with the respective items shown in the Trading and Profit and Loss Account and Balance Sheet.

Vouching of Outstanding Assets

While preparing the Profit and Loss Account all the profits or losses, incomes or expenditures, etc. related to that particular year only should be included in it. Nothing should be taken into account which relates to the previous or the following year. In practice, in every business there are some outstanding assets or liabilities which have to be adjusted into the accounts. All such outstanding assets or liabilities, not brought into accounts so far, for some reason or the other, must be brought into account to ascertain the true profit or loss for the year under consideration.

Adjusting entries for such items are passed through the journal. Sometimes a Memorandum Book is used to maintain such records. The auditor should obtain a certificate from some responsible official to the effect that all such outstanding items have been included in the books. It will make him familiar with the usual items for adjustments and facilitate the comparison of figures of such items for two given periods. He should see that such outstanding assets and liabilities are shown as assets and liabilities respectively in the Balance Sheet. Records for such adjusting items are made twice in the final accounts if the adjustment is made after balancing the accounts and preparation of the trial balance. The outstanding assets include following types of items:

A. Prepayments. Expenditures which might have been paid in advance. Some part or whole of an expenditure may relate to a period subsequent to the date of the balance sheet.

B. Accrued Incomes. Items accrued or due, not recorded in the books, which will ultimately be received in cash. To state profit and loss, only expenditure relating to the period under review should be included, and all incomes accruing that is reasonably certain to be received, is brought into account.

C. Prepaid Expenses. These have been paid in advance and represent working capital. These are usually the items which will be converted into expenses in a short time. These should be excluded from the Profit and Loss Account, but shown in the Balance Sheet as assets.

A. Pre-payments

1. Insurance premium paid in advance. Insurance premium on policies taken are usually payable in advance, part of premium paid may, belong to the period subsequent to the date to the Balance Sheet. The auditor should do the following to vouch this item:

(i) He should vouch the amount with the help of premium receipt;

(ii) He should inspect the actual policy taken if necessary;

(iii) He should see that the premium is properly recorded in the Profit and Loss Account and the Balance Sheet.

2. Rents paid in advance. Regarding rents paid in advance the auditor should make calculations to note what part of the amount paid in advance for the period subsequent to the date of Balance Sheet. He should check that proper apportionment is made between two periods and shown in the Profit and Loss Account and the Balance Sheet accordingly. He should also inspect agreements, leases and receipts, etc. so as to note the correct position.

3. Prepaid taxes and rates etc. Usually the tax period does not coincide with the accounting period. While accounts may be closed on 31st December the taxes may be paid upto 31st March. This may include prepayment of taxes. The auditor should do the following about prepaid taxes:

(i) He should make himself thoroughly familiar with all types of taxes,
(ii) He should scrutinise the copies of tax returns and tax bills,
(iii) He should consult the cash book for the taxes paid, so as to find out the amount of taxes paid in advance,
(iv) He should see that these payments have been correctly apportioned between the periods and correctly treated in the accounts.

4. Prepaid Interest. For vouching some interest which might have been paid in advance at the date of Balance Sheet the auditor should do the following:

(i) He should trace if interest and discounts are prepaid by comparing the agreements, rate of interest, conditions of payment of interest, actual amount of interest paid as shown in the cash book.
(ii) He should see that such amount of interest has been shown correctly in the final accounting statements.

In short, while vouching the prepaid expenses the auditor should examine the nominal accounts, the demand notes, receipts, etc. He should ensure that proper adjustments have been made in the books at the date of Balance Sheet. He should satisfy himself that a correct calculation has been made for the part of the expenditure which is unexpired on that date.

B. Accrued Incomes. Accrued incomes may be defined as those incomes which are accrued or due or earned but have not been received during the year under audit. They will be ultimately received by the concern. These should be included in the Profit and Loss Account and shown as assets in the Balance Sheet. Those incomes should not be credited in the Profit and Loss Account which are not likely to be received. Examples of certain accrued incomes include rent not received for a part of the current year, interest, dividend, commission not received before the date of Balance Sheet, etc. Accrued incomes may be vouched as follows:

1. Rents receivable. If the rent is due from the tenants but is not received till the date of Balance Sheet, the auditor should ensure the following:

(i) That the portion of the rents receivable which may not be recoverable or is doubtful, is not taken into account and a proper provision is made in the Profit and Loss Account.
(ii) That the copy of the receipt given to tenants and agreements, if any, to ascertain the balance of rents receivable.

2. Interest and dividends. Interest on debentures or other investments which are accrued but not received should be taken into account. Dividends on shares, which are due but not received, should also be taken into account.

However, the dividends on ordinary share cannot be vouched unless information about the amount of dividend is available.

DEFERRED REVENUE EXPENDITURE

Meaning

According to Arnold Johnson, Deferred Charges are "non-recurring expenditures which are expected to be of financial benefit to several accounting periods of indeterminate total length." Deferred revenue expenditure is a type of non-recurring item of expenditure which is incurred with a view to have financial benefit spread over many accounting years. The entire amount as such should not be charge to the Profit and Loss Account of the year in which it is incurred since the benefit is expected to be derived over a number of years. Examples:

1. Cost of removal of the business to a more convenient locality.
2. Cost incurred for dismantling, removing and erecting of plant and machinery.
3. Expenses incurred by way of exceptional repair of non-recurring nature.
4. Abnormal advertisement expenses incurred for heavy sale campaign.
5. Experimental expenditures.
6. Expenditures incurred on business researches.
7. Preliminary expenses in connection with the establishment of a new concern.
8. Development expenditures.

Auditors, Duties

1. The auditor should note that only the genuine deferred revenue expenses are written off over a number of years.
2. The auditor should guard against the writing off of the illegitimate expenses over a number of years just to inflate the profits of the organisation.
3. The auditor should check calculations and examine all related vouchers to ascertain the correct amount to be amortised.
4. The auditor should see that all such expenses have been correctly and properly spread over a number of years and debited to Profit and Loss Account.
5. The auditor should see that the balance of such expenditures (not written off) are shown on the asset side of the Balance Sheet until they are written off fully.

VOUCHING OF OUTSTANDING LIABILITIES

Certain outstanding liabilities exist on the date of the Balance Sheet in every business concern. All such liabilities belonging to the period for which the final accounts have been prepared, should be adjusted in the books of account. This is necessary to ascertain the correct amount of net profit for the year. Extension of such outstanding liabilities will inflate profit and to that extant the Balance Sheet will not present the true state of affairs of the concern. Hence the auditor should ascertain that all outstanding liabilities are dealt with. These should be brought into account before ascertaining the net profit or loss for the current year otherwise the dividends will have been paid out of capital as was stipulated in the case of the *Westminster Road Construction and Engineering Company Ltd.* 1932.

To ascertain the existence of such liabilities by thorough checking the auditor should to fall upon his own wisdom and experience. Most of the outstanding liabilities are of common nature in different concerns. These may be of two types: (A) the unpaid expenses, and (B) the unearned income.

A. *Unpaid Expenses.* Unpaid expenses are those which have already been accrued but not paid on the date of the Balance Sheet. These must be shown as expenditure in the Profit and Loss Account and as liability in the Balance Sheet. Such expenses are as follows:

1. Wages and Salaries. The auditor should see that outstanding wages and salaries have been adjusted into the accounts and shown as expenditure in the Profit and Loss Account of the year, on the liability side of the Balance Sheet.

2. Freight and Carriage. It the accounts by the agents are not submitted in time, the freight and carriage due on the goods purchased or otherwise may remain unpaid at the close of the accounting period. The auditor should do the following in this connection:

(i) He should ascertain the amount of freight and carriage unpaid;

(ii) He should see that such expenses are brought into accounts;

(iii) He should see that such expenses are debited to the Profit and Loss Account and shown in the Balance Sheet as liabilities;

(iv) He should compare such outstanding expenditure with that of the previous year so as to note any abnormal changes—increases or decreases;

(v) He should see that the whole of outstanding freight and carriage for the year has been taken into account.

3. Rent, Rates, Electricity etc. If these have remained unpaid on the date of the preparation of final accounts, the auditor should do the following:

(i) He should ascertain such outstanding expenses by examining the relevant documents;

(ii) He should examine the rent agreement or lease, the amount paid so far from the cash book and the receipts issued by the landlord;

(iii) He should examine the water, electricity and telephone bills so as to note the amount paid or unpaid till the date of Balance Sheet;

(iv) He should scrutinise the tax bills, tax returns and the demand notes for rates and taxes;

(v) He should see that all such outstanding expenses have been shown in the Profit and Loss Account and also in the liability side of the Balance Sheet.

4. Purchases. If the invoices relating to purchases of goods that have been taken into stock are received too late to be included in the Purchase Day Book, if any before the accounts are closed and may consequently have been entered in the succeeding period, the auditor should do the following:

(i) He should call for a schedule of such purchases;

(ii) He should see that their total is debited to the Purchases Account and credited to outstanding liabilities account;

(iii) He should compare the Goods Inwards Book with the Purchase Book for the few days of the closing month of the year; and

(iv) He should compare the creditors statement with their accounts in the Bought Ledger.

5. Commissions. If commissions payable to various agents and salesmen might not have been paid up to the Balance Sheet date the auditor should do the following :

(i) Examine and test the travellers' commission account in the impersonal ledger and compare the entries with statements relation to each other.

(ii) See that before setting the account of the agent, the commission payable is calculated after deduction any advance commission already paid.

(iii) Similarly, if the account section collects the amount directly from the customers and sets off their commission against the amounts thus realised, proper safeguards should be resorted to against it.

(iv) When the commission is to be paid to the *del-credere* agent such commission should also be taken into account. Commission to him is not payable if the customer does not pay the money due to the concern. The commissions on the amounts to be received from the customer whose financial position is doubtful or who have become insolvent need not be taken into account.

B. *Unearned Incomes or Incomes received in Advance.* Certain incomes received during the year under audit might not have been earned during that period, but will be earned only in the following year. These include the amount of rent, commission, dividends, interest, discounts, etc., received in advance. Such incomes belonging to the period subsequent to the date of the Balance Sheet, should not be credited to the Profit and Loss Account as income. These should be shown as liabilities in the Balance Sheet.

ALLOCATION BETWEEN CAPITAL AND REVENUE

If no distinction is made in expenses incurred of revenue nature or capital nature, it will affect the profit or loss of the concern and ultimately the balance sheet. The auditor as well as the directors of the company might be held responsible for the payment of dividend out of capital, if on account of wrong allocation, more profit is paid to the shareholders of a company.

Definition of Capital Expenditure

Capital expenditure is incurred in purchase new property which will help the production of goods or which will increase the earning capacity of the business or acquiring a valuable right or increasing the life of an asset. It is "incurred in acquiring assets for the purpose of earning income, or increasing the earning capacity of the business". If the existing property is permanently improved or enlarged or extended in order to increase the earning capacity of the business or its efficiency or reduce the normal expenses of production or administration, it is capital expenditure, for example, construction of a new shed, adding more looms and spindles in a textile mill, purchase of motor lorries to replace horse carts, initial expenditure incurred or losses suffered in the development of a plantation; interest paid out of capital during the course of construction of works subject to the conditions laid down under Section 208 of the Companies Act. The benefit of the capital expenditure extended over a number of accounting periods. Earning capacity of the asset is increased either by effecting large output or be reducing the cost. Other examples of capital expenditure are installation of fans and lights, acquisition of patent, copyrights, patterns, designs, etc. Such an expenditure is of capital nature if heavy expenditure is incurred on repairs which ultimately increase the efficiency of the plant or machinery. Expenses incurred in erection plant and machinery should be capitalized as such expenses increase the cost of machinery. It is only after taking into consideration all the relevant facts that the correct allocation between capital and revenue is determined

Sometimes it is conceived that if a heavy expenditure is incurred it is capital expenditure while a small expenditure is revenue expenditure. Depending upon the circumstances of each particular case it may or it may not be so. If repairs are effected in the ordinary course of business, it is revenue expenditure. If such repairs are effected to increase the life of the asset it is capital expenditure.

Therefore, the auditor should examine the basis on which the expenditure has been allocated between capital and revenue. He should not be guided by the amount of expenditure alone.

(b) Definition of Revenue Expenditure

Revenue expenditure is periodically incurred to maintain the revenue earning capacity of the business. This includes the following expenditure:

i) Those incurred to maintain the value of any existing asset, e.g. ordinary repairs, white-washing of the building, etc.

(ii) Those incurred in the ordinary conduct and administration of the business, e.g., rent, advertising, salaries, wages, etc.

(iii) Those incurred in connection with the administration and distribution of the goods manufactured or sold, e.g. commission, travelling expenses and so on.

(iv) Those incurred exclusively in earning the revenue of a particular accounting period, and are wholly consumed and written off during that period, e.g. the expenditure incurred for the purchase of goods for resale.

Distinction between Capital and Revenue Expenditure

The correct allocation of expenditure between capital and revenue affects the Profit and Loss Account and Balance Sheet of a concern. However, it is not easy to classify a particular expense and revenue expenditure. for example, wages during the ordinary course of a manufacturing business will be of revenue nature, while wages paid for erection and fitting a new machinery in the same manufacturing business will be of capital nature. In the capital expenditure the General Wages Account should be credited and the machinery account debited, if the regular workers of the concern were directed to erect or fit the new machinery and their wages had been debited to the general Wages Account. If this is not done, the Profit and Loss Account will be unduly burdened and less profit will be shown. Therefore, proper data should be obtained about the number of workers employed for the erection of the plant and machinery, number of days they worked rate, and so on. This should be certified by the wages clerk regarding the calculation of wages; by the foreman of the works regarding the nature of the work done and by the works manager about the correctness of the allocation. If such a certificate is not obtained, the auditor may not known the correct allocation of the expenditure between capital and revenue. Similar considerations apply to materials used for a particular asset, e. g., in case of building contractor, if cement or steel has been used out of the stock for construction his own building, personal account of the contractor should be debited and Materials Account should be credited. The Store-keeper and the Works Manager should certify the proper allocation and the cost of the materials. Expenses paid for buying a new machinery, interest paid during the construction of works, legal charges incurred in purchasing a building, etc., should be considered as expenses of capital nature and should be debited to the particular asset account. On the other hand, carriage expenses, interest on money borrowed or debentures, etc., will be classified as revenue expenditure and will be debited to the Profit and Loss Account.

If a new plant is purchased to replace and old one, the expenses incurred on pulling down the old plant will be treated as revenue expenditure whereas cost of erection the new one will be treated as capital expenditure .

If capital expenditure is debited to profit and loss account, the particular asset will be undervalued and a secret reserve will be created to the extent of the undervaluation of that asset. The creation of secret reserve by a public company is prohibited under the Companies Act. Moreover, the profit and loss account is unnecessarily burdened and show less profit or shown even a loss.

If revenue expenditure is debited to the capital account, profit will be inflated. Dividend will be paid out of capital which is against the provisions of the Companies Act. The auditor will be held responsible for such payment and might be asked to refund it.

Improper allocation of expenditure between capital and revenue will have far-reaching result on the accounts of a concern. The auditor should get a certificate regarding the allocation of expenditure between capital and revenue from a responsible official and mention that fact in his report, especially when the expenditure involved is very heavy. He should state in his report that he has relied upon the certificate from a responsible official about the allocation of expenditure between capital and revenue.

CONTINGENT LIABILITIES

Definition

1. Montgomery. "The term 'contingent liability' should be used in the accounting sense to designate a possible liability of presently determinable or indeterminable amount which arises from past circumstances or action which may or may not become a legal obligation in the future, and which, if paid, gives rise to a loss or an expense or an asset of doubtful value."

There may be certain liabilities which may or may not arise after the preparation of the balance sheet. Provision should be made for such unknown liabilities, called contingent liabilities. A contingent liability may be defined as one which may or may not arise at a future date. A contingent liability in a balance sheet is a possible future liability arising form one or more business acts preceding the date of the balance sheet". Examples of contingent liabilities are the result of a litigation; about the assessment of damages; a bill receivable which has been discounted may; be dishonoured on the due date and hence it may amount to a liability because the amount will have to be paid to the banker with whom the bill was discounted; calls on partly paid shares which have been purchased; liability under a contract of guarantee; liability in respect of unfinished contracts; forward contracts, etc.

2. Prof. Walter B. Meigs. "Contingent liabilities may be defined as potential obligation which may in the future develop into actual liabilities or may dissolve without necessitating any outlay." The uncertainty about legal obligation differentiates a contingent liability from an actual liability. A contingent liability may or may not involve the payment of money. If a bill receivable has been discounted with the banker, one is not sure whether the liability will arise or not. The question of liability will not arise, if the bill is honoured.

Kinds of Contingent Liabilities

1. A liability involving an ultimate loss. For example: a liability in a disputed case where damages may have to be paid; guarantee given by a company for loans or overdrafts granted to managed companies; speculative transactions on the stock exchange; forward contracts, etc.

2. A liability which will involve in the acquisition of an asset of corresponding value. Some examples are : when goods have been purchased for future delivery or under an agreement of service. No note should be made in the balance sheet in respect of this type of contingent liability but if the amount involved is considerable, a note should be inserted at the foot of the balance sheet.

The amount of the contingent liability may be definite or indefinite. The example of definite liability is that of a bill received which has been discounted and which might be dishonoured at the date of maturity. The example of the indefinite contingent liability is of a suit for damages against the company which is pending at the date of the balance sheet. Similarly a contingent liability may be certain or uncertain.

Duties of the Auditor

1. He should see that the necessary provision has been made for contingent liabilities. In order to ascertain the existence of contingent liabilities, he should examine the minutes of the meetings of the Board of Directors and other concerned correspondence.
2. He should enquire from the legal official of the client about possible losses from pending law suits.
3. He should ask the bank to supply a list of all the bills discounted and also the number of bills which have not matured as yet.
4. He should find out the amount of dividend payable to cumulative shareholders.

5. Divide the contingent liabilities into two main groups according to Part I of Schedule VI to the Companies Act, which are as follows:
   (i) The liabilities in respect of which a provision has been made in the Balance sheet, e. g. where the management thinks that the liability will definitely arise though the amount may be uncertain. These are shown under the heading "Current Liabilities and Provisions".
   (ii) The liabilities in respect of which no provision has been made in the Balance Sheet. These are shown by way of a footnote in the Balance Sheet. For example, if there are a number of suits pending against the company but according to the legal officers of the company the ultimate financial responsibility with regard to such cases is very negligible in relation to the total assets of the company, a note in the Balance Sheet will serve the purpose.
6. He should see that the above provisions of the Companies Act regarding the contingent liability have been complied with the Balance Sheet.

QUESTIONS FOR EXERCISE

1. Explain the meaning of "Deferred Revenue Expenditure". Give example of deferred revenue expenditure and describe the Auditor's duty with regard to this item of expenditure.
2. Write short notes on Vouching of outstanding Liabilities.
3. How do you define (a) Capital Expenditure, and (b) Revenue Expenditure ? As an auditor how would you deal with structural alterations?
4. You note in the course of your audit that the accountant has treated the following transactions as capital expenditure:
   (i) The construction of a new staircase by replacing the old one;
   (ii) Interest paid for delay in payment of acquiring a lease of a colliery;
   (iii) The cost of repairs to a Plant incurred during the course of its removal to a new and convenient site.
5. What are the principles of allocation expenditure between capital and revenue? Describe how you would apply such principles to each of the following items:
   (a) Additions to factory buildings.
   (b) Repairs to plant.
   (c) Heavy advertisement expenses.

(d) Renewals of licences.

6. Explains the meaning of the word "Contingent Liability". As auditor how would you consider the same for treatment in account? Name some items you will regard as "Contingent Liability" giving reasons for the same.

7. What are the auditor's duties regarding contingent liability? Illustrate your answer with two examples explaining their treatment and verification.

8. It is said that the contingent liabilities may be divided conveniently into two main classes. Give your view and if you also think so, state an example of each class. State also how each of them should be dealt with in the Balance Sheet of a company.

9. What are the contingent liabilities? Give five examples of such liabilities. What is the method by which you would satisfy yourself at the time of audit that all contingent and outstanding liabilities have been disclosed in the balance sheet.

10

Verification and Valuation of Assets and Liabilities

1. Arthur Holmes. "Verification is the proof of accuracy of extension, footings, posting, existence and ownership of assets."

2. Lancaster. "The verification of assets is a process by with the auditor substantiates the accuracy of the right hand side of the balance sheet and must be considered as having three distinct objects: (a) verification of the existence of assets, (b) the valuation of assets and (c) authority of their acquisition."

3. Spicer and Pegler. "Verification of assets implies an inquiry into the value, ownership and title, existence and possession and presence of any charge on the assets."

4. Institute of Chartered Accountants of India. "It aims at establishing, (a) existence (b) ownership (c) possession (d) freedom from encumbrances (e) proper recording (f) proper valuation."

5. Batliboi. Auditor must satisfy himself that the assets really existed at the date of the Balance Sheet and were free from any charge and that they have been properly valued. In verification of liabilities, he has to see that all liabilities have been inserted at their proper figures and that no liability has been omitted.

Activities in Verification

1. To compare the ledger accounts of assets with the Balance Sheet.
2. To verify physical existence of assets as on the date of Balance Sheet.
3. To confirm that assets were acquired for business purposes and by a duly authorised officer.
4. To confirm that the assets really owned by the business concern.

Items of Verification

Verification of Assets shows the following:

1. Existence. Assets are in existence at the date of Balance Sheet.

2. Valuation. Valuation of the assets as to the Balance Sheet is correct.

3. Ownership. Legal ownership rests with the concern.

4. Possession. Possession of the assets lies with the concern.

5. Charge. The assets are free from any charge or encumbrances.

6. Use. Assets are purchased for the business and Balance Sheet shows it.

Objects of Verification

1. Correct valuation of assets and liabilities. To ascertain whether the assets and liabilities have been shown in the Balance Sheet at their correct, value, the valuation should have been made on the principles of accounting.

2. True and fair financial position. To certify whether the Balance Sheet exhibits a true and fair financial position and for this he has to verify the assets and liabilities.

3. Existence of Assets. To ascertain the existence of the particular asset appearing in the Balance Sheet.

4. Ownership and title of the assets. To certify the ownership and title of the assets appearing in the Balance Sheet.

5. Detection of fraud and irregularities. To detect the fraud and irregularities in the books of accounts.

6. Arithmetical Accuracy. To ensure the arithmetical accuracy of the accounts books.

Verification means confirming the truth. The auditor has to see that entries coming in Balance Sheet of a concern are under proper categories of assets and liabilities. Existing assets are really present as shown in the balance sheet. Entry does not mean that the assets are possessed by the concern. Verification satisfies the auditor by real inspection or as to the existence, possession, ownership to the valuation and accuracy of the different items cited in the balance sheet.

VOUCHING V/S VERIFICATION

Vouching tells that an assets ought to exist. But its real existence is neither proved nor is it in the possession of the firm on the balance sheet date. It may be out, lost, destroyed, pledged or misappropriated. Hence verification is required to verify the existence of the assets stated in the balance sheet. Following are the main points of difference between vouching and verification:

1. Nature. While Vouching examines the entries relating to different transactions recorded in the books of accounts, Verification examines the assets and liabilities appearing in the balance sheet of the concern.

2 Basis. While Vouching is based on the documentary examination, Verification is based on physical inspection as well as documentary examination.

3. Time. While Vouching is done for the transactions of a whole year, Verification is done at the end of the year when the Balance Sheet of the concern is prepared.

4. Utility. While Vouching indicates that a particular assets must by possessed by the concern, Verification certifies the existence of assets and liabilities at balance sheet date.

5. Scope. While Vouching does not primarily concern with valuation, Verification includes valuation in its scope.

6. Personnel. While Vouching of books of accounts is done by juniors known as audit clerks, Verification is done by auditor himself. But verification should not be confused with vouching the expenditure in connection with the acquisition of an asset. Both differ in scope. Verification includes vouching. Its scope is greater than that of vouching. The Institute of Chartered Accountants of India in its *Statement of Auditing Practices* lays down that verification of assets should be aimed at establishing their (i) existence, (ii) ownership, (iii) possession, (iv) freedom from encumbrances, (v) proper recording, and (vi) proper valuation.

SCOPE OF VERIFICATION

1. Evidence with regard to the existence of the assets on the date of the Balance Sheet.
2. Evidence with regard to ownership of assets.
3. Evidence with regard to possession of the assets.
4. Evidence with regard to proper valuation of the assets in accordance with generally accepted accounting principles consistently followed.
5. Evidence with regard to proper accounting of the assets.
6. Evidence with regard to proper classification of assets in the Balance Sheet as per the provisions of the Companies Act.

VALUATION OF ASSETS

Definition

1. Joseph Lancaster. "The valuation of assets is therefore an attempt to equitable distribution of the original outlay on the period of the assets' usefulness."

2. J.R. Batliboi. "A company's balance sheet is not drawn for the purpose of showing what the capital would be worth if the assets were realised and liabilities paid off but rather to show how the capital stands invested."

Thus valuation implies, critical examination and the testing of determined values of assets by the auditor based on generally accepted accounting principles. Some of the problems of valuation are as follows:

(i) Whether the assets should be valued of replacement or realisable value.

(ii) How to value the assets during the inflationary period.

(iii) Break up value or scrap value of asset.

The prices used in valuation of assets are as follows:

(i) Cost price.

(ii) Market price.

(iii) Book value.

(iv) Replacement value.

(v) Scrap value.

(vi) Going concern value.

Objects of Valuation

1. To assess the correct financial position of the concern.
2. To assess the true position of the assets at the date of the Balance Sheet.
3. To enquire about the mode of investment of the capital of the concern.
4. To assess the goodwill of the firm.
5. To know about the difference in the value of the assets at the date of its purchases and at the date of the balance sheet and also to ascertain the reasons for the difference.
6. To satisfy the auditor about the accuracy of the Balance Sheet.

Importance of Valuation

Valuation of assets is one of the important duties of an auditor since the accuracy of assets and liabilities. It determines the correctness of Balance Sheet and profit and loss account. Though the valuation is done by responsible officers but ultimately it is the auditor who checks that valuation has been done on the basis of some scientific principles as the Balance Sheet must represent true and fair view of the financial state of the business. The auditor must not permit under valuation or over valuation of assets and liabilities. He should not allow creation of secret reserves. Final statements must be fair to all the parties interested in the affairs of the business concern.

Though not an expert valuer, the auditor must be cautious and take all relevant facts and evidences into consideration while ascertaining fair valuation of assets and liabilities.

Thus as the correctness of Balance Sheet and Profit and Loss Account depends upon the correctness of valuation of Assets and Liabilities, valuation of assets and liabilities is quite important.

Steps in Valuation

Following steps are recommended for proper valuation of Assets:

1. Collect all the relevant information for the valuation.
2. Check the valuation made by management of the business concern.
3. Confirm that valuation has been done on the basis of generally accepted conventions and principles of accounting.
4. Check that same basis of valuation has been followed from year to year.

VERIFICATION V/S VALUATION

According to Lancaster, "The verification of assets is a process by which the auditor substantiates the accuracy of the right hand side of the Balance Sheet, and must be considered having three distinct objects:

(i) The verification of the existence of the assets;

(ii) The valuation of the assets; and

(iii) The authority of their acquisition."

Thus Verification includes the following:

(i) Existence of the assets;

(ii) Valuation of the assets;

(iii) Ownership of the assets with the concern;

(iv) Possession lies with the concern;

(v) The assets are free from any charge or mortgage or lien; and

(vi) Assets are purchased for the business.

Again, according to Lancaster, "The valuation of assets is, therefore, an attempt to ensure the equitable distribution of the original outlay over the period of assets usefulness." The valuation shows the financial position of the concern.

Following are the main points of difference between verification and valuation:

1. Scope. While verification is the process by which the auditor satisfies the accuracy of the assets and liabilities appearing in the Balance Sheet by inspection of documentary evidence available, valuation is critical examination and the testing of determined values of assets by the auditor based on generally accepted conventions and accounting principles.

2. Responsibility. While verification is done by the auditor himself or by his senior assistant, valuation is made by the managers of the concern.

3. Advice. While the work of verification of assets is done by the auditor himself, in the case of valuation, the auditor may seek assistance and opinion of the technical personnel for ascertaining the value of any particular asset.

4. Basis. While verification is based on physical verification as well as documentary evidence, very few direct evidences are available for valuation. The auditor has to depend upon the estimates of managers to a large extent.

5. Guarantee. While the auditor is entirely responsible for the verification of the assets, in case of valuation, he does not give any guarantee.

6. Implication. While verification has a broader implication, valuation is just a part of verification.

PROBLEMS IN THE VALUATION OF ASSETS

The accuracy of the balance sheet and the estimated profits of a concern depend upon the correct valuation of the assets and liabilities, which are made by the proprietors or officials of the company or the firm. The auditor has to apply certain tests regarding the valuation of the assets, relying upon the certificates of competent persons such as valuers, surveyors, etc. He is not expected to possess the technical knowledge to find out the value of the assets. He should refer to the invoices to find out the price at which such assets were acquired. He cannot guarantee the correctness of the valuation of the assets.

Types of Valuation

'Replacement value' is the amount which would be required to purchase another asset of the same type to replace the existing one. 'Reliable value' is the amount which the existing asset would fetch if it is sold in the open market. 'Break-up value' or 'Scrap value' is the amount which would be realised if a particular asset is sold when it has become unserviceable. The assets are valued taking into consideration (a) their original cost, (b) the probable working life of the assets, (c) the wear and tear of the assets, (d) break-up value of the assets, and (e) the chances of the assets becoming obsolete. The auditor has to see that the basis of valuation and the calculations are correct and that all contingencies are provided for. The object of the valuation of assets is to show that the balance sheet represents a *true and fair view* of the state of affairs of the concern and that there is no manipulation of accounts to inflate to profits. For this purpose, the assets are generally classified into 'fixed assets', and 'circulating assets' or 'floating assets' or 'current assets.' Some writers divide the assets into (a) 'intangible assets' such as goodwill, copyrights, trade marks, etc., which cannot be seen or touched, (b) 'wasting assets' such as mines, quarries, etc., a part of which is extracted and sold during the period of their operation, and (c) 'fictitious assets' such as payment made in advance or heavy expenditure incurred while launching a campaign, e.g. heavy expenditure incurred to advertise an invention or new article introduced in the market and the expenditure of which is to be spread over a number of years.

Others classify the assets as fixed, current and unrealisable assets. They define unrealisable assets as "items of expenditure or a capital nature, such as discount and commission of the issue of shares and debentures, preliminary expenses and pre-acquisition losses."

Problems of Valuation of Assets During Inflationary Period

1. The value of stock may not be sufficient to meet the cost of replacing the same quantity of stock.
2. The depreciation charges based on the historical cost of the fixed assets may not provide sufficient amount required to meet the cost of replacing those assets if they are needed to be replaced later on.
3. If depreciation is provided on the historical cost of the assets and similarly if the stock-in-trade is also valued accordingly, the profits shown by the profit and loss account may not reflect an increase or decrease in terms of the purchasing power of the money.

Suggestions for Solution

1. The replacement cost method of dealing with the fixed assets should be followed, i.e., the fixed assets should be valued at replacement cost.
2. The fixed assets should be written up according to the market price of the assets prevailing on the balance sheet date.
3. The stock-in-trade should be valued at the market price and depreciation should be provided on the value of the stock so arrived at.
4. The index method of adjusting the accounts to reflect the changes in the purchasing power of money should be followed.

Verification and Valuation of Different Assets

Assets can be classified into the following groups: (i) fixed assets, (ii) intangible assets, (iii) floating assets, and (iv) fictitious assets.

1. Fixed Assets. Fixed assets are those purchases for permanent use in the business to earn more income. The whole business is carried on with the help of these assets. Their sale means the closure of the business. As these assets are acquired neither for resale nor for earning a profit on their sale, they are usually valued at the going concern value, i.e., cost price less depreciation. While valuing these assets, market value is not taken into account.

In case of valuation of fixed assets, the auditor is more concerned with the adequacy of provision of depreciation. He should see that fixed assets are not over-valued or undervalued. Under the Manufacturing and other Companies (Audit Report) Order, 1975 issued under Sec. 227(4A), an auditor is required to make a specific statement on whether the company is maintaining proper records to show particulars including quantitative details and situation of fixed assets; whether the fixed assets have been physically verified by the management and whether serious discrepancies noticed in the course of physical verification, have been properly dealt with in the books of account. The auditor is required to certify whether an adequate system of internal control exists or not commensurate with the size of the company and the nature of the business, for the purchase of these assets.

PROCEDURE OF VERIFICATION

(A) *Fixed Assets*. An auditor must satisfy himself with regard to the following points while verifying fixed assets:

1. The record of the fixed assets has been maintained in a proper manner and the complete inventory of all the fixed assets is available.
2. The fixed assets bear proper marks of identification.
3. The management planned detailed procedure regarding frequency and coverage for the physical verification of fixed assets by competent persons, preferably having some technical background.
4. All fixed assets are verified periodically and regularly and the physical existence is reconciled with records. In case of discrepancies, if any, what actions have been taken ?
5. There is a written procedure for the verification of fixed assets.
6. Verification is usually carried out by those who are familiar with the assets.
7. That the procedure for the verification of fixed assets is checked in the possession of third parties.
8. That the reports of internal verification of fixed assets indicate any damaged or obsolete assets.
9. That the fixed assets are properly insured. If there been any claim during the year how has it been dealt with in the accounts ?
10. That the fixed assets have been properly valued after depreciation and disclosed in the Balance Sheet according to the requirement of Schedule VI to the Companies Act.
11. That a proper system of authorisation and approval regarding the acquisition and disposal or replacement of fixed assets is followed in the organisation.
12. That the documentary evidence has been checked to ensure actual receipts of the purchased assets and the supplier's invoices have been traced into fixed assets records.

Classification of Fixed Assets

1. Assets which are not subject to depreciation or depletion, e.g. land.
2. Assets which are subject to depreciation, e.g. building, plant, tools, equipments, etc.
3. Assets which are subject to depletion, e.g. mineral, oilwells etc.

Principles and Practices of Recording Fixed Assets

1. Depreciable fixed assets are carried in the records at original net acquisition costs, less separate and proper accumulations for depreciation,
2. Fixed assets subject to depletion are carried in the records at original net cost less accumulated depletion, and
3. Non-depreciable fixed assets are carried in the records at original net cost (or other basic acquisition figure).

According to Spicer and Pegler, in recent years the following changes have resulted in purchasing power of money.

(a) Fixed assets appear in Balance Sheet at values far below their current replacement values, and

(b) Where depreciation has been provided on such book values, profits are distorted because turnover is in terms of depreciated rupees.

(c) Inadequate amounts are accumulated out of profits for replacement.

Due to these reasons, it is said that fixed assets should be written up to their current replacement values, capital reserve being credited with the surplus. Depreciation should be provided on such amended values. The Institute of Chartered Accountants in England and Wales recommends, "Any amount set aside to finance replacements (whether of fixed or current assets) at enhanced costs should not be treated as a provision which must be made before profit for the year can be ascertained, but as a transfer to reserve. If such a transfer to reserve is shown in the Profit and Loss Account as a deduction in arriving at the balance for the year, that balance should be described appropriately." The provision for depreciation should continue to be made on the basis of historical cost. But an additional amount should be set aside to provide further funds which will eventually be required for replacement, where it is anticipated that the cost of replacing a fixed asset will be greatly in excess of its original cost.

Owing to the continued occurrence of inflation and its consequences certain companies have now adopted the practice of revaluing their assets periodically, usually by reference to published indices and recalculating the accumulated depreciation thereon to counteract the illusory effect on account of loss of purchasing power. A substantial understatement of the real capital resources employed will result if this is not done. The longer the physical life of a company's assets, the greater is the understatement. This understatement can result in the erroneous conclusion that the company's assets are more profitable than they really are. It is primarily for this reason that there has been widespread adoption amongst large companies of what is now known as "purchasing power accounting," as opposed to conventional historical cost accounting.

(B) **Intangible Assets.** Assets having no concrete form and not capable of being perceived especially by the sense of touch, are known as intangible assets. Goodwill, patents, copyrights trade marks, etc. are examples of intangible assets. Their valuation is done more or less in the same manner as that of fixed assets.

(C) **Floating/Current/Liquid Assets.** This group of assets refers to cash and bank balance, including, such other assets or reserves as are expected to be realised in cash, sold, or consumed within a period of not more than twelve months in the ordinary course of business stock-in-trade, amounts due from sundry debtors for sale of goods and for services rendered, advance tax payments and bill receivable. But sums credited to a provident fund, pension fund, gratuity fund or any other fund for the welfare of employees receivables arising from unusual transactions such as the sale of capital assets, or loans or advances to affiliate officers, or employees, which also are not expected to be collected within twelve months are not floating assets. Book debts and bills receivable are generally valued at book value. In the case of the book debts a provision may be made for bad and doubtful debts. Raw materials and semi-produced goods are valued at cost. In case of closing stock, valuation at the Balance Sheet date is done at "lower of cost or market price": (i) it prevents the taking into account of anticipated profits and likely distribution of dividends therefrom, the same being detrimental to business, if profits do not materialise as anticipated, (ii) it recognises the probable loss of carrying value whether from change of style, shifting of market, deterioration or spoilage or for any number of reasons which may have no direct relation to market price.

(D) **Fictitious Assets.** Like an intangible asset, an asset which does not have a concrete form but which, unlike it, is not realisable in cash, is a fictitious asset. A fictitious asset represents capitalisation of expenditure which is essentially of a capital nature and the benefit thereof is expected to be available in future years. Examples of fictitious assets are preliminary expenses, special advertising expenses, expenses on issue of debentures and discount thereon and development expenses.

AUDITOR'S DUTY IN VALUATION OF ASSETS

According to Lancaster, "The auditor is not a valuer and cannot be expected to act as such. All that he can do is to verify the original cost price and to ascertain as far as possible that the current values are fair and reasonable and are in accordance with accepted commercial principles.

The auditor must determine that fixed assets have been properly valued. He should verify (1) original cost, (2) repair and maintenance costs, (3) additions and improvement costs, and (4) retirement or replacement cost of any part of the asset

1. Original Cost. While verifying the original cost of an asset the auditor should check that : (i) the company's object clause in the Memorandum of Association authorise the purchase of the asset, and (ii) the expenses have been incurred with the specific authority of the Board of Directors.

Cost of the assets can be vouched:

(i) by looking at the supplier's invoices;

(ii) where construction has been done by contractors or engineers, by verifying the receipts for part-payment and balance payable;

(iii) by referring to architect's or engineer's certificate where the company has constructed it itself. The auditor can also verify the wages and salaries paid to the workers;

(iv) when the asset is purchased under hire-purchase system, the hire-purchase agreement can be referred to ascertain cash price of the asset; and

(v) by vouching and examining the vouchers relating to the expenses, which have been capitalised.

2. Repair and Maintenance Cost. Every asset is subject to repair which is done to maintain the earning capacity of the business. While the former is termed as revenue expenditure the latter is known as capital expenditure. The auditor should see that the distinction is followed. The capital expenditure after capitalisation is subject to depreciation.

3. Additions and Improvement Cost. In broader terms the word additions involves the acquisition of new assets, improvement of existing assets and overhauling or replacement of parts of existing assets—resulting in an increase in the expected useful life of an asset. Such expenditure is capitalised and is subject to depreciation. The auditor should analyse all related expenses which should have been capitalised and depreciation charged on them while verifying the additions.

4. Depreciation. Allocation of the asset cost is the last phase of asset valuation. Among the many methods of depreciation, the type of method of depreciation to be used depends upon the type of the asset and the method allowed under the Income-tax Act. The auditor should see that depreciation on the various assets has been properly provided for.

VERIFICATION OF FIXED ASSETS

A. Verification of Plant and Machinery

1. Schedule. The auditor should start the process of verification by obtaining a schedule of plant and machinery certified by some responsible officer of the business. This schedule will help him in verifying plant and machinery.

2. Internal control system. The auditor should ascertain the efficiency of the system of internal control particularly with regard to the authority of purchase and sale, custody and recording of various items. If the auditor finds that register of plant and machinery is maintained disclosing original costs, additions and disposals and the final balance of asset, he should examine receipts and invoices for the additions and disposals of machine during the year. These include suppliers invoices, hire purchase agreements and payments receipts. He should test-check a few items from the certified inventory of plant and machinery with the entries in the plant register. Company management is bound to physically verify plant and machinery. Hence, the auditor should call for the related working papers for his examination.

3. Valuation

(i) *Depreciation.* The auditor should value plant and machinery on the basis of cost less depreciation. He should discuss the whole question of depreciation with the management. He should ascertain the basis of their estimates and provisions, and whether they have acted upon proper advice. Generally, the provisions for depreciation are fixed haphazardly, and without having regard to any of the considerations and principles governing the question. If the auditor is not satisfied that the depreciation is sufficient he should point this out clearly in his report.

(ii) *Expenditure.* The auditor should verify new purchases with the help of invoices, cash-receipts, agreements with the vendors, etc. Expenditure on a machine built in the client's own factory should be properly allocated between capital and revenue. The auditor should ascertain that expenditure on repair and renewals has not been wrongly adjusted as capital expenditure.

He should not agree to the writing up of the cost of such work to a higher figure outside the estimate or for capitalising any part of the overhead charges of the business where these have not been incurred by the business on account of installation work.

(iii) *Cost*

(a) The auditor should check the acquisition cost of the plant and machinery by referring to the invoice and receipts of the vendor.

(b) He should check the cost of additions and improvements to the asset and see that they have been properly added to the value of the asset and charged to depreciation.

(c) He should check the expenses incurred on repairs and renewals and see that they are not improperly capitalised.

(iv) *Machinery*

(a) The auditor should check the machines sold during the year and ascertain that the profit or loss thereon has been correctly recorded.

(b) He should check the certificate obtained from the foreign engineer or agent regarding the plant and machinery in use abroad.

(c) He should see that the plant and machinery has been properly stated in the Balance Sheet as per Companies Act, 1956.

(d) In the case of equipment purchased under a hire-purchase agreement or an agreement to pay by instalments, the auditor should see that the depreciation has been calculated on the cost price and not on the amount of instalments paid to date.

Due to the following reasons the realisable or replacement values of similar machinery are commonly disregarded:

(i) The plant of a manufacturing company is employed solely for the purpose of manufacturing for the whole of such asset's working life and this period is unaffected by fluctuations in the realisable and replacement values.

(ii) As a rule, portion of the plant and machinery has very little realisable value, for example, shafts, if pulled out, realise a very small proportion of the original cost.

(iii) Machinery specially manufactured for patent process might be of no value to any other concern.

The auditor should call for certified valuations if plant and machinery is revalued for Balance Sheet purposes.

Depreciation is normally provided on the basis of cost minus scrap or residual value divided by the estimated working life of an asset. This is not an easy job. It requires technical knowledge to fix this period. Therefore, in this respect the auditor has to largely depend upon engineers.

Verification of Imported Machinery

The auditor should verify the following in cost of imported machinery:

(i) *Agreement.* The agreement with the foreign supplier includes the terms and conditions on which the machinery has been supplied, the terms and conditions of payments, the number of instalments and the amount of each instalment.

(ii) *Import licence.* The import licence covers the plant imported.

(iii) *Invoice.* Copy of the invoice, documents relating to payment of customs duty.

(iv) *Instalments.* This includes installation charges and their recording in accounts.

(v) *Instalments.* Payment of instalments to the foreign supplier according to the agreement against the supply of machinery and the permission of the Reserve Bank of India authorising the remittance.

6. Cost. The total amount treated as cost of the machinery should comprise the amount payable to the supplier in terms of Indian Rupees, the import duty, transport and insurance, transit charges and amount spent on installation.

7. Entry in the Fixed Assets Register.

B. Verification of Investments

The auditor should do the following for verification of investments:

1. Checking of Schedule. The auditor should check the schedule of investments if there are a large number of investments as in the case of banks and insurance companies. The schedule should disclose full particulars of the investments, e.g. name of the investment, the cost price, the market price, book value, date on which the investment was acquired, rate of interest payable and the dates of the payment of interest, tax deducted and so on and compare these with the records in books of his client.

2. Checking of Transfer Deed. The transfer deed is a good evidence in the case of purchase of stocks and share for which no certificate has been issued till the date of verification. The receipt for the application money or the allotment letter should be examined when new shares have been applied for.

3. Comparison of investments with schedule. The auditor should compare all the investments with the schedule. If the number of the investments is large and they cannot be inspected at one sitting the investments which have been checked must be locked and sealed in a box so that they may not be produced again at the time of the next inspection. The auditor should retain the key and the seal.

4. Examination of trust deed. If investments are held by any trustee on behalf of the company, the trust deed should be examined. If trust deed is not available the auditor should get a certificate from the trustee that the latter holds those securities in trust and that they are free from any charge, and are in favour of the nominee or any other person. Further, the auditor should advise his client that a trust deed should be obtained as soon as possible.

5. Checking of securities with Bank. If the securities have been entrusted to a bank the auditor should get a certificate from the bank about the number of securities held by it for safe custody and to check that they are free from any charge of the securities.

The auditor must examine the date of *certificate* and find out, whether it is usual to deposit such securities with such companies for safe custody.

6. Checking of custody of secretary. Sometimes some securities are kept in the custody of the secretary of the company. The auditor should ensure that they are held by him jointly with some other officer of the company. These securities should be registered in the name of the company as is required by Sec. 49 of the Companies Act. These securities should be compared with schedule showing the particulars of securities, their numbers, cost price, etc. at the end of the year.

7. Vouching sales. If some of the investments have been sold since the date of the Balance Sheet but prior to the date of audit, the auditor should vouch the proceeds either in the Cash Book or the Bank Pass Book.

8. Auditing of Investment. While auditing the investments of a banking company, the auditor should inspect investment of the bank and the securities lodged with the bank against loans and advances. If the bank has lodged its investments with some other party, receipt given by such a party for investment lodged should be examined paying special attention to the following:

(i) That the certificate or the receipt states that the securities lodged are free from any kind of charge.

(ii) That the provisions of the Banking Companies (Regulation) Act, 1949, are complied with.

(iii) That the details of the investments are comparable with the Investment Register maintained by the bank.

(iv) That if the investments are held by the nominee of the bank, the former has clearly stated that he holds these investments on behalf of the bank.

(v) The investment are properly valued and shown in the Balance Sheet according to the Banking Companies (Regulation) Act, 1949.

9. Classification of Investment. Along with nature of the investment and mode of valuation of investments the different classes of investments must be shown under separate headings as follows:

(i) Investments in government or trust securities.

(ii) Investments in shares, debentures or bonds showing separately shares fully paid up and partly paid up, and also distinguishing the different classes of shares and showing also details of investments in shares, debentures or bonds of subsidiary companies.

(iii) Immovable properties.

10. Mention of quoted and unquoted investments. The auditor should mention the aggregate amount of company's quoted investment and also the market value thereof along with the aggregate amount of company's unquoted investments. A list of investments separately classifying Trade Investments and other Investments should be attached to the Balance Sheet stating the names of bodies corporate (with the names of their managing agent or secretaries and treasurers, if any) in whose names shares, debentures, bonds or investments have been made and also stating the amounts in respect of each item. It shall not be necessary to give such particulars (a) in respect of investments made by Managing Agency companies in managed companies' shares, debentures or bonds, or (b) in respect of investments made by investment companies. However, particulars in respect of investments in shares of private companies shall be given. The amount in respect of the holdings by investment companies in unquoted shares of private limited companies shall be separately stated, specifying the name of each company and the amount invested therein.

While "quoted investment" means an investment in respect of which there has been guarantee, a quotation or permission to deal on a recognised stock exchange and the expression "unquoted investment" is construed accordingly.

11. Mention of Interest accrued on Investments. Any interest on investments calculated from the date up to which it was last received to the date of the balance sheet will be mentioned under this head.

12. Mention of Investments in Shares or Debentures of a Subsidiary. These should be verified with the help of documentary evidence, e.g., share certificates or debentures deeds or lodgement certificates. If the securities have been pledged with anybody, like bankers etc. the reasons for such lodgement and competence of the party keeping the securities in its safe custody should be inquired. Their existence should be verified from the receipt of dividend or interest thereon. The investment should be valued at cost. The auditor should see that unless there is a substantial fall in the value of shares, the method of valuation is consistently followed from year to year. Securities must also stand in the name of the client.

13. Interest paid out of capital during construction. Under Sec. 208 of the Companies Act the interest paid on the share capital of company during the construction of its works, can be capitalised to plant or construction of works provided that such company is authorized to do so by its Articles or by special resolution. It should he checked that previous sanction of the central government has been obtained, and the rate of interest does not exceed four per cent, and that such payment is not made beyond the period as is determined by the central government. The item of interest, if any, paid out of capital during construction should be separately shown on the assets side of the Balance Sheet which must also indicate the share capital and the rate at which such interest has been paid during each period. Where such interest is paid, all the requirements of the Act, in this connection, should be duly complied with.

C. Verification of Property

(i) *Verification of Landed Property.* The verification procedure for landed property is as follows:

1. The auditor should see that land is shown in the Balance Sheet at original cost basis. Its method of valuation is the same whether it is freehold land or leasehold land.
2. The auditor should check the cost with reference to the original purchase contract. He should see the minutes of the Board of Directors authorising the purchase.
3. The auditor should verify that land is not subject to any charge or mortgage, etc.
4. As the auditor is not competent to check the title deeds, the purchaser's note etc. therefore, he should get a certificate about their validity from the solicitor.
5. Cost of land will increase due to broker's commission, title examination fees, improvement expenses, etc.
6. If the land has been given on rent the auditor should examine the agreement and other relevant data. The ground rent receivable should properly accounted for.

(ii) *Land and Buildings.* The auditor should do the following while verifying land and building:

1. Obtain sufficient evidence with regard to the ownership of the land and buildings; and
2. Determine the valuation in conformity with the method of acquisition.

For verification of land and buildings, the properties can be classified into freehold property and leasehold property.

(a) ***Freehold Property.*** The following is the procedure for verification of freehold property:

1. Examination of title deeds. The auditor should ascertain that the property is recorded in the name of the client. He should examine the deeds for verification of ownership. As he is not competent to examine the title deeds, he should depend upon the client to get a certificate regarding their validity from the solicitor. A certificate from the architect, surveyor, or an engineer may also serve the purpose for the valuation of the property.

2. Determination of valuation. The auditor should state Building in the Balance Sheet at cost less depreciation. He should examine in detail the method and rate of depreciation. He should verify calculation and see that the method of depreciation is followed consistently.

3. Vouching of expenses and credits. The auditor should check the various expenses which have been capitalised and credit to the property by reference to original documents such as contracts, invoice, and authorisations of shareholders, Boards of Directors or any other appropriate body. He should check that they are included in the value of the property for the purpose of computing depreciation.

4. Verification of rental income. If certain part of the freehold property is leased, the client is entitled to receive rent. The auditor should examine the agreement and other relevant data and see that the rent receivable has been properly accounted for.

(b) *Leasehold Property.* The auditor should adopt the following procedures while verifying leasehold property:

1. The auditor should verify leasehold property by an inspection of the lessee, and the terms of lease. If the client is not the original lessee, the assignment thereof should be inspected: He should ensure that all conditions have been duly complied with, the non-fulfilment of which might involve forfeiture of the lease such as prompt payment of ground rent, maintenance of fire insurance, etc.
2. If property has been mortgaged, the title deeds should be in the possession of the mortgage, from whom a certificate to that effect should be obtained.
3. If the leasehold property has been sublet, the counterpart of the tenant's agreement should be examined.
4. The auditor should physically inspect the properties if possible.
5. The auditor should also check that proper provision has been made for depreciation of leases and for any possible claims for dilapidations arising thereunder.
6. The auditor should see that lease rent has been charged to the revenue account. The amount of premium or rent payable and its terms must be ascertained.
7. The auditor should verify that the lease has been duly registered, particularly if it extends for more than a year.
8. The auditor should see that the lease money and legal expenses incurred in the acquisition of the leasehold property have been capitalised and written off over a number of years.

(iii) *Motor Lorries and Vans.* The verification procedure regarding motor lorries and vans is the same as that of plant and machinery. It is as follows:

1. Vehicles Register. A register, like the Plant Register, be maintained where the number of vehicles owned is large. It may be called the Vehicles Register. The auditor should obtain a schedule of all motor vehicles by the company together with the registration books and insurance policies. The balance brought down in the Motor Vehicle Account should be clearly shown by indicating the registration marks and cost of each vehicle comprising it.

2. Log Books. The Auditor should also go through the log book to carry out physical inspection of the vehicles. He should examine the Registration Book for each vehicle. Road tax and insurance premium receipts should be examined while comparing it with the ledger account of the Vehicle Register.

3. Unregistered Vehicles. On examination, if it is found that some vehicles are not registered in the client's name, the auditor must ascertain the reasons for this and obtain a written confirmation from the person named in the registration book that the vehicle is the property of the client and that no charge is claimed thereupon.

4. Wear and Tear. Where the original cost of these assets is appreciably high there will be heavy wear and tear. The auditor should ensure that the rate of annual depreciation applied is adequate. He should carefully scrutinise all additions during the year to ascertain that only actual additions by way of new acquisitions are capitalised, and that repairs and replacements have been charged off to revenue.

(iv) ***Furniture and Fittings.*** Following is the audit procedure for furniture and fittings:

1. Verification of purchases. The auditor should verify all original purchases from the invoices received from the dealers.

2. Depreciation. This asset should be depreciated in the same manner as plant and machinery. A higher percentage of depreciation should always be provided for fixtures and fittings of the nature of shelves, partitions, electric fans, fittings, etc. which have very little break-up value.

3. Fresh asset. If any fresh furniture is added during the period under audit, the auditor must scrutinise the item to see that it represents some fresh wrongly capitalised.

4. Balance sheet. All additions or deductions during year should be shown in the Balance Sheet as per the Companies Act.

D. Assets Acquired on Hire Purchase or Instalment

(i) The auditor should see that the asset account is not charged with anything beyond its each cash purchase price.

(ii) He should ensure that the interest attributable to each year is duly brought into that year's account.

(iii) Depreciation should be calculated on the full cash price of the asset in question from the first year of equation.

(iv) The hire purchase or instalment deeds agreement should be inspected in order to ascertain the terms and conditions of purchase. In case of hire purchase agreement, only the instalments paid from year to year need be brought into account. If the full cash price is brought into record from the first year, and shown as an asset, then the unpaid instalments should be shown as a liability or deducted from the asset. All instalments, to date of Balance Sheet, should be paid.

VERIFICATION OF INTANGIBLE ASSETS

Intangible assets are those which have no physical or intangible form. These include goodwill, patents, copyrights and trade-marks. These are verified as follows:

1. Goodwill. Goodwill is an intangible asset. Its value depends upon the earning capacity of the business and does not decrease or diminish with use. It is not valued on the Balance Sheet date. Like other assets it is normally shown as an asset in the Balance Sheet on the following conditions:

(i) The amount paid for the purchase of a business is in excess of its net assets.

(ii) The company has made revaluation of its assets and raised a goodwill account in its books.

(iii) Goodwill once written off is later brought back in the books to write off the debit balance of the Profit and Loss Account or capital losses that the company might have suffered.

(iv) Heavy expenditure is incurred in introducing a new product in the market or in rendering service to the customers.

(v) The company has established a special reputation in the market due to its increasing sales and profits.

Verification procedure

1. The auditor should verify it by referring to the contract with the vendors to find its value.
2. The vendor's agreement and the resolution of the Board of Directors would provide the auditor with sufficient evidence. If goodwill has been purchased as an asset, the auditor should see that the sum paid for goodwill does not exceed the difference between that total purchase consideration and the value of the net tangible assets acquired. He should not comment upon the price paid for goodwill even though he considers it to be excessive. He cannot insist on writing off this asset or bringing down its value. However, should financial policy would require the amount of goodwill to be gradually written off over a reasonable period of time.
3. The auditor should see that deferred goodwill must be clearly shown in the Balance Sheet to differentiate it from the 'purchased goodwill'

and written off within a reasonable time.

4. The auditor should see that the goodwill is shown separately in the Balance Sheet stating its valuation method clearly and valuing at cost. The writing, down of this asset may be treated as creating a secret reserve. If this asset has been raised apart from the actual purchase, the auditor should see that if reasonable ground for the creation of fictitious asset existed. He should examine the resolution regarding such raising of an intangible asset or writing it back in the books.

5. If goodwill has become fictitious due to contained heavy losses or sale of major part of the undertaking, the auditor should advise his client to write off the amount of goodwill so that the financial accounts disclose true and fair position of the business. According to the judgement in the *Wilmer* v. *McNamara* case goodwill need not be written off but from the sound financial point of view, it must be written off within a reasonable period out of the current profits or reserves, etc. It should never be shown never be shown at appreciated value in the books of a company.

2. Patents. Following is the audit procedure regarding patents:

(i) ***List.*** The auditor should insist on procuring his client a list giving the description of each patent, their registered number, date, and number of year to run.

(ii) ***Certificate.*** The auditor should check the certificate of grant of patent or the assignment of the interest in it and should also verify the cost and any subsequent expenditure of further protection of it.

(iii) ***Renewal fees.*** The auditor should see that renewal fees has been charged to revenue.

(iv) ***The cost of patent.*** The auditor should see that the cost of patent is written off in the course of its life.

(v) ***Valueless patent.*** If a patent becomes valueless due to obsolescence or failure to create a demand of the patented article, the auditor should see that its value is written off even before expiry of the period covered by the patent.

3. Copyrights. The verification procedure of copyrights in a Balance Sheet will be on lines similar to those in the case of patents. The best method is to revalue copyright at the end of each financial year. Where the copyright in respect thereof loses its value any publication ceases to command sales therefore, the cost of publication of such work should be written off as a loss.

4. Trade-marks

(i) The auditor should verify the Trade-marks by examining the assignment deed duly endorsed by the office of the Registrar of trade-marks.

(ii) He should see that the trade-marks are registered in the name of the client.

(iii) He should vouch the payment in case the trade-marks have been treated as a capital expenditure, while the renewal charges have been treated as revenue expenditure. All research expenses in this connection should also be capitalised.

(iv) The effect of obsolescence on the trade-mark should also be noted.

(v) Trade-marks should be disclosed in the Balance Sheet at the original cost less depreciation.

VERIFICATION OF FLOATING ASSETS

Meaning

Floating assets are those in which the firm deals in normal operation of the business and which are subject to constant changes and rotation. They are convertible into cash within a relatively short period of time. They include the circulating of liquid assets or current assets, such as stock in trade, cash, bills receivable, debtors, short-term securities and pre-payments etc. While valuing such assets, the convention of conservation is taken into account. They should be valued at cost or market price, whichever is lower. Valuing them at more than cost price will mean recording unrealised profits as they have not been sold and the profit may not be realised when assets are sold. Any expected loss should be taken into consideration at the time of the valuation of current assets. Floating assets are valued at the Balance Sheet date.

Verification of Floating Assets

1. ***Cash in Hand***

(i) The auditor should verify that the balance shown by the Cash Book does exist. Where cash in hand amounts to a fairly large sum, the auditor should verify it by actual counting on the last day of the period under audit.

(ii) Where several cashiers are employed, it is necessary that the cash of each one should be counted simultaneously.

(iii) The auditor should satisfy himself that cheques or IOUs are genuine by making inquiries from some person in authority.

(iv) If all cash balance of the closing date deposited in the bank, the auditor would be saved of the trouble of counting cash not in a position to attend to the actual counting of cash on the closing date, the auditor should count it later at the earliest and check up all the transactions from the closing date to the date on which cash is actually counted.

2. *Cash at Bank*

(i) If the balance of the bank column of the client's Cash Book is not in agreement with the balance shown in the Bank Pass Book, the auditor should reconcile the balance shown by the Pass Book with the bank account or the bank column of the Cash Book and obtain a certificate from the bankers.

(ii) If the audit, takes place after a long time from the date of the Balance Sheet, it is advisable to reconcile both right up to such date.

(iii) The auditor would vouch remittances from branch to the head office bank account from the branch returns. He should see that the cash collections have been regularly banked on the day following the receipts and that the last day's takings were duly banked on the first day of the next period.

(iv) He should verify the cash balances on the last day of the accounting period from the certificate of the branch manager.

(v) Teeming and Lading. While verifying cash balance the auditor should check that the employer has not committed the frauds of teeming, lading and kitting types. In such practising the dishonest employee makes entries in such a way that the cash book balances agree with the cash ledger balances. The auditor must match bank deposit certificates or memos or tickets with entries in the receipt side of the Cash Book in detail. Failure to record a bank deposit in the Cash Book is an indication of the lading process. Later on, there will be an entry in the Cash Book and no matching amount on a deposit ticket.

(iv) Kitting. The auditor must ensure that void or paid or dishonoured cheques are not made available to the cashier who had the opportunity to overstate. A bank transfer of funds through cheques should be fully investigated. The duplicate tickets obtained directly from the bank should be compared with the entries in the Cash Book or a surprise count and reconciliation of cash at a date later than the end of the period, will reveal such practice. Sometime the unscrupulous cashier withdraws for his use the balance of cash in hand and at bank and deposits in a day or two before the counting of cash by the auditor. To detect such a fraud, the auditor should have surprise counting. If this is not possible, he should supplement his last day's counting with one conducted a week or month later.

3. *Cash in Transit*

Following are duties of an auditor with regard to cash in transit :

(i) ***Evidence.*** Documentary evidence in the form of correspondence or advices etc. should be checked to ascertain that cash was actually remitted before the date of the closing of the accounts. Cash in transit must have been received when the year is over.

(ii) ***Receipts.*** The auditor should check up the receipts and also confirm that on the closing date of the year it was in transit.

(ii) ***Remittances Authorised.*** An auditor should see that remittances are made under proper authority and in the ordinary course of the business. To locatc discrepancies one should compare the date and amount of remittance mentioned in the statement of account with the date and amount of the remittance in transit.

STOCK-IN-TRADE

Meaning

Stock-in-trade comparises a variety of items including (i) stores and spare parts, (ii) loose tools, (iii) raw materials, (iv) work-in-progress, (v) finished goods, and (vi) scrap or by-products. Disclosure of these items in the financial statements often poses complex problems of an accounting nature to a management.

As the correctness of the profit of a business depends to a great extent on the accuracy of the valuation placed on the closing stock, the verification of this asset forms one of the most important part of an auditor's duty. It should be consistently applied from year to year to maintain uniformity in net incomes of various years. The auditor should give a note if the method of valuation is changed.

Difficulties in verification

Due to the following reasons, verification of the stock-in-trade is more difficult than that of any other asset:

1. It constitutes the largest current asset of a business.
2. There are many methods of pricing the stock-in-trade.
3. The determination of its value directly influences the sales and income of the year.
4. It is exposed to greater risks of defalcation and manipulation.
5. If stock-in-trade is overvalued it may lead to payment of dividends of other expenses based on inflated profits. If it is undervalued secret reserves will be crcatcd and it may also lead to a fall in the share-values due to disclosure of low profits. In this case, the auditor may not be able to avoid liability to the client or to interested third parties who act on the basis of audited accounts.

Audit Objectives

1. Ensuring that the stock is represented by physical goods and a reasonable care has been taken while determining their physical quantities and conditions.

2. Ensuring that the client owns the goods and any encumbrance etc. has been properly reported in the financial statements.
3. Ensuring that all the items of stock-in-trade have been valued according to the generally accepted accounting principles. The generally accepted principle of valuation of stock is cost or market price whichever is less. This principle ensures to take into account all possible losses but not the unrealised profits.

Verification

The auditor has the following duties in this connection:

1. Ascertaining the method of stock-taking and the basis of valuation.
2. Ensuring that the stock-sheets have been subjected to a good internal check, e.g., they are certified as to have taken prices, extensions and additions while determining the stock and also generally approved as correct by the managing director.
3. Checking calculations and additions.
4. Checking a few of the important items with actual invoices as to prices.
5. Examining some of the quantities in stock-sheets with those as shown by the stock books, if such books are kept.
6. Ascertaining that the stock is valued on the same basis as in the previous year.
7. Ascertaining that obsolete and unsalable stock is shown at fair market prices.
8. Comparing the percentage of grow profit on turnover with that of the previous period and enquire into the cause of any notable fluctuation.
9. Ensuring that the goods entered as sold and not delivered are not included.
10. Ensuring that the goods bought and not entered in the Invoice Book are not included.
11. (a) Ascertaining that the value of unfinished goods is taken at actual cost and the basis of valuation is the cost of the materials consumed and the wages spent thereon upto the date of the Balance Sheet. Sometimes a percentage is added in the above to cover the factory cost, such as foreman's wages, fuel, power, lighting, heating, deprecation of plant, etc.

    (b) Seeing that the financial statements show the authorities who have certified the stock if a reasonable percentage in respect of office cost has also to be added to the works cost. As per the Companies Act the Balance Sheet must show the mode of valuation of stock. For example, in case of the wine and timber trades where the stocks appreciate in value from year to year due to their maturing in quality, the auditor should see that a reasonable percentage to the original cost at periodic intervals has been added to cover the burden in respect of interest on the portion of capital thus locked up. Such value should not exceed the then market value of similar class of goods.

Heads of departments or managers of branches, should be held responsible for their individual stock-taking. They should be asked to sign their stock sheets, certifying the same as correct. If the auditor has reasons to believe that the stock is not correct, he should qualify his report to the shareholders accordingly.

Physical inventory

(i) ***Need.*** Necessitated by the fact that its valuation will affect the financial position and operating results, stock-taking will also reveal how efficient the various departments are in using the inventories and in accounting for them. Effective planning and proper system of internal control for the stock-in-trade are essential for the accuracy of stock-taking.

(ii) ***Time.*** Physical counting of the stock-in-trade is usually carried out on the last day of the financial year. The work of stock-taking should be planned and supervised by a person acquainted with the different phases of the business operations. Usually a responsible officer of the company should lay down a standard procedure and issue written instructions to be followed by the clerks, entrusted with the work of stock-taking.

(iii) ***Personnel.*** Precautions against errors and frauds in stock-taking is normally done by members of the staff of the client. Stock-taking personnel are divided into two categories: **(i) counters** who physically count, weigh or measure the goods, and **(ii) checkers,** who record the results of the physical count on specially designed sheets called stock sheets. The stock sheets are then priced, extended and added by the administrative staff and each sheet signed by a responsible official, to ensure the stock-taking free from errors or frauds. The auditor should take the following precautions :

1. The purchases which have been despatched by the vendors prior to the stock-taking date and included in the stock records though not actually received, should be included in the stock sheets. Again, goods actually received though not entered in the stock records due to not-receipt of supporting invoices should be excluded from stock-in-trade.
2. Goods held by own branches, agents or sent to customers on "sale or return" basis, are included in the stock sheets.

3. Goods sold and entered in the stock records as such, though not despatched to the buyers, are excluded from the stock sheets.
4. The goods held on behalf of others as an agent are not included in the stock sheet.
5. The store keeper has no role in the stock-taking in his own area. The auditor should ensure that the stock-taking staff is wholly independent and that there is no basic conflict of purpose in their assignment.

Auditor's duties

According to the Recommendations of the Institute of Chartered Accountants of India as contained in the Statement on Auditing Practices, the auditor should act on the following lines to carry out a test verification of the stock inventories :

1. Before commencement of the actual verification, the auditor should suggest to the management that instructions be issued to the staff entrusted with the work of verification. He should examine these instructions, as also programme of verification to satisfy himself that the work is properly organised to adequately cover the different types and location of the stocks.
2. The auditor should review the original physical verification sheets and trace selected items, including the more valuable items into the final inventories.
3. By special arrangement with the client, the auditor should be present for at least part of the time, when the physical verification is done and also to carry out a test check of the work performed. He may be present in rotation, say once in every few years, in respect on major items of stocks held at locations not normally visited by the auditor.
4. When the management carries out the annual verification of stocks, not at the end of the year but at some earlier date, the auditor should inspect the verification sheets and satisfy himself that the stock records are duly adjusted to take into account the shortages and excesses notified on verification. The auditor should ensure that proper and reliable stock records have been kept.
5. The auditor should do the following where inventories have been verified by means of a system of continuous stock-taking.

   (i) He should suggest to the management that the persons entrusted with the verification (a) should be reasonably competent for the purposes, (b) do not have other duties which would not leave them sufficient time for carrying out the verification, and (iii) do not have custody of the stocks and or are not responsible for maintenance of stock records;

(ii) He may review the records of the stocks showing all the items verified (and not merely the discrepancies) and enquire whether the physical verification carried out during the year has covered a substantial par of the inventories;

(iii) He should test check the list of discrepancies to ensure that the same have been adjusted in the stock records;

(iv) He should whenever possible carry out a test check during the year of the physical existence of the stocks in order to satisfy himself the stock records do in fact correctly reflect the stocks in hand; and

(v) He must test check the annual inventories with the stock records.

6. The auditor must obtain confirmations from the parties holding the stocks in respect of stock which are not in the client's possession, e.g. goods sent on consignment, goods pledged with banks, etc.

A physical verification by the auditor may not possible in all cases regarding work-in-progress. He should, therefore, satisfy himself that the statements, submitted by the management and the basis of valuation is reasonable.

Common Errors

Often certain errors creep in while counting stock physically, of which the following are the most important :

1. No proper listing of name, size, or part number on the count tags.
2. Mistakes committed in identifying the stage of completion of a particular product.
3. Wrong listing on the tags regarding unit of measure etc.
4. Some items of the stock escaping counting and some counted items not recorded on verification sheets.
5. Discrepancies in stock uncorrected through adjustment in the stock records.

Duties of Auditor About Goods sent out on Consignment

1. Scrutinising the basis of valuation such stock.
2. Ensuring that in valuing such stock, freight and all other charges incurred by the consignor (i.e. the company) have been included.
3. Verifying the stock certificate obtained from the consignee.
4. Ensuring that in case the consignee's certificate discloses that any goods have been damaged or deteriorated, proper allowance has been made in this respect from the cost.
5. Ascertaining that the market price of such goods is not lower than the cost.

6. Ensuring that none of such goods is old, obsolete or unsalable, if it is so then they are not counted in stock.
7. Ensuring that the necessary adjustment has been made in respect of consigned goods which remain unsold at the Balance Sheet date to bring them at actual cost where goods are sent out on consignment at proforma invoice price including percentage above cost.
8. Scrutinising long-standing debit balance on Consignment or Consignee's Accounts, to ensure that they are not doubtful or bad, otherwise, ample provision should be made for all likely bad debts.

Auditor's duties about Goods on Sale or Return Basis

1. The auditor should require a schedule to be prepared of goods not approved of and lying in the hands of customers at the close of the financial period and have an adjustment entry passed with the total amount thus ascertained, debiting the Sales Account and crediting debtors in Suspense Account. The effect of this entry will be to bring down the sales to their correct figure.
2. The credit balance of debtors in suspense will be deducted from the total amount of sundry debtors with the result that the item of sundry debtors will also be brought down to its proper figure.
3. The stock of goods in the hands of customers should then be valued at cost, and shown on the credit side of the Trading Accounting and also as an asset in the Balance Sheet.

Methods of Valuation

Valuation of stock-in-trade means the assignment of rupee value to the items of the stock-in-trade, determined by physical counting. As the units of the goods are purchased at varying cost prices and only a part of them is sold, the accountant is faced with the question as to whether the remaining goods should be shown at cost or at the price at which they could be sold in the market. Secondly, which costs should be assigned to the units of the stock-in-trade at the end if priced at cost or at market price, replacements cost or net realisable value.

it is a general practice to value the closing stock at 'lower of cost net realisable value or replacement cost.' This practice is based on the conservation principles. Any loss in 'value' must be accounted for, but not the unrealised profit. Loss in value should be recorded if the market price is lower than the original cost of the stock. If the market price is higher and stock is valued at it, this will amount to the recording of the unrealised profit. Conservatives believe that profit should not be recorded unless realised since it is possible that the price may decline and the goods may be sold at loss next year.

The principle of 'lower of cost or market price' whichever is less may be applied either in respect of each items separately or globally to all the items of stock-in-trade.

Following methods are adopted in valuation of stock in trade.

1. Pick and Choose Method. Under this method every item is shown at cost and market price, both, the lower of two is aggregated and that is the balance of closing stock.

Items of Stock	Cost	Market price	Lower of Cost or Market Price
1.	200	300	200
2.	400	380	380
3.	1000	940	940
4.	800	1050	800
5.	400	300	300
Total	2800	2970	2620

∴ Closing stock = Rs. 2620.

2. Global Method. Under this method cost and market price of all type of the stock are aggregated separately instead of picking the lower value for each category of the stock and then aggregating all lover values. The stock-in-trade is shown at the valuation. Whichever aggregate is lower, in the above illustration under this method Rs. 2800 will be taken as the valuation of stock-in-trade.

The application of 'lower of cost or market price' requires the identification of cost and its computation and the determination of the market price.

The elements of the cost of stock normally are the following :

(i) Direct expenditure. This is on the acquisition of the goods for resale and of raw materials to be used in the manufacture of finished goods.

(ii) Other expenditures. These are directly attributable to the acquisition of the stock.

(iii) Overhead expenditure. Examples are factory overheads, office overheads, etc.

Generally, although production overheads may be added to the stock values, it is not always prudent to add overheads in respect of administration and distribution is decided by the nature of the business, this is done as follows whether the fixed overheads should be added or not.

(i) Smooth flow. When a smooth flow of production and sales takes place, profits will not be greatly affected by the inclusion of overheads and *vice versa.*

(ii) Unpredictable sale. Where it is not possible to predict the nature of sales it would be wise to exclude overheads.

(iii) Contract Business. In the case of contract business, the inclusion of overhead affects the profit in the initial years.

(iv) Fixed Overheads. As fixed costs are proportionately high in the business holding maturing stocks (e.g. wine, timber), so to add fixed overheads would cause heavy risks to be incurred in respect of future sales.

(v) Time Basis. If fixed charges accrue purely on time basis rather than the variation in the production, there is justification in their exclusion.

3. Methods of Computing Cost. As the units of stock are purchased at varying costs, therefore, the problem arises as to which cost to be assigned to the unsold units of stock following the various methods of computing costs.

(i) *Unit Cost Method.* It involves each item or batch on hand at the actual cost of the consignment to which they belong. If different lots of goods have been purchased, the stock in hand can be easily identified and the invoices or the cash memos can help in finding out the cost price. The cost price of unsold stock will be the cost price at which such a lot is acquired.

(ii) *First-in-First-out Method (FIFO).* This involves the assumption that the quantity held in stock represents the latest purchases, i.e. the goods are issued in the order in which they are purchased. Therefore the stock is valued at the rate at which the most recent purchases were made.

(iii) *Last-in-First-Out Method (LIFO).* It is assumed that the quantity held in stock represent the earliest purchases, i.e. the latest purchases are sold first. Therefore the stock is valued at the rate at which the earliest purchases were made.

(iv) *Average Cost Method.* In this method the cost is computed by taking the average of the amount at which stock was brought forward in the beginning with the purchase prices. The cost of consumption is deducted on the basis of average cost so ascertained. During the times of rising prices, the method tends to give a lower amount than the cost of unsold stock ascertained on a FIFO basis and higher amount in times of falling prices.

(v) *Standard Cost Method.* Under this method a predetermined or budgeted cost per unit is used. It is particularly convenient where goods pass through a number of processes or are manufactured on a large scale production basis.

However, it does not result in a fair approximation of actual cost unless there is regular review of the standards.

(vi) *Adjusted Selling Price Method.* In this method the cost of stock is estimated by calculating it in the first instance at selling prices and then deducting an amount equal to the normal margin of gross profit on such stock.

(vii) *Base Stock Method.* In this method, the quantity of stock is predetermined (called the base-stock) and is valued at a fixed price each year. The price fixed is below the original cost of the 'base-stock'.

Which Method to Choose ?

It is pertinent to ask here as to which method is to be chosen. The most fair basis to establish cost in the year's average cost. Where it is impracticable, the cost should be established on the FIFO basis. In all cases, the cost figure should be increased by any direct expenses such as freight, duty, landing, dock and reasonable warehouse charges, etc. All trade discounts and allowances should be deducted.

Addition of Overheads

In the case of work-in-progress and finished stock, it is necessary to consider that addition should be made in respect of overheads. According to De Paula's *The Principles of Auditing,* following alternative methods are used to determine this addition :

1. The percentage for the last quarter or month of the accounting year.
2. The percentage actually applied at the time the goods were manufactured.
3. The average percentage for the year.
4. A standard percentage based on the normal value of production.
5. To exclude from the addition for overheads all "fixed charges".
6. To exclude overheads altogether.

The method to be used will depend entirely on the circumstances of the case. To quote Lord Reid in the *Duple Motor Bodies Case* (1961) :

"We have been invited to decide between these methods as a broad matter of principle, but this is very difficult. If the accountancy profession cannot do that, I do not see how I can. The real question is what method best fitted the circumstance of a particular business."

Different Bases of Calculating Market Price

1. Net Realisable Value Method. It is the price at which the goods can be sold in the market after deducting the necessary expenses.

2. Replacement of Cost Method. The goods may be valued at price at which similar types of goods can be presently purchased from the market.

Choice of Method

The Institute of Chartered Accountants in England and Wales as well as the Institute of Chartered Accountants in India have suggested the 'Net Realisable Value' as the true representative of the market price.

As the valuation of assets for Balance Sheet purpose is upon the 'going concern' basis, in the case of stores and raw materials the basis would be, not their saleable value as stores and raw materials, but as component parts of the manufactured goods. For example, in the case of manufacture of bread, *maida* (flour) is taken as its conversion into and sale as bread and as a rule only in the event of liquidation would *maida* be sold as *maida.*

To conclude in assessing the Balance Sheet valuations it is the net realisable value of the finished product that should be measured against the cost value of all classes of inventories.

VALUATION OF DIFFERENT ITEMS OF STOCK

1. Raw Materials. These are purchased to manufacture goods and not for resale purpose, thus they should be valued at cost. This will include all incidental expenses, such as carriage, freight, etc. But when market price has gone down they will be valued at reduced price. If raw materials were purchased at different time intervals, the average price may be taken to value them.

According to conservative accounting policy raw materials should not be valued at price higher than the market price. However, in case of goods such as wine, tobacco, rice, etc., which appreciate in value with the passage of time and are resold at high prices if actually sold in the market, goods may be valued at a higher price than the cost or market price.

2. Semi-finished Goods. These should be valued at the cost price of raw material plus the proportionate cost of manufacture. However, any amount in respect of selling, distribution and office expenses should be excluded. The unrealised profit on the work-in-progress should be taken into account, while valuing work-in-progress in case of contracts extending for many years. However, full credit of the unrealised profit should not be taken but rather provision should be made in some part of the profit for future contingencies and possible losses.

3. Finished Goods. This will include the cost price of raw materials plus all manufacturing expenses excluding distribution and office expenses. If the cost price of the manufactured goods is higher than market price, they must be valued at market price. If the goods have been manufactured under a contract, they will be valued at contract price excluding delivery expenses. However, obsolete, substandard products etc. should be valued at scrap price, if any.

4. Goods on Consignment. If in whole or part of goods remain unsold on the Balance Sheet date, goods sent to consignees to be sold for and on behalf of the client (consignor), the auditor should ensure that these are valued at lower of the cost or market price after satisfying himself that there in no deterioration in quality. The cost should also include a reasonable proportion of the expenses incurred on transshipment to the consignee, e.g. freight, duty, godown rent, etc. However, expenses properly relatable to sales such as commission should not be included in the cost. If goods sent on consignment have been priced above the cost price, so that the consignee may not know the cost thereof, the auditor should see that a reverse entry in the accounts has been passed at the time of account-closing such that the unsold stock is valued at cost alone.

5. Goods with Customers under Hire-Purchase Agreements. In this case the ownership on the goods is retained by the seller till the last instalment is paid by the customer. The instalment receipts are treated as sales for the accounting purposes, the instalments outstanding must be included in the stock-in-trade of the client. Goods sent for approval to customers should be included in the stock-in-trade. These will be valued at cost price or market price whichever is lower. Provision should be made for the damaged goods.

6. Verification of Loose Tools. By actually checking some of the items with the list provided to him the auditor will verify loose tools. A schedule of loose tools signed by some responsible officer of the business or the engineer-in-charge should be prepared at the end of the year. Detailed inventories of loose tools must also be signed by the persons concerned after comparison with the actual stock-taking sheets.

The auditor should ensure that the inventories contain no items of plant and machinery, the cost of which has been separately adjusted. Loose tools are revalued every year at their current price by a competent officer of the business or they are valued at actual cost, less provision for wear and tear. Reasons for abnormal variations in the items as well as their values should be ascertained. Physical examination of some of the loose tools included in the inventory may be carried to ascertain that the tools included are in serviceable condition. The auditor should not accept the practice of capitalisation of purchase of loose tools with the deduction of a periodical percentage for depreciation.

AUDITOR'S DUTY AS REGARDS STOCK-IN-TRADE

1. Examination of the accuracy and validity of accounting records. The auditor should verify the accounting work performed in connection with the stock-in-trade to ensure himself that totals, castings, calculations and summarizations are correct. He is liable for damages if he fails in his duty, as was held in *Henry Squire (Cash Chemists) Ltd.* v. *Bal, Baker Co.* (1911) case. The scope of verification will depend upon the system of inventory control, the size of inventory and its physical composition to ascertain the correctness of stock-taking system. The auditor should examine the stock sheets. To ascertain any discrepancy he should check a few items of the stock sheets and compare them with the stock records. About the purchase and sale of the goods during the year, the auditor must examine the Purchase Book, the Sales Book and the Cash Book, and the relevant documents. He should see that proper records exist for the goods sent on consignment, the goods sold on approval basis or under hire-purchase system. It should be ensured that the tools and other spare parts etc. have not been included in the stock. Proper records should be maintained for damaged, obsolete or otherwise wasted goods.

2. Physical verification of the stock-in-trade. As the physical examination of the items of the stock-in-trade is complicated and technical, different views are held as to whether the auditor is responsible for the physical verification of the stock-in-trade or not.

The case of *Kingston Cotton Mills* in 1896 and that to *Irish Woollen Co. Ltd.* v. *Tyson and Others* (1900) serve as guide about auditor's duty of physical verification. *Kingston Cotton Mills* case laid down the following principles in this connection :

1. The auditor has no duty to take stock. He must rely on other people for details of the stock in hand.
2. The auditor is not a valuer, he could rely on the certificates given by responsible officials of the client for materials necessary to enable him to enter the stock at its proper value in the Balance Sheet.
3. The auditor is not an insurer. His duty does not extend beyond exercising reasonable care and skill in the tasks performed by him which depends on the facts and circumstances of each case.

Practice in America

The principles laid down in the *Kingston Cotton Mills* case decision came under fire in the *McKesson and Robins* case. It was found in *McKesson and Robins* case that the audited Balance Sheet showed stock at $10 million which was completely non-existent. The decision in this case was that the auditor was responsible for the physical verification of the stock-in-trade. The duties of the auditors in America in connection with stock-taking have been expressed by the American Institute of Certified Public Accountants (AICPS), USA, in their, "Statement on auditing Procedure" which is as follows :

"Where the inventories are material in relation to the company's financial position, it is necessary that the auditor, in addition to making audit test and checks of the inventory account and records, shall, wherever practicable and reasonable, be present at the inventory-taking and by suitable observation and inquiry satisfy himself as to the effectiveness to the methods of inventory-taking and as to the measures of reliance that may be placed upon the client's Representation to the inventories and upon the records thereof. In doing so he may require physical tests of inventories to be made under the observation."

It is customary for the foregoing procedure to be followed at the time where the inventory is determined solely by means of a physical inventory at the end of the accounting period (or at a date before or after but reasonably close to that date, with adequate records supporting the changes during the intervening period).

This procedure may not be followed at the time of stock-taking where well-kept and controlled perpetual inventory records are maintained, supported by the following :

(i) A complete physical inventory at a date coincident with the balance sheet; or

(ii) Physical inventories of individual items taken from time to time so that the quantity of each item on hand is compared with the relative inventory records at least once in each year.

Direct confirmation in writing from the custodian is acceptable in the case of inventories/records which are in the hands of public warehouses or other outside custodians, provided that, where the amount involved shows a significant proportion of the current assets or of the total assets, supplemental inquiries are made to satisfy the independent auditor as to bona fide of the situation. Supervision of the inventory is entirely the province of the management."

Practice in England and India

The rulings of the *McKesson and Robins* case and the directions of the *A.I.C.P.A.* are not strictly followed in England as well as in India though the judgement of the *Kingston Cotton Mills* case is respected in these countries. However, the *Westminster Road Construction and Engineering Co. Ltd.* (1939) case in England and the *Deputy Secretary, Ministry of Home Affairs* v. *S.N. Das Gupta* (1955) case in India caused the judges, the accountants and the professional practitioners consider again the auditor's duty in connection with the verification of the stock-in-trade. Against the *Kingston Cotton Mills* case it is argued that the auditor may qualify his report with regard to the stock-in-trade (or any other asset) and absolve from the responsibility. However, it was very clearly stated by Justice Chakravarti in the case of *Deputy Secretary, Ministry of Home Affairs* v. *S.N. Das Gupta* that "Mr. Sen (lawyer) contended that since the respondent stated in his special report that he had not verified cash, he absolved himself from the liability. I am afraid the argument was entirely misconceived. If Mr. Sen's arguments were correct, an auditor might do nothing and assume no responsibility whether for any inaccuracy or untruth in the Balance Sheet or Profit and Loss Account. The absurdity of such a contention if advanced would be obvious."

Contemporary Practice

The decision of *Kingston Cotton Mills* case has no significance in auditing at present. The auditor is now required to state in his report whether the Balance

Sheet gives a true and fair view of the financial position of the company or not. This is not possible without physically verifying the stock-in-trade. It is also argued that "If the auditor were to accept, say, the officers' certificate without, in anyway checking or testing the stock, the audit will be of a little use, for although every other item in the Balance Sheet may by tested and checked in every way, yet if the auditor merely relies upon certificate as regards the stock, it means that the official responsible for the valuation of the stock can make the accounts show whatever results he pleases."

To conclude, the decision in the *Kingston Cotton Mills* case, where it was decided that "it is no part of an auditor's duty to take stock... he must rely on other people for the details of the stock-in-trade in hand..." has no relevance in the present circumstances. The auditor must take the stock or at least present himself when the stock is counted by the company's staff. As rigid adherence as to the physical counting of the items of the stick by the auditor will be very difficult and impracticable task for him, therefore, the obligation of the auditor should be to verify the accounting records and the system of stock-taking with the utmost care and diligence. Before this, he must examine the effectiveness of the system of inventory control. He must select a few items and count them as a test check to ensure the correctness of stock-taking by the client's employees. He must be present at time the stock-in-hand is counted by the client's staff. In technical matters as to the nature and quality of goods he can rely upon the certificate of the experts and management/official. The practice of sending a representative by the auditor at the time of taking stock is becoming popular in India.

Verifying the Valuation of Stock-in-trade

In the *Westminster Road Construction and Engineering Co. Ltd.* case, it was decided that the auditor was guilty of negligence if the work-in-progress was overvalued in the Balance Sheet. The auditor must apply tests to see that the stock-in-trade has been appropriately and correctly valued.

As to the cost figures the auditor must satisfy himself that they have been derived by some acceptable method applied consistently. If the method of pricing the inventory has been changed by the client as compared to the previous year, the auditor may reflect this fact in his report and show the results of changed method on the financial position. He should not forget to see that generally accepted accounting principles have been fully complied with in the valuation of the stock-in-trade.

Present position in India

Under the Companies Act, 1956 the auditor is supposed to make following report to the shareholders:

1. Whether the Balance Sheet and Profit and Loss Account prepared by the company exhibits a true and fair view of the state of affairs of the company.

2. Whether according to Part II Schedule IV to the Companies Act, the figures of opening and closing stock are shown in the Balance Sheet.
3. Whether the company's Balance Sheet and Profit and Loss Account are in agreement with the books of account and various returns. The Companies Act, 1956 clearly empowers the auditor :
   (i) to have access to books of accounts and vouchers of the company, at all times, and
   (ii) to acquire from the officers of the company such information and explanations as he may think necessary for the performance of his duties as the auditor of the company.

Thus the auditor must satisfy himself not only with regard to quantity of the stock held but also that it is properly valued. The Institute of Chartered Accountants of India has issued a booklet entitled, "Statement of Auditing Practices" to guide auditors for verification of stock-in-trade as well as other assets.

VERIFICATION OF DEBTORS

An auditor has to carry out verification of debtors including Book debts, Loan and Advances, Bills, Instruments, advance payments and typical assets.

1. Book Debts

It is an important duty of the auditor to see whether the debts as shown in the Balance Sheet are recoverable. Adequate provision has to be made for them if they are doubtful. They are not shown on the assets side when they are bad, i.e. they are irrecoverable. The Balance Sheet which the auditor certifies to show a "true and fair view" may be wrong and he might be held liable for damages if he does not pay any attention to these points.

Objectives. The objectives of verification of debtors is to establish: (i) accuracy, (ii) validity as claims against the recorded debtors, (iii) collectibility and determination of its realisable value, and (iv) fair disclosure in the financial statements in accordance with legal provisions. Verification of debtor's balances is carried out by employing the following procedures:

(i) Year-end scrutiny and checking of balances,

(ii) Test checking of subsequent recoveries,

(iii) Direct confirmation procedure.

The test is the best evidence in support of outstanding balances. Such confirmations however are not always available and will not bring to light suppressed debtor's balances, resulting from the suppression of sales.

Through its *Statement on Auditing Practices,* The Institute of Chartered Accountants of India recommends that the direct confirmation of balances should be based on the following:

1. Confirmatory letters. These should be obtained from the debtors directly by the auditor. The client should send out these letters to the debtors. Confirmation procedure should be carried out within a reasonable period from the end of the year. The date should be settled in consultation with client. Books written up to the date should be selected for confirmation of balances so that the correct balances are confirmed by debtors.

2. Debtors ledger trial balance. The auditor should see that the debtors' ledger trial balance is extended by clients and agreed with the control account, if any. All of them may be circulated where the number of debtors is small but this could be done on a test basis if they are numerous. The auditor should ensure that the method of selection of the customers to be circularised is not revealed to the client until the debtors ledger trial balance is handed over to the auditor. A list of debtors selected for confirmation should be prepared in duplicate and a copy handed over to the clients for preparing request for confirmation which should be properly and fully addressed, enclosing stamped enveloped bearing the auditor's name and address for confirmation so that all undelivered letters would be returned to the auditor and not to clients.

3. Checking on prevention of despatch. The auditor should see that client's staff is not given any opportunity to prevent despatch of the confirmatory letters to any particular debtors. The confirmation letter should preferably be posted by the auditor's own staff. Replies received should be carefully gone through. Clients should be asked to investigate in case where balances are not agreed. Reminders may be sent to customers who have not sent replies.

4. Negative confirmation. In appropriate cases, e.g. where there is a larger number of small balances due from customers, as in an electricity supply undertaking, a negative confirmation procedure may be followed:

In case of non-response to confirmation request, verification of subsequent realisation is the most widely used alternative procedure. This is valid only if the documents emanating from the debtor (e.g. correspondence, cheques, forwarding letters) identify the bill in respect of which the payments are made. The auditor should recognise the fact that as payment has been made, it does not provide proof that the debtor has no claims against the company at the confirmation date. If a reply is not received a reminder may be sent and in suitable cases the auditor may also correspond with the party.

The Research Committee of the Institute of Chartered Accountants of India in its publication *A Guide to Company Audit* has suggested the following detailed guidelines for the company auditors with regard to the valuation and verification of debtors.

1. Have you seen that sundry debtors have been classified for the Balance Sheet purposes as under ?

Rs.

(a) Debts outstanding for a period exceeding 6 month ....
(b) Other debts ....

Total Rs. ....

Less provision Rs. ....

Rs. ....

Further, have you ensured that the following particulars are stated separately ?

(a) Debts considered good and in respect of which, the company is fully secured.

(b) Debts considered good for which the company holds no security other than the debtor's personal security.

(c) Debts considered doubtful or bad.

Out of the above, indicate separately in the inner column :

(i) Debts due by the directors or other officers of the company.

(ii) Debts due by the directors or other officers of the company or any of them jointly with any other person or persons.

Note. The term 'officer' includes any director, manager or secretary but does not include an auditor of the company for this purpose.

(iii) Debts due by the firms or private companies respectively in which any director is a partner or a director is a member as the case may be.

(iv) Debts due from other companies under the same management. These should be disclosed with the names of the companies concerned (*vide* Sec. 370 for the definition of companies under the same management).

(v) Maximum amount due by the directors or officers of the company at any time during the year.

2. Have you ascertained that the amounts shown under Sundry Debtors include the amounts due in respect of goods sold or services rendered in respect of other contractual obligation, but do not include any amounts which are in the nature of loans or advances ?

3. Has the provision for bad or doubtful debts been shown as a deduction from sundry debtors ?

Note. The provision to be shown under this head should not exceed the amount of debts stated to be considered doubtful or bad and any surplus of such provision, if already created, should be shown at every closing under "Reserves and Surplus" (on the liabilities side) under a separate subhead "Reserve for Doubtful or Bad Debts".

4. Where Control Account is in the use for Sundry Debtors Ledger, have you ascertained that the balance in the Control Account at the end of the accounting period has been tallied with the total of all balances in the subsidiary ledger ?

5. Have you seen that the company's accountant has prepared a statement, analysing the age of all sundry debtor's balances to enable you to decide the extent of doubtful debts ?

Note. It should not be assumed that any balance which is confirmed is necessarily realisable.

6. If confirmatory letters are obtained, have you test-checked them ?

7. Have you obtained full information from the management about each account which you consider doubtful ?

8. Have you seen that credit balance, if any, in the debtor's ledger, are not deducted from the list of sundry debtors but shown as liabilities ?

9. Have you enquired about the position of goods sent out on VPP ? Are these amounts correctly included in sundry debtors and properly verified by you with the VPP register ?

10. Does the company follow a system of issuing cash memos for goods which are not immediately paid for ? If so, have you verified that all such uncollected cash memos are accounted for as debtors ?

11. Have you obtained the Board's resolution for bad debts written off and for debts considered doubtful ?

12. Have you paid particular attention to any big items of sales passed through at the close of the accounting year to ascertain that they are genuine? Have you seen that such sales are not subsequently reversed or shown as goods returned, if so, have they been deducted from the figures of sales ?

13. Have you enquired whether sales include any items of transactions for future delivery of goods ?

2. Verification of Loans and Advances

The verification procedure for loans and advances is almost the same as for debtors with the following additional points for verification of this item.

1. Sanction. The auditor should pay special attention to the sanctioning of loans by the Board of Directors, the purpose of the loans, and the provision of Secs. 292, 295 and 370 of the Companies Act which place restrictions on the giving of loans by companies.

2. Amount. If there are any debtors for loans granted by the company, the auditor should see that the amount of such loans is not included in the list of sundry debtors but is shown separately.

3. Secured. If such loans are secured the auditor should inspect the securities and obtain letters from the debtors acknowledging the amounts owned by them on the date of the Balance Sheet. If the loans are unsecured, the auditor should enquire if the amount is recoverable in full.

4. Competency. The auditor should examine all the documents relating to the loan and satisfy himself about the competency of borrower to receive the loan. This would include perusal of the borrower's constitution and opinion of legal counsel, where applicable. In the case of a company, the auditor should find out whether the lending company has satisfied itself about the compliance by the borrower which the provisions of Secs. 293 (where applicable), 292 and 58A of the Companies Act, 1956 as also the Reserve Bank of India's sanction under Sec. 26 (7) of the Foreign Exchange Regulation Act, 1973, is applicable.

5. Loans by officers. Where loans are owned by the directors or other officers of the company, a clear statement to that effect should be made on the face of the Balance Sheet.

6. Within power. The auditor should satisfy himself that loans, advances or deposits made by the company are within the powers of the company as laid down in its Memorandum and Articles of Association.

7. Sec. 370. As far as loans to companies are concerned, the auditor should specifically note that the provisions of the Sec. 370 are complied with. These are as follows :

(a) Loans given to bodies corporate, not under the same management should not exceed 10% of the capital and free reserve of the lending company.

(b) In case of loans in excess of the above limit the prior approval by special resolution of members of the company should be obtained. Approval of the central government must have been obtained in case the loans made to the bodies corporate exceed (i) 20% of the capital and free reserves of the lending company (where the borrowing and lending companies are under the same management) and (ii) 30% of the capital and free reserves (where the companies are not under the same management), in addition to the special resolution.

8. Loans of Employees. Sometimes loans are made by firms and companies to their employees to assist them to purchase houses or meet other occasional expenditure. In such cases the loan agreements or other documents signed by the employees acknowledging such loans must be inspected by the auditor and the terms in respect of interest, if any, and repayment noted. Normally such loans are unsecured. However, if any security has been provided, it must be examined. Where it has been arranged with the employee that the loan shall be repaid over a period by the deduction of a fixed monthly deductions sums from his salary, the auditor should see that the appropriate deductions have been made. A certificate should be obtained from each employee setting forth his indebtedness to the firm or company and shown as loan account in the Balance Sheet.

3. Verification of Bill Receivable

The auditor should do the following :

1. He should compare the schedule of bills in hand at the date of the Balance Sheet with the Bill Receivable Book.
2. He should verify Bills on hand by actual inspection of the bills, care should be taken to see that no overdue bills are included.
3. If any bills have been met subsequent to the period but prior to the date of audit, he should trace the same through the Cash Book.
4. If the bills are lodged with the bankers for collection, he should obtain a certificate from the bank stating the bills on hand at the date of the Balance Sheet.
5. In regard to bills that have been discounted or endorsed away and remain unmatured on the date of audit, he should ensure that the contingent liability in respect thereof has been shown at the foot of the Balance Sheet and a proper reserve has been made in regard to overdue bills.

4. Verification of Investments in Subsidiary Companies

Investments in subsidiary companies and indebtedness to and by subsidiaries should be shown separately in the holding company's Balance Sheet. In order to ensure that a true and fair view is given the auditor must satisfy himself that the values shown are true. He should examine the Balance Sheet and accounts of the subsidiaries. If, after enquiry, he is not satisfied he should qualify his report accordingly. He should ensure that dividends received after acquisition of controlling interests, if paid out of pre-acquisition profits, are credited against the cost of the shares, thereby reducing their value, as the holding company has since received part of the value which it originally purchased.

5. Advance Payments

The objective of verification of advance payment are :

(i) To establish the validity of the expenditure originally debited to an asset account,

(ii) To determine that definite benefits will be received in future periods from any unexpired cost being carried forward as an asset,

(iii) To determine the reasonableness of amortisation programme being applied to such an asset.

These objectives are accomplished through a variety of audit procedures, designed to fit the widely differing items included in the prepayment category. The following general techniques are adopted in most audit programmes for prepaid expenses :

(i) Analysis of the prepayment accounts to determine their contents.

(ii) Examination of supporting, evidences, such as insurance policies, and rent receipts, contracts etc. to prove the correctness of the costs separated as assets.

(iii) Review of the procedure followed by the client for the allocation of costs to the periods benefited and to determine the overall reasonableness and propriety of the amortisation programme.

(iv) Computing the unamortised balances to be carried as assets and the expired amounts to be charged to the expense accounts.

(v) Finding out the weakness of the system of internal control for expenses of theses types and develop suggestions for its improvement.

6. Verification of Some Typical Assets

According to the Statement on Auditing Practices issued by the Institute of Chartered Accountants of India the following procedure is adopted for verification of some typical assets:

1. Assets Acquired of Hire Purchase. In such cases ownership does not legally vest in the company. But such assets should be recorded at their cash value. It should be calculated by assuming an appropriate rate of interest if cash value is not readily available. They should be shown on the Balance Sheet with an appropriate narration to indicate that the company does not have full ownership.

2. Jointly Owned Assets. If a company owns assets jointly with others (other than as a partner in a firm), the auditor should ensure that the extent of the company's share in such assets and its proportion of the original cost, accumulated depreciation and written down value have been stated in the Balance Sheet. Alternatively, he may check that the *pro rata* cost of such jointly owned assets has been grouped together with similar fully owned assets. He should ensure that the details of such jointly owned assets are indicated separately in the fixed assets register.

3. Purchases in Lot. If several assets are purchased for a consolidated price, the auditor should see that consideration has been apportioned to the various assets in the ratio of their respective market value on the date of purchase as assessed by expert valuers in addition to the other considerations discussed above.

VERIFICATION OF LIABILITIES

Verification of liabilities is as much important as the verification of assets. The Balance Sheet will not reveal a true and fair view of the state of affairs of a business concern if liabilities are not properly verified and valued.

Types of Liabilities

The items appearing on the liability side of the Balance Sheet and requiring verification can be grouped under the following four headings :

1. Capital or Owner's Equity
2. Reserves—Capital and Revenue
3. Loan Capital
4. Liability and Provisions.

Duties of the Auditor

Proper valuation and verification of liabilities means that the auditor should see that: (i) the liabilities shown in the Balance Sheet are actually payable, (ii) all liabilities have been correctly recorded, (iii) the recorded liabilities are payable for the legitimate operations of the business, (iv) in the case of liabilities created by some charge, the nature and extent of such charge has been disclosed, and (v) the nature and extent of contingent liabilities has been disclosed in the Balance Sheet.

Duties of the auditor on First Audit

The duties of auditor at the time of first audit are the following :

1. To note the authorise capital of the company, the auditor should read the different clauses of Memorandum and Articles of Association of the company.
2. He should go through the Cash Book, Minute Book of the Board of Directors to know: (i) the number and the different classes of shares issued, (ii) the amount received on each share, and (iii) any balance due from the shareholders in respect of calls.
3. He should examine the various clauses of the contract between vendor and the company where some of the shares have been issued for consideration other than to vendors.

Duties of the Auditor on subsequent Audit

In case of the subsequent audit the duties of the auditor are to see that the share capital is same as at the end of the last year. If he finds that the capital stands altered by issued of fresh shares etc., he should ensure that the relevant provision of the Company Act have been complied with.

The Institute of Chartered Accountants of India in its publication. *A Guide of Company Audit* suggest the following steps with regard to audit of share capital:

1. See that the 'authorised capital' has been shown separately in the Balance Sheet.
2. Ensure that particulars in respect of each class of issued and subscribed capital have been shown regarding "Preference Share Capital", their preferential right.
3. Ascertain the amount called up in respect of each class of shares.
4. Ascertain as to how many shares of each class are allotted as fully paid up pursuant to a contract without payment being received in cash.
5. Enquire whether cash has actually been received in respect of shares and if no cash has actually been so received, whether the position as stated in the account books and the Balance Sheet is correct, regular and not misleading.
6. Find out as to how many shares of each class have been allotted as fully paid up by way of bonus shares and also specify the source from which bonus shares are issued, e.g. capitalisation of profits or reserves or from share premium account.
7. Calculate the total amount of calls unpaid on share by the directors and others.
8. Obtain from the management, a list of calls in arrears made out from the Register of members and reconciled with the debit balances in the Share Allotment or Share Call Accounts in the Financial Ledger.
9. Ensure only one class of shares has been issued by the company, if it has been styled as Equity Capital in the Balance Sheet.
10. Find out whether the company has issued Redeemable Preference Shares, see that the terms of redemption or conversion, if any, have been clearly shown together with the earliest date of redemption or conversion.
11. Ensure that the full particulars of the option on unissued share capital, if any, have been given.
12. Vouch that the amount originally paid up in respect of forfeited shares, if any, has been added to the share capital and separately shown.
13. Ensure that any capital profit, on reissue of forfeited shares, has been transferred to Capital Reserve.
14. *Forfeiture of Shares.* While verifying this item the auditor should do the following:
    (i) Ascertain that the detailed procedure as laid down in the Articles of the company and the Companies Act has been observed,
    (ii) Ensure that forfeiture is permitted by the Articles,

(iii) Examine the Director's resolution forfeiting the shares,

(iv) Check the entries in the books of accounts for the forfeiture, and

(v) Where forfeited shares are sold or reissued, verify that such shares have not been reissued at a price less than the difference between the called up value of shares and amount, if any, actually realised from the defaulting shareholders.

15. *Issue of New Share Capital.* In this connection the auditor should ensure that where any fresh capital has been issued during the period under audit, the principles embodied in Section 81 have been complied with.

16. *First Audits.* In the first audit after every new issue of shares, the auditor should specifically check the following:

(i) The capital issued does not exceed the Authorised Capital;

(ii) Wherever necessary the permission of Controller of Capital Issue has been acquired;

(iii) Wherever necessary permission of the Reserve Bank of India in regard to allotment to non-residents has been obtained;

(iv) Check the share applications with the Application and Allotment Book to see that the shares allotted have been actually applied for;

(v) Examine the Board's resolution regarding allotment of shares;

(vi) See that copy of the return of allotments;

(vii) Vouch the moneys received on application and allotment with the counterfoil receipts or other relevant, evidence;

(viii) If any calls have been made, see the Director's resolution for the same;

(ix) See that the total cash received on account of share capital agrees with the credit balance on share capital account less debit balance on Allotment and Call Account, if any, in the Financial Ledger;

(x) Note whether the directors have taken up their qualification shares and have paid for them to the same extent as the other shareholders;

(xi) Where shares are allotted for consideration other than cash, examine the contract constituting allottee's title to the shares with the director's minutes and mentioned in the prospectus or statement in lieu thereof, if any, authorising the allotment;

(xii) Where shares are issued at a premium, see that premium is shown distinctly under the head "Reserves and Surplus", and not under share capital;

(xiii) See that all moneys received from applicants for shares at the time of first public issue are placed in a Scheduled Bank till the certificate of the commencement of business has been obtained or if the certificate is already obtained, till minimum subscription is received; and

(xiv) If shares have been issued is exercise of an option see that the terms of the option have been duly complied with.

17. Particulars of shares held by holding company or the ultimate holding company. In the case of subsidiary companies, ensure that the number of shares held by the holding company as well as ultimate holding company and its subsidiaries are shown separately in the Balance Sheet. The auditor is not required to certify the correctness of the above shareholdings. He should obtain a certificate from the management and keep it in his file.

18. Capitalisation of Profits:

(i) See that it is authorised by the Articles;

(ii) See that the provisions in the Articles regarding capitalisation of profits have been duly complied with;

(iii) See that the sanction of the Controller of Capital Issues has been obtained;

(iv) Obtain a copy of the resolution for his records;

(v) See that a proper return of allotment has been duly filed with the Registrar as per the Companies Act.

Debentures

A debenture is a written acknowledgment under the seal of the company for a debt due by the company undertaking to pay the debt and interest on debt. Debentures can be of various types. Following are the duties of the auditor in auditing debentures:

1. Ascertain the company's borrowing powers. Whether a company has power to borrow or not depends upon its objects, and the auditor must refer to the Memorandum and Articles for this purpose. A power to borrow, need not be express but implied. All trading companies have an implied power to borrow, as the same is regarded as incidental to the carrying on of their business. If there is any limit placed on the borrowing powers of the directors or the managing agents, the auditor should see that such limit is not exceeded.

2. See that all the requirements of the Act in connection with loans on mortgage are rigidly carried out.

3. See that the assets mortgaged or charged are clearly indicated in the Balance Sheet.

4. See that where debentures are issued at a premium, the premium has been used towards reduction or writing off of goodwill or other fixed assets, or has been credited in the Debentures Redemption Fund or in the Capital Reserve Fund.

5. See that where debentures are issued at a discount and are repayable at par, the total amount of liability represented but the face value of the debentures has been shown on the liabilities side. The Discount on Issue of Debentures, being a loss has to be written off during the term of the debentures, the unwritten balance being shown on the assets side for the mean time.
6. See that where debentures have been issued at par and are repayable at a premium, the provision for the loss on account of premium has been provided proportionately out of the profits each year.
7. Ensure that the terms of issue of the debentures have been complied with.

Loans Secured and Unsecured

While verifying loans the auditor has the following duties:

1. He should check the existence of the loans with reference to the agreement and correspondence for getting the loans.
2. He should check payments on account of interest on loans. Where any interest due has not been paid he should see that it is shown as a liability.
3. He should call for confirmation letters from the parties who have advanced the loans. He should seek information not only about the amount of the loan but also about the interest due and the security offered.
4. He should check the power of the company to borrow with reference to the Memorandum and Articles of Association and the Companies Act.
5. He should ensure that where any properties have been mortgaged by the company, mortgage has been registered with the Registrar of Companies and an entry has been made in the Register of Mortgages.

According to Section 125 of the Companies Act, 1956, every mortgage or charge by the company under any of the following heads should be properly filed with the Registrar within 30 days from the date of its creation, viz.:

(i) Mortgage or charge, for the purpose of securing any issue of Debentures,

(ii) Mortgages or charge on uncalled share capital of the company,

(iii) Mortgages or charge on any immovable property whether situate, or any interest thereon,

(iv) Mortgage or charge on any book debts of the company,

(v) Mortgage or charge, not being a pledge on any movable property of the company,

(vi) Floating charge on the undertaking or property of the company, including stock-in-trade,

(vii) Charge or calls made but not paid,

(viii) Charge on ship or any share in a ship, or

(ix) Charge on goodwill, patent, licence under a patent, trade-mark, copyright or licence under a copyright.

Liabilities and Provisions

1. Examine these as follows the copy of application executed for obtaining the loan to ascertain the terms and conditions of the loan.
2. Examine the agreement concerning the creation of the charge and this fact must be disclosed in the Balance Sheet if any security has been provided for it, by creating a charge on some asset.
3. Verify the borrowing powers of the client and ensure that loan was raised under proper authority.
4. See that the amount of interest accrued till the balance sheet date should either be paid or provided for.
5. Confirm by obtaining a statement from the bank the amount of interest remaining unpaid at the close of the year.
6. Examine in case of bank overdraft :

   (a) the agreement with the bank,

   (b) the Bank Pass-book, and

   (c) the statement of mortgaged assets.

Trade Credit

The auditor should do the following :

1. Obtain a certified schedule of creditors from the client and check it with the individual creditor's accounts in the purchases ledger.
2. Ensure that all purchases, including those made at the year-end, have been included in the purchases and duly credited to the accounts of the creditors concerned.
3. Check Purchase Ledger with the books of original entry, invoices, credit notes, etc. According to the case of *Westminster Road Construction & Engineering Co. Ltd.* the auditor has a duty to determine unrecorded liability in respect of goods received prior to the period under audit which, though included in stock, do not have a corresponding entry under liabilities.
4. Send confirmation requests to a selected number of creditors concerning the balances as standing at the end of the year, particularly in case of suppliers with whom the client has begun to have dealings in the year

under audit, because it may be that non-existent goods may be shown as having been purchased and the proceeds shared by suppliers and dishonest employees.

5. Enquire if any debit is found unpaid for a long time, since it is possible that instead of paying the creditor, the amount might have been misappropriated.

Amount Received in Advance

(i) To verify amounts received in advance the auditor should obtain a certified schedule thereof from the company or organisation.

(ii) He should further ensure that the entire amount so received has been shown as a liability in the Balance Sheet.

Outstanding Expenses

(i) The auditor should obtain a certificate from a responsible official to the effect that all outstanding expenses have been included in the current year's accounts. Examples of expenses which should be debited to the current year are rent of twelfth month or salaries payable or electricity charges for the last month, etc. Further,

(ii) The auditor should check entries for some weeks after the Balance Sheet date to ensure that they are not related to the under audit.

(iii) The auditor should ensure that outstanding expenses have been subsequently paid.

Bill Payable

Following are the duties of auditor in connection with verification of bills payable :

1. Obtain a schedule of bills payable and compare the same with the Bills Payable Book and Bills Payable Account.

2. Certify with the Cash Book the bills that have already been paid.

3. Examine the Cash-Book of the succeeding year to see that the payment has been made in respect of bills payable to ensure that no fictitious bills have been included in direct confirmation from the drawers of the bills in the case any foul play is suspected.

4. Note that where any charge has been created on any asset of the concern by accepting the bill, note to this effect has been stated in the Balance Sheet.

CONTINGENT LIABILITIES

What are contingent liabilities ?

Certain liabilities may or may not arise after the preparation of the Balance Sheet. These are called contingent liabilities. In the words of Montgomery,

"The term 'contingent liability' should be used in the accounting sense to designate a possible liability of presently determinable or indeterminable or indeterminable amount which arise from past circumstances or action which may or may not become a legal obligation in the future, and which, if paid, gives rise to cost or an expenses or an asset of doubtful value." A contingent liability is different from an actual liability.

Types of Contingent Liabilities

1. Liabilities on Bills Receivable Discounted and not Matured. If the bills receivable are discounted with a bank and the money so received from it is made use of, the entire money will be refunded to the bank if the acceptor does not make payment on the date of its maturity. Hence such a contingent liability is distinctly shown in the Balance Sheet by way of a note at the foot.

2. Liability for Calls on Partly Paid Shares. The amount called on shares held and paid should be verified from the Cash Book and the liability for the amount uncalled should be ascertained.

3. Liability under a Guarantee. The auditor should ascertain the liability for a guarantee given by the client for a loan or overdraft to his friend, or partner. In case of non-payment of such loan, the possible liability should be ascertained.

4. Liability for Cases against the Company not Acknowledged as Debts. This is a liability in a disputed case where damages may have to be paid. A contingent liability should be ascertained and note should be made at the foot of the Balance Sheet.

5. Liability for Penalties under Forward Contracts. If losses arise in case of purchases or sales made under forward contracts, a proper provision should be made for such losses.

6. Liability in respect of Arrears of Dividend on Cumulative Preference Shares. The auditor should examine the Articles of Association which should contain rules in this regard and due provision should be made for such a liability.

Auditor's Duties

(i) Check the various contingent liabilities named above.

(ii) Some liabilities may have no provision made in the books but merely a note made at the foot of the Balance Sheet, e.g., bills receivable which have been discounted and which have not matured at the date of the Balance Sheet, arrears of fixed accumulated dividends, etc. In case for liabilities in respect of which provision has to be made on the Balance Sheet, e.g., liability which may arise in connection with a suit, etc., the auditor should examine such cases and ascertain the amount to be specifically reserved for the purpose.

(iii) Examine the Directors Minute Book, correspondence made with the legal advisers and the information obtained from the officials of the business. Ensure that proper provision has been made for all such liabilities and if he is not satisfied mention the fact in the report. The requirements of the Companies Act regarding the contingent liability should be complied with in the Balance Sheet on the liabilities side.

Contingent Assets

Following are some of the examples of contingent assets :

(i) Option to apply for shares in another company on favourable terms;

(ii) Refund of octroi paid for goods sent out later on;

(iii) Claim for money from a previous endorser of a bill receivable discounted but might be dishonoured;

(iv) Uncalled Share Capital;

(v) Legal action for infringement of a copyright, etc.

Usually, contingent assets are not shown at the foot of the Balance Sheet on the assets side. The Companies Act does not require the contingent assets to be disclosed as such.

QUESTIONS FOR EXERCISE

1. What is meant by the term "Verification of Assets" ? How does it differ from the term "Valuation of Assets"? State the importance of verification and valuation of assets from the point of view of an auditor of a Limited Company.
2. How and in what ways does verification of assets and liabilities differ from vouching? Discuss the scope of Verification.
3. After vouching has been done to the satisfaction of the auditor of a public limited company, do you think it is necessary for him to consider the question of valuation and verification of assets? What consequence might follow if valuation and verification are not carried out by auditors in respect of the assets appearing in the Balance Sheet to be certified.
4. What do you mean by valuation of assets? What are its objects? Also discuss its importance.
5. "An auditor is not a valuer." Explain fully how these two statements can be reconciled.
7. Point out the difference between "verification" and "valuation" of assets. Examine in detail the considerations that govern the valuation of different types of assets.

7. What are the Auditor's problems in the valuation of assets?
8. Valuation of investments depends largely upon the objects for which they are held. Discuss the statement describing the principles of verification and valuation to be adopted for different assets.
9. "An auditor is not a valuer and yet he is intimately connected with valuation". Comment.
10. On what basis should assets be valued for Balance Sheet purposes? Will the basis for valuation of fixed assets be different from the basis of valuation of floating assets? If so, how is such a distinction made? Do you know anything about replacement basis of valuation of assets?
11. How would you verify the following intangible assets :
    1. Goodwill
    2. Patents
    3. Copyright
    4. Trademark
12. What are Floating Assets? Explain their verification procedure.
13. A Cotton Mill Company places before you their Stock Sheets showing the stock at the end of the year. State how would your proceed to check them and what information would you call for before including the figures of the Stock in the balance sheet before you are called upon to sign.
14. Discuss various methods of valuation of stock in trade, computing and calculating world price.
15. How will an auditor value different items of stock?
16. What are the duties of an auditor regarding the valuation and verification of stock-in-trade of a manufacturing concern? State the facts and judgement in Kingston Cotton Mill Co. case bearing upon the duties of an auditor in regard to stock-in-trade.
17. In auditing the Balance Sheet of a limited company, state what steps you would take to verify Sundry Debtors and what are your duties regarding these.
18. What is the importance of verification of liabilities? How would you verify the different liabilities?
19. What are the Contingent Liabilities? Give five examples of such liabilities. What is the method by which you would satisfy yourself at the time of audit that all contingent and outstanding liabilities have been disclosed in the Balance Sheet?
20. Write short note on Contingent Assets.

11
Depreciation

The word "Depreciation'' has been derived from the Latin word 'Depretium' meaning decrease in the value of fixed or capital assets on account of natural wear and tear of effluxion of time. The depreciation is the gradual diminution, loss or shrinkage in the utility value of an asset due to wear and tear in use, effluxion of time or obsolescence. Depreciation accounting is a system which aims at distributing the cost or basic value of tangible capital assets, less salvage over the estimated useful life of the unit in a systematic and rational manner. It is not fluctuation since while it is due to internal causes, fluctuation is due to external causes. It is a charge against the profits of the year. It does not entail any actual expenditure. Initially capital expenditure is incurred on the acquisition of the asset and no further sum is spent thereafter. And yet, the business suffers a real loss in the years during the useful life of the asset while it is fit to render service. It is therefore necessary that the entire cost of the asset be allocated to the years of the expected useful life of the asset.

Definition

1. ***L.C. Cropper.*** "Depreciation is the diminution in the financial value of an asset owing to wear and tear, effluxion of time, obsolescence or similar causes, the suggestion being rather that of gradual deterioration than sudden loss or diminution in value."

2. ***Carter.*** "Depreciation is the gradual decrease in the value of an asset from any cause."[1]

3. ***F.R.M. de Paula.*** "In practice, the term 'depreciation' is commonly used in a very wide sense, covering diminution in the values of assets caused by outside fluctuations in realisable and replacement values, and also the amortisation of the cost of an asset over the period of its use."[2]

4. *Spicer and Pegler.* Depreciation is defined "as the measure of the exhaustion of the effective life of an asset from any cause during a given period."[3]

---

1. Carter, *Advance Accounts,* p. 645.
2. F.R.M. de Paula, *The Principles of Auditing,* Eleventh edition, p. 135.
3. Spicer and Pegler, *Practical Auditing,* Eleventh edition, pp. 115-16

5. *The Institute of Chartered Accountants in England and Wales.* (Recommendation No. (9) Depreciation as "that part of the fixed asset to its owner which is not recoverable when the asset is finally put out of use by him. Provision against this loss of capital is an integral cost of conducting the business during the effective commercial life of the asset and is not dependent upon the amount of profit earned."[4]

It will be clear from the above definitions that the authorities on the subject differ widely and a logical and workable concept, is yet to emerge. Charles Smith has written : "I have long struggled with a definition of depreciation. In fact I have been a member of the National Committee which have been studying the subject of depreciation for many years. That committee of the National Association of Railroad and Utilities Commission, 1943 finally give up the attempt and substituted instead a *description* of depreciation."[5]

Depreciation and Fluctuation

Fluctuations refer to the decrease or increase in the market price of a commodity. Depreciation is applicable to fixed assets whereas fluctuations are usually related to the floating assets. It is permanent, gradual and continuous decrease in the value of the fixed assets whereas fluctuation is temporary in nature depending upon the market conditions. Its provision as a charge against the Profit and Loss Account is essential to ascertain the true and fair estimate of Profit and Loss whereas fluctuations are ignored. It is because "Fluctuations in the value of assets have no relationship to the fact that all fixed assets, except land, are constantly wearing out and approaching a zero value." Fixed assets depreciate by use or otherwise and at the same time fluctuations in their value do also take place. But since fluctuations or increase or decrease in the market value of the fixed assets do not affect the earning capacity or working life of such assets, they are not taken into account.

Object of Charging Depreciation

Depreciation should be charged against the Profit and Loss Account as a loss in order to recoup the capital invested in the purchase of fixed assets, specially the wasting ones. Such assets are utilised to earn income. In this process they lose value gradually due to wear and tear or obsolescence. Then their earning capacity is lost and they become valueless for the business concern. All the capital invested in the purchase of these assets is lost. Such expired capital outlay is a revenue loss. Hence, it has to be provided as a loss in the Profit and Loss Account.

---

4. Quoted by Spicer and Pegler, *op. cit.*, p. 119
5. Charles Smith, "What concept of depreciation for fixed assets is most useful today." *Journal of Accountancy,* August 1951, p. 169.

If no provision is made for depreciation, the Profit and Loss Account will not show the correct profit for the period and this will result in the return of part of capital by way of dividend which is legally prohibited and commercially unsound. The Balance Sheet will also not exhibit the true and fair state of affairs because the assets will appear at their original value whereas it has, in fact, depreciated. This would result in over-stating the value of such assets.

Arguments Against Depreciation

The clients may object to making provision for depreciation on the following grounds:

1. the asset, say machinery, has been maintained through repairs and is as good as new; or

2. that market value of asset is more than the original cost on the Balance Sheet; or

3. that it will prevent the declaration of dividend if depreciation is charged; or

4. that in the past excessive depreciation has been charged.

Counter arguments

1. To say that no depreciation is needed since constant repair has been undertaken is wrong because repairs are necessary to keep the asset in good working condition, whereas depreciation is necessary to provide for loss in its value due to its being utilised in the business. Therefore, both should be charged Profit and Loss Account to arrive at correct profit or loss for the given period.
2. The *second argument* also does not hold good since market value of a fixed asset has nothing to do with depreciation, as explained earlier.
3. About the *third argument* it should be emphasised that the question of dividend arises when profit has already been arrived at and the correct profit cannot be ascertained unless provision for depreciation has been made.
4. About the *last argument*, it should be mentioned that the depreciation for current year must be charged to revenue and excessive depreciation charged in the past may be transferred to a Reserve Account.

Characteristics of Depreciation

1. It signifies that the value of a particular asset has fallen.
2. It is not concerned with the cost price or sale price but with its book value.
3. Fall in value due to depreciation is permanent.
4. Fall in value due to depreciation is constant.
5. It is concerned with fixed assets only.

Causes of Depreciation

The causes of depreciation may be divided into two classes:

1. Internal Causes, and
2. External Causes.

1. Internal Causes. These relate to the nature of the asset itself. These are the following:

(i) *Wear and Tear.* Some assets decrease in value by constant use to which they are put. These include building, plant and machinery, motor, etc. Although they are kept in order by providing for their repairs, a time comes when they are of no value.

(ii) *Exhaustion.* With the passage of time assets like plantations, animals, etc., gradually lose their value. They have their definite age, after the expiry of which these exhaust in value and become useless.

(iii) *Depletion.* Examples of Depreciation by Depletion are oil-wells, mines, etc., which lose their value if the oil or mineral is extracted out of them.

(iv) *Deterioration.* Depreciation by deterioration is found in case of those assets, which have temporary or short life e.g., food articles, etc., Repairs make up the loss caused by deterioration.

2. External Causes. External causes are those factors which arise from causes outside the assets. These are as follows:

(i) *Effluxion of Time.* Decrease in the value of asset is caused by the effluxion of time such as patents, leasehold property, etc. An asset acquired on lease becomes valueless after the expiry of the period of lease.

(ii) *Obsolescence.* Loss in the value of an asset which arises out of new inventions which may produce goods better and cheaper as old machines become out of date due to discovery of new machines and change of fashion, a businessman has to purchase the latest models and sell the old ones. He thus, suffers a loss. Hence, obsolescence is totally an external factor. It has no definite time of its occurrence.

(iii) *Accident.* Examples of depreciation by accident are that the assets such as works, machines, motors, furniture, etc., become valueless duc to an accident, like fire, flood or similar other havocs.

(iv) *Permanent fall in the Market Value.* Examples of permanent or temporary loss in value due to market fluctuation, include assets like investments which lose their value by a permanent fall in their market value.

Necessity of Depreciation

1. Use. Every asset is purchased in a business for use. Its constant use however, causes depreciation or decrease in its earning capacity. Such decrease in value is like any other business expense which must be debited to Profit and Loss Account. Correct profits cannot be calculated, if it is not done. Again, when the asset becomes a mere scrap, it would be a heavy charge on the Profit and Loss Account if the whole of the loss, *i.e.,* the entire cost of the asset is charged to the Profit and Loss Account of that year. This is totally unfair, unjustified and against business principles.

2. Overhead figure. If provision is not made for depreciation for a particular asset, it appears in the Balance Sheet as an overhead figure *i.e.,* at a higher value than its real value. Thus, the Balance Sheet do not exhibit the true and fair view of the state of affairs of the business.

3. Showing correct value of the asset. Depreciation on a particular asset is provided to keep the capital intact and show the correct value of the asset in the Balance Sheet. Hence, the entire loss is distributed over a number of years for which the asset remains in use.

For example. Suppose, the expenses of the goods manufactured are:

1. Raw Material used	1000
2. Wages	200
3. Indirect Expenses	100
	Cost Rs. 1300

Also suppose machinery worth Rs. 2000 has been acquired to manufacture those goods which are consumed in the process of manufacture and scrap value is Rs. 400 only. Thus, the net cost of the machinery, *i.e.,* Rs. 2000 — 400=1600 also be included in the cost of goods manufactured which will now be Rs. 2900 and not Rs. 1300 only.

4. Making sum available. Another purpose behind providing for depreciation for an asset is to make a certain sum available at a time when that asset becomes totally valueless for its replacement.

5. Checking over-valuation. If depreciation is not provided for, the asset will be shown at an over-valued figure and profits would be higher than the actual ones. If so, dividend will be paid out of capital and thus, a part of the capital will be returned to the shareholders.

Bases or Principles of Depreciation

1. Original Cost of the Asset. The books of accounts may reveal facts about the original cost of the asset. If the business has been purchased from the vendors, the price at which it has been acquired should be inquired into, in order to know about its cost.

2. Estimated Working Life. The assets differ in their nature and character. The exhaustion in their value depends upon their use in business. Some business employ experts to assess the probable life for which an asset will remain in use and in proper working order. However, much depends upon the conditions under which an asset is maintained and preserved. Thus, the working life of an asset should be considered carefully.

3. Provision for Repairs and Renewals. Proper provision for repairs helps in maintaining an asset in good order. Through proper attention, an asset works well for the stipulated period otherwise it becomes useless after a few years. This should be considered before providing of depreciation.

4. Capital Expenditure. Additions and extensions are made whenever necessary throughout the life of an asset. Thus improvements are affected in a way that the asset maintains its earning capacity as normal as it could be. Such an expenditure is of capital nature. If it is incurred in large amounts, the working life may be extended and depreciation will have to be provided for accordingly.

5. Loss of Interest on Capital Investment. Interest could be earned if the capital involved in purchasing an asset would have been invested elsewhere. As a part of capital is blocked in a particular asset, the loss of interest on that account should be taken into account before depreciation is provided for.

6. Residual or Scrap Value. The value which an asset brings when it is sold as scrap should be considered before making provision for depreciation.

7. Depreciation in Case of Obsolescence. More amount of depreciation should be provided for before making provision for depreciation. If an asset is likely to be of no value due to some new inventions the possibility of new developments and inventions should be given due weight as new inventions make asset valueless.

8. Provision for Depreciation in Previous Years. A business may not provide a huge amount for depreciation during the current year.

9. Legal Provision or any Change therein. It should be noted whether the legal provisions have been complied with if there is some legal provision for providing depreciation on assets or there has been some amendment to change in the existing law in this regard.

METHODS FOR PROVIDING DEPRECIATION

1. Fixed Instalment Method,
2. Diminishing Balance or Reducing Instalment Method,
3. Annuity Method,
4. Depreciation Fund Method,
5. Insurance Policy Method,
6. Revaluation Method,
7. Compound Interest Method,
8. Depletion Unit Method,

9. Use of Kilometre (Mileage) Method,
10. Efficiency Hour Method,
11. Single Charge Method,
12. Global Method.

1. fixed Instalment Method. This is also called 'fixed Percentage Method,' 'Straight Line Method' or 'Original Cost Method'. Under it a fixed percentage of the original cost of the assets is written off each year till the asset is ultimately reduced to nil or its break-up value. Thus, the entire cost less the scrap value is written off during the estimated working life after which the asset becomes valueless.

This method is simple in calculation. However as the charge of repairs increases with the passage of time, the effects on net profits are not steady every year. A lot of calculations are involved in case of additions made to the asset.

2. Diminishing Balance Method. It is also known as 'Diminishing Value Method' or 'Written Down Value Method' or 'Decline Balance Method'. Under it a fixed percentage is written off every year on the reduced balance of the asset. The percentage of depreciation is not applied to the original cost but only to the balance which remains after charging depreciation in the beginning of a year. It remains fixed for all the years of the working life of an asset. However, the actual amount of depreciation written off every year goes on decreasing with the reduction in the value of the asset till after the expiry of the working life, the value of the asset is brought down to its scrap value by and by.

In the case of assets which have fairly long life and which require plenty of repairs, e.g., plant and machinery, it is a useful method. However, it is not of much use for assets having short life for which depreciation has to be charged at a uniform rate.

3. Annuity Method. Under this method the asset is treated like an interest bearing investment. The money invested in the asset is retained in the business and is expected to earn interest at a fixed rate. Thus, an amount equivalent to the estimated loss of interest is written off in the Profit and Loss Account throughout the useful life of the asset. A certain fixed amount of depreciation is provided for every year as shown by the annuity table. The asset account is debited with interest at a fixed rate. A fixed sum is written off the asset account so that the value of the asset plus interest comes to nil at the end of its working life.

This is applied in case of assets which have a definite span of life, *e.g.*, lease etc. For assets to which additions are made every year it is not of much value. Hence this method is not much popular.

4. Depreciation Fund Method. This method is also known as 'Sinking Fund Method' or 'Reduction Fund Method' or 'Amortization Fund Method'. According it a depreciation fund is created every year and credited with the amount charged to the Profit and Loss Account. Simultaneously, an equivalent sum is invested outside the business to bring interest every year while the asset remains at its original cost in the books of accounts. The instalments are fixed in a way so that the whole investment accumulates at the compound interest and provides a sum equivalent to the replacement cost of the asset at the end of its working life.

Thus, the asset is written off after a fixed interval of time and the money is available to replace it at the end of its useful life. The cash is usually invested in gilt-edged securities. Thus under this method no inconvenience is caused to the business. Money becomes available from outside to replace the asset after the expiry of its working life.

5. Insurance Policy Method. Under this method, the fund, instead of being invested in gilt-edged securities, is applied in taking out an Insurance Policy so that after the expiry of the working life of the asset, the insurance company pays the sum assured to replace the asset.

This method is superior to the Depreciation Fund Method. There are little chances of loss on realization. However, it is more expensive. It is not applicable to assets whose life cannot be calculated and determined precisely.

6. Revaluation Method. Under this method the asset is valued at the end of the each year when the Balance Sheet has to be prepared and the fall in its value is charged as depreciation. Occasions are rare on which there are profits on revaluation. Assets are usually revalued by technical experts. Their value is determined as the value to the business as a going concern. This method is useful in case of assets such as loose tools, horses, patterns, models, designs, bottles, trade-marks, etc. It is the most scientific method of calculating depreciation. However, as competent men are needed to revalue the assets it is costly.

7. Compound Interest Method. This method is usually adopted for charging depreciation on fixed assets of the electric supply undertakings. It is like the Depreciation Fund Method with the only difference that investments are not made outside the business and the interest is also calculated on the increasing balance of depreciation each year. The depreciation provided for each year is so adjusted that it becomes equivalent to 90% of the value of the asset accumulated at the rate of 4% per annum compound interest.

This method enables to retain enough of the working capital in the business. It involves no risk of loss on realization as in the case of the depreciation Fund Method.

8. Depletion Unit Method. It is also known as the 'Production Unit Method'. It is used in case of wasting assets such as mines, quarries, etc. In order to find out the amount of depreciation, the value of the mine is reduced to the extent to which the output is obtained from it. Thus, it is based on factual data and not so much on calculations. For example, if the estimated output of a mine is 5,000 tonnes of coal and the total cost is Rs. 2500, the depreciation will be 50 p. per tonne. If the coal drawn out is 100 tonnes, depreciation will be Rs. 50. The amount of depreciation should be written off to the account according to the amount of output raised.

9. Use of Kilometre (Mileage) Method. This method is simple in nature but difficult for adoption in practice. It is adopted in case of asset whose use may be measured in terms of kilometres, e.g., cars, buses, motor cycles, etc. If a car costing Rs. 40,000 is estimated to run for about 1,60,000 kilometres and on an average, it runs for about 16,000 kilometres each year, it will be valueless after the expiry of 10 years. But it runs 32,000 kilometres in the first year, 24,000 kilometres in the second year, 28,000 kilometres in the third year and so on, the depreciation charged calculated at the rate of 25 paise per kilometre will be Rs. 8,000, Rs. 6,000 and Rs. 7,000 respectively.

10. Efficiency Hour Method. It also known as 'Machine Hour Method' or 'Unit of Production Method' or "Hour of Service Method'. It is like the Kilometre Method with the only difference that the working life of the asset is calculated in terms of hours instead of calculation it in terms of kilometres. It is applied in case of machines, the working life of which can be measured in terms of hours. It is used for costly machines.

11. Single Charge Method. In it a fixed sum of money equivalent to the amount of depreciation and repairs over the working life of the asset is charged to the debit of the Profit and Loss Account and credited to a depreciation and Repairs Reserve Account. Repairs effected in the following years are charged to this account.

12. Global Method. In it a flat rate of depreciation is charged every year on all the assets taken together. It is practically not much in use. Its use is not permissible under the Companies Act as the fixed assets have to be distinguished from one another for this purpose.

DEPRECIATION AND OBSOLESCENCE

What is Depreciation?

Depreciation is a charge against the profits of the business and not an appropriation of profits. It is charged regardless of the fact whether the business makes any profit or runs into loss. Provision for it is to be made even if the market value of the asset increases. It should be provided on some uniform basis consistently used form year to year. Any increase in the market value of the asset should be ignored for the reason that the asset was not purchased for resale but for the use in the business. It should be distinguished from obsolescence or loss in the value of any asset on account of fluctuations in its market price.

What is Obsolescence ?

Obsolescence is due to loss in the value or reduction in the ability of an asset on account of external factors which render the asset useless for efficient working and economical earnings. Due to invention of new, better and cheaper machines, the old machines greatly lose their value. Thus, loss can be actually determined only when the asset is replaced by a new model. Obsolescence is totally an external factor. It has no definite time of its occurrence.

DEPRECIATION AND FLUCTUATION

Fluctuation means changes in the market price of any asset, which may be temporary or permanent and sudden or abnormal and therefore no estimate can be formed in advance. Depreciation is the process of allocation and not the process of valuation. It represents loss of capital and therefore it must be provided. Fluctuation differs from depreciation on the following points:

1. Causes. While depreciation is mainly caused by internal forces like regular use, wear and tear, fluctuations are due to market forces such as changes in the market prices.

2. Nature. While depreciation is always permanent, gradual and continuous, a fluctuation may be temporary, sudden change in the value of any asset.

3. Value. While depreciation always implies decrease in value of an asset, fluctuation is increase or decrease in the value of the asset.

4. Charge. While depreciation is a charge against the profits, fluctuation does not affect profits and hence it is ignored.

PROVISIONS BY COMPANIES ACT

According to Companies Act, an auditor should render his opinion about the truth and fairness of financial statements. He must carefully examine whether adequate depreciation has been provided on all depreciable assets of the company. Section 205 of the Companies Act makes it mandatory for a company to provide depreciation before any dividend is declared or paid. Section 205(2) lays down the following methods for providing depreciation:

(i) To the extent specified in Section 350 i.e., the amount calculated with reference to the written down value of the assets, as shown by the books of account of the company, at the rate specified in Schedule XIV to the Companies Act.

(ii) In respect of each item of depreciable asset, for such an amount as is arrived at by dividing 95% of the original cost thereof to the company by the specified period in respect of such respect.

(iii) On any other basis approved by the Central Government which has the effect of writing off by way of depreciation 95% of the original cost to the company of each such depreciable asset on the expiry of the specified period.

(iv) As regards any other depreciable asset for which no rate of depreciation has been laid down in Schedule XIV, on such basis as approved by Central Government.

Thus Companies Act recognises Straight Line Method and written down value method of depreciation. It permits the reducing balance method of providing depreciation under both Secs. 205 and 350. Under it, the rate of depreciation in respect of any asset would be the rate as prescribed in the case of that asset in Schedule XIV to the Companies Act or Rules made thereunder. The Schedule gives separate rates in case of reducing balance method and straight-line method. In case of certain assets which are worked for more than one shift, higher rates have been provided for double and triple shift working thereof.

According to Part II of Schedule VI "the Profit and Loss Account must give information as to the amount provided for depreciation, renewals or diminution in value of fixed assets. If such provision is not made by means of depreciation charge, the fact shall be stated and the quantum of arrears of depreciation computed in accordance with Section 205(2) of the Companies Act shall be disclosed by way of note."

Most of the companies are required to follow the rule and provisions of the depreciation as provided in the Companies Act. The auditor should prepare the accounts primarily to fulfil the requirements of the Companies Act. An auditor is bound to obey the instructions of the Companies Act. If the company has not made necessary provisions for depreciation, the auditor must disclose the fact in the report. Moreover, the amount of depreciation should be specifically shown in the books of the company and in the auditor's report.

Following are the important assets and rates of depreciation as given in Schedule XVI:

Nature of assets	Single shift * WDV ** SLM	Double shift * WDV ** SLM	Triple shift * WDV ** SLM
1	2	3	
I. Buildings (other than factory buildings)			
NESD	5%	1.63%	
Factory buildings	10%	3.34%	
II. Plant and machinery:			
General rate	15%	5.15%	22.5%
Special rates for certain categories	8.09%	30%	11.31%
III. Furniture and fittings,			
General rate:	10%	3.34%	

1	2	3	4
NESD *** Special rate in certain cases: NESD	15%	5.15%	
IV. Ships			
Ocean going ships:			
(i) fishing vessels with wooden hull (NESD)	27.05%	10%	
(ii) Dredgers, tugs, etc. Ships operating on inland waters.	19.8%	7%	
(i) Speed boats (NESD)	20%	7.07%	
(ii) Other vessels (NESD)	10%	3.34%	

Notes: * WDV means written down value.
** SLM means straight-line methods
*** NESD means no extra shift depreciation.

NECESSITY FOR PROVIDING DEPRECIATION

1. To find out the correct cost of production. When an asset is purchased for the purpose of using it during the course of business in order to earn profits, it loses its value when it is used. Therefore, such a decrease in value is like any other expense which must be debited to profit and loss account before divisible profits are arrived at. It is a kind of loss to the business. Hence, consumption of the asset must be provided for every year during the life of the asset. If it is not done, the asset will become a mere scrap and will have no value after a few years. The profit and a loss account of the year in which the asset has become a mere scrap should not be debited with the whole of the loss, i.e., the total cost of the particular asset. As all the previews years in which that asset was used took fair advantage of it those years should be debited with a part of the loss caused by the consumption of the asset. This wear and tear is just like any other expense and must be debited to profit and loss account. Moreover, if depreciation is not provided, the profits of the year will be inflated.

2. Proper evaluation of assets. If depreciation is not provided, the asset will be shown at a higher value in the balance sheet than its real vale. It will be over-valued in the Balance Sheet which will then not represent a true and fair view of the state of affairs of the concern.

3. To keep the capital intact. This is done distributing the loss in its value over a number of years when it is in use. To take an example, suppose a machinery worth Rs. 2,000 is purchased. Suppose that the machinery lasts only for one year. Its scrap value is Rs. 4,000. Suppose, the expenses for the manufacture of goods are (a) raw materials, Rs. 2,000 (b) wages, Rs. 1,000 (c) overhead charges, Rs. 400, the cost of the goods manufacture will not be only (a) Rs. 2,000 plus, (b) Rs. 1,000, plus (c) Rs. 400 but it will be more. The net cost of machinery consumed during the process of manufacture will have to be taken into consideration. Therefore, the cost of the goods manufactured will be Rs. 2,000 plus Rs. 1,000 plus Rs. 400, plus Rs. 1,600 (the net value of the machinery), i.e., Rs. 5,000. The goods manufactured will have to be sold at not less than Rs. 5,000 otherwise it will not be possible to purchase new machinery next year and the business will have to be closed down for want of capital. Thus in order to keep the capital intact, when an asset has been used for earning income, the reduction in the value of the asset by its use should be entered into the cost of the production and regarded as an expense.

4. To set aside a certain sum of money every year to replace that asset later on when it breaks down. When the machinery does break down, more capital will be required to replace the asset. If depreciation is not provided a part of the capital is returned to the shareholders in the form of profit without making provision for replacing the capital. In the case of a company reduction of capital without going through certain legal formalities is against law. In cases when no provision was made for depreciation the business had either to be closed down or money had to be borrowed to replace the asset when the asset broke down and as no provision had been made for replacement of the asset.

5. To replace the old plant and machinery with the latest model. Latest model is usually an improvement on the older one. It enables a company to compete favourably with other companies using the latest models.

6. According to Section 205 of the Companies Act. It is also necessary to make provision for depreciation on fixed assets before a company can distribute its profits. This is so case of proprietary concerns. But from the sound financial point of view, it is necessary to provide depreciation in order, (i) to arrive at the exact cost of production per unit of the goods manufactured, (ii) to arrive at true profits, (iii) to show the correct state of affairs of a concern, (iv) to keep the capital intact, and (v) to make provision for the replacement of the asset.

Auditor's Duties Concerning Depreciation

1. Dividing amount of depreciation. The object of accountancy is to know the exact profit or loss by debiting the revenue account with all legitimate expenses whether actually paid or not. Therefore, it is necessary that the exact amount of depreciation should be debited to revenue account. The object of providing for depreciation is to set apart a sum of money for the purpose of replacement of an asset at the end of its life. But it is difficult to calculate the amount required at the end of the life of the asset. The auditor cannot forecast the value of the asset which will have to be purchased especially when there are changes in the prices.

According to Section 227 of the Companies Act the auditor should state in his report to the shareholders whether the profit and loss account gives a true and fair view of the profit or loss of the year under review. He cannot give such a report unless he is satisfied that the amount of depreciation provided for is adequate. The Companies Act has laid down the measure of depreciation according to Section 205(2). The Electricity (Supply) Act, 1948, provides the rates at which depreciation is to be calculated on different assets. The Income Tax Act, 1961, provides the rate of depreciation on different kinds of assets. Therefore, the auditor should take the law into consideration along with the following factors:

1. The original cost of the asset.
2. The additions to the asset during the year, taking into consideration the dates on which these additions were made for the purpose of calculations.
3. The interest that could be earned if the sum spent in the purchase of the asset had been invested outside.
4. The estimated efficiency of the life of the asset.
5. The scrap, break-up or the residual value of the asset.
6. Obsolescence, i.e., the chance of the asset going out of fashion.
7. The working hours of the asset concerned.
8. The repair and renewals or the maintenance policy.
9. The skill of the operators who handle the asset.
10. Depreciation should be provided according to the Income Tax Act and the Companies Act.
    (i) Income Tax authorities will not agree to the higher rate of depreciation than what has been prescribed by the Income Tax Act and the Companies Act.
    (ii) No suitable basis has been determined to find out the replacement cost because the value of the currency fluctuates violently.
    (iii) If depreciation is to be charged according to the price level each year, it would not be possible to compare the Profit and Loss Accounts of several years.
    (iv) The aim of providing depreciation is to find out the actual cost of production and hence only the actual expense should be debited to the revenue account. This is possible only when the original cost of asset is spread over the useful life of the asset.

(v) The managing agents, directors and employees will object to raising the amount of depreciation because in that case the net profits will be reduced on which they are to get commission or bonus.

(vi) It is not a simple method to calculate the rate of depreciation where there is a violent fluctuation in the price level of the fixed assets.

(vii) If Replacement Method is followed there will be no need to provide depreciation in some cases if the cost of machinery has been considered reduced due to mass production.

(viii) If depreciation is charged on inflated price of the asset due to inflation, the rate of dividend and value of shares will go down because of less distributable profits.

(ix) Providing depreciation on inflated value of the asset will amount to creation of secret reserves which is prohibited.

(x) Replacement cost cannot be defined, as the owner may not purchase the same type of plant. Moreover, due to improvement in the manufacture of plant and machinery, a new model may be available.

(xi) If the assets are to be revalued, the liabilities will also have to be revalued.

2. Cost of Rehabilitation. It is suggested that depreciation should be provided on the purchase price, plus the Rehabilitation Cost. While appraising the property, market fluctuations should be ignored until the prices have stabilised.

3. Interest during Construction. Interest paid on debentures, loan, etc., should be added to the cost of the building or machinery as the case may be, and depreciation should be provided over the total cost of building, machinery, etc., plus the interest so paid.

4. Cash Discount. Same system should be followed if cash discount is allowed on the purchase of machinery provided the amount of interest is substantial.

5. Property acquired in exchange of Company Stock or Bonds. Cost of such property should be determined by the market value of the consideration given or by the fair market value of the property acquired whichever is more clearly evident.

6. Property acquired as a Contribution or Donation. It should be valued when received at the appraised amount.

7. Change in method. The Institute of Chartered Accountants of India has recommended. "There is no bar either from accounting point of view or legal point of view to make a change in the method of providing depreciation... The auditor should see the proper depreciation has been provided for under the changed method."

"However, a disclosure should be made in the report regarding the change in the method of accounting. It is mandatory... Different methods of depreciation may be used for different classes of assets. If the change results in a surplus, such may be transferred to General Reserve through the appropriation part of the Profit and Loss Account. Similarly, deficiency may be made up from the General Reserve Account, through the Appropriation part of the Profit and Loss Account."

8. Plant Register. It is not an easy thing to estimate the working life of an asset. It would be better if a "Plant Register" is maintained.

The Plant Register contains the following information for each type of asset:

(i) Opening balance of the plant and machinery.

(ii) Additions during the year.

(iii) Nature of the plant, e.g., lathe, boiler, drilling machine, etc.

(iv) Original price.

(v) Estimated life of the plant.

(vi) Estimated scrap value.

(vii) The rate at which depreciation is to be charged.

(viii) The number of non-working hours, e.g., breakdown of plant, strike, lack of work or lock-out, etc.

(ix) Repairs effected during the year.

(x) Sale of any part of any plant.

The Plant and Machinery account in the General Ledger should be adjusted accordingly.

The advantages of Plant Register are as follows:

(i) The auditor can be sure that the depreciation charged is fair and that the book value of the asset shown in the balance sheet is correct.

(ii) The depreciation allowances can easily be checked by the Income Tax authorities.

(iii) An exact amount for depreciation can be ascertained easily and, therefore, the exact cost of article manufactured can be known.

(iv) Un-economic repairs are revealed.

However, due to following reasons it is not easy to measure exactly the amount of depreciation during the year on a particular asset:

1. It is not possible to know the scrap value of the asset.

2. One is not in a position to estimate the life of an asset in most of the cases.
3. It is only a fair estimate which can be formed with the help of technical experts and experience. Hence, the auditor should see whether the provision made for depreciation is reasonable or not. If he finds that the amount is inadequate, he must ask the management to increase it and if he is unsuccessful, he must refer the matter in his report.

QUESTIONS FOR EXERCISE

1. What do you mean by depreciation ? What are its characteristics ?
2. What are the causes of depreciation ? Explain their necessity and basis.
3. State the objectives of providing depreciation.
4. Discussion various methods for providing depreciation.
5. Distinguish depreciation of assets from losses due to obsolescence and fluctuations in the prices of the assets.
6. Specify the provisions of Companies Act as regards provision for depreciation.
7. Discuss if it is necessary for a company to provide for the depreciation in respect of fixed assets both from commercial and legal points of view. State also the auditor's duties in this respect.

12

Provisions and Reserves

In order to save the business from risks and uncertainties, it is necessary to make provisions and reserves in every business. This has become a normal practice in all business concerns. Sometimes, provisions and reserves are used interchangeably but they are different from each other.

According to American Institute of Accountants, "The use of the term 'Reserve' be limited to indicate that an undivided portion of the assets is being held or retained for general or specific purpose."

Thus reserve is part of the profit, which is set aside for any known or unknown contingencies, liabilities or diminution in the value of an asset. It is that portion of the current profits or of accumulated profits which is not distributed as dividend, but is kept separate for purposes of meeting some known or unknown liabilities or for fulfilment of future needs.

What are Provisions?

Provisions are always a charge against Profit and Loss Account. They are meant to meet some ascertained, estimated and expected contingencies or losses. They can be used only to meet the specific liability for which they have been created while reserves can be used to meet any contingency excepting capital or specific reserves. The term 'provision' means any amount written off or retained by way of providing depreciation, renewals or diminution in the value of assets retained by way of providing for any known liability the amount of which may not be determined with substantial accuracy. Some examples are: provision for depreciation, provision for bad and doubtful debts, provision for taxation, provision for repairs and renewal, provision for contingencies.

The main purpose of provision for repairs and renewals is to give a uniform charge to Profit and Loss Account in respect of machinery. This is necessary as the usefulness of the machinery is also uniform from year to year. The total repairs over the life of the asset are estimated and then average is found. This amount is debited to the Profit and Loss Account of every year and credited to the provision for repairs and renewals account. The actual amount of repairs and renewals is debited to the provision for repairs and renewals account, the balance of the account appears on the liabilities side in the Balance Sheet. As soon as the life of the assets is over, the account is automatically closed.

PROVISION V/S RESERVE

1. Nature. While provision is a charge to profit and loss account, reserve is an appropriation of profit. Thus while provision must be charged to profit and loss account before calculation the net profit or loss reserve can be made only when there is profit.

2. Need. While provision is made because of legal necessity, creating a reserve is a matter of financial prudence and to save the concern from prospective losses and liabilities.

3. Objects. While provision is created for some specific object and must be utilised for the object for which it is created, reserve is created for probable losses and can be used for any future liability or loss.

4. Use. While provisions cannot be distributed as profits or transferred to any general reserve, reserves can be distributed as profit if these remain unutilised for some period. Some amount out of reserves can be transferred to provisions, if needed.

5. Investment. While provisions reduce the net profit and are not invested in outside securities, reserves reduce divisible profits and can be invested in outside securities.

KINDS OF RESERVE

1. Capital Reserve;
2. General Reserve;
3. Specific Reserve; or to be more appropriate "provision";
4. Sinking Fund;
5. Secret Reserve.

1. Capital Reserve. This is the reserve which is created out of capital profits as against trading or revenue profits and is not readily available for distribution as dividend among the shareholders. Profits prior to incorporation, premium on the issue of shares or debentures, profit on the reissue of shares, profit on redemption of debentures, profits on the sale of undertaking or a part of it and any profit of exceptional or abnormal nature which is not meant for distribution as dividend to shareholders. While, some of the capital profits can be distributed as dividend among the shareholders under certain conditions other capital profits can be disposed only in accordance with the provisions of the Companies Act. When a profit becomes available for dividend it should be transferred to General Reserve. Premium on shares can be utilised only for the specified purposes as given in section 78 of the Companies Act. Sanction of the court will be necessary if it is to be dealt in any other manner. Amount utilised out of profits to redeem redeemable preference shares can be utilised for issuing bonus shares to the members of the company. The profits prior to incorporation, premium on debentures and profit on redemption of debentures may be utilised to declare a dividend in absence of clear cut legal provisions regarding disposal of profit. The profit on the sale of fixed asset can be utilised to declare a dividend only if (i) the articles of the company do not prohibit such a distribution, (ii) the profit has actually been realised in cash and (iii) the profit exits after a revaluation of all assets and liabilities of the company. [Vide decision in *Lubbock* vs. *The British Bank of South America Ltd.*] However, profits arising from revaluation of fixed assets cannot be distributed as dividend among shareholders. Capital profits should not be distributed as dividend, but should be retained in the business as reserve to strengthen the financial position of the concern.

2. General Reserve. General reserve is an amount set aside out of the profits or surplus of a business with the objects (i) to provide additional working capital (ii) to strengthen the liquid resources of the business (iii) that they may be available for any unknown contingency (iv) to equalise dividend or for expansion of business, etc. An appropriation of profit, it is usually treated as a revenue reserve. It is also known as a "free reserve" or a "Revenue". It is not created to meet any known liability, contingency or commitment. It may be considered as the "undistributed profit". It can be created only when there is profit. Therefore, there cannot be a debit balance of Profit and Loss Account and a General Reserve at the same time. A businessman saves money out of profits for any unknown contingency, which is called "Reserve". The whole of the profit is not distributed. A part of the money which would have been withdrawn from the business and paid to the shareholders, is not paid to them but is retained in the business. It is the surplus over the asset, minus the liabilities and the capital. It improves liquid resources of the business. It can be utilised or it may be distributed later on, provided the articles of Association of the company do not prohibit such course. According to Binnie and Manning, "A general reserve, in effect, differs only in name from the 'carry forward' or 'surplus' as the balance remaining at the credit of Profit and Loss Account (after deducting dividends) is commonly called. The transfer of part of the profits to general reserve has the effect of setting aside a sum which thereupon ceases to be regarded as profit available for distribution under ordinary circumstances."

Distinction from Capital Reserve

Part III of Schedule VI to the Companies Act indicates the nature of the terms "reserve" and "capital reserve" as follows:

1. (a) The expression "provision" shall be subject to sub-clause (2) of this clause, means any amount written off or retained by way of providing for depreciation, renewals or diminution in value of assets, or retained by way of providing for any known liability of which the amount cannot be determined with substantial accuracy.

(b) The expression "reserve" shall not, subject as aforesaid, include any amount written off or retained by way providing for depreciation, renewals or diminution in value of assets or retained by way of providing for any known liability.

(c) The expression "capital reserve" shall not include any amount regarded as free for distribution through the profit and loss account ; and the expression "revenue reserve" shall mean any reserve other than a capital reserve.

And in this sub-clause the expression "liability" shall include all liabilities in respect of expenditure contracted for and all disputed or contingent liabilities.

2. Where—

(a) any amount written off or retained by way of providing for depreciations, renewals or diminution in value of assets not being an amount written off in relation to fixed assets before the commencement of this Act;

(b) any amount retained by way of providing for any known liability; is in excess of the amount which in the opinion of the directors is reasonably necessary for the purpose, the excess shall be treated for the purposes of this Schedule as a reserve and not as a provision.

Conversely, if there is a heavy loss in future, the General Reserve can be utilized for the purpose of wiping of the debit balance of Profit and Loss Account and the balance, if any, may be shown in the Balance Sheet.

The profits so withheld from distribution may be retained in the business if the turnover on such amount in the business itself is higher than if they were invested outside the business and provided further if there is any scope of expansion.

It is not obligatory to set aside a certain sum of money for general reserve. If the profits permit and the management thinks it advisable, it may make provision for general reserve. It is not compulsory to do so. It is an appropriation of the profit and not a charge against it. It depends upon the discretion of the management. However, if there is any particular law to set aside a certain sum of money out of the profits, e.g. in case of banking companies or co-operative societies, a part of the profits, according to the particular law, has to be carried to reserve account. Similarly, the company must create a reserve if the articles of association lay down that a particular amount has to be carried to reserve account before distribution of the profit.

The value of such a reserve depends upon the value of other assets. It will have no value if they are over-valued because no or inadequate provision had been made for depreciation on the assets or doubtful and bad debts in the past. It may be inflated or it may not be in existence at all if other assets are over-valued.

Reserve Account and the Reserve Fund

While Reserve Fund denotes that the sum set aside out of the profits of the business is invested in readily realisable securities, Reserve Account denotes that the sum set aside out of the profits is retained in the business itself and the Reserve Account is represented by the general asset of that concern.

Duties of the Auditor

An auditor need not see the adequacy or inadequacy of a reserve. He need not insist upon its creation if the directors do not wish to provide for such a reserve. However, he may be called upon to advise the directors on the desirability of creating such a reserve or whether the reserve be invested inside or outside the business.

3. Specific Reserve or Provision

Specific reserve is the reserve which is a charge against revenue for the purpose of providing for losses and contingencies which are known or expected at the date of making provision for such a contingency to occur at a future date. It must be created whether there is any profit or not and even if there is a loss. Its exact amount involved is not fixed. It is provided before the profits are distributed.

Objects. Specific reserve may be for the following objects:

(i) To meet a known loss, such as depreciation, heavy repairs, and renewals, etc.

(ii) To meet an expected contingency, such as doubtful debts, discount on sundry debtors, liability for a disputed claim, contingent liability under Workmen's Compensation Act, etc.

(iii) To meet an outstanding liability for expenses already incurred, such as salaries and wages, commission, income tax and other accrued expenses.

Nature. Specific Reserve is not a surplus. It is not represented by any asset. It is not available for distribution amongst the shareholders. Its amount is only an estimate at the date of making a provision. If according to the directors its provision is in excess of the need the excess amount may be treated as reserve. It is deducted from the assets as in the case of depreciation, Reserve for Bad and Doubtful Debts, etc. Reserves for outstanding liabilities are shown on the Liabilities side of the Balance Sheet. Both General Reserve and Specific Reserve are known to the accountancy profession in modern times as Reserve and Provisions respectively.

Distinction between "General" and "Specific" Reserves or Reserve and Provision

1. While "Reserve" or General reserve is an appropriation of profits provision or specific reserve is a charge against profits.

2. General Reserve is created by debiting Profit and Loss Appropriation Account for the redemption of a known liability or to strengthen the liquid resources of the Company or for the equalization of dividends or for the redemption of debentures, etc. A Provision or Specific Reserve is made by debiting the Profit contingency or expected loss, e.g., Provision for Bad and Doubtful Debts or Provision for Depreciation, etc.
3. General Reserve is created without taking into consideration the actual amount required except in the case of redemption of debentures when a definite sum is set aside. A Provision of specific reserve is made to a definite amount and, therefore, a definite sum is set aside every year to meet the known contingency.
4. In General Reserve, the standing credit balance may be carried to Profit and Loss Account or may be distributed amongst the shareholders except in the case of Debenture Redemption Reserve which cannot be touched before the debentures are redeemed when it is carried to General Reserve Account. Provision Account is debited when the loss occurs.
5. General reserve is usually shown on the liability side of the Balance Sheet as it is not Specific Reserve. The provision or specific reserve is generally shown of the assets side of the Balance Sheet by way of deduction from the Asset concerned, e.g., Reserve for Doubtful Debts is deducted from the Sundry Debtors Account.
6 Making of a General Reserve is discretionary and is matter of financial prudence except, (a) when the articles of the company so provide; or (b) in case of companies of special nature, e.g., in the case of a banking company where the Banking Companies Act, 1949, provides that 20 per cent of the profit must be credited to the General Reserve Account every year, or (c) when the terms and conditions of the issue of debentures provide that a Debenture Redemption Fund must be created and so on. Making of provision or specific reserve is compulsory.
7. General Reserve is created not with a view to meeting any definite liability and hence it is left to the Directors to make any provision or not to make any provision at all. The auditor need not interfere except when the articles definitely lay down that the reserve must be created, or according to the term of the issue of the Debentures, a provision for redemption has to be made. In connection with the provision it is the duty of an auditor to see that adequate provision is made to meet the loss. If it has not been done and he has not been able to persuade the directors to made adequate Provision, he should refer the matter in his report. He must, therefore, consult the Articles, Minute book and the recommendations of the Directors.

8. The amount allocated for General Reserve depends upon the profits of the company. Provision or specific reserve does not depend upon the profits of the company.

Kinds of Specific Reserves or Provision

(i) ***Reserve for Bad Debts.*** If the debtors fail to pay the whole or a part of the debt owing by them created to meet any future loss, provision is made for the exact amount. The revenue account is debited and the account of the particular debtors is credited. This procedure may be objected to on the ground that a loss will occur in future and hence the revenue account of the year in which the loss will actually occur, should be debited and not the revenue account of the year in which it is created. However, the future liability may be provided for out of the profits of the current year. It is argued, that the debts were incurred during the current year and hence the reserve for any such bad and doubtful debt should be provided for out of the profits of the current year. The profit and loss account and the balance sheet will not be correct if it is not provided. A fair estimate formed on the basis of past experience, should be made about the amount of the future loss and expense. Adjustment should be made when the actual loss occurs.

This is not the case with accrued expenses which have already been incurred and the amount ought to have been paid during the current year in order to show a correct statement of profit made or loss suffered during the year. It is not the duty of the auditor to see the adequacy or inadequacy of reserves. However, if he thinks that the reserve is inadequate and he cannot bring round the client to raise the amount, he may refer the matter in his report. If no or inadequate provision for bad and doubtful debts has been made a balance sheet cannot be said to exhibit a true and fair view of the state of affairs of a company.

(ii) ***Reserve for Discount on Debtors and Creditors.*** In some business houses, it is customary that when the debtors make payment within the prescribed period, a certain amount of discount is allowed to them. When making payment to creditors, a business house earns discount at the date of closing the books, the book debts shown may not be worth the amount mentioned as some discount will have to be allowed to the debtors. Hence the debts should not be shown at their book value but on the actual amount realisable from that. The balance sheet will not show the correct position of the concern if this is not done. Therefore, discount payable to the debtors should be deducted from the total debts and net realizable figures should be shown in the balance sheet. Some accountants argue that it is not necessary that provision should be made for discount at the close of the year as the debtors may not take advantage of the discount and thus the full amount may be realized. A cash discount is granted to the debtors who make payment before the due date. Hence the year in which such payment is made should bear the loss as that year has taken advantage of the cash payment. Both the arguments appear to be sound. However, as an auditor has to certify the sundry debtors to be correct, he has to show the net worth of such debtors, i.e., whatever amount is expected to be realised at the date of the balance sheet. The balance sheet will not represent the correct state of affairs of the concern if such a reserve is not provided. If it is decided to provide for discount on debtors, the amount can be calculated on the basis of past experience. The discount should be calculated on the debtors after deducting Bad Debts Reserve from the total debtors. The auditor should see that if no reserve for discount on debtors has been provided for in the past, it should not be done during the current year. Otherwise such a step will affect the comparison of the profit and loss accounts of the two periods.

4. Sinking Fund

Objects

The objects of Sinking Fund are as follows:

1. to reduce a liability, e.g., redemption of debentures or repayment of a loan, or
2. to replace a wasting asset, e.g., a mine; or
3. to replace a depreciation asset; or
4. to renew a lease, etc.

Definitions

1. Lancaster. ''Any fund which is created by the regular investment of such an amount as, with compound interest earned thereon will accumulate to a given sum at the end of a stated period."

2. Binnie and Manning. "A Sinking Fund is a form of specific reserve set aside for the redemption of a long-term debt or the replacement of a wasting or a depreciation asset."

The main purpose of creating a Sinking fund is to have a certain sum of money accumulated for a future date by setting aside a certain sum of money every year. It is a kind of specific Reserve.

Method of Creation

The Sinking Fund is created by the following methods:

1. By debiting the profit and loss account every year. This is done with a certain sum of money inverted in gilt ledged securities to ensure the safety of capital and a regular rate of interest. Its object is to provide against a loss which should naturally fall on revenue, e.g., in the case of a Depreciation Sinking Fund. It is a charge against profit. Provision must be made for such a fund.

2. By debiting the Profit and Loss Appropriation Account every year. It is done with a certain sum of money which is vested in gilt-edged securities. Its object is the reduction of a liability or repayment of a liability. It is created by allocation of profits.

Investment of Sinking Fund

Whatever the object or the method of creating sinking fund may be, a certain sum of money is invested every year in such a way that with compound interest, the exact amount will be available to wipe off the liability or replace the wasting asset or to meet the loss. The amount to be invested every year may be known from the compound interest annuity tables. Alternatively, an endowment policy may be taken out which matures on the date when the amount required will be paid by the insurance company. Thus a definite amount will be available. In the case of investment of funds in securities the exact amount may not be available on account of fall in the value of securities. The following steps should be taken if it is decided to take out a policy.

(i) Profit and Loss Account should be debited with the amount of the annual premium.

(ii) A Sinking Fund Policy Account should be debited each year with the amount of the premium and a Sinking Fund Account credited, the respective balances being included in the Balance Sheet.

Money will have to be borrowed or certain assets will have to be sold to repay the loan to redeem the debentures at the time of maturity if no provision is made to meet the liability or the loss. Therefore, it is advisable to set aside a part of the profits, when it is desired to redeem a liability or to charge the revenue account every year to meet a loss. Provision for depreciation for the wasting asset should be made by debiting the revenue account as it represents provision for the depreciation of the asset.

The Profit and Loss Appropriation Account is debited when any provision is made for the redemption of debentures or to repay the loans. It is not a charge against the revenue account. It is an allocation of the profits for the redemption of the debentures. If any profit is made on selling the investments representing the Sinking Fund, it should be transferred to General Reserve. If any loss is incurred, it may be debited to Profit and Loss Account.

Redemption of a Liability and Replacement of an asset

1. While provision for the former is made out of the divisible profits it is made by debiting the revenue account in the latter case.

2. After the liability is redeemed, the Sinking Fund is no longer required and as it is the undistributed profit, it may be distributed to the shareholders or may be transferred to the General Reserve Account. In replacement of asset the Sinking Fund no longer exists as it is transferred to the original assets, to close that asset account.

3. After the expiry of the period, the gilt-edged securities are sold and the cash so realised is applied for the payment of the liability or debentures. In the case of replacement of the asset, the cash realised by the sale of the securities is used to replace the existing asset.

Duties of an Auditor

Though there is no legal obligation to create a Sinking Fund to meet a liability on a loan or debenture, but it is incumbent to do so if the Articles of Association of a company or the Debenture Trust Deed lay down that such a reserve should be created. In such a case it is the auditor's duty to see that such a provision is made accordingly. If he fails to do so, he will be held liable as was decided in the case of *Davar Sons Ltd.* v. *M.S. Krishanaswami* (1952). Sometimes the Articles are silent in regard to such a provision, but Sinking Fund has to be created for the redemption of debentures according to the terms of the issue of debentures. Referring to the Debenture Trust Deed, the auditor should not only see that Sinking Fund is created but that adequate provision is made every year. Investment against Sinking Fund should be clearly marked in the Balance Sheet to distinguish them from ordinary investments.

4. Capital Reserve

What is Capital Reserve?

The term "Capital Reserve" has been defined in a negative way in Part III of Schedule VI to the Companies Act. It has been defined as "any reserve which cannot legally be distributed amongst the shareholders". But Capital Reserve may be distributed amongst the shareholders under certain circumstances. It is just like a General Reserve except that it is *generally* not distributable amongst the shareholders and that is not created by debiting the Profit and Loss Appropriation Account.

Reserve Capital v/s Capital Reserve

Reserve capital denotes the uncalled capital which the shareholders cannot be called upon to pay unless the company goes into liquidation. According to Section 99 of the Companies Act, "A limited company may, by special resolution, determine that any portion of its share capital which has not already been called up, shall not be capable of being called up except in the event and for the purposes of the company being wound up, and thereupon that a portion of its share capital shall not be capable of being called up except in that event and for these purposes." Reserve Capital is also known as Reserve Liability.

Profits of Capital Nature

Capital reserve is created out of following profits of a capital nature :

1. If there has been an appreciation in the value of a fixed asset, the difference between the book value and the appreciated value is transferred to Capital Reserve provided other assets have been revalued and necessary adjustment has been made.
2. If a fixed asset is sold for a higher price than its book value is not credited to the revenue account but is transferred to Capital Reserve Account as it is not regular profit.

3. Premiums received on the issue of shares and debentures.
4. Profit made on the Redemption of debentures in the market at a discount.
5. The balance standing to the credit of Forfeited Shares Account after such shares have been re-issued.
6. Profits of an exceptional nature which have not been earned in the regular course of business.
7. Profit made in purchasing a business, i.e., when the purchase price is less than the net assets acquired.
8. Profit earned prior to incorporation of a limited company.
9. Any profits including revenue profits, which are not represented by liquid assets or which cannot be distributed amongst the shareholders according to the Article of Association of a Company.
10. Asset Replacement Reserve Fund.

These profits are either not earned in the regular course of business or are prohibited to be distributed amongst the shareholders. They are set aside to strengthen the financial position of the company or to meet capital losses. They are carried either to Capital Reserve Account or to Capital Reserve Fund according to whether the amount is retained in the business or is invested in securities respectively. If such a course is not resorted to, the capital reserve may be utilized in the following ways:

1. Issue of Bonus Shares subject to Articles of Association of the company; or
2. Writing of intangible assets, such as Goodwill, Preliminary Expenses, Cost of the Issue of Debentures; or
3. The Premium received on the issue of shares, though credited to Capital Reserve Account, may be utilised only for the purposes mentioned in Section 78 of the Companies Act, i.e.
   - (i) In paying up un-issued shares of the company to be issued to members of the company as fully paid bonus shares; or
   - (ii) in writing off Preliminary Expenses; or
   - (iii) in writing off commission or expenses or discount, etc., on the issue of debentures or shares; or
   - (iv) in providing for the premium payable on the redemption of redeemable preference shares or debentures.

Duties of Auditor about Capital Reserve

1. Seeing that those capital profits which have been transferred to Capital Reserve Account are really surplus of capital over the assets and liabilities;

2. Checking that the capital reserve is utilized according to the Articles and law;
3. Growing that capital profits may be transferred to revenue account and distributed or utilised in writing off previous losses provided it is made clear in the accounts to distinguish such a profit from ordinary trading profits of the business, as was decided in the cases of *Foster* v. *The New Trinidad Lake Asphalte Company Ltd.* (1901) and *Lubbock* vs. *The British Bank of South America Ltd.* (1882). They may be distributed as dividends only,
   (i) when the Articles of Association permit such a distribution;
   (ii) the surplus is realised; and
   (iii) such surplus remains after a revaluation of other assets.
4. Showing Capital Reserve distinctly in the Balance Sheet and distinguishing it from the Revenue Reserve Account. Showing any additions and deductions since the last Balance Sheet.
5. Seeing that capital reserve may be invested either in he business itself or may be invested outside the business in easily realisable securities.

5. Secret Reserve

Secret Reserve has been defined as "any reserve which is not apparent on the face of the Balance Sheet." It is called "Hidden Reserve" or "Internal Reserve" or "Inner Reserve". According to Simon & Kareenbrook, "Secret Reserves are an under statement of assets or an over-statement of liabilities accompanied by a corresponding under-statement of capital." It represents the surplus of assets over liabilities and capital. It is not disclosed although the existence of such a reserve may be inferred from an intelligent perusal of the accounts of the concern even though the amount cannot be ascertained. However, it does appear in the ledger. It is created usually by Joint-Stock Companies especially the banking, insurance and financial concerns. Its creation may not always be looked upon with suspicion.

Methods of Creating Secret Reserve

1. Writing down the assets much below their cost or market value, such as investments, stock-in-hand, land and buildings, plant and machinery, etc.
2. Not writing up the value of an asset, the price of which has permanently gone up.
3. Providing more reserve than necessary for bad and doubtful debts or discount on sundry debtors.
4. Providing excessive depreciation on fixed assets.
5. Writing down the goodwill to a nominal value.

6. Omitting some of the assets altogether from the balance sheet.
7. Charging capital expenditure to revenue account and thus showing the value of the asset to be less than its actual value.
8. Over-valuing the liabilities.
9. Inclusion of fictitious facilities.
10. Showing contingent liabilities as real liabilities.
11. Grouping dissimilar items on the liabilities side of the balance sheet, e.g., reserves, provisions and creditors, under a general heading, as "Sundry Creditors and other Credit Balances."

Objects of Creating Secret Reserve

1. To meet Extraordinary loss. The reserve may be used in future to meet any extraordinary loss without disclosing this fact to the shareholders or the outsiders. If a very heavy loss occurs and consequently no dividend is declared, the value of the shares will go down in the market. In case of a banking company, there may be a "rush" on the bank for withdrawals and the bank might go into liquidation.

2. To withhold information of the progress of the company from trade competitors. If the true earning position of the company is shown, it is possible that more rival companies may come into the field and compete with it, thus bringing down its profits.

3. To be utilized in a lean year. This is a case where the company has made an abnormal profit in a year and when it is intended that the whole of it should not be distributed.

4. To utilize profit. The profits which have been utilised for the payment of dividend, remain in the business and increase the working capital and financial stability of the concern.

5. To equalise the payment of dividends.

Dangers or Objections against Secret Reserve

1. The balance sheet does not show the correct financial position of the concern. Though this objection appears to be valid the position of the company is *not shown better than* what it actually is. If it is shown better than what it is, then there can be a charge of fraud or manipulation. Therefore, the objection is feasible. The balance sheet does not show a true and fair view of the state of affairs of the company as is expected under the Companies Act, if Secret Reserve is created.

2. The shareholders do not get their due share of the profit. This may not always be correct. The shareholders are entitled to the reserve later on. But if a shareholder ceases to be so by selling his shares, he loses the profit he would have got, had the Secret Reserve not been created.

3. Value of the shares goes down in the market. This may not happen if the dividend paid is the same as in the previous year.

4. Low dividends and supposed bad position of the company may lead the company into crisis. This is so especially in case of banking concern. Secret reserve may not be created when the profits are insufficient. Thus the question of "supposed bad position" will not arise.

5. Speculation encouraged. By creating Secret Reserve and thus lowering the dividend, the directors may indulge in speculation in the shares of the company.

6. Loss in reclamation. If the fixed assets are undervalued for the purpose of creating Secret Reserve, and if there is a fire, the company will not be able to claim the full value of the assets because the insurance company will pay according to the book value of the asset destroyed or damaged and hence cause a loss to the company.

7. Improper use. Secret Reserve may be used improperly by the directors to conceal their own weakness. For example if there has been a loss due to their negligence, such a loss may be drawn upon the Secret Reserve by appreciating the value of an asset which had been under-valued in the past for the purpose of creating Secret Reserve. If the position of the company is worse than it appears from the balance sheet due to the creation of Secret Reserve, the directors' policy of concealment cannot be upheld, *vide Newton* vs. *Birmingham Small Arms Co. Ltd.* (1906). If such a reserve is utilized, the shareholders should not only be informed that such a step has been taken but the amount should also be disclosed to them. This change in the opinion of the accountants is due to the decision in the case of *Rex.* vs. *Kylsant* in 1931. Others argue that if this is done the object of creating a Secret Reserve will be frustrated. If an asset is altogether omitted from the Balance Sheet the auditor might omit to verify the asset and, in course of time, the asset might be spirited away. If, however, it is desired at all to reduce the value of an asset considerably, it may be reduced to a nominal amount rather than omit it altogether from the books of account.

8. Prohibition. According to the Companies Act, except in the case of banking, insurance or finance companies:

(i) The Act requires the full disclosure of the accounts relating to the reserve and provisions.

(ii) The Profit and Loss Account and the balance of a limited company must show a *true and fair* view of the state of affairs of the company. This is possible only when the accounts are not misleading, i.e., there is neither under-statement nor over statement of the assets and liabilities of the company. According to the proforma of the balance sheet prescribed by the Companies Act, it must show the reserves and provisions. Therefore, no secret reserve can be created now except by banking, insurance, electricity, finance companies, etc.

Duties of an Auditor about Secret Reserve

1. In case of Other Companies. The position of the auditor is clear as far as the audit of public companies other than banking, insurance, finance, electricity companies is concerned. He has to disclose the fact that secret reserve has been created. He would be making a false statement if he does not disclose the fact that there is a reserve of such a kind and certifies the balance sheet as showing a *true and fair view* of the state of affairs of the company. It will leave some of the assets under-valued while some of the liabilities are over-valued.

2. In case of Banking Companies etc. In case of companies such as banking companies, etc., the auditor should carefully enquire into the necessity of creating such a reserve. If he finds that it is in the best interest of the company to create a Secret Reserve, and that the amount is reasonable, he need not qualify his report. He may make a statement: "The value of the assets is understated." Such a statement will indicate the existence of a Secret Reserve, but the extent of the reserve will not be shown. If the shareholders so desire, they may eke out the information by putting questions to the directors. The auditor cannot be accused of making a false statement because the statement which he makes does not mislead any person as was decided in the case of *Newton* v. *Birmingham Small Arms Co. Ltd.* (1906) where the learned judge said, "The purpose of the Balance Sheet is primarily to show that the financial position of the company is at least as good as there stated, not to show that it is not or may not be better." Again the Balance Sheet does not show the position of the company as better than what it is. If any person deals with the company, which has created Secret Reserve, on the basis of the Balance Sheet he does not suffer any loss. He may gain if he purchases shares on the strength of such a balance sheet as the intrinsic value of the shares is more than what is indicated by the balance sheet. This argument is sound but the balance sheet does not represent the *true and fair view of the state of affairs* of the company. If the auditor finds that the intention of the directors is to fabricate improper dealings in the shares of the company, he must disclose the fact in his report. A company cannot by its Articles of Association restrain its auditors from reporting to the shareholders the creation of Secret Reserve as was decided in the case quoted above. If any part of a Secret Reserve is utilised by the directors to meet bad and doubtful debts, it must be shown in the Balance Sheet and should not be concealed from the shareholders as was decided in the case of *Shamdasani* v. *Pochkhanwala* in 1927, when their Lordships said: "If any part of secret reserve is availed of to meet bad and doubtful book-debts, it must be revealed in the Balance Sheet and not concealed." To quote from *Lord Kylsant's* case, 1931 "A very heavy or long, protracted utilization of the secret reserves, in order to keep the company going, is a serious matter which ought to be disclosed to the company."

AUDITORS DUTIES

1. Provisions. An auditor should adopt following procedure:

(i) Consider carefully what types of liabilities are likely to exist.

(ii) Examine the various decuments to determine the quantum of claims outstanding against the enterprise.

(iii) Seek assurance from the directors that the adequate provision has been made in the financial statements in respect of all known liabilities.

(iv) Obtain written confirmations from third parties of representations made by the directors.

2. Specific Reserve. The auditor must ascertain whether the reserve is adequate and reasonable having regard to the objects for which it has been created, though the extent of adequacy and reasonableness will differ from business to business.

3. General Reserve. Creation of a General Reserve is not a legal necessity. Only a management endowed with foresight and a sense of judgement will create and maintain it. If reduces the work of an auditors as he has only to ascertain whether the creation of General Reserves is in the interests of the business and that if the company has framed certain rules in this regard, they are duly adhered to. If his advice is solicited on the question of adequacy or reasonableness of the reserve, he may oblige but he should not on his own offer any advice as to creation of reserve.

4. Capital Reserve. The auditor should see capital reserve is invested either in easily realisable securities or may be invested in the business itself. He should check that the capital reserve has been utilised in conformity with the provisions of the Articles of Association of the company. The capital reserve should be shown separately in the Balance Sheet after meeting all adjustments. The auditor should ensure that capital reserve is shown separately in the Balance Sheet and not mixed up with any revenue or general reserve. He should ascertain that it is used only for the writing off capital or abormal losses.

5. Reserve Fund. The auditor should ascertain that a reserve fund is separately shown in the Balance Sheet and that it is represented by earmarked securities or other assets realisable as and when required, at less than the amount of the reserve fund.

6. Sinking Fund. The auditor should see that Sinking Fund has been shown separately in the Balance Sheet. The auditor should familiarise himself with the terms and conditions of creation of a Sinking Fund and ensure that these are being adhered to.

QUESTIONS FOR EXERCISE

1. Distinguish between Reserve and Provision and state your duty as an auditor in relation thereto.
2. Explain different kinds of reserves along with duties of the auditor concerning them.
3. Describe and contrast:
   (a) A Reserve which is a charge against Profits, and
   (b) A Reserve which is an appropriation of Profits.
4. What do you understand by 'Capital Reserves' and 'Revenue Reserves' ? Give illustrations. To what purposes may a capital reserve be applied ?
5. Distinguish between the following:
   (a) A General Reserve and a Specific Reserve.
   (b) Capital Reserve and Revenue Reserve.
6. What do you understand by the following, and what are the duties of an auditor in respect of these ?
   (a) Reserve Fund.
   (b) Specific Reserve.
   (c) Depreciation Fund.
   (d) Sinking Fund.
7. What do you mean by 'Sinking Fund' ? Explain the difference between a Sinking Fund to replace an 'Asset' and a 'Sinking Fund to repay a liability'. What is the duty of an auditor in respect of Sinking Fund ?
8. What is meant by Capital Reserve and Revenue Reserve ? Give illustrations. To what purpose may Capital Reserve by utilized by a joint stock company ?
9. What do you understand by "Secret or Internal Reserves" ? How are they created in the books of a limited company ? Give illustrations. Can such reserves be created under the Companies Act, 1956 ? What are the auditor's duties in this matter ?
10. What are the objects of Secret Reserves ? State how they are created and give a few reasons in support of and against them respectively. Explain the duty of an auditor regarding their verification and disclosure.

13

Auditing of Limited Companies

Today limited companies are carrying on business of a very large scale. The inherent complex nature and constitution of a company necessitates the compulsory audit of its accounts. The shareholders, the real proprietors, are in general the absentee owners of the company. They invest the capital and vest the management and control of the company in the hands of directors. An individual, shareholder is not in a position to ascertain whether the capital invested by him is properly utilised by the directors or misappropriated by them for their private gains. Being in complete control of the company the directors are in a position to misutilise these funds. To prevent this, the law has come to the rescue of the shareholders. It provides adequate protection to them through various provisions, including the compulsory audit of company accounts.

As independent professional auditor, conducts the audit of the books and accounts of the company on behalf of the shareholders by thoroughly examining them and reporting thereon. He disclosed whether the directors are carrying on the affairs of the company well or there is any irregularity on their part. He ensures that the legal provisions have been duly complied with, the Balance Sheet and the Profit and Loss Account have been drawn in the manner required by law and exhibit the true and fair view of the state of financial affairs and earnings of the company. He also ensures that the company did not enter into any business transactions without appropriate sanction or authority. He detects and prevents frauds, errors and other irregularities on the part of the employees of the company. It has been rightly stated that "In fact, an examination of the affairs of the company by an independent agency like the auditor is practically the only safeguard which the shareholders have against the enterprise being carried on in an unbusiness like manner or their money being misapplied or misappropriated without their knowing that it has been so done."[1]

PRELIMINARIES OF AUDIT

An auditor should go through the following preliminaries before he begins his actual work.

1. *Dy. Secretary to Government of India, Ministry of Finance* v. *S. N. Das Gupta.*

1. To see that his appointment is in order. If the auditor has been appointed as the first auditor of the company by the directors before the annual general meeting, he should get a copy of the resolution by the directors about his appointment. If he is appointed in place of a retiring auditor, he should see whether due notice was given to the previous auditor. He should also require from the retiring auditor the circumstances under which he retired. If he is appointed by the shareholders at the annual general meeting he should get a copy of the shareholder' resolution. Within 30 days of his appointment he should inform the registrar whether he has accepted or refused to accept the appointment. If his appointment is casual to fill the vacancy caused by the death of the previous auditor he should get a copy of the minutes of the Board. In case the vacancy was caused by the resignation of the previous auditor, the Board has no power to fill that vacancy.

2. Inspection of the Documents and Books. Before commencing his work the auditor should examine the following documents:

(i) ***Memorandum.*** To see whether the company is carrying in the work according to the object clause of the Memorandum, the issue of the share capital is within the authorised limit.

(ii) ***Articles of Association.*** To ascertain the issue of share capital and its sub-division, the payment of under writing commission and brokerage, and the amount of minimum subscription etc.

(iii) ***Prospectus.*** To examine the prospectus to ascertain all the points which have been mentioned under the Articles of Association.

(iv) ***List of Books.*** He should ask the authorities to give him a list of all the books of accounts, statistical and statutory books maintained by the company. A limited company is under statutory obligation to maintain the following:

1. Register of investments which are held in the name of its nominees [Section 49(7)].
2. Register of mortgages and charges (Section 142).
3. Register of members (Section 150).
4. Register and Index of Debenture holders (Section 152).
5. Foreign Register (Sections 157 and 158).
6. Register of Contracts with Companies and Firms in which the Directors are interested (Sections 297, 299 and 301).
7. Register of Directors, Managing Agents, Secretaries etc. (Section 303).
8. Register of Director's shareholding (Section 307).

3. Inspection of Contracts. The auditor should examine the contracts which have been entered into between a company and parties, e.g.:

(i) Contracts with the vendors of any property.

(ii) Contracts with the brokers and underwriters.

(iii) Contracts with the promoters for the preliminary expenses, etc.

Brief particulars about such contracts are given in the prospectus of a Company. The auditor should see that the statement of particulars is correct and transactions relating to such contracts have been properly recorded in the books of account.

4. Study of previous year's Balance Sheet and Auditor's Report. When the auditor is appointed in place of a retiring auditor, he should examine the balance sheet of the last year to be familiar with any relevant matter raised by the previous auditor. He should ensure that the objections or qualifications raised in the previous audit report have been duly met by the company. He may also examine the director's report to the members containing the recommendations of the directors in respect of the appropriations of profits made last year.

5. Obtaining a schedule of books and persons handling them. The auditor should get a list of the persons employed to maintain accounts of the company and also books maintained by them. This helps him in the successful conduct of the audit whenever he needs some information and explanations.

6. Study of internal check system. This will enable him to note down the shortcomings of the accounting system and the procedure followed by the company.

7. Certificate of Incorporation and Commencement of business. The auditor should examine the certificate and see that the company has commenced business after it is granted. A public limited company is not allowed to commence business unless a certificate entitling the company to commence business is not granted. A private company is entitled to commence business and exercise borrowing powers immediately after incorporation.

INSPECTION OF DOCUMENTS, BOOKS AND REGISTERS

Documents: 1. Memorandum of Association

1. Under the provisions of Section 13 of the Company Act, the Memorandum of every company shall state:

(a) the name of the company with 'Limited' as the last word of the name in the case of a public limited company and with 'Private Limited' as the last words of the name in the case of a private limited company;

(b) the state in which the registered office of the company is to be situated;

(c) in the case of a company in existence immediately before commencement of the Companies (Amendment) Act, 1956, the objects of the company.

(d) in the case of a company formed after such commencement:

   (i) the main objects of the company to be persued by the company on its incorporation and objects incidental or ancillary to the attainment of the main objects.

   (ii) other objects of the company not included in sub-section (i); and (e) in the case of companies (other than trading corporations), with objects not confined to one State, the States to whose territories the objects extend.

2. The Memorandum of a company limited by shares or guarantee shall also state that the liability of its members is limited.

3. The Memorandum of a company limited by guarantee shall also state that each member undertakes to contribute to the assets of the company in the event of its being wound up while he is a member or within one year after he ceases to be a member, for payment of the debts and liabilities of the company, or of such debts and liabilities of the company as may have been contracted before he ceases to be a member, as the case may be, and of the costs, charges and expenses of winding up, and for adjustment of the rights of the contributors among themselves, such amount as may be required, not exceeding a specified amount.

4. In the case of a company having a Share Capital—

(a) unless the company is an unlimited company, the Memorandum shall also state amount of Share Capital with which the company is to be registered and the division thereof into shares of a fixed amount;

(b) no subscriber of the Memorandum shall take less than one share; and

(c) each subscriber of the Memorandum shall write against his name the number of shares he takes.

Under Section 17, a special resolution should be passed for alteration of Memorandum so as to change the place of its registered office from one state to another or with respect to the objects of the Company the alteration shall not take effect until and except in so for as it is confirmed by the Company Law Board on petition. It has to be registered within three months from the date of the order and be filed by the company with the Registrar as provided by Section 18 of the Act.

Auditor's Duties

1. Examine the 'Object Clause' of the Memorandum to ensure that the company is carrying on the work as specified.
2. Check the 'Capital Clause' and see that the issue of share capital is within the 'Authorised Capital'.
3. Verify and trace the Authorised Capital that has been increased according to law.

4. Check that the Memorandum has been altered, within the provision of Sections 17 and 18 of the Companies Act.

2. Articles of Association

(i) ***Section 26.*** Every company is required to have the articles of Association. The Articles of Association of a company limited by shares may adopt all or any of the regulations of Table A in Schedule I. These contain regulations to control the internal administration of the company, viz., regulation for day-to-day work, relationship between its members, their rights and responsibilities, etc. The Articles of Association may be altered by a special resolution as and when necessary, subject to the provisions of the Companies Act and to the conditions contained in its Memorandum.

(ii) ***Section 30.*** The Articles will be printed and divided into paragraphs, numbered consecutively and signed by each subscriber of the Memorandum of Association (who shall add his address, description and occupation, if any) in the presence of at least one witness who shall attest the signature and shall likewise add his address, description and occupation, if any.

(iii) ***Section 31.*** A special resolution subject to the provisions of this Act and to the conditions contained in its Memorandum, has to be passed to alter the Articles of Association when such an alteration has been approved by the Central Government.

A printed copy of the Articles should be filed by the company within one month of the date of receipt of the order of approval.

(iv) ***Section 33.*** Thus, the Memorandum of the company, its articles., if any, and the agreement, if any, which the company proposes to enter into with any individual for appointment as its managing or whole-time director or manager, shall be presented to the Registrar of the State in which the registered office of the company is situated.

(v) ***Section 36.*** Memorandum and Articles shall, when registered, bind the company and the members thereof to the same extent as if they respectively had been signed by the company and by each member and contained covenants on its and his part to observe all the provisions of the Memorandum and of the Articles. All moneys payable by any member to the company under the Memorandum or Articles shall be a debt due from him to the company.

Auditor's Duties

He should examine the Articles of Association of the company for the following matters.

(i) Issue of Share Capital.
(ii) Calls on shares.
(iii) Calls in advance.
(iv) Calls in arrear.

(v) Forfeiture and re-issue of shares.

(vi) Transmission of shares.

(vii) Payment of commission on shares.

(viiii) Rights of various classes of shareholders.

(ix) Appointment, remuneration, rights and duties of Managing Director or Manager.

(x) Appointment, remuneration, qualification, shares, rights and duties of directors.

(xi) Alteration of Share Capital.

(xii) Dividends and Reserves.

(xiii) Borrowing powers of the company and directors.

(xiv) Appointment, rights and duties of the auditor.

(xv) Account and Audit of the Company.

(xvi) Under-writing of Shares.

(xvii) Meetings and their procedure.

(xviii) How to inform Shareholders.

(xix) Voting powers of the Shareholders.

(xx) Payment of interest out of capital.

(xxi) How far Table A has been followed in framing the Articles of Association?

In the case of *Leeds Estate Building and Investment Society Ltd.* v. *Shepherd* (1887), it was held that an auditor has no defence with him to say that he could not see the Articles of Association when he knew of their existence.

3. Prospectus

Section 56 of the Companies Act provides matters to be stated and reports to be set out in Prospectus. A Prospectus is issued with the objective of inviting public to purchase the shares of the company. All matters dealt with above in the Articles of Association are found in the Prospectus.

Auditor's Duties. He should examine the prospectus for the following matter:

(i) Amount of capital to be issued, classification of shares and rights of shareholders attached therewith.

(ii) Amount payable on allotment and calls,

(iii) Amount of minimum subscription,

(iv) Particulars of any contract entered into with the vendors for the purchase of business,

(v) Amount payable for underwriting commission on shares or debentures,

(vi) Amount of preliminary expenses paid or payable,

(vii) Qualifications, remuneration, etc., of Managers,

(viii) Appointment, remuneration, etc., of Managers,

(ix) Particulars of any material contracts entered into within two years of the date of issue of the Prospectus.

4. Books and Registers

Section 209 of Companies Act stipulates that every company shall keep at its registered office proper Book of Account with respect to:

(i) all sums of money received and expended by the company and the matters in respect of which the receipt and expenditure take place;

(ii) all sales and purchases of goods by the company;

(iii) the assets and liabilities of the company; and

(iv) in the case of a company pertaining to any class of companies engaged in production, processing manufacturing or mining activities, such particulars relating to utilization of material or labour or to other items of cost as may be prescribed if such class of companies is required by the Central Government to include such particulars in the Books of Account.

All or any of the Books of Account may be kept at such other place in India as the Board of Directors may decide. When the Board of Directors so decides the company shall, within seven days of the decision, file with the Registrar a notice in writing giving the full address of that other place.

Where a company has a Branch Office, whether in or outside India, proper Books of Account relating to the transactions effected at the Branch Office should be kept at that office and proper summarized returns, made up-to-date at intervals of not more than three months, should be sent by the Branch Office to the company at the registered office or the other place referred to earlier.

For the purposes of sub-sections (1) and (2), proper books of account shall not be deemed to be kept with respect to the matters specified therein,—

(i) if there are not kept such books as are necessary to give a true and fair view of the state of affairs of the company or branch office, as the case may be, and to explain its transaction; and

(ii) if such books are not kept on accrual basis and according to the double entry system of accounting.

During business hours of Books of Account and other books and papers shall be open to inspection by any director.

The Books of Account of every company relating to a period of not less than eight years immediately preceding the current year shall be preserved in good order. If a company incorporated less than eight years before the current year, the Books of Account for the entire period preceding the current year shall be preserved.

The Managing Director or Manager is held responsible for maintaining and preserving the Books of Account. If there is no Managing Director or Manager, the Board of Directors of the company will be responsible for maintaining the books. In default anyone responsible will be punishable with imprisonment for a term which may extend to six months or with fine which may extend to one thousand rupees or with both.

Kinds of Books and Registers

1. Register of Members. Under section 150 every company will keep in one or more books a Register of its Members and enter therein the following particulars:

(i) the name and address, and the occupations, if any, of each member;

(ii) the shares held by each member, the amount paid thereon, etc.

(iii) the date at which each person was entered in the register as a member; and

(iv) the date at which any person ceased to be a member:

Provided that where the company has converted any of its shares into stock and has given notice of the conversion to the Registrar, the register shall show the amount of stock held by each of the members converted instead of the shares so converted which were previously held by him.

In case of default the company and every office of the company who is in default shall be punishable with fine which may extend to fifty rupees for every day during which the default continues.

2. Register of Charges. Under section 143 every company is required to keep at its registered office a Register of Charges and enter therein all charges on the undertaking or on any property of the company giving in each case:

(i) a short description of property charged,

(ii) the amount of the charge, and

(iii) except in the case of securities to bearer, the names of the persons entitled to the charges.

If any officer of the company knowingly omits, or wilfully authorizes or permits the omission of any entry required to be made, he shall be punishable with fine which may extend to five hundred rupees.

3. Minute Books. Under section 193, every company shall prepare minutes of all proceedings of every meeting of its Board of Directors or of every committee of the Board, to be kept by making within thirty days of the conclusion of every such meeting concerned, entries thereof in Minute Books with their pages consecutively numbered. Minute Books are statutory books, and are of three types:

(i) Shareholders, Minute Books to record the proceedings of Shareholders Meetings,

(ii) Directors, Minute Books to record the proceedings of the Meetings of the Board of Directors.

(iii) Committees' Minute Books to record the proceedings of the Meetings of the committees appointed by the Board of Directors.

It was held in the case of *Hearts of Oak Insurance Co. Ltd.* v. *Flower,* 1935, the Minute Books should be in the form of a bound book and not loose sheets that can be removed or substituted. The Minutes recorded in the Minute Books have to be certified by the Chairman of the meeting concerned. The minutes of proceedings of a meeting shall not be attached to any other book by pasting or otherwise.

The Chairman shall exercise an absolute discretion in regard to the inclusion or non-inclusion of any matter in the minutes on the grounds specified. In case of default every officer of the company who is in default shall be punishable with fine which may extend to fifty rupees.

The auditor shall inspect the *Shareholders' Minute Book* to examine the following matters:

(i) Issue of shares at a discount;

(ii) Issue of Redeemable Preference Shares;

(iii) Issue of further shares to persons other than the existing equity shareholders;

(iv) Alteration of Share Capital;

(v) Adoption of Annual Accounts;

(vi) Declaration of Dividends;

(vii) Appointment and remuneration of Auditors;

(viii) Appointment and remuneration of Directors;

(ix) Increasing the powers of the Board of Directors;

(x) Increasing the remuneration of Directors, with the sanction of the Central Government;

(xi) Investments in Shares and Debentures of other companies;

(xii) Reduction of Share Capital;

(xiii) Payment of interest out of capital;

(xiv) Authorizing remuneration to an ordinary Director on the basis of a percentage of the net profit;

(xvi) Appointing a Director, his relative or associate to an office of profit under the company;

(xvii) Granting any loans, etc., to a company under the same management; etc.

The auditor will examine by *Directors' Minute Book* to obtain confirmation of the following:

(i) Issue of capital and allotment of shares;
(ii) Calls made by the company;
(iii) Forfeiture of shares;
(iv) Approval of contracts;
(v) Adoption of Annual Accounts;
(vi) Appointment, remuneration, rights and duties, etc. of Managers Auditors, etc.;
(vii) Sanction of borrowing powers;
(viii) Exercising of borrowing powers;
(ix) Declaration of interim dividend and recommendation for final dividend;
(x) Purchase of Fixed Assets;
(xi) Transfer to General Reserves;
(xii) Alteration of Articles;
(xiii) Payment of travelling expenses to officials and Directors of the company;
(xiv) Redemption of Debentures; etc.

4. Register of Directors, etc. Under section 303 of the Companies Act, every company is required to keep at its registered office a register of its Directors, Managing Director, Manager and Secretary containing their names, addresses, nationality, father's or husband's name in full, occupation and his business or occupation, if any.

In case of the company and every officer of the company in default shall be punishable which may extend to fifty rupees for everyday during which the default continues.

5. Register of Directors' Shareholdings, etc. Under section 307, a separate register has to be maintained by every company to record the number, description and amount of any shares or debentures of the company or any other body corporate being the company's subsidiary or holding company, or a subsidiary of the company's holding company, which are held by him or in trust for him or of which he has any right to become the holder whether on payment or not.

6. Register of Contracts, Companies and Firms in which Directors are interested. Under section 301, every company is required to keep one or more registers in which separate particulars of all contracts or arrangements, e.g., dates of contracts and arrangements, names of the parties, principal terms and conditions and the date of the meeting of the Board of Directors on which the contract is considered, will be entered. The auditor has to see whether the register is kept as per requirement of the Act and is in order.

7. Index of Members. Under section 151, every company having more than fifty members shall, unless the Register of Members is in such a form as in itself to constitute an index, keep an index (which may be in the form of card index) of the names of the members of the company and shall, within fourteen days after the date on which any alteration is made in the Register of members, make the necessary alteration in the index.

The index will contain a sufficient indication to enable the entries relating to each member and will be kept at the same place at which the Register of Members will be kept. In case of default, the company and every officer who is in default, shall be punishable with fine which may extend up to fifty rupees.

8. Register and index of Debenture-holders. Under section 152, every company shall keep in one or more books a Register of the holders of its Debentures and enter therein the particulars relating to the names, addresses, occupation, etc., about the Debentures-holders.

In case of default, the company and every officer of the company shall be punished with fine which may extend to fifty rupees.

9. Register of all investments made by the Company in shares. Under section 372(6), every company shall keep a Register of Investments made by it in shares of any other body or bodies corporate showing names of such corporate bodies in which investment has been made, date of investment, date on which body corporate came in the same group and the names of all body corporate in the same group as investing company.

10. Register of Loans. Under section 370(1C) of the Companies Act, every lending company shall keep a register in respect of loans made, guarantees given and the date on which the loans have been made.

11. Register of Public Deposit. Under section 58(A) every company shall maintain a separate register in which all public deposits are to be recorded.

12. Register of Investment. Under section 49 of the Companies Act, it is provided that "all investments of a company shall be made and held in its own name." If the company's nominee or director in another company on its behalf and is required to hold qualification shares, they may be held jointly in the name of the company and such person. A separate register shall be maintained by the company for such investment.

5. Contracts

The auditor should examine the following contracts entered into between a company and other parties, e.g.,

(i) Contracts with the vendors of any property.

(ii) Contracts with the brokers and underwriters.

(iii) Contracts with the promoters for the preliminary expenses, etc.

Usually, brief particulars about such contracts are given in the Prospectus of a Company. The auditor should see that the Statement of Particulars is correct and transactions relating to such contracts have been properly recorded in the Books of Accounts.

6. Previous Year's Balance Sheet and Auditor's Report

If the auditor is appointed in place of retiring auditor, he should examine the Balance Sheet of the last year and also the Report of the auditor appointed last year to be familiar with any relevant matter raised by the previous auditor. He should ensure that the objections or qualifications raised in the previous Audit Report have been duly met by the company. He may also examine the Director's Report to the members containing the recommendations of the Directors in respect of the appropriation of profits made last year.

7. Schedule of Books and Persons Handling them

The auditor should get a list of the persons employed to maintain accounts of the company and also of books maintained by them. It will help him in the successful conduct of the audit whenever he needs some information and explanations, and difficulties can, thus, be met easily.

8. Internal Check System

The auditor shall obtain a detailed statement from the Directors of the Company about the system of the internal check in operation to enable him to note down the shortcomings of the accounting system and the procedure followed by the company.

9. Certificate of Incorporation and commencement of business

A public limited company is not allowed to commence business without a certificate entitling the company to commence business. A private company is entitled to commence business and exercise borrowing power immediately after incorporation. The auditor should examine the certificate and see that the company has commenced business after it is granted.

PRELIMINARY EXPENSES

What are preliminary expenses ?

Preliminary Expenses are those which are incurred in the creation, flotation or incorporation of a company. These are sometimes called promotion, Flotations or Foundation Expenses. These may be written off by and by in subsequent years, although it is not obligatory for a company to do so unless its regulations lay it otherwise. If share capital or debentures are issued in subsequent years, expenses incurred in the issue of such shares and debentures are not to be debited to Preliminary Expenses Account but are debited to 'Capital Issue Expenses Account'. These are shown separately from the Preliminary Expenses. The Capital Issue Expenses Account is also written off in subsequent years or written off against the premium, if any, if the shares have been issued at a premium. If any loss has been incurred in the first year of the life of the company, it should to be debited to preliminary expenses. After the company has begun to earn revenue, the current expenditure should not be debited to preliminary expenses.

Types of Preliminary Expenses

1. Legal expenses incurred for drafting the Memorandum and Articles of Association, the Prospectus, and the Contracts entered into with the vendors, managing agents, etc.
2. Fees of accounts, the valuers, surveyors, engineers, etc.
3. Stamp duty, registration fees, etc., which is according to nominal capital.
4. Company sales's, Statutory Books and Original Books of Accounts.
5. Cost of printing, stamping, etc., of the memorandum of and articles of association, prospectus, debentures and debenture trust deeds, if any, share certificates, etc.
6. Expenses incurred in entering into agreement, together with stamps duties thereon.
7. Cost of advertising the Prospectus, etc.

Auditor's duty in connecting with the Preliminary Expenses

(i) Only expenses of incorporation. The auditor should check that only those expenses are debited to preliminary expenses account which are connected with the incorporation of the company. In order to show more profit in the very first year of the life of the company, the directors may debit the ordinary revenue expenses to Preliminary Expenses. According to the case of *Baidya Nath Biswas* v. *Emperor* (1935), the preliminary expenses are not to be debited to Profit and Loss Account of the first year because the benefit of such expenses will be derived by subsequent years also and, therefore, it is but fair that those years must also bear the burden. Moreover, if the very first year of its incorporation is debited with such expenses, the result will be that very little or no profit will be left for distribution amongst the shareholders. The shares, therefore, might be quoted at a discount at the Stock Exchange. Again, these expenses are of non-recurring nature. To avoid all these consequences, the preliminary expenses are written off within three, five, or seven years.

The auditor should vouch as usual the cash payments in connection with these expenses by referring to vouchers, receipts, bills, etc. He should also examine the contract with the vendors of the business to find out whether they have to bear the preliminary expenses. If this is the case, their account should be debited with the amount. Sometimes the preliminary expenses are born by the promoters and sometimes they are divided amongst the vendors, promoters and the new company. He should, therefore, see that such expenses are properly allocated. For this purpose he should refer to various contracts, agreements, correspondence, etc.

If the company has issued prospectus or a statement in lieu of prospectus and has stated the amount of preliminary expenses therein, the auditor should see that this amount is not exceeded. If the preliminary expenses have exceeded the amount stated in the prospectus, he should see whether the shareholders have sanctioned the excess amount.

The auditor should see that brokerage, commission, etc. for selling or underwriting or for placing shares is not debited to preliminary expenses but is shown as a separate item on the assets side of the Balance Sheet as per Schedule VI, Part 1 of the Companies Act.

Premiums received on the issue of shares may be utilised in wiping off the preliminary expenses (Section 78).

In the case of banking companies, the Banking Companies Act of 1949, prohibits the payment of dividends until all the Preliminary expenses incurred have been written off.

The statutory report should set out, *inter alia,* an account or estimates of the preliminary expenses of the company.

PUBLIC DEPOSITS

In order to protect the interest of depositors, two new sections, 58A and 58B, have been added to the Companies Act by the Companies (Amendment) Act in 1974, which empower the Central Government to frame rules in consultation with the Reserve Bank of India, regarding the terms and conditions for inviting or accepting deposits either from its members or the public. Some such terms and conditions are given below:

1. A company, whether a private or a public company, is prohibited to invite or accept public deposits or from its members except in accordance with the rules prescribed by the Central Government in consultation with the Reserve Bank.
2. If, however, it is allowed to invite deposits, it should
   - (i) issue an advertisement inviting deposits from the public and its members;
   - (ii) advertise in the prescribed form;
   - (iii) receive deposits in conformity with the provisions of the Companies Act, namely relating to the issue of a prospectus.

The deposits which have already been made, before the commencement of the Companies (Amendment) Act, 1974, under the directions of the Reserve Bank in November, 1972, must be repaid in accordance with the terms of such deposits unless renewed according to the new rules framed under the Companies (Amendment) Act, 1974, within 30 days. In case of the officers in default heavy penalty and even imprisonment up to five years may be imposed. The penalty will not be less than twice the amount equal to the amount not repaid.

Section 43 MA of the Reserve Bank of India Act, lays down that it would be duty of the auditor of the non-banking company to see whether or not the company which has received funds through fixed deposits has forwarded the necessary particulars to the Reserve Bank. The auditor should accordingly make suitable mention in his report under Sec. 227(2) of the Companies Act. If he is not satisfied with the particulars furnished to the Reserve Bank by the company, he should mention the aggregate amount of such deposits held by the company. In the case of a non-banking company under Sec. 227(1) the auditor shall give the contents of the report which he has made or intends to make to the Reserve Bank of India as mentioned above.

Any person who contravenes any of the above provision or any other order, regulation, condition, etc., made in this behalf, under the Companies Act or the Reserve Bank of India Act, shall be punished with a fine of two thousand rupees and where the contravention or default is continuing one, with a further fine which may extend to one hundred rupees for every day, during which the contravention or the default continues under Sec. 58B of the Reserve Bank of India Act, 1934. This provision does not apply to the banking companies and financial institutions except the provision relating to the advertisement. The Central Government may exempt any company from these provisions in consultation with the Reserve Bank of India.

Interest paid out of Capital

Where a company has been formed to undertake some construction work or the provision of any plant or any other work where it will not be possible to earn any profit for some years, it may pay interest on the paid up capital according to Section 208 of the Companies Act, and may debit the same to construction account, etc., provided:

1. the payment of such an interest is authorised by the Articles or a special revolution;
2. the prior sanction of the Central Government has been obtained for this purpose. Such a sanction will be the conclusive evidence that the shares of the company have been issued for the purpose of construction, etc.;
3. the period for which interest is paid does not exceed the period sanctioned by the Government but in no case shall it exceed beyond the close of the half-year next after the half-year during which the works have actually been completed or the plant provided, etc;

4. the rate of interest does not exceed four per cent or such other rate which may be prescribed by the Central Government by notification in the Official Gazette;
5. the payment of such interest and the rate at which it has been paid is clearly shown in the Balance Sheet of the year in which such interest is paid if it has not been shown in the Profit and Loss Account;
6. the payment of such interest shall not operate as a reduction of the paid-up capital of the company.

The above provisions do not affect any company to which applies the Indian Railway Companies Act, 1895, or the Indian Tramways Act, 1902.

Interest paid on the debentures issued for the purpose of construction, etc., may also be treated as started above.

The auditor should see that all the legal formalities have been complied with and that the interest so paid is mentioned separately in the balance sheet of the company under a distinctive head "Miscellaneous Expenditure" unless it has already been debited to the Construction, Plantation Account, etc.

Statutory Meeting, Report and Audit

Section 165 of the Companies Act stipulates that every company limited by shares, and every company limited by guarantee and having a share capital, shall hold a general meeting of the shareholders within six months but not before one month after the company is entitled to commence business. This is called the Statutory Meeting. A private company need not hold such a meeting, even if it is converted into a public company.

The Companies Act, further lays down that the directors shall forward to the shareholders and the Registrar twenty-one days before the holding of the Statutory Meeting, a report, called the Statutory Report, and is required to be drawn up in Form 22 printed as annexure to the Company Rules. The report must contain the following:

1. The number of shares allotted as fully paid and partly paid.
2. The amount received in respect of such shares.
3. The number of shares which have been allotted for consideration other than cash and the consideration thereof.
4. An abstract of cash receipts in respect of shares, debentures and other sources and payments thereout up to seven days before the submission of the Statutory Report and balance in hand on that date.
5. The names and addresses and occupation of the directors, managing agents, auditors, managers and secretary of the company and any change which might have occurred in the names, addresses, etc., since the date of the incorporation of the company.

6. The particulars of contracts which are to be submitted to the shareholders at the meeting for their approval.
7. The extent, if any, to which each underwriting counteract, if any, has not been carried out, and the reasons thereof.
8. An account of the commission and brokerage paid or to be paid to any manager, director or agents in connection with the sale or issue of shares or debentures.
9. An account of estimate of preliminary expenses.
10. Arrears of calls, if any, due from the directors, managing agents, every partner of the managing agents, the secretaries, treasurers, etc.

The report has to be certified by not less than two directors, one of whom shall be a managing director, if any, and the auditor has to certify as correct the report so far as it relates to the shares allotted by the company, the cash received in respect of such shares and the receipts and payments of the company. Such an audit is termed as Statutory Audit.

In connection with the report the auditor has to give a certificate as follows:

We hereby certify as correct so much of the report as relates to the shares allotted by the company and to the cash received in respect of such shares and to the receipts and payments of the company.

....
Auditors

Dated this......... day of .... 19........

Thus the auditor has to certify the cash book entries, and he will have to examine a number of books and documents to enable him to do so.

He will have to consult the following in certifying the numbers of the shares allotted, and cash received and payments made thereout, etc.,

(i) The Memorandum of Association.
(ii) The Articles of Association.
(iii) The Prospectus.
(iv) The Cash Book.
(v) The Bank Pass Book.
(vi) The Minute Book of the Board of Directors/
(vii) The contracts entered into with the Vendors, Brokers and the Underwriters.
(viii) The application and Allotment Books, Register of Shereholders, ect.

In connection with the Statutory Report an auditor is to certify the receipts and payments contained in it with regard to-

(i) the shares allotted by the company;

(ii) the cash received on such shares; and

(iii) the miscellaneous items of the receipts and the payments, e.g., on account of debentures, brokerage and underwriting commission, etc.

PROFITS PRIOR TO INCORPORATION

A company comes into existence only when incorporated and, can act only then through its officers.

It may so happen that the company might have entered into contract with the vendors of a business which has been purchased as from a date before the company was incorporated. The business might have made a profit since then but before the company was incorporated. Such a profit cannot be legally distributed in the form of dividends as it could not have earned anything before incorporation. Such profits are carried to Capital Reserve. These cannot be distributed to the shareholders but utilised in the following ways:

1. In the payment of interest. If any, which was to be paid to the vendors for the purchase price calculated only up to the date of incorporation. The interest payable to the vendors after the date of incorporation should be debited to profit and loss account.
2. The balance, if any, may be utilised in wiping off goodwill, if any, which has been taken over from the vendors. Goodwill is the extra amount paid over and above the price of the net assets taken over.
3. The remaining balance, if any, may be utilised in writing down fixed assets.
4. The balance, if any, should be carried to a capital reserve which is not available for distribution.

When the stock of the business purchased is not taken on the date of incorporation, the profit may be apportioned between the two periods, viz., ante-incorporated and post-incorporated periods on the following basis :

(i) Gross profit on the basis of turn-over of the two periods;

(ii) Direct expenses such as advertising, commission, etc. on the turn-over basis;

(iii) Indirect expenses, e.g., salaries, rent, taxes, etc., on the basis of the time of each period.

If there is any loss prior to incorporation on such business it may be:

(i) debited to goodwill; or

(ii) transferred to suspense account, which may be written off out of the capital profits later on or premium on the issue of debentures or forfeited shares account or any other capital profit.

The date of division of the profit or loss should be the date of incorporation of the company and not the date entitling the company to commence business.

Duties of Auditor

The auditor should examine the methods of apportionment. He should see that it is apportioned on the principles described above, and also see that such profits are not distributed to the shareholders as they are in the nature of capital profits.

QUESTIONS FOR EXERCISE

1. Discuss the preliminaries to be gone through before the actual work of audit is begun by the auditor.
2. You are appointed an auditor of a public limited company. Before starting an annual audit what formalities you should attend to? Give a detailed programme for the main audit work.
3. What legal documents of company should an auditor examine prior to the commencement of the first audit and to what points should his special attention be directed in the examination?
4. What are preliminary expenses? Elaborate auditor's duties about them.
5. Explain rules and regulations concerning Public Deposits, Interest and Statutory meetings pointing out the duties of the auditors in this connection.
6. What is meant by "Profits and Losses prior to the Incorporation"? State how you would determine them and deal with them in the final accounts of a company.

14

Company Directors and Managerial Remuneration

COMPANY DIRECTORS

The Companies Act provides that the business of a company shall be managed by its directors. They can do anything unless otherwise provided for by the Articles or by the Companies Act itself clarifying the position of the directors of a company. Lord Selbourne said in *G. E. Rly. Co.* v. *Turner* (1872), "The directors are the mere trustees or agents of the company—trustees of the company's money and property; agents in the transactions which are entered into on behalf of the company." As was decided in *The Union Bank of Allahabad Ltd.* case, in 1925, Directors of a company are its trustees.

Dual Position

Thus the directors hold a dual position— that of the trustees and of agents. As agents the directors cannot sell to or purchase goods from the company whose directors they are. They cannot make any profit out of any transaction entered into by them on behalf of the company. However, it is open to the company to ratify such acts of the directors provided these are not *ultra vires* the company, i.e., have contravened the provisions of the Companies Act.

Contracts with the Company

Sometimes provision is made in the Articles of Association of the company permitting the directors to enter into contracts with the company provided they make it clear at the time the contract is entered into. However a director is not entitled to vote when a question about the contract to be entered into with him is being discussed, nor is he counted for the purpose of forming a quorum at the meeting of the Board. According to Sec. 301, company is required to maintain one or more registers of contracts in which directors are interested. This register is open for inspection to the shareholders. According to Section 297 of the Companies Act, the following restrictions are imposed on the directors who to enter into contracts with the companies whose directors they are :

1. Except with the consent of the Board of Directors of a company, a director of the company or his relative, a firm in which such a director or relative a partner, and the partner in such a firm, or a private company of which the director is a member or director, shall not enter into any contract with the company-

(a) for the sale, purchase or supply of any goods, materials or services; or

(b) after the commencement of this Act, for underwriting the subscription of any shares in, or debentures of the company provided that in the case of company, having a paid-up share capital of not less than rupees one crore, no such contract shall be entered into except with the previous approval of the Central Government.

2. Nothing contained in clause (a) of sub-section (1) shall affect—

(a) the purchase of goods and materials from the company, or the sale of goods and materials to the company, by any directors, relative, firm, partner or private company as aforesaid for cash at prevailing market price; or

(b) any contract or contracts between the company on one side and any such director, relative, firm, partner or private company on the other for sale, purchase or supply of any goods, materials and services in which either the company, as the case may be, regularly trades or does business:

Provided that such contract or contracts do not relate to goods and materials the value of which exceeds five thousand rupees in the aggregate in any year comprised in the period of the contract or contracts; or

(c) in the case of a banking or insurance company any transaction in the ordinary course of business of such company with any director, relative, firm, partner of private company as aforesaid.

3. Notwithstanding anything contained in sub-sections (1) and (2), a director, relative firm, partner or private company as aforesaid may, in circumstances of urgent necessity, enter without obtaining the consent of the Board, into any contract with the company for the sale, purchase or supply of any goods, materials, the value of which exceeds five thousand rupees in the aggregate in any year comprised in the period of the contract; but in such a case, the consent of the Board shall be obtained at a meeting within three months of the date on which the contract was entered into.

4. Every consent of the Board required under this section shall be accorded by resolution passed at a meeting of the Board and not otherwise; and the consent of the Board required under sub-section (1) shall not be deemed to have been given within the meaning of that sub-section unless the consent is accorded before the contract is entered into or within three months of the date on which it was entered into.

5. If consent is not accorded to any contract under this section, anything done in pursuance of the contract shall be voidable at the opinion of the Board.

6. Nothing in this section shall apply to any case where the consent has been accorded to the contract before the commencement of the Companies (Amendment) Act, 1960.

The auditor is to see that the directors have not entered into any contract with the company unless they are authorised to do so by the Articles of Association, the Board and the Statute. He should examine the director's minute book to find out whether the director had made it clear at the time of the meeting when the question of the contract was being discussed that he was interested in the contract, and whether he voted at such a meeting. He should inspect the register of contracts as mentioned above, and see that the directors hold the qualification shares, according to the Articles of Association.

Loans to and from Directors

(i) ***Section* 295.** It prohibits a company to advance loans or give a security or guarantee a loan made to its director or to a firm of which such a director is a director or a member except when such a private company is a subsidiary company of the public company, or to any relative of a director without the approval of the Central Government.

(ii) ***Section* 296.** This restriction of advancing loans to Directors, etc. shall also apply to any transaction represented by a book debt which was from its inception in the nature of a loan or an advance. It does not apply to a company whose business is to lend money in the ordinary course of business or where the money has been advanced to a director to incur expenses on behalf of the company or to a private company, not being a subsidiary company of a public company or by a holding company to its subsidiary company or by a company which is the managing agent or secretaries or treasurers to the managed company.

The auditor should see that such loans or advances to directors have been made according to law and are clearly mentioned on the assets side of the balance sheet. He should see that rate of interest charged from the directors is no less than what is usually charged. If a director has borrowed money from the company and repaid it before the date of balance sheet, the fact must be mentioned in the footnote of balance sheet. The maximum amount due by directors or other officers of the company at any time during the year is to be shown by way of a note, even though the loan might have been repaid during the course of the year.

When a director has advanced any loan to the company, that must be shown separately on the liability side of the balance sheet and not shown by way of deduction from the "Loan to Directors and Officers of the company." The auditor should see that the company has the power to borrow and the rate of interest charged is not excessive.

MANAGERIAL REMUNERATION

Sections 198, 309, 310, 311, 348, 349, 350, 351, 352, 381, 387 and 687AA of the Companies Act specify the rules and the amount of remuneration payable to the managerial personnel. Managerial personnel include (a) Directors, (b) Managing Director, (c) Managing Agent, (d) Secretaries and Treasurers, (e) Managers.

1. Remuneration Payable to the Director

The directors are not entitled to any remuneration as a matter of right unless an agreement to that effect has been entered into, or the Articles of Association provide such payment or the shareholders at the general meeting decide to pay them any remuneration.

According to Section 314, except with the previous consent of the company in general meeting accorded by means of a special resolution, (a) no director of a company shall hold any office or place of profit, and (b) no partner or relative of such a director, no firm in which such a director or relative is a partner, no private company of which such a director is a director or member, and no director, managing agent, secretaries and treasurers, or manager of such a company shall hold any office or place of profit carrying a total monthly remuneration of five hundred rupees or more. This section will not apply to manager directors, managing agents, secretaries and treasurers, manager, legal technical adviser, bankers or trustees for the debenture-holders of the company.

It is the duty of the auditor to examine the agreement or the Articles and the Minute Book of the Shareholders to find out if any resolution had been passed sanctioning such a payment. The remuneration of the directors may be in the form of fees, percentage of profits, travelling expenses or special allowances or fees, etc. They may be paid in the following forms:

According to Section 309(2) of the Companies Act, the directors are now paid their remuneration in the form of fees for attending the meetings of the Board or a Committee of the Board. The maximum fee payable to a director for attending the meetings of the Board of Director or any committee thereof has been fixed at two hundred and fifty rupees per meeting. The Amendment Act further provides that if fees have been paid to the directors in the form of a monthly salary before the commencement of the Companies (Amendment) Act, 1960, such a salary small continue to be paid for a period of two years or for the remaining term of office of the directors, whichever is less but not longer.

The auditor should vouch the payment as usual by referring to the Director's or Committee's Minute Books to see as to how many meetings were attended by such a director. The Articles should also be referred to find out the amount to be paid for each meeting. He should also examine the vouchers. He should inspect the register of the director to find out the names of the directors.

A director, who is either in the whole-time employment of the company or a managing director, may be paid remuneration either by way of a monthly payment or at a specified percentage be of the net profits of the company or partly by one way and partly by the other. Such remuneration shall not exceed five per cent of the net profits for one such director. If there is more than one such director, it should not exceed ten per cent for all of them together except with the approval of the Central Government.

In the case of a director who is neither in the whole-time employment of the company nor a managing director and whose remuneration does not include anything by way of a monthly payment, the company may by way of a special resolution authorise payments to such a director, or where there is more than one director, all of them together—

(i) if the company has a whole-time director, managing agent, etc., on a commission not exceeding one per cent of the net profits of the company;

(ii) in any other case on a commission not exceeding three per cent of the net profits of the company.

It is the duty of the auditor to examine the Articles and see that the computation of profits is correct according to Sections 349, 350 and 351. He should also examine the vouchers. If the commission has been paid in excess of the amount prescribed by the Companies Act the auditor should see whether a special resolution had been passed and whether the previous approval of the Central Government has been taken. If any director draws or receives any remuneration in excess of the amount mentioned above without the prior approval of the Central Government, he shall refund such sums to the company and untill such sum is refunded, hold it in trust for the company. The company has no power to waive the recovery of any such refundable sum, unless permitted by the Central Government.

The net profits referred to above are computed according to Sections 349, 350 and 351.

No director who is in receipt of any commission from his company and who is either a managing or whole-time director can receive any commission or any other remuneration from any subsidiary of such company.

No director is entitled to any pension or gratuity, etc., for the services rendered by him to the company.

The remunerations payable to directors are subject to the provisions of Section 198 of the Companies Act as amended in 1960, i.e., the total managerial remuneration payable to the director and treasurer or manager of a public company or a private company which is the subsidiary of a public company shall not exceed eleven per cent of the net profits of the company. This percentage shall be exclusive of any fees payable to directors under sub-section (2) of Section

309 of the Companies Act. These provisions do not apply to a private company unless it is a subsidiary of a public company.

Where special remuneration is paid to a director for some special work performed by him, the auditor should refer to the Director's Minute Book to check up the resolution sanctioning the special payment and vouch the payment by examining the receipt issued by such a director.

The directors are not entitled travelling expenses for attending the meeting unless the Articles of Association so provide, or if Table "A" is applicable. If the Articles are silent, the shareholders may pass a resolution sanctioning such payments. However, if the journey was undertaken by the director for the work of the company, the directors may sanction such a payment. The auditor should inspect the Minute Book of the Board of Directors and vouch the payment by inspecting the receipt issued by the directors concerned. He should see that the travelling expenses incurred by the directors were in the interest of the company and were incurred according to the rules and regulations of the company. He should vouch the payment as usual.

According to Section 310 any amendment in the articles, or memorandum, or an agreement entered into by it, or any resolution passed by it in its general meeting or Board's meeting in regard to increase in the remuneration of any director or managing director or whole-time director, shall be void unless approved by the Central Government.

On 14th September, 1970, the Government announced guidelines for the Company Law Board regarding the remuneration and perquisites payable to the directors of a public company. A public company cannot pay more than ninety thousand rupees per annum or seven thousand five hundred rupees per month including dearness allowance and all other fixed allowances, as remuneration to Managing Director, whole-time or part-time director or the manager of the company. Incentive commission can be paid up to one per cent of the net profit subject to a ceiling of forty-five thousand rupees or fifty per cent of the approved salary.

If a company pays remuneration to the directors in the form of commission only the ceiling has been fixed now at one lakh and thirty-five thousand instead of one lakh eighty thousand which was fixed according to the Companies (Amendment) Act of 1960.

Formerly, no maximum limit except on certain items of perquisite in addition to salary had been fixed but now perquisites have been fixed at thirty thousand rupees per annum or one-third of the remuneration payable, whichever is less. Companies have been given the choice to fix the different items of perquisites within the limit specified above. The perquisites limit one-third of the salary does not include employer's contribution to Provident Fund, contribution to pension, etc., which are not taxable subject to certain limits. The reimbursement of medical expenses actually incurred subject to the present ceiling of five thousand rupees annually or one month's salary whichever is less are excluded from the ceiling on perquisites. The ceiling regarding the perquisites does not include passage benefits at reasonable intervals and leave salary admissible within one-eleventh of duty period. Exceptions to the ceiling will be considered in individual cases where higher remunerations have already been drawn or in cases of expatriate directors of Indian subsidiary companies.

Exceptionally higher fee may be allowed in case of Indian companies, having foreign collaboration arrangements, provided the appointment is justified and the director concerned had been drawing higher emoluments prior to his appointment.

According to the new Section 637AA which has been added by the Companies (Amendment) Act, 1974, the Central Government is empowered to fix such amount or percentage of profits of the company, within the maximum limit stated above, as it deems fit. While fixing such remuneration, the Central Government shall have regard to—

(i) the financial position of the company;

(ii) the remuneration or commission drawn by the individual concerned in any other capacity, including his capacity as a sole selling agent;

(iii) professional qualifications and experience of the individual concerned;

(iv) public policy relating to the removal of disparities in income.

While vouching the remuneration paid to the directors and managing directors, etc., the auditor must take into consideration the above facts.

Such remuneration to be paid to the directors must be mentioned in the prospectus and the profit and loss account. If no payment has been made to the directors at the date of the balance sheet, the auditor should see that necessary adjustment is made and the amount payable is shown as a liability.

Sometimes the directors waive their right of remuneration. In such a case, the auditor should refer to the Directors' Minute Book to examine the resolution to that effect. He should also find out whether they have foregone the right to claim the fees or merely foregone their immediate payment. In the latter case such fees should be shown as a liability in the balance sheet of the company.

It may be mentioned here that remuneration payable to the directors is a debt owing by the company to such directors. Even if the company suffers a loss, the amount is payable to them. Remuneration payable to a director being a debt, can be paid out of capital. Section 200 of the Companies Act prohibits the payment of director's remuneration fee of income-tax. The annual accounts and balance sheet must show sums paid to directors for remuneration.

2. Remuneration to Managing Director. The company in a general meeting or the Board may appoint one of the directors as managing director to look into the day-to-day affairs of the company for a period not exceeding five years and fix his remuneration or if authorised by the Articles of Association of the company and provided the approval of the Central Government is obtained. It may be on the basis of a monthly payment or a percentage of profits which should not exceed five per cent of the net profit of the company. If there are more than one managing director, the percentage of the net profit payable to all of them should not exceed 10 per cent. Under Sections 310 and 311 if during the course of the year there has been an increase in the remuneration of the managing director, the auditor should see that it has been confirmed by the Central Government.

It is the auditor's duty to examine the Articles of Association or the Directors' Minute Book regarding his appointment and remuneration and see whether the approval of the Central Government has been obtained. He should vouch the payment of such remuneration by examining the vouchers. He should see that the 'Net profit' is properly calculated according to Sections 349, 350 and 351 of the Companies Act. A managing director cannot receive any commission or remuneration from a subsidiary company. He can claim compensation if his services are dispensed with before the due date. It should not exceed average remuneration for the previous three years of his retirement for the unexpired period of his service or three years whichever is less. Under Section 318 he is not entitled to get compensation if he resigns or attains the age of 65 years or he is guilty of fraud, negligence, etc.

3. Remuneration to the Manager. A manager is an individual whom subject to the superintendence, control and direction of the Board of Directors, has the management of the whole, or substantially the whole, of the affairs of a company, and includes a director or any other person occupying the position of a manager, by whatever name called, and whether under a contract of service or not. Subject to the provisions of Section 198, he can be paid either a monthly salary or by a percentage of net profits not exceeding five per cent or both calculated according to the Sections 349, 350 and 351. If the company has not made any profit or inadequate profit, he may be paid the minimum amount of Rs. 50,000.

QUESTION FOR EXERCISE

1. Explain the rules concerning duties, loans and remuneration of the director.

15.

Audit of Share Capital Transaction

REORGANISATION OF CAPITAL

If authorised by its Articles a company may alter the share capital as mentioned in the Memorandum of Association in any of the following ways:

1. Increase of Capital. This may be effected:

(i) by the issue of new shares;

(ii) consolidation of all or parts of its capital, i.e., divide its share capital into shares of larger amount;

(iii) conversion of all or a part of its fully paid-up shares into stock;

(iv) reconversion of all or a part of its stock into paid-up shares of small amounts; and

(v) sub-division of all or a part of its capital into shares of small amounts; and

(vi) cancellation of any unissued shares (Section 94).

Such an alteration should be stated in the Memorandum and Articles of Association after the alteration has been made. Notice of such an alteration must be filed with the Registrar within one month of doing so. If the share capital has been increased beyond its authorised capital, information must be sent to the Registrar within 15 days of passing the resolution to that effect.

Under Sec. 81(4) of the Companies Act, the Central Government can order the conversion of debentures issued by a company and the loan obtained by it, into the shares of such a company.

Under Sec. 94A added by the Companies (Amendment) Act, 1974, the conversion of debentures or loan under the direction of the Central Government will have the effect of increasing the nominal share capital of the company equal to the amount of the value of the shares into which the debentures or loans or part thereof has been converted.

If any public financial institution wishes to convert its debentures or loan into shares of the company in pursuance of the option exercised by it, the Central Government may direct that it may be done. This will have the effect of increasing the share capital of the institution equal to the amount of such debentures and shares converted. The Central Government shall send a copy of such an order to the Registrar and also a copy of the order to the company which in its turn will file a return with the Registrar regarding the increase of the share capital who will make the necessary changes in the memorandum of the company. The return shall be filed within 30 days of the receipt of the order.

2. Reduction of Capital. This may be effected in the following ways:

(i) extinguish or reduce the liability on any of its shares in respect of share capital not paid up; or

(ii) either with or without extinguishing or reducing the liability on any of its shares, cancel any paid-up share capital which is lost, or is unrepresented by available assets; or

(iii) either with or without extinguishing or reducing liability on any of its shares, pay off any paid-up share capital which is in excess of the wants of the company (Section 100).

Capital can be reduced only (a) if authorised by the Articles, (b) by passing a special resolution, and (c) by confirmation of the resolution by the Court.

Duties of an Auditor

1. Examine the Memorandum and Articles of Association and the resolution for the alteration of capital and see whether the resolution was passed according to law.
2. Examine the confirmatory order of the court sanctioning the reduction of capital.
3. Examine the Registrar's certificate which is a conclusive evidence that the legal requirements regarding the reorganisation have been complied with.
4. Verify the old share holdings and surrendered share certificates, if any, with the new holdings and certificates.
5. Vouch Journal entries with other documentary evidence available.
6. Examine the record in the register of members.
7. See that the legal requirements have been complied with.
8. See that the provisions of Sections 100, 101, 102 and 103 have been complied with according to which if the capital has been reduced, the court may order the company to use the words "and reduced" after its name.

PROCEDURE OF AUDIT

The Pubtary Sastri Committee mentions that the company auditor should see that "The share capital of a company must be supported by and be reflective of the existence of cash or other valuable assets and should not represent mere book adjustments based upon promissory notes or the taking over by another of the liability to pay. Auditors must enquire, wherever it is stated that cash has been paid towards subscriptions to share capital, whether that cash has in fact passed, and if the cash has not been passed, they should satisfy themselves that the position as stated in the accounts book and that in the balance sheet is correct, regular and not misleading."

Share Capital Audit for a New Company/First Issue

Audit involves three stages, namely the application share capital of a new company in the first issue stage, the allotment stage and the call stage. However, the company is required to fulfil a lot of formalities before actually going for public subscription. The auditor should examine compliance of provisions.

Verification of Capital

1. The auditor should confirm that the permission of the Controller of Capital Issues has been obtained in case the issue exceeds Rs. one crore.
2. He should study the terms and conditions of issue contained in the Memorandum and Articles and Prospectus or Statement in lieu of Prospectus and see that these have been fully complied with.
3. He should ensure that the prospectus contains a provision in terms of Sec. 68A that any person who
   - (a) makes, in a fictitious name, an application to a company for acquiring or subscribing for, any shares therein, or
   - (b) otherwise induces a company to allot or register any transfer of shares therein to him, or any other person in a fictitious name, shall be punishable with imprisonment for a term which may extend up to five years.
4. He should verify that preliminary contracts, if any, entered into for the purchase of a property or business, for creating an organisation for management of the company etc., have been carried out strictly as laid down in the prospectus.
5. He should ascertain that there exists an internal check on receipts of amount along with the application.
6. He should examine shares issued for cash and shares issued for consideration other than cash, if any.

Verification of Shares issued for Cash

1. Application stage. The auditor should undertake the following checks:

(i) Checking of the original applications with the application and allotment sheets.

(ii) Checking and comparing entries in the application and the allotment books as regards deposit of money at the time of application with those in the cash book.

(iii) Checking that the application money was money deposited in scheduled bank till the grant of the 'Certificate to commence business' or these were returned as per the provisions of section 69(5).

(iv) Vouching that amounts pertaining to rejected applications, non-allotted application or any excess amount there to have been returned by comparing entries in the cash book with that of application and allotment sheets (books) or letters of regret, if any.

(v) Examining that the issue is within the limits authorised by the Memorandum and Articles of Association.

(vi) Examining that the minimum subscription fee, the amount received on application being not less than 5% of the nominal value of shares, has actually been received before making the allotment.

(vii) Checking the balance on the application and allotment sheets (book) and verify the total capital issued.

2. Allotment Stage. Following steps may be taken in this stage:

(i) Examining the Director's Minute Book to verify approval of allotment which may be in stages as spreading over a number of days. He should note that recording at each stage was properly initialled by at least one director. He should also see that the allotment was legally in order.

(ii) Comparing copies of letters of allotment/letters of regrets with entries in the application and allotment sheets (book).

(iii) Vouching money receipt on allotment by comparing the entries in the application and allotment sheets with the cash book or bank statement.

(iv) Confirming the journal entries regarding allotment money, examining the ledger accounts and comparing the balances in the ledger accounts with the number of shares allotted.

(v) Verifying the entries in the Register of Members by comparing these with a separate summary of shares allotted. Verifying that the amounts of the shares allotted do not exceed the authorised or nominal capital of the company.

(vi) Seeing that returns of allotment have been filed with the Registrar of Companies.

3. Calls stage. The auditor should take the following steps:

(i) Examining the Director's Minute Books regarding decisions about calls.

(ii) Seeing that the calls as resolved are within the provisions in the Articles of Association and statement in the prospectus issued by the company.

(iii) Vouching amounts received against calls with the counterfoils of receipts.

(iv) Checking postings of the amount received from the calls book (for calls due) and the cash book (for cash money received) into the share register.

(v) Comparing the application and allotment books with the schedule of calls in arrears showing the difference between calls due and calls received. He should confirm that the call in arrears figure is correct.

(vi) Checking the calls received in advance either in the cash book or through the journal and seeing that these are transferred to a separate account not meant up with the share capital of the company.

General Precautions

1. Under written Issue. The auditor should study the contracts with the underwriter and examine the Directors' Minute Book, selling or allotting to underwriters the unsubscribed portion of the issue. He should verify that the underwriting commission paid does not exceed the statutory maximum, i.e. 5 % on the nominal value of the share.

2. Payment of Brokerage. The auditor should check the amount paid with stamped or marked application forms.

3. Balances of Shareholders. The Auditor should determine balances of shareholders' accounts contained in the Share Register and tally the total with the balance in the Share Capital.

4. Return of Application money. The auditor should see that the company has to return this application money received if:

(i) the minimum subscription is not received, and

(ii) the permission to deal in and for quotation for shares of any stock exchange is not received where the directors have stated in the Prospectus that such permission would be obtained.

Subsequent Audits

After the audit of share capital in the first year or after incorporation, the auditor should simply compare the total of the individual balances in the share register with the issued share capital of the company in subsequent years till a new issue is made. He should verify transfers of shares registered during the year and reconcile the total number and value of shares held by different shareholders with the total paid-up capital of the company.

Audit of Fresh Capital

The auditor should take the following steps to audit fresh issue of capital:

1. He should see whether the fresh issue is within the limit of the authorised capital of company. If it exceeds, he should ascertain that all legal formalities regarding increase of capital have been fully complied with.
2. If the fresh issue warrants permission from Controller of Capital Issues, he should see that such a permission has actually been received and not simply applied for.

Shares Issued for Consideration Other Than Cash

A company may issue certain shares for consideration other than cash. Checks by the auditor under different situations are as follows:

1. Issue of Shares to a Vendor as Purchase Consideration. The auditor should vouch it by reference to the contract between the company and the vendor, and the Director's minutes recording the allotment. He must see that such contracts have been filed with the Registrar of Companies within thirty days after allotment. If the vendor's nominees are issued shares under a supplementary agreement or a written nomination thereto, these are the basic documents for the audit purposes.

2. Issue of Shares to Underwriters. The auditor should study the Prospectus and verify that it does contain the right for the payment of the commission. He should study Articles of Association to determine the procedure of payment. He should check the resolution of Allotment from Directors' Minute Book and the contract to see that the issue is in terms of these documents.

3. Issue of Shares to Promoters. The auditor should study the documents such as the contract, the Articles of Association and the Prospectus.

4. Issue of shares to shareholders of an old company on amalgamation or reconstruction. The auditor should see the amalgamation agreement, duly approved by a competent High Court and if required, check that the allotment has been made in accordance with the agreed arrangement.

5. Issue of bonus shares to existing shareholders. The audit process in regard to bonus shares is dealt with, under heading 'Issue of Bonus Sheres'.

Steps in Auditing Non-Cash Share Issue

1. Checking that the company has filed with the Registrar of Companies within one month of the allotment, all copies of contracts as required under Sec. 75(1) (B) along with a return stating the number and nominal amount of shares so allotted, the extent of their being paid-up and the consideration for which they have been allotted.
2. Vouching the Journal entries thereto to ensure their proper recording.

3. Examining that such shares have been separately shown on the liabilities side of the Balance Sheet.
4. The decision in *Spargo's case* reminds an auditor that when the allotment is made in lieu of a *bona fide* debt payable in money at once, the allotment should be considered as against cash. This will be of great help in determining duties under Sec. 227(1-A)(7).
5. If the shares are allotted on a cash basis, even when the amount is actually paid later, such an allotment will be deemed to be against cash.

ISSUE OF SHARES AT A PREMIUM

Section 78 of Companies Act does not restrict the issue of shares at a price higher than its face value though it requires that sum equal to the issue of shares at a premium, whether for cash or otherwise, shall be transferred to a separate account called the 'Share Premium Account'. The amount of the share premium shall not be mixed up with the share capital of the company. It is a capital profit which cannot and should not be transferred to Profit and Loss Account, neither can it be carried either to Capital or Capital Reserve Account.

Uses of Premium

A company can use the share premium account for the following purposes:

1 To issue unissued shares of the company to the members of the company as fully paid bonus shares.
2. To write off the preliminary expenses of the company.
3. To write off the expenses, or the commission paid or the discount allowed on any issue of shares or debentures of the company.
4. To provide for the premium payable on the redemption of any redeemable preference shares or any debentures of the company.
5. To write off the capital losses when shares are forfeited while the premiums received on such shares is not forfeited.

Auditor's Duties

1. He must examine the Prospectus, Articles and the Directors' Resolution in the Minute Book to verify that this is not only permissible but properly authorised also.
2. He should vouch the amount of premium received and its transference to the Share Premium Account.
3. He should see that this amount has been utilised only for the purposes mentioned in Sec. 78. He cannot object if the utilisation is within law. If the premium is used for an unauthorised use, this amounts to reduction of capital.

4. He should see that this amount has not been credited to profit and loss account but shown as 'Reserves and Surplus' on the liabilities side on the Balance Sheet.
5. He should note that provisions regarding reduction of share capital apply to share premium account as well.

As was held in the case *Head and Henry and Co. Ltd.* v. *Ropner Holdings Ltd.* where shares are issued at a premium for consideration other than cash, an amount equal to the amount of premium must be transferred to Share Premium Account.

ISSUE OF SHARES AT A DISCOUNT

Conditions of Issue

Under Sec. 79 of the Companies Act, a company can issue its shares at a discount on the following conditions:

1. The issue is of a category of shares already issued.
2. A period of one year has at the date of the issue, elapsed since the date on which company was entitled to commence business.
3. The issue is authorised by an ordinary resolution passed by the company in a general meeting and sanctioned by the Company Law Board.
4. The resolution specifies the maximum rate of discount at which the shares are to be issued. This cannot be more than 10% unless the Company Law Board is of the opinion that higher percentage of discount may be allowed in special circumstances.
5. Shares are issued within two months after the date on which the issue is sanctioned by the Company Law Board or within such extended time as the Company Law Board may allow.
6. Prospectus relating to the issue of shares contains the particulars of the discount allowed on the issue of shares or of so much of that discount as has not been written off at the date of the prospectus. Shares issued are shown at their nominal value and not the value at which issued. Though the discount is written off over a short period it should be shown as 'Miscellaneous Expenditure' on the assets side of the Balance Sheet.

Auditor's Duty

The auditor must examine compliance with requirements under Sec. 79 and its presentation and disclosure in the Balance Sheet. The company is not obliged to write off the discount. This will be treated as in the case of preliminary expenses, underwriting commission etc.

ISSUE OF BONUS SHARES

If there is a big gap between the paid up capital and the capital actually employed due to high reserves, it needs to be filled up. Further payment of dividend at a high rate is linked to excessive divisible profits with the company which may not announce a higher rate due to the fear of attracting competitors to business, a resentment from employees and customers etc. The management may opt to regularise dividend payment by announcing a lower rate of dividend along with a bonus issue of shares. Issue of bonus shares is a good method of capitalising large profits or reserves. Instead of paying high dividends a company may capitalise its profits, if the Articles of Association permit by issuing fully paid shares. These are called bonus shares. These cannot be issued in lieu of dividends. Bonus shares serve as a technique to adjust high dividends and not to substitute payment of dividend. These are allotted to existing members in a fixed and declared proportion to their shareholdings.

Bonus shares may also be issued out of the Share Premium Account and the 'Capital Redemption Reserve Fund'.

Use of Reserves

When a company has accumulated disproportionately large reserves in relation to its share capital and profits such an amount can be applied towards:

1. paying up any amount for the time being unpaid on any shares held up members;
2. paying up any in full, unissued shares of the company to be allotted and distributed as fully paid up, to and among such members in the aforesaid proportion;
3. partly in the way specified in (1) and partly in the way specified in (2) above. In any case bonus shares cannot be partly paid up.

Guidelines for the Issue of Bonus Shares

1. Provision. Bonus shares can be issued only when there is a provision in the Articles for the captalisation of reserves. In alternative a general meeting resolution providing for the same in the changed articles should be produced.

2. Sanction. Bonus shares cannot be issued without the sanction of the Controller of Capital Issues. The application in this regard should be made to him. It must contain a resolution passed in the general meeting for the bonus issue.

3. Dividends. No bonus issue can be made in lieu of dividends.

4. Norms. The bonus issue is subject to the following norms:

(i) Free reserves built out of genuine profits or the share premium collected in cash only are available for capitalisation.

(ii) Reserves created by the revaluation of fixed assets are not permitted to be capitalised.

(iii) The development reserve is treated as a free reserve for calculating residual reserves test and can also be capitalised.

(iv) The existing capital redemption reserve if any, cannot be included in computing the minimum reserve of 33-1/4%,

(v) The residual reserve after the proposed capitalisation should be 40% of the increased paid up capital.

(vi) All contingent liabilities disclosed in the annual accounts, which have a bearing on the profits should be considered in the calculation of the minimum residual reserve of 33-1/4%.

5. Return. 30% of the average amount of pre-tax profits for the preceding three years should yield a return of 7% on the expanded capital base of the company.

AUDIT OF UNDERWRITING COMMISSION

Section 76 of the Companies Act permits joint-stock companies to pay commission to any person who subscribes or agrees to subscribe to or who procures or agrees to procure subscription for any shares in or debentures of the company provided the following conditions are fulfilled:

1. The Articles must permit such a payment.
2. The commission should not exceed 5 % of the price of the issued shares and 2.5% in case of debentures or the amount or rate authorised by the Articles.
3. It should be disclosed in the Prospectus. A copy of the contract with each underwriter must be filed with the Registrar of Companies at the time of filing in the prospectus.

Non-compliance of the above provisions will make the company and its officer in default liable to be punished with fine which may extend up to Rs. 5,000.

Auditor's Duties

1. To examine the agreement with the underwriters and see the compliance of the terms and conditions thereto.
2. To compare the receipts given by the underwriters with the payments made as commission.
3. To examine the Articles to see authorisation and see that it is shown on the assets side of the Balance Sheet under 'Miscellaneous Expenditure'.
4. To ascertain that the provision of Sec. 76 has been complied with.

5. To mention it in his report if the underwriter calls or payments on allotments are in arrears.

AUDIT OF BROKERAGE

Companies brokerage as commission to brokers and bankers for shares subscribed through them. The application form has a separate column for the name or seal of the broker which is the evidence of shares being subscribed through them. Brokerage is different from underwriting as Sec. 76 is not applicable to it. Whereas underwriting commission can be paid to any person, brokerage can be paid only to stock brokers or to bankers. In *Andrecc* v. *Zinc Mines of Great Britain* case, it was held that brokerage must not only be reasonable but also paid only to broker and not to a private person.

Auditor's Duties

1. To see that the Articles authorise payment of such brokerage.
2. To see whether the directors have resolved and confirmed the arrangement.
3. To examine the applications and ascertain that they are stamped by the agents.
4. To examine the prospectus to verify disclosure of brokerage paid or payable.
5. To check the calculation and show it separately on the assets side under the head 'Miscellaneous Expenditure'.

AUDIT CONCERNING CALLS (SECTIONS 1-92)

Section 36(2) of the companies stipulates that "all money payable by any member to the company under the Memorandum or Articles shall be a debt due from him to the company. However, the liability to pay debt does not arise until a valid call has been made. Thus, a call is a demand by the company on the shareholders to pay whole or part of the balance remaining unpaid on each share, made at any time during the life of the company."

Auditors Duties

1. To examine that the provisions of the Articles have been fully complied with;
2. To inspect Director's Minute Book and note that the decision was taken by the Board and not by a sub-committee or one/two directors;
3. To examine that the call resolution does state the time and place of payment as it will be invalid otherwise;
4. To ensure that the directors acted as trustees and the power to call is exercised for the benefit of the company;

5. To see that the calls are made on a uniform basis as regards all shares falling under the same class.

Types of Calls

1. Calls-in-Arrears. The sums of call money due from shareholders is known as calls-in-arrears. Its amount should be verified by reference to the share register. Calls due from director etc. must be shown separately in the balance sheet. It should be deducted from the amount of called up amount and shown in the liabilities side. The Articles provide that interest is to be charged on calls-in-arrears. Therefore, the auditor should verify the interest adjustment.

Calls-in-Advance. The rules permit the company to accept money from shareholders in either the whole or part of the amount remaining uncalled on any shares held by them as calls in advance. This amount does not become a part of the capital for the purpose of voting right. Under Sec. 93, a company may, if so authorised by the Articles, pay dividends in proportion to the amount paid on each share where a larger amount is paid upon some shares than on others. In terms of clause 88(2) of Table A, no amount paid or credited as paid on a share in advance of calls shall be treated for the purpose of paying dividends. The shareholders making advance payment of calls are entitled to receive interest at the specified rate which can be paid out of capital when profits are not available for such a payment. If the company is wound up, calls in advance are repayable along with interest accrued thereon before any part of the capital is returned to shareholders. Under clause 18 of 'Table A' power is bestowed on the company to pay interest at a rate not exceeding 6% on amounts so advanced.

The auditor should go through the Articles to find out that it permits calls in advance. He should ensure that the interest does not exceed the rate stated in the Articles. He should vouch the entries both for receipt of calls in advance and payment of interest thereon. He should compare the entries on the share register with those in the cash book.

FORFEITURE OF SHARES

When shareholders do not pay the amount due on calls the directors do not have an implied power in this regard as forfeiture basically is a penal proceeding carried out lawfully under certain conditions. The directors have to observe the following rules in case of forfeiture of shares:

1. Authorisation. Forfeiture can be exercised only if authorised. As per 'Table A' shares can be forfeited only against the non-payment of calls duly notified. In *Naresh Chandra Sanyal* v. *The Calcutta Stock Exchange Association Ltd.* it was held that the Articles may lawfully incorporate any other grounds of forfeiture.

2. Notification. 'Table A' also requires that a notice requiring payment of the amount due with any interest accrued and period of 30 days is generally served on the defaulter to pay his dues. This time should not be less than 14 days from the service of the notice on or before which the payment is to be made.

3. Resolution and bona fide intentions. No shares can be forfeited unless so resolved by the directors. The resolution must not reflect a breach of trust *vis-a-vis* the shareholder-applicant. It should be exercised in the interest of the company. In the case *Kanshi Ram* v. *Kishore Chandra* it was held, "The right to forfeit shares must be pursued with the greatest accuracy, it must be exercised by the proper parties, that is by the directors properly appointed, and by the requisite number of them and in the proper manner and for the proper cause."

Usually, the amount standing to the credit of forfeited shares account is applied to the discount on the reissue of shares. Balance if any may be utilised in educating or writing of fictitious assets like goodwill, preliminary expenses are carried to Reserve Account. Legally, it can be transferred to P &L A/c, provided Articles do not prohibit such a transfer.

Re-issue of Forfeited Shares

In the case *Naresh Chander Sanyal* v. *Ramnikant T. Roy*, it was held that forfeiture of shares, otherwise than non-payment of call, does not amount to an illegal reduction of capital in contravention of the provision of the Companies Act. It does not mean the purchase of its own shares by the company. If the shares are not re-issued, forfeiture thereto results in reduction of capital as forfeited shares become the property of the company. The reissue is the usual affair.

Reissue of forfeited shares may be made at any price provided that the total of sum paid by the former holder of the shares, together with the amount paid on reissue and the amount remaining unpaid on shares is not less than the face value. If it were so, that will amount to an issue at a discount and the provisions of Sec. 79 shall become relevant. The reissue may be at a discount which cannot exceed the actual amount forfeited on these shares. In the case of *Morrison* v. *Trustees, Executors and Securities Insurance Corporation Ltd.*, it was held that forfeited shares may be issued as paid up to an amount not exceeding the amount paid by the previous holder and may be reissued in consideration of a sum less than the sum credited as paid on them.

If the shares are reissued at a price more than face value, the excess is a premium which must be transferred to the 'Share Premium Account'. According to Sec. 75 the company need not file a return of allotment of the reissued shares. It was held in the case of *Bishambhar* v. *Agra Electric Store Ltd.*, that though forfeited shares are normally reissued, the directors are not bound to do so.

Auditor's Duties

1. To examine the Articles to verify authorisation and compliance of the Provisions of the Articles. The fact that Articles authorise the

company to expel a member is not sufficient to enable the company to deprive the expelled members of the shares also.

2. To examine the Directors Minute Book to see the resolution forfeiting the shares. The auditor must see that the forfeiture has been correctly accounted for and that necessary adjustments have been made in the Register of Members.
3. To inspect the directors' resolution about the forfeited shares reissued. To trace the receipt of money and to verify that the amount of discount, if any, does not exceed the amount already received thereon from the defaulter shareholders.
4. To vouch the cancellation by reference to the Directors' Minute Book and the Register of Members, in case the forfeiture is cancelled by the directors.
5. To see that any premium received on the original issue of the forfeited shares is not transferred to 'Forfeited Shares Account' but remains in the 'Share Premium Account.'
6. To examine that in case some excess money has been realised, it should be transferred to the Capital Reserve Account as it represents capital profit and not divisible profits.

ISSUE OF SHARES

Certificate of Shares (Sec. 113)

Within three months of allotment and within three months after the application for registration of the transfer every company must have ready for delivery the certificates of all shares, debentures and the certificates of debenture stock, allotted or transferred. Share certificates must be issued within the provisions of the Companies (Issue of Share Certificate) Rules, 1960.

The following points should be noted in this regard:

1. A share certificate is a document certifying that the allottee is the holder of the specified number of shares in the company.
2. A share certificate is a *prima facie* evidence of the title of the member to shares specified therein. The company cannot deny his title to the shares.
3. Where the certificate states that the shares are fully paid, the company cannot deny it later as against a person who has acted *bona fide* on the faith of the statement.

Issue of Share Warrants to Bearer (Secs. 114-115)

If so authorised by its Articles public company, limited by shares may, with the prior approval of the central government, issue under its common seal, share warrant in respect of fully paid shares, stating that the bearer is entitled to the shares therein specified, and may provide by coupons or otherwise for payment of dividend shares specified therein. These shares, become transferable by mere delivery of the share warrant. Every share warrant is a negotiable instrument.

A share warrant holder ceases to be member as his name has been struck off the Register of Members. If Articles permit, the bearer of share warrant may surrender it for cancellation to the company which may enter his name as member in the Register of Members, thus, restoring all membership rights.

The auditor should study the Articles. He should check the prior approval of the central government. He should ensure that provisions of Secs. 114 and 115 have been complied with. He should compare the entries in the Register of Share Warrants with the cancelled entries in the Register of Members.

Redemption of Preference Shares

Under Sec. 80, a limited company may issue redeemable preference shares whose amount and the terms of their redemption or conversion and the earliest date of redemption or conversion must be disclosed in the Balance Sheet.

Such shares cannot be redeemed unless they are fully paid. They can be redeemed only (i) out of the proceeds of a fresh issue of shares made for the purpose, or (ii) out of profits otherwise available for dividend. The redemption may be made on such terms and conditions, in such manner as may be provided in the Articles.

New shares may be issued up to the nominal value of the shares redeemed without being, for the purposes of capital duty, deemed to have increased its share capital. Where the new shares are issued before redemption, they are not exempted from capital duty unless the redeemable preference shares are redeemed within one month. If preference shares are to be redeemed out of the proceeds of a fresh issue of shares, there is no restriction except that any premium payable on redemption must be provided out of profits or out of the company's Share Premium Account before the shares are redeemed. If the redemption of preference shares is made out of profits otherwise available for dividend, a sum equal to the nominal value of shares redeemed must be transferred to the 'Capital Redemption Reserve Account'. It can be used for issuing fully paid bonus shares.

Where the profits of a company are applied in redeeming preference shares, the effect of the amount of the issued capital is reduced. In order that a breach of Sec. 100 may note happen, the share capital which has been redeemed must be replaced by an equivalent capital reserve which, for purposes of Sec. 100 is to be regarded as if it were paid up share capital of the company. The balance of the Profit and Loss Account gives a misleading picture of the profit available for dividend unless a transfer is made from the Profit and Loss Account of an amount equal to the amount of the Shares redeemed.

Auditor's Duties

1. To examine that the Articles permit issue of redeemable preference shares.
2. To verify that the shares redeemed were fully paid up.
3. To examine the Articles and Directors' minutes to see authorisation and execution, if the shares are redeemed out of a fresh issue.
4. To ensure that a sum equal to the nominal value of the shares redeemed was transferred to a 'Capital Redemption Reserve Account' in case the shares were redeemed out of divisible profits.
5. To confirm that the premium paid on redemption, if any, was provided out of profits or Share Premium Account only, even where the redemption was carried out by issue of new shares.
6. To vouch the entries passed to materialise redemption.

TRANSFER OF SHARE

Procedure of Effecting Transfer (Sec. 108)

1. Execution by both. The instrument of transfer must be executed both by the transfer and transferee. It must be duly stamped and delivered to the company along with the share certificate.

2. Prescribed form. The instrument of transfer must be executed in a prescribed form. It should be presented to the prescribed authority before it is signed by the transferrer and before any entry is made therein.

3. Period of Transfer. Transfer may be made at any time before the date on which the Register of Members is closed or within two months whichever is later in case of shares dealt in or quoted on a recognised stock exchange. In other cases, presentment should be made to the prescribed authority within two months except for shares held by the scheduled banks and other financial institutions as security for any loans and the shares held by central or state government in the name of a nominee.

4. Partly paid shares. Where the application is made by the transferrer and relates to partly paid shares, the transfer must not be registered unless the company gives notice of the application to the transferee and the transferee makes no objection to the transfer within two weeks from the receipt of the notice [Sec. 110(2)].

5. Registration and Endorsement. After scrutinising these formalities the Board of Directors can register transfer by recording and making an endorsement on the back of share certificate.

Auditor's Duties

1. To verify the Articles of Association of the company to know the procedure to be followed for the transfer of shares.

2. To examine the Directors' Minute Book to confirm approval of transfers and authorisation of issuing new share certificates.
3. To verify that transfer forms are duly completed, duly stamped and signed by transferrer.
4. To ensure that no forgery is committed.
5. To vouch the transfer fee with the Cash Book or Bank Statement. It should be credited to Profit and Loss Account. To make an enquiry where the consideration for transfer appears to be inadequate.
6. To check transferrer names and class, number and distinctive numbers of shares as stated in the transfers and that the old certificates have been cancelled.
7. To inquire whether a notice as required under Sec. 110(2), was given to the transferee in the case of partly paid shares and find out whether the 'no objection' letter has been received from the transferee within two weeks from the receipt of the notice.
8. To inquire whether the transferee is in any way disqualified to be a member of the company.
9. To see whether a notice was given to the mortgagee and whether the shares, which are mortgaged, are lodged for transfer.
10. To check the transfer with the Share Register and to see whether shares have not been transferred twice.
11. To verify the number of share certificates issued with their counterfoils kept with the company.
12. To see the indemnity bond obtained by the company where duplicate share certificates are issued in the absence of the old certificates which are lost or destroyed. To inspect the consent of the Board.
13. To see that if shares have been transferred in favour of an incorporated company, it is authorised to hold such shares.
14. To ensure that a duplicate certificate in place of the one lost or destroyed was issued with the consent of the Board of Directors.
15. To examine the letter of indemnity where shares have been issued in the absence of old share certificates.
16. To verify the issue of Balance Certificates to the transferrer if only a part of the shares have been transferred out of those stated in a share certificate also to confirm that the distinctive number of shares are correctly recorded.
17. To verify that all new share certificates in replacement of old certificates contain the original numbers, i.e. the fact of these being replaced must be enlisted on the face of the new certificates.

18. To see that a separate certificate relating to the share transfer audit, may be worded as below:

"I have audited the share books of ... Co. Ltd, for the year ended ... and certify that all transfers have been correctly recorded therein, that the relative share certificates have been properly authorised, and that the balances in the Register of Members agree with the issued share capital as shown in the Balance Sheet."

Transmission of Shares

If shares have been transmitted on account of the death or the bankruptcy of a shareholder the auditor should examine the following:

1. The Article of Association of the company to see whether the regulations have been complied with;
2. The succession certificates granted by the Court or the order of the Court of insolvency, as the case may be;
3. The 'will' in the case of death of a shareholder;
4. The certificate issued by the Controller of the Estate Duty that estate duty has been paid;
5. The application from the executor or the legatee that the shares may be issued.

Shareholder's Right to Transfer his Shares

A shareholder's right to transfer his shares is subject to the following limitations:

1. Section 3(1)(iii). A private company should restrict the right of a member to transfer his shares.

2. Under Sec.42(1). Except in certain cases, a company cannot be a member of its holding company, and any transfer of shares in a company to its subsidiary is void.

3. Section 77(1). A company limited by shares and a company limited by guarantee and having a share capital, cannot buy its own shares. A member company cannot transfer its shares to the company.

4. Under Section 250. The Company Law Board has the power to ban the transfer of certain shares for a period not exceeding three years.

5. Section 372. A company cannot purchase shares in another company belonging to the same group except in certain circumstances.

6. Section 395. Under certain circumstances the majority members of a company shall have the right to insist that the minority shall transfer their shares to the persons to whom they have transferred their own shares.

7. Section 84 of the Estate Duty Act, 1953. Where a company has knowledge of the death of any member, it cannot register a transfer of his shares except where the transferee acquired such shares for valuable consideration without the production of certificate from the Controller of Estate Duty to the effect that the duty in respect of the value of such shares has been paid or will be paid or that no duty is due.

8. Foreign Exchange Regulation Act, 1973. A transfer of shares to a non-resident is not allowed without the permission of the Reserve Bank.

9. Power to decline. The directors of a company may decline to register any transfer of shares to a person whom they do not approve.

Blank Transfers

The idea of a transfer is that the creditor gets equitable interest in the shares and may sell them on failure of the mortgagor to pay the debt after giving him reasonable notice. It is an instrument of transfer in which transferrer fills in his name and signature only and in which the transferrer fills in his name and signature only and in which the transferee's name and signature and the date of transfer are not filled in. The advantage of giving such a blank transfer is that the transferee will be at liberty to sell the shares again to a subsequent buyer without disclosing his own identity and without paying for the transfer stamp.

Evils of blank transfer system

1. It conceals the identity of the real beneficial owners behind their nominees.
2. It leads to evasion of tax by suppression of secret profits invested in holdings on blank transfers.
3. It facilitates window-dressing of Balance Sheet of company by re- shuffling of shares held on blank transfers between associated companies with the object of replacing inter-company loans by investments at the time of the closing of accounts.
4. It brings into existence fictitious or anti-dated transactions in the book of companies in order to create fictitious losses in investments for the purposes of reducing the taxable profits.

Restrictions on the period of currency

Section 108(1A) has imposed the following restriction on the period of currency of blank transfers:

1. Every instrument of transfer of shares shall be in the prescribed form and presented to the prescribed authority (being a government employee) before it is signed by the transferrer and before any entry is made therein, and the prescribed authority shall stamp thereon the date on which it is so presented.
2. The said instrument with the date of such presentation stamped thereon shall, after it is executed by the transferrer and completed in all other

respects, be delivered to the company for registration within the period stated below:

(a) In the case of listed shares, at any time before the date on which the Register of Members is closed for the first time after the date of the presentation of the prescribed forms to the prescribed authority or within two months from the date of such presentation, whichever is later; and

(b) The instrument of transfer duly completed in all respects is delivered to the company for registration within two months of the date so stamped.

Under Section 153, no notice of any trust, expressed, implied or constructive, may be entered on the Register of Members.

2. Any share deposited by any person with (i) the State Bank of India, (ii) any scheduled bank, (iii) any other banking company or financial institution approved by the central government or (iv) the state government or a government company, by way of security, if the following conditions are fulfilled:

(a) The depositor stamps on the form of transfer the date on which such share is returned to the depositor, or, in case of default on the part of the depositor, the date on which such share is released for sale, or, where the depositee intends to get such share registered in its own name, the date on which the instrument of transfer relating to it is executed by it; and

(b) The instrument of transfer in such form, duly completed in all respects, is delivered to the company for registration within two months of the date so stamped.

3. Any share which is held by the central government in the name of its nominee.

Forged Transfer

This may happen in the case of following types of shares :

1. Fully paid-up Shares. In a forged transfer the Transfer Deed is signed by a person other than the transferrer and the transferee. For safety purposes the Companies draw the attention of the transferrer, the fact of such a transfer and invite objections, if any. This, however, does not give any protection to the company as the transferrer is not legally bound to reply to the company. If the true owner's name is removed from the Register of Members because of a forged transfer he can get his name re-enrolled as an existing member. If the company has issued a new certificate to the alleged transferee, it cannot deny his title to the share as the certificate stops the company from doing so. The person or broker lodging the transfer must indemnify against loss by forgery. The share certificate is not a representation that the transferrer has a title. According to Sec.

112(2) if any person acts on the faith of a false certification which has been made by the company negligently, the company will be under the same liability to such person as if certification has been made fraudulently.

2. Partly Paid Shares. Sometimes the true owner may himself forge the transfer of shares in the name of a fictitious person to escape liability, in case of partly paid share, particularly when the company is in a loss. He himself signs as usual but forges the signatures of the transferee who in fact will never be traceable by the company to send call notices and to receive money from him. He also avoids realisation of call money by the company through the Court by attachment of his assets. The Companies Act provides that even the previous shareholder may be held liable to pay as contributory of the company for non-payment of the calls by the existing shareholders. One way is to focus attention on the acknowledgment of the transferee because if nothing could be delivered at a wrong address how could that be a valid transfer.

ALTERATION OF CAPITAL

1. Section 94. It deals with powers of a limited company to alter share capital. A limited company having share capital may alter the capital clause of its Memorandum by passing an ordinary resolution, in any of the following way:

1. Increase its share capital by issuing new shares;
2. Consolidate and divide all or any of its share capital into shares of a larger amount;
3. Convert all or any of its fully paid-up shares into stock and reconvert the stock into fully paid shares;
4. Sub-divide its shares into shares of smaller amount in such a manner that the proportion between the amount paid and the amount, if any, unpaid on each reduced share shall remain the same as before;
5. Cancel the unissued shares thereby diminishing the amount of the share capital.

2. Section 949(A). It provides that where the central government has by order, under Sec. 81(4), directed that any debenture or loan or any part thereof shall be converted into shares and where such order has the effect of increasing the nominal share capital of the company, the conditions in the Memorandum stand altered by an amount of the value of shares into which such debentures or loans have been converted.

3. Section 94(2). The company can alter its share capital without the confirmation of the Court.

4. Section 94(3). Cancellation of shares in such a manner is not to be regarded as reduction of capital.

5. Section 95. Within thirty days of altering the capital in such a manner the company has to give a notice to the Registrar of Companies after seeing whether the shares were consolidated, divided, converted, sub-divided, redeemed or cancelled or the stock reconverted, The Registrar will issue orders for necessary alterations in the company's Memorandum or Articles or both.

Auditor's Duties

1. To verify the Articles to see the company's power to alter its capital and that the provisions are observed.
2. To see that requirements as in Secs. 94 and 95 are complied with.
3. To verify that Minutes of the Directors and the minutes of the shareholders' authorising the alteration.
4. To verify the necessary entries in the books of accounts and other registers including the Register of Members.
5. To verify that due intimation to Registrar of Companies has been given, as in Sec. 95, and that he has ordered the alteration of the Memorandum or Articles or both.
6. To verify and compare the cancelled share certificates with the counterfoils of new certificates issued, in case of a consolidation or sub-division of shares.
7. To obtain allotment lists with details of new shares or stock-holdings by each member and verify the same with the entries.
8. To verify that the share capital account is correctly shown in the Balance Sheet.

REDUCTION OF SHARE CAPITAL

Objects of Reduction

Provisions regarding reductions of share capital are contained in Secs. 100 to 105. A company limited by shares or a company limited by guarantee and having a share capital may, if so authorised by the Articles, by special resolution, reduce its capital subject to confirmation by the Court.

1. To extinguish or reduce the liability on any of its shares in respect of the share capital not paid up; or
2. To cancel the paid-up share capital which is lost or is unrepresented by available assets; with or without extinguishing or reducing liability on any or its shares.
3. To pay off any paid up share capital which is in excess of the wants of the company with or without extinguishing or reducing liability on any of its shares.

Articles may be altered by special resolution giving authorisation to the company which must be passed before the resolution to reduce is dealt with, by the meeting. There must be separate resolutions for the power and the sanction though can be passed in the same meeting.

Reduction with consent of the court

1. Section 101(1). The company must apply by petition to the Court for an order confirming the reduction. The Court may hear the creditors' objection, if any and if satisfied with the logic of reduction, may make an order confirming the reduction of the capital on such terms and conditions as it deems fit. It may require the company to add to its name as last words 'as reduced' which will form part of the name of the company for the specified period.

2. Sec.103. The company shall produce to the Registrar of Companies, a certified copy of the Court order and minutes approved by the Court. The Registrar will register the order and the minutes and issue a certificate which is a conclusive evidence of all the legalities being already performed and that other share capital of the company is such as stated in the minutes. The minutes when registered are deemed to be the corresponding part of the company's Memorandum and shall be valid and alterable as if it had been originally contained therein. The Registrar's certificate is conclusive even where it is found afterwards that the company's Articles contained no clause empowering reduction of capital or that the resolution for reduction was invalid.

Reduction with Consent of the Court

A company may reduce its capital without the consent of the Court by doing the following:

1. Forfeiture. By forfeiting shares, if the Articles permit cancelling the forfeited shares;

2. Surrender. By accepting a surrender of shares under circumstances where forfeiture is justified;

3. Redemption. By redeeming redeemable preference shares, subject to the provision of Sec. 80;

4. Cancellation. By cancelling unissued shares.

Auditor's Duties

1. To examine the Articles to verify that reduction of share capital is authorised and if not, a special resolution is passed altering the Articles.
2. To examine that the convening of the meeting and the resolution passed there were proper and valid.
3. To examine the order of the court and the minutes thereto as approved by it.
4. To see that a copy of the same was filed with the Registrar of Companies.
5. To inspect the Registrar's certificate regarding reduction of capital.
6. To verify the adjustment made with reference to the Register of Members, audits ensure that new shares were issued only after cancelling the old certificates.

7. To vouch the Journal entries made to reduce the capital and to write down the assets by referring to shareholders' resolution and other documentary evidence.
8. To see that the requirements of Schedule VI, Part I regarding reduction of the value of fixed assets have been complied with.
9. To confirm that the revaluation of assets has been properly disclosed in the Balance Sheet.
10. To ensure that the company did comply with all the terms and conditions laid down by the Court.
11. To see that the words 'as reduced' form part of its name, if so decided by the court.
12. To ensure that the Memorandum of Association had been accordingly altered and no legal formalities are pending.

Condition of Further Issue of Capital

According to Sec. 81, where a company proposes to increase its subscribed capital by allotment of further shares after the expiry of two years from the formation of the company or at any time after the expiry of one year from the first allotment of shares after is formation, whichever is earlier, such shares must first be offered to holders of equity shares in proportion, as nearly the circumstances permit, to the capital paid-up on those shares. The company must send a notice to all the shareholders stating the number of shares offered, the time within which to accept, and power to renounce all or any of the shares offered to them in favour of their nominees. These provisions, however, will become inapplicable under the following conditions:

1. After the time limit the directors have decided to dispose of the shares offered in such manner as they think most beneficial to the company; or
2. If a special resolution is passed by the company in general meeting to allot the new issue in a different manner than that provided in Sec. 81; or
3. If any ordinary resolution to that effect has been passed and the central government is satisfied on the application of the Board that the proposal is most beneficial to the company [Sec. 81(1A)).

Interest paid out of Capital

According to section 208 a company may pay interest out of capital in special circumstances. Interest can be paid where any shares in a company are issued for the purpose of raising money to meet the expenses for the construction of any works or building or the provisions of any plant which cannot be made profitable for a long period. Interest may be paid on that part of the share capital which for the time being is paid up. Such a charge of interest can be debited to the capital as a part of the cost of construction of the work or building or provision for the plant. Interest on debentures issued or amount borrowed for similar purpose can be charged to capital during the period of construction.

Conditions under Section 208

1. Articles of Association of the company must authorise such a payment of interest. The rate of interest shall in no case exceed 4% p.a. or such other rate as may be notified by the central government in the Official Gazette.

2. Sanction of the central government must have been obtained. The government may at the expense of the company appoint a person to inquire into and report to it the circumstances of the case, and may, before making the appointment require the company to give security for the payment of cost of such an inquiry.

3. The payment of such interest shall operate as reduction of the amount paid up on shares in respect of which it is paid.

PRELIMINARY EXPENSES

Preliminary expenses are those which concern the creation, flotation incorporation of a company. These include the following:

1. All expenses concerning the basic documents. This includes drafting charges of the legal solicitor, stamp duty, registration fee, fees paid to valuer and other experts, printing charges of such documents and cost of advertising and issuing the prospectus.

2. All costs concerning stationary etc. These include :

(i) The cost of paper and printing of share application forms, letters of allotment and share certificates etc.

(ii) The cost of seal of the Company.

(iii) The cost of necessary set of Statutory Books, Registers and Books of Accounts.

1. Auditor's Duties. To verify the following on the basis of documentary evidence and to see that preliminary expenses do not include these:

(i) loss incurred in the first year of the life of the company;

(ii) brokerage, commission etc. for selling or underwriting or for placing shares;

(iii) once the company begins to earn revenue, the current expenditure should not be debited to preliminary expenses account (*Baidya Nath Biswas* v. *Emperor*).

2. To see that the company is charged only with expenses appropriately payable by it.

3. To examine the contracts relating to these expenses and vouch the mode of payment.

4. To see that expenses of capital nature but unsupported by available assets, be written off as soon as possible out of the revenue. According to Sec.78 such expenses can be charged against share premium.
5. To see that these are disclosed in the prospectus, statutory report and balance sheet.
6. To see that the preliminary expenses not written off yet have been shown separately under 'Miscellaneous Expenditure' in the Balance Sheet.

PROFITS PRIOR TO INCORPORATION

A company is born on the date mentioned in the Certificate of Incorporation issued by the Registrar of Companies. It may take over a business as and from a date prior to its own incorporation. In the process, it may earn some profits which are legally not available for dividend distribution. Such profits are of a capital nature and can be used for the following purposes only.

1. To pay interest, up to the date of incorporation, to the vendors on the amount of purchase consideration. Interest payable in respect of any period after the date of incorporation can be debited to the company's Profit and Loss Account.
2. Writing off goodwill, if any.
3. Writing off some other fixed assets.
4. Any balance left after such utilisation is to be carried forward as a capital reserve and in no case available for revenue purposes.

Gross profits may be apportioned according to the turnover of the pre-incorporation and post-incorporation periods, indirect expenses on the basis of time covered by the respective periods and direct expenses in proportion to the turnover of these periods. Apportionment of a loss occurring in the pre-incorporation period cannot be made. Such a loss is either added to the goodwill amount or adjusted or written off out of the subsequent capital profits.

The auditor should ensure that an equitable division of profits has been materialised, that profits prior to incorporation are not paid as dividends and that any pre-incorporation loss has been properly dealt with.

STATUTORY AUDIT

Statutory audit is that which is required to be by the auditor prior to the statutory meeting of the company. According to Sec. 165, every public company limited by guarantee and having a share capital, must hold a general meeting of its members, to be called the 'Statutory Meeting,' within six months but not before one month from the date on which the company is entitled to commence business.

At least twenty-one days before the day of the meeting, the Board of Directors must forward to every member and to the Registrar, a report along with the notice of the meeting.

This is the Statutory Report drawn up in Form 22 stating the following :

1. The total number of shares allotted, distinguishing between share allotted as fully or partly paid up and the shares allotted for consideration other than cash.
2. The total amount of cash received by the company in respect of all the shares allotted.
3. The number of shares allotted for consideration other than cash and the consideration thereof.
4. The receipt of cash receipts in respect of the other payments made by the company, up to date within seven days before the submission of the statutory report and the balance in hand on that date.
5. The receipt of cash from shares and debentures and other sources and the balance remaining in hand.
6. An account of estimate of preliminary expense.
7. The names, address and occupations of directors, auditors, manager and secretary of company and any changes which have taken place in the names, addresses and occupations of directors, auditors and others since the date of incorporation.
8. The particulars of any contract, or its modification to be placed before the shareholder for their approval.
9. The extent to which any underwriting contract has not been carried out and the reasons thereof.
10. The arrears due on call from every director, secretary etc.
11. The particulars of any commission or brokerage paid or to be paid, in connection with the issue or sale of shares or debentures to any director.

At least two directors, one of whom must be managing director, if there is one must certify that statutory report as correct. The auditors of the company should certify it as correct so far as it relates to the shares allotted by the company, the cash received in respect of such shares and the receipts and the payments of the company. This certificate is worded as under:

We hereby certify as correct so much of the report as relates to the shares allotted by the company and to the cash received in respect of such shares and to the receipts on payments.

Dated this day of Auditors

Auditor's Duties

1. To examine the Memorandum of Association and the Articles of Association to know the terms of issue of shares.
2. To examine the Prospectus and the Minute Book of the Board of Directors to know the resolution regarding the allotment of shares and calls made thereon.

3. To examine the Cash Book and Bank Pass Book to verify the accuracy of all cash receipts and payments.
4. To examine the application and allotment book, register of shareholders, etc.
5. To examine the contracts entered into with the vendors, underwriters and brokers.
6. To vouch all the receipts and payments as usual.
7. To carry out a complete audit of the issue of share capital with special regard to
   (i) the shares allotted by the company,
   (ii) the cash received on such shares, and
   (iii) miscellaneous receipts and payments.

DEBENTURES

Definition

According to Sec. 2(12) of the Companies Act, debenture includes debenture stock, bonds and other securities of a company, whether constituting a charge on the assets of the company or not. It is an acknowledgment of a debt which is given under the common seal of the company and which contains a contract.

1. For the repayment of the principal sum at a specified date,
2. For payment of interest at a fixed rate per cent till the principal sum is repaid.
3. Debenture includes 'debenture stock'. A debenture may or may not give a charge on the assets of the company as security for the loan. It mentions the conditions as to security and the repayment of the loan, the payment of interest and as to the redemption of the loan.

Power of Directors to Issue Debentures

1. Section 293(1). The Board of Directors of a public company, or of a private company which is a subsidiary of a public company, shall not, except with the consent of the company given in a general meeting, borrow money, where moneys borrowed together with the moneys borrowed already, will exceed the aggregate of the paid-up capital of the company and its free reserves. Temporary loans obtained from the company's bankers in the ordinary course of business will not be considered for such a limit.

2. Section 293(5). Debts incurred by the company in excess of the limits shall not be valid or effective unless the lender proves that he advanced the loan in food faith and without the knowledge that the limit imposed had been exceeded. If the company wants to borrow in excess of this limit, it must pass in a general meeting an ordinary resolution empowering the directors to borrow in excess of the limit prescribed by Sec. 293(1).

3. Section 292(1). The Board of Directors of a company shall exercise the power to issue debentures only by means of a resolution passed at the meeting of the Board.

Procedure of Issue

This is similar to that of issue of shares. It is as follows:

1. Resolution. A resolution authorising the issue of debentures must be passed at a meeting of the Board of Directors of the company.

2. Meeting. If the proposed borrowing under the debentures, together with any money already borrowed by company exceed the aggregate of the company's paid up capital and free reserves, then, in the case of public companies and their private subsidiaries, a meeting of the members must be called and their consent for the issue must be obtained by an ordinary resolution.

3. Consent. The consent of the central government must be obtained for the issue, if the aggregate of the company's capital issue (both shares and debentures) during the year exceeds Rs. 2.5 million.

4. Debentures to non-Residents. The issue of debentures to non-resident must be permitted by the Reserve Bank of India.

5. Convertible Debentures. If the debentures carry an option of conversion into shares, the issue must be approved by central government and also authorised by a special resolution of the company.

6. Prospectus or statement. When the debentures are offered to the public, a prospectus containing all the statutory informations must be filed with the Registrar on the same date on which it is issued. If a prospectus is not issued, a statement in lieu of prospectus must be filed with the Registrar at least three days before the first allotment of debentures.

7. Date of Allotment. No allotment of debentures can be made until the beginning of the fifth day from the day on which the prospectus is issued or such later time as specified in the prospectus itself.

8. Application to Stock Exchange. Where the prospectus states that an application is being made to a stock exchange for permission to deal, any allotment made will be void if the application is not made or the permission is refused.

9. Debenture Certificates. It is not necessary to file a return of allotment of debentures with the registrar, but the debenture certificates should be completed and be ready for delivery within three months of the allotment.

10. Register of Debenture Holders. After the allotment, the necessary particulars relating to each debenture holder must be entered in the Register of Debenture-holders.

11. Particulars of the Charge. If the debentures create a charge on the company's property, particulars of the charge must be filed with the Registrar within 30 days after the execution of the deed containing the charge. A certificate registration should be obtained from the Registrar and a copy of the certificate should be endorsed on every debenture certificate. Particulars of the charge should also be entered in the Company's Register of Charges.

12. Interest. Interest is always payable at the nominal value of the debenture even when debenture is issued at a discount or at a premium. It is a revenue expenditure and should be so audited.

13. Section 117. After 1st April, 1956, a company cannot issue any debentures carrying voting rights at any meeting of the company.

14. Decree for specific performance. A contract with a company to take and pay for any debentures of the company can be enforced by a decree for specific performance.

Rules About Types of Debentures

1. Debentures Issued at a Premium. In this case the Companies Act does not specify the treatment of premium amount. However, being a capital profit it is available for purposes of writing off debenture issue expenses or redemption of debentures or even writing off fictitious assets like preliminary expenses. It is classified in the Balance Sheet as capital reserve which will appear as a liability at their nominal value.

2. Debentures Issued at a Discount. This is subject to the provision of Sec. 76(2). The discount represents the consideration of tenders for accepting a lower rate of interest then what would have been payable, had the debentures been issued at par. The debentures will appear in the Balance Sheet as liability at their nominal value. The discount amount will be written off over a period of years, the balance remaining at any date being carried forward as separate item in the Balance Sheet. The following guidelines may be observed in this connection:

(i) The discount should be written off as early as possible.

(ii) An equal amount of the discount should be written off each year, if the amount is carried over for a longer period without forming a sinking fund for the purpose of repaying the debentures which are repayable at the end of given period.

(iii) The discount should be written off in relative proportion to the amount of debentures outstanding each year, if debentures are repayable by annual drawings, without the provisions of a sinking fund.

(iv) The discount must be shown in the Annual Returns.

3. Debentures Repayable at a Premium. These debentures will appear in the Balance Sheet as a liability at their nominal value but with a note of the amount at which they are repayable. The premium at which the debentures are redeemable is a loss which should be spread over a number of years for which debentures are to run. If a sinking fund is formed to provide for repayment, this should include provision for the payment of the premium on redemption If no sinking fund is formed, the premium should be provided from the Share Premium Account or out of profits over the term of the debentures.

4. Debentures Issued as Collateral Security for a Loan. These are issued in terms of Sec. 121(4) against a loan or overdraft from a bank or other parties. Such debentures shall not be deemed to have been redeemed by reason only of the account of the company having ceased to be in debit whilst the debenture remained so deposited. A note stating the fact of debentures being issued must be shown on the Balance Sheet. The loan against which they are issued will appear as a liability. The nominal value of such debentures is invariably more than the loan amount. It is a sort of additional or secondary security without any cash receipts. If the loan is not repaid when due, the collateral security becomes effective. The debentures are automatically released as the loan is repaid.

5. Debentures Issued at a Discount but Redeemable at a Premium. The difference between the actual amount received and the amount payable at redemption, should be spread over the life of debentures. The nominal value of the debentures will be shown as a liability and the discount on issue and the premium on redemption of debentures appears as asset in the Balance Sheet.

Auditor's Duties

1. To ascertain the company's borrowing powers from its Memorandum and see that they have not been exceeded having regard to the restrictions laid down in Sec. 293(d).
2. To see that the consent of the central government has been obtained for the issue, if the amount of the issue exceeds Rs. 2.5 million.
3. To note that the issue of convertible debentures is approved by the central government and authorised by a special resolution of company.
4. To see that requirements of law relating to the allotment of debentures have been complied with and that the allotment of debentures to non-residents has been permitted by the Reserve Bank of India.
5. To examine the Director's Minute Book regarding the issue of debentures and mortgage of the company's property.
6. To vouch the proceeds when debentures are issued for cash.
7. To examine the contract under which debentures have been issued.
8. To inspect the debenture trust deed (if any) or an actual debenture to find out the exact terms and conditions of issue, and see that they are complied with.

9. To see that the charge created on the company's assets has been entered in the company's Register of Charges and that the necessary particulars have been filed with the Registrar. To see the Registrar's certificate of registration.
10. To see that they are properly shown in the Balance Sheet issued as security for a loan.
11. To check the amount of debentures outstanding with the balances shown in the Register of Debenture-holders.
12. To see that the remuneration of debenture trustees has been paid or provided for.
13. To examine the company's Articles to see that they do not prohibit the procedure, where debentures have been issued at a premium and the company wants to take credit for it in its Profit and Loss Accounts.
14. To check the amount of interest paid or accrued on debentures.
15. To see that all debenture transactions have been correctly entered in the books and properly shown in the Balance Sheet.
16. To see that the Balance Sheet shows the nominal amount of the debentures and the amount at which they are stated in company's books, even when held by a nominee or a trustee for the company.

Redemption of Debentures

Following are the three ways of redeeming debentures according to the terms of the issue:

1. By payment to the holders at the expiry of the period stated. A Sinking Fund Account is created by debiting the Profit and Loss Appropriation Account. The amount so credited is invested in the gilt-edged securities. These securities are sold on the date of the redemption of debentures.

2. By payment year after year of a certain portion of the total debentures by drawings. The revenue account is debited with the annual drawings and the 'Redemption Fund' account is credited. When debenture-holders are paid, their accounts are debited and cash account is credited. Finally, the Redemption Fund Account is debited and General Reserve is credited to close down the former.

3. By payment being made by the company to the debenture-holders. In this case a proper notice should be given by the company about its intention to such holders.

Auditor's Duties

1. To examine the terms of the issue and redemption of debentures or the Debenture Trust Deed, if any, and see their compliance.
2. To vouch the redemption with the Minute Book, the counterfoil of the cheque book, entries in Pass Book and the Cash Book.

3. To examine the cancelled debenture bonds or registered certificates.
4. To examine that provision for redeeming the debentures has been made in the books every year, in case a sinking fund had been credited for their redemption.
5. To vouch the receipt of cash by the sale of investments with the Sold Note when sinking fund investments have been sold for the redemption of debentures.
6. To examine the disposal of the credit balance of Debenture Redemption Fund or Sinking Fund Insurance/Endorsement Policy. The balance is accumulated profits but represent general assets of the business which had previously been subject to the charge of the debentures. The amount of such fund should be transferred to General Reserves. Financially as a rule the balance is not used for the payment of dividends but legally it can be so distributed if cash is available and the Article permit it.
7. To see that when debentures have been redeemed by purchasing these in the market at a discount, the profits so made have been transferred to Profit and Loss Account or preferably, to reserve account.
8. To see that where no sinking fund has been provided, profits on redemption have been taken to reserve and not credited to the Profit and Loss Account.

QUESTIONS FOR EXERCISE

1. Write short note on Reorganisation of Capital.
2. Explain procedure of share capital audit for a new company, first issue.
3. Explain the procedure of issue of shares under premium and at a discount. Point out auditor's duties in this connection.
4. Explain the procedure and guidelines in the case of issue of Bonus Shares.
5. What are the auditor's duties in connection with underwriting commission, brokerage and calls.
6. What is the procedure of forfeiture and re-issue of forfeited shares? Point-out the auditor's duties in this connection.
7. Explain the procedures of issue and transfer of shares and point out the auditor's duties in this connection.
8. Explain legal provisions concerning alteration and reduction of share capital.
9. Write short note on:
   (i) Preliminary expenses.
   (ii) Profits prior to Incorporation
   (iii) Statutory Audit.
10. Define debenture and discuss the procedure of its issue.
11. What are the rules concerning various type of debentures. Enumerate Auditor's duties in this connection.

16

Financial Statements

CONTENTS OF BALANCE SHEET

Section 211 of the Companies Act contains the form and contents of the Balance Sheet and Profit and Loss Account. It stipulates these as follows:

1. True and fair Balance Sheet. Every Balance Sheet of a company should give a true and fair view of the state of affairs of the company, at the end of financial year. It should be in the form set out in Part I of Schedule VI or as near thereto as the circumstances permit or such other form as many be approved by the central government either generally or in any particular case. The general instructions for the preparation of Balance Sheets, under heading "Notes" and at the end of the Part should be followed.

2. True and fair Profit and Loss Account. Every Profit and Loss Account of a company should give a true and fair view of the profit and loss of the company for the financial year and should comply with the requirements of Part II of the Schedule VI, so far as they are applicable thereto.

The above mentioned Sec. 211 is not applicable to an insurance or a banking company or a company engaged in the generation or supply of electricity or any other class of company for the Schedule VI, so far as they are applicable thereto.

The above mentioned Sec. 221 is not applicable to an insurance or a banking company or a company engaged in the generation or supply of electricity or any other class of companies for which a form of the Balance Sheet or the Profit and Loss Account has been specified in or under the Act covering such class of companies. Under Sub-Sec.(3) the central government is authorised to exempt any class of companies from compliance with any of the requirements in Schedule VI, by a notification in the Official Gazette if, in its opinion, it is necessary to grant the exemption in public interest, unconditionally or subject to such conditions as may be specified in the notification. On the application of or with the consent of the Board of Directors of the company, the central government by order, modify in relation to that company any of the requirements of the Act as to the matters to be stated in the company's Balance Sheet and Profit and Loss Account for the purpose of adapting them to the circumstances of the company.

To attain true and fair view of the state of affairs of a company, it is necessary that the statements of accounts of a company may exhibit the information required by law and the same be displayed in the manner required.

Form of Presentation of Financial Statements

Schedule VI to the Companies Act permits presentation of financial statements either in the traditional form (T form)/horizontal form or in the vertical form/columnar form. Keeping in view the fact that the vertical form of presentation is more clear and educative to a layman the Company Law Board has permitted it and also prescribed a form for it.

Merits of Vertical Presentation of Financial Statements

1. Easy Comprehension. A layman can easily and readily comprehend the financial position of the company when the financial statements are drawn in this form.

2. Trading and Non-trading Profit. The Profit and Loss Account discloses clearly the amount of trading and non-trading profit made during the year, that is brought forward from the previous year, and the appropriations made out of the total profits recommended by the Board of Directors.

3. Debt and Equity. The Balance Sheet discloses the amount of debt and equity very distinctly. It further discloses the position of assets held against them segregated into fixed assets and working capital.

4. Easy financial analysis. As this form is capable of presenting together the comparative figures of a number of years financial analysis becomes easier.

5. Ratios. The relationships between the various balances can be easily worked out.

Presentation in a Summary Form

Unduly loaded by too many figures the horizontal and the vertical form of presentation of financial statements were found to be out of reach of ordinary public. It was felt that figures of income and expenditure, assets and liabilities must be properly grouped or categorised and the totals shown in a summary form. To fulfil legal requirements the details and other information requiring disclose are relegated to schedules attached to them. Obviously, the schedules form as integral part of the Profit and Loss Account and the Balance Sheet.

Merits of Summary Form Presentation

1. Overall View. It enables the readers to have an overall view of the financial position and the working results at one glance. One can ascertain the final position very easily and quickly.

2. Interesting. It maintains their charm and sense as readers do not lose interest therein.

3. Schedules. Persons who are interested in further details can go through the supporting schedules. Details are systematically tabulated under different heads in the schedules.

Devices to Make Financial Statements more Informative

1. Statistics. To make the accounting data more meaningful and comparable modern accountants use statistics. These are published in respect of the following matters:

(i) The value of shareholders' equity, i.e. net worth per share,

(ii) Percentage of net profits after taxes, to the shareholders equity,

(iii) Number of employees,

(iv) Number of shareholders and break-up thereto,

(v) Dividend paid per share.

2. Charts, graphs and diagrams. Presentation of financial information in a pictorial form is an effective method of communication. Some examples are given below:

(i) Use pie-chart diagram to present break-up of earnings into constituent items of expenditure.

(ii) Use pie-chart or rupee-break-up diagrams to show break-up of sales percentages of different products sold.

(iii) Use bar diagrams or graphs to show the increase in production, sales, profit, etc. from year to year.

(iv) Use the statistical technique of tabular presentation to show dividend declared and the percentage of dividend to invested capital.

(v) Use pie-charts or graphs to show distribution of divisible profits as dividends, retained profits, taxes and other appropriations.

Schedule VI to the Companies Act

Section 211 requires that every Balance Sheet and Profit and Loss Account should fulfil the requirements of Schedule VI to the Companies Act, as far as they are applicable. Schedule VI has three parts given as follows :

Part I. It contains the form of the Balance Sheet and states the information about different assets and liabilities to be disclosed therein. It categorises all assets and liabilities and lists them in their order of preference. It contains general instructions which should be followed in the preparation of the Balance Sheet.

Part II. This part contains provisions about information relating to items of income and expenditure which should be disclosed thereto. Companies may adopt any form depending on its suitability and convenience provided that all the disclosures required by this part are clearly carried out. It must disclose every material feature, including credits or receipts and debits or expenses in respect of non-recurring or exceptional transactions.

Part III. It defines and interprets 'provision', 'reserve', 'capital reserve', 'revenue reserve' and 'quoted investments'. It provides that in the case of a provision or liability the excess should be treated as a reserve and not as a provision.

As the Act does not dwell upon the accounting practices that should be followed in order to generate the information required to be disclosed, professional bodies like ICAI, formulate various accounting standards in order to harmonise the diverse accounting practices and policies.

REQUIREMENTS REGARDING BALANCE SHEET

The Balance Sheet must be prepared and presented in accordance with the requirements of Part I of Schedule VI to the Companies Act.

A. Liabilities. Liabilities should be classified into the following five main categories:

1. Share capital,
2. Reserves and surpluses,
3. Secured loans,
4. Unsecured loans,
5. Current liabilities and provisions.

Contingent liabilities and certain other items should be disclosed by way of a note to the Balance Sheet.

Auditor's objectives about liabilities

1. The credit balances appearing in the books are real liabilities;
2. The liabilities remaining unrecorded whether by accident or design are brought into books;
3. They are properly valued;
4. They are properly classified and disclosed.

B. Assets. Assets should be classified into following five categories:

1. Fixed assets,
2. Investments,
3. Current assets and loans and advances,
4. Miscellaneous expenditures, and
5. Profit and Loss account.

Auditor's objectives about assets

1. They exist;
2. They belong to the client;
3. They are in the possession of the client or persons authorised by him;
4. They are not subject to undisclosed encumbrances or lien;

5. They are stated in the balance sheet at properly valued amounts in accordance with sound accounting principles; and
6. They are recorded (including scrap and waste) in the accounts.

Notes to Part I of Schedule VI contain general instructions for preparation of the balance sheet. The figures of the previous year should also be shown along with the figures of the current year. The information required to be given under any of the items of the balance sheet may be given in separate Schedules to be annexed to and form part of the Balance Sheet.

REQUIREMENTS ABOUT PROFIT AND LOSS ACCOUNT

Part II of Schedule VI contains general instructions for preparation of the Profit and Loss Account. These apply to the Income and Expenditure Account [Sec. 200(2)] as well as Profit and Loss Account.

(i) The Profit and Loss Account shall be so made as to clearly disclose the results of the company during the period covered by the account, and

(ii) It shall disclose every material feature, including credits or receipts and debits or expenses in respect of non-recurring transactions or transactions of an exceptional nature.

GENERAL DISCLOSURE

1. Items of Income and Expenditure. These must be disclosed in the most convenient form disclosing the following:

(i) the turnover, i.e. sales amount of each item with quantities thereto;

(ii) commission paid to other selling agents within the meaning of Sec. 234;

(iii) commission paid to other selling agents;

(iv) brokerage and discounts on sales other than the usual trade discount:

(a) If it is a manufacturing company the income and expenditure must show the value of the raw materials consumed giving item-wise breakup in respect of each class of goods traded in by the company and indicating the quantities thereof.

(b) If it is a company rendering or supplying service the income and expenditure should not show income and expenditure, but the gross income derived from services rendered or supplied.

(c) If it is a company falling under more than one category, account must show the total amounts in respect of the opening and closing stock, purchases, sales and consumption of raw material with values and quantitative breakup and the gross income from services rendered and in the case of other companies, the gross income derived under different heads.

(d) In the case of all concerns having work-in-progress the income and expenditure must show the amounts for which such work has been completed at the commencement and at the end of the accounting period.

2. The Profit and Loss Account

(i) *Provision for depreciation renewals or diminution in value of fixed assets.* If such a provision is not made by means of depreciation charge, the method adopted in making such a provision must be clarified. If no provision is made for depreciation, the fact shall be stated and the quantum of arrears of depreciation computed in accordance with Sec. 205(2) must be disclosed by way of a note.

(ii) *Interest.* The Profit and Loss Account must include the amount of interest on the company's debentures and other fixed loans, such as loans of fixed periods, stating separately the amount of interest, if any, paid or payable to the managing director and the manager, if any.

(iii) *Income Tax.* Profit and Loss Account must show the amount of charge for Indian income-tax and other Indian taxation on profits, including where practicable with Indian income-tax any taxation imposed elsewhere to the extent of the relief, if any, from Indian income-tax and distinguishing where practicable, between income-tax and other taxation.

(iv) *Reserves.* The Profit and Loss Account must show the amounts reserved for :

(a) repayment of share capital, and

(b) repayment of loans.

(v) ***Aggregate.*** The Profit and Loss Account must show the aggregate, if material of any amounts set aside or proposed to be set aside, to reserves but not including provisions made to meet any specific liability, contingency or commitment known to exit to the date as at which Balance Sheet is made up. It should mention the aggregate, if material, of the amounts withdrawn from such reserve and also the aggregate, if material, of the amounts set aside to provisions made for meeting specific liabilities, contingencies or commitments.

(vi) *Expenditure.* The Profit and Loss Account must show expenditure incurred on consumption of stores and spare parts, power and fuel, rent, repairs to buildings, repairs to machinery and salaries, wages and bonus, contribution to provident funds and other funds, workmen and staff welfare expenses to the extent and adjusted from any provision or reserve, insurance, rates and taxes including tax on income. It should show the miscellaneous expenses provided that any item under which the expenses exceed 1% of the total revenue of the company or Rs. 5,000, whichever is higher, shall be shown as a separate and distinct against and appropriate account head in the Profit and Loss Account and shall not be combined with any other item to be shown under Miscellaneous Expenses.

(vii) *Other Disclosures.* The Profit and Loss Account must also show the following :

(i) the amount of income from investment, distinguishing between trade investments and other investments;

(ii) other income by way of interest, specifying the nature of the income;

(iii) the amount of income-tax deducted if the gross income is stated under income.

(viii) *Detailed and Separate Disclosure.* The Profit and Loss Account must also contain a note including detailed information regarding the following :

(i) Managerial remuneration under Sec. 198 of the Act, paid or payable during the financial year to the director, managing director or manager, if any;

(ii) Other allowances and commission including guarantee commission with details;

(iii) Any other perquisites or benefits in cash or in kind;

(iv) Pensions, gratuities and payments from provident funds, in excess of own subscription and interest thereon;

(v) Compensation for loss of office; and

(vi) Consideration in connection with retirement from office.

If the central government is satisfied that the information relating to depreciation, renewal or diminution in value of assets should not be disclosed in the public interest and would prejudice the company but subject to the condition that in any heading stating an amount arrived at, after taking into account the amount set aside as such, the provision shall be so framed or marked as to indicate that fact.

1. Relevance. As the statement of account should reflect only the profit or loss of the year on the working of the concern, capital profits should be shown separately from revenue profits. These are not available for distribution as dividends and are credited to Capital Reserve Account. Any change in the value of fixed assets should be disclosed and their effect must be adjusted in the Capital Reserve Account. In order to have certain relevance the loss or profit on a transaction in the previous year is segregated from those of the current year. Any changes in the purchasing power of money should be accounted. If such a change is material, it can distort the financial picture as disclosed by the statement of account.

2. Accuracy and Reliability. Assets should be valued according to the universally accepted objective bases. For example, fixed assets are valued at cost or market price whichever is less. A provision is made for any loss that has arisen or is anticipated due to occurrence of bad debts and on other accounts, but no credit is made for a profit unless the same has been realised.

3. Intelligibility. The presentation of accounts should be simple, precise and accurate.

(i) ***Clarity.*** The accountant should use concise expression and simple words except necessary legal or technical terms/words. Items may be simplified by means of notes in statements, annexed to the accounts.

(ii) ***Significance.*** The accounts should be so presented as to enable significant descriptions to be applied to the figures. The presentation should be in a composite way. Immaterial items should be minimised. Appropriate descriptions are give for all significant sub-totals. It is desirable to avoid the sub-totals having no significance.

QUESTIONS FOR EXERCISE

1. What are the contents of financial statements? Explain its form and devices.
2. State the requirements regarding Balance Sheet, Profit and Loss Account and General disclosure.

17

Statutory Report and Audit

Statutory Meeting

The auditor is mainly concerned with the audit of Statutory Report. He should be familiar with the provisions of section 165 of the Companies Act, 1956 which deal with the Statutory Meeting, Statutory Report and Audit thereof.

It provides that every company limited by shares or limited by guarantee and having a share capital, shall hold a general meeting of the members of the company, within a period of not less than one month and not more than six months from the date the company is entitled to commence business. The meeting is called the "Statutory Meeting".

STATUTORY REPORT

The Board of Directors shall send to every member of the company a report known as "Statutory Report", at least 21 days before the date of the meeting. A private company is not required to forward the Statutory Report to its members or file it with the Registrar.

Particulars of Statutory Report

There is following express provision in section 165 with regard to the particulars to be mentioned in the Statutory Report :

1. Total number of shares allotted, distinguishing shares allotted as fully or partly paid-up otherwise than in cash. In the case of shares partly paid-up, stating the extent to which they are so paid-up.
2. The consideration for which the shares have been allotted.
3. Total amount of cash received by the company in respect of all the shares allotted.
4. An abstract of the receipts and payments of the company up-to-date within seven days of the date of the Report and particulars concerning the balance in hand.
5. An account for estimate of the preliminary expenses of the company showing separately any commission or discount paid or to be paid on the issue or sale of shares and debentures.

6. Names, addresses and occupation of the directors, auditors, managing agents or secretaries and treasurers, manager and secretary of the company and changes therein, if any, since the date of the incorporation of the company.
7. Particulars of any contracts and proposed modifications of such contracts, if any modification has to be made, which are to be submitted to the meeting for its approval.
8. The extent to which any underwriting contract has not been carried out and the reasons therefor.
9. Arrears due on calls from every director, managing agent, secretaries and treasurers, and, manager.
10. Particulars of any commission or brokerage paid or to be paid in connection with, the issue or sale of shares or debentures to any director, managing agent, secretaries and treasurers or manager.

The Statutory Report with the above particulars in a form given below-Form 22 of the Companies (Central Government's) General Rules and Forms, 1956— must be certified as correct by not less than two directors of the company, one of whom shall be a managing director, where there is one. Its copy must be filed with the Registrar for registration forthwith after copies thereof have been sent to the members of the company.

No. of company.

Form No. 22
Filing Fee.....

THE COMPANIES ACT, 1956

Statutory Report
Pursuant to Section 165

Name of Company
Statutory Report of the..Limited,
Certified and filed pursuant to section 165(5).
Presented by....................................

The Board of Directors submits the statutory report to the members in pursuance of section 165.

1. Shares allotted and cash received upon........(a)

No. of shares	*Nominal value of each share*	*cash received upto (a)*

(a) Allotted subject to payment thereof in cash :
(i) Equity

(ii) Redeemable Preference Shares
(iii) Preference shares other than Redeemable preference Shares

(b) Allotted as fully paid up otherwise than in cash and the consideration for which they have been allotted :
(i) Equity
(ii) Redeemable Preference Shares
(iii) Preference Shares other than Redeemable Preference Shares

(c) Allotted as partly paid up to the extent of Rs.........................
Per share, and the consideration for which they have been so allotted :
(i) Equity
(ii) Redeemable Preference Shares
(iii) Preference Shares other than Redeemable Preference Shares

(d) Allotted at a discount of Rs......per share :
(i) Equity
(ii) Redeemable Preference Shares
(iii) Preference Shares other than Redeemable Preference Shares

2. Abstract of receipts and payments upto (a)—

Receipts	*Rs.*	*Payment*	*Rs.*
Shares		***Preliminary expenses***	
Equity		Commission on issue or sale of shares..............................	
Redeemable Preference Shares		Discount on issue or sale of shares	
Preference Shares other than Redeemable Preference		***Capital Expenditure***	
Shares		Land..	
Advance payment for Shares		Building..................................	
Debentures................................		Plant.......................................	
Loans..		Machinery..............................	
Deposits..................................		*Other Items to be specified*	
Other sources (to be specified)...............		Balances	
		In Hand..............................	
		At Banks..............................	
		At Post Office	
		Savings Bank..................	
Total		Total	

(a) The date should be a date within 7 days of the Report.

3. Preliminary expenses as estimated in the prospectus or Statement in lieu of Prospectus*..

	Preliminary expenses actually incurred upto aforesaid date Rs.	Preliminary expenses estimated to be incurred after the aforesaid date Rs.
Law Charges		
Other charges in connection with the preparation of the Memorandum and Articles of Association		
Printing expenses		
Registration charges		
Advertisement charges		
Commission on issue or sale of shares		
Discount on issue or sale of shares		
Other initial Expenses (to be specified as far as possible)		
Total Rs.		

*Strike out the portion which does not apply.

4 . Names, addresses and occupation of the company's Directors, Auditors, Manager and Secretary.

Name(s)	Address(es)	Occupation(s)	Particulars of change(s); if any, in entries in columns (1) (2) and (3)since the date of incorporation	Date of the change*
A. Directors				
B. Auditors				
C. Manager				
D. Secretary				

**These particulars must include dates of changes.*

5. *Particulars of any contract which is to be submitted to the statutory meeting for approval*

   (If any modification or proposed modification of a contract and particulars of modification or proposed modification should be given).

6. *Underwriting Contracts*

   Brief description of each contract.

   If contracts are carried out fully, extent to which it has not been carried out and reasons thereby.

7. *The arrears, if any, due on calls from Directors, and Manager.*

Names	Amount due
Directors	
Names	Amount due
Manager	

8. *Particulars of any commission or brokerage paid or to be paid in connection with the issue or sale of shares to any director or manager.*

Name	Commission or Brokerage paid or to be paid on shares, on Debentures
Directors	
Directors	
Manager	

Dated this day of 19

We hereby certify that the above report is correct. Signatures of two or more directors.*

We hereby certify as correct so much of the report as relates to shares allotted by the company to the cash received in respect of such shares and to the receipts and payments.

Auditors

Dated this day of 19

* *Where there is a managing director, he should be one of the signatories.**

STATUTORY AUDIT

The audit of Statutory Report under section 165 is commonly known as Statutory Audit. The auditor of a company has to certify the Statutory Report as correct in certain specified respect after it has been certified by the directors etc., but prior to holding of Statutory Meeting by the company. Its audit and issue of certificate on the Report are limited to the following items of the Report only—

(i) Shares allotted by the company;

(ii) Cash received in respect of such shares; and

(iii) Receipts and Payments of the company.

Checking of Share Capital Transactions

To *certify* the above items of the Report as correct, the auditor will have to carry on exhaustive checking of the share capital transactions and the system of internal check in use with regard to the receipts, payments and other transactions and recording thereof. He will vouch in detail the Cash Book for entries made therein with regard to the receipts and payments, which may be on capital as well as revenue account. He must examine and verify the balance in hand.

Verification of Shares Allotted

So far as the *verification of shares allotted* by the company and cash received in respect thereof is concerned, the auditor should see that all the provisions of law in this connection have been duly complied with. He should refer to the Memorandum and Articles of Association of the company and the Prospectus issued etc., and see that various terms provided therein have been duly followed. He should refer to the Directors Minute Book for the allotment of shares. He should examine the Cash Book and Register of Members etc.

Verification of Receipts and Payments

For the *verifications of receipts and payments* of the company, the auditor should see that all the receipts and payments are within the scope of the company and have been duly and properly authorised. They should also be supported by adequate vouchers. The auditor should proceed as follows :

1. Vouch carefully the cash received on account of shares and debentures as appearing in the Ledger with the Application Book, Allotment Book and Register of Members, Debentures, etc.;
2. Vouch in detail the commission and brokerage paid for the issue of shares of debentures;
3. Vouch payments to vendors with reference to the contracts entered into and the Directors Minute Book;
4. Vouch the preliminary expenses thoroughly and check that the amounts recoverable from the promoters or vendors on account of preliminary expenditures have been duly collected and that they do not exceed the limit laid down in the Prospectus and the Articles;
5. Vouch the purchase of fixed assets, if any, with the help of Directors' Minute Book and the contract with supplies and the receipts given by them;
6. Vouch all the receipts and payments of the company in detail upto a date not more than seven days before the date of the Report;
7. Examine and compare the records in Bank Pass Book and reconcile them with the Cash Book. Also obtain a certificate from the bankers about the balance in the Bank. Verify carefully the balance in hand also;
8. See that all the receipts and payments of the company have been shown in the Report under appropriate heads.

AUDITOR'S CERTIFICATE

On being satisfied about the correctness of the above mentioned particulars of the Statutory Report, he should furnish a certificate to the directors of the company as follows :

> "We hereby certify that the Statutory Report so far as it relates to the shares allotted by the company and to the cash received in respect of such shares and to the receipts and payments of the company is correct."
>
> Auditors

Reliability of Audit Report

Lancaster defines a report as, "a statement of collected and considered facts, so drawn up as to give clear and concise information to persons who are not already in possession of the full facts of the subject-matter of the report."

Audit report can be relied upon as an expression of opinion based on facts and not as something guaranteeing or insuring the subject matter. It is a tangible proof of the financial state of affairs of the company. It indicates how the interests of the shareholders are being looked after by the management. An auditor is neither an insurer nor a guarantor. When he gives 'clean report' he does not guarantee that all the entries or details/particulars in the company's books of accounts are accurate and real. There is nothing in the Companies Act which specifically places a duty upon an auditor to search for material irregularities or to examine the books and accounts with the object of discovering whether there have been defalcations or other irregularities by directors or employees of the company.

Contents of an Audit Report

The auditor's reporting requirements are contained in Sub-sec.1(A), (2), (3), (4) and (4A) of the section 227 of the Companies Act.

Being basically verificatory, auditing is an 'attest' function. Audit's report has two parts or categories.

A. a fact content implying a statement of facts; and

B. an opinion content implying the formed opinion on the basis of the facts contained.

The entire reporting requirement hinges on the ascertainment of fact and the formation of opinion by the exercise of judgement.

A. Fact Content

Sub-secs. (2) and (3) require that the audit report include statements of facts about the following :

1. Whether the auditor has obtained all the information and explanation

which to the best of his knowledge and belief were necessary for the purposes of his audit.

2. Whether the report on the accounts of any branch office audited under Sec. 228 by a person other than the company auditor has been forwarded to him as required by Sec. 228(3) (C) and how he has dealt with the same in preparing the auditors' report.

3. Whether the companys' Balance Sheet and Profit and Loss Accounts dealt with by the report are in agreement with the books of accounts and the returns.

These three statements constitute the fact content of Audit report. An auditor is required to opine on the following :

B. Opinion Content

1. Whether proper books of accounts as required by law have been kept by the company so far as it appears from the examination of books and proper returns adequate for the purposes of his audit have been received from branches not visited by him;
2. Whether the accounts give the information required by the Act in the manner so required;
3. Whether the accounts give a true and fair view, in the case of Balance Sheet of the state of the company's affairs, and in the case of Profit and Loss Account of the profit and loss for the year.

These three statements constitute the opinion content.

Utility of the two parts

The fact part and the opinion part of Audit Report have distinct utility and necessity. A part from their own significance which probably accounts for their distinct disclosure the facts are complementary to the opinion. When facts are adverse or negative, the opinion cannot be favourable or clean. Sub-sec. (4) of Sec. 227 states that if any of the matter as referred to in Sec. 227(2)(3) is answered in the negative or with a qualification, the audit report should state the reasons for such a qualification.

Necessary Inquiries

Over and above these normal legal requirements of reporting, Sec. 227 (IA) imposes extra obligation on the audit report to include the following inquiries and report thereon :

1. Loans and Advances. Whether loans and advances made by the company on the basis of security have been properly secured and whether the terms on which they have been made are not prejudicial to the interests of the company or its members.

2. Transactions. Whether transactions of the company which are represented merely by book entries are not prejudicial to the interests of the company.

3. Securities. Where the company is not an investment company within the meaning of Sec. 372 or a banking company, whether a part of the assets of the company as consist of shares, debentures and other securities have been sold at a price less than that at which they were purchased by the company.

4. Deposits. Whether loans and advances made by the company have been shown as deposits.

5. Personal expenses. Whether personal expenses have been charged to revenue accounts.

6. Cash. Where it is stated in the books and records of the company that any shares have been allotted for cash, whether such cash has actually been so received.

7. True and Fair. Whether the position as stated in the books of accounts is correct, regular and not misleading.

Guidelines for the Auditor

1. Legal Requirements. Sec. 227(4) makes an auditor obliged to comply with directions issued by the central government. The central government may, by a general or special order, direct that in the case of such class or description of companies as may be specified in the Order, the auditor's report shall also include a statement on such matters as specified therein. The central government may consult the Institute of Chartered Accountants of India before making any such order.

2. Professional requirements. While reporting, an auditor has also to observe certain professional requirements along with the legal ones. His report should contain his professional opinion as an expert. He should look at his professional guidelines, conventions and practices. As he has to disclose all material facts adequately with a view to discharging his duty towards the shareholders, the law and the company, he must pay special attention to the following considerations :

(a) *General report.* An auditor must keep in mind that his report has a general use for many persons or groups and as such the report must be a general one and not confined to a particular person or group to help the competitor in any way.

(b) *Statement of Facts.* In certain cases largely legal in nature, the auditor must state facts as they are without any inference or interpretation. Facts must be distinguished from opinions.

(c) *Disclosure.* The auditor must disclose all that must be known to others and need not bother for what others may not know. He need not disclose the following :

(i) the general and external economic information,

(ii) the internal managerial decisions not having a material content or impact, unnecessary and injurious information.

The following aspects must be properly disclosed :

(i) *Special contractual obligations requiring disclosure.* These include contracts with creditors, debenture-holders or lease-holders.

(ii) *Scope, limitations and restraints on audit.* For example, the auditor must express whether he enjoyed free access to books or not.

(iii) *Material uncertainties and contingencies.* All taxation disputes and court cases on other counts where the company seems to be on the loosing side, must be expressly disclosed.

(iv) *Inconsistencies and irregularities.* Any deviation from the uniform or generally accepted pattern, say, depreciation policy or rate must be disclosed.

(v) *Examination.* Character and nature of examination of books and other records.

(vi) *Disclaimer of Liabilities.* A disclaimer of opinion and the attached liabilities is justified only when the auditor fails to obtain sufficient information to form an opinion.

(vii) *Disclosure of events after the date of the Balance Sheet.* Though the auditor is required to disclose and give his opinion for the accounts prepared, yet he can and should report subsequent happenings, after the date of the Balance Sheet, if he thinks that those matters or events are crucial so as to warrant the attention of the shareholders.

(viii) *Reports Under Sec. 227.*

(a) The accounts examined;

(b) Every Balance Sheet and Profit and Loss Account;

(c) Every other document declared by the Act to be forming part of or annexed to the Balance Sheet and Profit and Loss Account, which are laid before the company in the annual general meeting during the tenure of his office as statutory auditor of that particular company.

(d) *Clear Relevant Report.* An audit report, though brief, must convey clear and relevant information and not means of information. It should be so worded that the average person gets the idea or the message in the direct way.

The auditor has to submit his report to the shareholders even if appointed by the Board as in the case of the first auditor of a company, or a casual vacancy has been filled by the Board. He should send his report, addressed to the shareholders to the secretary or a responsible executive officer of the company. However, according to *Allen Craig & Co. (London) Ltd.* (1934) it is not his duty to send the report to each and every shareholder. Before signing the report, he should satisfy himself that the accounts had been approved of by the directors by referring to the minute book of the directors. His report is to be read and discussed at the annual general meeting of the shareholders before whom are placed the audited Profit and Loss Account, Balance Sheet and any other document declared by the Act to be part of or annexed to the Balance Sheet.

While making a report, he has a right of access to the "books" which include not only the books of account but all records and all statistical and memorandum books, such as minute books, cost books, stock registers, share ledger, etc. He may require to see "voucher" as documentary evidence of contracts, correspondence, invoices, etc. Further, he is entitled to secure from the directors and officers of the company any information and explanation in connection with the examination of any voucher, books, contracts, etc. if any of the point therein is not clear to him.

Characteristics of Good Report

1. Based on factual information.
2. Convincing.
3. Forceful.
4. Unbiased.
5. Point out the mistakes.
6. A constructive criticism and not reprimanding in tone.
7. Offer constructive and timely suggestions to the management.
8. Brief.

If no action had been taken on auditor's previous reports, it may be that these have not been presented properly. Hence it should be written in a better way.

Section 227(2), requires every auditor to make a report to the shareholders on the accounts examined by him and every balance sheet and profit and loss account and on every document declared by law to be annexed to the balance sheet and profit and loss account which are placed before the shareholders of the company at the general meeting. Section 215 requires that the balance sheet and the profit and loss account should be first approved by the directors and signed by them before they are submitted to the auditor for his report thereon.

True and Fair view of Company Affairs

On examining the accounts, the Balance Sheet and Profit and Loss Account and other documents annexed as required by the Act; must state in his report:

(i) That in his opinion and to the best of his information and according to the explanation given to him, the accounts give the information required by the Act and give a *true and fair view* of the state of the company's affairs in the case of the Balance Sheet as at the end of the financial year and in the case of the Profit and Loss Account for the financial year;

(ii) That he has obtained all the information and explanation which to the best of his knowledge and belief were necessary for the purpose of his audit;

(iii) That in his opinion, proper books of accounts as required by Section 209 have been kept by the company so far as appears from his examination of those books, and proper returns adequate for purposes of his audit have been received from branches not visited by him; and whether the report on the accounts of any branch office audited under Section 228 by a person other than the company's auditor has been forwarded to him as required by clause (c) of sub-section (3) of that section and how he has dealt with the same in preparing the auditor's report; and

(iv) That the company's balance sheet and profit and loss account dealt with by the report are in agreement with the books of returns.

The auditor's report shall state the reasons for the answer if it is in the negative or with a qualification.

Meaning of true and fair view

The phrase "true and fair view" has been used in Section 221 of the Companies Act. It means that the profit and loss account state clearly and correctly the result of the working of the company for the year under audit. There is no manipulation of accounts. The balance sheet shows the honest position, i.e., there is neither over-valuation nor under-valuation of assets or liabilities.

Loopholes in True and Correct

Before the enactment of he Companies Act in 1956, the works "true and correct" were used in Section 145 of the Companies Act, 1913. There were a few loopholes in the expression. Hence the words "true and fair" were substituted in 1956 on the model of the English Companies Act of 1948. The following were the loopholes of the phrase "true and correct" :

(i) If the assets were under-valued by providing more depreciation or otherwise by passing the entries in the books of account, strictly speaking, the balance sheet was correct according to the books of the company and therefore the auditors could not be hauled up for a wrong statement even though the balance sheet did not give a fair picture of the state of affairs to either the shareholders or to the public.

(ii) The expression indicated exactitude or precision though in fact the balance sheet is based on estimates, e.g., the depreciation is provided by mere estimates.

Advantages of True and Fair

If the accounts give all the information which is disclosed according to Schedule VI to the Companies Act, they will be presumed to give a true and fair view of the state of affairs of the company. The auditor should see that (a) the statements or accounts are not only arithmetically correct but substantially accurate, and (b) that provision had been made for depreciation, bad and doubtful debts, outstanding liabilities and expected losses.

Commenting about *"True and Fair View"*, under the English Companies Act, 1948 W.G. Campbell said, "The question is sometimes raised to whom the presentation is to be fair, and the answer seems implicit in the Act, that the scale ought to be fairly held between the interests of the companies as a whole and the interests of those who are concerned with the accounts the shareholders and the creditors at the date of the accounts." In the case of *Deputy Secretary, Ministry of Finance* v. *S.N. Dasgupta,* P. Charkravarty, C.J., observed : "It is the duty of the auditor to verify not merely the arithmetical accuracy of the balance sheet, but it is substantially accurate and to see that it includes the particulars required by the articles and the statute and contains the correct representation of the state of company's affairs."

Thus a greater responsibility has been thrown on the shoulders of the auditor who has to report that the accounts show that the position of the company is not misleading by overstating or understating the assets liabilities of the company, e.g., (a) neither inadequate provision for depreciation nor more provision for depreciation has been made, (b) that all the contingent assets and liabilities are shown in the balance sheet, and (c) that the stock is valued properly on a consistent basis.

Distinction between Report and Certificate

While the report means and expression of opinion, a certificate means that the person issuing or signing it vouchsafes the truth of the statement he makes, i.e., what he states is cent per cent true and correct. If the certificate was found wrong later he will be held responsible while in the case of a report, which is merely an opinion it is possible that he may be wrong in holding it. An auditor is not required to 'certify' the accounts but is required to 'report' that the balance sheet and profit and loss account are properly drawn up in accordance with the Companies Act so as to give a 'true and fair view' of the state of the company's affairs and that the accounting and other records are properly maintained. While he never certifies that the accounts depict a true and fair view, he reports that, in his opinion, the accounts represent a true and fair view of a company's affairs. Thus audit is only a test and not a guarantee. The auditor is not expected to examine each and every transaction especially in the case of a business where the number of transactions run into millions. When he checks each transaction, it would be difficult for him to detect an ingenious fraud committed by an employee, e.g., when a document is concealed from him. He is not expected to guarantee the accuracy of the company's books. He cannot assume that frauds and errors have been committed in the books of account. He is watch dog and not a blood hound. His duty is to see that the financial position of the company is truly exhibited to the shareholders. He should thoroughly check the internal check system in operation and apply test checks. He can be responsible if it is proved that he could have discovered the fraud or error had he been reasonably careful.

Conditions not barriers true and fair view

The Companies Act has laid down that the balance sheet and profit and loss account of a company do not bar a true and fair view of the state of affairs of the company, if they do not disclose the following :

(i) Insurance company. Any matters which are not required to be disclosed by the Insurance Act, 1938;

(ii) Banking company. Any matters which are not required to be disclosed by the Banking Companies Act, 1949;

(iii) Company governed by any other special Act. Any matters which are not required to be disclosed by that special Act; or

(iv) Any company. Any matters which are not required to be disclosed by virtue of the provisions contained in Schedule VI or by virtue of a notification issued under sub-section (3) or an order issued under sub-section (4).

Under Section 229 only the person appointed as the auditor of the company, or a partner in the firm of auditors (if all the partners of the firm are entitled for practice in India) may sign the auditor's report, or may authenticate any other document of the company required to be signed or authenticated by the auditor. If it has been signed by a partner of the firm of auditors, he should inform the Registrar that he has done so, preferably within seven days after the date on which the audit report was signed under sections 233. If a report or any document of the company is signed or authenticated, otherwise than in conformity with the requirements of Sections 227 and 229, the auditor concerned and the person, if any, other than the auditor who signs the report or signs or authenticates the document, shall, if the default is wilful, be punishable with fine which may extend to one thousand rupees.

Under Section 216, report of the auditor (including the auditor's separate, special or supplementary report, if any) shall be attached to every balance sheet placed before every annual general meeting while the report is to be annexed to every annual returns.

The Canadian Audit and Research Committee has given the following guidelines to the auditor for drafting the Report :

1. He should specifically state in his report the area covered by him while engaged in auditing the accounts.
2. He should state whether the financially statements were prepared in accordance with the generally accepted accounting principles on a basis consistent with that of the previous year.

3. Where he found some discrepancy in the financial statements, he should state that fact.

Events Subsequent to the Balance Sheet Date

An auditor audits the accounts of a concern sometimes after the last date of the financial year on which date the balance sheet and the profit and loss account have been prepared by the client. Subsequent to the Balance Sheet date an auditor has to take note of those events which may have a material effect on the final accounts but which took place after the preparation of the balance sheet and profit and loss account but before the actual audit. These events may be of two types :

(i) Events occurring after the balance sheet date which have no direct bearing on the accounts but are nevertheless important from the point of view of the true position.

(ii) Events occurring after the balance sheet date which have a direct bearing upon the items appearing in the balance sheet, e.g., the decision of the directors regarding the proposed dividend and the appropriation of the profits to be shown in the accounts. Schedule VI to the Companies Act requires that such events have to be taken into accounts. Liabilities, provision for liabilities or contingent liabilities existing on the date of the balance sheet, information of the events occurring after the balance sheet date may be taken into account in order to provide a guide. Any event occurring after such a date should be shown by way of a footnote or by the directors in their report to the shareholders. For estimating liabilities, guidance may be obtained from the developments which have taken place since the balance sheet. Such events may be the following :

1. a heavy and apparently permanent fall in the market value of stock-in- trade;
2. any unforeseen calamity such as earthquake, fire, etc. which might have caused heavy loss to the plant, machinery, buildings, etc., and which property might not have been insured against such a risk.
3. filtration in the rate of exchange, e.g., devaluation of rupee announced by the Indian Government on 6th June, 1966; the Council of the Institute of Chartered Accountants of India had made recommendations in 1967, regarding the treatment of accounting problems created in such a case;
4. alteration in the rate of Income Tax where it is required by law to make provision for Income Tax in the accounts;
5. accidents to the employees of the company and consequently a claim against it if the event was not covered by insurance;

6. an apparently permanent fall in the value of investments by the company;
7. disposal or destruction of fixed assets like sinking of a ship of a shipping company;
8. ascertainment of the amount of the contingent liabilities;
9. an award by the Labour Tribunal for increase of minimum wages or in the rate of bonus payable to the workers and which might have been given with retrospective effect provided the amount involved is substantial and so on.

It is the duty of the management to disclose these facts as the auditor does not know about them but he has to report on the fairness of the statements of accounts. His responsibility is limited to only those facts which are shown to him or which he ought to have known. However, he should remember that there may have been such events and that it may be necessary or desirable for him to see that appropriate information is given in or with the accounts on which he is reporting. It would be advisable if he gets a certificate form the management regarding such subsequent events which effect the balance sheet and the profit and loss account.

Some accountants argue that the auditor is concerned with the books of account and he need not take note of those events. He has to report on the balance sheet and profit and loss account on the date on which they are supposed to have been prepared and hence he should ignore those events which take place thereafter even though the accounts are audited later on.

In article in *The Accountants Journal of New Zealand,* December 1964, the auditor is recommended the classification of the events subsequent to the balance date into the following categories:

1. Those which require adjustment. For example, settlement and determination of liabilities on a basis substantially different from that previously anticipated, major variations is realised value of the assets such as debtors, stock, directors' recommendations as to dividend or any alteration to taxation which have been made retrospective.

2. Those which do not require adjustment. These should perhaps be disclosed in some form, e.g. capital explanation, mergers or acquisition or damage by fire or fraud. Such events might be covered in the Directors' Report or otherwise.

3. Events which do not require disclosure. These items should not affect auditors' report, e.g., changes in the management, changes in production or trading policies, change in directors, loss of important customers, etc.

The auditor should refrain from referring to these items in his report even though a pressure might be brought upon him by the management. He should confine his report to those matters essential to proper interpretation of the accounts being reported. Others believe that since the auditor is to sign his report sometimes after the balance sheet date after having audited the accounts he must take into account any event, affecting the accounts before he signs the audit report. The Institute of Certified Public Accountants of America (C.P.A.) has issued guidelines on disclosure of subsequently discovered facts. It has recommended that if an auditor becomes aware of significant facts previously unknown to him, he should advise his client company to issue revised financial statement provided the disclosure is not delayed. If the financial implications of the newly discovered facts are not readily determinable, the company should report that the statement should be relied on and that revised statement will be issued after further investigation. If the company fails to make appropriate disclosures, the auditor should notify each member of the Board of Directors and take action to prevent further reliance on his report. He should also notify to such agency as the Securities and Exchange Commission.

There seems to be weight in both the above mentioned views. However, the trend amongst the accountants today is that events subsequent to the balance sheet date should be considered by the auditor if such events substantially affect the accounts, e.g., events which require adjustments like settlement and determination of liabilities on a basis substantially different from those previously anticipated, variations in realised values of assets such as debtors, etc., or any alterations in the rate of taxation which have been made retrospectively and so on. This view is supported by the Council of the Institute of Chartered Accountants of England and Wales. According to Statement of Auditing Practices if the Institute of Chartered Accounts of India, it would be better of the auditor gets a certificate from the client that all the events subsequent to the balance sheet date have been disclosed to the auditor.

Under Section 227(1)(d) events which do not substantially affect the balance sheet, e.g., capital extension, acquisition of other business, damage by fire etc., need not be taken note of by the auditor as they can be covered by the directors in their report.

In order to know of the events occurring after balance sheet date the auditor should reasonable care and do the following :

(i) Inspect the accounts to the date of inspection and not merely confine himself up to the date of the preparation of the final accounts;

(ii) Inspect the bank pass book after the date the balance sheet date as to the correctness of the bank balance;

(iii) Inquire from his client whether any significant event has taken place after the accounts had been closed;

(iv) Inquire about the contingent liabilities, forward purchases or other commitments, etc.;

(v) Get from his client a certificate in regard to any event after the balance sheet date which might have any substantial effect on the accounts.

QUALIFIED REPORT OF AN AUDITOR

Whenever an auditor is not satisfied with any explanation or information given to him or if he thinks that the profit and loss account and the balance sheet do not exhibit a true and fair view of the state of company's affairs or if the accounts presented by the directors call for further elucidation, he must ask the directions to set the matters right and if he is unsuccessful in persuading the directors to do so he must mention the fact in his report. As distinct from a "Clean Report," this report is called a "Qualified Report". It is normally not necessary unless the amount involved is substantial. The Companies Act does not lay down the manner in which the qualified report should be worded. But the auditor should discuss the points with the directors before giving a qualified report.

1. Clear and unambiguous. The readers should understand what the auditor wants them to know should not be they are left in doubt as to the implications of the report.

2. Concise. This should not be at the cost of sacrificing clarity.

3. Specific and to the point. The amount involved if any should be clearly stated.

4. Analytic. The report should state the effect of the matter under report on the accounts.

5. No misinterpretation. The opinion of the auditor expressed in the report should not be capable of misinterpretation.

Auditor's Responsibility

The directors may try to persuade the auditor to desist from giving a qualified report as it is a slur on their work for the year under review. Moreover, it leads to bad consequences, e.g., fall in the value of shares in the market, non-renewal of the appointment of the directors, appointment of investigators and so on. The auditor is appointed by the shareholders to check the accounts prepared by the directors so that he may inform them that the accounts have been properly maintained and that the balance sheet and profit and loss account exhibit a true and fair view of the state of the company's affairs. Thus he has to safeguard the interests of the shareholders. If he fails to do so and falls a prey to the persuasion of the directors, he will not be performing his duty honestly and may be held liable civilly and criminally. Under such circumstances, the whole of the object of the appointment of the auditor will be frustrated. Sometimes the auditors do not mention some facts in their report to the shareholders, just to soften the tone of the report. In this connection it would be instructive to note the letter dated 27th October 1967 from the Under Secretary to the Government of India, in the Department of Company Affairs, to the Secretary of the Institute of Chartered Accountants of India, New Delhi, and published in the *Chartered Accountants's Journal* on page 346 of its December 1967 issue.

"I am directed to say that it has been brought to the notice of this Department that the auditors usually fail to remark in their reports on the balance sheet of the company about the following contraventions of the Companies Act, 1956:

(a) Contravening the provision of Section 210(4) of the Companies Act, 1956. Balance Sheet prepared beyond 15 months without the approval of the Registrar of Companies.

(b) Mode of valuation of stock-in-trade omitted to be pointed out in the Balance Sheet.

(c) Nature of securities not disclosed for the secured loans shown in the Balance Sheet.

(d) Nature of Account and Bank not disclosed as required under Schedule VI.

(e) The word 'income' used instead of 'profit' in the audit report.

(f) Classification of unsecured loans not given in the audit report.

(g) Depreciation not provided on fixed assets.

(h) Investment not classified.

(i) Non- compliance with item 7B Part I and 3(I) (b) of Part II, Schedule VI.

(j) Sundry Debtors not classified.

(k) Fines imposed on directors are actually paid by them and not out of the funds of the company not checked by the auditors.

The auditor should be very careful while drafting his report that he should not omit to mention the facts required by the Companies Act to be included in the audit report.''

In the case of *London and General Bank,* the bank had advanced loans on insufficient securities. Knowing the inadequacy of the security the auditor qualified his report in these words: "The value of the assets as shown on the Balance Sheet is dependent upon realisation." He was held liable to pay damages as the phrase with regard to the securities did not convey the true meaning. Part of the judgement reads as follows:

"It is mere truism to say that the value of loans and securities depends upon their realisation. We are told that a statement to that effect is so unusual that the mere presence of so many words is enough to excite suspicion. But as already stated, the duty of an auditor is to convey information, not to arouse enquiry, and although an auditor might infer from an unusual statement that something was seriously wrong, it by no means follows that ordinary people would have their suspicion aroused by the similar statement if, as in the case, its language expresses no more than any ordinary person would infer without it."

The auditor should make the report very clear and no ambiguous words should be used. In *London & General Bank* case it was stated that:

"A person whose duty is to convey information to others, does not discharge that duty by simply giving them so much information as is calculated to induce them or some of them to ask for more. Information and means of information are by no means equivalent terms an auditor who gives shareholders means of information instead of information in respect of a company's financial position, does so at his peril and runs the very serious risk of being held judicially, to have failed to discharge his duty."

Matters in Qualified Report

Using appropriate words or phrases the auditor should report the following matter in qualified report:

(i) Insufficient provisions have been made for depreciation.

(ii) Inadequate provision has been made for bad and doubtful debts.

(iii) The investment have been valued at cost price which is in excess of the market price.

(iv) The stock-in-trade has been valued at market price which is more than the cost price.

(v) There is a contingent liability in respect of bills discounted for Rs. 1,00,000 which has not been disclosed.

(vi) No provision has been made for taxes payable to the extent of Rs.....

If the auditor wishes to report on other points he should write a separate report and attach it to the balance sheet. He should make a mention of such a separate report below the balance sheet as under:

"The Balance Sheet and the Profit and Loss Account of....Co. Ltd., above set forth and dated....19....should be read in conjunction with my report to the shareholders dated....19...attached herewith."

THE AUDIT OF PRIVATE LIMITED COMPANY

Definition

1. A private company consists of at least two members;
2. It limits the number of its members to fifty exclusive of its past or present employees who have been or are its members;
3. It prohibits any invitation to the public to subscribe for shares in, or debentures of, the company; and
4. It restricts the right to transfer its shares, if any.

Privileges

1. Section 12. The minimum number may be two instead of seven as in the case of a public company.

2. Section 26. It must register Articles of Association with the Memorandum of Association.

3. Section 70. It need not file a statement in lieu of prospectus before shares are allotted.

4. Section 149. The question of minimum subscription does not apply as the shares are not offered to the public.

5. No restrictions. Restrictions as to the issue of different classes of shares, or shares with different kinds of rights in respect of dividends or voting, etc., as are applicable to public companies, do not apply to private companies.

6. Directors. Minimum number of directors is two instead of three as in the case of public companies. Certain provisions which are applicable to public companies do not apply to private companies. These include appointment of directors, limit of 20 companies which can be directed by a director, prohibition of loans to directors without the approval of the Government, voting by the interested directors at Board meetings, provisions in regard to remuneration, acquiring of qualification, shares by the directors, etc.

7. Section 165. It need not hold the Statutory Meeting and submit the Statutory Report to the shareholders.

8. Section 149. It can commence business or exercise borrowing powers as soon as it is incorporated.

9. Section 219. As regards the right of members to have copies of Profit and Loss Account and Balance Sheet these provisions do not apply to private companies.

10. Sections 189, 219(1- 4), 309, 311, etc. These are not applicable relating to the provision of amount payable as remuneration to managing agents, directors, etc.

11. Consent. It need not file the written consent by the directors to act as directors.

12. No Restrictions on directors. Restrictions such as a person cannot act as managing director or managing agent of more than so many companies or for more than so many years do not apply.

13. Directors' shares. The directors are not required to hold any qualification shares.

The above privileges cannot be enjoyed by a private company which is the subsidiary of a public company. The private company shall cease to be a private company and will not be entitled to enjoy the privileges as mentioned above. If not less than twenty-five per cent of the share capital is held by one or more bodies corporate, it would be treated as a public company under Section 43A. Where the average annul turnover of a private company, whether in existence at the commencement of the Companies (Amendment) Act, 1974, or incorporated thereafter, is not, during the relevant period, less than rupees one crore, the private company shall irrespective of its paid-up share capital, become a public company by virtue of Sec.43A(1A) on and from the expiry of a period of three months from the last day of the relevant period during which the private company had said average annual turnover.

According to the Companies (Amendment) Act, 1974, where not less twenty-five per cent of the paid-up share capital of public company is held by a private company, such a company will become a public company.

Even after the private company has so become a public company, its articles of association may include provisions relating to the matters specified in clause (iii) of sub-section (1) of Sec. 3 and the number of its members may be or may at any time be reduced, below seven. Such a company may continue to have only two members and two directors. Within three months of its becoming a public company, it must inform the Registrar about this fact. This provision will not be applicable to a private company the major portion of capital of which is held by another single private company or by one or more bodies corporate incorporated outside India.

Audit of private Company

As there is no deference in the audit of the accounts of a private company and a public company a private company must get its accounts audited by a Chartered Accountant. If a private company is deemed to be a public company under Section 43A as aforesaid, the auditor will have to bear in mind that most of the provisions of the Act relating to public companies will apply to such a company.

THE AUDIT OF A HOLDING COMPANY

What is Holding Company?

Holding Company is that which

(i) controls the composition of the Board of Directors of another company; or

(ii) holds more than fifty per cent of the equity capital of another company or where the other company having equity as well as preference shares with the same voting rights, holds more than half of the total voting power.

It is also called a Parent Company, which holds the shares of a Subsidiary or an Associate Company. Holding company is deemed to control the composition of the Board of Directors of another company as it has the power to appoint or remove all or the majority of the directors of the other company. A company, whose principal business is to invest funds in the purchase of the shares of other companies, is not to be considered as a Holding Company even through it holds more than fifty per cent of the shares of another company. Such companies are called Trust companies and shares, etc. purchased by such companies are treated as fixed assets. Their object is to average the profits and to divide the risk. Again, a company which has lent money to another company on the security of the shares is not to be considered as a Holding Company.

According to the Companies Act Sec. 212 a Holding Company must disclose certain particulars relating to the Subsidiary Companies into report, Profit and Loss Account and the Balance Sheet so that the shareholders of the Holding Company may know the exact position.

A Subsidiary Company may in its turn hold more than fifty per cent of the shares of another company or more than fifty per cent of the voting power, etc., of another company. It is called a subsidiary Company of the Holding Company. A Subsidiary Company may be a Subsidiary Company of two or more different companies at the same time. Mr. De Paula uses the words, "Children," "Grandchildren" and "Great-grandchildren," when he writes, "It will be appreciated that the holding company may have a large family including children, grandchildren and even great-grandchildren."

Documents in Balance Sheet of the Holding Companies about Subsidiary Company

According to Sec. 212 of the Companies Act the following documents about subsidiary company should be attached to the Balance Sheet of the Holding Company.

(i) a copy about the latest balance sheet;

(ii) a copy of the latest profit and loss account;

(iii) a copy of the report of the auditors;

(iv) a statement of the Holding Company's interest in the Subsidiary Company;

(v) a statement showing the changes which have occurred in respect of (i) the Subsidiary's fixed assets; (ii) its investments; (iii) the money lent by it; (iv) the money borrowed by it for any purpose other than that of meeting current liabilities since the last financial year of the Subsidiary and where it does not coincide with the financial year of the Holding Company;

(vii) a report where the Board of Directors of the Holding Company could not obtain information about Subsidiary's profit or loss.

The balance sheet of the Holding Company must show about Subsidiary Company separately secured loans and advances, unsecured loans and advances current liabilities due to advances and loans and investment in the shares and debentures to Schedule VI Part I of Companies' Act. However, the Central Government may, on the application of the Holding Company, permit it to forego provisions of Section 212 set out above.

The documents referred to in clauses (v), (vi), and (vii) above be singed by the persons who are required to sign the Balance Sheet of the Subsidiary Company.

When the financial years of the Holding Company and the Subsidiary Company do not coincide, the following information must be given in respect of the Subsidiary.

Where during the same period any material changes have occurred in respect of fixed assets, investments or loans of the Subsidiary.

If the Subsidiary Company has been incorporated outside India, its profit and loss account and the balance sheet must be drawn up according to the Companies Act for the purpose of the above requirements by passing a resolution.

A Holding Company may authorise its representative to inspect the books of account kept by its Subsidiary. The Holding Company may apply to the Government to appoint a person to investigate into the affairs of the Subsidiary.

The signatories of the Balance Sheet of the Holding Company should state how the profits or losses of the Subsidiary Company have been delt with in the Profit and Loss Account of the Holding Company. They must make a statement if the report of the Subsidiary Company is a qualified one.

According to Section 212(6) the Board of Directors of the Holding Company is unable to obtain information on any of the matters required to be specified relating to the Subsidiary's profit or losses, a report in writing to that effect shall be attached to the balance sheet of the Holding Company.

Duties of an Auditor of a Holding Company

1. Pay attention to the inter-company transactions and verify such transactions.
2. Examine the contracts for the purchase of the shares of the Subsidiary companies.
3. Examine the share certificates.
4. See that the shares of the Subsidiary Company are held in the name of the company.
5. See that the Holding Company may hold shares of the Subsidiary Company in the name or names of its nominees to ensure that the number of members of the Subsidiary is not reduced, where it is a public company, below seven, and where it is a private company, below two.
6. Vouch as usual the receipt of dividends from the subsidiary company.
7. See that if any dividend has been declared by the Subsidiary after the preparation of the balance sheet of the Holding Company, it should not be included in that balance sheet.
8. See that the profit and loss account of the Holding Company shows the dividends received from the Subsidiary and losses, if any.

9. See that if a consolidated Balance Sheet has been prepared, proper grouping, classification and valuation of the assets and liabilities has been done. In regard to valuation of the shares of the Subsidiary Companies they should be valued at cost price or the market price whichever is lower.
   (i) If they are quoted on the Stock Exchange, there will be no difficulty in the valuation of the shares of the Subsidiary Company.
   (ii) If they are not quoted on the Stock Exchange, the auditor should examine the Balance Sheet of the Subsidiary Company and form an idea of their value.
   (iii) If he finds that the position of the Subsidiary Company is worse than when the shares were purchased, then such shares must be written down.
   (iv) He should examine the Articles of Association as regards the method of valuation of the Subsidiary company.
   (v) If the shares of another company are held by way of permanent investment as in the case of a Trust Company, such investments are considered as fixed assets and, therefore, depreciation on such assets must be provided.
10. See that in the Balance Sheet of the Holding Company, the number of the shares of the Subsidiary Company is clearly mentioned.
11. See that the amount of indebtedness to and from the Subsidiary Companies should be stated in the Balance Sheet of the Holding Company.
12. See whether the Holding Company has made any provision for the losses of the Subsidiary Company; also whether the Balance Sheet of the Holding Company represents true and fair view of its state of affairs.
13. Make reference to them in the report if not satisfied on any the above points.

QUESTIONS FOR EXERCISE

1. What is an audit report? How far is it reliable? Give its contents in detail.
2 What are the characteristics of a good report? Discuss the implication of the phrase "True and fair" as applied to audit report.
3. Enumerate and evaluate events subsequent to the Balance Sheet Date.
4. Write short note on - Qualified Report of an Auditor.
5. Explain the legal provisions concerning audit of a Private Limited Company.
6. What is holding company? What provisions have been made for its Balance Sheet? Explain Auditor's duties in this connection.

18

Criticism of Published Accounts

PUBLISHED ACCOUNTS AND STATEMENTS

The Published Accounts of a company are the accounting records which are released to the public. These include the following :

A. Published Profit and Loss Account

(i) Manufacturing Account
(ii) Trading Account
(iii) Profit and Loss Account
(iv) Profit and Loss Appropriation Account

B. Published Statements

1. Balance Sheet
2. Directors' Report
3. Auditor's Report
4. Chairman's Speech delivered at Annual General Meeting

C. Published Account of a Holding Company

The Published Accounts of a holding company include the Balance Sheet, Profit and Loss Account, Auditor's Report, Directors' Report of each of the Subsidiary and Sub-subsidiary Companies.

These are valuable to the management for the formulation of its correct policies and also to the outsiders including shareholders, debenture-holders, etc. Study of these accounts can help them in making an assessment of the company's financial position and its progress. These are also known as 'Annual Accounts'. The Companies Act, 1956 has provided for the disclosure of all essential information relating to the financial affairs of a company.

1. Profit and Loss Account. It includes Manufacturing Account, Trading Account, Profit and Loss Account and Profit and Loss Appropriation Account. It explains the position of expenses incurred and of incomes earned during the course of a year by a company since the publication of the last Balance Sheet. It reveals the position of profit or loss for a particular year. It is prepared in different forms in accordance with the nature and circumstances of a business.

2. Balance Sheet. It exhibits financial position existing at the close of a financial year. It discloses the sources from which capital has been acquired and also other liabilities on the one side and the position of assets on the other. As shown in the Balance Sheets, assets are recorded at their proper value after making provision for depreciation at specified rates. The Companies Act, 1956 has laid down the specific form in which the Balance Sheet should be prepared by a company. If the principles of accountancy are not followed in framing the Financial Records and Statements, the results are likely to be misleading.

3. Directors' Report. It has to be appended to every Balance Sheet indicating specifically the state of the company's affairs including its financial position and also proposals for the disposal of profits, i.e., transfer to reserves, recommendation for dividends, etc. The subject-matter of such a Report will depend upon the discretion of Directors and the nature of a company's business. The Directors' Report will include all such matters as they want to report to the shareholders.

4. Auditor's Report. Prepared at the close of a financial period the auditor's report includes the comments of an auditor on the Annual Accounts of a company. It covers all the irregularities and errors which are found in the course of audit of the accounts.

5. Chairman's Speech. Made on the occasion of the Annual General Meeting of the company it includes almost every major point concerning the progress and prospects of the company. Although there are no hard and fast rules for such a speech, yet efforts are made by the Chairman to analyse the working of the company during the course of the year. The speech provides some very important and valuable information for the present and prospective shareholders and creditors. As an important document, it is expected to be lucid and precise.

Criticism of Published Accounts

In the lines of action to be covered in the criticism of Published Accounts, there are three P's— Progress, Position (i.e., financial position) and Prospects.

1. Progress. It is judged by the earning capacity of the company. The earning capacity can be measured by a peep into the trends of earnings of a company for which a study of the Profit and Loss Account, Directors' Report and Chairman's Report for a few years will be necessary. A comparative analytical summary should be prepared on the basis of information revealed by these accounts. Following are the points of examination in the Trading Account.

1. Amount of Sales,
2. Percentage of Credit Sales to Total Sales,
3. Percentage of Closing Stock to Purchases,
4. Percentage of Gross Profit to Total Sales.

Bases of examination of Profit and Loss Account :

1. Percentage of Secondary Income to Gross Profit,
2. Percentage of Selling Expenses to Total Sales,
3. Percentage of Distributive Expenses to Total Sales,
4. Percentage of Management Expenses to Total Sales,
5. Percentage of Total Expenses to Total Sales,
6. Scrutiny of Management Expenses,
7. Percentage to Net Profit to Total Sales.

By examining the Profit and Loss Account in the manner specified above, the auditor can easily form a reliable opinion about the company's future earnings, dividends or yields per share.

2. Position. The present position of a company can be disclosed by its Balance Sheet which is a statement of assets and liabilities of a business at a particular date. The financial position of a business on a particular date can be disclosed by a careful study and critical examination of the assets and liabilities as shown in the Balance Sheet which contains a mass of details. For this purpose it has to be broken into pieces so as to analyse its important segments in the following form to arrive at a definite conclusion:

Paid-up Share Capital	Gross Block
Reserves and Surplus	*Less:* Depreciation
Debentures and other Loans	Net Block
(secured and unsecured)	Investments
Current Liabilities and	Store and Stocks
Provisions	Bad Debts
Contingent Liabilities	Loans and Advances
Profit and Loss	Cash and Bank Balances
	Profit and Loss

Norms of judging a sound financial position

(i) ***Adequate Reserves.*** Strong reserves denote a sound financial position. These must always be backed by liquid assets.

(ii) ***Balance between Block Account and Paid-up Capital.*** A proper balance should be maintained between Block Account and Paid-up Capital. It is not sound and proper if there is a big gap between the two represented by huge reserves.

(iii) ***Position of Current Assets and Liabilities.*** The proportion of current assets to current liabilities is called the liquid position. From an analysis of a very large number of concerns it has been concluded that if current assets are twice the current liabilities, the financial position can be said to be quite sound.

(iv) ***Current Assets being Mostly Liquid***. If a company is not in a position to meet out its current liabilities as and when they fall due, it will have to close down its business. Hence, liquid position should always be strong.

(v) ***Working Capital Trend.*** It should always show an increasing trend. If more contributions are made to the General Reserve Fund, there are more additions to the working capital. If the percentage of General Reserve Fund to paid-up capital shown a rising tendency over a number of years, there is an expansion in business and a policy of 'Ploughing back the profits' is being adopted in the business.

(vi) ***Investment Position.*** To make a company progressive and prosperous the investment position should always be sound. This has to be ascertained from a critical perusal of the assets side of the Balance Sheet. The present position should be judged in the light of the past trends in the investment position.

(vii) ***Fixed Assets Position.*** Fixed assets must always be adequately depreciated. The adequacy or otherwise of depreciation will depend upon the policy of the management prepared in the light of the principles of accountancy and past experience of the business in this respect. The whole situation has to be judged in this light and conclusion should be arrived at accordingly.

3. Prospects. This requires a reference to the Directors' Report and the Chairman's Report. It should be enquired into whether the management of the company is quite efficient, economical and honest.

(a) ***The Directors' Report.*** It should be examined for the disposal of profits and transfer to reserves and distribution by way of dividends. It should be ensured whether they have kept in view the following points :

(i) Provisions of Law,

(ii) Permanent interests of the Company,

(iii) Rate of dividends (which must have a reasonable relation to the extent of the net profits earned by the company), and

(iv) Cash Position of the Company.

The future prospects of the company are quite bright if they have followed these norms in deciding the disposal of profits.

(b) ***The Chairman's Report.*** Chairman's speech should have no scope for arousing suspicion in the minds of outsiders, especially the prospective shareholders. It should contain details about the present difficulties of the company and its future prospects.

Principles of Criticism

The criticism can be of three classes :

1. Criticism from Point of View of Short-term Creditors
2. Point of view of Debenture-holders
3. Point of view of Shareholders.

1. Criticism from Short-term Creditors' Point of View

The short-term creditors are those who are to be paid after a short time. A company must have adequate resources and good liquid position to pay them off. Its current assets must be more than its current liabilities. By paying off the short-term creditors, the working capital should remain in its hands at a level so that the company may be in a position to meet out its present requirements.

The purpose to which the credit is put, may be noted comparing the Balance Sheet for a number of years. It is usually unwise to utilize the short-term credit for capital development where it will be blocked for a long period.

Another important thing is the value of the purchases and sales in each of the forthcoming months till the month in which repayment to the short-term creditors is due. Much will depend upon the nature of a business, being of a seasonal character or otherwise.

2. Criticism from the Debenture-holders' Point of View

The Debenture-holders or creditors are primarily interested in the following :

(i) Ability of the company to pay interest regularly,

(ii) Ability to redeem debentures, and

(iii) Nature of business and the financial policies of the company.

(i) Ability to Pay Interest. Interest on debentures has to be paid and hence, it is a charge on Profit and Loss Account. If the business suffers a loss, interest has still to be paid even out of capital. This will reduce not only the working capital but also the security available to the Debenture-holders.

(ii) *Ability to Redeem Debentures.* If the value of security to Debenture-holders is 1-1/2 times the amount of debentures, it is said to be quite adequate.

Following two points may be noted in this connection :

(a) If there is a Sinking Fund for the repayment of debentures, the balance (i.e., amount of debentures-amount of Sinking Fund) will be treated as liability.

(b) If the security to Debenture-holders is less than the amount of debentures, they will rank for the balance *pari passu* with the unsecured creditors.

(iii) ***Nature of Business and Financial Policies.*** To criticize the Published Accounts on behalf of the Debenture-holders, if the financial policies are sound and satisfactory, the accounts can be criticized in the light of bases discussed.

3. Criticism from the Shareholders' Point of View

The preference or equity shareholders are always interested in the soundness of the financial position of a company. Their criticism of Published Accounts may be based on the following five factors :

(i) ***Prospects of dividend.*** Out of the net profit of the company appropriations are made and then divisible profits are arrived at.

(ii) ***Yield on Shares.*** The yield per share should be calculated on the basis of the market price of a share and not so much on its paid-up value.

(iii) ***Prospectus of Return to Capital.*** A statement should be prepared in the name of a 'Statement of Return of Capital to Shareholders' to signify the amount which the shareholders are likely to get in the event of the winding up of the company.

(iv) ***Net Worth of Shares.*** The net worth of shares can be calculated by dividing the security available to shareholders by the number of shares held by them. The market value of shares should also be taken into consideration.

(v) ***Careful Study of Published Accounts.*** A careful and analytical study of the records and accounts can reveal the position and prospects of the company.

QUESTION FOR EXERCISE

1. What are the published accounts and statements ? Explain the line of action in the criticism of the published accounts of a company ?

19

Profits and Divisible Profits

Concept of Profit

Like the term "value" in economics, accounts have used the word 'profit' without assigning a definite meaning to it. This has given rise to much uniformed criticism of accountants and their work. Added to this is the difficulty caused by the divergence that exits on the concept of "profit" between an economist and an accountant for the purposes of a business.

What is profit?

1. Economist's Concept. According to Increased Net Worth Theory of Profit, profit is the increase in the value of total net assets of a business over a period of time after making an allowance for any withdrawal or introduction of capital. Profit is ascertained by determining the market value, at the two accounting dates of all the assets reduced by the amount of liabilities incurred. The increase or reduction in the net worth is the profit or loss for the intervening period.

2. Accountant's Concepts. From the accountant's point of view profit is the margin between operating income and associated expenses as related to a given period of time. The accountant's business is a continuing operation. Its wheels do not cease to grind, as is assumed for the purpose of preparing the periodical statements of account. So, while these should be prepared in order that proprietors may have periodical reports of the stewardship, they are subject to limitations. Hence the accountant is continually striving to perfect this method to evaluate the expenditure which has not resulted in an income so that, on its exclusion, the accounts may become more accurate and meaningful. To quote George O. May, an American Accountant, "Accounts essentially are historical records and as is true in history, in general, correct conclusion cannot be reached by a hurried survey of temporary conditions but only by a large retrospect and a careful distinction between permanent tendencies and transitory influences." Some of the ideas which have dominated the thinking of accountants in the past are : the necessity of preserving the monetary value of the proprietary capital originally contributed, the unpredictable nature of the future course of events and sale as an essential step to the emergence of profit. In due course, these ideas have developed into a complicated fabric of accepted accounting practices."

3. Rushden Heel vs. I.R. (1946). The term 'profit' may be described as "the increase in the net value of the assets of a business over their net value at the commencement of a given period which has arisen other than by capital adjustment."

4. Spanish Prospecting Co. Ltd. (1991). "If the total assets of the business at the two dates be compared, the increase which they show at the later date as compared with the earlier date (due allowance, of course, being made for any capital introduced into or taken out of the business in the meanwhile) represents in strictness the profit of the business during the period in question. The strict meaning of the word 'profits' is rarely observed in drawing up the accounts of firms or companies. Certain assumptions have become so customary in drawing up Balance Sheets and Profits and Loss Accounts that it may almost be said to require special circumstances to induce parties to depart therefor. For instance, it is usual to exclude gains and losses arising from causes not directly connected with the business of the company. The value assigned to trade buildings and plant is usually fixed according to an arbitrary rule, by which they are originally taken at their actual cost and are assumed to have depreciated by a certain percentage each year. Though it cannot be pretended that any such calculation necessarily gives their true value either in use or exchange. It is better to under-rate than to over-rate the profits, since it is impossible for you to see all the risks to which a business may in future be exposed. But though there is a wide field for variation of practice in these estimations nor profits, this liberty ceases at once when the rights of third parties intervenes. In the absence of certain stipulations to the contrary, 'profits' in cases where the rights of third parties come in, mean actual profits, and they must be calculated as closely as possible, for you to see all the risks to over-rate the profits, since it is impossible for you to see all the risks to which a business may in future be exposed. But though there is a wide field for variation of practice in these estimations or profits, this liberty ceases at once when the rights of third parties intervene. In the absence of certain stipulations to the contrary, 'profits' in cases where the rights of third parties come in, mean actual profits, and they must be calculated as closely as possible, in accordance with the definition to which I have referred."

Thus there is no unanimity among the accountants on the meaning of the term "profit". But the concept is important since profit is determined every year to determine the claims of various parties and to compute bonus, income tax, dividend and managerial remuneration etc. on the basis of the annual profits of the company.

DIVISIBLE PROFITS

Definition of Divisible Profits

1. Common Definition. The term 'divisible profits' relates to those profits which can be legally distributed amongst the shareholders of the company by way of dividend.

2. Fisher v. Black and White Publishing Company (1901). "Profits available dividend" mean "net profit after making any deductions which the directors can duly make." Thus, all profits cannot be divisible profits. A part of this is set aside for reserves etc. and only the remainder is divisible. Profits may consist of profits arising out of trading as well as from other sources. They may be capital profits that may be distributed as dividends under certain situations.

3. Section 205 of the Companies Act, 1956. "No dividend shall be declared or paid by a company for any financial year except out of profits of the company for that year arrived at after providing for depreciation in accordance with the provisions."

Principles for Divisible Profits

1. Capital shall not constitute part of divisible profits.
2. Only *bona fide* surplus profits should be divisible amongst the shareholders.
3. This should be with reference to Memorandum, Articles and Provisions of Companies Act.

Determination of Divisible Profits

1. Principles of accountancy,
2. Provisions of Memorandum of Association and Articles of Association,
3. Legal decisions,
4. Provisions of the Companies Act, 1956.

Factors influencing Divisible Profits

1. Capital profits,
2. Capital losses,
3. Depreciation,
4. Past losses,
5. Transfer of Reserves,
6. Profits prior to incorporation of the company.

1. Capital Profits. Capital profits are not to be distributed. Though the Companies Act does not prohibit their payment as dividend still there must be distinction as to capital profits to be distributed as bonus shares and cash dividends. Capital profit may be distributed as bonus shares as it does not affect the assets of the company in any circumstances. In a case in England it was held : "A profit made on the sale of a part of the undertaking of a company is available for dividend, if the Articles so permit. Here the company sold its branches and later on repurchased them at a profit. It gained in the transaction. In another case it was held that "A realized appreciation in the value of a Book debt taken over by a company at its formation is not profit available for dividend, unless such surplus remains after a revaluation of the whole of assets." The conditions given below should be fulfilled if the capital profits are to be made available:

(i) The Articles of the company do not prohibit distribution in this way.

(ii) The capital profit should have been realised.

(iii) The surplus profit remain even after the revaluation of all the assets of the company.

(iv) All the capital losses have been met and their distribution to the shareholders does not affect the payment of the company debts.

Payment of capital profits to shareholders does not mean payment of dividends out of capital. It is better to keep the distinction between capital and capital profits. As Lord Lindley puts it, "Moreover, when it is said and said truly that dividends are not to be paid out of capital, the word 'capital' means the money subscribed pursuant to the Memorandum of Association or what is presented by the money. Accretions to that capital may be realised and turned into money which may be divided amongst shareholders."

2. Capital Losses. Losses on capital may arise due to depreciation of capital assets or loss on the sale of such assets. If a company has lost part of its capital it may declare or pay dividend without making good the capital which has been lost. Legally, profit is divisible out of current profits to the shareholders without making good the loss on capital, but according to Section 15 of the Banking Companies Act, 1949, it is not applicable to Banking Companies.

3. Depreciation. It is compulsory for all the Companies to charge depreciation before it can pay dividends to the shareholders. Section 205 of the Companies Act, 1956 specifically provides that no dividends can be declared or paid except "out of profits of the company for that year arrived at after providing for depreciation according to the provisions of Sections 205(2)". According to section 205(1)(c) the Central Government may, in the public interest, allow any company to decare or pay dividend out of the profits of the current year of any previous financial year or years without providing for depreciation.

4. Past Losses. Legally, there is no need for making good a debit balance of the Profit and Loss Account on account of the losses in the previous years before and distribution of current profits. In the case of *Ammonia Soda Company* vs. *Chamberlian and other* (1918) it was said that "It is not necessarily illegal for directors of a company to pay dividends out of the profits of the company during a current year without making good existing deficiencies in paid-up capital, or without writing off a debit to the Company's Profit and Loss Account occasioned by losses in the previous years."

5. Transfer of Reserves. Directors are free to create reserves out of profits of the current year before the distribution of dividend provided the Articles of Association of the company so need. In one of the cases it was held, "The preference shareholders cannot claim dividends as a matter of right before the provisions of reserves which the directors thought necessary, were duly made, provided the articles give power to create reserves before the payment of dividends." According to Section 205(2A) after 18th February, 1975, no dividend shall be declared or paid for any financial year out of the profits for that year arrived at after providing for depreciation in accordance with Section 205(2) except after the transfer to the reserves of such percentage of its profits for that year, not exceeding 10% as may be prescribed. Section 205(A) does not prohibit the voluntary transfer of a higher percentage of the profits to the reserves in accordance with the rules prescribed by the Central Government.

6. Profits Prior to incorporation of the Company. Profits before incorporation of the company cannot be legally distributed amongst the shareholders, as the company had not come into existence till that date in law even if it was purchased before. As legal existence was not there, there is no problem of distribution of profits before incorporation.

GUIDELINES AND GENERAL RULES REGARDING DIVISIBLE PROFITS

1. Divisible profits will depend upon the particular position of each case.
2. Company need not distribute whole of its profits calculated in the particular year.
3. Dividends should be paid out of trading profits. These can be paid from capital profits in few circumstances.
4. Directors should be held responsible to repay the excess if they authorise to pay out of capital.
5. Breach of trust will be applicable to directors jointly and severally for such acts if done.
6. The Companies Act prohibits giving a part of capital to shareholders by way of dividends.
7. Capital profits may be given to shareholders as dividend if Articles so allow. These should be separately shown in Profit and Loss Account so that they are not taken as trading profits.
8. For manufacturing Company, depreciation of plant and machinery

must be provided before dividends are paid out of the company profits.

9. Loss on the floating or circulating assets should be provided before such distribution.
10. Circumstances and regulations of the company will decide the replaced capital loss. The company can retain for the payment of debts and other liabilities before declaring dividends.
11. Provision for depreciation of fixed assets is not required legally but it is necessary for company purpose.
12. Revaluation of assets is allowed if shareholders approve.
13. Increase in the value of fixed assets may be distributed as dividend provided liabilities are also taken into account. As it is realised in cash, dividends cannot be prohibited by Articles.
14. Past losses need not be adjusted before the payment of dividends out of current profits.

Duties of the Auditor

1. To see that Memorandum and Articles are followed, besides statutory provisions.
2. To satisfy that facts are properly presented in the company accounts. If he finds any defects, he will show these to the shareholders.
3. To point out if provisions for depreciation are not made before dividends are distributed or a part of the capital has been returned to shareholders. These matters must be reported to share holders. If he finds any deficiency regarding accounts, his responsibility ends with his report to the shareholders.

CAPITAL PROFITS

Capital profits are profits which are not earned through trading. Non-trading profits are capital profits. These profits are not earned in the regular course of business characteristics of profits:

(i) These are non-trading nature.
(ii) These are not certain and don't arise again and again.
(iii) These do not refer to the efficiency of the business.
(iv) These do not appear in the credit side of the Profit and Loss Account. Non-trading profits are capital profits. Examples of capital profits are the following :
  (a) Premium received on the issue of shares.
  (b) Profits made from a business which has been purchased and before the certificate of commencement of business has been granted to the company.
  (c) Profits made on the resale of the forfeited shares.

(d) Profits made on the redemption of debentures in the open market, i.e., purchasing them at a discount.

(e) Profit made on the sale of a fixed asset.

Can capital profit be distributed as dividend?

Ordinarily, such profits should not be distributed because these are not the trading profits, i.e. normal profits. In certain circumstances, however capital profits can be distributed among the shareholders of the company. The courts have allowed that a company can distribute capital profits under the following conditions :

1. Lubock v. The British Bank of South America. Dividends can be paid out of realised capital profits provided the Articles of the company do not prohibit.

2. Foster v. The New Trinidad Lake Asphalte Co. Ltd. The capital profits cannot be distributed as dividend without having regard to the result shown by the accounts as a whole.

Conditions of capital profits distribution

1. Articles of Association of the company must authorise to distribute such capital profits as dividends.
2. Such capital profits must have been realised, i.e. the company has the cash funds generated from such capital profits.
3. Revaluation of all assets and liabilities has been done and the capital profit is the actual surplus of assets over liabilities.
4. All revenue and capital losses has already been adjusted.
5. The company is financially sound to pay off all his debts.
6. The capital profit has not been transferred to capital reserve account.

   According to section 205 of the Companies Act, dividend can be declared only out of profits of the company which include capital profits also. However, as a commercial policy, companies do not opt for the distribution of capital profits as it is not a prudent. They prefer to utilise the capital profits for the following purposes:

   (i) Writing off capital losses, extraordinary losses.

   (ii) Writing of preliminary expenses, underwriting commission etc.

   (iii) Transfer to Capital Reserve Account.

   (iv) Implementation of expansion programmes.

Capital profits are usually not distributed as it affects:

(i) Requirements of working capital.

(ii) Future financial commitments.

(iii) Expansion and Improvement programmes.

Capital profits are utilised to strengthen the financial position of the company. These are capitalised by issuing Bonus Shares rather than distributing the cash resources of the company.

CONDITIONS OF DIVISIBLE PROFITS

Capital profits are not treated as divisible profits for the purpose of distribution of dividends to the shareholders. But from legal point of view a company is authorised to pay dividends both out of capital and revenue profits.

According to the decisions of the cases, it held that following conditions should be fulfilled if the capital profits are to be made divisible:

(i) The Articles of the company do not prohibit such distribution.

(ii) The capital profits must have been realised.

(iii) The surplus profits remain even after the revaluation of all the assets and liabilities of the company.

(iv) Not transferred to the 'Capital Reserve Account' by the directors.

(v) All the capital losses have been met and their distribution to the shareholders does not effect the payment of the debts of the company.

Dividend out of capital

The payment of dividend is based on the principle that dividends can never be paid out of capital. If there are any provisions in the Memorandum or Articles of Association of a company, it is void, and invalid. Following acts of the company amount to the payment of dividends out of capital:

1. Payment of dividend out of sale proceeds of the company's assets out of capital receipts.
2. Payment of dividend out of overstated profits in case of revenue expenditure charged to capital expenditure.
3. Profit and Loss Account do not deal with any profit and there are no undistributed past profits, but the dividends are proposed to be paid.

Reasons for Restrictions

1. Illegal. Under the provisions of Section 100 a company cannot reduce its capital without the permission of the court. Therefore distribution of dividend out of capital is illegal. If dividends are paid out of capital, it would result into depletion of the assets of the company.

2. Dangerous. Distribution of dividend out of capital is a serious danger to the security of the creditors and debenture holders of the company because they agree to deal with a company only on the basis of the capital of the company. The company holds the limited liability. Therefore, reduction of capital amounts to reduction in their security.

3. Prohibited by Law. According to the 94the Article of 'Table A' dividend cannot be distributed out of capital. If the Memorandum of Association or its Articles give such power to the company it is invalid.

4. Director's Liability. If the directors of the company have distributed dividends out of capital, they will be personally liable to return the money to the company along the interest at the rate of 5% per annum.

5. Fraud. Fraudulent promotors may cheat the publicly taking big loans and later on take back their capital in the form of dividends. Thus the money lenders are put to a great loss.

QUESTIONS FOR EXERCISE

1. What do you understand by "divisible profits"? What points are to be taken into account while determining the divisible profits?
2. Define divisible profits. Is the entire amount of profits of a company divisible among its shareholders?
3 What are the guidelines about divisible profits from the auditors point of view? Explain his duties in this connection.
4. What are capital profits? Are such profits available for distribution as dividend?
5. Can dividends be paid out of capital profits? Discuss.
6. "Capital profits may be used for the payment of dividends but dividends must not be paid out of capital". Examine this statement critically.

20

Dividend and Interest

According to *Lamplough* vs. *Kent Waterworks,* in the ordinary sense the word dividend means the sum paid and received, or the quotient forming the share of the divisible sum payable to the recipient. The director's power to recommend dividend is discretionary. They may refuse to recommend the payment of dividend, if they think it is in the interest of the company even if there are profits. The directors may transfer profits to a depreciation fund or to a reserve fund and the minority of shareholders cannot object to the majority of the shareholders agreeing to such funds or to capitalisation of profits [*Dinshaw M. Petit* (1926)]. They know the financial position of the company and decide what should be paid to the shareholders. They make a recommendation that such and such amount may be paid to the shareholders. They decide whether the income tax at the standard rate is or is not to be deducted from the dividends without the consent of the ordinary shareholders or unless originally the preference shares were 'free of income-tax shares'. It is the right of the shareholders to declare dividend except when the directors have a right sometimes to declare dividend on preference shares and declare interim dividends on all shares.

Dividend vs. Interest

'Dividend' is a portion of the amount of profit of the company. It is distributed amongst the members in proportion to their shares. On the other hand, 'interest' is the consideration paid to the moneylender by the borrower for the use of borrowed money. The payment of interest is a charge on the profit and loss account of the borrowing concern. It is to be compulsorily paid whether there is a profit or not. Dividend is declared only out of divisible profits of the company. If no profit is earned, the question of declaring dividend does not arise. However, under special circumstances, the Central Government may authorise a company to pay dividend even when there are no profits. Following are the points of distinction between dividend and interest.

(1) While dividend is paid out of profits of a company and can be regarded as mere appropriation of profits, interest is a charge on the profits of a company.

(2) While the question of paying dividend will arise only when profits are earned, the interest is paid irrespective of the profits made by a company.

(3) While the dividend arrears carry no interest, interest on debentures in arrears necessarily carries interest unless there is an agreement to the contrary.

(4) While the directors, if allowed by articles, may declare an 'Interim Dividend', it is not possible to expect interest to be accrued before its fixed date of payment. In other words, the directors cannot pay 'Interim interest.'

(5) While declaration of dividend is left to the discretion of the Board of Directors, the payment of interest must be made whether the board likes it or not. Hence, the declaration of dividend is voluntary, while payment of interest on debentures etc., is compulsory.

(6) While the dividend is paid to the registered shareholders of the company, the interest is paid to the debenture-holders or other creditors of the company.

(7) While the dividend is not paid on call money received in advance, interest is paid on all loans received from debenture-holders and other creditors of the company.

(8) While the dividend is treated as a liability of the company only when it is declared, the interest payable is always treated as a liability of the company.

(9) While the dividend can be declared as free of income-tax or less income-tax, the interest is payable always less income-tax. Hence, only in the case of dividend the income-tax is deducted at the source.

(10) While the dividend on shares is declared by the Board of Directors and approved by the shareholders at the annual general meeting, the payment of interest on debentures neither requires recommendation of directors nor approval of the shareholders as it is already fixed before hand in accordance with the terms of the contract.

STATUTORY PROVISIONS

The Sections 93, 205, 206 and 207 of the Companies Act, 1956, make legal provisions as to the declaration, manner and time of payment of dividend and they are as follows:

(1) Any public company may, if it is authorised by its articles, pay dividend in proportion to the amount paid on each share where a large amount is paid-up on some shares than on others. [Sec. 93]

(2) The company cannot declare or pay dividend except out of its profits, out of moneys provided by the Central or a State Government for the payment of dividend in pursuance of a guarantee given by such Government for the payment of dividend. [Sec. 205]

(a) Where dividend has been declared by a company but has not been paid within forty-two days from the date of the declaration, the company shall within seven days from the date of expiry of the said period of 42 days, transfer the total amount of dividend unpaid to a special account to be called "unpaid dividend Account of .....Co. Ltd."

If the default is made in transferring the total amount, the company shall pay from the date of such default interest at the rate of twelve per cent per annum. Where any part of dividend declared before the commencement of Companies (Amendment) Act, 1974, remains unpaid at the commencement of the said Act, the company shall within six months from the commencement of the Act transfer the unpaid amount to the unpaid dividend Account.

(b) Any money transferred to the unpaid dividend account of a company and unclaimed for a period of three years from the date of such transfer, shall be transferred by the company to the general revenue account of the Central Government.

(c) The company shall be entitled to a receipt from the Reserve Bank of India for any money transferred by it to the general revenue account of the Central Government. On defaults the company and every officer of the company who is in default shall be punishable with fine which may extend to five hundred rupees for everyday during which the failure continues.

(d) Any person claiming any money transferred to the general revenue account of the Central Government, may apply to the Central Government for an order for payment of the money claimed and the Central Government may, if satisfied, make an order for the payment to that person of the sum due to him after taking such security from him as it may think fit.

(3) No dividend can be paid by any public company in respect of any share therein except:

(a) to the registered shareholder or to his order or to his bankers; or

(b) to the share warrant holder where share warrant has been issued in respect of such shares. [Sec. 206]

(4) Where a dividend is declared by a company, it must be paid or the warrant in respect thereof must be posted to the shareholders within forty-two days from the date of its declaration failing which a party to the default is liable to a simple imprisonment for a term not exceeding seven days and may also be liable to a fine. [Sec. 207]

Conditions under which Payment of Dividend may not be made

Under the following conditions, no offence shall be deemed to have been committed and therefore the party responsible for the payment of dividend may not have to pay a fine or undergo imprisonment, even though the payment of dividend is not made within three months of his declaration:

(a) where dividend could not be paid by reason of the operation of any law;

(b) if the shareholder has given certain directions as to the payment of the dividend and those directions cannot be complied with;

(c) if there is a dispute as to who has to receive the dividend;

(d) if the amount of dividend is adjusted by the company towards the amount due from the shareholders; and

(e) where the company's failure to pay the dividend or post-dividend warrant is not due to any fault on its part. (Sec. 207)

Regulations of Table 'A' Regarding Dividend

Regulations from 85 to 94 of Table A pertain to the declaration and payment of dividend. They are explained as below:

1. A company in general meeting may declare a dividend, but no dividend shall exceed the amount recommended by the Board. [Reg. 85]

2. The Board may, from time to time, pay to the members such interim dividends as appear to justified by the profits of the company. [Reg. 86]

3. (a) The Board may, before recommending any dividend, set aside out of the profits of the company such sums as it thinks proper as a resource or reserve which shall, at the discretion of the Board, be applicable for any purpose to which the profits of the company may be properly applied, including provision for meeting contingencies or for equalising dividends, and pending such application, may, at the discretion of the Board either be employed in the business of the company or be invested in such investment (other than shares of the company) as the Board may, from time to time, think fit.

   (b) The Board may also carry forward any profits which it may think prudent not to distribute, without setting them aside as a reserve. [Reg. 87]

4. (a) All dividends shall be declared and paid according to the amounts paid subject to the special rights of persons as to dividends.

   (b) Where nothing is paid upon any of the shares in the company, dividends may be declared and paid according to the face value of the shares.

(c) Amount paid as advance on uncalled calls will not be treated as money paid on the shares for the purpose of paying dividend.

(d) All dividends shall be apportioned and paid proportionately to the amounts paid on the shares. But if any share is issued on terms providing that it shall rank for dividend as from a particular date, then such shares shall bank for dividend accordingly. [Reg. 83]

5. The Board may deduct such sums of money from the dividend payable to any member if that member has to pay to the company on account of calls or otherwise in relation to the shares of the company. [Reg. 89]

6. (a) The general meeting is authorised not only to declare a dividend or bonus, but also to direct payment of such dividend or bonus, wholly or partly, by the distribution of specific assets.

(b) The Board of Directors is expected to give effect to the resolution of the general meeting.

(c) If any difficulty arises in regard to such distribution the Board is allowed to settle it as it thinks proper.

7. (a) Any dividend, interest or other moneys payable in cash in respect of share may be paid by cheque or warrant sent through the post directed to the registered address of the holder.

(b) In the case of joint holders, it will be paid to one of the joint holders whose name appears first on the register of members, or to one as joint holders may direct the company in writing.

(c) Lastly, every such cheque or warrant shall be made payable to the order of the person to whom it is sent.

8. Any one of two or more joint holders of a share can give effectual receipts for any dividends, bonuses, or other moneys payable in respect of such a share. [Reg. 92]

9. Notice pertaining to the declaration of dividend should be given to the person entitled to share in the manner prescribed by the Companies Act, 1956. [Reg. 93]

10. No dividend that may have been declared shall bear interest against the company. [Reg. 94]

THE COMPANIES (TRANSFER OF PROFITS TO RESERVES) RULES, 1975

The Central Government under Sec. 205(2A) of the Companies Act notified these rules in the Gazette of India Extraordinary dated 24th July, 1975, and these rules were further amended and published on 24-7-1976. The amended rules regarding transfer of profits to reserves are as follows:

Percentage of Profits to be Transferred to Reserves (Rule I)

The company cannot declare or pay dividend out of the profits arrived at after providing for depreciation during the financial year except after the transfer of specified percentage of profits to reserves as mentioned below:

(i) Where the proposed dividend is more than 10% but less than 12.5% of the paid-up capital, the amount to be transferred to the reserves shall not be less than 2.5% of the current profits.

(ii) Where the proposed dividend is more than 12.5% and less than 15% of the paid-up capital, the amount to be transferred to the reserves shall not be less than 5% of the current profits.

(iii) Where the proposed dividend is more than 15% and less than 20% of the paid-up capital, the amount to be transferred to the reserves shall not be less than 7.5% of the profit.

(iv) Where the proposed dividend is more than 20% and of the paid-up capital, at least 10% of the current profits should be transferred to the reserves.

Voluntary Transfer of Higher Percentage (Rule II)

The above mentioned rules regarding transfer of profits to reserves will not prohibit the company from voluntarily transferring more than 10% of its profits to reserves provided it fulfils the following conditions.

(i) Where a dividend is declared:

(a) the minimum rate of dividend is ensured equal to the average of the rates of dividends declared during the three years immediately preceding the financial year, and

(b) the minimum rate of dividend is ensured equal to the average of the rate of dividend declared during the three years preceding the financial year in which the bonus shares are issued and also the dividend is declared.

Such minimum distribution of dividend may not be ensured where the net profits after tax or lover by 20% or more than the average net profits after tax of the two immediately preceding financial years.

(ii) Where no dividend is declared, the amount to be transferred to reserves from the current profits shall be lower than the average amount of dividends declared over the three years preceding the financial year. The company and every officer shall be fined up to Rs. 500 in default and Rs. 50 per day till the default continues.

Declaration of Dividend out of Reserves

The Central Government under Sec. 205A(3) has enacted the Companies (Declaration of Dividend out of Reserves) Rules, 1975 and they provide as follows:

The company is empowered to pay dividend out of the accumulated profits earned in the past and transferred to the reserves when it finds inadequate profits or in the year of no profit subject to the following conditions:

(i) The rate of dividend declared shall not exceed the average of the rate at which the dividend was declared by it in the five years immediately preceding that year on 10% of its paid-up capital, whichever is less.

(ii) The total amount to be withdrawn from the reserves for the payment of dividend should not be more than one-tenth of the paid-up capital and its free reserves.

(iii) The amount so drawn should first be utilised in setting off the losses incurred in the financial year before any dividend is declared on preference or equity shares.

(iv) The balance of reserves after such withdrawals, should not be less than 15% of its share capital.

Procedure of Declaration and Payment of Dividend

The Secretary will convene a meeting of the Board of Directors as soon as the final accounts (profit and loss account and balance sheet) are ready. In this meeting will be discussed the director's report prepared by the secretary showing the progress of the company during the period under review. If the Board thinks that the financial position of the company is sound, it may pass a resolution recommending dividend payable at a particular rate per cent on the paid-up value of the shares or a certain stipulated amount on every share depending upon the circumstances. Decision as to the closure of the register of transfers is taken at this meeting and necessary instructions are given to the secretary for making the payment of dividend so declared. After getting these instructions from the Board the secretary sends a notice to all the members of the company inviting their attention to the general meeting at which the declaration of dividend as recommended by the Board is to be passed. To facilitate the work of the secretary in preparing the list of shareholders to whom the dividend may be payable, the register of transfers will remain closed during this period.

Dividend List

The secretary would prepare a final dividend list of shareholders as they stood on the closing day of the register of transfers.

The *"Dividend List"* is prepared by the secretary with the help of information already given in the register of members. It is the responsibility of the secretary to see that the total amount payable, tax deducted, etc., are calculated correctly and before handing over this list to the banker of the company, it should be carefully checked to ensure the arithmetical accuracy.

The *"Dividend List"* gives the following particulars:

(a) Names and addresses of shareholders eligible to receive dividend recommended by the Board;

(b) Number of shares held by such shareholders;

(c) Amount paid by them on shares;

(d) Amount of gross dividend due;

(e) Amount of income-tax to be deducted;

(f) Net amount of dividend payable to each member.

Dividend Warrants

After completing the dividend list, the secretary will take up the work of completing dividend warrants. A dividend warrant is generally divided into two parts: the top part and the cheque part. In the top part of warrant, information regarding the dividend amount due is given in the form of a letter addressed to a shareholder. The cheque part is a form of cheque drawn on a banker with whom the arrangement for paying dividend warrant is made. Such dividend warrants are generally signed by the secretary and the banker will be informed accordingly. Sometimes the signature of director is printed on the warrant. Such warrants should be countersigned by the secretary. Under instructions received from the company the banker will honour all such dividend warrants presented by members to whom they were despatched by the secretary. Before despatching dividend warrants to members the secretary should see that all are properly checked and initialled by the auditors.

INTERIM DIVIDEND

Interim dividend is usually declared in between the two annual general meetings of the company. If the directors feels that there are adequate funds to meet all the company's requirements, and the prospects of earning profits are bright, then such a dividend is declared. It is generally paid half yearly. It may be paid even quarterly. Declaration of such a dividend depends upon the financial position and earning capacity of the company. In this respect Reg. 86 of Table 'A' provides that the Board may, from time to time, pay to members such interim dividends as appear to it to be justified by the profits of the company. The articles should confer such authority on the Board of Directors and then alone dividend can be declared. In the absence of such a provision in the Articles of Association of a company, the Board cannot declare the interim dividend. But where it is allowed, the Board can declare it without consulting the shareholders at a general meeting. If the Board is confident that it can conveniently declare an interim dividend out of the profits of the company, it should get the accounts made up-to-date. Now, the secretary will be asked to close transfer books of the company in order to find out the names of members that appear in the Register of Members. This declaration of dividend will be passed by a Board resolution as follows:

> *"RESOLVED that an interim dividend of 4 per cent (free of tax) be and is hereby declared on the equity shares of the Company payable on or after 20th June, 19.... and the dividend be initialled warrants, bearing the printed signature of Shri. B.K. Acharya by the secretary of the company."*

Now, subject to the articles of the company, dividend warrants will be issued to those members whose names appear on the Register of Members on a specified date. The interim dividends are generally declared on a conservative basis as they are closely connected with the total amounts of profits of the company. The rate of interim dividend is fixed at a lower rate so that the rate of final dividend is always higher. This precaution is taken as a matter of business policy.

DECLARATION OF INTERIM DIVIDEND

SHIVENDRA & CO. LTD.

Notice is hereby given that in compliance with the provision of the Preference Share (Regulation of Dividends) Act, 1960, the Board of Management has sanctioned the payment of an Interim Dividend on 5% Cumulative Preference Shares for the half year ending 31st October, 1989 at the rate of Rs. 3.25 per share subject to deduction of tax in accordance with the Finance Act currently in force.

The Preference Share Transfer Register will be closed from 12th December, 1989 to 16th December, 1989, both days inclusive.

Dividends will be paid only to the shareholders whose names are registered in the Books of the Company on the 16th December, 1989, or to their Mandates.

By Order of the Board

R.N. Sharma

Secretary

63, Netaji Subhash Road, Calcutta,
November 27, 1989

DIVIDEND MANDATES OR REQUESTS

"Dividend Mandate" means the special request made by shareholders of the company to pay dividend due to them direct to their bankers. This generally done by those shareholders who hold shares of different companies. Such requests are also called Dividend Requests or Dividend Authorisations. When such mandates are received, the secretary should keep a separate file and immediately make a note in the register of members. Now the dividend warrant should be prepared in the name of the bank as per conditions of respective dividend mandates and not in the name of the member. It is not the responsibility of the

members' bank to inform the member about the total amount of dividend collected on his behalf. On receipt of dividend warrant the bank will credit the members' accounts.

In the situation of paying dividend to one bank on behalf of a large number of members of the company, only one cheque amounting to the total amount to be paid to that bank is sent to the office of the bank, instead of sending different cheques in the name of different members at different places. The head office of the bank will receive, list of members to whose accounts the amounts are to be credited and dividend warrants. It distributes the top parts of warrants to its branches which will accordingly credit the accounts of the respective members. This is a special device adopted by many companies to save expenses to be incurred on postage of different dividend warrants and stamp duty.

Loss of Dividend Warrants

After receiving a request its members who have either lost or mislaid or destroyed it the company is authorised to issue a duplicate dividend warrant. As soon as such application is received by the secretary, he should collect all the facts pertaining to the loss of dividend warrant. He should also inform the bank not to honour the specified dividend warrant which has been claimed by the members as lost or mislaid. He should obtain a letter of indemnity from the member. Now, the secretary will place the matter before the Board for getting the necessary approval of the issue of duplicate dividend warrant, after which a duplicate warrant is issued to the member, in the same form in which the previous one was issued; but with the number different from the original one. Lastly, the duplicate dividend warrant will be issued only after the lost cheque becomes '*stale*' or '*out of date*' *i.e.* after the expiry of six months from the date of its issue.

Revocation of Declared Dividend

Generally any company cannot revoke a dividend once declared at the annual general meeting after it is approved by the shareholders. Hence, any revocation of such a declaration of dividend can be made only with the consent of shareholders who, on such declaration, become creditors of the company to the extent of declared dividend. The Board of Directors will be justified in revoking the declaration of dividend when it thinks proper to conserve the remaining assets under following conditions: when,

(1) the company's property has been destroyed;

(2) there is outbreak of war; or

(3) heavy tax has been imposed; or

(4) it is felt that the assets of the company are likely to diminish; or

(5) it is realised that the dividend has been illegally declared.

Interim dividend

The Board may rescind the resolution at any time before the payment is made provided it is satisfied that the prevailing circumstances do not justify such payment.

If the payment of dividend is illegally declared the directors are jointly and severally liable to make good the loss caused to the company.

PAYMENT OF INTEREST ON DEBENTURES

(1) Bearer Debentures

1. *Procedure:* It is through coupons attached to bearer debenture that the payment of interest is made. The mode of payment of interest is stated in the debentures. Generally such interest is payable half-yearly on the stipulated dates or on such terms and conditions mentioned in the debenture.

As and when the interest falls due, the company through the press notifies this fact requesting the debenture-holders to lodge their respective coupons with the company for verification and payment.

2. *List*: Now, the company will prepare a list of bearer debentures showing therein:

(a) the number of value of each debenture;

(b) the amount of gross interest payable on each debenture;

(c) the amount of income-tax to be deducted on each debenture; and

(d) the net amount of interest payable on each debenture.

3. *Banker's duty:* The list is then sent to the company's banker along with other statements such as (a) list of coupons payable, (b) completed interest warrants, (c) listing forms and coupons receipts. The banker thereon will be instructed to open a special 'Interest Account' to which the amount sufficient to pay interest will be transferred from the company's account. The debenture-holders claiming the interest form the company's banker will have to obtain the listing form together with the interest coupon, on receipt of where the banker will issue a coupon receipt bank will carefully examine all such interest coupons and listing forms received from debenture-holders. If coupon receipts are found in order, the banker will take up the interest warrants one by one and will complete them on the basis of the information given in the listing forms. Now the banker will give interest warrants to debenture-holders who in exchange are expected to part with their coupon receipts. After the completion of the issue of interest warrants, all statements are returned by the banker to the company.

2. Register Debentures

1. *Procedure :* In this case, the necessary interest is paid through interest warrants without any declaration as it is fixed before hand. The transfer books

will remain closed for a specified period in order to ascertain the total holding of each debenture-holder. Interest warrants are prepared with the help of the list. The amount of interest is paid in the same manner as it is done in the case of dividend warrant. But all joint debenture-holders are required to jointly sign the interest warrants issued to them before payment.

Payment of Interest out of Capital

The capital of the company once raised by way of shares cannot be repaid to its members during the life time of the company unless and until the company is wound up. But Sec. 208 of the Companies Act, 1956, permits the company to pay interest out of capital under the following conditions:

(1) Where a company has issued shares to raise money for meeting the expenses of the construction of a building or the installation of a plant which is not likely to prove profitable or remunerative for a pretty long period, it may pay interest on such shares out of capital by charging such amounts to the capital as a part of the cost of construction or provision of the plant installed.

(2) Such amount of interest is payable only when the company is authorised by its articles or by passing a special resolution at a general meeting.

(3) The prior sanction of the Central Government is also necessary in this respect although the articles authorise the company to do so.

(4) The rate of interest fixed as per terms and conditions specified in the sanction of the Central Government; if not, the company can pay at any rate not exceeding four per cent per annum.

(5) The Central Government, before sanctioning such payment, may appoint a person to inquire into the affairs of the company and make a report. Such a person is appointed by the Government at the cost of the company seeking permission. The Central Government will also demand a security for the cost of the inquiry from the company and unless and until the Government obtains security, no appointment of any person is made to make the necessary inquiry in the matter.

(6) The sanction to pay interest out of capital will be given by the Central Government specifying the period for which such interest is to be paid.

(7) The payment of interest out of capital is not a reduction in the paid-up capital on the shares in respect of which it is paid.

Dividend and Income-tax

As income-tax is paid by the company on its total net profits, so when dividend is declared, it is generally declared less tax. A holder of shares will receive less than the actual amount of dividend declared as the company will deduct the amount of income-tax. He can claim a refund of tax if he finds that more amount is paid by the company on his amount of dividend than what he is expected to pay as an individual. He can get the refund of excess money provided he sends an application stating all facts and a dividend warrant notice to show to the income-tax authorities the amount declared as dividend less tax.

As once income-tax paid it is very difficult to get it refunded, therefore, those who are not liable to pay income-tax, (except companies) may submit an Income-tax Exemption Certificate issued on application, by the Income-tax Officer concerned. When the company is in receipt of this certificate from its member, it will pay him dividend without deducting income-tax.

However, as per the amended provision for deducting income-tax at source with effect from 1st October 1977, if the dividend amount payable to the shareholder on or after 1st October 1977, is not more than Rs. 250, companies have been exempted from the liability to deduct tax at source provided:

(i) the shareholder, not being a company, is a resident in India, and

(ii) he furnishes a statement to the company in duplicate, in the prescribed form and declares therein that his estimated total income of the previous year in which the amount of dividend declared is liable to be included in his total income does not exceed the exemption limit.

Unclaimed Dividend

If the dividend, when declared, is not claimed by some shareholders, such amount of dividend is called "unclaimed dividend". It appears on the liability side of the company's balance sheet. This amount is usually transferred to "Unclaimed Dividend Account". Under the provisions of Section 205 of the Companies (Amendment) Act, 1974, if any amount remains unclaimed in the unpaid Dividend Account of the company for more than three years, such unclaimed amount should be transferred to general revenue account of the Central Government.

Sections. 205A and 205B provide that "Unclaimed Dividend Account" should be opened with any scheduled bank within seven days of the expiry of 42 days within which the dividend declared has not been paid. Unclaimed dividend amount should be transferred to the above Account within six months from such commencement. The company will be liable to pay interest on the amount not so transferred at 12% from the date of such default and the interest so accrued shall be paid to the shareholders in proportion to the amount not paid to them. These Sections further provide that if the dividend warrants are not cashed, amount equal to such uncashed warrant should be deposited in the "Unclaimed Dividend Account" within seven days of the expiry of the said 42 days.

If the unclaimed dividend amount thus transferred to the Unclaimed Dividend Account remains for a period of three years from the date of its transfer, such amount to the General Revenue Account of the Central Government, furnishing all the details of such transfer in a prescribed form to an officer appointed by the Central Government in this behalf. On completion of this procedure, the Reserve Bank of India is supposed to issue a receipt for the money so transferred by the company.

For any default regarding any of the foregoing provisions, the company and every officer who is in default shall be punishable with fine which may extend to Rs. 500 for every days till the default continues.

RULES, 1978, REGARDING TRANSFER OF UNPAID DIVIDEND TO GENERAL REVENUE ACCOUNT

1. Transfer of Moneys: Any amount of unclaimed dividend required to be transferred to General Revenue Account of the Central Government should be transferred to any of the branches of the Punjab National Bank within fourteen days from the date it falls due for transfer.

2. Statement to Registrar: (a) After transferring the amount to "G.R. A/c" of the Central Government, the company is required to file a statement in the prescribed Form 1 mentioning therein all the particulars regarding such transfer made with the Registrar of Companies. (b) Every company so transferring the unpaid dividend amount finally to G.R. A/c of the Central Government from Unclaimed Dividend A/c where it was lying for three years is also required to furnish a certificate along with its Annual Returns to the Registrar.

3. Maintaining Account by the Registrar: The Registrar is expected to maintain in his office separate accounts for each company thus transferring its unclaimed dividend to G.R. A/c of the Central Government.

4. Claim for Payment: The rules for claiming the unpaid dividend which stands transferred to General Revenue A/c are as follows:

(i) The person claiming such amount or any other person holding the power of attorney should first apply to the Registrar of Companies concerned in duplicate in the prescribed Form II.

(ii) The Registrar on receipt of such an application in Form II should verify from his records whether the applicant can claim the amount or not.

(iii) If the Registrar is satisfied as to the title to the aforesaid money, he will ask the claimant other than the Government claimant to execute an indemnity bond with or without surety in Form III.

(iv) On receipt of the indemnity, the Registrar will issue a payment order in Part B of Form II sanctioning the payment of the amount claimed by the applicant.

(v) The order for payment will be issued to Pay and Accounts Officer of the Department of Company Affairs who will issue a cheque in favour of the claimant. The cheque thus drawn will be sent to the concerned Registrar of companies.

(vi) Where the claimed amount is not more than Rs. 500 and the Registrar is fully satisfied as to the title of the claimant, payment may be made without production of the indemnity bond.

(vii) On receipt of the cheque, the claimant should give a stamped receipt bearing signatures of two witnesses to the Registrar of Companies.

(viii) Finally the Registrar will record this payment in the relevant books of account and the amount thus paid will be put under the special category called "Deduct Refunds".

Lien on Dividend

Under Reg. 9 of Table 'A', the company shall have a first and paramount lien on every share for all moneys called in respect of that share provided such a share is not fully paid. The company's lien on a share shall also extend to all dividends payable thereon. The company is empowered to deduct any dividend payable to any member, all sums of money presently payable, by him to the company on account of calls, or otherwise, or the company can also withhold the amount of dividend payable to a member till such time the debt is paid. The company has a right to withhold the amount payable to a member till such time he clears his dues.

Dividend and Depreciation [Sec. 205]

The following points must be remembered while declaring dividend:

(1) Necessary provision for depreciation must be made for the year in question before the dividend is declared.

(2) Dividend is to be declared only out of net profits arrived at after the provision for depreciation is made.

(3) A company can declare dividend out of profit earned during the previous years provided necessary amount of depreciation for those previous years concerned was already deducted.

(4) When a State or Central Government has given a guarantee for payment of dividend, pursuant to such a guarantee, a company may pay dividend out of moneys earmarked for this purpose.

(5) If a company incurred loss in the previous year after 31st December, 1963, and now intends to declare dividend out of profits, before declaration of dividend, it can deduct the amount either equal to the loss or equal to the amount of depreciation, whichever is less from the profits out of which the dividend is to be declared.

The Central Government can allow any company to pay dividend without making any provision for depreciation if it is convinced that declaration of such a dividend is really in the interest of the public. A company, however, need not set aside any amount of depreciation if it is to declare dividend out of profits earned before the commencement of the Companies (Amendment) Act, 1960.

Rules About Non-Resident Shareholder and Payment of Dividend

(1) No dividend can be paid to non-resident shareholder without the permission of Reserve Bank of India.

(2) Till such time, the dividend will be treated as unpaid and the same should be transferred to a separate account viz., ''unpaid dividend A/c.'' to be opened by a company in a scheduled bank.

(3) It is only after obtaining the necessary permission from the RBI, the dividend amount so transferred to "unpaid dividend account" can be paid to such non-resident shareholders by the company.

(4) Any director, who is a resident abroad and not concerned with the day-to-day affairs of the company cannot be regarded as officer in default unless so specified by the Board of Directors.

THE DUTIES OF AN AUDITOR

1. He should examine the Memorandum and Articles of Association to ascertain the rights of different classes of shares in respect of which the dividends have been paid.
2. He should see that the profits available for dividends are really available according to Section 205 of Companies Act and legal decisions.
3. He should check the Minute Books of the directors and the shareholders in order to find out the rate of dividend and that the payment of dividends has been properly recommended by the directors and resolution for their payment has been passed by the shareholders.
4. He should check the Bank Pass Book of dividend account with the Dividend Warrants, which have been returned duly cancelled. Check the amount transferred from the General Bank Account to the Dividend Account. Usually the total amount to be paid on account of dividends is transferred to a separate bank account called "Dividend Account". When the shareholders present the Dividend Warrant to the bank for payment of dividend, the bank debits the "Dividend Accounts" of the company. From the scrutiny of this account the auditor can know the amount of the unclaimed dividend.
5. He should examine the list of shareholders which has been prepared from the Register of Members. The list should show (a) the gross amount payable, (b) deduction of income tax at full rate, provided the dividend has not been declared "Free of Income-tax", and (c) the net amount payable. The total of the net dividend payable according to this list should agree with the Dividend Account and the outstanding dividends with the balance of the "Dividend Account" in the Pass Book.

6. He should check the unclaimed dividend amount from the Dividend Account Pass Book, the returned Dividend Warrants, etc.
7. He should see dividends are paid *pro rata* according to the amount paid on shares if the Articles so provide.
8. He should see whether dividend is payable with or without the deduction of income tax, from the Minute Books or the resolutions passed by the directors. Payment of Dividends on Preference Shares without deduction of income tax is illegal.
9. He should examine the Articles and the Directors Minute Book, if the directors have forfeited the unclaimed dividends.
10. He should see that the Articles authorise the payment of dividend in the form of 'Scrip' and whether the unissued capital just covers this amount in case of Bonus shares.
11. He should see whether the provisions of Section 205 regarding (a) the provision for depreciation, (b) transfer to reserve, (c) writing off of the past losses, etc., have been complied with.

QUESTIONS FOR EXERCISE

1. Discuss the various kinds of dividends and the provisions of the Companies Act, 1956 regarding them.
2. "Dividends cannot be paid out of capital." Explain it and discuss the auditors duties in this connection.
3. Explain the auditor's duties regarding the unclaimed dividends and 'arrears of dividends on preference shares'.
4. When can it be said that the dividends have been paid out of capital ? Describe the auditor's duties also in this connection.
5. "A company cannot declare dividends without making provisions for depreciation." Explain it and discuss the legal and commercial viewpoints in this connection.
6. Do you agree with the statement that "Capital profits may be used for payment of dividends but dividends must not be paid out of capital."
7. Describe the various sources from which the dividends can be paid by a company. Explain the auditor's duties with regard to payment of dividends.
8. Explain the auditor's duties regarding payment of final dividends by a company.

21

Liabilities of An Auditor

MEANING OF LIABILITIES OF AN AUDITOR

According to De Paula, ''the subject of the exact legal position of an auditor is one of considerable complexity and difficulty. An audit is an audit whether paid or unpaid. An honorary auditor is as much liable as a paid auditor. He cannot just plea protection under 'no consideration, no contract'. If audit were to be void on that count, everybody in the profession will have an escape rout. As can be seen the liabilities of an auditor begin with his signing the report and not with the start of audit itself. Secondly, it must be cleared that he is responsible when appointed as an auditor and for audit work. An auditor's liability co-exists with his authentication of a statement. Any audit has a specific social purpose behind it and an auditor who disputes this is actually not aware that his professional liability has to be ever on the increase as society expects more of him."

An auditor's job is responsible as well as accountable not only to his client but to others as well. His liability may arise from contractual engagement or statutory obligations. He is presumed to carry out the assigned professional job completely and with the care and diligence expected of a member of his profession. Though the Companies Act does not provide an exact, comprehensive or clear picture of the liabilities of an auditor, he is expected to discharge his duties according to generally accepted auditing standards obtaining at the time when the professional work is carried out. His audit must be done with reasonable care and skill and in accordance with the statutory or contractual requirements. He may be held liable and called upon to pay the damages for any loss suffered by his client on account of his negligence, his act of dishonesty or for breach of duty. The third parties can also claim damages if they prove auditor's fraud and wilful or intentional misconduct.

CIRCUMSTANCES OF LIABILITIES

1. Negligence in Law. According to the general dictum of law where a person is under a legal duty to take care whether imposed by specific contract or otherwise, the failure to exercise a reasonable standard of care will make that person liable for any resultant damage or loss to those whom the duty is owed. As agent of the client an auditor becomes liable to the client if he suffers a loss due to auditor's negligence. This liability is only towards certain parties suffering loss from such a negligence, i.e., when a reasonable degree of skill and care is not exercised in discharge of duties which a man of ordinary prudence will do.

According to Lamphier Phipos, "Every person who enters into a learned profession undertakes to bring to exercise of it a reasonable degree of care and skill, he does not undertake, if he is an attorney, that at all events you shall gain your case. A surgeon does not undertake that he will perform a cure; nor does he undertake to use the highest degree of skill. There may be persons who have higher education and greater advantages than what he has but he undertakes to bring a fair, reasonable and competent degree of skill." It follows, therefore, that either (i) absence of the requisite professional skill or (ii) the failure to exercise it, gives rise to an action of damages for negligence against a professional accountant.

Thus negligence in law means a breach of duty one person owes to another who pays him to render certain services. There is negligence on the part of an auditor who does not perform his job with reasonable skill and care. Judicially the test must always be whether, in addition to the failure to do the duty, partial or entire, there had also been a failure to act honestly and reasonably.

2. Professional Negligence. Professional negligence means failure to perform duties according to "accepted professional standards" resulting in some loss or damage to a party to whom the duty is owed. Culpable negligence consists of three elements:

(i) existence of duty or responsibility owed by one party to another to perform some act with certain degree of care and competence,

(ii) occurrence of a breach of such duty,

(iii) loss of retirement, being suffered by the party to whom the duty was owed as a result of negligence.

3. Negligence with reference to Audit. These may be as follows:

(i) The dividend is paid out of capital (*Leads Estate and Investment Society Ltd.* v. *Shepherd*).

(ii) The provisions of the Articles have not been complied with.

(iii) Cash or stock has been misappropriated by the officers of the company, which could have been discovered with ordinary skill e.g., the case *Armitage* v. *Brewer & Knot.*

(iv) The accounts show overstated or understated results either through an error or by deliberately done falsification.

(v) Liquidity problems are concealed.

(vi) There occurs non-disclosure of fictitious receivables or overvaluation of accounts receivables.

(vii) Liabilities/assets are verified as existing when they do not actually exist.

(viii) There exists non-discovery of misappropriation of the petty cash balance *London Oil Storage Co.* v. *Sears Hasluck & Co.*

(ix) e.g., There is non-disclosure of a bad debts schedule which in itself was inaccurate.

Test of Negligence. The test of negligence may depend upon the circumstances of each case. However, if the auditor omits to do certain work which is within the terms of his contract with the client or which is required by the Companies Act, 1956 or if he performs such work without the enquiry or care, he may be discharged of negligence, and may be held responsible to make good to his clients the resulting loss therefrom.

LIABILITY TO THIRD PARTIES

Who is Third Party ?

A third party, who is not a privy to the contractual engagement between the clients and the auditor, may suffer a loss by depending on audited documents and the auditor's report. In such cases the auditor may hold the view that he cannot be made liable to those whom he owes no duty. However, the relevance of third parties, is implied in social recognition and public usefulness of financial statements audited by the auditor.

A variety of users study audited financial statements which are specially designed to serve common purposes. These include creditors, bankers, tax authorities, investors and the government. Users like the owners, creditors and suppliers, potential owners, management, taxation authorities, employees and consumers have direct economic interest in the concerned enterprise. Users may be with indirect interests like financial press, trade associations, financial analysts and advisers, stock exchanges, lawyers, regulatory authorities and labour unions. All such parties are without any brevity with the auditor.

1. The Traditional View. To hold a negligent auditor liable "in an indeterminate amount for an indeterminate time to an indeterminate class will be expanding the limit too far. It tantamounts to saying that a man is entitled to be as negligent as he pleases towards the entire world if he owes duty to none." The courts had held that in the absence of a contractual relationship, a plaintiff cannot hold a suit against the auditor. The fact that the plaintiff is a member of the society or that he has suffered damages by relying on the auditor's skill does not make the auditor liable to him.

2. Modern view. Starting with the *Ultramares Corporation case* the modern view got settled in *Hedley Byrne & Co.Ltd* v. *Heller and Partners Ltd.*, which decided that an action for negligence can be brought against the auditor in tort by persons with whom the auditor is not in contractual relationship but to whom he owes a duty even indirectly. Modern view rests on the principle that though the action for negligence cannot be brought against the auditor, negligence may sometimes amount to fraud and he may be sued for that.

3. Hedley Byrne Principle. In the *Hedley Byrne & Co.* v. *Heller & Partners Ltd.* case, Lord Morris observed, "I consider that if someone possessed of a special skill undertakes, quite irrespective of the contract, to apply that skill for the assistance of another person who relies on such skill, a duty of care will arise....Furthermore, if in a sphere in which a person is so placed that others could reasonably rely on his judgement or his skill or on his ability to make careful enquiry, a person who takes it on himself to give information or advice to, or allows his information or advice to be passed on to another person who, as he knows or should know, will place reliance on it, then a duty of care will arise." While dissenting with other judges in the case of *Candler* v. *Crane Christmas & Co.* Lord Denning felt that an auditor has a social responsibility. He observed : "The accountant who certified the accounts of his client is always called upon to express his personal opinion whether the accounts exhibit true and correct view of his client's affairs; and he is required to do his not so much for the satisfaction of his client but more for the guidance of the shareholders investors, revenue authorities and others who may have to rely on the accounts in serious matters of business. If we could decide this case in favour of the accountant there will be no reason why accountants should ever verify the word of one man in a one-man-company, because there will be no one to complain about it. In my view accountants owe a duty of care not only to their clients, but also to all those whom they know will rely on their accounts in the transactions for which these accounts were prepared."

4. Reasonable Foresight Test. The Hedley Byrne special relationship principle has been recently substituted by a reasonable foresight test. In the case *Jeb Fasteners Ltd.* v. *Marks Bloom & Co.* Justice Woolg established that auditors did have a duty of care but were not held liable because the areas in which they were negligent did not have any bearing or proximity to the loss. This judgment just gives weightage to notion of proximity which may not be the final solution. Establishing the rule that chartered accountants are liable to third parties for deceit but they cannot be held liable to unidentified third parties for negligence, Justice Cardozo observed in *The Ultramares Corporation* v. *Touche* case "It would be wrong for accountants to be exposed to liability in an indeterminate amount for an indeterminate time to an indeterminate class. The amount involved could indeed be almost infinite, and the fact of reliance very difficult to prove objectively. Furthermore, it is the directors who should really take primary responsibility for loss through misleading accounts. Yet so often they are 'men of straw'. So there is no point in pursuing them; the auditors, with their insurance cover, will prove a much better bet." In the case of *State Street Trust Co.* v. *Ernest,* the court observed, "Accountants, however, may be liable to third parties even when there is lacking of deliberate or active fraud. A representation certified as truc to the knowledge of the accountants when in knowledge there is none, a reckless misstatement or an opinion based on grounds so flimsy as to lead to the conclusion that there was no genuine belief in its truth, are all sufficient upon which to base liability. A refusal to see the obvious, a failure to investigate the doubtful, if sufficiently gross, may furnish evidence leading to an inference of fraud so as to impose liability for losses suffered by those who rely on the Balance Sheet. In other words, heedlessness and reckless disregard of consequence may take the place of deliberate intention." In the case of *Ryan* v. *Kanne* third parties were given the right to recover against auditors for ordinary negligence if (a) the auditor knew the engagement was for the benefit and guidance of the third party and (b) the third party was identifiable before the statement or report was submitted by the auditor.

5. Doctrine of Holding Out. In all those employments where peculiar skills are required, if a person offers his services, he is understood as holding himself out to the public as possessing the degree of skill commonly possessed by others in the same employment. If a person holds out to the public that he possesses certain skills and makes other people rely on him he must use reasonable skill and care in discharging his duties. Whenever one person is, by circumstances, placed in such a position in relation to another that if that one person knows that by not using ordinary care and skill in his own conduct, he would cause danger or injury to the person or property of the other, a duty arises to use ordinary care and skill to avoid such a danger. This is a duty which one owes to the large body or interest which may be affected by the acts of a professional man.

The traditional view based on doctrine of brevity has been replaced the modern view based on the doctrine of holding out (specialised relationship test).

6. Doctrine of Proximity. According to the doctrine of proximity the liability arises only when auditor's job is the most proximate cause of the loss that have accrued. Lord Atkins observed, "You must take reasonable care and skill to avoid acts or commissions which you can reasonably foresee, would be likely to injure your neighbours— persons who are closely and directly affected by the act." The Council of the Institute of Chartered Accountants in England and Wales states that liability to third parties may arise "whenever a professional person does work for his client in circumstances where he knows or ought to know:

1. that his work is liable to be relied upon by third party;
2. that the third party may suffer financial loss if the work question has been done negligently. Liability will rise when the work in question

is of a kind which it was reasonable for the third party to rely on for his particular purpose."

To conclude, an auditor is liable to the third parties under the following circumstances :

1. In all cases. In all cases, to his clients with whom he is in a contractual relationship.

2. To any Person. To any person, if his report is fraudulent.

3. To third parties. In case of only negligence, to third parties if he knows or ought reasonably to know that his report would be shown to the third parties and the third party concerned is relying on his skills and judgement.

Liability for Negligence

This may be held in the following cases :

1. When the auditor does not take reasonable degree of skill and care while performing his duties as a professional account.
2. When the auditor does not prove himself worthy of what he holds himself out to the public as an expert. Every audit has a social purpose and every auditor is socially accountable.
3. The absence of the requisite professional skill or the failure to exercise it in an auditor.
4. Civil or criminal liability for professional negligence may arise either under a statute or an agreement. Disciplinary action for professional misconduct (under Sec. 21 of the Chartered Accountants Act) may also be taken against a negligent auditor.
5. No liability arises if there is negligence which does not involve any damages or when there are damages without negligence.
6. When the auditor owes a duty to a person or persons and fails to perform or performs it negligently.
7. To third parties when a fraud is involved.
8. In discharge of his duties in tort by persons with whom the accountant is not in a contractual relationship but to whom he owes a duty.

Legal Decisions on Auditor's Negligence

The following court cases in England, USA and India on liabilities arising out of the auditor's negligence, give a bird's eyeview of the main parts of the judgement.

1. Torts by Cooly. No man, whether skilled or unskilled, undertakes that the task he assumes shall be performed successfully and without fault or error; he undertakes for good faith and integrity, but not for infallibility, he is liable to his employer for negligence, bad faith or dishonesty but not losses consequent upon errors of judgement."

2. Dery v. Peek. A false statement made through carelessness and without reasonable ground for believing it to be true could be evidence of fraud. However, if it was made in the honest belief that it was true, it remains unfraudulent and could not render the person liable in deceit.

3. Athur E. Green & Co. v. Central Advance and Discount Corporation Ltd. An auditor is guilty of negligence when he accepts a schedule of bad debts from some responsible officer although it is clear from the list that some of the debts are doubtful and irrecoverable. "If there were circumstances which seemed to call for enquiry, the auditor must make the proper enquiry and if he did not fulfil the duty he owed to the company as one of the officers."

4. Hedley Byrne and Co. Ltd. v. Haller and Partners Ltd. Persons accepting specialised jobs accept a legal duty to exercise such a care as the circumstances require; and for failure to exercise that care an action of negligence will lie if damage results.

To Conclude. There is no immunity from third party liability to an accountant unless he is acting judicially. Even if the auditors act as arbitrators, they cannot claim immunity in case of negligence. Immunity stems from the origin of the appointments and not from the way the duties are performed.

CIVIL LIABILITIES UNDER THE COMPANIES ACT

The Companies Act puts civil liabilities on an auditor in a number of situations. For instance :

1. Section 2(30). The term 'officer' includes an auditor for the purposes of Secs. 437, 438, 539, 543, 545, 621, 625 and 633. It implies that an auditor is liable under these sections as an officer of the company.

2. Section 62. An auditor is liable for misstatements in the Prospectus.

3. Section 233. An auditor is liable to penalties for non-compliance with certain provisions concerning the audit of company's accounts, i.e. non-compliance with Secs. 227 and 229.

4. Sections 477 and 478. A court of law has powers to prosecute an auditor.

5. Section 539. An auditor is subject to a criminal liability whenever fraudulent falsification of books is carried out by the officers of the company including the auditors.

6. Section 628. An auditor is liable for penalty for false statements.

7. Section 545. In the course of winding up, delinquent officers, the auditors and the members of a company may be prosecuted.

8. Section 621. Except the offences under Sec. 545, an offence under the Companies Act will be cognizable only on a complaint in writing by the Registrar of Companies, a shareholder of the company, or a person authorised by the central government.

Civil Liability for Misfeasance

'Misfeasance' means a breach of duty or trust involving the company in a loss. Under Sec. 543, when a company is in liquidation, its past and present directors, promoters and auditors are liable to make good all losses sustained by the company on account of their negligence of duty or breach of trust. It is only when it goes into liquidation that a liquidator has the alternative right to institute misfeasance proceedings against the auditor. The proceedings under Sec. 543 do not take away the general right of action from the liquidator. Though Sec. 543 is enforceable within a time-limit (6 years) yet it is preferred to a common action because all the evidences obtained in the liquidation is available against the delinquent directors and auditors etc. If any document or report is authenticated or signed otherwise than in conformity with the requirements of Sec. 227(5) and Sec. 229, the auditor is held liable to pay a fine which may extend to Rs. 1,000. A good number of court cases illustrate the liability under misfeasance.

Liability for Misstatements in Prospectus

Under Sec. 62, an auditor will be liable to pay compensation to every person who subscribes for any shares or debentures on the faith of the prospectus for any loss or damage sustained because of an untrue statement made by him as an expert. The term 'expert' under Sec. 58(2) includes amongst others an accountant and any other person whose profession gives authority to a statement made by him. It should be noted that under Sec. 55 of the Act a statement may be considered to be untrue, not only because it is so, but also if it is misleading in the form and context in which it is included. The liability, however, will not arise if :

1. the prospectus was issued without his knowledge or consent of which he has already notified the public through newspapers; or
2. his consensus was withdrawn in writing before delivery of the prospectus for registration; or
3. he, on realisation, after registration but before allotment of shares debentures, that the statement was untrue, withdrew his consent in writing and gave reasonable public notice of the withdrawal; or
4. he was competent to make the statement and that on reasonable ground he believed and has continued to believe up to that time of allotment of shares or debentures that the statement was true.

Legal Cases

1. London & General Bank Case. The auditor who does not report to the shareholders the facts of the case, when the Balance Sheet is not properly drawn up, is guilty of misfeasance. It was held that "A person whose duty is to convey information to others does not discharge that duty by simply giving them so much information as is calculated to induce them, or some of them, to be asked for more. Information and means of information are by no means equivalent terms. An auditor, who gives shareholders means of information instead of information in respect of the company's financial position, does so at his peril, and runs the very serious risk of being held, judicially, to have failed to discharge his duty."

2. The Kingston Cotton Mills Case. It is not the duty of the auditor to take stock and that he is not guilty of negligence of the certificate if a responsible officer is accepted in the absence of suspicious circumstances.

3. The Irish Woollen Co. Ltd. v. Tyson and Others. An auditor is liable, if dividends have been improperly paid out of capital due to such understatement of liabilities of the company as could have been discovered by the exercise of reasonable care and skill. He is always liable for any damages sustained by a company by reasons of falsification of accounts which might have been discovered by the exercise of reasonable care and skill in the performance of audit.

4. Republic of Bolivia Exploration Syndicate. In general the auditor is *prima facie* liable if the audited Balance Sheet does not show the true financial conditions of the company. When *ultra vires* payments are made on the faith of the Balance Sheet, the onus is on the auditors to show that this is not the result of any breach of duty on their part.

5. The City Equitable Fire Insurance Co. Ltd. An auditor is not justified in omitting to make personal inspection of securities that are in the custody of a person or a company with whom it is not proper that they should be left. The *obiter dicta* made by the learned judge was : "I think the auditor must take a certificate from a person who is in the habit of dealing with, and holding securities, and who, on reasonable grounds, rightly believes to be, in the exercise of the best judgement, a trustworthy person to give such a certificate. The auditor's defence of not being guilty particularly in view of the indemnity clause existing in the Articles was rejected by the court." Sec. 201 of the Companies Act, 1956 now prohibits any indemnity clause in the Articles or Memorandum of Associations.

6. The Westminster Road Construction and Engineering Co. Ltd. Overruling the decision in the *Kingston Cotton Mills* case, the Auditor was charged in respect of overvaluation of work-in-progress and omission of liabilities. As there were no profits out of which dividend could be paid it was paid by understanding the company's liabilities and overstating the work-in-progress. Commission on profit was also paid to a director. When there is a time lag between the incurring of a liability and the receipts of bills and at the time of audit, sufficient time has not elapsed for the invoices relating to such a liability to have been received, it is the duty of the auditor to make specific enquires as to the existence of such liabilities. He must also check the value of the work-in-progress at which it is included in the Balance Sheet.

7. Continental v. Ending Case. Though in ordinary disposition of funds advanced by the client to its affiliates need not be disclosed by the auditor, it becomes necessary in cases of : (i) looting, (ii) known dishonesty by a high official, (iii) corporation being operated to a material extent for the private benefit of its President, and (iv) dishonest diversion of funds. An auditor's approach should not necessarily be limited to the mere compliance with the accepted standards but should primarily be governed by the objective to establish an honest and fair representation of financial facts.

CRIMINAL LIABILITIES OF AN AUDITOR

Meaning of Criminal Liabilities

Criminal liabilities are those which arise because of offences against the statutory provisions. These may emerge because of criminal neglect, actual fraud or conspiracy of the auditor. These may emerge due to some criminal acts on the part of auditor or gross neglect of some provisions of the Companies Act. In all such cases, the auditor is liable not only to the shareholders but to the State as well. When charged with a criminal liability, an auditor is punishable with fine or imprisonment or both.

Criminal offence of an Auditor

A company auditor may be guilty of criminal offence under the following sections of the Companies Act.

1. Section 63. An auditor is criminally liable for any untrue statement in the prospectus. He shall be punishable with imprisonment for a term which may extend to two years or with fine which may extend to Rs. 5,000 or with both unless he proves that either the statement was immaterial or that he had reasonable grounds to believe, and did, up to the time of the issue of the prospectus, that the statement was true.

2. Section 233. If the audit report does not give the required information as under Sec. 227 or if it is not signed as in accordance with Sec. 229, the auditor or any other signatory is punishable with fine up to Rs 1,000, if the default is wilful.

3. Section 240. If the auditor does not give the required assistance to an inspector appointed by the central government, the auditor is punishable with imprisonment up to six months or with fine up to Rs. 2,000 or with both.

4. Section 242. If on the report of an inspector, the central government prosecutes any person connected with the company, the auditor should assist in the prosecution, otherwise punishable as if he were guilty of contempt of court.

5. Section 477. When a company is wound up by the court, the auditor is supposed to be present and subject himself to a private examination by the court and is also liable to return to the court any books or documents concerning the company in his possession. If he does not comply accordingly, he may be arrested.

6. Section 478. The auditor of a company in liquidation can be publicly examined in the High Court if so applied by the Official liquidator. The notes so signed by the auditor in the court may be used in evidence against him in proceeding—civil or criminal.

7. Section 539. An auditor can be held criminally liable, if with the intent to defraud or deceive any person, he (a) destroys, mutilates, alters, etc. any books, papers or securities, or (b) makes or is privy to the making of any false or fraudulent entries in any register or books of account or document belonging to the company. And if convicted, he can be imprisoned for a term which may extend to seven years besides being also liable to a fine.

8. Section 545. The court may direct the liquidator of a company which is wound up by or under supervision of the court to prosecute the auditor, if he has been found guilty of any criminal offence.

9. Section 628. An auditor is liable for criminal prosecution, if he in any return, certificate, Balance Sheet, prospectus, statement or other document required by or for the purpose of the Act, makes a statement (a) which is false in any particular material knowing it to be false; or (b) which omits any material fact knowing it to be material. If convicted, he can be punished with imprisonment for a term extending to two years and also with a fine. This section is applicable only to false statements which are not specifically punishable under any section of the Act. It penalises the making of a false statement in any document required by or for the purposes of complying with the provisions of the Act.

Legal Decisions on Criminal Liabilities

1. Rex v. Lord Kylsant and Another. The directors and the auditor were charged for making a deliberate false representation to the shareholders that the company was making a trading profit when, in fact, it was making a trading loss. Drawing upon the secret or hidden reserves, the company paid its debenture interest and dividends on both the preference and ordinary shares. While acquitting the directors the Court held the auditor liable to pay damages for the dividends which were paid out of capital. It held that it is the duty of the auditor to mention the fact either of creation of excessive reserve or where there is a suspicion that such a reserve will be improperly utilised. This decision led to change of phraseology of the auditor's report from 'true and correct' to 'true and fair.'

2. Rex v. Hinds, Musgrave and Steven. Inflated statements and a forecast regarding profits were made in the company's prospectus to invite people to apply for preference shares. There was a trading loss when the prospectus was issued and there was no basis whatsoever for an estimate of the profit. As forecasts were not a part of auditor's report, he was not held to be liable.

3. Dumbell Banking Co. Ltd. The directors and auditors of the Dumbell Banking Company were criminally prosecuted and sentenced for issuing a false Balance Sheet by showing an overdraft from another bank as cash in hand.

While the auditors had drawn the manager's attention regarding overdrafts they failed to report to the shareholders.

4. Official Liquidator of Karachi Bank Ltd. It was stated, "Where the directors of a bank show in the Balance Sheet a cash profit for the year by ending bad debts or doubtful debts which were never paid and which are never likely to be paid, it amounts to making a false statement and a very material one. The fact that no dividend is declared makes no difference."

Liabilities under the Indian Penal Code

1. Section 197. Whoever issues or signs any certificate required by law to be given or signed of relating to any fact which such certificate is by law admissible in evidence, knowing or believing that such certificate is false in any material point, shall be punishable in the same manner as if he gave false evidence.

2. Section 177. It prescribes simple imprisonment up to six months and/ or fine up to Rs. 1,000 for furnishing false information.

3. Sections 188 and 199. A false statement on oath and false declaration may attract the provisions of these sections.

4. Section 193. It prescribes imprisonment up to seven years and a fine for giving false evidence in judicial proceedings.

5. Section. 107. Abetment of the various acts covered above attracts the same penalty.

6. Section 470A. An auditor can be prosecuted for falsification of accounts even when the company is not being wound up.

Liability under Income Tax Act

1. Section 288. A person who has been convicted of an offence connected with any income tax proceedings or on whom a penalty has been imposed under this Act except under clauses (i) and (ii) of Sub-sec. (1) of Sec. 271 is disqualified from representing an assessee for a period to be decided by the Commissioner of Income Tax.

2. Section 278. It prescribes rigorous imprisonment for a person who abets or induces, in any manner, another person to make and deliver to the income-tax authorities false account, statement or declaration relating to any income chargeable to tax which he knows to be false.

3. Section 277. Where the Chartered Accountant files tax returns on his client's behalf, under Rule 12A of the Income Tax Rules, he is expected to submit a report of his examination and which is a statement within the meaning of Sec. 277 of the Income Tax Act, if this report contains any information which is false and which the chartered accountant either knows or believes to be false or untrue, he would be liable to rigorous imprisonment which may extend to two years.

Liability of an Honorary Auditor

An honorary auditor has no defence under absence of consideration whenever he is charged to be responsible for negligence or misfeasance. An audit work whether paid or unpaid remains an audit. An auditor cannot be given the licence to escape his liability on the grounds that the contract is void in view of his not charging anything from the client for his audit work.

Liability of Auditors for Libel

Though authorised to make a *bona fide* libelous or slanderous statement, if the auditor, while making such a slanderous statement, has actually crossed the scope of his duties, he would be liable even for a *bona fide* libelous statement.

QUESTIONS FOR EXERCISE

1. "An auditor's duty is to convey information". Explain how you would distinguish between "information" and "means of information".
2. Discuss the liabilities of auditor under the Companies Act, 1956.
   Is an auditor personally liable or is it subsequently proved that his audit assistants were negligent and as a result the accounts he has certified are false or fraudulent.
3. What is the liability of an auditor of a public limited company with regard to stock-in-trade of a manufacturing business? Quote legal decisions.
4. "An auditor has no liability for negligence in the conduct of an honorary audit". Discuss.
5. Discuss the liability of an auditor under the Companies Act, 1956.
   Is an auditor personally liable if it is subsequently proved that his audit assistants were negligent and as result, the accounts he has certified are false or fraudulent.
6. Enumerate briefly the conclusion which you would draw from the various cases on the subject of the legal liability of auditors as decided by the courts.
7. "An auditor is to convey information." Explain how you would distinguish between "Information" and "Means of information".
8. When can an auditor be held liable for damage to third party? What are the points that the third party should prove to hold the auditor liable when the third party has not appointed the auditor?
9. Discuss the auditor's liabilities to third parties for (a) fraud, (b) negligence, (c) misfeasance.
10. What are the various civil liabilities of an auditor under different statutes?

11. (a) "An auditor is not an insurer, he does not guarantee that the books do correctly show the true position of the company's affairs, he does not guarantee that the balance sheet is accurate according to the books of the company."

    (b) "An auditor is a watchdog and not a bloodhound."

    Elucidate the above statement quoting legal cases.

12. (a) What do you understand by 'Criminal Liability' of an auditor? Name the criminal offences of which an auditor may be guilty under the Indian Companies Act, 1956.

    (b) In the Kingston Cotton Mills case (1896), in the course of his judge ment, the learned judge remarked : 'An Auditor is not bound to be detective, or as was said, to approach his work with suspicion or with a foregone conclusion that there is something wrong. He is a watch-dog but not a bloodhound.'

    In the *Armitage* v. *Brewer and Knott* case (1932), in the course of hearing, the learned judge declared 'that it was the duty of auditors to be suspicious : that was what they were therefor. If everybody was honest and careful, there would be no need for auditors.'

    How would you reconcile the two conflicting views?

22

Cost Audit

DEFINITION OF COST AUDIT

1. Smith and Day. "Cost Audit is the detailed checking of the costing system, technique and accounts to verify their correctness and to enquire adherence to the objective of cost accountancy."

2. I.C.W.A. London. "The cost audit is the verification of cost records and accounts and a check on the adherence to cost accounting plan."

3. Harper. "Cost audit is the verification of the correctness of the cost accounts and of the adherence to proper cost accounting procedures."

4. I.C.W.A. of India. "Cost audit is an audit of efficiency of minute details of expenditure while the work is in progress and a *post-mortem* examination. Cost audit is mainly a preventive measure, a guide for management policy and decision, in addition to being a barometer of performance."

5. J. G. Tikhe. "Cost audit would apparently mean an examination of cost books, cost accounts, cost statements and subsidiary and prime documents with a view to satisfy the Auditor that these represent a fair and true view of the cost of production. This will naturally mean an examination of the appropriateness of the cost accounting system adopted by the business and effectiveness of its implementation."

Thus Cost audit is a detailed checking as well as verification of the correctness of costing techniques, systems and cost accounts. It ensures the adherence of the cost accounting plans. The cost auditor has to see that the cost accounting plan is in accordance with the objectives set by the organisation and the system of accounting is geared towards the attainment of the objectives behind the cost accounting system.

OBJECTS OF COST AUDIT

1. To determine whether cost accounts have been correctly prepared according to the systems and techniques employed by the organisation with a view to enforce cost control and proper cost ascertainment.

2. To ensure that cost accounting plan is adhered to and the routines laid down are carried out.
3. To detect and prevent errors and frauds in preparing cost records.
4. To ensure the integration of cost accounting system and technique into the total system of the organisation.
5. To verify that proper process of cost accounting has been maintained by the management as per the requirements of the industry.
6. To ensure that the process of cost accountancy is adequate to the management for taking effective decisions.

PHASES OR ASPECTS OF COST AUDIT

1. Efficiency Audit. Efficiency audit or profitability audit may be described as the critical assessment of performance of the cost plan, i.e., the expenditure and results obtained are as planned or budgeted. Variations, whether shortfalls or excesses, are investigated into. Following are the aims of efficiency audit :

(i) To give optimum return on investment.

(ii) To determine that opportunity for each area of investment and product mix is changed as suggested by such an analysis.

(iii) Cost-benefit analysis to determine whether some of the variable costs are worth incurring.

2. Propriety Audit or Higher Audit. It is the scrutiny of such actions and plans of management which concern the expenditures and finances of the organisation. The cost auditor has to determine:

(i) Whether the channels or size were designed to produce the best results.

(ii) Whether the planned or budgeted expenditure could give optimum results.

(iii) Whether the return from investments in certain channels could be improved by using an alternative plan of action.

COST AUDIT V/S FINANCIAL AUDIT

The functions of cost audit and financial audit are the same. The basic principles and techniques applicable to both types of audit are common but the approach and the objectives with which they are carried out are quite different. Following are the distinction between these :

1. Nature. While cost audit is concerned with cost accounts the financial audit is concerned with financial accounts.

2. Objectives. While cost audit aims at analysing figures to establish the cost of each operation activity or product, financial audit is to ascertain whether the financial statements reveal a true and fair view of the state of affairs of the business or not.

3. Reportage. While the cost auditor is nominee of the management and as such reports to management, financial auditor's report is addressed to the owners (the shareholders) and he acts as the nominee and watchdog of the shareholders.

4. Regularity. While cost audit report has to be completed within 120 days of the close of the financial year; and the company is bound to supply such cost accounting records, cost statements and other books that are required for conducting cost audit within 90 days from the close of the year, the financial audit is conducted on regular annual basis and thus it tends to become a continuous process.

5. Approach. While cost audit deals with standards and budgets and thus is forward-looking, financial audit is a *post-mortem* check to find out whether expenditure incurred has been really incurred or not. It checks and verifies historical data.

6. Issues. Cost audit and financial audit differ on many issues, such as valuation of inventories, interest on capital and depreciation, etc.

7. Scope. While the scope of cost audit is not specified in the Companies Act but outlined by the Board of Directors or the Central Government as the case may be the scope of financial audit is specified for every company by the Companies Act, 1956 and it remains the same every year.

8. Compulsory. While the cost audit is not compulsory for all the companies but only for some specified category of companies, financial audit is compulsory in case of all the companies.

9. Responsibility. While the cost auditor is responsible to the management of the company the financial auditor is responsible to the shareholders.

MANAGEMENT AUDIT

Management audit is the process of auditing the quality of managers through appraising them as the individual managers and appraising the quality of the total system of managing in an enterprise. It aims at assessing how mangers perform different functions of management e.g. planning, coordinating, motivating etc.

OPERATIONAL AUDIT

Operational audit is the regular and independent appraisal of the accounting, financial and other operations of an enterprise.

Although both the management audit and operational audit have similar aims (of appraising managerial efficiency) yet the two must be considered as two different processes. For example, in a seller's market, the factory or marketing department may function profitably, yet there may be lack of management efficiency. Operational audit may not reveal much. Cost audit is operational audit and is different from management audit. Thus, if we are to Cost audit, we must also management audit an organisation. The two audits— management and cost—are a parallel and continuous process.

TYPES OF COST AUDIT

1. Statutory Cost Audit. Statutory cost audit is that which is conducted by the orders of the Government under any of the following situations :

(i) When three are reasons to believe that the organisation or industry is indulging in profiteering or production is hampered due to inefficient or dishonest management.

(ii) When the industry needs protection.

(iii) When the orders are placed under cost plus contract system, e.g. in the case of defence sub-contracts or civil works contracts etc.

(iv) When fair prices of some basic materials are to be determined, the cost records of units producing petroleum products, cloth, paper, sugar etc. can be examined by the cost accounts offices of the Tariff Commission to determine their cost price.

Under the provisions of Companies Act, 1956, The Cost Audit (Report) Rules were framed in 1967, and cost audit was made compulsory for 27 industries including cement, cycles, caustic soda, tyres and tubes, refrigerators, electric fans, motor vehicles etc.

2. Voluntary Cost Audit

(i) ***Labour Tribunals.*** An industrial tribunal may ask for voluntary cost audit for some special purposes, e.g. to fix bonus, share in profits and fair wages etc.

(ii) ***Management.*** Internal cost audit can be instituted as a continuing means of controlling managerial performance. Its objectives are as follows:

(a) to check the veracity and reliability of cost data.

(b) to measure in cost terms, the performance of different departments, divisions and units of the enterprise.

(c) to prepare future plans.

(iii) ***Trade Association.*** Trade association may ask for cost audit of member firms to determine whether the costing procedure is followed as mutually agreed upon.

(iv) ***Customer.*** The customers may insist on a cost audit to satisfy about the correct ascertainment of cost. This may require voluntary cost audit.

ADVANTAGES OF COST-AUDIT

1. Advantages to Management

(i) ***Detailed Insight.*** It gives management a detailed insight into the costing of various operations of the company. The management can control the affairs of cost of production on the valuable advice and suggestions of the cost auditor.

(ii) ***Fixation of Price.*** It helps in the fixation of price especially when tenders or quotations are sent during competition.

(iii) ***Planning.*** By cost audit the management can abandon the less economic units of production and pay more attention to the more profitable units of production.

(iv) ***Cost of production.*** It helps to find out the correct cost of production.

(v) ***Improvement in cost procedure.*** It can improve the efficiency of cost procedure introduced to avoid leakage of resources of the Company, their theft, fraud and negligence.

(vi) ***Test and Evaluation.*** It can test the effectiveness of cost control techniques and help to evaluate their advantages to the enterprise.

(vii) ***Checking Wastage.*** It would check wastage of materials and labour.

(viii) ***Fixing Responsibility.*** Individual responsibility can be fixed for individuals in case of efficiency, less productivity, wastage, pilferage or theft. It can fix the responsibility of an individual or of the management wherever inefficiency or wastage is found.

(ix) ***Test Checking.*** It can test check important items of cost to find accuracy of the items, cost figures and their reliability.

(x) ***Evaluation of inventory and work.*** It can be useful to check the evaluation of inventory and work in progress at various stages of completion especially at the close of the financial year.

(xi) ***Internal control and check.*** It can help internal control and check that may in their turn be helpful to the financial auditor.

(xii) ***Information.*** It can give the up-to-date information whenever required for any purpose.

2. Advantages to Consumers

(i) ***Direct Benefit.*** The direct benefit accrues where a statutory cost audit has been done to fix a reasonable price for the consumers.

(ii) ***Reduced prices.*** Since cost audit aims at ensuring efficiency in the organisation, this may also get reflected in reduced prices to the consumers.

3. Advantages to Labour

(i) ***Bonus and other benefits.*** If cost audit is done thoroughly, labour also stands to gain through increased profitability in the shape of bonus and other benefits.

(ii) ***Role of labour.*** It brings into focus the role of labour in improving efficiency in terms of increased productivity.

4. Advantages to Shareholders

(i) ***True picture.*** If there is correct valuation of all kinds of inventories this may project a true picture of the organisation before shareholders and other investors and help them to assess its performance.

(ii) ***Fact finding.*** External cost audit highlights efficiency or inefficiency, utilisation of manpower and other resources and adequacy of return etc.

5. Advantages to Government and Economy

(i) ***Settle Accounts.*** Cost audit helps the government to settle accounts where cost-plus contracts have been made.

(ii) ***Intervention.*** The government can intervene to protect the interests of the consumer, labour, shareholders and investors from exploitation or inefficient managements.

(iii) ***Cost Consciousness.*** At the national level, cost audit promotes cost consciousness and overall efficiency. This means that every rupee invested produces the maximum quantity of goods and services.

Criticisms against Cost Audit

1. Interference. It is an interference with the management over matters on which the management is the best judge.

2. Unnecessary. There is no necessity of cost audit when the accounts are audited by an independent auditor who checks the accounts including the manufacturing account of a company. An internal auditor may be appointed if there is a necessity of detail checking of the cost accounts.

3. Overlapping. Cost audit is overlapping or superimposing on the existing system of financial audit or statutory audit. When the cost accounts are prepared by a cost accountant, there is no necessity of appointing a cost auditor whose work will be the same as that of the cost accountant. If the same cost accountant is to act as cost auditor, he will never point out his own mistakes and shortcomings.

4. No Statutory Recognition. No Government in any country of the world has given a statutory recognition to cost audit. Therefore, there is no necessity of taking such a step in this country. This is not a good argument. If no country has given recognition to cost audit that is no reason why should India follow other countries as every country has its own problems.

5. No demarcation. The field of financial audit and cost audit cannot be demarcated. This argument does not hold good as there is sufficient distinction between financial audit and cost audit.

6. Objective not achieved. The amendment to the Companies Act introducing the cost audit has not achieved its objective as is clear from report submitted by the Institute of Cost and Works Accountants of India to the Parliament, which states that the scope of cost audit should be enlarged so as to include inventory audit, cost control, stocks issue procedure, audit's capacity utilisation, overhead and indirect expenditure etc. The Government has accepted some of these suggestions. However, Cost audit has been conducted in public sector undertakings and, therefore, it is but fair that is should be extended to industries in the private sector. It is a special branch of audit to which the cost auditor can do more justice than a financial auditor.

To conclude, cost audit is an effective tools of control in the hands of management. It keeps check and safeguards the interests of shareholders, consumers and the Government. It brings forth efficiency at all levels of the management. It is necessary from the point of view of corporate social responsibility.

COST AUDIT MANUAL

It would be ideal to prepare a Cost Audit Manual for the purpose of outlining procedure and the framework within which the cost audit programme is to operate. This will include the following:

1. The objectives of cost audit.
2. The organisation for cost audit, the authority and responsibility of the staff.
3. Definition of inter-relationship of cost audit with management accounting, cost accounting and financial accounting.
4. Cost audit procedure based on cost accounting system and the management systems in general.
5. Cost audit programme integrated with the cost audit procedure.
6. Cost Audit Report.
7. Follow-up of Cost Audit Report.

Cost audit procedure

1. Vouching. Vouching is the examination of documentary evidence to support and substantiate a particular transaction. It implies that the transaction is properly authorised, recorded and entered in the books of accounts. For example, where overtime work is allowed, the authorisation, the allocation to the job concerned, etc. should be properly recorded in the books.

2. Checking and ticking. The auditor puts check marks or tick marks in pen or coloured pencil to confirm that totals, calculations, postings, etc., have been checked. Rubber stamps can also be used in place of signed ticks if provided in the cost audit procedure.

3. Test Checking. In a large organisation, with numerous products, divisions or department, it is almost impossible to check each and every item of cost. The detailed checking may be left to the internal audit staff while a random sampling check should be made by cost auditor. The size of the sample would depend upon the nature and importance of the items.

4. Working Papers. The cost auditor should obtain the organisation manual/ chart, costing manual, uniform costing manual (if any), cost audit manual, and other such related documents and accounts which are essential for conducting cost audit.

5. Audit Notes. The auditor should record facts in the audit notes in order to seek clarifications from the concerned executives and to make suggestions for improving cost accounting and management accounting organisation.

6. Questionnaires. The cost auditor should frame suitable questionnaires to be included in the cost audit manual to collect information about cost elements. The auditor would do well to make use of them, and even check their suitability in the context of changing cost audit needs. These questionnaires should be brief, adequate and seek answers in a very brief form, say, 'yes' or 'no'.

7. Audit Report. After the cost audit has been completed, the cost auditor has to prepare cost audit report incorporating a certificate regarding correctness of the accounts. This report should also contain suggestions, if any, for improvement in the system. It is not to be sent to the Registrar of companies or to the shareholders. It is not to be disclosed in the annual reports.

PROVISIONS IN THE COMPANIES ACT

1. Compulsory Audit. According to Section 209(1)(d), companies engaged in following activities may be asked to maintain cost accounts:

(i) Production, (ii) Processing, (iii) Manufacturing, (iv) Mining.

2. Additional and Independent Audit. Audit of cost accounts is to be in addition to, and independent of the normal and regular financial audit of the company accounts.

3. Appointment. The cost auditor shall be appointed by the Board of Directors with the prior approval of the Central government.

4. Qualifications. Cost auditor must be a Cost Accountant as per Cost and Works Accountants Act, 1959. Following persons cannot be appointed as cost auditor:

(i) a body corporate,

(ii) an officer or employees of the company,

(iii) a partner or employee of any officer or employee of the company,

(iv) any person indebted to the company for a sum more than Rs. 1000 or has given any guarantee or provided any security in connection for a sum more than Rs. 1000,

(v) Any person disqualified for the appointment as auditor of a subsidiary or holding company of such company.

5. Rights and Duties. In the case of Cost Auditor these are same as that of an auditor of the company.

6. Report. As per Cost Audit (Report) Rules 1968, the cost auditor is to report to the Central Government regarding the company in a specified form within 120 days since the end of the relevant accounting year of the company.

7. Remuneration. Where the Central Government orders for the special cost audit of any company or class of companies, all expenses and remuneration of the special auditor as determined by the Central Government shall be borne by the company.

COST AUDITOR

Qualifications of Appointment

Section 233 B of the Companies Act prescribes following provisions with regard to appointment of a cost auditor:

1. The cost audit is to be done by a cost accountant only within the meaning of Cost and Works Accountants Act, 1959.
2. In the event of sufficient cost accountants not being available the Central Government may by notification in the Official Gazette, direct that the chartered accountants possessing the prescribed qualification may be permitted to do cost audit.
3. With the prior approval of the Central Government only the Board of Directors is competent to appoint cost auditor.
4. The qualifications and disqualifications prescribed for a statutory auditor under Section 226(3) and (4) are applicable to the cost auditor. No relative of a director can be appointed as the cost auditor of the company.
5. If a person appointed as cost auditor becomes subject to any of the disqualifications specified in the Act, he shall cease to conduct the audit of the company.
6. On receipt of an order from the Government for the appointment of a cost auditor, it shall be the duty of the company to render every assistance to such a cost auditor to conduct the cost audit.
7. The cost auditor has to submit his report to the Central Government instead of the company. The Government may send a copy to the directors of the company.
8. The company must furnish such information and explanations within 30 days of the receipt of the copy of the report if called upon to do.
9. The Central Government may allow the company to circulate the audit report.
10. If any default is made by the company, it shall be punishable with a fine upto Rs. 5,000 and every officer of the company who is in default is also liable to punishment with simple imprisonment which may

extend to three years or with a fine which may extend to Rs. 500 or both.

Powers, Duties and Liabilities

1. According to Section 233B(4), a cost auditor shall have the same powers and duties in relation to an audit conducted by him under this section as an auditor of a company has under Sub-section (i) of Section 227.
2. He shall submit his report to the Company Law Board in such form and within such time as may be prescribed.
3. He shall forward a copy of the report to the company within 60 days before the date fixed for annual general meeting.

Functions of Cost Auditor

The Institute of Cost and Works Accountants of India has brought out a booklet *"Cost Audit— its significance"* which spells out the functions of a cost auditor in relation to different items, these are as follows:

1. Inventory. The cost auditor should examine the following regarding inventory:

(i) Is the size of the inventory excessive or adequate in view of the production plan ?

(ii) Is the drill of providing it economical ?

(iii) Does it take into account the cost of storage *vis-a-vis* the cost of carrying ?

(iv) Does it ensure optimum order size for each item ?

(v) Does it take into account lead time of different items or groups of items.

(vi) Are there too many forms and records ?

(vii) Are bottlenecks in production caused by the receipt and issue system ?

(viii) Is there a possibility of reducing inventory cost consistent with production needs ?

(ix) Is the inventory certified by the management as physically correct and priced as per the store ledger ?

(x) Are the expenditures on consumable stores within the standards ? If not so why ?

(xi) Are the raw material issues as per production schedule and standards, or covered by authorised schedules ?

(xii) Is same type of attention and care given to money changed into inventory and tangibles as is given to cash ?

2. Opening and Closing Stocks. The cost auditor should examine the following regarding opening and closing stocks :

(a) Opening Stocks

(i) Its volume should be consistent with the volume of output during the year.

(ii) The opening stock against different jobs physically exists in the stocks and is not merely an accounting figure.

(iii) The shop foreman/supervisor/engineer maintains proper account of consumption *vis-a-vis* withdrawals from the stock, and he is personally responsible for every aspect of stock in the shop.

(b) Closing Stocks

The cost auditor will examine and certify :

(i) that the physical verification is carried out;

(ii) that the valuation is correct with reference to the actual cost of production and recognised policy for valuation;

(iii) that the volume of closing stock is commensurate with the volume of production and that it does not reflect any failure or bottleneck in sales budget or production budget;

(iv) that the volume of unmoved stores is not abnormal in comparison with the normal rate of yearly consumption. The Cost Auditor will recommend disposal of such unmoved stores with consequent release of capital unnecessarily locked up to the advantage of the financial resources of the concern.

3. Store Issue Procedure in Stocks. The Cost Auditor will see :

(i) that withdrawal of material stores to production shop is scientific or covered by authorised schedule and permits receipts to be located;

(ii) that there is no possibility of loss or pilferage of stock lying in the production section;

(iii) that surplus materials and scraps arising in production shops are returned to stores correctly and without delay for which necessary credit is given to unit cost of production. If transferred to other jobs, proper transfer voucher has been prepared and copies sent to the accounts, stores, etc.

4. Working in Progress. The Cost Auditor will see :

(i) that the work-in-progress has been physically verified and that it agrees with the balance in the incomplete cost card;

(ii) that valuation of the work-in-progress is correct with reference to the stage of completion of each job or process and the value job cost cards or process cost sheet;

(iii) that there is no over-valuation or under-valuation of opening work-in-progress or closing work-in-progress, thereby artificially pushing up and down net profits or net assets as the case may be;

(iv) that the volume and value of work-in-progress is not disproportionate compared with finished out-turn.

5. Labour

(i) Proper utilisation of labour and increase in productivity are now receiving attention. Several productive teams have emphasised importance of higher productivity. Therefore, it is essential to assess the performance efficiency of labour and compare it with the standard performance, so that labour utilisation could be progressively improved. Compared to similar types of industries in other developed countries, the labour force in Indian industries is generally very high. Our aim should be to reach that level, though not immediately but over some time. Cost audit would give an idea where the inefficiency lies so that timely and adequate steps could be taken to ensure maximum utilisation of labour to reduce that labour cost.

(ii) Cost of labour is allocated to different jobs with reference to time of job cards.

6. Capacity Utilisation. The Cost Auditor will see :

(i) that the capacity of any production work shop or of transport facilities for distribution is not excessive :

(ii) the production volume and overall machine time utilised are commensurate. The machine hours utilised should give the optimum out-turn.

7. Overhead and Indirect Expenditure. The Cost Auditor will see and certify :

(i) that allocation of indirect expenditure over production, sales and distribution of logical and correct;

(ii) that compared with the value of production in a production workshop, the overhead charges are not excessive;

(iii) that the actual expenditure does not exceed budgets or standard expenditure significantly and that any variations are satisfactorily explained and accounted for;

(iv) that the relation of indirect expenditure in keeping with the load on individual production workshop is appropriate;

(v) that the appropriate allocation of overhead expenditure correct.

(vi) that allocation of overheads between finished products and unfinished products is in accordance with correct principles.

For determining the scope and the extent of cost audit, the cost auditor will have regard to the relevant costing records required to be maintained according to Section 209(1)(d). He will also pay special attention to the reporting requirements laid down under the Cost Audit (Report) Rules.

REPORT OF COST AUDITOR

Characteristics of the Report

After completion of the audit of cost accounts, the cost auditor is to submit his report in terms of Section 233(B)(4) of the Companies Act to the Central Government. It is not submitted to the Registrar of the Companies. It may contain confidential and secret matters which should not be disclosed to anyone. A copy of the report is also sent to the company concerned but not to the members. It should be precise, concise and clear. The cost auditor should give his independent opinion. He should not hesitate to report irregularities and deficiencies coming to his notice.

Contents of the Report

1. The cost auditor should report if a large quantity of raw-materials were stocked and which remained unutilised for a long time and thus locking up of the working capital of the company.
2. He should report if the machines and labour remained idle during the year because of the shortage of raw materials.
3. He should report whether the cost records maintained by the company were adequate for the purpose of audit.
4. He should report whether the broad policy laid down by the management was faithfully followed.
5. His report should concentrate more on the cost of production, comparative profitability and operating efficiency of different lines in which the company is engaged rather than the routine statistical or financial information.
6. He should report if there has been a rise in the cost of production as compared with the previous year. He should analyse the causes of such a rise which might have been due to lapses or negligence on the part of the management or because of rise in the price of raw materials of labour costs or reasons beyond the control of the management e.g., imposition of import duty on raw materials, if used in production etc.
7. He should report if there has been any wastage during the process of manufacture and how could it be avoided.
8. He should mention the areas in which it is possible to reduce the cost of production.
9. He should report whether or not the cost statement reveals a true and

fair view of the cost of production. He should see whether the cost accounts maintained by the company are correct or not and whether the policy laid down by the management has been or has not been followed.

Duties of Cost Auditor

The auditor should not sit in judgement on the policy matters of the management. He should not bother about technical matters such as the company should have used electric power instead of steam power to reduce the cost of production; or it would have been better to run two shifts rather than asking the workers to put in overtime and so on. No definite duties of the Cost Auditor have been laid down by the Companies Act except that he has to submit his report to the Central Government and the company concerned.

Cost Audit Report Rules

1. Report. The cost auditor has to submit his report to the Central Government in the form prescribed by the Cost Audit Report Rules, 1971 and proforma of which is given later on.

2. Copy. He shall forward a copy of the report at the same time to the company within 120 days from the end of the company's financial year to which the cost audit report relates.

3. Records. The company and every officer of the company shall make available to the cost auditor within 90 days from the end of the financial year of such cost accounting records, costing statements and other books and papers that would be required for conducting the cost audit and render any assistance required by the cost auditor so as to enable him to complete the audit and his report within 120 days.

4. Default. In default by any cost auditor, he is punishable with fine upto Rs. 500.

5. Certification. In his report, the cost auditor shall mention whether proper records of fixed assets in detail are maintained, assets have been physically verified and revalued during the year.

6. Form. Cost Audit Report Rules (1968) framed by the Central Government state that the Cost Audit Report should be in the following form :

I/We .... having been appointed as auditor(s) under Section 233B of the Companies Act, 1956 (1 of 1956) hereinafter referred to as the "Cost Auditor(s)" of Messrs .... Ltd. (hereinafter referred to as the company), have examined the books of accounts prescribed under clause (d) of sub-section (1) of Section 209 of the said Act and other relevant records for the year ended .... relating to .... maintained by the company and report that :

(a) I/We have obtained all the information and explanations which to the best of my/our knowledge and belief were necessary for the purposes of this audit;

(b) Proper cost accounting records as required under clause (d) of sub-section (1) of Section 209 of the Companies Act, 1956 (1 of 1956) have been kept by the company;

(c) Proper returns adequate for the purpose of my/our cost audit have been received from branches not visited by me/us;

(d) The said books and records give the information required by the Companies Act, 1956 (1 of 1956) in the manner so required; and

(e) In my/our opinion the company's cost accounting records have been properly kept so as to give a true and fair view of the cost production, processing, manufacturing or mining activities, as the case may be and marketing of the product under reference.

The matters contained in the Annexure to this report form part of this report which is also subject to my/our observations made therein.

Dated this .... day of .... 19 at ....

.... Cost Auditor(s).

7. Annexure. Under the Cost Audit (Report) Rules, 1968 an Annexure has been provided to be filled by the cost auditor and annexed to the report. The matters contained in the Annexure form part of the cost auditor's report. These matters are as follows:

(i) General information; (ii) System of costing accounting;

(iii) Financial position of the company; (iv) Production;

(v) Process of manufacture; (vi) Raw materials;

(vii) Fuel and Power; (viii) Wages

(ix) Stores and spare parts; (x) Depreciation;

(xi) Overhead charges; (xii) Sales;

(xiii) Abnormal expenditure etc.

The cost auditor has also to state his own observations and conclusions in the report such as what matters appear to him to be wrong in principle etc. He should make his suggestions and recommendation in order to improve the working of the company, reducing the cost of production, increasing production and improvement of the inventory policy.

QUESTIONS FOR EXERCISE

1. Define cost audit. What are its objects and important aspects?
2. Explain the differences between cost audit and financial audit.
3. How is the cost audit related to management audit and operational audit ? Explain the various types of cost audit.
4. What are the advantages of cost audit ? On what grounds the introduction of cost audit is opposed?
5. Describe the procedure you would adopt with regard to cost audit as a cost auditor of a large organisation.
6. State the provisions of Companies Act regarding cost audit in the case of limited companies.
7. What are the qualifications prescribed for the appointment of Cost Auditor? What are the rights and powers of cost auditor?
8. What are the functions of cost auditor while conducting a cost audit?
9. Write a note on the report of the cost auditor.

23

Special Audit

AUDIT OF RAILWAY COMPANIES

1. Statutory Provisions. Examine the provisions of the Special Act of Parliament under which the railway company has been established. Make a special study of the provisions affecting the accounts. Acquaint oneself with the system of internal check and the internal audit existing in the company.

2. Verifying Traffic Summary Book. Verify the entries made in the Traffic Summary Book which relates to the various traffic receipts, with the help of the Returns of the Station Masters.

3. Checking Cash. Check the remittances of cash by the Stations in the Returns of Cash and Subsidiary Cash Book. Also check their entry in the Cash Book proper.

4. Verifying Clearing House Journal. Verify the entries made in the Clearing House Journal with the help of the Railway Clearing House Statements.

5. Verifying Ledger Accounts. Ledger Accounts should be verified specially for the receipts in respect of passengers, goods, minerals etc.

6. Examining Vouchers. Examine the original vouchers to check the various items of expenditures.

7. Checking Expenditure. Ascertain whether proper distinction has been made in the allocation of expenditures between revenue and the capital. For the capital expenditures be ascertain and examine the certificate from the proper authority.

8. Verifying Investment. Verify all the investments with the help of securities and the Title Deeds etc.

9. Checking Liabilities. Outstanding liabilities with reference to the certified Returns from the Stations.

10. Verification of unearned Amounts. Unearned amounts by way of the unexpired portion of season tickets should also be and it should be seen that it is carried forward.

11. Certification of Stock and Stores. Ascertain that the stock and the stores on hand are duly certified by the responsible officials.

12. Examine Provisions. Examine the provisions made with regard to depreciations and other contingencies.

13. Checking Balances. Check the balances from the General Ledger to the Final Accounts.

14. Examining Final Accounts. Examine the Final Accounts in detail and see that they have been drawn as required by the Statute.

AUDIT OF SHIPPING COMPANIES

1. Articles of Association. Examine the Articles of Association and any other contract entered into with captains etc.

2. System of Internal Check. Examine the system of internal check existing in the company.

3. Ledger Account. See that Separate Ledger account is maintained for each ship and separate account is maintained for each voyage.

4. Voyage Account. See that voyage account has been debated with all items of expenses and each voyage is properly charged with the expenditures on stores. Such account should be duly credited with the freight and passage money received.

5. Liabilities. See that all the outstanding liabilities with regard to each voyage are duly adjusted and brought into account.

6. Freight Accounts. Vouch the freight accounts with the help of manifests from the agents and advices from the receiving offices. Also check that the provisions have been made for outstanding rebates.

7. Foreign Exchange. See that the foreign exchange has been correctly adjusted.

8. Insurance Policies. Vouch the insurance policies taken to cover the fleet and the freight in detail. See that the premiums have been properly apportioned over each voyage. In case of the time policy it sees that the proportion unexpired has been carried forward. Carefully vouch amount received in respect of claims from the insurance companies.

9. Depreciation. See that proper depreciation has charged in respect of each ship.

10. Purchase. Vouch the purchase of the ships and any addition made therein with the help of the contract of sales.

11. Capital Expenditure. Scrutinise the items of capital expenditure and see that it has been capitalised and no revenue expenditure has been capitalised. See that all the expenditures incurred by way of repairs and renewals have been charged to revenue.

12. Charter Parties. Examine the charter parties with particular attention to brokerage, commission, and rates of freight and it should be seen that credit has been taken of the agreed returns.

AUDIT OF COAL COMPANY

1. System of Internal Check. Enquire into the system of existing internal check with special reference to the recording and payment of wages.

2. Capital Expenditure. Examine all the capital expenditures. See that proper allocation of expenditures has been made between revenues and capital as certified by the Mining Engineer and the Mine Manager.

3. Lease. Examine the lease or agreements to see the conditions with regard to the royalty, shortworking and the minimum rent etc. Vouch the royalty from the sub-lessee.

4. Short-working. Examine the condition for the recoupment of the short-working out of the future surplus. See that the Balance of the shortworking is shown in the Balance Sheet as an asset until totally recouped.

5. Sales. Verify all the sales must be with the help of the Sales Agents' Accounts. Ascertain the rates charged the contracts with the consumers, such as railway company, electric companies etc. should be examined.

6. Provision of Depreciation. Consult the Articles of Association and see that adequate provisions for depreciation has been made as required by the Articles.

7. Stock. Verify the stock of coals and stores at the end of the year and the basis for their valuation should be duly ascertained.

8. Output. Compare the figures of output of the coal of the current year with that of the previous year.

9. Liabilities. Ascertain that no liabilities have been omitted from being brought into the accounts.

10. Wagons. If the wagons utilised by the company have been obtained on hire purchase system. See that the instalments paid have been correctly apportioned between the revenue and capital, and depreciation on such wagons has been charged on the total cash value of the wagon and not on their instalment value.

AUDIT OF BUILDERS AND CONTRACTORS

1. Internal Check. Enquire into the system of internal check prevailing in the concern, specially with regard to the preparation of the wage-sheets and the payment of wages to the workers.

2. Cost Accounts. Ascertain whether any system of cost accounts is being used by the concern, specially the system of dealing with expenditure on stores, materials and allocation of indirect expenses. If proper cost accounts are maintained see how far they agree with the Financial Accounts.

3. Stores and Materials. Enquire into the system of issue of stores and materials to the various contracts. Find out how the records of such receipts and issue of stores and materials are maintained. Ascertain the system of dealing with the materials returned from such contracts or jobs.

4. Contract. See that separate account is opened for each contract and there is proper allocation of amount of wages, materials and stores and other charges.

5. Transfer of Machinery. See that the transfer of machinery from one contract to another is properly recorded. If any particular plant is used exclusively for one job, the depreciation should be charged to that particular Contract Account.

6. Wages. See that there is proper allocation of wages to the different contracts as certified by some responsible officials.

7. Work-in-Progress. See that the work-in-progress, representing the value of uncompleted contracts at the date of the Balance Sheet, has been properly valued. Obtain a certificate of the official concerned in his connection or verify it carefully if that is not available.

8. Profit. See whether the profit has been taken into account with regard to the uncompleted contracts and if it is so, see that it has been done on the conservative basis. It will be safe if no credit is taken with regard to the uncompleted contracts. However, if the profit has been taken into account it should be done after giving due allowance to the contingencies and at least one-third of the profit should be carried forward. Due regard should also be given to the proportion of cash paid on account.

9. Amounts Received. Vouch the amounts received on account of contracts with the help of Architects' Certificates.

10. Basis of Valuation. Examine the basis of valuation of the stock on hand and see whether only certificate for it is available from some responsible official.

11. Depreciation. Ascertain whether the provision for depreciation on Plant and Machinery has been adequately made or not.

AUDIT OF TRUST AND FINANCE COMPANIES

1. Provisions. Examine the various provisions of the Memorandum and Articles of Association of the Company specially with regard to the object of the company and restrictions of investment of the funds of the company.

2. Purchase and Sales. Vouch the purchase and sales of the investments very carefully with the help of the brokers' contract notes.

3. Interest and Dividends. Ascertain that all the interest or dividends receivable have been duly received and recorded in the books properly.

4. Investments. Verify all the investments very carefully.

5. Valuation. Enquire into the basis of valuation of the investments. As far as possible it should be valued at cost and if the market price happens to be lower, it should be brought down to the same value. However, a Trust Company is under no legal obligation to provide for the fall in the value of the investments. See that the basis of valuation has been clearly indicated in the Balance Sheet.

6. Principal and Interest. Ascertain that the principal and interest on the sale or purchase of the investments have been properly accounted.

7. Investment. See that the loss on the sale or investment has been properly accounted for. It may be charged to revenue or treated as capital loss depending upon the nature of the investments. If the investment has been held as fixed asset with a view to earn income from them, any loss on it would be a capital loss and not be charged to revenue account. On the other hand, if the investment has been held with a view to resell, it will be in the nature of floating asset and any profit or loss on the sale of such investment should be transferred to Profit and Loss Account.

8. Partly Paid Shares. Ascertain whether the company holds any partly paid shares and see that the contingent liability in respect of calls not yet made has been stated on the Balance Sheet.

9. Underwriting Commission. See that the underwriting commission earned by the company, if any, has been set against the cost of the shares which it had to take to fulfil the commitments and that it has not been taken into account as profit.

10. Depreciation. Ascertain that the provision for the depreciation of investments has been adequately made. Due regard should be given to the provision of Section 205 of the Companies Act, 1956. Provision of depreciation of the investment, if held as fixed asset by a trust company, is not legally necessary, though it is financially necessary to depreciate it. But the provision for depreciation must be made on the investment held as floating or current asset and it must be valued in such case either at cost or market value whichever is lower at the date of the Balance Sheet.

AUDIT OF NEWSPAPERS, PERIODICALS AND PUBLISHERS

1. Advertising Day Book. Vouch the Advertising Day book very carefully and ascertain that no dummy advertisement has been included in it. Vouch the amount received by way of advertisement and the subscription.

2. Agents. Ascertain the details of arrangement made with the agents with regard to charging out the copies sent to them and copies returned from them when they have not been sold. See that proper check is enforced with regard to the unsold copies returned and that proper records have been made for the same or provisions have been made for those estimated to be outstanding.

3. Subscriptions. Ascertain that all the unexpired subscriptions and the amounts received with regard to the advertisement in advance have been duly included and carried forward.

4. Authors. Examine agreements entered into with the authors, specially with regard to the payment of royalties to them.

5. Payment. Vouch the payment made to the contributors with the help of the acknowledgment received from them.

6. Establishment Account. Examine the Establishment Account maintained, if any, very carefully and see that all the items in it have been properly dealt with.

7. Production Account. See that Production Account has been properly maintained with regard to the publication work. Separate Production Account should be opened for each work. It should be debited with the cost of the copyright; provided it has been purchased, together with the prime cost of production such as editing, compiling, indexing, setting up type and blocks etc.

8. Royalties and Commission. See that provisions have been made for all outstanding royalties, commission to selling agents or amounts due to the contributors. In case advance payment of royalty has been made to the sale resulting into loss, it should be written off, as customarily it is not returnable by the author.

9. Suit for Libel. Ascertain that due provision has been made in respect of any suit for libel etc., pending against the company.

10. Unsold Stock. See that the stock of unsold books has been valued at cost but if the publication fails to command sales, it should be written down considerably.

11. Copyright. See that the copyright has been valued from year to year. It should never be written up but if the publications for which the copyright has been obtained are not saleable, it should be written off.

12. General Stock. If the publication has been done at the author's risk, see that the unsold stock of such books should not be included in the general stock.

13. Old Types and Papers. See that the amounts received on sale of the old types or papers etc., have been duly certified.

14. Depreciation. See that the provision for depreciation on types and printing machinery has been adequately made.

AUDIT OF CHARITIES

1. Constitution. Examine the constitutions of the charitable institution its legal status and rules and regulations governing it. If the charity is a public one the provisions of the State legislations should also be carefully noted.

2. Minute Book. Inspect the minute book of the trustees or the executive body to ascertain the transaction affecting the accounts.

3. Cash Book. Vouch all the receipts and subscriptions entered in the Cash Book with the help of the counterfoil Receipt Book and also with the help of the printed Donation and Subscription Lists, if any.

4. Fund. Ascertain whether any fund was remarked for any specific purpose and see whether it was duly complied with.

5. Trust Deed. Examine the Trust Deed to see the provisions with regard to the investment or the utilisation of the funds and ascertain that they have been faithfully observed.

6. Legacy Register. Vouch the receipts from the legacies with the help of the Legacy Register and the correspondence entered into in this connection.

7. Investments. Vouch the purchase of the investments, and see that it has been done according to the prescribed rules, if any.

8. Incomes. See that the incomes from the investments in the form of interest and dividends etc., have been properly brought into account.

9. Income Tax. See that no income-tax has been paid on the incomes of the charities since usually their incomes are not liable to tax.

10. Assets and Liabilities. Verify the assets and liabilities of the charities at the date of the Balance Sheet carefully.

11. Annual Accounts. See that the annual accounts of the charities have been prepared in the prescribed manner, if any.

AUDIT OF LANDED ESTATES

1. Acquisitions. Vouch all the acquisitions with the help of the Conveyance Deeds and the Solicitor's Bills of Costs. Examine the Agreements of the Lease if the acquisitions are leaseholds. On subsequent audit, examine the new acquisition or leases only.

2. Rent Rolls. Examine the Register of Tenants or the Rent Rolls with a view to vouch the rents collected and entered in the Cash Book. See that any deductions or allowances have been granted by the proper authority.

3. Sale of Products. Vouch all the receipts from the sale of the products from the Estate such as stock, timber or game etc., with the help of the counterfoil receipt books or other records available.

4. Rent Arrears. Enquire into arrears of rents, specially those which are due for a long period. Such arrears should be checked from one period to another with the help of List of Arrears made out from the Rent Rolls.

5. Expenses. Vouch all the expenses such as insurance, municipal expenses, commissions etc., with the help of the relevant receipts.

6. Repairs. Vouch expenditure incurred for the repairs of building etc., see that it is duly authorised.

7. Outstanding Rents. See that all the outstanding rents have been properly brought into account and carried forward in the Rent Rolls.

8. Sale of Property. In case of the sale of any property of land by the Estate, the Sales Deed should be inspected.

AUDIT OF SOLICITORS' ACCOUNTS

1. Partnership Deed. Examine the Partnership Deed, if it is a partnership firm, specially with regard to those provisions which affect the accounts. The rules and regulation laid down by the High Court and in force at the time should also be ascertained.

2. Separate Accounts. See that separate accounts have been maintained for the client's moneys and the funds of the firm.

3. Cash disbursements. Vouch all the cash disbursements made on behalf of the client and entered in the Client's Disbursements Cash Book with the help of the original vouchers.

4. Cash Balances. Compare the total of the cash balances of the client's money as appearing in the accounts with that of the balance shown in the client's bank accounts and any difference in the balance must be reported.

5. Petty Cash Disbursement. Scrutinise Petty cash disbursements on account of the clients and see that it has been properly brought into the accounts.

6. Register of Bills Delivered. Examine the Register of Bills Delivered.

7. Clients Register. Check the Clients' Ledger very carefully and see that allowances to customers have been properly recorded.

8. Liabilities. See that all the outstanding liabilities in respect of the fees to be paid to the counsel on behalf of the clients, though charged to the clients, have been brought into account.

9. Premiums. See that the premiums received from the articles clerks have been properly apportioned over the terms of the articles.

10. Costs of Incomplete Matters. See that estimated costs of incomplete matters not charged to clients have been taken into account on a conservative basis. In case they have not been taken into accounts, see that a note to this effect has been given in the Balance Sheet.

AUDIT OF RETAIL STORES

1. Internal Check. Enquire into the system of internal check in use with regard to purchases and sales, specially with regard to the handling of cash.

2. Purchases. Vouch all the purchases made with the help of invoices and stock records and correspondence entered into in this connection.

3. Cash Book. Vouch the Cash Book exhaustively and carefully. If the bills are given to the customers for the payment to be made at a separate counter, make a test checking in the assistants' books with the cashier's daily summary.

4. Customers Account. Check the balances of the customers account exhaustively particularly when no proper credit control system exists therefor.

5. Debts. See that adequate provisions have been made for all the bad and doubtful debts.

6. Profit. Calculate the percentage of gross profit to the sales for the previous two to three years and compare it with that of the current year and make proper enquiry if there is material variation in the percentages.

7. Expenditures. Vouch all the expenditures incurred very carefully.

8. Stock. Verify the stock at the date of the Balance Sheet and seek proper explanations for any shortage in it.

AUDIT OF WHOLESALE TRADERS

1. Internal Check. Enquire into the system of internal check in operation with regard to the purchases and sales and maintenance of stock.

2. Purchases. Vouch all the purchases made very carefully with the help of the invoices and other relevant documents and see that purchases returns have been duly accounted for.

3. Sales. Vouch the sales also exhaustively with the copy of the invoices and see that the sales returns and the allowances given to the customers have been duly accounted. In case of foreign sales, see that the conversion of foreign currency into rupees has been correctly made.

4. Discounts. See that the trade discounts allowed to the customers are at the agreed rate only.

5. Sales. Ascertain the procedure of dealing with the goods sold on sale or return basis or goods sent on contingent etc., and see that it has been properly adjusted into the accounts.

6. Expenses. Vouch expenses such as godown rent, clearing charges, damages paid etc.,

7. Debtors. Find out the balances of the debtors at the end of the period and check it. See that debts are not outstanding for a long period; if it is so, enquire into the matter. See that adequate provisions have been made on bad and doubtful debts.

8. Stock. Verify the stock at the end of the financial year very carefully with the help of the stock records maintained. Examine particularly the purchase, sales and returns of the last month very carefully. See that the stock has been valued on the consistent basis and there is no shortage in it.

9. Profits. Find out the percentage of the gross profit to the sales for the last three years at least and compare it with that of the current year and see if there is any material variation in it. If it is so, seek explanations for the same.

AUDIT OF BRANCH ACCOUNTS

1. System of Accounts. Acquaint himself with the system of accounting employed in the branches and the way it is incorporated in the head office books. Ascertain whether there is uniformity in the system of accounting employed by the different branches. Also find out the system of internal control applied for recording of various transactions in the branch books.

2. Terms of Engagement. Ascertain the terms of engagement precisely specially whether he will have to visit the branches personally or to examine the returns submitted by the branches duly certified by the local auditors.

3. Cash. Vouch all the cash remitted from the branch, as shown by the branch accounts into the head office books and similarly vouch all the cash remittances from the head office to the branches into the branch accounts.

4. Sales Moneys. Check the sales moneys collected by the branches locally, in detail. See that all the cash collected has been duly accounted for. In case the branch does not collect the sales money and simply reports the matter to the head office, see that all the sales by the branch have been properly reported to head office and for this purpose check the Despatch Book exhaustively.

5. Records. Ensure if the branch maintains complete set of books for the purposes of recording all the transactions carried on by it, the head office maintains simply the Current Account in respect of cash branch. Trial Balance or the Final Account of the branch will be available. See that proper vouchers are available in respect of the transactions recorded. If the local auditor has certified them, there will be no need for the same. It should be noted that balance of the current account of the branches will show the capital employed by them and it should be shown as such in the Balance Sheet and should not be included in sundry debtors.

6. Remuneration. Vouch the branch manager's remuneration very carefully specially when his remuneration has been linked with the profits of the branch and see that the profits have been inflated wrongly with a view to earn more remuneration.

7. Expenses. See that the expenses of the branch are met by the cheque drawn by the head office. The head office, should remit necessary amounts to the branch for petty cash transactions. The Petty Cash Accounts should be maintained on the Imprest System.

8. Stock. See that the closing stock of the branches has been properly valued. The goods may be sent to branches at cost price or at cost price plus a fixed percentage or at marked price or selling price. If the goods have not been sent at cost price, it should be ascertained that the stock at the end of the year has been reduced to cost. Branch Adjustment Account may be prepared for the purpose.

9. Debtors. With regard to the branch debtors at close, obtain a certificate from the branch official and see that it has been duly incorporated in the head office books. Also see that all the liabilities at the branch have been duly accounted in the head office books.

10. Transactions. See that all the inter-branch transactions have been properly recorded in the books.

11. Cash or Goods in Transit. Examine the adjustments made in the books in respect of cash or goods in transit, and verify that it was subsequently received.

12. Valuation. If the certificates from the branch officials are accepted in respect of the valuation of stock, quantity of stock, balance of the sundry debtors, reserve for bad and doubtful debts etc., see that it is mentioned in the reports to limit his responsibility.

13. Foreign Exchange. See that conversion of foreign currency into rupee has been correctly made. The difference in value of exchange has also to be seen and checked. If the exchange rate is stable, the conversion may be made at the fixed rate, but if the exchange rate is fluctuating see that the following rule has been adopted for conversion; fixed assets are converted at the rate prevailing when they were purchased; current assets and liabilities are converted at the rate prevailing at the close of the financial period; revenue items are converted at the average rate; remittances are converted at the actual rate; the balance of the Head Office accounts should be replaced by the balance of the Branch Accounts as shown in the Head Office Books.

14. See that all the instructions given by the head office have been duly followed by the branch.

AUDIT OF DEPARTMENTAL STORES

1. System of Accounts. Enquire into the system of accounts employed by the stores. See whether it is maintained on the column system or not. Enquire into the system of internal check prevailing with regard to cash sales, purchases and payment of wages and salaries etc. Acquaint himself with the general organisation and control of the stores.

2. Vouching Cash Sales. Vouch the cash sales with the Cash Memo Books into the Daily Sales Summaries. Make a test checking if the sales are enormous.

3. Checking General Cash Book. Check the General Cash Book exhaustively with the help of the Sales Summaries.

4. Vouching Purchases. Vouch all the purchases made with the help of invoices. See that payment has been made only when the invoices have been duly authorised by some responsible official. See that all the allowances and discounts obtainable on the purchases made have been taken advantage of.

5. Vouching Salaries. Vouch the salaries and wages paid, specially when the commission is payable on the basis of the sales.

6. Inter-departmental Transactions. See that all the inter-departmental transactions have been properly brought into the account.

7. Checking Distribution of Expenditure. Check the basis of the distribution of the common expenditures between the different departments. See that the basis adopted for the purpose is just and equitable and is followed consistently from year to year.

8. Ascertaining Percentage of Selling Expenses. Ascertain the percentage of the selling expenses to the total sales in the previous year and seek explanation in case there is material variations in the percentages.

9. Applying Gross Profit Test. Apply the gross profit tests also.

10. Verifying Stock. Verify the stock on the date of the Balance Sheet and see that it has been properly valued. Obtain a certificate from the General Manager of the stores in this respect.

11. Seeing Depreciation. See that adequate depreciation has been made to the building, if owned by the stores, and furniture and fixtures etc.

BANK AUDIT

Banking Companies Regulation Act, 1949

In India banks or banking companies are controlled by the Banking Companies Regulation Act, 1949. The State Bank of India and its subsidiaries are governed by their own Act. There are many enactments, rules, regulations, bye-laws which are found relevant while auditing the financial accounts of the banking company. Considering a large number and complexity of business transactions, it is practically impossible for an auditor of a bank to perform detailed audit. He has to rely considerably on the system of internal control and internal check. Before doing auditing of banks, the auditor should be well acquainted with these acts and provisions.

1. Section 29. A banking company is required to prepare at the end of the year a Balance Sheet and Profit and Loss Account.

2. Section 30. The Balance Sheet and Profit and Loss Account of a banking company shall be audited by a person qualified to be an auditor of the companies.

Internal Check.

The Research Committee of the Institute of Chartered Accountants of India has made the following suggestions for internal audit of a bank :

(i) The internal auditor should fix the audit programme in consultation with the external auditor to derive the maximum amount of advantage.

(ii) The programme so adopted should be changed from time to time according to circumstances and the experience gained.

(iii) The external auditor may call for the internal auditor's report to the management and go through it. This will be of great help to the statutory auditor as well as to the management.

The statutory auditor can eliminate or reduce his work of audit in view of the existence of internal audit. He should note the following in this connection.

(i) The efficiency of the internal auditor.

(ii) Whether the internal auditor is under the influence and subject to interference by the management.

(iii) Whether the standard procedures were followed by the internal auditor.

(iv) The action taken by the management on the report of the internal auditor.

Procedure of Bank Audit

(i) The auditor will ask for internal check before commencing audit as he cannot do detailed checking. If he finds it satisfactory, he will begin the audit work.

(ii) He will deal with assets and liabilities on Balance Sheet and income and expenditure on Profit and Loss Accounts.

(iii) He must attend at the bank on the closing date of the financial year on the date of Balance Sheet with a view to check the cash balances in hand on the date. He may count or weigh cash, notes, postal orders, cheques etc. that may remain with the bank.

(iv) He should confirm with the Reserve Bank of India or any other bank for the cash deposit made by them.

(v) He should verify and reconcile with other banks in Banker's ledger with the balances. Certificates should be verified for balances.

(vi) He should verify cheque and drafts received later on the Balance Sheet date for clearing. He should ascertain that they come later on within few days in due course.

(vii) He should verify money at call and short notice with the call deposit receipts.

(viii) He should check the securities for this purpose with the schedules attached to the borrowing notes.

(ix) He should check unmatured bills and see that they agree with the general ledger and that they are not over due for payment with the maturity date of the bill.

(x) He should see that appropriate provisions are made for dishonoured bills.

(xi) He should see that bills discounted and purchased have not crossed the limits of limitation.

(xii) He should examine the rebates on bills discounted and see that right proportion of rebate for discount on bills due has been carried forward to the subsequent year.

(xiii) He should check current fixed and savings bank accounts' balances with the help of schedules.

(xiv) He should check loan ledgers.

(xv) If the investments are made in the banks, a certificate must be had for such amount.

(xvi) He should ensure that same security is not produced again for the investments.

(xvii) He should check the investments in government securities, debentures and shares by real inspection on the Balance Sheet date.

(xviii) He should see that banks provide confirmation certificates for investments they had.

(xix) He should see that balances in investment ledgers agree with Investment Accounts in the General Ledger.

(xx) He should see that if the book value of investments is more than market value, it should be properly provided for.

(xxi) He should see that hypothecated investments should be disclosed in the Balance Sheet as needed.

(xxii) He should see that provisions of Section 19(2) are properly observed.

(xxiii) He should see that income from investments are vouched.

(xxiv) He should see that customer's securities deposits must be examined for loans and overdraft.

(xxv) He should ensure that loans are covered properly.

(xxvi) He should see that for unsecured advances, bank has confidential reports for the good financial position of borrower.

(xxvii) He should see that only bad doubtful debts have been properly provided.

(xxviii) He should see that secured and unsecured loans have been distinguished in Balance Sheet.

(xxix) He should see that the balance sheet shows properly classified loans, advances, cash credits and overdrafts.

(xxx) He should that all the interests payable on various accounts of the customers have been duly accounted till the date of Balance Sheet.

(xxxi) He should ascertain that interest recoverable from the debtors is being regularly received from them.

(xxxii) He should test some Banks pass books and see that they tally with ledger accounts.

(xxxiii) He should check general ledger balances with trial balance and final accounts.

(xxxiv) He should verify the assets with the bank for their existence value, title and possession.

(xxxv) He should see that all assets and securities written off specially with a view to create a secret reserve.

(xxxvi) He should ensure that branch returns are incorporated in the Head Office books and return is duly certified by branch managers.

(xxxvii) He should ascertain that foreign currency transactions are scrutinized and incorporated in accounts.

(xxxviii) He should see that all liabilities of bank are rightly brought into account.

(xxxix) He should verify the liabilities on account of letters of credit and guarantees given by the bank or on behalf of the constituents with the help of documents and registers and it should be seen that proper margin is held.

(xl) He should verify the centre items in connection with Bills for collection or acceptances, endorsements and other obligations. He should check them with the registers maintained by the bank for recording these transactions.

Auditor's Report

As per Section 30(3) an auditor has to give statement of affairs to shareholders of the banking company in his report as under Section 227 of the Companies Act, 1956, if the Banking Company is incorporate in India. This includes the following :

1. Whether or not the information and explanations required by him have been found to be satisfactory.
2. Whether or not the transactions of the company which have come to his notice have been within the powers of the company.
3. Whether or not the returns received from branch offices of the company have been found adequate for the purpose of his audit.
4. Whether the Profit and Loss Account shows a true balance of profit and loss for the period covered by such account.
5. Any other matter which he considers should be brought to the notice of the shareholders of the company.

Special Liabilities

1. Qualifications. In the case of a banking company incorporated outside India, the accounts of such a company must be audited by an auditor duly qualified under the Companies Act or by a person who is duly qualified to be an auditor under the law of the country in which the company has been incorporated.

2. Powers, Duties and Responsibilities. The auditor of a banking company will have the same powers, duties, responsibilities and is subjected to the same penalties as that of an auditor appointed under Section 227 of the Companies Act.

3. Debts, Loans and Reserves. The auditor of a banking company is deemed to be a public servant under Chapter IX of the I.P.C. He should examine the provisions of bad and doubtful debts as the advances and loans in the case of a bank are other than those considered bad and doubtful. Since a bank is permitted to create secret reserves, the auditor should see that such reserves are not misused by it.

4. Penalties. If an auditor wilfully makes a false statement in any statement, return, Balance Sheet or wilfully omits to make a material statement, he is liable to be imprisoned upto a period of three years and is also liable to be fined.

SPECIMEN OF THE AUDITORS' REPORT

(i) We have audited the foregoing Balance Sheet of the ...... banks as at 31 December 19.... and also the foregoing Profit and Loss Account of the Bank for the year ended upon that date in which are incorporated the audited returns from all the branches of which 101 branches by other auditors.

(ii) We report that :

(a) We have got all the information and explanation, which to the best of our knowledge and belief were necessary for the purpose of our audit and have found to be satisfactory.

(b) The transactions of the bank that have come to our notice have been within the powers of the Bank.

(c) In our opinion proper accounts as needed by law have been kept by the bank so far as appears from our examination of those books and proper returns adequate for the purposes of our audit have been received from all the branches of the Bank.

(d) The report on the accounts of branches, audited by other auditor have been forwarded to us and the same have been considered in preparing this report.

(e) The Banks' Balance Sheet and Profit and Loss Account dealt with by this Report are in agreement with the books of account and the audited returns.

(f) In our opinion and to the best of our information and according to the explanation given to us, the said account gives the information required by the Companies Act, 1956, in the manner so required by Banking Companies Act and on such basis the Balance Sheet gives a true and fair view of the state of affairs of the bank as at 31st December 19.... and the Profit and Loss Account give a true and fair view of the profit for the year ended upon that date.

New Delhi Signatures

Dated....... 19.......... ....

Chartered Accountant

AUDIT OF INSURANCE COMPANY

According to Section 227 of the Companies Act, 1956, the auditor shall have the powers of exercising the functions vested in and discharge the duties and be subject to the liabilities on auditors of companies. He shall proceed as follows :

(i) Premiums. Vouch the premiums received with the copies of the insurance policies, covernotes, premium receipts etc. Check the premium receipts with the Register of Policy. Total income should be checked from premium with the Premium Register. Check all the adjustments with the premiums. For extra premiums, vouch with the premium receipts issued to the insured. Vouch refund vouchers with refunds of premiums. As prohibited according to Section 41 see that no rebate to premium has been given.

(ii) Interests and dividends. Check these through receipts and if they are duly checked upto date, check that outstanding interest and dividends have been entered into account properly.

(iii) Claims. Check claims paid or payable by the company by the Register of claims, the Survey Report, receipts given by the insured and the copy of the policy. Check circular from the concerned company with Survey Report for re-insurance claims. Check money received from the re-insurance. Check all the adjustments for the claims-outstanding and payable with the entries in the books.

(iv) Commission. See that commission payments have been vouched with commission vouchers and the receipts given by the agents with agents' accounts. Rate of commission should agree with prescribed limit. Reconcile the premiums received on such business for further checking. Check all the outstanding commissions duly adjusted in the accounts. Check received and paid re-insurance commission with the receipts, statement of accounts received from the re-insurance companies and treaties.

(v) Expenses. Examine managements expenses carefully and see that provisions of the Act are duly observed in this connection. See that such expenses have been charged to Revenue Account only duly classified. Check that the common expenses have been allocated between various departments (fire, accident, marine and general). Ensure that such allocation is based on accounting principles and made reasonably and equitably.

(vi) Re-insurance. Check all the re-insurance in detail. They may be ceded or accepted. They may be ended if a part of the risk is passed on the other companies. In that case, examine the treaties with the ending companies. Vouch all payments and recoveries with care. All the outstanding liability or asset should be duly provided for. Ensure that in revenue accounts commission or re-insurance accepted and ended have been disclosed separately on its debits or credit side as the case may be. Some treaties incorporate a provision entitling the ceding company to provide commission on the profits realised by each of the re-insuring companies from its share of the treaty. If it is so, see that provision is made in the accounts for outstanding profit commission.

(vii) Investments and Cash Balances. Verify all the investments made and cash balances. An auditor of an insurance company has to state in his report that he has verified the cash and bank balances, investments and the securities relating to them.

(viii) Branch and Agency. Scrutinise carefully the outstanding branch and agency balances to determine that they are recoverable. Check that sufficient provision has been made against all doubtful accounts.

(ix) Reserve. See that sufficient amount has been set aside for reserve for unexpired risks. A reserve of 40% of the premium income is considered sufficient.

(x) Contingent liabilities. Make sure that all the contingent liabilities have been duly ascertained and properly disclosed in the Balance Sheet as required.

(xi) Code of conduct. Check that the provisions of code of conduct have been duly observed.

(xii) Annual Accounts. See that the annual accounts of the insurance company has been prepared in accordance with the prescribed forms and regulations for their preparations have been duly observed.

(xiii) Loans and advances. See that no loans or temporary advances have been made to any director, manager, auditor or any other officer of the company.

(xiv) Qualified auditors. See whether the accounts of the branches have been audited by qualified auditors. If not, they should be checked by him at the Head Office when all vouchers should be produced.

(xv) Deposits. See that other needs of the Insurance Act have been properly fulfilled, e.g. deposits with the Reserve Bank and presentation of annual accounts are prescribed by the Insurance Act.

(xvi) Report. Submit report to the shareholders of the Insurance company.

Specimen of Auditor's Report

We have audited the annexed Balance Sheet of the ...Company Ltd. as at .... 19... and the Revenue account, the Profit and Loss Account and the Profit and Loss Appropriation Account of the company for the year ending upon that date in which are incorporated the returns from various branches and agencies and we report that :

1. We have obtained all the informations and explanations which we have required.
2. In our opinion, the annexed Balance Sheet, Revenue Account, Profit and Loss Account and Profit and Loss Appropriation Account are drawn up in conformity with the law.
3. Such Balance Sheet exhibits a true and fair view of the state of the company's affairs according to the best of our informations and explanations given to us and as shown by the books of the company.
4. In our opinion, the books of account have been kept by the company for the year under report as required.
5. We have verified the cash balances and investments by actual inspection or by the production of certificates or vouchers and have also verified the securities relating to the loans.
6. All the expensed of management incurred in respect of the general insurance business have been fully debited as expenses in the respective Revenue Accounts.

Signatures

New Delhi ....

Dated .... 19..... ....

Auditors.

AUDIT OF EDUCATIONAL INSTITUTION

1. Acts etc. Examine the charters trust deeds, University Act etc., containing rules and regulations and those rules which relate to accounts in particular.

2. Accounts. Ascertain the system of keeping the accounts and go through the proceedings of the minutes of the governing body or managing committee, specially those related with the accounts.

3. Budget. Obtain a copy of the budget sanctioned or the financial statements. Acquaint with the different heads of income and expenditures of the institutions.

4. Receipts. Vouch all the receipts through students monthly fees with the help of the carbon copy of the receipts and the Registers of students into the Cash Book. See that the cash received is deposited in bank daily.

5. Fees. See that the fees received in advance have been properly dealt with.

6. Grants-in-Aid. Verify grants-in-aid from the government.

7. Extra fees. Examine that extra fees for laboratory, library, examination and games have been charged properly.

8. Admission fees. Verify the admission fees with the register of newcomers.

9. Particular money. Check that the money received for a particular purpose has been utilized for the same.

10. Freeships and concessions. Examine that freeships or concessions granted to the students are duly authorized and any charges irrecoverable have been written off.

11. Donations. See that donations received from different charitable bodies or persons have been duly acknowledged and recorded properly in the accounts.

12. Incomes. Vouch the incomes from the properties, buildings and other lands.

13. Hostel fees. Vouch the hostel fees and deposits received from the students with the counterfoils of the receipts from the students. The outstanding amount at the date of balance sheet should agree with the schedules.

14. Expenses. Vouch all the establishment expenses and the capital expenses in detail.

15. Stocks. Verify the stocks of furnitures, equipments, stationary, provisions etc. very carefully give. Special attention to the stock of books and equipments in the laboratories.

16. Provision. Confirm that adequate provision is being maintained for contingencies.

17. Scholarships. Check the payments made on account of scholarships with the help of receipts from the students and the scholarships Register.

18. Assets and liabilities. See that the assets and liabilities are brought into account.

19. Provident fund. Check the provident fund of the staff and see that it has been properly invested.

20. Salaries. Vouch the amount of salaries paid to staff through salary register.

AUDIT OF COOPERATIVE SOCIETY

Privileges

Cooperative societies are established under the provisions of Cooperative Societies Act. They enjoy following privileges :

(i) It has privileges of a body corporate.

(ii) It has perpetual succession and a common seal.

(iii) It has power to hold property.

(iv) It has power to enter into contracts with others.

(v) It has power of suing and being sued by others.

(vi) It has shares no-attachable and non-stable under any decree or order of the court for any debt or liability incurred by members.

(vii) The Central Government may exempt a cooperative society or remit income-tax payable in respect of the profits of the society of the dividend or other payments received by the members of the society on account of profits.

(viii) The Central Government exempt a registered society from any fee or stamp duly payable in respect of certain documents as per Section 28.

(ix) It has a prior claim as against other creditors for the recovery of any amount due from a member or a past member in respect of debts.

(x) Its shares are not liable to be attached or sold against any decree or order issued by a court or by an assignee or official recover under the Insolvency Act.

According to Section 17 of the Co-operative Societies Act, 1912, the responsibility of audit accounts of cooperative institutions rests with Cooperative Department of the State Government. Auditors are appointed by the members except under certain conditions.

Duties and Rights of the Auditor

(i) To study the Co-operative Societies Act, 1912 and byelaws of the society.

(ii) To see that a member should not hold more than 10% of capital of society.

(iii) To vouch receipts of cash on accounts of deposits with the cash books and counterfoils of the receipt book and check them with relevant accounts. Some societies permit non-members to deposit money with the society.

(iv) To vouch the money borrowed from the Central Co-operative Bank with Cash Book, check correspondence and resolution passed by Managing Committee of the society to borrow money, the period and the rate of interest.

(v) To vouch interest received from borrowers or return of loan from them with the agreement entered into between the society and the borrower, regulations of the society, counterfoils of the receipt books and cash book.

(vi) To check loans to the members with the agreement regulations and resolutions passed by the Managing Committee. Receipt issued by the member concerned, cash book etc. permission of Registrar is a necessary if non-member is given a loan. If loan is given to a cooperative society by the Central Cooperative Bank, it should be within the prescribed limits.

(vii) Vouch expenses as usual.

(viii) Give priority to Reserve fund 25% and Welfare Fund 10% after that.

(ix) Check cash in hand with actual counting of cash and by comparing it with the Cash Book.

(x) Verify investments by inspecting the ledger for investment Account.

(xi) See that surplus funds of cooperative society are invested only in Government Saving Bank. If approved by the Registrar they may be invested in securities mentioned in Section 20 of Indian Trust Act, 1882 or in shares and services of other cooperative societies with limited liability. The investments should be as per rule.

(xii) Check the sales summaries with the sales in a consumers' society. Check the purchases with Order Book, and the Stock Book. Verify the stock and examine the method of valuation.

(xiii) See if accounts of Society are prepared as per Cooperative Societies Act and Income Tax Act as applicable to cooperative societies.

(xiv) See that Balance Sheet and Profit and Loss Accounts are to be prepared as per Part V. Third Schedule, Section 56 of Bank Regulation Act, 1945.

(xv) The Registrar of cooperative societies of few states have prescribed a proforma for drawing up the auditor's Report and the final accounts. See that report is according to the proforma.

(xvi) See that the Cash Reserve is according to Section 50(f) of Banking Regulations Act.

(xvii) See that the Balance Sheet and the Profit and Loss Account are drawn as per Section 56(2) of Banking Regulation Act or as near thereto as possible unless the Registrar of cooperative societies has prescribed another form.

(xviii) Verify furniture and stationary physically and compare with the Stock Registrar.

There is no internal check system in the Cooperative Banks.

AUDIT OF HOSPITAL

1. Examine the letter of the appointment and ascertain whether it in any way enlarges the scope of his responsibilities.

2. Carefully go through the Charter or Trust Deed under which the hospital has been set up and take a special note of the provisions affecting the accounts.
3. Examine and evaluate the system of internal check and control and devise his audit procedures taking in view its weaknesses.
4. Vouch the entries in the Patients' Bill Register with copies of the bills issued. Issued bills pertaining to a selected period should be test-checked to see if these have been correctly prepared taking into account the period of stay of each patient as recorded on the Attendance Sheets.
5. Ascertain whether bills have been issued to all patients from whom charges are due, and whether the same has been done according to the established rules and procedure.
6. Vouch collection from patients with copies of their bills and entries in the Bills Register. Arrears of dues should be properly carried forward and where these are deemed to be irrecoverable, they should be written off after due authorisation from the Trustees or the Managing Committee, according to the predetermined criteria.
7. Vouch shares and securities settled on the hospitals in case of income by way of interest/dividends as recorded in the Investment Register and dividend and interest warrants. Where dividends/interests has accrued but not yet received, he should ascertain whether appropriate entries have been passed in the books and the respective amounts duly disclosed in the annual statements.
8. Vouch the rent rolls and counterfoils of rent receipts for rental income from landed property settled on the hospital, as shown in the Property Register. In case of arrears or advance payment of rents, he should confirm whether appropriate entries have been passed and the respective sums duly disclosed in the annual statements.
9. Ensure that legacies and donations received for a specific purpose, or the income therefrom, as the case may be, are not applied for any other purpose.
10. Check actual collection of subscriptions with Subscribers Register and the difference, whether due to arrears or advance payments is carried forward and properly disclosed in the annual statements.
11. Verify grants-in-aid received from the Government or a local body by reference to the correspondence with the authorities concerned and entries in Cash Book.
12. See that a clear distinction has been made between capital and revenue expenditure.
13. See that expenditure of capital nature is duly authorised by the valid resolution of the Managing Committee.

14. Vouch payments for the purchases of stores, drugs, linen, clothes, instrument etc.
15. Vouch the payment of salaries to the members of the staff and other expenses also.
16. Verify the assets including closing stock.
17. Ascertain that proper depreciation has been provided for.
18. Ensure that expenditures of different categories do not exceed the amounts budgeted.

AUDIT OF CLUB

A club is not an institution which earns trading profits. It collects subscriptions from its members and provides for their amusements. The following is the procedure of audit of accounts of a club :

1. Study the rules and regulations including the Memorandum and Articles of the club, if any, note down special points with regard to accounts.
2. Examine the minute books of the club.
3. Go through the system of internal check in vogue in respect of receipts in dining room etc., and confirm that it is quite effective.
4. The income from subscriptions is the main source of revenue for a club. Vouch the receipt of cash on account of admission fees and subscriptions by reference to the counterfoils in the receipt books and the list of members. Check the subscriptions in arrears with the help of a schedule received from the client and it should be seen that it is duly certified by the committee managing its affairs.
5. Ascertain that the subscriptions received in advance are carried over and adjusted subsequently in the accounts.
6. Vouch if a canteen is running under the club receipts, similarly, if some property of the club has been let out, the income therefrom should be verified.
7. If some special donation is received by the club, see that it is utilized for the purpose for which it is meant.
8. See that the heavy expenses are spared over a number of years instead of their being charged to the years concerned. See that all purchases of the club are duly sanctioned.
9. Ensure that proper distinction has been made between capital and revenue.
10. Vouch the expenditure incurred by the club.
11. Verify the assets including stock in hand and see that they are properly valued.

12. Check minutely the inventory of wines, provisions and similar other materials.

AUDIT OF ELECTRICITY SUPPLY COMPANY

1. Study the provisions of the Electricity (Supply) Act, 1948 and Indian Electricity Act, 1910 relating to the accounts of the company.
2. Enquire into the internal check system regarding the records of the consumption of electric current by the consumers.
3. Go through the Memorandum and Articles of Association, if any, specially noting the provisions relating to accounts.
4. The main source of income of electric supply companies is the money that they receive from the consumers of electric current. Inspect the necessary contracts, if any, and vouch the cash so received by reference to the counterfoils of receipts.
5. See that arrears are properly arrived at and subsequently received and entered in the books of accounts.
6. Ascertain that wages are properly allocated between capital and revenue and are also certified as such by the engineer.
7. Confirm that salaries paid to the staff are allocated between management, generation and distribution departments on proper basis.
8. See that the cost of replacement has been properly allocated and repairs and renewals are charged to revenue.
9. See that allowances granted to consumers are duly authorized by some responsible officer and do not exceed the limits.
10. See that proper depreciation in respect of power house, plant and machinery, meters, mains, stores, etc., has been provided.
11. Check entries in consumer's ledger and also their postings to the impersonal ledger.
12. Ascertain that account and specially annual accounts are prepared according to the prescribed forms as given in the relevant Acts.

AUDIT OF AN INDUSTRIAL CONCERN

1. Examine the system of internal check in force. See that there is proper control over the purchases, issue of materials and stores.
2. Enquire into the system of payment in respect of purchases. Vouch the invoices with special attention to discounts and allowances.
3. Enquire into the system of effecting sales with particular attention regarding the delivery of the finished products. Vouch the sales invoices with care so that fictitious entries could be detected.
4. Make an examination with regard to the total material consumed in the production and the total amount of goods produced. It will give

an idea of total wastage and loss in production. See that adequate records are maintained to record all these items.

5. Examine the records concerning empties.
6. Give special attention in respect of the payment of wages. Vouch the payment of wages carefully.
7. See that proper allocation is maintained between capital and revenue expenditures.
8. See that the physical verification of stock has been done by a responsible officer and the valuation is done on the basis of generally accepted accounting principles.
9. Examine the system of issuing samples and stock records in itself.
10. Examine the ratio of gross profits to sales and compare the same with previous year's records in order to know the reasons of variations.
11. Check the provisions for depreciation and see that a proper method is adopted to charge depreciation for different assets.
12. See that proper provisions have been made in respect of bad doubtful debts and other items like trademarks, tools, patents etc.
13. Ensure that proper provisions have been made in the books for contingent liabilities.
14. See that Balance Sheet has been drawn up properly and all items have been properly shown.

AUDIT OF STOCK BROKER'S FIRM

Stock Broker's firm deals in shares and securities in a recognised stock exchange. Normally the firm deals on behalf of its clients but in some cases it also deals in its own account. Dealings in a Stock Exchange may be either on the basis of

1. Ready delivery or on the spot.
2. Through the Clearing House of the Stock Exchange.
3. Regular delivery.

1. Ready delivery. The shares or securities are delivered within three days of the transaction and the payment is made.

2. Regular delivery. The shares and securities are delivered as per rules of the stock exchange which normally extends upto ten days.

3. Transactions settled through the Clearing House of the stock exchange. Delivery of shares and securities are not made but the accounts are settled by receiving or paying the difference of accounts. Every transaction is recorded on the contract notes which are exchanged between the brokers and on this basis the transactions are recorded in the contract journal and then posted to the clients account or the Investment Account of the firm.

Audit Programme

1. Examine the system to transact for the sale and purchase of shares and securities adopted in the broker's firm i.e. who is authorised to transact and upto what limit ?
2. Examine the system of internal check adopted in the firm.
3. Examine the process and procedure to record the transaction in the books of accounts.
4. Check the procedure of delivery of the stock exchange and the way the periodical settlement is made with different customers.
5. Vouch the journal entries with contract notes and simultaneous confirmation by the clients or the other brokers.
6. Verify the calculations with regard to:
   (i) Commission receivable.
   (ii) Total amount payable or receivable for the sale or purchase of shares.
   (iii) Service charges including transfer fees, stamp fees etc.
7. Check vouchers for the receipt of payments from clients and different brokers to the delivery of shares or the amounts due against settlement of accounts.
8. Verify from the counterfoils for the proper payments being made to different clients or brokers against the receipt of delivery of shares and securities.
9. Physically examine the securities in hand or get certificate from the Stock Exchange authorities or the bank if they are lodged with them. Care should be taken to check securities deposited by the clients as guarantee for the payment of any due balance against them.
10. Evaluate securities held as investments at cost or market price whichever is less.

AUDIT OF CINEMA COMPANY

1. Examine the Internal check system with regard to:
   (i) Receipt of cash,
   (ii) Maintenance of unissued tickets,
   (iii) Daily returns of tickets of different shows.
2. Make surprise check to confirm that entrance to the shows are only through printed and duly numbered tickets.
3. Check that the daily collections are deposited in a bank.
4. Verify that entertainment tax is duly charged and paid to the authorities within the prescribed time.

5. Check sundry receipts from:
   (i) Advertisers
   (ii) Hire charges
   (iii) Allottees for display of goods
   (iv) Sellers supplying refreshments and confirm these amounts with the terms of agreements between the parties.
6. Check various payments made from:
   (i) terms of contract to show films.
   (ii) operating expenses and the maintenance of Cinema hall.
7. Check that different expenses have been duly allocated between capital and revenue.
8. Check that adequate provisions have been made for:
   (i) Outstanding liabilities.
   (ii) Depreciation on building, furnitures, machines etc.
   (iii) Pensions and gratuity for employees.

Audit of Company Engaged in Financing Hire Purchase of Motor Vehicles

Such a company operates as follows:

1. Purchases the vehicle from the motor dealer.
2. Gets the motor vehicle registered in its own name.
3. Delivers the motor vehicles to the hire purchaser after receiving a specific amount as initial deposit from the hire purchaser.
4. The amount of loan advanced is repayable in specific number of instalments.
5. The company transfers the ownership of the motor vehicle to the hire purchaser on the payment of last instalment.

Audit Programme

1. Check the agreement entered between the company and the hire purchaser to know the following:
   (i) Amount of loan advanced against the motor vehicle.
   (ii) Rate of interest.
   (iii) Clause of panel interest.
   (iv) Discount or rebate to be allowed for earlier payments of instalments.
   (v) Terms of repayment.
   (vi) Amount of hire charges.
2. Check that the proper records are maintained after allocating the amounts received as principal amounts, amount earned as interest and as hire charges.

3. Check that the entries have been duly posted in proper ledgers.
4. Vouch the entries for payment of cash charges to the motor vehicle dealer and receipts of cash or cheques with the counterfoils of receipts issued to the hire purchaser.
5. Ascertain the amount of instalments remaining unpaid.
6. Inquire the reasons for the non-recovery of amount due and repossession of goods.
7. Verify the value of repossessed motor vehicle and confirm that the value as shown in Balance Sheet etc. is not more than its proportionate cost.
8. Check that the expenditures incurred for the repairs on the repossessed vehicles has been added to the cost of the vehicles.
9. Ascertain that adequate reserve for bad debts are provided on the instalment outstanding from the hire purchaser, where the motor vehicle has been repossessed.
10. Verify the payments of interest and repayments of loans, where the finance company accepts loans, deposits from outsider, public etc.

AUDIT OF A TRANSPORT COMPANY

1. Examine the system of internal check particularly in respect of passengers and goods.
2. Vouch the fare received from passengers with the summary of tickets sold.
3. Check the freight receipts with the copies of the bills maintained for this purpose.
4. Vouch the purchases of trucks and buses in the usual manner.
5. Carefully check all the repairs and maintenance charges. All such charges must have the approval of the chief engineer.
6. See that sufficient depreciation has been made on the vehicles.
7. See that a proper register of buses is maintained.
8. See that there is a proper system of wages payments to the drivers, conductors and other staff.
9. Verify the stock of stores, spare parts, patrol and tyres etc.

MISCELLANEOUS BALANCE SHEETS

SCHEDULE VI

(PART I—FORM OF BALANCE SHEET OF A COMPANY)

(See Section 221)

The balance sheet of a company shall be either in a horizontal form or vertical form

A. Vertical Form

Balance Sheet of....(Here enter the name of the company)

As at.....(Here enter the date as at which the Balance Sheet is made out)

Instructions in accordance with which liabilities should be made out	Liabilities Figures for the previous year	Liabilities Figures for the current year	Assets Figures for the previous year	Assets Figures for the current year	Instructions in accordance with which assets should be made out
1	2		3		4
	Rs. (b)	Rs. (b)	Rs. (b)	Rs. (b)	
*Terms of redemption or conversion (if any) of any Redeemable Preference Capital to be stated, together with earliest date of redemption or conversion. Particulars of any option on unissued share capital to be specified. * Particulars of the different classes of Preference shares to be given.	* Share Capital Authorised.... shares of Rs..........each Issued (distinguishing between the various classes of capital and stating the particulars specified below, in respect of each class) ....shares of Rs.....each Subscribed (distinguishing between the various classes of capital and stating the particulars specified below in respect of each class), (c)....shares of Rs....each.		*Fixed Assets:* Distinguishing as far as possible between expenditure upon (a) Goodwill, (b) land, (c) buildings, (d) leaseholds, (e) railway sidings, (f) plant and machinery, (g) furniture & fittings, (h) development of property, (i) patents, Trade-marks and designs, (j) livestock and (k) vehicles, etc.		*Under each head the original cost and the additions thereto and deductions therefrom during the year, and the total depreciation written off or provided up to the end of the year to be stated. "Where the original cost aforesaid and additions and deductions thereto, relate to any fixed asset which has been acquired from a country outside India and in consequence of a change in the rate of exchange at any time after the acquisition of such asset, there has been as increase or reduction in the liability of the company, as expressed in Indian Currency for making payment towards the whole or a part of the cost of asset or for repayment of the whole or

	Rs.....called up......of the above shares, shares are allotted as fully paid up pursuant to a contract without payments being received in cash.		a part of monies borrowed by the company from any person directly or indirectly, in any foreign currency specially for the purpose of acquiring the asset (being in either case the liability existing immediately before the date on which the change in the rate of exchange takes effect, the amount by which the liability is so increased or reduced during the year, shall be added to, or as the case may be, deducted from the cost, and the amount arrived at after such addition or deduction shall be taken to the cost of the fixed asset. *Explanation 1.* This paragraph shall apply in relation to all Balance Sheets that may be made out as at the 6th day of June, 1966, or any day thereafter and where, at the date of issue of the notification of the Government of India, in the Ministry of Industrial Development and Company Affairs (Department of Company Affairs), G.S.R. No. 129 dated the 3rd day of January 1968, any Balance Sheet, in relation to which the paragraph applies, has already been made out and laid before the company in annual General Meeting, the

1	2		3		4
	Rs. (b)	Rs. (b)	Rs. (b)	Rs. (b)	adjustment referred to in this paragraph may be made in the first Balance Sheet made out after the issue of the said notification. *Explanation 2.* In this paragraph, unless the context otherwise requires, the expressions 'Rate of Exchange', 'Foreign Currency' and' Indian Currency' shall have the meanings respectively assigned to them under sub-section (1) of section 43-A of the Income-tax Act, 1961 (XLIII of 1961), and *Explanation 2* and *Explanation 3* of the said sub-section shall as far as may be, apply in relation to the paragraph as they apply to the said sub-section (1)" * In every case where the original cost cannot be ascertained without unreasonable expense or delay, the valuation shown by the books shall be given. For purposes of this paragraph, such valuation shall be the net amount at which an asset stood in the company's books at the commencement of this Act after deduction of the amounts previously provided or written off or depreciation

* *Specify the source from which Bonus Shares are issued, e.g., capitalisation of Profits or Reserves or from Share Premium Account.*	*(Of the above shares.....shares are allotted as fully paid-up by way of Bonus Shares). Less Calls unpaid : ** (**)		or diminution in value, and where any such asset is sold, the amount of sales proceeds shall be shown as deduction. Where sums have been written off on a reduction of capital or a revaluation of assets, every Balance Sheet (after the first Balance Sheet), subsequent to the reduction or revaluation shall show the reduced figures, and with the date of the deduction in place of the original cost. Each Balance Sheet for the first five years subsequent to the date of the reduction, shall show also the amount of the reduction made. Similarly, where sums have been added by writing up the assets every Balance Sheet subsequent to such writing up shall show the increased figures with the date of the increase in place of the original cost. Each Balance Sheet for the first five years subsequent to tho date of writing up shall also show the amount of increase made. *Explanation.* Nothing contained in the preceding two paragraphs shall apply to any adjustment made in accordance with the second paragraph.
	(ii) By Directors. (iii) By Others.		
* *Any capital profit on reissue of forfeited shares should be transferred to Capital Reserve.*	* Add. Forfeited shares (amount originally paid up)		

1	2	3	4
* Additions and deduction since last Balance Sheet to be shown, under each of the specified heads. [1]The word 'Fund' in relation to any 'Reserve' should be used only where such Reserve is specifically represented by ear-marked investments. Loans from Directors,** *(***) Manager should be shown separately*	Rs. *(b)* Rs. *(b)* * *RESERVES & SURPLUS*; [1]1. Capital reserves 2. Capital Redemption Reserve. 3. Share Premium A/c (cc). 4. Other reserves specifying the nature of each reserve and the amount in respect thereof. Less Debit Balance in Profit and Loss Account (if any) (h). 5. Surplus, i.e., balance in Profit and Loss A/c after providing for proposed allocation, namely : RESERVES SURPLUS Dividend, Bonus or Reserves. 6. Proposed additions to Reserves. 7. Sinking Funds.	Rs. (b) Rs. (b) INVESTMENTS ; Showing nature of investments and mode of valuation, for example, cost or market value and distinguishing between. *1. Investments in Govt. or Trust Securities. *2. Investments in shares debentures or bonds showing separately shares, fully paid-up and partly paid-up and also distinguishing the difference. INVESTMENTS : Classes of shares and showing also in similar details investments in shares Debentures or bonds of subsidiary companies. 3. Immovable properties. 4. Investments in the capital of partnership firms (Added by G.S.R. 494 (E) dated 30.10.1973).	Aggregate amount of company's quoted investments and also the market value thereof shall be shown. Aggregate amount of company's unquoted investments shall also be shown.

Interest accrued and due on secured loans should be included under the appropriate sub-heads under the head 'Secured Loans.'[1] The nature of the security to be specified in each case. Where loans have been guaranteed by** (***) manager and/or Directors, a mention there of shall also be made and also the aggregate amount of such loans under each head. $ Terms of redemption or conversion (if any) of debentures issued to be stated together with earliest date of redemption or of conversion.	SECURED LOANS *1. Debentures *2. Loans & Advances from Banks. *3. Loans and Advances from Subsidiaries. *4. Other Loans and Advances.	CURRENT ASSETS, LOANS AND ADVANCES : (A) Current Assets : 1. Interest accrued on Investment. $$2 .Stores and Spare Parts. 3. Loose Tools 4. Stock-in-trade. **5. Works in Progress. $6. Sundry Debtors- (a) Debts outstanding for a period exceeding six months. (b) Other Debts. Less : Provisions— (7-A) Cash Balance in hand (7-B) Bank balance- (a) With Scheduled Banks, and (b) with others. (G.S.R. No. 78, dated 4th January, 1963)	** Mode of valuation of stock shall be stated and the amount in respect of raw materials shall also be stated separately where practicable. ** Mode of valuation of work-in-progress shall be stated. $ In regard to Sundry Debtors particulars to be given separately of— (a) debts considered goods and in respect of which the company is fully secured; (b) debts considered goods for which the company holds no security other than the debtor's personal security; and (c) debts considered doubtful or bad. Debts due to Directors or other officers of the company or any of them either severally or jointly with any other person or debts due by firms or private companies respectively in which any Director is a Partner or a Director or a Member to be separately stated.

1	2		3		4
	Rs. (b)	Rs. (b)	Rs. (b)	Rs. (b)	
					Debts due from other companies under the same management with in the meaning of *sub-section (1-B)* of *section 370* to be disclosed with the names of the companies.
*Loans from Directors, **() Manager should be shown separately.*					The maximum amount due by directors or other officers of the company at any time during the year to be shown by way of a note.
Interest accrued and due on unsecured loans should be included under the appropriate sub-head under the head un-secured loans.					The provisions to be shown under this head should not exceed the amount of debts stated to be considered doubtful or bad and any surplus of such provision, if already created, should be shown at every closing under 'Reserves and Surplus' (in the Liabilities side) under a separate sub-head 'Reserve for Doubtful or Bad Debts.'
					In regard to Bank Balances, particulars to be given separately on (a) the balances lying with Scheduled Banks in Current Account Call Accounts and Deposit Accounts; (b) the names of the bankers other than Scheduled Banks and the balances lying with each such banker on Current Accounts, Call

			Accounts and Deposit Accounts and the maximum amount outstanding at any time during the year from each such banker; and (c) the nature of the interest, if any, of any Director or his relative **() any associates of the latter in each of the bankers other than Scheduled Banks referred to in (b) above. (G.S.R. No. 78, dated 4th January, 1963).
Where loans have been guaranteed by ** ()Managers, and/or Directors, a mention thereof shall also be made and also the aggregate amount of such loans under each head.	UNSECURED LOANS 1. Fixed Deposits. $2. Loans and Advances from Subsidiaries $$3. Short-term Loans and Advances : (a) From Banks (b) from others. $$4. Other Loans and Advances : (a) From Banks (b) From others.		
* See note (d) at foot of Form	CURRENT LIABILITIES & PROVISIONS [1](A) Current		$ The above instructions regarding 'Sundry Debtors' apply to 'Loans and Advances' also.
		(B) Loans & Advances	

1	2	3	4
	Rs. (b) Rs. (b)	Rs. (b) Rs. (b)	Rs. (b)
	Liabilities 1. Acceptances. 2. Sundry Creditors. 3. Subsidiary companies. 4. Advance payments and unexpired discounts for the portion for which value has still to be given, e.g., in the case of the following classes of companies : (Newspaper, Fire Insurance, * Theatres, Clubs, Banking, Steamship Companies etc.) 5. Unclaimed dividends. 6. Other Liabilities (if any). 7. Interest accrued but not due on loans. (B) Provisions : 8. Provisions for Taxation. 9. Proposed Dividends. 10. For Contingencies. 11. For Provident fund Scheme. 12. For Insurance, Pension and similar Staff Benefits Schemes.	8. (a) Advances and Loans to Partnership Firm in which the company or subsidiaries is a Partner added by G.S.R. 494 (E) dated 30-10-1973. 9. Bill of Exchange. 10. Advances recoverable in cash or in kind or for value to be received, e.g., Rates, Taxed. Insurance, etc. 11. ** ($$) 12. Balance with Customs, Port Trust, etc. (where payable on demand).	

** The period for which the dividends are in arrears of if there is more than one class of the dividends on each such class are in arrears, shall be stated.

The amount shall be stated before deduction of Income tax, except that in the case of tax-free dividends for the amount shall be shown free of Income-tax and the fact that if it is so shown shall be stated.

$$- The amount of any ** guarantees given by the company on behalf of Directors or other officers of the company shall be stated and where practicable, the general nature and amount of each such contingent liability, if material, shall also be specified.

13. Other provisions: footnote to the Balance Sheet may be added to show separately.

1. Claims against the company not acknowledged as debts.
2. Uncalled liability on shares partly paid.
**3. Arrears of fixed cumulative dividends.
4. Estimated amount of contracts remaining to be executed on Capital account and not provided for.

**5. Other money for which the company is contingently liable.

MISCELLANEOUS EXPENDITURE (to the extent not written off or adjusted)[1]

1. Preliminary Expenses.
2. Expenses including commission or brokerage on underwriting or subscription of shares or debentures.
3. Discount allowed on the issue of shares or debentures.
4. Interest paid out of capital during construction (also stating the rate of interest).
5. Development Expenditure not adjusted.
6. Other items (specifying nature).

$PROFIT & LOSS A/c.

$ Show here the debit balance of Profit and Loss Account carried forward after deduction of the uncommitted reserves, if any.[2]

2. THE THIRD SCHEDULE (THE BANKING COMPANIES REGULATION ACT Section 29)

FORM A

Form of Balance Sheet

Capital and Liabilities	Rs.	Rs.	Property and Assests	Rs.	Rs.
1. Capital (a) Authorized Capital ....shares of Rs. .... Each Issued Capital ....shares of Rs. .... Each Subscribed Capital : . ...shares of Rs. .... Each Amount called up at Rs....per share *Less* : Calls unpaid *Add* : Forfeited shares.			1. Cash : In Hand and with Reserve Bank (including foreign currency notes.) 2. Balance with other Banks (showing whether on Deposit or Current Account): (i) In India (ii) Outside India 3. Money at call and short notice. 4. Investment stating mode of valuation, e.g. cost of market value (f)		
2. Reserve Fund and other Reserves (b) 3. Deposits and other Accounts : Fixed Deposits Saving Bank Deposits Current Accounts and Contingency Accounts. 4. Borrowing from other Banks, Agents, etc. (i) in India (ii) outside India			(i) Securities of the Central and State Governments and Trustee Securities including Treasury Bills of the Central and State Governments. (ii) Shares (classifying into preference, ordinary, deferred and other classes of shares and showing separately share fully paid up and partly paid up). (iii) Debentures or Bonds (iv) Other investments (to be classified under proper heads) (v) Gold		

Particulars :			5. Advances		
(i) Secured (stating the nature of Security)			(i) Loans, Cash Credits and Overdrafts (other than bad and doubtful debts for which provision has been made to the satisfaction of the creditors)		
(ii) Unsecured			(a) in India		
5. Bills Payable			(b) outside India		
6. Bills for Collection being Bills Receivable (As per contra)			(ii) Bills discounted and purchased (e) other than Treasury Bills of the Central and State Governments)		
(i) payable in India			(a) Payable in India		
(ii) payable outside India.			(b) Payable outside India		
7. Other Liabilities to be specified (c) Pension or Insurance fund, Unclaimed Dividends, Advance Payment, Rebate on Bills Discounted, etc.			(i) Debts considered good in respect of which the bank is fully secured.		
			(ii) Debts considering good for which the bank holds no other Security than the debtors, personal security.		
8. Acceptances, Endorsements and other Obligations per contra.			(iii) Debts considered good secured by the personal liabilities of one or more parties in addition to the personal security of the debtors.		
9. Profit and Loss A/c (As per last Balance Sheet)			(iv) Debts considered doubtful or bad not provided for.		
Less : Appropriation			(v) Debts due by Directors or officers of the bank or any of them either severally or jointly with any other person.		
Add : Profit for year brought forward from P.& L. A/c.					
10. Contingent Liabilities			(vi) Debts due by companies or firms in which the Directors of the bank are interested as Directors, Partners or Managing Agents or, in the		

			case of private companies, as members.		
			(vii) Maximum total amount of loans, including temporary advances made at any time during the year to Directors or Managers or officers of the company.		
			(viii) Maximum total amount of loans including temporary advances granted during the year to the companies or firms in which the Directors of the Bank are interested as Directors, Partners or Managing Agents or, in the case of private companies of private companies as members.		
			(ix) Due from banks		
			6. Bills for collection being Bills Receivable as per contra :		
			(i) payable in India		
			(ii) payable outside India.		
			7. Constituents Liabilities for Acceptances, Endorsements and other Obligations.		
			8. Premises *less* Depreciation (g)		
			9. Furniture and Fixtures *less* Depreciation (h)		
			10. Other Assets including Silver (to be specified)		
			11. Non-Banking Assets of claims (standing mode acquired in satisfaction of valuation) (i)		
			12. Profit and Loss		
Total			Total		

Notes :

(a) Capital :

(i) The various classes of capital, if any, should be distinguished.

(ii) Shares issued as paid-up pursuant to any contract without payments being received in cash should be stated separately.

(iii) Where circumstance permit, Issued and subscribed capital and amount called up may be shown as one item, e.g., Issued and Subscribed Capital......shares of Rs......paid-up.

(iv) In the case of banking companies incorporated outside India, the amount of deposit kept with the Reserve Bank of India, under sub-section (2) of section 11 of the Banking Companies Act, 1949 should be shown under this head. The amount, however, should not be extended to the outer column.

(b) The Reserve Fund maintained under section 17 of the said Act should be shown separately.

(c) Under this heading are to be included such items as following to be shown under separate heading suitably described : Pension or Insurance Funds, unclaimed dividends, advance payments and unexpired discounts, liabilities to subsidiary companies and any other liabilities.

(d) These should be classified under the following categories :

(i) Claims against the banking company not acknowledged as debts.

(ii) Money for which the bank is contingently liable showing separately the amount of any guarantee given by the banking company on behalf of Directors or officers.

(iii) Arrears of cumulative preference dividends.

(iv) Liabilities on Bills of Exchange rediscounted.

(v) Liabilities on account of outstanding Forward Exchange Contracts.

(vi) Partly paid shares—uncalled amount.

(e) Particulars as under Loans, Advances, Cash, Credits and Overdrafts are to be shown under this heading.

(f) Where the value of the investments shown in the outer column of the Balance Sheet is higher than the market value, the market value shall be shown separately in brackets.

(g) Bank premises wholly or partly occupied for the purposes of business should be shown against Premises less Depreciation. In the case of fixed capital expenditure the original cost and additions thereto and deductions therefrom during the year should be stated, as also the total depreciation written off. Where sums have been written off on reduction of capital or revaluation of assets, every Balance Sheet after the first Balance Sheet subsequent to reduction or revaluation should show the reduced figures with the date and amount of the reduction made. Furniture, fixtures and other assets which have been completely written off need not be shown in the Balance Sheet.

(h) Under this heading may be included such items as the following which must be shown under heading suitably described : preliminary formation and organization expenses, development expenditure, commission and brokerage on shares, interest accrued on investments but not collected, investments in shares of subsidiary companies and any other assets.

(i) Value shown shall in no case exceed market value.

FORM B

Form of Profit and Loss Account

Profit and Loss Account for the year ended......March, 19....

Expenditure	Rs.	Income (Less Provision made during the year for Bad and Doubtful Debts)	Rs.
1. Interest paid on Deposits 2. Salaries and allowances showing separately salaries and allowances to Managing Director or Manager. Contribution to Provident Fund		1. Interest and Discount 2. Commission, Exchange and Brokerage.	
3. Directors' Fees and allowances, Local Committee Members' Fees and allowances.		3. Rents	
4. Rent, Taxes, Insurance, Lighting, etc.		4. Net Profit on sale of investments, gold and silver, land premises and other assets.	
5. Law Charges		5. Net profit on revaluation of investment, gold and silver, land premises and other assets.	
6. Postage, Telegrams and Stamps		6. Income assets, non-banking assets and profits from sale of or dealing with such assets.	
7. Auditor's Fees 8. Depreciation on Bank's Property and Repairs to Bank's Property. 9. Stationary, Printing, Advertisement, etc. 10. Loss from sale of or dealing with non-banking assets. 11. Other Expenditure 12. Balance (Net Profit) subject to taxation.		7. Other receipts 8. Loss (if any)	
Total		Total	

3. Form 'A'
Form of Balance-Sheet of an Insurance Company
Balance-Sheet of.....Insurance Co. Ltd. as at....19

Liabilities	Rs.	Previous Year Rs.	Assets	Rs.	Previous Year Rs.
Shareholders capital (each class to to be stated separately).			Loans :		
Authorised : ....shares of Rs............each Rs.			On mortgages or within India.		
Subscribed : ....shares of Rs............each Rs.			On mortgages of property outside India.		
Called up : ....shares of Rs.............each Rs.			On security of municipal and other public dates.		
Less Unpaid calls Rs.			On Stocks and Shares.		
Reserve or ContingencyAccount (a) :			On insurers policies within their surrender value		
Investment Reserve Account.....			On personal security		
Profit and Loss Appropriation Account Balance......			To subsidiary Companies.		
Balance of Funds and Accounts :			Reversions and Life Insurance purchases		
Fire Insurance Business Account			Loans and Reversions and Life Interests.		
Miscellaneous Insurance Business Account (m)			Debentures and Debenture stocks of subsidiary Reversionary Companies (f)		
Other accounts, if any (to be specified) (i)			Ordinary stocks and shares of Subsidiary Reversionary companies (f)		
Pension or Superannuation Accounts (a)			Loans to Sudsidiary Reversionary Companies (f)		
Debenture Stock per cent......			Investments :		
			Deposit with the Reserve Bank of India (securities to be specified).		
			Indian Government Securities.		
			State Government Securities.		
			British, British Colonial and British Dominion Government Securities.		

Liabilities	Rs.	Previous Year Rs.	Assets	Rs.	Previous Year Rs.
Loans and Advances (c)			Foreign Government Securities.		
Bills Payable (c)			Indian Municipal Securities.		
Estimated Liability in respect of outstanding claims, whether due or intimated (d)			British and Colonial Securities.		
Annuities due and unpaid (d)			Foreign Securities.		
Outstanding Dividends			Bonds, Debentures, Stocks and other Securities whereon interest is guaranteed by the Indian government or a State Government.		
Amount due to other persons or bodies carrying on Insurance Business (c)			Bonds, Debentures, Stocks and other securities whereon interest is guaranteed by the British or any Colonial Government.		
Sundry Creditors [including outstanding and accruing expenses and Taxes (c)]			Bonds, Debentures, Stock and other Securities whereon interest is guaranteed by any Foreign Government.		
Other sums owing by the Insurer [Particulars to be given (c)]			Debentures of any railways in India.		
			Debentures of any railways out of India.		
Contingent Liabilities (to be specified) (c)			Preference or guaranteed Shares of any railway in India.		
			Preference or guaranteed Shares of any railway out of India.		
			Railway Ordinary Stocks (i) in India (ii) out of India.		
			Other Debentures and Debentures Stock of Companies incorporated. (i) in India (ii) out of India.		
			Other guaranteed and Preference Stock and Shares of Companies incorporated.		

Liabilities	Rs.	Previous Year Rs.	Assets	Rs.	Previous Year Rs.
			(i) in India (ii) out of India. Other Ordinary Stocks and Shares of Companies incorporated. (i) in India (ii) out of India. Holdings in Subsidiary Companies (f) House Property. (i) in India (ii) out of India. Freehold and Leasehold ground rents and rent charges. Agent's Balances. Outstanding Premiums (g) (d). Interest, Dividends and Rents outstanding (d). Interest, Dividends and Rent accruing but not due (d). Amounts due from other persons or bodies carrying on Insurance Business (h). Sundry Debtors (i). Bills Receivable. Cash : At Banker on Deposit Account. At Banker on Current Account and in hand. At call and Short Notice (j). Other Accounts (to be specified) (k).		

Assets and Liabilities, shareholders, Capital and Reserves, not allocated to any class of business specified in column (1) must be shown in column (2).

NOTES

(a) The reserves or Contingency Accounts must be separately stated.

(b) If the insurer has not full and unrestricted control of the assets constituting the Pension or Superannuation Accounts either those Accounts and assets and liabilities relating thereto must be omitted from the balance-sheet or the assets of which the insurer has not such control must be clearly indicated on the face of the balance-sheet.

(c) If the insurer has deposited security as cover in respect of any of these items, the amount and nature of the securities so deposited must be clearly indicated on the face of the balance-sheets.

(d) These items are or have been included in the corresponding items the Revenue or Profit and Loss Account. Outstanding and accruing interest, dividends and rents must be shown after deduction of income-tax must be provided for amongst the liabilities on the other side of the balance-sheet.

(e) Such items as amount of liability in respect of bills discounted, uncalled capital of subsidiary companies, uncalled capital of other investments, etc., must either be shown in their several categories under the heading "Contingent Liabilities" or the appropriate items on the assets side must be set out in such details as will clearly indicate the amount of the uncalled capital.

(f) Such items as amount of liability in respect of bills discounted, uncalled capital of subsidiary companies, uncalled capital of other investments etc., must either be shown in their several categories under the heading "Contingent Liabilities" or the appropriate items on the assets side must be set out in such details as will clearly indicate the amount of the uncalled capital.

(g) As regards life and annuity business full particulars of holding in and loans to subsidiary companies must be stated, giving the name of each company, the number and description of each class of shares held, the amounts paid up thereon and the value at which the holding in each company stands in the balance-sheet.

(h) Either this items must be shown net or the commission must be provided for amongst the liabilities on the other side of the balance-sheet.

(i) The aggregate amount owing by a subsidiary company or subsidiary companies is to be shown separately from all other assets and the aggregate amount owing to a subsidiary company or subsidiary companies is to be shown separately from all other liabilities.

(j) Amounts due from directors and officers must be shown separately.

(k) No amounts must be entered under this heading unless fully secured. If not fully secured, the amounts must be included under the heading "Sundry Debtors".

(l) Under this heading must be included such items as the following, which must be shown under separate heading suitably described : Office-furniture, goodwill, preliminary, formation and organisation expenses, development expenditure account, discount on debentures issued, other expenditure carried forward to be written off in future years, balance being loss on Profit and Loss Appropriation Accounts, etc. The amounts included in the balance-sheet must not be in excess of cost.

(m) Under the head, ''Other accounts, if any (to be specified)", on the left hand side, fines realised from the staff and their contribution towards the provident fund, if any, should be shown under separate sub-heads.

(n) Where the insurer is required to maintain a separate account in respect of sub-class of miscellaneous insurance business this heading is to be split up accordingly.

(The First Schedule)

Form 'AA'

Classified Summary of the Assets in India of the......Insurance Co., Ltd., as on.....19..........

Class of Asset	Book value as per (a) below	Market value as per (b) below	Remarks as per (c) below
1. Government of India Securities.			
2. Indian State Government Securities.			
3. Indian Municipal Port and Improvement Trust Securities including Debentures.			
4. Debentures on Indian Railways			
5. Guaranteed and Preference shares of Indian Railways.			
6. Ordinary Shares of Railways in India.			
7. Other Debentures of concerns in India.			
8. Other Guaranteed and Preference Shares of concerns in India.			
9. Other Ordinary Shares of concerns in India.			
10. Loans on the Company's policies effected in India and within their surrender value.			
11. Loans on Mortgage of property in India.			
12. Loans on Personal Security to persons domiciled and resident in India.			
13. Other loans granted in India (particulars to be stated).			
14. Land and House property in India.			
15. Cash on Deposit in Banks in India.			
16. Cash in hand and on current account in banks in India.			
17. Agent's balances and outstanding premiums.			
18. Interests, dividends, and rents either outstanding or accrued but not due.			
19. Other assets in India (to be specified).			

The statement shall show :

(a) the value for which credit is taken in the balance-sheet for each of the above-mentioned classes of assets,

(b) the market value of such of the above-mentioned classes of assets as has been ascertained from published quotations after deduction of accrued interest included in market prices in those cases, where accrued interest is included elsewhere in the balance-sheet,

(c) how the value of such of the above-mentioned classes of assets as has not been ascertained from published quotations has been arrived at, and

(d) the rates of exchange at which the values of the assets other than in rupee currency have been converted into rupees.

The market value need not be shown separately where they are not less than the book values and a certificate to that effect is appended to the statement.

The amounts on account of any of the following items may be entered in the statement :

Goodwill.

Preliminary, formation, organisation or development expenses.

Commission or discount on shares or debentures issued.

Commuted commission.

Expenditure carried forward to be written off in future years.

(The Second Schedule)

REGULATIONS AND FORMS FOR THE PREPARATION OF PROFIT AND LOSS ACCOUNTS

PART I— Regulations

1. The items on the income side of the Profit and Loss Account and the Profit and Loss Appropriation Account must relate to income whether actually received or not, and the items on the expenditure side must relate to expenditure whether actually paid or not.
2. Deduction from Interest, Dividends and Rents to be shown in respect of income-tax must include all amounts in respect of Indian (Central) Inocme-tax whether or not it has been or so is to be deducted at source or paid direct.
3. The Interest, Dividends and Rents, *less* income-tax thereon shown in the Revenue Accounts for any classes of business other than life insurance business, including annuity busisness may, if the insurer so desires, be included with the corresponding items in the Profit and Loss Account.

Part II—Forms

FORM 'B'

Form of Profit and Loss Account

Profit and Loss Account of....for the year ended 19....

	Rs.		Rs.
Indian (Central) Taxes on the Insurer's profits (not applicable to any particular Fund or Account)		Interest, Dividends and Rents (not applicable to any particular Fund or Account) Rs..... *Less*—Income-tax thereon. Rs.....	
Expenses of Management (not applicable to any particular Fund or Account)		Profit on realisation of Investments(not credited to Reserves or any particular Fund or Account)	
Loss on Realisation of Investments (not charged to Reserves or any particular Fund or Account)		Appreciation of investments (not credited to Reserves or any particular Fund or Account)	
Depreciation of Investments (not charged to Reserves or any particular Fund or Account)		Profit transferred from Revenue Accounts (details to be given)	
Loss transferred from Revenue Account (details to be given)		Transfer Fees	
Other Expenditure to be specified.		Other Incomes (to be specified)	
Balance for the year carried to Appropriation Account.		Balance being loss for the year carried to appropriation Account.	
		Rs.	

FORM 'C'

Form of Profit and Loss Appropriation Account

Profit and Loss Appropriation Account of....for the year ended 19....

	Rs.		Rs.
Balance being loss brought forward from last year.		Balance brought forward from last year Rs....	
Balance being loss for the year brought from Profit and Loss Account (as in Form 'B')		*Less*— Dividends since paid in respect of last year (to be specified and if 'free of tax' to be so stated). Rs....	
Dividends paid during the year on account of the current year (to be specified and if 'free of to' be stated).			
Transfers to any particular Funds or Accounts (details to be given).		Balance being loss at the end of the year as shown in the Balance Sheet.	
Balance at the end of the year as shown in the Balance Sheet.			
Rs.		Rs.	

(The Third Schedule)
FORM 'F'
Form of Revenue Account applicable to Fire Business, Marine Insurance Business and Miscellaneous Insurance Business
Revenue Account of.....for the yar ended....19....
In represent of....Business

	Rs.		Rs.
Claims under policies, Less Reinsurances : (a) (d) Paid during the year Rs.... Total estimated liability in respect of outstanding claims at the end of the year whether due or intimated Rs.... Total..... *Less*— Outstanding at the end of Previous year *(b)* Rs.... Commission on direct Business Commission on RE-insurances accepted Expenses of management *(c)*.... Bad debts ...... United Kingdom Indian, Dominion and Foreign Taxes .... Other expenditure (to be specified) .... Profit transferred to Profit and Loss Account...... Balance of Account at the end of the year as shown in the Balance-Sheet. Reserve for Unexpired Risks, being....per cent of premium income of year Rs...... Additional Reserve (if any) Rs....		Balance of Account at beginning of the year. Reserve for Unexpired Risks Rs....... Additional Reserve (if any) Rs....... premiums, less re-insurances *(d)* Interests, Dividends and Rents Rs...... *Less*— Income-tax thereon Rs....... Commission on Re-insurances ceded. Other Income (to be specified) *(e)* Loss transferred to Profit and Loss Account...... Transferred from Appropriation Account....... Rs.	

NOTES

(a) This heading must include all expenses directly incurred in setting claims.

(b) If in any year the claims actually paid and those still unpaid at the end of that year in respect of the previous year or years are in excess of the amount included in the previous year's Revenue Account as provision for outstanding claims, then the amount of such excess must be shown in the Revenue Account.

(c) If any sum has been deducted from this item and entered on the assets side of the balance-sheet the amount so deducted must be shown separately.

(d) Where the account is furnished under the provisions of section 11 of the Insurance Act, 1938, separate figures for claims paid to claimants in India and claimants outside India, and for premiums derived from business effected in India and effected outside India must be given.

(e) All the amounts received by the insurer directly or indirectly whether from his head office or from any other source outside India shall also be shown separately in the revenue account except such sums as properly appertain to capital account.

* Where the account is furnished under the provisions of clause (9b) of sub-section (2) of section 16 of the Insurance Act, 1938, by an insurer to whom that section applies, separate figures for business within India and business out of India must be given against the items marked with an asterisk. Against all other items the total amount for the business as a whole may be given.

4

THE THIRD-SCHEDULE

FORM A

Form of Balance Sheet of a Co-operative Bank

Capital and Liabilities	Rs. P.	Rs.P.	Property and Assets	Rs. P.	Rs.P.
1. Capital :			1. Cash		
(i) Authorised Capital.... Shares of Rs....each.			In hand and with Reserve Bank, State Bank of India, State Cooperative Bank and Central Cooperaative Bank.	———	
(ii) Subscribed Capital.... Shares of Rs....each.					
(iii) Amount called up on... Shares of Rs....each.	———		2. Balance with other Banks:		
Less calls unpaid of (iii) above, held by			(i) Current deposits		
(a) Individuals			(ii) Savings bank deposits.		
(b) Co-operative Institutions					
(c) State Government.			(iii) Fixed Deposits.	———	

CAPITAL AND LIABILITIES	Rs. P.	Rs. P.	PROPERTY AND ASSETS	Rs. P.	Rs. P.
2. Reserve Fund and other. Reserves :			3. Money at Call and Short Notice.		
(i) Statutory Reserve			4. Investments :		
(ii) Agricultural (Credit stabilization Fund)			(i) In Central and State Governments securitie (at book value)		
(iii) Building Fund			Face Value Rs.....		
(iv) Dividend Equalization Fund			Market Value....		
(v) Special Bad Debts Reserves.			(ii) Other Trustees Securities		
(vi) Bad and Doubtful Debts Reserve			(iii) Shares in co-operative institutions other than in item (5) below.		
(vii) Investment Depreciation Fund.			(iv) Other investments		
(viii) Other Funds and Reserves (to be specified)		———	(to be specified)		———
3. Principal/Subsidiary State Partnership Fund Account :			5. Investments out of the Principal Subsidiary State Partnership Fund :		
For share capital of :					
(i) Central Co-operative Banks.			(i) Central Co-operative Banks		
(ii) Primary agricultural credit societies.			(ii) Primary agricultural Credit Societies		
(iii) Other societies.		———	(iii) Other Societies		———
4. Deposit and Other Accounts:			6. Advances :		
(i) Fixed deposits**			(i) Short-term loans, cash credits, over-drafts and bills discounted.		
(a) Individuals**			Of which secured against :		
(b) Central Co-operative Banks			(a) Government and other approved securities		
(c) Other Societies			(b) Other tangible securities@		
(ii) Savings Bank Deposits					
(a) Individuals**					
(b) Central Cooperative Banks			Of the advances amount due from individuals		
(c) Other societies					
(iii) Current Deposits			Of the advances, amount overdue :		
(a) Individuals**					
(b) Central Cooperative Banks			Considered bad and doubtful of recovery		
(c) Other deposits			(ii) Medium-term loans		
(iv) Money at call and short notice.			Of which secured against :		
5. Borrowings			(a) Government and other approved securities.		
(i) From the Reserve Bank of India/State/Central/ Cooperative bank :			(b) Other tangible securities@		
(a) Short-term loans,cash,					

CAPITAL AND LIABILITIES	Rs. P.	Rs. P.	PROPERTY AND ASSETS	Rs. P.	Rs. P.
credits and over drafts.			Of the advances, amount due from individuals		
Of which secured against :			Of the advances, amount overdue :		
(A) Government and other approved securities.			Considered bad and doubtful of recovery.		
(B) Other tangible securities			(iii) Long-term loans		
(b) Medium-term loans of which secured against :			Of which secured against :		
(A) Government and other approved securities			(a) Government and other approved securities		
(B) Other tangible securities @			(b) Other tangible securities @		
(C) Long-term loans			Of the advances, amount due from individuals		
Of which secured against :			Of the advances, amount overdue		
(A) Government and other approved securities.			Considered bad and doubtful of recovery		
(B) Other tangible securities @			Interest Receivable : of which overdue		
(ii) From the State Bank of India			Considered bad and doubtful of recovery.		
(a) Short-term loans, cash credits and drafts			8. Bills Receivable being Bills for Collection as per *contra*.		———
Of which secured against :			9. Branch Adjustments		———
(A) Government and other approved securities.			10. Premises less Depreciation		
(B) Other tangible securities @			11. Furniture and Fixtures less Depreciation		
(b) Medium-term loans			12. Other Assets (to be specified)		———
Of which secured against :			13. Non-Banking Assets acquired in satisfaction of claims (Stating mode of valuation)		———
(A) Government and other approved securities.			14. Profit and loss		
(B) Other tangible securities @					
(c) Long-term loans					
Of which secured against :					
(A) Government and other approved securities					
(B) Other tangible securities @					
From the State Government					
(a) Short-term loans					
Of which secured against :					
(A) Government and other approved securities					
(B) Other tangible securities @					

CAPITAL AND LIABILITIES	Rs. P. Rs. P.	PROPERTY AND ASSETS	Rs. P. Rs. P.
(b) Medium-term loans			
Of which secured against:			
(A) Government and other approved securities			
(B) Other tangible securities @			
(b) Long-term loans			
Of which secured against:			
(A) Government and other approved securities			
(B) Other tangible securities			
(iv) Loans from other sources (Source and security to be specified)			
6. Bills for collection being Bills Receivable as *per contra*			
7. Branch Adjustments			
8. Overdue Interest Reserve			
9. Interest Payable			
10. Other Liabilities			
(i) Bills payable.			
(ii) Unclaimed dividends			
(iii) Suspense			
(iv) Sundries			
11. Profit and Loss Profit as per last balance sheet Less appropriations add profit for the year brought from the Profit and Loss Accounts.			
Contingent Liabilities			
(i) Outstanding Liabilities for guaranting issued			
(ii) Others			
Total			

NOTES

* "Fixed deposits" will include reserve fund deposits of societies, employees fund deposits, staff security deposits, recurring deposits, cash certificates, etc.

** Under the item "individuals" deposits from institutions other than co-operative banks and societies may be included.

\+ "Borrowing" and "Advances"— Short-term loans will be for periods up to 15 months, medium-term from 15 months to 5 years and long-term loans over 5 years.

@ "Other tangible security" will include borrowings against gold and gold oranaments, repledges of goods, mortgage of land, etc.

General Instructions. The corresponding figures (to the nearest rupee, if so desired) for the years immediately preceding the year to which the balance sheet relates should be shown in separate columns.

Form B

Form of Profit and Loss Account of a Co-operative Bank

Profit and Loss Account for the Year ended.....

Capital and Liabilities	Rs. P.	Rs. p.	Property and Assets	Rs.P.	Rs. P.
1. Interst on deposits, borrowings, etc.			1. Interest and discount		
2. Salaries and allowances and provident fund.			2. Commission, exchange and brokerage.		
3. Directors' and local committee members fees and allowances.			3. Subsidies and donations		
4. Rent, taxes, insurance, lighting etc.			4. Income from non-banking assets and profit from sale of or dealing with such assets.		
5. Law charges			5. Other receipts		
6. Postage, telegrams and telephone charges.			6. Loss (if any)		
7. Auditor's fees					
8. Depreciation on and repairs to property					
9. Stationary, printing and advertisement, etc.					
10. Loss from sale of or dealing with non-banking assets					
11. Other expenditure					
12. Balance of profit					
	Total			Total	

General Instructions. The corresponsing figures (to the nearest rupee, if so desired) for the year immediately preceding the year to which the profit and loss account relates should be shown in separate columns.

QUESTIONS FOR EXERCISE

1. What are the special features of Bank Audit ? What are the special points to be kept in view while auditing the bills of a commerical bank ?
2. Discuss the special points to which you will give your particular attention while auditing the accounts of a banking company.
3. State the special points to which you will pay particular attention while auditing the final accounts of an insurance company.
4. Describe the procedure for auditing the accounts of a big educational institution.
5. What points will receive your special attention while auditing the accounts of a school or a college ?
6. Outline the special features of the audit of a cooperative society. Draft an audit programme for a District Cooperative Bank.
7. As auditor of an approved hospital, outline the steps you would take while examining its accounts.
8. How would you audit the accounts of a club ? Discuss the special points that arise in such an audit ?
9. Draft the procedure to be adopted in auditing the accounts of an electricity supply company.
10. Mention the special points in auditing the acconts of an industrial concern.
11. Discuss the special points that arise in the audit of accounts of a Stock Broker's firm.
12. Discuss the special points to which you will give your particular attention while auditing the accounts of a cinema company.
13. State the points to which you will pay special attention as an auditor in the audit of a company engaged in financing hire purchase of motor vehicles.
14. What are the special points to which you, as an auditor would direct your attention while auditing the accounts of the transport company ?

24

Investigation

Definition of Investigation

1. Dicksee. "An investigation is an examination of accounting records undertaken for special purpose. Its object is usually to discover and display the facts in such a manner as will enable the parties for whom it is undertaken to draw conclusions and make their decisions accordingly."

2. Lancaster. "An investigation may be defined as an examination of an inquiry into the accounts of a business with a view to disclose the true position of affairs in relation to the special matters falling within the scope of investigation".

3. Spicer and Peglar. "The term investigation implies an examination of records for some special purpose."

4. Taylor and Perry. "Investigation involves an enquiry into the facts behind the books and accounts into the technical, financial and economic position of the business house or organisation."

5. I.R. Batliboi. "An investigation may be defined as enquiry into the resultant profit or loss of any business for the past several years in order to ascertain the normal profit-earning capacity of the business and necessary average working capital required in earning such profits, or with a view to ascertain the true financial condition of business for a particular object in view."

CHARACTERISTICS OF INVESTIGATION

1. It relates to a special and specific objects only.
2. Its scope may be extended or curtailed according to its objectives.
3. It is critical examination and verification of specific records for a specific period.
4. It is started with a suspicious mind and propose as future course of action along with the report on the existing situation.
5. Its report is analytical, descriptive and exhaustive, so that relevant and correct conclusions may be drawn and action initiated.

6. It may involve the personal examination of the directors, auditors and other officers of the company to ascertain the real facts behind the situation under investigation.

OBJECTS OF INVESTIGATION

1. To ascertain the financial position and the earning capacity of a concern on behalf of an individual or a promoter of a joint stock company who wishes to take-over or purchase the concern.
2. To assess the financial position of the concern and whether it is advisable to become a partner, on behalf of an incoming partner who wants to know the earning capacity of the firm.
3. To investigate on behalf of a client who wishes to lend money to a concern to know its financial position.
4. To investigate where fraud is suspected by the proprietor.
5. To investigate on behalf of a client who wishes to purchase the shares of a company.
6. To investigate under the Indian Companies Act.
7. To investigate to ascertain the amount of compensation payable on the compulsory removal of business.
8. To investigate for claims under an Insurance Policy covering consequential losses, e.g., in the case of fire, burglary etc.
9. To investigate on behalf of the company or an individual for alleged negligence or lack of skill by the auditors.
10. To investigate on behalf of the liquidator of a company where the directors are suspected of fraud or misfeasance.
11. To investigate on behalf of beneficiaries where trustees are suspected of fraud or misappropriation.
12. To investigate on behalf of Income-tax authorities for tax liability or for detection of undisclosed income.

INVESTIGATION V/S AUDIT

1. Meaning. An investigation means an enquiry or examination with a fixed object, e.g., detection of a suspected fraud, ascertainment of causes of low productivity, continuing losses, high labour turnover, inadequate working capital, etc., or evaluation of the worth of a running business on behalf of the owners, prospective investors, and in case of a company, also the Central Government. Audit, on the other hand, is checking of financial matters and preparing audit report.

2. Scope. The scope of an investigation is determined by the objects sought to be accomplished by the party on whose behalf it is to be undertaken. An investigation to evaluate the worth of a business will only be concerned with the value of the assets, reserves and liabilities of the business, together with its potential and prospects. Investigation on behalf of the owners into the causes of low productivity may only focus on the related factors such as availability and quality of raw materials, competence, morale and stability of tenure of workers, and so on.

On the other hand, an audit examination extends to all the facts asserted in the financial statements of the business with a view to ascertaining their truth and fairness. The scope of audit examination cannot be curtailed in case of statutory audit, where this is done in an optional audit the auditor cannot be held liable for any fraud or error lying outside the purview of his examination.

3. Aims and Objectives. Investigation aims at ascertaining some facts, such as fraud, tax liability, value of shares, or causes of an existing situation such as low productivity, high labour turnover, inadequate working capital, continuing losses, etc. It may be made with the object of evaluating the worth of the business from the point of view of a prospective buyer, investor, etc. On the other hand, the object of an audit is to critically examine and made a report on the truth and fairness of the assertions made in the financial statements as to the results of operations (profit or loss) and the state of affairs of the business (position of assets and liabilities).

4. Time Coverage. While an audit examination covers the accounting year of the client, the period to be covered by an investigation is determined with reference to its objectives. It may be as short as a few days or may extend to several years.

5. Approach to work. The auditor examines and reviews the financial statements as prepared by the client, with a general objective namely, to express his opinion on the authenticity of the financial statements. The standards of strictness of enquiry are not as demanding as in the case of an investigation. An investigator, on the other hand, is required to be more skilled, critical and cautious. The information required for his work may not be available readymade. His enquiry for the necessary evidence will have to go beyond what appears in the books and records. He must possess an alert, open eyed quality to distinguish the clues which may help him in getting at the truth. He does not accept any factor figure at its face value but subjects it to a close scrutiny.

6. Work Programme. As the work programme is generally fixed in an audit, it is not possible to provide a standard work programme for an investigation. There cannot be an identical programme for two specific investigations of the same nature. It will depend on the variability of the required information which will be determined only as the work proceeds. The very logic of the programme may have to be reviewed at the completion of each stage of work.

7. Disclosure Requirements. While there are no legal requirements as to disclosure of information in an investigation the auditor is required under the law to ensure complete disclosure of the information as prescribed. The investigator may, at his discretion, rearrange the existing data, redraft the accounts, develop new data and provide support for a particular viewpoint.

8. Report. An investigator reports to the persons on whose behalf he has undertaken his work, in the form of a summing up of the conclusions drawn by him after an inquiry into the specific facts and circumstances. He may not adhere to any standard form or pattern in the matter or reporting. He need not render any opinion of his own. But he should provide adequate material for a correct judgement by his client. For example, in an investigation on behalf of an intending buyer of business, it is necessary for him to say whether the business is worth pursuing, or whether it is worth the price demanded, as these questions are to be decided by the buyer himself. But as the investigator's report will form an important basis for judgement by the buyer, he should present his conclusions and the evidence supporting them in a clear and cogent manner so that the buyer may be able to form a correct judgement as to the prospects of the business.

An auditor, on the other hand, reports to the owners of the business, in a standard form. He is concerned with facts and circumstances which, in case of an optional audit, are stated in the letter of his appointment and in case of statutory audit, in the statute concerned. He expresses his opinion as to the authenticity of assertions made in the financial statements. He is not required to cite evidence in support thereof.

TYPES OF INVESTIGATION

1. Evaluations. Evaluatory investigation may be either with a view to determine the worth of a business proposed to be bought or sold, or to determine the ability and efficiency of the personnel or machinery, etc. It relates to valuing the assets and liabilities, and determining the current earning potential and future prospects of the business. In case of a business proposed to be bought, it relates to determining the net worth of the business. In case of sale of a business, investigations about evaluation of personnel or machinery deal with determining their ability and efficiency as against the projected performance on their part.

2. Reviews. Investigation by way of review may be conducted either to ascertain the compliance with the terms of a contract or to determine the reliability of business data. For example, the secured creditors of a company may engage the auditor either to investigate the company's compliance with the deed creating a charge on the assets of the company in their favour; or to interpret the technical terms in the deed. Persons entitled to payments of royalty or commission as a percentage of the output or turnover, may appoint the auditor to investigate the correctness of the relevant data furnished by the company.

3. Surveys. Investigation by way of survey may be undertaken to measure and map out a wide range of matters such as the accounting and cost systems, employees of the business, etc.

(i) Survey of the accounting system. It may be undertaken as a follow-up of the audit report pointing to the weaknesses of the system. It may be ordered with a view to installing an effective budgetary control system.

(ii) Survey about the cost system. It may be undertaken to study the inadequacies of the existing procedures of inventory pricing or allocation of various overheads, and to determine suitable alternatives.

(iii) Survey about employees of the business. It may be undertaken to identify their personality traits such as experience, aptitude, initiative, leadership, etc., and to determine a suitable incentive scheme to promote individual land departmental efficiency.

4. Analysis. An investigation through analysis of the available data and information may be undertaken to facilitate decision-making by the management in certain vital areas such as determination of the price or cost products. It calls for a great deal of research to identify the factors responsible for increase in price or cost and determination of the ways in which these may be controlled.

5. Special Audits. These are usually undertaken to determine frauds, losses caused by fire or machinery breakdown calling for filing of claim with the insurers. Cash and inventory records are the most susceptible to the frauds. An investigations in this area generally covers a period of three to six months. Investigations about losses are concerned with determining the factors responsible for it as also computing the amounts for filing of claims with the insurers.

6. Statutory Investigation. According to Sections 235 to 251 of the Companies Act, the affairs of a company may be investigated by the Central Government. It includes an investigation of all its business affairs such as profit and losses, assets including goodwill, contracts and transactions, investigations and other property, interests etc.

DUTIES OF INVESTIGATOR

1. To find out the nature, objects, scope and extent of investigation. The investigator should obtain written instructions from his client about the following:

(i) the special object and general purpose of enquiry.

(ii) the period to be covered by enquiry.

(iii) the extent or scope of enquiry.

(iv) the restrictions placed by his client upon the scope of his work.

2. Method of Work. Taking into consideration the nature of business, the efficiency and reliability of accounts maintained and the internal check in operation. The investigator should determine the method of work to be followed.

3. Impartiality. The investigator should use the best of his skill in the best interests of his client. He should maintain his independence of views so as not to be influenced by any interested party.

4. Enquiry into Status of Personnel of the business. The investigator should enquire into the character and position of the persons connected with the business.

5. Careful and cautious. The auditor should be careful in gathering, analysis and evaluation of evidence. He should seek expert opinion from outside. In areas where he lacks adequate competence such as valuation of assets and liabilities, he should not hesitate in collecting data from sources other then the records of the business.

6. Discussion with the auditor. Where he has been asked to enquire into the accounts and records already audited by an auditor, an investigator should carry out a brief discussion with the auditor of the firm to ascertain the extent of his audit and his opinion about the business.

7. Adequate Reporting. The report of the investigation should be a clear-cut indication of the character of the examination carried out and the degree to which the auditor is prepared to own responsibility. It should present the conclusions clearly and precisely and give adequate evidence to justify them.

INVESTIGATION FOR PURCHASE

Where the investigation is to be done on behalf of a limited company desiring to buy another established concern, the investigator will be required to examine the following things:

1. The earning capacity of the concern,
2. Real Profits,
3. Values of the assets,
4. Extent of liabilities,
5. Reasonability of the purchase price,
6. Estimation of value of goodwill,
7. Any other general points that may have bearing in this respect.

1. Earning Capacity. The future earning capacity of the concern can be determined on the basis of past achievements. The past achievements can be traced back with the help of Profit and Loss Account of the past years. If the books of account are properly audited the investigator will be at ease with the work. He will collect Profit and Loss Account of previous years in tabular forms to compare them. The turn over percentage can be known various items. The causes of variation should be determined. He should give satisfactory explanations thereof.

He should investigate to find out the true and net effective sales by preparing a sales statement. If there are variations in sales volume its cause must be known. He must also note if he has seen the sales high due to exceptional contracts entered into by the vendor or by his personal influence, as such chances may not be available to the purchaser.

He should examine the item of stock in trade at the end of each period. He should compare the stocks of the past years and check the variations. He should make comparison of expenses for series of years to ensure that there is no omission of the expenses.

2. Real Profits. (A) Inflation. The concern's profit may be inflated by the following usual methods which should be investigated to know real profit:

(i) Inflation of closing stocks.

(ii) Inclusion of fictitious sales.

(iii) Omission of purchases.

(iv) Including goods sale or return or consignment as completed sales.

(v) Omitting wages, manufacturing and other expenses.

(vi) Taking capital income as revenue income and capitalizing the revenue expenses.

(vii) Making less provision for depreciation and reserves.

(viii) Trading and Profit and Loss Account should be scrutinised to ascertain the true amount of profit. The adjustments in net profits have to be made to ascertain the amount of profit that the intending purchaser will be able to earn in changed circumstances.

(B) Additions. Then following items should be added to the profits of the vendors:

(i) *Salaries.* Partner's salaries over the fair amount of remuneration to the management.

(ii) *Interests.* Interest on partner's capital and current account. Interest on loans and overdrafts, if any. If the purchaser has assumed certain loans interest should not be included.

(iii) *Rent.* If the buyer is buying the trade premises that was being used by the vendor who paid rents in past.

(iv) *Discount.* On purchases and excessive cash discounts on sales.

(v) *Exceptional losses.* Those which do not arise in ordinary course of business at low costs, damages and defalcation.

(vi) *Capital losses.* Those on the sale of fixed assets.

(vii) *Additions in Capital.* Any addition or improvements of capital nature which might have been changed to the Profit and Loss Account.

(viii) *Provisions.* These include provisions for bad/doubtful debts or other contingencies in excess of the usual normal provisions required.

(ix) *Depreciation.* Excessive provision for depreciation.

(x) *Charges.* Any charges not incidental to the business as donations and subscriptions.

(C) Deductions. The following items should be deducted from the profits of the vendors:

(i) Income, from those assets that have not been purchased by the purchaser.

(ii) Rent, if purchaser has not acquired the premises used by the vendors and no charge has been made for the same in the Profit and Loss Account.

(iii) Exceptional profits, not arising in the usual course of business as speculation profits or insurance profits.

(iv) Capital profits, arisen on account of the sale of fixed assets.

(v) Depreciation, if not properly provided.

(vi) Remuneration amount for the management expected to be incurred by the purchaser. The should be deducted if the reasonable management remuneration has not been charged for in Profit and Loss Accounts.

(vii) Any known additional expenses that the purchaser will have to incur in earning the same gross income.

3. Values of the Assets. The investigator should do the following:

(i) Ascertain the value of various assets shown in the Balance Sheet.

(ii) Find out the value of the assets as correctly as possible.

(iii) Take the help of experts, if necessary.

(iv) Pay special attention to the adequacy of the amount of depreciation shared to fixed assets.

(v) Prepare a statement of assets of past few years and make a comparison year-wise.

(vi) Examinc whether adequate provisions have been made for discount, and bad and doubtful debts.

4. The Extent of Liabilities. The investigator should do the following:

(i) Prepare a statement of liabilities of past few years and make a comparison year-wise.

(ii) See that there is no omission of the liabilities specially the outstanding liabilities.

(iii) Pay special attention to those contingent liabilities which may be expected to become real ones.

(iv) Intensively examine the creditors.

5. The Reasonability of the Purchase Price

(i) Purchase consideration can be determined on the basis of Balance Sheet of the concern.

(ii) The investigator should examine the fairness of purchase price by making calculations on the basis of available facts and figures.

6. The Goodwill. If the amount of goodwill has already been agreed upon, the investigator will not have to worry about it. There are different methods of calculating goodwill. It should be calculated on the basis of Super Profits of the business concern.

7. General Points. The investigator should remember the following points:

(i) Find out the reason for the proposed sale by the vendor of the business concern.

(ii) Evaluate the impact of personality of the vendor upon the business of the concern.

(iii) Study the future demand of the commodity with the concern deals.

(iv) Study the terms of contracts with the employees of the concern.

(v) Consider the responsibility of the purchase price agreed and the value of goodwill estimated.

(vi) Carefully weigh the burden of the contracts or other commitments undertaken by the concern.

(vii) Try to ascertain the period and terms on which the business premises have taken by the vendors.

INVESTIGATION OF PARTNERSHIP

The investigator should take the following points into consideration:

1. Enquire about the reasons as to why a new partner is being taken in by the existing partners.
2. Ascertain whether the firm will be put to some loss by the absence of partner, if the new partner is taking the place of a deceased or retiring partner See if the loss so caused will be made good by the availability of skill and experience of the new partner.
3. Locate the use to which the capital to be introduced by the new partner will be put. It may be utilized for paying off any liability or paying back the capital balance of the retiring or deceased partner or for providing additional working capital. See whether this amount of capital will be sufficient for the purposeful expansion of the business.
4. Compare the capital of different partners with their proportion of share in the profit or loss of the firm.

5. Enquire into the financial position of the business. If it is under heavy financial strain, diagnose whether such a situation will adversely affect the interest of the new partner.
6. Study the balance sheet to ensure that assets and liabilities have been correctly shown therein.
7. Scrutinise the Draft Partnership Deed, specially the clauses which are connected with the entry of the new partner.
8. Enquire whether the amount of goodwill to be paid by his client is a reasonable one. Ordinarily, a new partner is asked to bring in a specific amount of goodwill. See as to how this amount is to be shared by the existing partners.
9. Pay special attention to the earning capacity of the business so that he may be in a position to make an idea of the future prospects of the business.
10. Enquire whether any specialized technical knowledge is necessary for the successful conduct of the business; and, if so, how far the new partner will be in a position to fill up the gap.
11. Submit report to the client and deal with all these matters freely and clearly in the reports.

INVESTIGATION OF FRAUD

Bases of Procedure

The procedure to investigate a fraud depends upon the following:

1. Accounting system adopted in the business.
2. Effectiveness of internal control system.
3. Nature of fraud suspected.

Types of Frauds

Frauds may be of following types :

1. Misappropriation of cash,
2. Misappropriation of goods,
3. Misappropriation of securities,
4. Manipulation of accounts.

1. Misappropriation of cash. This may be done in any of the following ways:

(i) Omitting to enter the receipts of cash.

(ii) Entering less amount in the cash book than what has been received.

(iii) Entering fictitious payments.

(iv) Entering more amount than what has actually been paid.

Steps to detect misappropriation of cash

(i) Enquire into the weaknesses of accounting system.

(ii) Ascertain the inefficiencies in the Internal Control System.

(iii) Enquire reasons for defalcations.

(iv) Determine the extent and form of misappropriations.

(v) Scrutinize the duties and functioning of different employees.

(vi) Check Cash Book, Vouchers, correspondences, counterfoils, traveller's advices, memos and all other similar evidences.

(vii) Enquire in details for such vouchers or receipts which appear to have been altered or defaced.

(viii) Vouch Bank reconciliation statement to detect frauds as to the amounts deposited or withdrawn.

(ix) Scrutinize discounts and allowances allowed and amounts written off as bad debts.

(x) Confirm balances of debtors and creditors from their statements and correspondences.

(xi) Make comparative statements of Orders Received Book with Orders Placed Book, Sales Book with Purchases Book and Goods, Outward Book with Goods Inward Book. Critically assess the differences discovered between them.

(xii) Count cash in Hand and check with the Cash Book the reason. Enquire if there is any difference.

2. Misappropriation of Goods or Stock. Take the following steps:

(i) Scrutinize Receipts and Issues of goods.

(ii) Check reliability of Stock Control System.

(iii) Ascertain defects in the recording system of movement of stock.

(iv) Check in details goods returned and goods sent on approval.

(v) Scrutinize the procedure to purchase qualitative goods and the manner they are approved and maintained in the godown.

(vi) Compare sales invoices and the outward stock register.

(vii) Check the physical closing stock with the balance of Stock Register.

3. Misappropriation of Securities. This is affected by selling or pledging the securities fraudulently and misappropriating the cash proceeds. It is normally done by those who have the custody of the securities or have the access to these securities. To detect misappropriation of securities scrutinise the following:

(i) Number of securities held by the responsible officer of the business concern.

(ii) Method of recording these securities in the books of the business concern.

(iii) Method of keeping these securities in the safe custody of the responsible officer.

(iv) Probability of others to have access to such securities.

The investigator should do the following :

(i) Find out defects in the procedure of recording, keeping in safe custody and releasing the securities as maintained in the business concern.

(ii) Ascertain the amount of the securities that must be held by the business concern so that he comes to know to what extent and which particular security is running short of the figure.

(iii) After preparing a list of all the securities held by the business concern as per the general ledger, check these securities personally in the presence of the officer responsible to keep these in safe custody.

(iv) Where the securities are in the custody of some outside agency, insist for a certificate from such agency as having the custody of security on behalf of the business concern and the reasons for keeping the securities in their custody.

4. Manipulation of Accounts. This can be done only by responsible officers of the business concern, for some specific purpose such as follows:

(i) To disclose fancy rather than true position of the business concern, for some specific purpose such as follows:

(a) To disclose fancy rather than true position of the business concern.

(b) To conceal some serious mistakes in the functioning of the business concern or of any particular official.

(c) To deceive partner, creditor or prospective buyer or financier.

(d) To defraud tax authorities.

(e) To declare dividends, bonus etc.

(f) To secure promotion, larger commission etc. by the responsible officers.

(g) To earn speculative profits through the manipulation of share prices.

B. Methods. Accounts are manipulated by following methods:

(i) Overvaluation of Assets and Liabilities.

(ii) Undervaluation of Assets and Liabilities.

(iii) Overcharging expenses or understanding incomes to show less profits.

(iv) Over-stating incomes to show higher profits.

v) Charging capital expenses to revenue expenses or *vice versa* to increase or decrease profits.

No hard and fast rule of procedure can be laid down to detect window dressing and manipulations of accounts by senior officials. The investigator should adopt procedure relevant to a particular case and its circumstances. As an expert he should move very carefully to detect errors, frauds and manipulations committed by the senior and responsible officials of the business concern.

INVESTIGATION ABOUT FINANCIAL STATUS

Before extending a loan to a customer a bank examines the Balance Sheet of the customer so as to satisfy itself as regards his sound financial position. In case of loans involving sizeable sums, the bank may call for a detailed investigation by an auditor. The investigator will examine the following points in his investigation.

1. In case of loan for a new project

(i) **The gestation period,** i.e., the time it would take the project to start commercial production and be financially viable;

(ii) **The activity schedule,** i.e., the maximum time during which different phases of the project would be completed;

(iii) **Estimated cost of the project** including cost of each item involved therein;

(iv) **Estimated profit-earning potential** as worked out by accounting ratios;

(v) **Estimated liability** as regard taxes, dividends, managerial expenses, interest on borrowing, etc.;

(vi) Working capital;

(vii) Adequacy of security offered.

2. In case of an on-going concern

(i) **Book debts** with reference to the period of credit extended;

(ii) **Amounts due** from directors, partners, employees, branches, subsidiaries, etc.

(iii) **Adequacy of provision** for bad and doubtful debts;

(iv) **Valuation** as per generally accepted and consistently followed method of valuation of stock-in-trade, including finished goods, work-in-progress, raw materials, etc.

(a) **Book debts** with reference to the period of credit extended;

(b) **Amounts due** from directors, partners, employees, branches subsidiaries, etc.

(c) **Adequacy of provision** for bad and doubtful debts;

(d) **Existence of charge** in respect of any of the amounts against any loan.

(e) **Valuation** as per generally accepted and consistently followed method of valuation of stock-in-trade, including finished goods, work-in-progress, raw materials, etc.

(f) **Cost and market value of fixed assets** such as buildings, plant, machinery, and other fixtures, the adequacy of depreciation provided, including creation of any pledge in respect thereof.

(g) **Cost and market value of investments,** including provision for fluctuation in prices and creation of any pledge in respect thereof.

(h) **Long-term liabilities** including the amounts involved, interest payable, repayment schedule, mortgages and charges involved, etc. The auditor should not loose sight of any existing or contingent liabilities such as guarantees, warranties, present commitments, etc. He should also state whether there are sufficient grounds for seeking the loan, and whether the amount of loan is going to be profitably employed in business so as to make for meeting of interest and repayment obligations.

INVESTIGATION FOR DISCLOSURE

When accountants are called upon to compute the income of an assessee which has escaped assessment, to settle his income-tax liability, the investigation is undertaken in two circumstances:

1. Where the assessee has maintained accounts but the accounts do not fully disclose his income ; and
2. Where no accounts have been maintained.

1. Where accounts have been maintained. When accounts are maintained in an irregular way, profits are amassed either by the proprietor or his employees by withdrawing money from the business or by switching over the profits of one year to another by adopting one or more of the undermentioned devices:

(i) Understatement of sales.

(ii) Inflation of expenses.

(iii) Undervaluation of closing stock.

(iv) Good debts being written off as bad, and subsequent receipts from the parties not being accounted for.

(v) Omission of a profitable transaction.

(vi) Non-disclosure of source of income, such as commissions or fees received for some advice given.

Procedure of investigation

(i) The investigating accountant should check his findings or estimates by computing the increase that has taken place, in the personal assets, as well as from the details of personal expenses of the assessee that were met but of undisclosed sources of income, during the period under investigation.

(ii) He should obtain from the tax-payer a complete statement of his personal assets including amounts held in different bank accounts, investments and any real property, along with the dates of their acquisition. On the basis of such data, he should prepare a statement showing the wealth of the individual concerned, as on 31st March, each your, throughout the period under enquiry. The increase in the wealth in the given financial period, after making due allowance for the tax-payer's living expenses, receipts from non-taxable sources, e.g., agricultural income share, of income from H.U.F., would represent his net annual income. On deducting from this figure, the income already disclosed, the resulting figure would represent the income which had escaped assessment.

(iii) In such a computation, not only he should include information in respect of tax-payer's assets but also those of his wife, other members of the family and persons holding property as benamidars. The estimate of living expenses should be drawn up carefully, having regard to the standard of living of the assessee. If large amounts have been withdrawn from the Bank Deposit Accounts, an explanation in respect of each of them should be sought. The wealth statement would indicate, positively, the amounts which the assessee had secretly withdrawn from the business from year to year. If the amount so computed is corroborated by the findings or estimates prepared on investigation of his accounts described above, the undisclosed income shown by the wealth statement could be taken as correct.

2. Where no accounts have been maintained

(i) It is necessary to construct the accounts by analysing bank statements, invoices, creditor's statements, receipts or invoices for expenditure and any other available documentary evidence or data. It is difficult to make an estimate of sales from analysis of cash takings and receipts from debtors shown to have been paid into the bank, but if the total purchases can be ascertained, it is possible to estimate the amount of sales by applying to the purchases the percentage of gross profit normally earned in the particular trade or by auditing to the amounts of sales deposited in the bank an estimate of cash-takings applied in payment of purchases and expenses and amounts withdrawn by the assessee for his personal expenses.

(ii) The results of investigation of accounts in the manner aforementioned should be checked by preparing the wealth statement as aforementioned.

(iii) While drawing up the report, the investigating accountant should indicate, without any reservation, any deficiencies in the data produced to him, or matters in respect of which he has been able to obtain satisfactory explanations. Further, he must state the extent of which he is in a position to accept responsibility for the accuracy of figures shown in the statement of wealth which he has prepared.

INVESTIGATION UNDER COMPANIES ACT

A. Purposes

The Central Government has been empowered to appoint inspectors for the purposes as mentioned below to investigate :

1. Section 235(a). On application either of not less than 200 members or members holding not less than one-tenth of the voting power therein, in case of a company having a share capital.

2. Section 235(b). On the application of not less than one-fifth in number of the persons on the company's register of members, in the case of a company not having a share capital.

3. Section 235(c). On a report by the registrar under Section 234 dealing with the power of Registrar to call for information or explanation, in case of any other company.

4. Section 237. If the opinion of the Central Government is that:

(i) The business of the company is being conducted fraudulently.

(ii) The company was formed with fraudulent and unlawful purposes.

(iii) The persons concerned in the formation of the company have been guilty of fraud, misfeasance or other misconduct.

(iv) Full informations have not been given to the members of the company regarding its affairs.

B. Conditions

Investigation must be conducted in the following cases:

(i) Special resolution. A company requires it by special resolution;

(ii) Section 237(a). The court passes an order for it.

(iii) Section 238. To investigate the affairs of the company, no firm, body corporate or association can be appointed as inspectors. Only an individual can be appointed for lit.

(iv) Section 239. The inspectors appointed by the Central Government for the purpose of investigation of the affairs of the company have also been given power to investigate the affairs of the related companies which include the company's subsidiary or holding company or a subsidiary to its holding company or a holding company of its subsidiary. They can also investigate into the affairs of any person who is or has at any relevant time been the company's manager or managing director.

(v) Section 240. The inspectors so appointed have been given wide powers to examine on oath all past and present officers and agents of the company and other specified persons. Agents include bankers, legal advisers and auditors. The officers or agents or other persons should produce all books and documents in their possession and generally to help in the investigation.

(vi) Section 240. The inspectors have been given power to seize the documents or the books etc. with the help of relevant authorities provided he has not sufficient reason to believe that they will be mutilated, altered, falsified or secreted.

(vii) Section 241. The Inspector must report to the Central Government on the conclusion of the investigation. He should submit an interim report too, is so required.

C. Action on the Report

The Central Government may take the following actions on the reports from the inspector.

(i) Prosecution. If it appears that any man has been guilty of an offence for which he is criminally liable, it may, after taking necessary legal advice, prosecute such persons for the offence.

(ii) Winding up. If it considers desirable, it may arrange to have the company or any related company wound up, or it may make application to the court for an order under Section 379 or 398 of the Act.

(iii) Recovery. If it appears in public interest, the Central Government may bring proceedings in the name of the company for recovery of the damages in respect of any fraud, misfeasance or misconduct in connection with the company's formation or management or for the recovery of any property misapplied or wrongfully retained.

D. Reimbursement of expenses

The investigation expenses by an inspector appointed by the Central Government shall be incurred by it in the first instance, but the persons specified in Section 245 will have to reimburse the Central Government in respect of such expenses.

POWERS OF GOVERNMENT INSPECTORS

Under Sections 235 and 237 of the Companies Act, the Central Government is empowered to appoint inspectors to investigate the affairs of a company.

Under the provisions of Section 238, only an individual can be appointed as inspector to conduct an investigation. His function is equivalent to the function of fact-finding mission.

Inspectors enjoy following powers according to the provisions of Section 239 of the Companies Act.

1. Section 239(2)—To investigate affairs of any other company in same group. If the inspector appointed to investigate the affairs of a company thinks it necessary for the purposes of his work also to investigate the affairs of any other body corporate, which is at the relevant time under the same management or group, he has the power to do so and to report on the affairs of the other body corporate to the extent it is relevant for the investigation of the first company.

However, in certain cases, prior approval of the Central Government is required for overstepping the brief [*Sahu Jain Ltd.* v. *Union of India* (1965) 2 Comp. L.J. 45]. Before according such approval, the Central Government shall allow the body corporate a reasonable opportunity to show cause why such approval should not be accorded.

2. Section 240(1)—To require officers of the company to produce books, etc., and to assist. It is the duty of all officers and agents of the company to preserve and produce to the inspector all books and papers of, and relating to, the company which are in their custody or power. They are duty-bound to give to the inspector all assistance in connection with the investigation which they are reasonably to give.

3. Section 240(1-A)—To require any body corporate to give information. The inspector may also, with the prior approval of the Central Government, require any body corporate to furnish such information or to produce to him such books and papers as he may consider necessary or relevant for the purpose of his investigation.

4. Section 240(3)—To keep books and papers in custody. The inspector may keep in his custody any books and papers produced before him for six months. Thereafter, he is bound to return the same to the person by whom or on whose behalf the books and papers were produced.

If any persons fails without reasonable cause or refuses:

(i) to produce to the inspector or any person authorised by him in this behalf with the previous approval of the Central Government, any books or papers which it is his duty to produce; or

(ii) to furnish any information which it is his duty to furnish; or

(iii) to appear before the inspector personally when required to do so or to answer any question which is put to him by the inspector; or

(iv) to sign the notes of any examination,

he shall be punishable with imprisonment for a term which may extend to six months, or with fine which may extend to Rs. 2,000 or with both, and also with a further fine which may extend to Rs. 200 for every day after the first during which the failure or refusal continues.

5. Section 240(2)—To examine officers on oath. With the previous approval of the Central Government the inspector may examine on oath any officers and employees of the company. He may also examine any other person and require any of these persons to appear before him personally.

Notes of any examination must be taken down in writing. These must be read over to or by, and signed by, the person examined, and may thereafter be used in evidence against him.

6. Sec. 240 A (1) To seize books and papers. If, in the course of the investigation, the inspector has reasonable ground to believe that the books and papers of the company may be destroyed, mutilated, altered, falsified, of secreted, then he may, with the permission of the Magistrate of the First Class or Presidency Magistrate, seize the books and papers. The Magistrate may also by order authorise the inspector:

(i) to enter, with such assistance as may be required, the place or places where such books and papers are kept;

(ii) to search that place or those places in the manner specified in the order; and

(iii) to seize books and papers he considers necessary for the purpose of the investigation [Sec. 240A(2)].

The books and papers so seized shall be kept in the inspector's custody for such period, not later than the conclusion of the investigation, as he considers necessary. Thereafter, he shall return the same to the company or any other persons from whose custody or power these were seized and inform the Magistrate of such return.

7. Inspector's report (Sec. 241). The inspector *may*, and if so directed by the Central Government *must*, make interim report to the Government and on the conclusion of investigation, *must* make a final report to the Central Government. The report shall be in writing or printed, as the Central Government may direct.

QUESTIONS FOR EXERCISE

1. What is meant by investigation of accounts of a business? Explain its features.
2. Distinguish between investigation and audit.
3. What are the types of investigation?

4. What are the duties of an investigator?
5. What special considerations an auditor must bear in mind while conducting an investigation?
6. An individual wants to buy a business and has asked you to conduct the investigation on his behalf. Explain how would you conduct the investigation.
7. What special points should be borne in mind while carrying out an investigation on behalf of a person who wants to purchase a business as a going concern.
8. You are asked, on behalf of a limited company to investigate into the financial position of a firm which is going to be purchased by the company. Five years of accounts are placed before you. Indicate the procedure of investigation.
9. Your client is contemplating joining an established firm as partner. He has handed to you a draft of the proposed terms. He has instructed you to make such an investigation of the affairs of the business as you think fit and to advise him generally. State the matters to which you would direct attention when carrying out the investigation.
10. A fraud is suspected in a business and you have been asked to investigate it. Explain the procedure you would adopt in this matter.
11. A bank appoints you to advise it as regards financial position of a customer who has asked for a sizeable loan. Show how would you go about your work.
12. State the procedure of investigation on behalf of an assessee desirous of disclosing his income which has escaped assessment.
13. What are the main features of investigation under Companies Act under Sections 235 and 237?
14. What are the powers of inspectors appointed by Central Government to investigate the affairs of a company?

25

Management Audit

As compared to statutory financial audit management audit is of quite recent origin. Its concept is still in its infancy. However, it has caught the attention of the management experts, the accountant and auditors all over the world. With the growing size and complexity of business organisation and more and more professionalisation of management, the need was felt for the review of performance of the management itself. This resulted in development of management audit.

Meaning

The management audit implies an attempt to evaluate the performance of various management functions and processes with a view to improve its efficiency and productivity, on the basis of certain pre-determined acceptable norms or standards. It involves a detailed and critical evaluation as to what has been done by the management. It is an audit "to examine, review the various policies and actions of the management on the basis of certain objective standards." It serves to improve the quality of management and thereby the overall performance of the organisation itself.

Definition

1. *William P. Leonard.* Management audit is "a comprehensive and constructive examination of an organisational structure of a company, institution, or branch of government, or of any component thereof, such as a division or department, and its plans and objectives, its methods of control, its means of operations, and its use of human and physical facilities."[1]

2. *H. Washbrook,* "The total examination of an organisation or part of it, include checks on the effectiveness of managers, their compliance with company or professional standards, the reliability of management data, the quality of performance of duties, and recommendations for improvement. These are variously termed as management audits, administrative audits, operations audits, or management and administrations audits."[2] He further stated that

---

1. Leonard William, P., *The Management Audit : An Appraisal of Management Methods and Performance,* Prentice Hall Inc. Englewood Cliffs, p. 35.
2. Washbrook H., *The Board and Management Audit*, Business Books Ltd., London, p.4.

"Management and Administration audit is an independent assessment of the soundness of the business unit and its ability to face the business problems of the future."[3]

3. *American Institute of Management,* "Management Auditing is a diagnostic appraisal process for analysing goals, plans, policies and activities in every phase of operation to turnover unsuspected weaknesses and to develop ideas for improvement in areas that has escaped management attention."[4]

4. *William F. Kelly,* "A management audit is a critical review of an organisational structure and administration. Its purpose is making recommendation for adjustment and improvement. An audit may involve a whole company structure or be restricted to one of its parts such as division or department."[5]

5. *Leslie R. Howard:* "The management audit may be more specifically defined as being an investigation of a business from the highest level downwards in order to ascertain whether sound management prevails throughout, thus facilitating the most effective relationship with the outside world and the most efficient organisation and smooth running internally."[6]

6. *Federal Financial Officer's Institute, Canada* . "A systematic independent appraisal activity within an organisation for a review of the entire departmental operations a service to management. The overall objective of operational auditing is to assist all levels of management in the effective discharge of their responsibilities by furnishing them with objective analyses, appraisals, recommendations and pertinent comments concerning the activities reviewed."[7]

7. *Michael Stephen R.* "The business counterpart of human physical examination is the management audit. In many ways, it is like a financial audit in which the financial operations of the company are tested against commonly accepted standards and practices. In the same way, Management Audit is an examination of the administrative operations and organisational arrangements of a company using commonly accepted standards of good management for evaluation."[8]

8. *Roy A. Lindberg and Theodore Cohn.* It is a "technique for regularly and systematically appraising units or function effectiveness against corporate

---

3. *Ibid,* p.5.
4. Paul Mali, *Improving Total Productivity* (The Management Audit, American Institute of Management, New York, 1966), John Wiley & Sons, New York, p. 134.
5. William F. Kelly, *Management Through Systems and Procedures,* John Wiley & Sons, New York, 1969.
6. Leslie R. Howard, *Taylor and Perry's Principles of Auditing,* p. 356.
7. Quoted in Kamal Gupta, *Contemporary Auditing,* Tata McGraw-Hill, Delhi, p. 324.
8. Michael Stephen R., *Appraising Management Practices and Performance,* Prentice-Hall, p. 23.

and industry standards by utilizing personnel who are not specialists in the area of study with the objectives of assuring a given management that its aims are being carried out and/or identifying conditions capable of being improved."[9]

Characteristics

1. It involves comprehensive examination of organisation or part thereof.
2. It is undertaken to check the operations of management and its effectiveness.
3. Such checking or examination has to be based on commonly accepted company or professional standards which are objective in nature.
4. Such examination is to be carried on independently by experts in the area.
5. It involves analysing goals, policies and activities in every phase of management operation.
6. The objective of such examination is to see whether operations of the management are being carried on in accordance with its plans or objectives or not.
7. It seeks to identify its weaknesses, if any, and suggest suitable measures and give recommendations to bring about necessary improvements so that overall improvement may take place and the management may be able to face or tackle any business problem in future effectively.

REASONS FOR MANAGEMENT AUDIT

1. *Improvement of Performance*. It helps in improvement of performance of the various managers as independent experts offer valuable and constructive suggestions for their improvement. The general manager or the managing director is not in a position to make such objective study and analysis independently, as he is too much involved in the organisation itself.

2. *Size and Complexity of Organisation.* The size and complexity of organisation is increasing day by day and often it is not possible to make such studies and find out the weaknesses or shortcomings leading to inefficient performance.

3. *Incentives.* Review of the performance of managers may become necessary when the management desires to provide some sort of incentives and link the same with performance.

4. *Improvement..* Such audit is necessary in case of sick, inefficient or less productive business units in able to give them benefits of the experts' opinion for bringing necessary improvements and efficiency.

9. Roy A. Lindberg and Theodore Cohn, *Operations Auditing,* American Management Association, New York, p. 9.

5. *Government's requirement..* The Government is often forced to undertake the management audit with a view to find out weaknesses and inefficiencies of the management. This has often become necessary in a country like India.

6. *Need of Financial Institutions.* The financial institutions and banks may require such management audit to be undertaken when they are either willing to lend huge funds to a concern or when they want to review the progress of the concern whom funds have already been given.

7. *Need of Foreign Collaborators.* Foreign collaborators of often undertake management audit periodically to assess the progress and performance of management of the concern with whom collaboration has been undertaken. They might be interested in seeing that their investment is being fully utilised and there is no wastage.

8. *Need of Public Enterprises.* There is growing need for undertaking management audit in case of public enterprises in India, specially where the management has been following bureaucratic approach and emphasis might be on following the rules and procedures rather than on achievement and results. They have to be suggested to change their outlook and improve the overall efficiency of the enterprises concerned.

9. *Defects of Managerial Operations.* The management audit may be necessary to reveal the defects or irregularities in the managerial operations. It has been rightly pointed that it is necessary to "determine actual and potential trouble-spots, deficiencies, bottlenecks, unsound performance, poor cooperation, irregularities, shortcomings, errors, failings, defalcations, excessive wastes, unnecessary losses, internal friction between executives and general lack of knowledge or disregard for good organisation."

10. *Greater Efficiency on Less Costs.* The management audit is needed to search better and improve methods and performance with a view to obtain greater efficiency, to reduce costs and to find better way of doing things.

MANAGEMENT AUDIT V/S STATUTORY FINANCIAL AUDIT

1. *Purpose.* While the purpose of management audit is to review the management operations with a view to bring about necessary improvements, the purpose of financial audit is to find out whether the accounts present true and fair financial state of affairs of the concern.

2. *Nature.* While the management audit is a preventive as well as curative check, the financial audit is a *post-mortem* examination. The former is evaluative and suggestive whereas the latter is verificatory in nature.

3. *Basis.* While the management audit is based on financial as well as non-financial data derived from internal and external sources, in financial audit, only financial data from internal sources are used for the purpose of examination.

4. *Statutory Provision.* While there is no statutory provision for undertaking the management audit, and it is not legally compulsory but discretionary financial audit is legally compulsory and legal rules and regulations have to be observed for that.

5. *Qualification.* While there is no prescribed qualification for the management auditor and any expert on the management may be asked to undertake it, in financial audit, it can be undertaken by the chartered accountants only. The former requires inter-discipline expertise whereas the latter requires accounting expertise.

6. *Process.* While management auditor examines the managerial activities and operations and adopts operations management technique for the purpose, the financial audit examines financial accounts, statements and schedules and generally accepted audit techniques are applied for the purpose.

7. *Norms for Evaluation.* While in case of management audit, the generally accepted management standards or norms are used for the purpose of evaluation and examination, in case of the financial audit, the principles, conventions and postulates are used as norms.

8. *Precision.* While in case of management audit, only relative precision is necessary, in case of financial audit, absolute precision is quite necessary.

9. *Area of Study.* While in management audit the study may be related to the entire organisation or part of it only in the financial audit, it is necessary to examine the accounts of the entire organisation.

10. *Periodicity.* While there is no fixed period for which the management audit has to be undertaken in financial audit, it has to be undertaken every year.

11. *Reporting.* While the management auditor is appointed by the management and hence, the report has to be submitted to the management only. In case of financial audit, the report has to be submitted to the shareholders, who appoint the auditor.

12. *Format and Use of Report.* While there is no set or standard form in which the management auditor has to submit the report and his report is mainly useful to management, the report of the financial audit has to be submitted in the standard or prescribed form and is mainly useful to the shareholders.

13. *Liability.* While the management auditor cannot be held criminally liable the financial auditor can be held criminally liable under the Companies Act, 1956.

APPROACH OF MANAGEMENT AUDIT

William L. Campfield has suggested the following three important approaches to the management auditing:

1. *Studying the Prescribed Organisation.* The management auditor has to review the formal organisation structure, personnel inter-relationship, policies, procedures, information systems and flows, and the decision centres in order to determine what management has established as optimum arrangements for running an entity.

2. *Evaluating the "Live Entity".* The management auditor has to review as to : what the operating people are really performing. How they are trying to accomplish various objectives set for them? What schedules and routines they have set to attain the given aims ? He has also to measure the results of their operations on the basis of establishment norms.

3. *Searching for Profit Inhibitors.* The management auditor has to examine and search for various obstacles which are on the way to better performance and more profits. He has to uncover the weaknesses in the organisational structure and responsibility assignments; breakdown in operations, programming and work flow, inadequate or ineffective communications, evaluation and measurement, and disclosing the results that are below the established standards.

BENEFITS OF MANAGEMENT AUDITING

William L. Campfield has suggested that the management auditor is helpful in the following main areas :

1. *Plans.* He can assist in establishing and reviewing the system of planning in the organisation. After reviewing the system of planning, he can assist in developing orderly planning system, allocating responsibility for planning. He can also help in reviewing the progress of planning and evaluate its effectiveness against accepted standards.

2. *Decision-making.* The management auditor may help in reviewing the mechanism of decision-making and find out whether sufficient information is available to the management for the purpose. He would help the management to bring about more objectivity in decision-making.

3. *Authority Structure.* The management auditor may help the management in proper designing of the authority structure including rendering assistance in strengthening and expending the flow of information between the responsibility centres.

4. *Effective Communication.* He can assist the management in establishment of effective communication network and bring about necessary improvement in this regard.

5. *Results Measurement.* The management auditor may assist the management in establishing acceptable standards to judge the results and pinpoint the key areas or functions in the profit-making process. He may also point out the inhibiting factors and the ways to remove them so that the results may improve.

6. *Overall improvement.* The management auditor may suggest suitable constructive measures to the management so that desirable change may be brought about. This would ultimately bring about better efficiency and overall improvement in the results obtained.

7. *Developing Human Resources.* In every organisation, it is the human resources which is quite crucial and important and sufficient measures must be taken to develop people. The management audit helps in improving the performance appraisal system and helps developing human resources.

8. *Relieves Pressure on Management.* The important job of review and appraisal is undertaken by the management auditor and the management is relieved of the pressure and thus it may give more attention to other important and special matters.

9. *Specialised Service to Management.* The nature of management audit is such that it offers a very specialised service to the management. "This service is designed to determine potential danger spots or conversely to highlight possible favourable opportunities to reduce and control costs ; to eliminate waste and unnecessary losses, to observe the performance and to evaluate the effectiveness of controls ; to assure management that company policies and procedures are complied with ; to have a check on overall plans and objectives of the enterprise, to provide management with better and more effective systems of recording and improve method of communication ; to study ideas, new developments and new types of equipment ; and to determine whether or not the business is operating as profitably as it should be and providing the society the desired benefits."

LIMITATIONS OF MANAGEMENT AUDIT

1. *Irregular.* The management audit is not undertaken regularly. Hence, it may not bring necessary improvements in the interval period.

2. *Lack of Expert Knowledge.* While the management audit is a highly complex job which requires inter-disciplinary knowledge and specialised skill on the part of such auditor, in practice, it is difficult to get competent and expert personnel to undertake such audit.

3. *Costly.* As the management audit is a very costly affair all business firms cannot afford it.

4. *Lack of Intensive Study.* As it is not possible to undertake intensive study of all the managerial operation, hence, the results obtained may not be very reliable.

5. *Degree of Independence.* The management auditor may not quite independent in the review and examination of the operations of the management audit. In practice, he may not be a position to assess the competence of other managers independently.

6. *Lack of Suitable Standards.* It is quite necessary to develop suitable acceptable standard for objective assessment. As it is not an easy task to develop such standards and with the result, the conclusions arrived at may not be acceptable.

7. *Controversy about Suggestions.* It is controversial whether the management auditor should give suggestions or recommendations to bring about changes. *Bradford Cadmus* has stated that "unless the auditor is assigned this project as a special study, he is not in a position to make definite recommendations as to change. His primary responsibility is fulfilled when he has brought the results of the policy to attention through his report— which should present the facts in such manner that the situation may not be overlooked or dismissed without adequate review at a appropriate management level."

8. *Ineffective recommendations.* The recommendations of Management Auditor may be given casually or carelessly. In that case, the desired results may not be obtained.

9. *Improper Implementation.* The job of the management auditor is over after submitting the report to the management. Its very objective may be jeopardise of the management does not implement the recommendations effectively.

10. *Competence Judgement Difficult.* The management auditor has to see how competently the management is getting the plans executed and implementing controls. In practice, it has been found that individual competence is not judged properly. In a study it was pointed that "a large majority of accountants interviewed said that their firms either made no recommendations on the competence of personnel or they did not commit such evaluations to paper. There was a strong feeling that a lack of management competence could best be pointed out indirectly."

SCOPE OF MANAGEMENT AUDIT

1. Review of objectives, goals, plans, and policies.
2. Appraisal of planning.
3. Review of organisational structure, particularly the job content, the grouping of jobs and assignment of authorities and responsibilities.
4. Review of systems and procedures of the organisation, such as rules, regulations and methods etc.
5. Review of office operations.
6. Review of management control systems, which may be direct or indirect or quantitative or non-quantitative.
7. Review of purchasing operations.
8. Review of manufacturing operations.
9. Review of selling and distribution systems.
10. Review of personnel policies.
11. Review of management information system.
12. Appraisal of physical processes and activities.
13. Appraisal of management decisions.

14. Appraisal of utilisation of financial, material and human resources.
15. Review of the results of various operations.

PRELIMINARIES IN MANAGEMENT AUDIT PROGRAMME

1. *Scope of audit.* The management auditor should discuss the scope of the audit with his employers. It must be determined keeping in mind the terms of appointment. He should finalise whether the operations of entire organisation are to be audited or one part/few parts only. He should decide whether the audit of systems in operation, utilisation of human and financial resources, all or a few of the functional management areas are to be covered.

2. *Discussion with the Management.* The management auditor would thoroughly discuss various issues related to the audit such about its cost, nature and results, participation and cooperation from the employees, duration, frequency of audit work, place of audit etc.

3. *Knowledge of Technical Aspects.* Before he actually starts the audit work the management auditor should try to familiarise with various technical matters of the unit which he is going to audit and which will affect his audit work.

4. *Recruitment and Training of Audit Personnel.* According to the requirements of the audit concerned, the management auditors will have to determine the type and skill of audit personnel required for the purpose. While describing the qualities required in a management auditor, *Francis C. Dykman* has rightly stated that "In order to analyse the information developed, the auditor must have a broad background of knowledge. This should include not only accounting principles and auditing techniques, but knowledge of organisation principles, budgeting and forecasting methods, office equipment, data processing equipment including computers, inventory control methods, statistics, compensation methods, work measurement, production scheduling, sales, and purchasing methods. He must have the ability to bring this knowledge to the problems he is investigating, not necessarily in an attempt to develop improved solutions, methods, or procedures, but with a sufficient level of understanding to identify areas where, with more intensive study and other technical support he can assist management in its search for improved methods. The auditor may then guide and assist line management in implementing the agreed-upon programme." He should then, determine the size and sources of audit personnel. Arrangement for their training is also quite essential if they are not properly trained. They should be thoroughly trained about the various aspects of management audit so that they may take up such audit with proper skill and ability.

QUALITIES OF MANAGEMENT AUDIT PROGRAMME

1. It should be objective.
2. It should be logical and flexible.

3. It should be clear, simple and easily understandable.
4. The object of such audit should be clearly outlined.
5. It should incorporate the various methods to be adopted for the purpose of audit.
6. It should have proper time schedule in which the audit work is to be completed.
7. It should mention the duties and responsibilities of audit personnel.
8. It should also lay down the responsibilities of the persons cooperating with the audit personnel.
9. It should not only contain the limits of time but also the limits of such audit.
10. There should be provision for the preparation and submission of the interim report.
11. It should contain the list of persons to be consulted for the purpose.

About the importance of management audit programme, *Stephen R. Michael* has very rightly pointed that "It is a statement of future action stating the purpose of the activities, what will be done, how things will be done, when activities will take place, who is responsible for the activities and who will participate."

PROCESS OF MANAGEMENT AUDIT

1. Review of Management Systems and Processes

(i) *Review of Objectives.* About objectives the management auditor will have to review whether the objectives have been clearly defined and stated in writing clearly, whether the objectives have been stated in quantitative terms and the targets have been formulated on that basis, whether the objectives are revised with the various changes which might have taken place, whether the goals, policies and sub-policies have been formulated on the basis of the objectives set for the concern.

(ii) *Review of Planning.* The management auditor has to review the system of planning as a whole and see whether there is any room for improvement in the same, whether the concern has carefully formulated the long range, and short range planning, keeping in view the objectives of the concern, whether the planning is financialised with active cooperation of the various persons at different levels concerned or not, what is the flexibility in planning, to what extent the changes in the planning has been made with the change in the circumstances, how are the plans translated quantitatively in terms of budget, in what manner the budget is formulated and how are the various budget estimates estimated, are they based on authentic information and data or not, whether the timing of budget formulation and communication to various operational managers is properly adhered to whether the various personnels involved are faithfully observing the various budget targets, to what extent the budget is flexible, and does the concern adopt flexible budgeting ?

(iii) *Review of Organisation.* The management auditor will have to review the managerial philosophy behind the organisational structure. He has to see to what extent that philosophy has been translated in practice. Whether the organisation structure of the concern is properly defined or not, on the basis of principles of organisation. He will have to see whether the levels of hierarchy are properly defined. Whether the lines of authorities are quite clear. He will have to see whether there is a unity of command and span of supervision well within the limit. He has to review the superior-subordinate relationship and see what improvement can be brought about in this area.

(iv) ***Review of Control Systems.*** The management auditor has to analyse the system of control to see to what extent the internal check and internal control system are effective. Weak points have to be identified and suggestions for improvement have to be given properly. He may review the internal control system with the help of well-formulated questionnaires, interviews with the related personnel, personal observation, and the flow chart. He has to see whether the control is duly related to the plan the basic philosophy of control which the concern is adopting and the extent to which it has been actually translated in practice. He has to review various methods of control adopted at different levels for different activities to find out the system of monitoring adopted in the concern. He are to find out whether the control systems clearly bring about the result after proper comparison of the planned data with the actual data and whether the variances are being properly worked out and reported. He has to see whether the control system is duly acceptable to the various persons involved or not. He has to find out the system of reward and punishment and see how effectively it is being enforced in the concern.

2. Review of Management Functions

Following are the important managerial functions which have to be reviewed by the management auditor:

(i) Production.

ii) Selling and Distribution.

(iii) Personnel and Industrial Relations.

(iv) Accounting and Finance.

(v) Legal, Secretarial and Administrative.

(vi) Research and Development.

(vii) General Management.

Let us discuss them briefly one by one.

(i) *Review of Production Function*

The management auditor has to examine following main aspects related to it reviewing the production function:

(a) Building and Layout;

(b) Buying process;

(c) Production Planning process;

(d) Production process;

(e) Storage and Inspection;

(f) Production Control Techniques;

(g) Quality Control.

(a) ***Building and Layout.*** The management auditor has to see whether the building and layout designed are used efficiently and effectively. He has to see to what extent the floor available is utilised and whether there is proper ventilation, lighting, heating and safety arrangements. He has to review the layout with the help of Process Flow Diagram, Machine Data Card and Scale Model Layout of the manufacturing process. If there is any lacuna he should properly note it and give suggestions for its improvement. He should also work out the cost involved in bringing about any change in the layout.

(b) ***Buying Process.*** The management auditor has to review the purchase policy thoroughly and point out the need for improvement in it. He has to see whether the policy is in accordance with the objectives set for the concern. He has to study whether the purchase department has been properly organised or not. He has to study the duties and responsibilities of the purchase officer. He has to review the system of determining the quantity level and whether that is determined on the scientific lines or not, the cost involved in it and the purchase procedure. He has to see that goods are purchased in the right quantities, at right time and at right price. He has to pay special attention to the order quantity so that only right quantity of goods is purchased, has to and to the storage system and procedure the system of issue from the stores. He should pay special attention to the following points:

(i) Purchase authorisation ;

(ii) Purchase requisition ;

(iii) Review of comparative statement ;

(iv) Review of purchase order ;

(v) Review of inspecting and testing of goods ;

(vi) Review of accounting procedure involved ;

(vii) Review of improvement, if any.

(c) ***Production Planning Process.*** The management auditor has to review the production planning process and see that an effective system has been evolved for the purpose. He has to examine whether some kind of link exists between the receipt of order and the despatch of goods. He has to review the past performance in this regard and make out a chart for the purpose to arrive at the conclusion whether the planning work is adequate or insufficient.

(d) *Review of Production Process.* The management auditor has to review the methods of production adopted in the organisation concerned such as Job Manufacturing Method, Process Manufacturing Method, Specialised Manufacturing Method or a combination of two or more methods. He has to see whether the method adopted for the production is alright. He has to review the manufacturing process which may be : Synthetic, Analytic, Conditioning or Extractive. In practice, one or more processes of production may be adopted in accordance with the needs and nature of organisation concerned. The auditor has to review the process and see whether there is any room for improvement. He has to examine whether the production is carried on with the minimum possible cost and, what changes can be brought to achieve this objective and minimise the wastes. He has to properly examine the process records to find out its strength and weaknesses. He has to satisfy himself whether the process of passing the materials from the raw state to the finished state is being carried on efficiently and with the lowest possible cost. In this review he may take the help of the technical persons, if required.

(e) *Review of Storage and Inspection.* The management auditor has to pay special attention to the following : (i) handling method inside stores; (ii) the method adopted for issuing material; and pricing of the material issues; (iii) the method adopted for recording and placing of returned materials; (iv) the method of stock-taking from time to time or perpetually; (v) the security of the goods in the store. For the purposes of inspection, he has to see the independence of the chief of the inspection department from the process department. He has to see the system of inspection and find out its effectiveness. He has to see whether the inspection is effectively carried on from the receipt of the material to the despatch of finished goods.

(f) *Review of Production Control techniques.* There are four important and recognised techniques of production control: Routing; Scheduling; Despatching; and follow up. The management auditor has to see how effectively these techniques are adopted to control the production process at minimum possible cost and acceptable quality. If the control technique not being adopted effectively, the cost of production is bound to increase. The auditor should examine it carefully and suggest measures to bring necessary improvements in the area.

(g) *Review of Quality Control.* The management auditor should see whether the quality standards have been fixed. How the quality deviations are ascertained and recorded ? What measures are taken to control such deviations ? What is the system of separation of defective goods from the quality goods ? Whether the continuous evaluation is being undertaken and necessary corrective actions are taken in the light of that. He has to see whether the goods produced are suitable for their purpose.

3. Review of Selling and Distribution

The purpose of management audit is "determining what is being done, apparaising what is being done, and recommending what should be done in the bear future." In the words of *Kotler* it is "an independent examination of the entire marketing efforts of a company, or some specific marketing activity, covering objectives, programme, implementation, and organisation." Thus, it involves review of following items:

(i) *Sales Policy and Planning.* The management auditor has to review the sales policy to find out whether the policy is conducive to the attainment of the objective and whether it is helpful in improving the sales. He has to analyse the policies regarding organisation, recruitment, training, remuneration of the sales force, fixing of quota, divisionalisation, grant of discount, sales campaign etc. He has to review the sales planning system methodology and see how far the plans formulated are duly implemented in practice. If the sales policies and plans are defective, it will not be possible to attain the objectives.

(ii) *Sales Organisation.* The management auditor has to review the sales organisation and see whether it is effective enough to attain the sales objective. He has to see whether there is any responsible officer to look after the sales and whether he has been assigned proper authority commensurate with his responsibilities. The sales organisation structure, proper coordination between the various sections concerned need for restructuring the organisation, have to be reviewed because only effective organisation can bring about the desired results.

(iii) *Publicity.* As, it is necessary to undertake advertisement campaign to push the sales in the competitive market, the management auditor has to see whether adequate budget has been provided for the purpose. He has to examine whether the amount actually spent on it is giving adequate result. He has to make constructive suggestions to improve the situation.

(iv) *Review of Sales Records.* The management auditor has to review sales records for a few years to find out the real position. He has to review the current records to see the result of the efforts made in this direction. He has to see whether adequate and proper records have been maintained. Based on ratio analysis and other techniques the records should be thoroughly reviewed to arrive at the conclusions.

(v) *Price Fixation.* The management auditor has to review the prince fixation policy and see that it has been adopted on a scientific line. He has to see whether due care and thinking is undertaken before the price is fixed. He has to examine the price fixation on the basis of cost of production, purchasing power of the consumers, sales at different price levels, the degree and nature of competition etc. and give proper suggestions for improvement in the system and policy of price fixation.

(vi) *Packing.* The management auditor has to examine the packing policy and practice of the organisation concerned. He has to see whether the packing is undertaken to protect the product concerned and is in accordance with the tastes and requirements of the consumers. The packing should quite attractive and protective besides being at reasonable cost.

(vii) *After Sales Service.* The management auditor has to see whether the concern is providing after sales service or whether the sales are affected for not providing efficient after sales service. If it is so, he has to suggest to take up this issue seriously.

(viii) *Sales Control.* The management auditor has to examine the various sales control measures adopted by the concern. He has to find out potency of the monitoring and reporting system. If the budgeted sales have been fixed, he has to compare it with the actual sales and find out the reasons for deviations, if any. He has to find out who is responsible for it and how effectively he is controlling the sales. He has to work out various related ratios and see whether they show favourable or unfavourable results. If they are unfavourable, he has to find out the factors for the same. If these factors are uncontrollable, he cannot do anything, but if they are controllable, he has to find out the facts and make constructive suggestions to improve the situation.

4. Review of Personnel and Industrial Relations

Every management auditor has to review systematically all the policies and activities of the personnel programme and the manner in which these activities are really undertaken in a firm. In this connection, *Dale Yoder* has suggested "Result Audit, Procedural Audit and Policy Audit." Thus the auditor has to review the results, procedures, and the policies related to the personnel of the concern. He has to review various aspects, such as, personnel department, selection policy and procedures, training, time recording and work load, wages, performance, appraisal, working conditions, morale and motivation, labour turnover, labour welfare, and labour relations.

(i) *Review of Personnel Department.* The management auditor has to review the organisation of the department and see whether it is manned by competent and experienced personnel manager assisted by well-trained employees. He has to scrutinise the authority and responsibility of the employees.

(ii) *Selection.* The management auditor has to review the selection policy and procedure and find out how far it is effective. He has to examine the selection procedure and see whether it is suitable for needs of the concern. He has to see whether right type of persons with reasonable salary are appointed.

(iii) *Training.* The management auditor has to examine the training policy and system adopted by the concern, the suitability of the training procedure and whether that is effectively implemented. He has to help in training the employees properly. He has to review the cost of training and find out whether the budget allocated for the purpose is adequate. Thus, the training policies and programmes should be thoroughly reviewed and proper suggestions should be given to bring about necessary improvement.

(iv) *Review of Time Recording and Work-load.* The management auditor has to examine the system of time recording of arrival of the employees. It should he made correctly and there should he no possibility of any mistake in such records. He has to see that correct record is maintained for those who come late and also for those who move out during the working hours. He has to review the method of deciding the workload of the employees, and see that there is neither over-staffing nor under-staffing. He has to see that the work is entrusted to those who are capable of doing it more efficiently.

(v) *Wages.* The management auditor has to review the wage policy, programmes, and method of wage payment properly as wages form an important part of the total cost. He has to examine the wage policy keeping in mind the equity, simplicity, economy, practicability and permanence etc. He has to see that the wage policy is being implemented properly. He has to see that the employees get their wages regularly and timely and do not have grievances against the wage payment.

(vi) *Performance Appraisal.* The management auditor has to examine whether the method adopted for performance appraisal is satisfactory. He has to see that method is adopted properly and the promotion or system of reward or punishment is properly based on the performance appraisal.

(vii) *Working Conditions.* The management auditor has to see that the working condition is congenial and suitable. If it is not so he has to find out its weaknesses and give constructive suggestions for amelioration.

(viii) *Morale and Motivation.* The management auditor has to see that the employees morale is up to the mark. He has to suggest the ways, on which management may motivate them for working more efficiently. He has to find out if there is excessive absenteeism, tardiness, labour turnover, slow pace of work, fall in the quality of work or the increase in the accidents etc. He has to analyse the reasons for the same and give constructive suggestions for their amelioration.

(ix) *Labour Turnover.* If, the labour turnover is more than reasonable, the management auditor should find out the reasons for the same.

(x) *Labour Welfare.* The management auditor has to see that welfare measures are taken by the management as a happier and more contented labour class is an asset to the organisation that is adequate or not and the workers are statisfied or not with them.

(xi) *Labour Relations.* The management auditor has to review the state of industrial relations prevailing in the organisation with the help of the number of strikes, go-slow measures, lockouts and number of man days lost etc. He has to analyse the causes of disputes and see whether these can be prevented by adopting certain measures. He has to suggest the management to adopt those measures to bring about lasting peace and higher production and profits.

5. Review of Accounting and Finance

The management auditor has to review the accounting and finance to see that they are playing the desired role in the organisation. His main objective is "to provide economic information for decision making at the various levels of management, to account for assets and liabilities and to manage the sources and application of funds." He has to see that the accounting system is efficient and is able to provide the necessary information timely and correctly. He has to review the cost accounting procedure and see that proper cost standards have been fixed and they are effectively used for the control purpose. He has to analyse the internal check, internal audit and internal control systems and find out their effectiveness. He has to see that the statutory audit is undertaken properly and the auditor is aware of his duties. He has to find out the relationship between the internal auditor and the statutory auditor and see that the statutory auditor has been appointed in accordance with the legal provisions and he has been able to discharge his duties well. He has to see that the estimation of long term capital and working capital is undertaken properly. He has to review the sources of capital and also the cost of capital. He has to review the budgeting and reporting system and see that the higher management receives the periodical reports properly and timely. He has to work out various financial ratios and ascertain the degree of efficiency with which the operations are carried on as compared to similar concern. He has to review the manual and flow chart system and find out their efficacy.

6. Review of Secretarial and Administrative Function

The management auditor has to review the various rules and regulations of administration and find out to what extent they are followed. He has to review the degree to which the various provisions of related laws are observed, such as Companies Act, 1956, Factories Act, 1948 etc. He has to examine the organisation structure of administrative office and its strength and weaknesses. He has to see that the secretarial work is being discharged by the secretary and its secretariat effectively. He has to examine the arrangement of filing etc. also. He has to review the arrangements of the meetings and see that the directors and shareholders meet frequently and the minutes are properly recorded. He has to review the various secretarial and administrative functions adopted by a concern.

7. Review of Research and Development

The management auditor has to see that the top managers are taking sufficient interest in this regard and adequate budget is approved for the purpose. He has to review the experimental development of new products and improvement of the existing products. He has to analyse the efforts made and expenditures incurred on product development and market or marketing research. The auditor has to see the effectiveness with which the research activities are being undertaken by those who are involved in it.

8. Review of General Management

The management auditor has to see that the top management is able to discharge its functions effectively. It should be engaged on the more important activities or engrossed unnecessarily on details. He has to review the process of decision making adopted by the higher level management and assets the objectivity with which these decisions are taken. He has to examine the reporting system for the internal as well as external matters undertaken effectively. The top management should be able to see the results at a glance and then provide effective leadership to others. The management auditor should satisfy himself as to what is submitted to the top management is really adequate. His reports should show the following items to the management:

(i) The activity of the business, Indicated by the orders received, the invoice issued, the orders outstanding etc.

(ii) The efficiency of the business indicated by the personnel data, the product cost, the equipment data, the data relating to development work etc.

(iii) The profitability of the business, indicated by the details set out in the profit and loss account of the concern.

(iv) The security of the business, indicated by the cash for cost and ratios based on balance sheet data.

The management auditor has to see whether the targets fixed by the top management are being timely and effectively achieved and to the efforts made for the cost control and cost reduction are sufficient. He has to review, the entire operations of the concern and assess efficiency of the management on the whole.

THE REPORT

After having reviewed the various management functions and general administration of organisation concerned, the management auditor has to submit his report, precise as well as concise, to pinpoint the strength and weaknesses of the organisation. He should clearly mention the practicable as well as the constructive suggestions to bring about the necessary improvements in the performance of the organisation concerned.

SPECIMEN OF REPORT [10]

To the Audit Committee of the Board of Directors and the Stockholders of XYZ Manufacturing Corporation:

We have investigated the management of XYZ Manufacturing Corporation for the year ended December 31, 1970. In carrying out our investigation, we focused on the following areas : the organizational structure of the company; the information system of managerial controls and procedures; and the managerial plans policies, and goals for the year under investigation. Our investigation did not include managerial forecasts of earnings and cash flows, or the projected results of planned projects, operations, and financial position in future years.

In conducting our investigation and evaluating managerial performance, we used objective research procedures and available standards, both absolute and comparative, which we considered necessary and appropriate in the circumstances.

In our judgement, XYZ Manufacturing Corporation was managed with reasonable efficiency during the year ended December 31, 1970, judged in the light of our findings and the circumstances in which the company operated during that year.

Your attention is called to the report on our examination of the financial statements of the company for the year ended December 31, 1970, on page 10 of this annual report.

A summary of the major findings of our investigation follows. First, the systems of informational, financial, and operational controls and procedures were found to be well established and working on a basis consistent with the organizational structure of the company. There were good relationships among the various levels of management, and the management personnel displayed mutual respect and empathy in their work. There was convincing evidence of satisfactory degree of motivation at all levels of management.

Second, the plans, policies, and goals of management for the year were evaluated and found to be reasonable and attainable. The organizational structure fostered the attainment of the goals, while the plans and policies were found to be efficiently designed and implemented.

Third, the most important opportunity for improving management was found in the areas of the information system. We found several cases in which information communicated from lower supervisory levels was either incomplete, irrelevant or so classified and summarized that it did not provide an adequate basis for decision making. As a result, additional costs were incurred to obtain adequate information, decisions were often delayed, and faulty decisions were

10. Extracted from Robertson, J.C., *Auditing*, Business Publication Inc, Dallas, p. 692.

made. We have provided management with a detailed description of this deficiency, a list of the actions we recommend to overcome it, and have been assured that they will be implemented immediately.

It will be understood that our firm assumes no responsibility for the activities of the management of the company or the results of such activities.

A B & Company

POSITION OF MANAGEMENT AUDITOR

1. Appointment. As the management audit is not prescribed by the law, a company is required to take its own decision in respect of selection and appointment of management auditor. The Directors on behalf of the shareholders can ask the firm of a Chartered Accountant or Cost Accountant to undertake the management audit of the firm.

2. Removal. The termination of the professional services of a management auditor can be done by the Board of Directors or by the shareholders. A proper notice is required to be served and explanatory statement must be submitted and circulated amongst the members to this effect. A resolution requiring special notice shall have to be passed in the members' meeting. The requiring special notice should be passed by 75 percent majority of the members present and voting in favour of the resolution. Thus, the management Auditor can be replaced.

3. Remuneration. While the rules prescribed under the Companies Act applicable on Financial Auditor and on Cost Auditor should be equated with the Management Auditor, certain variations in terms can be made, because it is a contractual agreement for a period of 3 to 5 years. It will always be in the interest of the undertaking to enter into specific contract with the Management Auditor in respect of the remuneration so that the undertaking can get the fruitful results of the advices of the Management Auditor and in turn the Management Auditor should also put in his professional talents for the betterment of the undertaking.

4. Qualifications. No particular qualification is prescribed for the management auditor but some important attributes should be possessed by him before he proceeds to the required investigation in the course and process of management audit. These justify the work of management auditor who improves the business both in its external and internal conditions.

5. Duties

(i) To verify statement of production.

(ii) To conduct enquiry.

(iii) To examine documents and records.

(iv) To confirm or cross-check the supplied information.

(v) To observe pertinent activities and conditions.

(vi) To correlate information.

(vii) To make comparisons.

(viii) To make an appraisal of these objectives.

(ix) To review the process of management by making appraisal of important activities.

(x) To be honest and faithful towards the concern.

(xi) To submit audit report.

(xii) To edit and review the audit report.

6. Rights

(i) To examine the records, books and various statutory books.

(ii) To claim his remuneration.

(iii) To make timely appraisal of various managerial policies and to review them.

(iv) To obtain statements with a view to verify and confirm the information.

(v) To adopt and use a number of techniques of verification audit.

(vi) To prepare and sign the audit report.

QUESTIONS FOR EXERCISE

1. Define management audit and distinguish clearly between management audit and financial audit.
2. What do you understand by management audit ? Discuss the benefits and limitations of management auditing.
3. "The importance of management audit is increasing in the competitive business world today." Explain this statement and discuss the need for management audit.
4. Discuss the importance and main features of a management audit programme.
5. As a management auditor, how would you review the production, accounting and finance of a large company ?
6. Explain briefly the various processes of management audit.
7. How would you, as a management auditor, review the management systems and procedures ?
8. "Reviewing personnel and industrial relations is not an easy task." Explain this statement and discuss how would you, as a management auditor, review the personnel and industrial relations of a company.

9. "The deficiencies of financial audit has led to the growth of management audit." Critically examine this statement.

10. Give essentials of a good purchase procedure. How would you review its efficiency ?

11. How would you, as management, auditor, examine that control over the receipt, inspecting and testing of goods is satisfactory ?

12. Write short notes on:

    (a) R & D audit

    (b) Scope of management audit.

    (c) Limitations of management audit.

    (d) Specimen of management audit report.

13. Discuss the various provisions with regard to the appointment, remuneration and rights and duties of a management auditor.

26

Auditing of Mechanised or Computerised Accounts

These days, due to many recent inventions, accounting in becoming more and more mechanised and computerised.

TYPES OF MECHANISED AND COMPUTERISED SYSTEMS

1. Accounting Machines. A ledger posting machine can perform a large number of accounting operations such as adding, subtracting, preparation of cash receipts, debtor's ledger cards, sales ledger etc. A transaction can be recorded at many places in a single operation on a specially designed continuous stationary through the use of this machine. Invoicing machine is capable of summarising and consolidating the figures. A ledger posting machine prepares a ledger card and a statement simultaneously which can be detached and sent to a customer. It is also used to prepare a control sheet.

2. Punch-card Installations. Punch card machines help in analysing voluminous data quickly and from various points of views. Each transaction is recorded on a separate punch-card punched at various places. A qualified verifier checks the correctness of punches. After a transaction is properly recorded on the punch card, the rest of the work can be done by machine. Punch-card installations are electro-mechanical in nature. Various machines are used to carryout sorting, punching, tabulations, verification and calculations.

3. Computers. Computers are used in keeping accounting and other records of business as well as for decision making and managerial purposes. It requires that a proper computer programme should be drawn up before any job may be performed on it. In order to obtain the correct results specific, clear and detailed instructions should be fed to the computer. The computer cannot work without it.

Various components of a computer can be classified as follows :

(i) Input devices

(ii) Storage devices

(iii) Control devices

(iv) Output devices

(i) *Input Devices.* These are the devices through which data are fed into the computer for example, punch-cards, paper tapes and magnetic tapes are input devices for feeding the computer.

(ii) *Storage Devices.* These devices provide memory to the computer Magnetic tapes, magnetic discs or magnetic drums store the data in such a way that they can reproduce the same as and when required.

(iii) *Output Devices.* These are the devices through which the computer can communicate the end product of any data processing exercise line printers. The line printer prints letters, numerals and special symbols which can be decoded later. Visual displays like graph can also be drawn.

(iv) *Control Devices.* These are control processes which perform the arithmetical, logical and control operations connected with input, storage and output devices to exercise an overall control over them.

Problems of Audit of Computerised Accounts

1. Loss of audit trial. Audit trial means the tracing of the transactions in sequence through the system from these sources to completion and *vice versa.* The auditor cannot trace the final impact of all transactions on the financial statements unless each item of the output could be traced back to the source document. He may not apply auditing in depth because the punch card system or EDP system affects the audit-trial as they eliminate the source document.

2. Lack of knowledge of computer programme. In India a majority of the auditors lack knowledge about computer programme.

3. Lack of knowledge of Input and output. The auditor does not have a complete knowledge of input and output documents.

INTERNAL CONTROLS

An auditor should familiarise himself with the accounting system and learn the environment of the computer, its capabilities, built in controls, programmes and processing techniques etc. He should review the system of internal control in existence. Most of the internal controls depend on the same principles as that in the case of manual system. However, there are many special controls which are applicable in punch-card installation system and electronic processing of accounting data. Controls in punched-card or electronic data processing system are the following :

1. Programme alterations. Alteration in the programmes should not be made by the machine operator in order to avoid manipulations in the accounts.

2. Documentation. In order to have an effective internal control system, there should be proper documentation of all programmes such as preparation of flow charts, descriptions of controls, procedures, detailed instructions to operators, listing programme instructions etc. Unauthorised alteration of the programmes should be avoided without the prior authorisation of the reviewing authorities. Documents should be numbered. A procedure for their movement should be strictly followed. All documents should be pre-listed by the source-department.

3. Hash Totals. Hash totals concern those figures which do not form the part of accounting data but are otherwise useful for control purposes. Through them it can be known if some document has not been posted or has been posted to a wrong account.

4. Introduction of Control Sheet/Proof Sheet. The ledger posting machine must bring out a control sheet bearing the posting to various accounts in the form of a carbon copy. If posting is correctly done, the debits and credits on the controls sheet will be equal. It ensures that the balances of the debtors and creditors accounts have been correctly picked up. Discrepancy will reveal presence of some errors.

5. Error rectification. Errors detected should be rectified by proper procedure.

6. Loose leaf stationary. As most of the stationary is in the loose leaf forms, it would be better if some control is exercised over the use of ledger cards and other items.

7. Input Controls. The quality of output depends on the quality of input, Accurate and complete data should be fed to computer. To detect and prevent all possible errors proper controls should be exercised on input.

8. Control over conversion of input data. As the original documents cannot be fed into the machine straightaway, they have to be converted into a machine readable form, i.e. punched cards or punched paper tapes. Certain errors may be committed in this process of conversion. Each punch card should be verified by an operator other than the one who did the punching.

9. Control over processing. Following are the controls which can be instituted during the processing of data :

(i) *File Label.* The programmer should check the file label to ensure that correct data are being read into the data processor. It is a record at the beginning and at the end of the file, recording identification and control information.

(ii) *Cross Checks.* A check on the processing of data can be exercised through cross footing test. The individual items showing an analysis of any item may be totalled separately. These may then be added together to check the total of the main column, showing the total of the item.

10. Output Controls. The output should be verified with reference to its relationship with the input. It should display a positive co-relation with the input. There should be proper control over the distribution of output.

11. Control over E.D.P. Equipment. Electronic Data Processing system includes a large number of electronic and mechanical parts. Errors can creep if any of these parts is not functioning properly. Therefore, there must be some inbuilt controls to keep all these parts in a preface condition for the efficient performance of the system.

The auditor has to review the internal controls. All the controls should be evaluated from time to time to the satisfaction of the auditor.

AUDIT OF COMPUTERISED ACCOUNTS

After the evaluation of the internal controls the auditor decides upon the extent of the detailed checking to be undertaken. He may obtain evidence regarding the reliability of the electronic data processing system and its output with or without the help of the computer. Following two audit approaches are used for the audit of computerised accounts.

(a) Audit around the computer

(b) Audit through the computer.

(a) Audit around the computer. This audit is conducted in a traditional manner by examining the print-outs of the computer, in the same way as in the case of manual systems of accounting. The computer is employed for the print outs as the end products. The auditor more or less ignores the computer and verifies the source documents with the computer output. Ignoring the detailed procedures within the computer this method concentrates on probing the initial input and checking that it is properly authorised and described ; that it has been properly coded and that it has been properly translated into computer input.

(b) Audit through the computer. In this approach, the computer is used to undertake certain verification procedures. If the auditor possesses a basic knowledge of computers and their working, he may make use of the capacities of the computer to test programmes through test packs or through controlled processing. He can also design his own computer programmes for testing and evaluating computer records. This calls for an expert knowledge of the computer techniques. To test EDP system the auditor should be able to adopt available audit techniques which are as follows :

(i) Compliance tests

(ii) Test packs

(iii) Reprocessing

(iv) Computer audit.

Both the above approaches should be combined in practice as they are not separate or contradictory.

PROCEDURE FOR THE AUDIT OF ACCOUNTS KEPT ON EDP SYSTEM

1. Pre-audit planning phase. It involves initial familiarisation with the EDP system of the client for the purpose of identifying the weaknesses and strength of the system.

2. Analysis phase. It involves designing of a specific audit programme with detailed check lists and procedures.

3. Phase relating to review. It involves transaction tests and compliance tests to determine effectiveness of controls and validity and reliability of records.

4. Guard against the possibility of computer frauds. The computer frauds and errors could be due to following reasons :

(i) Faulty selection and design of the system.

(ii) Intervention of the dishonest human agencies.

The EDP systems rely on the specialised work of computer experts. This leads to a reduction in the desired levels of checks and balances in the internal control system. The computers leave behind a less visible trial. The expert operator can also abuse the system so as to conceal evidence of fraud. Lack of basic intelligence in the computers renders it unable to spot obvious errors and anomalies.

Examination of the System of Internal Controls

The auditor should examine the system of internal controls to evaluate :

(i) the data processing system (EDP),

(ii) the records produced by that system.

(i) Evaluation of EDP. In order to evaluate the EDP system, the auditor should prepare the hypothetical test data and process it through the clients of EDP system taking care to include in the test data by comparing. He will ascertain the results with pre-determined tabulation whether the computer is programmed so as to reject the invalid data. The auditor may use a sample of the historical data processed by the clients' computer and compare it with data repossessed through controlled computer. He may also integrate test data with the client's "line data" and use the result of the tabulation to monitor the client's EDP system. He has to use his imagination in developing a programme which adequately evaluates the records produced by the computer. He can proceed on conventional lines where the audit trail left behind by the computer is adequate. Where the audit trail is insufficient, the use of computerised audit procedure is generally recommended.

ADVANTAGES OF COMPUTER

1. Detailed Records. Detailed records and accurate and up-to- date records are readily available for accounting purposes. This improves upon the over all control of the management and assists the auditor in testing.

2. Repetitive Ability. A small volume of compliance testing is more reliable.

3. Mechanical Ability. As compared to the human being, the computers have a high degree of mechanical ability. It needs less testing on this account.

4. Regular Reconciliations. The computer offers the facilities of more regular and frequent reconciliations which are otherwise performed only periodically.

5. Instant Rejection and Exception Reports. The computer instantly supplies both rejection and exception reports. The auditor knows the standard of input from the quantity of rejections. Exception reports facilitate management by exception.

6. Sophisticated Techniques. As a sophisticated technique the computer can be used by the auditor to assist himself in audit testing. He may use "test packs" to determine whether the client's programme controls are working effectively.

AREAS OF COMPUTER USE

Following is the list of some of the areas where the computers can be used to assist the auditor :

1. Selecting accounts receivables for confirmation, tabulating and analysing confirmation results.
2. Testing the analysis of accounts receivable and listing over due accounts for follow up and evaluation.
3. Price testing inventories and listing significant differences between test counts and book records.
4. Stores and stock inventory analysis on the "abc" return.
5. Verifying interest on investments against controlled amounts.
6. Preparing analysis of travels and relationships between income and expense amounts both within the same year as well as by reference to comparisons with earlier years.

The computer can compile the annual accounts and the statutory form. It can prepare schedules and analysis for year-end financial statements. It can assist the auditor in preparing tabulated statements, flow charting etc.

QUESTIONS FOR EXERCISE

1. Describe in brief the various types of mechanised and computerised systems of accounting.
2. Describe the problems in case of audit of computerised accounts. Suggest different internal controls in cases where the accounts are kept on EDP system.
3. Describe the approaches used for the audit of computerised accounts.
4. What do you understand by :
   (a) Audit around the computer, and
   (b) Audit through the computer.
5. Describe the procedure for the audit of accounts kept on EDP system.
6. What are the advantages of computer for audit purposes ? Mention the areas where the computers can be used to assist the auditor.

27

Audit of Public Accounts and Government Undertakings

Under the following articles of Indian Constitution, the legislature has a vast control over the revenue and expenditure of the Government.

LEGISLATURE'S FINANCIAL CONTROL ON GOVERNMENT

1. Article 265. No tax can be levied or collected except under the authority of the Act of the Legislature.

2. Article 266. The proceeds of all government revenues shall be part of the specified funds.

3. Articles 112 to 116. These deal with the procedure to be followed in Parliament for the supply or grant of money.

Thus in financial matters, the President in required to lay Annual Budget before both the Houses of Parliament. It is an annual financial statement. It gives the estimated income and expenditure for the year. The expenditure which charged to the Consolidated Fund of India is not submitted to the vote of Parliament through non-votable items can be discussed in either House of Parliament. Other expenditure is to be submitted in the form of demands for grant to the Lok Sabha which has power to assent or refuse to assent to any demand. After the grants have been made by the Lok Sabha, it takes up the Appropriation Bill for consideration and passing which specifies all the grants made by the Lok Sabha and the consolidated fund charges as shown in the Budget. The Financial Bill contains proposals for taxation.

Two Levels of Control

Thus, the financial control by Parliament is at two levels—proposals and results. There is an open and free debate of the fiscal policies of the Government and on its financial proposals for implementing them. It includes imposition of taxes and voting of expenditure for provision of public services. There is also scrutiny of the moneys spent and the manner of their spending. Through the Public Accounts Committee the Parliament examines the public accounts of the Government as well as the reports of the Controller and Auditor General in respect of these accounts.

CONSOLIDATED FUND

1. Article 266(1). All revenues received by the Government of India, all moneys raised by loan and all moneys received in repayment of loans, not including taxes which are assigned to the States, shall form one consolidated fund, called the Consolidated Fund of India. It is formed by all revenues received by the State, all moneys raised by it through loans and all moneys received in repayment of loans.

2. Clause (3) of Art. 266. No moneys out of the Consolidated Fund of India or that of a State shall be appropriated except in accordance with law, and for the purposes and in the manner provided in the Constitution.

3. The Annual Budget. The estimates of expenditure charged upon the Consolidated Fund of India and the sums of other expenditure required to be met out of it, are shown separately in the annual budget. Though forming part of the budget estimate of the first category of expenditure is not submitted to the vote of Parliament though it can be discussed by either House. The second category of expenditure, submitted to Parliament in the demands for grant, is discussed and debated and the Lok Sabha may also assent or refuse to assent to, or make reduction in any of them.

4. The expenditure belonging to the first category. Charged upon the Consolidated Fund, it consists of the following:

(i) the salary and allowances, etc., of the President;

(ii) debt charges, including interest, sinking fund and redemption and cost of raising loans;

(iii) salary, allowances and pension payable to the Comptroller and Auditor-General of India;

(iv) salaries, allowances and pensions of the Judges of the Supreme Court

(v) pensions of the Judges of High Courts;

(vi) salaries and allowances of the Chairman and Deputy Chairman of the Rajya Sabha and the Speaker and Deputy Speaker of the Lok Sabha;

(vii) the sums required to meet any judgment or award of any Court or arbitration tribunal; and

(viii) any other expenditure charged by the Constitution or any Union Act on the Consolidated Fund.

PUBLIC ACCOUNT

1. Article 266(2). It provides for the creation of Public Account into which all public moneys, other than those of the Consolidated Fund, shall be credited. The same will be the case with regard to the Public Account of a State.

2. Article 284. All moneys received by or deposited with any Union officer, other than revenues or public moneys raised or received by the

Government of India or deposited with any Court in India, shall be credited to the Public Account of India or of a State, viz. receipts from Posts and Telegraphs Departments.

CONTINGENCY FUND

Under Article 267(1). Parliament is empowered to establish a Contingency Fund in the nature of an impress by enacting a law to that effect. The fund shall be placed at the disposal of the President to enable advances to be made by him out of such fund for meeting any unforeseen expenditure pending authorisation by Parliament. A similar fund may be established by a State Legislature also. Parliament has enacted the Contingency Fund of India Act, 1950. Under this Act, Rs. 30 crores are paid out of the Consolidated Fund of India to Contingency Fund every year.

COMPTROLLER AND AUDITOR GENERAL OF INDIA

1. Appointment. According to Article 148(1), the Comptroller and Auditor General (C.A.G.) is appointed by the President of India. His status is that of a judge of the Supreme Court.

2. Remuneration. C.A.G. draws a salary @ Rs. 4000 p.m. equivalent to that of a judge of the Supreme Court and is also entitled to a rent-free official residence and travelling allowance.

3. Removal. According to Article 148(1), C.A.G. can be removed from Office by the President on the ground of proven misbehaviour or incapacity.

4. Duties and Powers. According to Art. 149, the C.A.G. shall perform such duties and exercise such powers in relation to the accounts of the Union and of the States and of any other authority or body as may be prescribed by Parliament by law. As amended in 1976, the Comptroller and Auditor-General (Duties, Powers and Conditions of Service) Act, passed by Parliament in 1971, lays down the duties and rights of C.A.G. as follows:

(i) to audit and report on all expenditure from the Consolidated Fund of India and each State and each Union Territory having a Legislative Assembly as to whether such expenditure has been in accordance with the law;

(ii) to audit and report on all expenditure from the Contingency Funds and Public Accounts of the Union and the States;

(iii) to audit and report on all trading, manufacturing, profit and loss accounts, etc., kept by any Department of the Union or a State;

(iv) to audit the receipts and expenditure of the Union and of each State to satisfy himself that the rules and procedures in that behalf are designed to secure an effective check on the assessment, collection and proper allocation of revenue;

(v) to audit and report on the receipts and expenditure of (a) all bodies and authorities "substantially financed" from the Union or State revenues; (b) Government companies; (c) other corporations or bodies when so required by the laws relating to such corporations or bodies.

According to Art. 150, as amended in 1978, the accounts of the Union and of the State shall be kept in such form as the President may, on the advice of the C.A.G., prescribe.

AUDIT FUNCTIONS BY C.A.G.

1. Audit of Appropriation Accounts. Its object is to ensure that the funds voted by the legislature are utilised by the executive for the objects for which these were intended, with due regard to economy and efficiency. Thus, it aims to verify (i) whether the final accounts present a true and complete picture of financial transactions; (ii) whether those who incurred the expenditure had the requisite authority to do so; (iii) whether the amounts voted by the legislature have been used for the purpose for which they were intended; and (iv) whether the expenditure conforms to the principle of propriety.

(i) ***Audit of Accounts.*** It seeks to check and detect technical errors or frauds by examination of vouchers and other related evidence as to expenditure and its booking against the appropriate head.

(ii) ***Audit of Authority.*** It aims at ascertaining whether or not expenditure has been incurred on the basis of proper authority. Cases of expenditure without authority or in excess of authority, are duly mentioned in the audit report.

(iii) ***Audit of Appropriations.*** It seeks to see that the amounts voted by the legislature are utilised for the purposes for which they were intended. It aims to bring to the notice of legislature, through the audit report, cases of over-spending, under-spending and unauthorised diversion of funds. It highlights the important aspects of current revenues and expenditure, financial performance of important public works and position of debts.

(iv) ***Audit of Propriety of Transactions.*** It involves expenditure and seeks to examine the transactions from the point of view of wisdom, faithfulness and economy. Thus, improper use of stocks and stores, or unsound principles of financial administration are the aspects to be highlighted here. Propriety audit is discretionary and not mandatory on the part of the C.A.G.

2. Audit of Public Undertakings. Both at the centre and in the States there has been a phenomenal increase in the number of public sector undertakings, e.g., statutory corporations and government companies. The funds employed in these undertakings belong to the people. In order to ensure effective accountability, they need comprehensive audit. In the case of some, the accounts are directly audited by C.A.G.. The C.A.G. may conduct supplementary audit even in the case of those which entrust the work of audit to the private firms of Chartered Accountants. These audit reports are submitted to the Committee on Public Undertakings or the Public Accounts Committee.

The reports of C.A.G. about the accounts of the Union shall be submitted to the President who shall cause them to be laid before each House of Parliament. Those relating to the accounts of a State shall be submitted to the Governor of the State who shall cause them to be laid before the Legislature of the State.

PUBLIC ACCOUNTS COMMITTEE (PAC)

What is PAC?

Public Accounts Committee (PAC) is an instrument of legislative control over the administration. It is a Standing Committee of Parliament consisting of 22 members of Parliament. It exercises vigilance over governmental spending and performance. It scrutinises the Appropriation Accounts of the Government and the report of the C.A.G. thereon.

Objects of PAC

1. whether due economy has been exercised in the financial transactions of the executive government;
2. whether public moneys have been spent by the executive government as Parliament intended them to be spent;
3. whether high standards of public morality have been observed in all matters of finance.
4. whether moneys shown in the accounts as having been disbursed were legally available for, and applicable to, the services or purposes to which they have been applied or charged;
5. whether the expenditure conforms to the authority which governs it; and
6. whether every re-appropriation has been made in accordance with the provision made in this behalf under the rules framed by the competent authority.

Functions of the PAC

1. To examine, in the light of the report of the Comptroller and Auditor-General, the statement of accounts showing in income and expenditure, together with Balance Sheets and Profit and Loss Accounts of :

(a) state corporations,

(b) trading or manufacturing schemes,

(c) concerns, or

(d) projects.

2. To examine the statements of accounts showing the income and expenditure of autonomous and semi-autonomous bodies, the audit of which may be conducted by the Comptroller and Auditor-General of India, either under the directions of the President or by a statute of Parliament.

3. To consider the report of the Comptroller and Auditor-General in cases where the President may have required him to conduct an audit of any receipts or to examine the accounts of stores and stocks.

4. To examine moneys spent on any service during a financial year in excess of the amount granted by Parliament for the purpose.

Working of PAC

The PAC may organise itself into sub-committees and working groups. After the reports of these smaller bodies are approved by the PAC, they become the reports of the PAC itself.

PAC has power to summon witnesses or require documents or records to be produced before it. The persons to be called before it to answer questions are generally the heads of departments or those vested with authority to incur expenditure. Even ministers of the Government may be required to appear before it in rare cases.

The Comptroller and Auditor-General may attend PAC meetings by invitation and also, with the permission of the chairman, put questions to the persons testifying before it. His expertise in financial matters helps the PAC in gaining insight into complicated technical issues. He is a friend, philosopher and guide of the PAC, and a right hand man of its chairman.

ESTIMATES COMMITTEE

Estimates Committee consists of 30 members of the Lok Sabha only. It serves as a means of parliamentary control over the administration by examining possibilities of economy and reform in financial administration.

Functions of the Estimates Committee

(i) to report what economies, improvements in organisation, efficiency or administrative reforms, consistent with the policy, may be effected.

(ii) to suggest alternative policies to bring about efficiency and economy in administration.

(iii) to examine whether the money is well laid out within the limits of the policy implied in the estimates.

(iv) to suggest the form in which the estimates shall be presented to Parliament.

The Estimates Committee is not a policy-making body although it looks whether the policies laid down by Parliament are being properly implemented. It seeks to ensure efficiency and economy in administration. If it finds any instance of extravagance or waste it brings them to the notice of the House along with its suggestions.

Working of Estimates Committee

The Estimates Committee may organise itself into one or more sub-committees. It is empowered to summon witnesses, interview officials and require documents to be produced before it. It may issue questionnaires to ministries and departments of the Government. It submits its report to the Lok Sabha in which it gives its recommendations on what economies and improvements in organisational efficiency or administrative reforms may be effected.

COMMITTEE OF PUBLIC UNDERTAKINGS

A large part of the investment in public undertakings has been made available by the Union Government out of Consolidated Fund of India. The Committee on Public Undertakings (CPU) is a parliamentary instrument to keep vigil over proper utilisaion to these funds and to seek measure of control and accountability. It is composed of 15 members 10 from the Lok Sabha and 5 from the Rajya Sabha. It is primarily concerned with evaluation of the performance of public undertakings in specific areas— implementation of policies, programmes, management, financial success etc.

Functions of CPU

1. To examine the reports and accounts of such public undertakings as have been specifically allotted to the CPU for this purpose;
2. To examine the report, if any, of the Comptroller and Auditor General as regards public undertakings;
3. To examine, in the context of the autonomy and efficiency of public undertakings, whether the affairs of the public undertakings are being managed in accordance with sound business principles and prudent commercial practices; and
4. To exercise such other functions vested in the Public Accounts Committee and the Estimates Committee in relation to the public undertakings specified for the committee as are not covered by clauses (a), (b) and (c) above, and as may be allotted to the Committee by the Speaker from time to time.

Sources of Information

The subjects and undertakings to taken up for examination by CPU are decided by it well in advance. These may be detailed in every aspect of the subject or working of the undertaking concerned, or lit may be limited to matters of topical interest only. The CPU uses following sources of information for the purpose of its examination:

1. preliminary and detailed information submitted by the Ministry/Department of the undertaking concerned, along with the subjects to be examined;
2. memoranda on the subjects under study submitted by non-official organisations, such as Chambers of Commerce, trade association, trade unions, etc.;
3. evidence given by officers of the Ministry/Department and the undertaking; and
4. audit reports of the Comptroller and Auditor General.

Working of CPU

The draft report of the CPU is sent to the undertaking, ministry/department, Ministry of Finance and the Comptroller and Auditor General for verification of facts stated therein. On receipt of factual information from them, the reports is finalised and presented to Parliament. Information about action on the basis of recommendations made in the report forms part of the Action Taken Report which is also presented to Parliament.

PROVISIONS ABOUT AUDIT OF PUBLIC UNDERTAKINGS

For commercial audit purposes, the various public undertakings can be divided into three categories:

1. Departmental Undertakings
2. Statutory Corporations
3. Government Companies.

1. Departmental Undertakings. Under the provisions of Article 149 of the Constitution of India, the Comptroller and Auditor General is empowered to conduct audit of departmental undertakings. The object of the audit is to ensure:

(i) that final accounts of the these undertakings present a true and complete picture of their financial transactions and that these have been prepared in accordance with generally accepted accounting principles.

(ii) that the persons who incurred expenditure on behalf of these undertakings had the requisite authority to do so.

(iii) that the amounts authorised by the legislature have been spent for the purposes for which they were intended.

(iv) that there has been no extravagance or waste even where an expenditure is well within the confines of legality and regularity.

This audit includes an examination of the working of the undertaking concerned and instances of malfunctioning or weaknesses are suitably highlighted in the report to be presented to Parliament.

2. Audit of Statutory Corporations. These are set up under the legislature, a wide range of variations is found pertaining to the maintenance of accounts and their audit. The statutory responsibility rest with the Comptroller and Auditor General of India, but in some cases the private practising Chartered Accountants are enrusted with this task of audit of their financial accounts. The financial accounts are audited by the professional Chartered Accountants subject to the approval of the Comptroller and Auditor General of India, in case of State Bank, Industrial Finance Corporation, Central and State Warehouse Corporation, Life Insurance Corporation. In all these cases, the professional Chartered Accountant is expected to be familiar with the provisions of the concerned Act applicable on the statutory corporation.

3. Audit of Government Companies. This audit procedure is different from the above two undertakings. Like other Companies, Government Companies are registered under the provisions of Companies Act. The provisions of Sections 224 and 233 are applicable in case of Government companies. The provisions of Section 619 supersede the provisions of routine working.

PROVISIONS ABOUT AUDIT OF GOVERNMENT COMPANIES

In case of audit of Government companies, set up under the Companies Act, the provisions of Sec. 619 supervene those of Secs. 224 to 233 which deal with audit and auditors of non-Government Companies.

1. Meaning of Government company [Sec. 617]. A Government company has been defined as "any company in which not less than 51% of the paid up share capital is held by the Central Government, or by any State Government or Governments, or partly by the Central Government and partly by one or more State Governments, and includes as company which is a subsidiary of a Government company thus defined."

2. Appointment of auditor [Sec. 619]. The auditor of a Government company shall be appointed or reappointed by the Central Government on the advice of the Comptroller and Auditor-General of India. The limit as to the auditorship as prescribed in Sec. 224(1-B) and (1-C) will apply in the case of such appointments.

3. C.A.G.'s power to direct audit and to conduct supplementary or test audit [Sec. 619(3)]. The C.A.G. has power to direct the manner in which a Government company's accounts have to be audited by the auditor appointed for the purpose, and to give him instructions in regard to any matters relating to the performance of his functions. He can also order supplementary or test audit of the accounts of the Government company by a person authorised by him and to this end, may require necessary or additional information to be furnished to such person.

His directions relate to systems of accounts, internal control, maintenance of Production and Manufacturing Accounts, Cost Accounts, Profit and Loss Account, Balance Sheet and their general review, townships, manpower, service units and analysis of accounts to show capital formation, growth and funds-flow of the company.

4. Audit report [Sec. 619 (4)]. A copy of the report of the Government company auditor shall be submitted to the C.A.G. who shall have the right to comment upon, or supplement, the audit report as he may think fit. These shall be placed before the annual general meeting as the audit report.

QUESTIONS FOR EXERCISE

1. Explain how legislatures in India exercise financial control over the revenue and expenditure of the Government.
2. Define Consolidated Fund, Public Account and Contingency Fund.
3. Describe the Provisions relating to appointment, duties and powers of the Comptroller and Auditor General of India.
4. Describe the scope of audit functions performed by Comptroller and Auditor General.
5. Discuss the functions and working of the Public Accounts Committee.
6. Discuss the functions and working of Estimates Committee.
7. What are the functions of Committee of Public Undertakings?
8. Explain the provisions with regard to audit of public undertakings.
9. Bring out the provisions of the Companies Act with regard to audit of Government Companies.

28

Professional Conduct and Ethics: Provisions of Chartered Accountants Act

Chartered Accountants Act, 1949 seeks to regulate the profession of Chartered Accountants through Institute of Chartered Accountants of India (ICAI) a corporate body set up thereunder.

INSTITUTE OF CHARTERED ACCOUNTANTS

Management Council

The affairs of the ICAI are managed by a Council whose membership consists of fellow Chartered Accountants elected from various regions and nominees of the Central Government. It is elected for a term of three years and every year it elects its President and a Vice-President. It functions are as follows:

1. conducting the various examinations relating to the chartered accountancy course;
2. regulating the engagement, training and theoretical education of the articles and audit clerks;
3. prescribing the qualifications for entry in the Register of Members;
4. granting certificates of practice;
5. enforcing discipline among the members; and
6. carrying out research and developmental activities in accounting and allied fields.

Standing Committees

From among its members, the Council constitutes three Standing Committees, namely Executive Committee, Examination Committee and Disciplinary Committee. It is empowered to constitute any other committees also.

Membership of ICAI

Any person who possesses the prescribed qualifications or who has passed the examinations and completed the training prescribed by the ICAI can become a member of the ICAI and have his name entered in the Register of Members (Sec. 4).

ICAI MEMBERS IN PRACTICE

Every member of the Institute is designated as a Chartered Accountant whether he practices the profession of accountancy or not. There is no distinction between members in practice and members not in practice. However, Section 2(2) of the Chartered Accountants Act clarifies the expression "to be in practice" as follows:

A member of the ICAI will be deemed to be in practice if, individually or in partnership with any Chartered Accountant (s) in practice, he in consideration of remuneration received or to be received:

1. engages himself in the practice of accountancy; or
2. offers to perform or performs services involving the auditing or verification of financial transactions, books, accounts or records or the preparation, verification or certification of financial accounting and related statements or holds himself out to the public as an accountant; or
3. renders professional services or assistance in or about matters of principles or details relating to accounting procedures or the recordings, presentation or certification of financial facts or data; or
4. renders such other services as, in the opinion of the Council, are or may be rendered by a Chartered Accountant in practice; and the words "to be in practice" with their grammatical variations and cognate expression shall be construed accordingly."

If an associate or a fellow of the Institute is employed by a practising chartered accountant or a firm of Chartered Accountants, he will be deemed to be in practice for the purposes of the training of the article clerk. A Chartered Accountant rendering part-time service will be deemed to be in practice under Regulation 167 of the Chartered Accountants Regulation, 1964. A member will be deemed to be in practice during the period he renders service with Armed Forces.

Any member, who sets up an establishment and performs various accounting functions will be considered as a "member in practice" even if he does not have any clients.

TYPES OF MEMBERS

1. Associates. An associate member is one whose name is entered in the Register of Members of the ICAI. An associate may use the letters A.C.A. after his name.

2. Fellows. An associate who has been in continuous practice in India for five years or more, and any other associate who has been a member of the ICAI for five years or more and possesses the qualifications as prescribed by the Council of the ICAI, may be enrolled as fellow of the ICAI and he may then use the letters F.C.A. after his name.

Entry of Names in the Register

According to Section 4 of the Chartered Accountants Act following provisions have been laid down for an entry of names in the Register.

1. Any of the following persons shall be entitled to have his name entered in the Register, namely:

(i) any person who is a registered accountant or a holder of restricted certificate at the commencement of this Act.

(ii) any person who has passed the examination and completed such training as may be prescribed for members of the institute.

(iii) any person who has passed the examination of the government diploma in Accountancy before the commencement of this Act and who, although not duly qualified to be registered as an accountant under the Auditor's Certificate Rules 1932, fulfils certain conditions as the Central Government may specify in this behalf.

(iv) any person, who at the commencement of this Act, is engaged in the practice of accountancy in any acceding State (Part B State) and who although not possessing the requisite qualifications to be registered as an accountant under the Auditor's Certificate Rules, 1932, fulfils certain conditions as the Central Government may specify in this behalf.

(v) any person who has passed such other examination and completed such other training without India as is recognised by the Central Government or the Council as being equivalent to the examinations and training prescribed for members of the Institute:

Provided that in the case of any person who is not permanently residing in India, the Central Government or the Council, as the case may be, may impose such further conditions as it may deem fit.

(vi) any person domiciled in India, who at the commencement of this Act, is studying for any foreign examination and who is at the same time undergoing training whether within or out India or who having passed such foreign examination is at the commencement of this Act, undergoing training, whether within or without India:

Provided that any such examination or training was recognised before the commencement of this Act, for the purposes of conferring the right to be registered as an accountant under the Auditor's Certificate, Rules, 1932, and provided further that such person passes the examination or completes the training within five years after the commencement of this Act.

2. Every person belonging to the class mentioned in clause (i) of sub-section (1) shall have his name entered in the Register without the payment of an entrance fee.

3. Every person belonging to the class mentioned in clauses (ii), (iii), (iv), (v) and (vi) of sub-section (1) shall have his name entered in the Register on application being made and granted in the prescribed manner and on payment of the prescribed fee, which shall not exceed rupees three hundred in any case.

4. The Central Government shall take such steps as may be necessary for the purpose of having the names of all persons belonging to the class mentioned in clause (i) of sub-section (1) entered in the Register.

Disabilities for Registration. According to section 8 of the Chartered Accountant Act a person shall not be entitled to have his name entered in, or borne on the Register, if he :

(i) has not attained the age of twenty-one years at the time of his application for the entry of his name in the Register; or

(ii) has been adjudicated by a competent Court to be of unsound mind; or

(iii) is an undischarged insolvent; or

(iv) being a discharged insolvent, has not obtained from the Court a certificate stating that his insolvency was caused by misfortune without any misconduct on his part; or

(v) has been convicted by a competent Court, whether within or without India, or an offence involving moral turpitude and punishable with transportation or imprisonment, or of an offence, not of a technical nature, committed by him in his professional capacity unless in respect of the offence committed he has either been granted a pardon or on application made by him in this behalf, the Central Government has, by an order in writing, removed the disability; or

(vi) has been found on enquiry to have been quality of conduct which renders him unfit to be member of the Institute.

Professional Misconduct

Failure on the part of a person to disclose the fact that he suffers from any one of the disabilities mentioned above would amount to professional misconduct and accordingly his name may be removed by the Council from the Register of Members (Sec. 20).

False Representation

If a person, who is not a member of the Institute, falsely represents that he is, or uses the designation "Chartered Accountant", or practises without obtaining a certificate of practice, he will be liable to be punished with a fine which may extend to Rs. 1,000.

More than one office India

If a Chartered Accountant in practice, or a firm of Chartered Accountants, has more than one office in India, each one of such office should be in the charge of a member of the Institute (Sec. 27).

PROFESSIONAL MISCONDUCT

Definition of Professional Misconduct

Professional Misconduct has been defined by Section 22 of the Act as follows: "For the purpose of this Act, the expression professional misconduct shall be deemed to include any act or omission specified in any of the schedules, but nothing in this section shall be construed to limit or arbitrage in any way the power conferred or duty cast on the council under sub-section (1) of Section 21 to enquire into the conduct of any member of the Institute under any circumstances." However, the Council of the Institute of Chartered Accountants of India is empowered to enquire into the conduct of a chartered Accountant under any circumstances which are not specified in the Schedules of the Act.

Distinction from Professional Negligence

The expression 'professional misconduct' is completely different from the expression 'professional negligence'. The latter refers to an auditor's failure to perform his duties according to accepted professional standards, which may result in loss or damage to the client. The party who has suffered a loss can sue the auditor and can claim damages. Similarly, negligence differs from gross negligence. The 'negligence' means carelessness or accidental or inadvertent failure to perform a particular work while 'gross negligence' means failure on the part of the auditor to perform a duty which he was entrusted to do.

Procedure of Enquiry

In regard to inquiries into the misconduct of the members: Section 21 has laid down the following procedure.

1. Prima Facie. On receipt of information by or on a complaint made to it the Council first decides whether a "Prima facie" case has been made out against a member for professional or other misconduct. The use of the words "or other" empower the council to inquire into any misconduct of a member even if it does not arise out of his professional work. A Chartered Accountant is expected to maintain the highest standards of integrity is his personal (non-professional) conduct and any deviation from this high standard would expose a Chartered Accountant to a disciplinary enquiry. If a Chartered Accountant is found to have forged the will of a relative, he would be liable to be excluded from membership of the Institute, even though this was not done in the course of his duties.

2. Reference to Disciplinary Committee. If the Council is satisfied that a "Prima Facie" case exists, then the matter is referred to the Disciplinary Committee which holds an inquiry and reports its conclusions to the Council.

3. If Guilty. If the Council finds the member guilty of professional misconduct as specified in the First Schedule to the Act, it must give to the member an opportunity of being heard. Thereafter, it may either reprimand the member, or remove his name from the Register for a period not exceeding five years.

Exceptions. The Council's decision on every case involving misconduct under the first Schedule, is final except under the following cases:

(i) When the aggrieved member prefers an appeal to the High Court.

(ii) When the High Court, on its own motion or otherwise; revises the order of the Council.

(iii) Where the Council decides to remove the member's name for a period exceeding five years or permanently.

4. Forward to High Court. If the misconduct of the member does not fall within the scope of the First Schedule to the Act, the Council must refer the case to the High Court with its recommendations, unless, on receipt of the Report of the Disciplinary Committee it finds that the member is not guilty of any misconduct. The High Court may make any of the following orders after hearing the case:

(i) reprimand the member;

(ii) direct that the proceedings be filed or dismiss the complaint as the case may be;

(iii) remove his name from the membership of the Institute either permanently or for such a period as it may think fit, and

(iv) refers the case to the Council for further enquiry and report.

5. Appeal to High Court. Under section 22 of the Act, any member of the Institute, can appeal to the High Court. The Court may entertain the appeal even after the expiry of 30 days, if it is satisfied that the member was prevented by sufficient cause from filing the appeal in time. The High Court also has the power to revise any order.

6. Enquiry of past member. The Council is entitled to enquire into the conduct of a person who was a member of the Institute but has ceased to be so at the time of the inquiry.

7. Powers of Civil Court. The Council and the Disciplinary Committee can exercise the same powers as are vested in a Civil Court, viz.

(i) to summon and enforce attendance of any person and to examine him on oath.

(ii) discovery and production of any document.

(iii) to receive evidence on affidavit.

PROVISIONS OF SCHEDULES IN PROFESSIONAL MISCONDUCT

Two schedules. In the Chartered Accountants Act, there are two schedules to see whether a member is guilty of misconduct or not; whether the Council or High Court is to punish the member guilty of misconduct; whether a member who is not in practice can be punished etc.

1. First Schedule. It deals with misconduct by a member whose case can be decided by the Council. It consists of three parts.

(i) Under Part I are enumerated various acts and omissions which amount to misconduct committed by 'members in practice',

(ii) Part II of this Schedule deals with 'members not in practice' and the last,

(iii) Part III deals with all members.

2. Second Schedule. It refers to certain other important rules of conduct, the breach of which requires a decision by the High Court after the Council has considered the case. The finding of the Council requires to be referred to a High Court for final adjudication.

Following are the implications of the different clauses in these Schedules.

FIRST SCHEDULE

Part One

It describes the circumstances in which members in practice may be held guilty of misconduct.

1. Clause 1. If he allows any person to practise in his name as a chartered accountant unless such person is also a chartered accountant in practice and is in partnership with or employed by himself.

This clause seeks to prevent unqualified persons from acting as qualified accountants at the behest or with connivance of the chartered accountant. A chartered accountant may have employees all of whom may not be chartered accountants themselves. An employee, even if not a Chartered Accountant himself, can work on behalf of his Chartered Accountant - employer if the former works directly under the supervision and control of the latter.

2. Clause 2. If he pays or allows, or agrees to pay or allow, directly or indirectly any share, commission or brokerage in the fees or profits or his professional business, to any person other than a member of the Institute, or a partner or a retired partner, or the legal representative of a deceased partner.

Sharing of fees is permissible in the case of a partner, or a retired partner, or even the legal representative of a deceased partner, if such share is payable to him/her in accordance with the provisions of the partnership agreement. This clause seeks to restrain a member from sharing his fees, whether directly or indirectly with any non-member.

3. Clause 3. If he accepts or agrees to accept any part of the profits of the professional work of a lawyer, auctioneer, broker, or any other agent who is not member of the Institute.

This clause restrains a member from sharing any fees, brokerage, etc. earned by a non-member, with the object to prevent him from exploiting his position as auditor of his client for whom the advice of his auditor as regards which lawyer, broker, etc. to engage for his work may be conclusive.

4. Clause 4. If he enters into partnership with any person other than a chartered accountant in practice, or person resident outside India who but for his residence abroad would be entitled to be registered as a member under Sec. 4(1)(v) of the Act, or whose qualifications are recognised by the Central Government or the Council for the purpose of permitting such partnerships, provided that the chartered accountant shares in the fees or profits of the business of the partnership both within and outside India.

According to this clause, a non-practising chartered accountant may be taken as a partner if— (a) he resides outside India; (b) he could be enrolled as member if he had been residing in India; and (c) the member shares with such person the fees and profits of the partnership earned in India or abroad.

5. Clause 5. If he secures, either through the services of a person not qualified to be his partner or by means which are not open to a chartered accountant, any professional business.

By this clause, a chartered accountant can secure professional business only through a person who is qualified to be his partner or through any other means open to a chartered accountant. Professional business secured through a non-member, i.e., a tout, will tantamount to misconduct.

6. Clause 6. If he solicits clients or professional work, either directly or indirectly, by circular, advertisement, personal communication, or interview or by another means.

This clause restrains a chartered accountant from soliciting clients by whatever means. It will be misconduct, if a professional work is sought through advertisement, contacting interviewing, sending circulars etc. The professional work should be obtained gradually inspiring confidence in his ability.

7. Clause 7. If he advertises his professional attainments or services or uses any designation or expression other than chartered accountant on professional documents, visiting cards, letter heads or signboards, unless it is a degree of a university established by law in India or recognised by the Central Government or a tile indicating membership of the Institute of Chartered Accountants or of any other Institution that has been recognised by Central Government or may be recognised by the Council.

This clause prohibits all forms of advertising one's attainments, except as approved. Only professional attainments permitted by the Institute or university degree may be mentioned on signboards, letter-heads, visiting cards, etc. Thus, while writing "B.Com. F.C.A." after one's name is all right, use of phrases such as 'Expert in Income tax,' 'Recognised Auditor of Banks' will tantamount to misconduct. Likewise, writing designation such as membership of a legislature or functionary of any organisation, falls under misconduct. However, there is no prohibition of advertisement for one's staff, or advertisement on behalf of client for recruitment of staff, or advertisement in the capacity of a trustee.

8. Clause 8. If he accepts a position as auditor previously held by another chartered accountant or a restricted state auditor without first communication with him in writing.

This clause seeks to prevent unscrupulous directors of company from removing honest auditors who refuse to toe their line because permitting them to do so could harm the interests of the shareholders besides lowering the image of the profession.

9. Clause 9. If he accepts an appointment as auditor of a company without ascertaining from it whether the requirements of Sec. 224 and 225 of the Companies Act, in respect of such appointment, have been duly complied with.

(i) ***Section. 224.*** It lays down that the first auditor of a company is to be appointed by the directors within one month of the registration of the company or, on their failure to do so, by the shareholders at their general meeting. While the directors could fill in a casual vacancy but a vacancy caused by resignation of an auditor can be filled up only by the shareholders in the general meeting. If an auditor is not appointed either by the directors or by the shareholders, the vacancy will be filled by the Central Government.

(ii) ***Section 225.*** It is concerned with fulfilment of certain requirements in case of appointment of an auditor in place of the existing auditor.

10. Clause 10. If he charges or offers to charge, accepts or offers to accept, in respect of any professional employment, fees which are based on a percentage of profits, or which are contingent upon the findings, or results of such employment, except in cases which are permitted under any regulations made under this Act.

Remuneration of an auditor should not be linked with the results of his work as that could be detrimental to the quality of work to be put in by him, besides compromising his independence. However, there are exceptions to this rule, such as fees payable to the liquidator who is a chartered accountant, being based on the amount distributed to the shareholders or the amount realised on sale of the company's assets.

11. Clause 11. If he engages in any business or occupation other than the profession of chartered accountants, unless permitted by the Council to so engage. Provided that nothing contained therein shall disentitle a chartered accountant from being a director of a company unless he or any of his partners is interested in such company as an auditor.

This clause seeks to ensure that a chartered accountant does not engage in any business or profession that may bring a bad name to the profession. He may act as director, liquidator, trustee, arbitrator, etc. He may take up specified occupations such as employment under a chartered accountant, private tutorship, authorship, part-time lecturership or tutorship, full-time or part-time employment, business or non-business concerns, proprietorship of an educational institution, editorship of professional journals, membership of any elected body, etc.

12. Clause 12. If he accepts a position as auditor previously held by some other chartered accountant or a restricted State auditor in such conditions as to constitute under-cutting.

This clause seeks to prevent competition among the chartered accountants such that they do not wangle an audit assignment at a fee lower than the charged by another chartered accountant in practice. However, charging of a lower fee may be justifies if there is decrease in work-load. Appointment of an auditor by the Government or by a nationalised bank at a fee lower than that paid to the previous auditor, will not tantamount to misconduct on the part of the auditor being appointed.

13. Clause 13. If he allows a person not being a member of the Institute, or a member not being his partner, to sign on his behalf or on behalf of his firm, any Balance Sheet, Profit and Loss Account, report of financial statements.

This seeks to ensure pinpointing of responsibility as regards documents signed by the chartered accountant. Financial statements of the client-enterprise can only be signed by a chartered accountant or by his partner who is also a chartered accountant.

First Schedule— Part Two

It contains decisions as regards cases of misconduct to be made by the Council of ICAI. According to it a chartered accountant not in practice (i.e, holding employment or otherwise) would be guilty of misconduct in the following circumstances :

(i) if he pays or allows or agrees to pay directly or indirectly to any person any share in the emoluments of employments undertaken by him;

(ii) if he accepts or agrees to accept any part of fees, profits or gains from a lawyer, a chartered accountant, or broker engaged by such company, firm or person or agent customer of such company, firm or person, by way of commission or gratification; or

(iii) if he discloses confidential information acquired in the course of his employment except as and when required by law or except as permitted by the employer.

These rules seek to enforce proper conduct among chartered accountants even if they are not in practice. They are prohibited from paying any share or commission from their own remuneration or gratification or from accepting fees, profits, etc. by way of commission or gratification. They are barred from disclosing confidential information acquired in the course of employment, except when it is duly permitted.

First Schedule— Part Three

According to Part III of the First Schedule, a chartered accountant, whether in practice or not, would be guilty of misconduct, if he:

(a) includes in any statement, return or form to be submitted to the Council any particulars knowing them to be false;

(b) not being a fellow, styles himself as a fellow; or

(c) does not supply the information called for, or does not comply with the requirements asked for by the Council or any of its committees.

This rule seeks to prohibit chartered accountant from deliberately supplying particulars to the Council, holding out as a fellow while not being one, or nor supplying the information as called for from him by the Council or any committee thereof.

SECOND SCHEDULE

Part One

It specifies circumstances in which a chartered accountant in practice would be deemed to be guilty of misconduct while Part II specifies circumstances in which any chartered accountant, whether in practice or not, would be guilty of misconduct. In either case, the Council of the ICAI is required to forward the case to the High Court along with its recommendations.

1. Clause 1. If he discloses information acquired in the course of his professional engagement to any person other than his client, without the consent of his client, or otherwise than as required by any law for the time being in force.

This seeks to restrain a chartered accountant from disclosing any information regarding the affairs of his client except with the client's consent or as required by any law. There would be no misconduct if disclosure of any information is required in the course of performance of professional duties, since the client himself requires such performance which, in turn, would mean that he has himself consented to disclosure.

2. Clause 2. If he certifies or submits in his name or in the name of his firm, a report of an examination of financial statements unless the examination of such statement and the related records has been made by him, or by a partner or an employee of his firm, or by another chartered accountant in practice.

This clause seeks to ensure that chartered accountant does not sign any report, financial statements or accounts examined by outsiders. He may submit a report in his name or in the name of his firm only if the relevant financial statements have been examined by him, or by his partner, or by his employee. He may also sign reports regarding financial statements examined by another chartered accountant in practice as in the case of conducting a joint audit.

3. Clause 3. If he permits his name or the name of his firm to be used in connection with an estimate of earnings contingent upon future transactions in a manner which may lead to the belief that he vouches for the accuracy of the forecast.

The object of this clause is to prohibit chartered accountants from certifying the accuracy of statements about future earnings, the same being subject to uncertainties of various kinds. However, a chartered accountant, can very well help in the preparation of cash flow forecasts, or budgets, etc. There will be objection only when the auditor certifies its accuracy.

4. Clause 4. If he expresses his opinion on financial statements of any business or any enterprise in which he, his firm, or a partner in his firm, has a substantial interest, unless he discloses the interest also in his report.

This clause restrains a chartered accountant from expressing his opinion on financial statements of any business in which he is directly or indirectly interested because the opinion might be biased in such a case. If he expresses an opinion, he must take his interest clear in the certificate. Disclosure of interest that an auditor may have in the organisation is essential to maintain independence of auditors.

5. Clause 5. If he fails to disclose a material fact known to him which is not disclosed in a financial statement, but disclosure of which is necessary to make the financial statement not misleading.

The auditor should ensure that there is full and complete disclosure of all material facts in the financial statements of the enterprise under the audit. He will be guilty of misconduct if any material act known to him is not disclosed in the financial statements and such non-disclosure could make the statements misleading in effect.

6. Clause 6. If he fails to report a material mis-statement known to him appear in a financial statement with which he is concerned in a professional capacity.

This clause seeks to reinforce the provision made in clause (5) in the sense that the auditor should not only point out the omission of a material fact from the financial statement but should also bring to the notice of the shareholders and all those who read the report, any material mis-statements in the financial statements. Thus, if the value of investments in the Balance Sheet of a bank is inflated and hence there was distortion in the Profit and Loss Account, non-reporting of this mis-statement will constitute misconduct on the part of the auditor.

7. Clause 7. If he is grossly negligent in the conduct of his professional duties.

This clause seeks to ensure that the auditor works will skill, care and caution of a responsible competent, careful and cautious auditor. Reasonable skill, care and caution would depend on the circumstances of each case. However, if the auditor does not use the degree of skill, care and caution expected of him in the circumstances of the case, he would be guilty of negligence and therefore, within the meaning of this clause, of misconduct.

8. Clause 8. If he fails to obtain sufficient information to warrant the expression of an opinion or his exceptions are sufficiently material to negate the expression of an opinion.

This clause ensures that an auditor must obtain all the information and explanations. If he fails to do so or the management did not supply him sufficient information even though he required it, he must not express any opinion about the correctness of the financial statements of the concern.

9. Clause 9. If he fails to invite attention to any material departure from the generally accepted procedure of audit applicable to the circumstances.

This clause ensures that if the auditor has not been able to follow the normal procedure of audit he must state this fact in his report. He will be guilty of professional misconduct if he does not do so.

10. Clause 10. If he fails to keep moneys of his client in a separate banking account or to use such moneys for purposes for which they are intended.

If a client entrusts his money to the auditor, it should be kept in a separate bank account and used only for purposes for which it is intended. However, where the auditor receives any advance against services to be rendered by him, or, against expenses to be incurred by him, it need not be kept in separate bank account as per the opinion of the ICAI.

Second Schedule— Part Two

1. Clause 1. A chartered accountant would be deemed to be guilty of professional misconduct, if he contravenes any of the provisions of the Chartered Accountants Act or the Regulations made thereunder.

The Chartered Accountants Act and the Chartered Accountants Regulations (1964) contain detailed provisions as regards engagement, registration, termination of articleship, auditship, receipt of premiums, payment of stipends, etc. Failure to comply with these provisions could tender a chartered accountant guilty of misconduct.

2. Clause 2. A chartered accountant would be deemed to be guilty of professional misconduct, if he is guilty of such other act or omission as may be specified by the Council on this behalf by notification in the Gazette of India.

The Council of the ICAI is empowered to notify in the Gazette of India any acts or omissions which may be deemed to constitute misconduct on the part of the chartered accountant. Following are the important acts or omissions so notified by the Council.

(i) A member of the Institute, whether in practice or not, who is employed by a chartered accountant in practice or by a firm of such chartered accountants shall be deemed to be guilty of professional misconduct, if he is grossly negligent in the conduct of his duties.

(ii) A member of the Institute shall be deemed to be guilty of misconduct if he expresses his opinion on financial statements of any business or enterprise in which one or more persons who are his "relatives" have a substantial interest unless he discloses his interest also in his report.

SOME LEGAL DECISIONS CONCERNING AUDIT

In Re G.M. Oka[1] (1952)

Allegation : *Auditor's Negligence in not verifying the securities before the issue of certificate for the same.*

Case : The Assurant Controller of Insurance required from the Trinity Mutual Assurance Company Ltd. a certificate duly certified by the auditor about the number of Government and approved securities held by the Company as on 31st December, 1949. Mr. G.M. Oka, the auditor, gave a certificate to that effect on 16th January, 1950 with regard to the point of the company as on 31st December, 1949. According to the certificate the face value of the securities held by the company was Rs. 5,98,400, but the book value and the market value of the securities were quite different. The book value of securities was Rs. 5,98,653-2-6 and the market value was Rs. 58,915-4-0 which is less than the book as well as the face value of securities. The company had not complied with the provisions of the Insurance Act, 1938, which required an assurance company to have a certain minimum value of the Government and approved securities. The company had already deposited Bombay Municipal debentures of the face value of Rs. 1,00,000 with the Saraswat Bank as security against an overdraft. These debentures were not part of the securities included in the list of securiting as they were encumbered with Saraswat Bank. To comply with the provisions of the Act, the management of the company had sold Conversion Loan 1946, on

1. C. A. No. of 1952.

13th January, 1950 and with the proceeds paid off the overdraft and redeemed the Bombay Municipal Debentures which had been pledged with the Saraswat Bank. The Managing Director of the company had shown the debentures to the auditor. The auditors put the following remarks against this form of security : "Purchased on 28th September, 1949. Lodged as security with bankers for overdraft; repaid in full on 13th January, 1949. Actual bonds seen." Due to under all these circumstances and due to the inclusion of the said Debentures as security, which was not correct, the certificate issued by the auditor of the company was false and misleading. It was sent to the Assistant Controller of Insurance who found it to be wrong and therefore made a complaint against the auditor to the Institute of Chartered Accountants of India. The Council found the auditor guilty in the performance of his duties in not verifying the securities. The case was taken to Bombay High Court. The Court also found Mr. Oka, the auditor, guilty.

Judgment : following is the part of the judgment given by Chagla, C.J.: "Now the only answer which the respondent (auditor) can give and has given through his counsel is that he was very credulous that he accepted the statement made by Mr. Nadkarni that the overdraft has been repaid from the company's other funds, and acting on his statement he did not verify whether all the securities were there on the 16th January but merely saw the Municipal Bonds which had been released from the Saraswat Bank and issued the certificate. The case of the respondent that he issued this certificate on a mis-representation made to him by Mr. Nadkarni rests solely on the word of the respondent. It is very easy when you are charged with misconduct to throw the blame upon someone else who is not present to defend himself. It is true that Mr. Nadkarni is convicted out of his own mouth by his letter he had written to the Assistant Controller of Insurance on the 18th January, 1950, but that letter does not show that Mr. Nadkarni made a false statement to the respondent. The other possibility has clearly to be taken into consideration, viz., that the letter was written and the certificate was sent in conjunction with and in consultation with the respondent. But even assuming that we have to eliminate that possibility which would convict the respondent of colluding with Mr. Nadkarni in deceiving the Assistant Controller of Insurance, the fact remains that as a responsible Chartered Accountant acting as an auditor of the Insurance Company, called upon to give a special certificate, he failed to verify the securities as on the 16th of January and issued a certificate, which admitted is an incorrect certificate. We fail to understand how any auditor can seriously put forward in his defence that he was gullible, that he accepted someone's statement at its fact value and failed to discharge his duty of verifying the securities. The very defence and the very explanation render the respondent unfit to continue as a member of the Institute of Chartered Accountants...His certificate, his signature, his verification carry great weight, and they are usually accepted as correct and genuine. In this particular case the Assistant Controller of Insurance accepted the certificate, did not prosecute the Insurance Company, and it was only when it was found not by the Assistant

Controller that the certificate was not genuine and that he had been misled and deceived that he preferred a complaint to the Institute of Chartered Accountants. In our opinion, this is a serious case and we agree with Sir Jamshedji Kanga, who is appearing on behalf of the Council and who asks us to take a serious view of the conduct of the respondent.

"Under the circumstances, we think that the proper order we should pass is that the name of the respondent shall be temporarily removed from Register of Chartered Accountants for a period of six months. The respondent should pay the costs of the case."

Devar & Sons Ltd. v. **M.S. Krishnaswami**[2] (1952)

The auditor held guilty for misfeasance

Case : Debentures issued by the Amalgamated Coffee Estate Ltd., Madras, were secured on the properties of the company by a Deed dated 8th January, 1945, executed by the company in favour of Mr. B.N. Vishwanathan, the managing agent, as trustee of the debenture-holders. The debentures were issued with a condition besides others that the company shall establish a special fund called sinking fund for the redemption of the debentures and shall each year provide a sum of Rs. 33,000 out of the profits of the company or other resources. The company's published accounts showed the profits but the sinking fund was not created. The Balance Sheet also did not show any sinking funds.

Allegation : The action was brought by Devar & Sons, who had purchased a number of the debentures. They alleged that in spite of the fact that the published accounts of the company showed profits during the financial year ending 30th April, 1945, it had not transferred anything to the contemplated sinking fund. Later on also the company made profits in 1946, 1947 and 1948, but sinking fund was not created at all. Thus, the Balance Sheet did not show the true and correct state of affairs of the company and was misleading.

Defence : The defendants, the auditors, pleaded that it was not their part of duty to see whether the company paid to its creditors or not, or whether the company set aside any sum for the redemption of debenture or not. It was for the debenture-holders to see that the terms of issue of the debentures were being duly carried out by the company.

Judgment : The auditors were held guilty by the Madras High Court. A part of the judgment is reproduced below : "We do not think it is necessary to decide the question whether the directors of the company were not under an obligation to create a sinking fund, though we are inclined to take the view that the true deed did contemplate such an obligation. But we are clearly of the opinion that it was the duty of the respondent as an auditor to have mentioned the fact that in spite of the company earning the profits no part thereof had been set apart towards the sinking fund and that on the other hand the company had

2. Referred Case No. 56 of 1951.

borrowed Rs. 33,000 from the managing agents for the purpose of sinking fund investments. A sinking fund primarily denotes 'moneys set aside for the purpose of sinking or wiping out a corporation's debt by degrees'. Such a fund is created by periodically debiting instalments against profits and crediting the amount of such instalments to the sinking fund account.

Having regard to the nature of the sinking fund and its purpose, it strikes us extremely strange that the company instead of allocating the prescribed sum from and out of the profits should have borrowed that amount from the managing agents...But surely it was incumbent on the auditor to have drawn the attention of the shareholders to this extraordinary action of the directors...It is taken as an axiom in auditing that no sum which is not set aside out of profits can properly be called a reserve.

We, therefore, hold that the respondent failed in his duty as an auditor in not drawing the attention of the shareholders to the fact that the sinking fund was not created as contemplated by the debenture true deed and in not making clear the fact that the amounts shown as towards the sinking fund were borrowed from the managing agents.

We agree with the finding of the committee that the respondent was guilty of gross negligence in accepting as correct during the course of his audit the Journal entries which were mere book entries and that he was guilty of passing the balance-sheet as on 30th April 1946, 30th April 1947, and 30th April 1948, which contain material defects and misleading entries as regards the sinking funds investments and the cash described as being with the debenture trustee or the managing agents. We hold that the respondent must have known or with the exercise of due diligence could have known that no investments existed and there was no cash of Rs. 33,000 with the managing agents as shown in the balance-sheet as on 30th April 1948 but nevertheless he certified to the correctness of the relative entries."

Commissioner of Income-tax, Madras v. G.M. Dandekar of Messrs. G.M. Dandekar & Co., Madras[3] (1952)

Auditors Held guilty of Negligence

Messrs. G.M. Dandekar, the Chartered Accountants, were engaged by A. Mohamed & Co. to audit the accounts of the firm.

The Income Tax Officer was informed of the appointment of Messrs. Dandekar & Co. by the company. The auditors examined the books of account of the company and signed a few statements including the Trading of the Profit and Loss Account, Profit and Loss Adjustment Account, and Balance Sheet. But the quantitative statement of stock, purchases, sales and closing stock was signed by A. Mohamed & Co. The company used to keep two separate sets of books account but the auditors were never told about this.

3. Referred case No. 57 of 1951.

Allegations : The action was brought by the Commissioner of Income Tax against its auditors with a charge that they were guilty of negligence in discharge of their duties. The following allegations were made against them :

(1) that their certificate that the books of account of A. Mohamed & Co., for the year ended 29th October, 1943, were kept in the usual course of business was unwarranted;

(2) that they failed to report the ommission of the cost which was debited in the main book and which was not accounted in sales or the closing stock; and

(3) that their subscribing to the unsubstantiated plea that some of the sales recorded in the separate book were from and out of the unaccounted purchases debited in the main book was misleading.

Defence : The auditors pleaded that they were not engaged with a view to audit the books of account. They took the examination of the books of account of the company with the view to present it to the Income Tax Officer and it was not a certificate but merely a opinion given about the books. According to the terms of appointment they were not expected to go beyond the books of account.

Decision : The case was decided in favour of the auditors and they were not held guilty for negligence.

Judgment : Part of the judgment given by Venkatarama Ayyar, J., is given here : "...The point for decision is whether on the facts mentioned the respondent can be held to the guilty of gross negligence. There can be no negligence unless there is a duty cast upon the person to do a particular act and he fails to do it.

"It is, therefore, necessary to ascertain what the duties of the auditors are as the auditors of Messrs. A. Mohamed and Co. It is contended by the respondent that when an assessee engages him for auditing his accounts and preparing the income tax return for him, his duty is only to prepare the statements on the basis of the accounts produced by the assessee and that he is under no obligation to go further and enquire whether the account books maintained by the assessee are reliable.

But the question is whether there is the same duty when the auditing relates to the accounts of individuals. In those cases the auditor acts only for those individuals and it is his duty to act on their instructions, and to audit the accounts produced by them and prepare statements from them. He is under an obligation to them to perform the auditing with the due skill and diligence and if he does that, it is difficult to see what further obligation he has in the matter and in favour of whom... In like manner the accountant is under a duty to prepare and present correct statements of the accounts of the assessee : and he should, of course, neither suggest nor assist in the preparation of false accounts. But he is under no duty to investigate whether the accounts produced by the assessee are correct or not.

"...But if the duty of the respondent was only to prepare a correct statement from the accounts of the assessee and not to investigate where those accounts are correct or not, this charge must fall on the ground. The respondent did not state that the figures mentioned in the statement represented the real profits made by the assessee. He only stated that the balance sheet represented the correct position according to the accounts of the assessee.

"There is no charge against the respondent that he connived at the assessees putting forward false statement or that he had in any manner associated himself with the attempt of the assessee to mislead the department. The charge is that he owed a duty to the department, to himself investigate the truth and correctness of the accounts of the assessee and not merely to act as their post office in transmitting them. We do not agree that the respondent is under any such duty to the department and, therefore, no question of negligence arises.

"In the result we hold that the respondent is not guilty of any conduct which renders him unfit to be a member of the Institute."

The Registrar of Companies v. P.M. Hedge[4] (1954)

The auditor held guilty for gross negligence

Case : The Rural Bank of India Ltd. had not complied with the provisions of the Companies Act, 1913 and cash in hand disclosed in its Balance Sheet was also not correct. The respondent had been appointed as an auditor of the company. The auditor did not act with reasonable care and caution and failed to discharge his duty to the shareholders.

Allegation : The main charges against the auditor were with regard to the following :

(a) He did not verify the cash in hand at the head office on the date of the balance sheet in each of the years, viz., 1945, 1946, 1947, 1948 and 1949; and

(b) he did not report to the shareholders that the company had not complied with the provisions of section 101(2-B) of the Indian Companies Act, 1913.

Defence : The auditor pleaded that he had verified the existence of cash in hand but the verification was carried on the dates other than that of the Balance Sheet. He stated that he had checked the amount of cash in hand on 5th December, 1945 for the Balance Sheet as on 31st October, 1945. Likewise, he had verified the cash in hand each year. However, he had not checked the cash in hand at the head office on the date of the Balance Sheet. He did not care to check the balance of cash in hand at the dates of counting and that of the Balance Sheet.

---

4. Chartered Accountant No.1-D of 1953.

Judgment : In the course of the judgment Their Lordships quoted Lord Alverstone in the case of *London Oil Storage Co., Ltd. v. Seear Hasluck & Co.* : "It cannot be disputed that when an auditor returns to the shareholders an entry of cash in hand, he must have taken reasonable steps to ascertain that the cash was in hand." He continued : "Cash in hand is verified either by production of actual cash balance or if the date of the accounts has gone by, exhaustively vouching the cash count up to the date of audit and then counting the balance of cash in hand. It is, of course, obvious that in the case of cash at distant branches a satisfactory certificate from responsible officers of the branches that the balance exists may generally be accepted in lieu of actual counting...In our opinion, it is the duty of the auditor, except in special circumstances, to verify the cash in hand on the material date. The respondent admittedly did not verify the cash on the material date, and even when at a later date he made a check he did not examine the intermediate transactions. We, therefore, agree with the finding of the Council that the respondent, who was required to satisfy himself by actual verification that the cash did exist on the date of the Balance Sheet and Profit and Loss Account exhibited a true and correct view of the Bank's affairs, had failed in his duty to satisfy that asset was there."

With regard to the second charge against the auditor, their Lordships said "Even assuming that the managing director did give this explanation, it was the duty of the respondent to have mentioned that there was non-compliance with the statutory direction...the very failure to deposit the monies should have aroused his suspicion, and very probably a searching enquiry would have revealed the fact that the major allottees of the shares had not paid a pie for the large number of the shares allotted to them."

"We therefore, agree with the Council of Institute of Chartered Accountants that the respondent failed to discharge this duty as an auditor of the Rural Bank of India Ltd. and he was guilty of gross negligence...."

Note : It may be mentioned here that the provisions of Section 101(2-B) were that all money received from applicants for shares should be deposited in a scheduled bank until the company is allowed to commence business or it is returned to the applicants for want of minimum subscription before a particular date.

Deputy Secretary to the Government of India, Ministry of Finance, *v.* S.N. Das Gupta[5] (1955)

The auditor held liable for not verifying the cash balance and for not giving informations to the members in unequivocal words. Found guilty of misconduct he was suspended from the membership of Institute of Chartered Accountants and from practice for two years from the date of order.

5. Matter No. 71 of 1955. In the matter of Chartered Accountant's Act.

Case : The respondent had acted as an auditor of the Aryan Bank for the years 1942, 1943 and 1944. The Bank went into liquidation later on. The auditor had failed to verify the cash in hand for the years 1942 and 1943. For the years 1942 and 1943 the auditor simply gave a certificate in accordance with the provisions of section 145(2) of the Indian Companies Act, 1913 and in it he simply answered the four specified questions in affirmative. He made certain reservations in special report but it turned out to be simply the means of information and not the information itself. For example, he gave the following statements in his special report :

"All the loans and overdrafts of branches are shown in the Balance Sheet as good."

"These have been granted to eight parties against the fixed deposit receipts of debtors."

These statements were found to be incomplete and vague by the Court and Disciplinary Committee. The Committee stated that his duty was to give information and not merely the means of information.

Judgment : In the judgment given by Chakravarti, C.J., it was stated : "......The Companies Act, therefore, provides for the employment of an auditor who is the servant of the shareholders and whose duty is to examine the affairs of the company on their behalf at the end of a year and report to them what he has found. That examination by an independent agency such as the auditor is practically the only safeguard which the shareholders have against the enterprise being carried on in an unbusiness-like way or their money being misapplied or misappropriated without their knowing anything about it. The Act provides the safeguard in two forms. It makes it the duty of the auditors to give an expression of opinion on certain specified matters of a vital character and it makes him liable, along with the directors, for misfeasance, if he fails to perform his duties as required by law and the approved audit procedure. It is now well settled that it is the duty of an auditor to verify not merely the arithmetical accuracy of the balance sheet but its substantial accuracy and to see that it includes the particulars required by the Articles and the statute and contains a correct representation of the state of company's affairs. And auditor's duty is to see what the state of company's affairs actually is and whether it is reflected truly in the accounts of the company upon which the balance sheet and the profit and loss account are based, but he is not required to perform the functions of a detective. As has been said, he is a watchdog and not a bloodhound and as, the same thing has been said without the aid of a metaphor, his duty is verification and not detection, although in performing the duty of verification he must employ reasonable care and skill. What is reasonable care and skill must depend on the circumstances of each case. Where there is nothing to excite suspicion and there is an atmosphere of complete confidence, based on the record of continued success in financial matters less care and less severity of scrutiny may be considered reasonable, whereas reasonable care and skill may be regarded as not exercised when, in spite of the presence of unusual features in the accounts or other *prima facie* reasons for believing that the affairs of the company may not be in order; the examination is perfunctory and not sufficiently detailed......If such circumstances, that is to say, when the subject matter is one which is not capable of direct verification and when to verify properly the results presented in the balance sheet, it would require investigation rather than checking and where there is nothing at all to excite suspicion, if in relying upon the statements in such circumstances, the auditor is himself deceived, he will not be held to have failed in the discharge of his duties.....

"The audit with which we are concerned in the present case the audit of a banking company. Such an audit has been called a balance sheet audit, meaning thereby that it is primarily confined to the verification of the existence of assets shown in the balance sheet because on account of the multitudinous character of the transactions of a bank, it is not ordinarily possible to examine everyone of them, nor is it usually done except with reference to matters, if any, which provoke enquiry ... *Vis-a-vis* the shareholders, the auditor holds a position of trust and it is his bounden duty to honour that trust being candid with the shareholders and telling them frankly and fully everything with regard to the affairs of the company which has come to his knowledge and which it is material for the shareholders to know......authorities, both legal and professional, are unanimous that in a bank audit, the cash balance claimed by the management, must be verified by the auditor, because otherwise the management might remove the greater part of the funds and show them falsely as lying in hand in cash and thereby relieve themselves of the necessity of even making up accounts, showing the disposition of money...... In spite of having felt these doubts and such uneasiness, the respondent did not inform the shareholders frankly and directly what the facts were which had caused misgivings in his minds, but he chose to employ some euphemistic or enigmatical language which might or might not be taken by the shareholders to be of any significance and which certainly conveyed no definite information."

Deputy Secretary to the Government of India, Ministry of Commerce and Industry *v.* Shadi Lal Batra[6] (1960)

Case : The respondent who was practising as a Chartered Accountant and was a member of the Institute of Chartered Accountants of India, was appointed liquidator of a company. He failed to file the annual statement prescribed under section 224 of the Indian Companies Act, 1913 for the years 1951 to 1955. Disciplinary proceedings were initiated against the respondent, who claimed that he did not file the statements as he was doubtful whether he had the necessary authority to do so. His appointment had been challenged in court but the Court upheld his appointment although it observed that there was some irregularity in his appointment.

6. (1961) 31 Comp. Cas., p. 271.

Decision : It was held that the failure of the respondent to comply with the provision of Section 224 of Indian Companies Act, 1913, amounted to misconduct and attracted the disciplinary jurisdiction of the Institute. The fact that there was some doubt in regard to the validity of his appointment as liquidator was not a sufficient ground for failure to comply with the section, particularly when, during the relevant, period, he was acting as liquidator of the company. This conduct, however, did not render him unfit to be a member of the Institute.

Registrar of Companies, Kerala v. P. Arunajatai[7] (1962)

Allegation :

(a) The first charge relates to the Balance Sheet of the year 1956. A sum of Rs. 11,90,081-5-7 was written off in the Profit and Loss Account of the company for the period ended 31st December, 1956. The sums in question consisted of six items and the auditor did not investigate the accounts to find out whether the various amounts that were transferred against the managing agents were properly done.

(b) The second charge relates to the failure of the auditor to investigate the existence of cash vouchers for payments made by company during the year 1956 to the extent of Rs. 37,000.

(c) The third charge relates to certain unauthorised loan made to Alagappa Chettiar College Endowment Trust.

(d) The fourth charge concerns the Balance Sheet of the year 1955 which showed that certain shares owned by the company in another company were fully paid up while in fact it was not so.

(e) There was a further charge in regard to the omission on the part of auditor to verify certain stock entries.

Decision : It was held that where large sums of money due from others are consolidated and written off as bad debts in the Balance Sheet of a company for one year while the very same debts in the Balance Sheets of previous year were shown as good ones, the auditor is bound to investigate into the circumstances leading up to the writing off of such debts, to ascertain whether there were vouchers for such debts and, if he is of the opinion from the vouchers, maintained in respect of those debts that they were to 'valueless' too disclose that fact in his report to the shareholders. He should not give a clean certificate to the Balance Sheet. Even if there are vouchers which are apparently regular, it is necessary for him to see that those vouchers are for the amounts received and were given by persons entitled to bind the debtor where the debtor is a company.

7. (1962) 32 Comp. Cas., p. 1153.

The writing off of debts as irrecoverable might be justified but, it is the auditor's duty to investigate why they came to be treated as bad. He should first check the existence of the debt itself and then enquire into the circumstances that led to its being treated as a bad debt.

Where a debt is shown as doubtful in one year, the same debt is shown as good for subsequent years and in a still later year it is written off, it is the duty of the auditor to enquire into the matter and make a reference to it in his report.

It is the duty of an auditor (i) to inquire into the circumstances under which transfers of liabilities are made and investigate the accounts to find out whether the amounts were properly transferred; (ii) to verify whether advances have been made with proper sanction; (iii) to verify the existence of assets and not to assume as true the particulars given in earlier Balance Sheets and the work of persons in management of the company.

The Attorney General of Kenya v. V.B. Joshi[8] (1968)

Case : The auditor, Shri V.B. Joshi, has been a Member of the Institute ever since it was established. For quite some time now he has been practising at Mombasa. The address of his place of business in India furnished by him is "Care of Messrs. Sapat & Co.,113, Cavel Street, Bombay-2." On 8th June, 1964, the Attorney General of Kenya forwarded a complaint against the respondent, complaining that the respondent has prepared a false Trading and Profit and Loss Account for Messrs. Mombasa Ration Stores for the year 1960, and that it was falsely prepared to the knowledge of the respondent. He had also prepared a false Balance Sheet for the said firm which was fictitious for the year 1960.

Decision : It was held that the Chartered Accountant was guilty of professional misconduct and that his name should be removed from the membership of the Institute for a period of three years.

Director of Accounts Gujarat State, Ahmedabad v. K.D. Patel[9] (1968)

Auditor found guilty of professional misconduct under Section 21 of Chartered Accountants Act, 1949.

Case : The respondent was engaged to prepare Balance Sheet of a public trust which runs Khadisabhai Maternity Home, Sidhpur, for the year ended 1956, 1957, 1958 and 1959, and in the course he submitted the Balance Sheet along with the reports in respect of the said years to the Charity Commissioner. Except for certain observation made by him for the year ending 31-12-1957, the reports which were submitted to the Charity Commission were clean reports. The Charity Commissioner, however, ordered special audit in respect of the four years by the firm M/s. C.C. Chokshi & Co., who were appointed Special Auditors. They

8. The Chartered Accountant, Vol. XVI, June 1968, p. 681.
9. The Chartered Accountant, Vol. XVI, Part X, April 1968, pp. 572-73.

submitted their reports in which they pointed out several discrepancies. On that a complaint was made to the Institute on 26th September, 1962.

Decision : It is held that none of the charges for which the respondent has been found guilty savours of moral turpitude and, therefore, it was ordered that the respondent be reprimanded in respect of the charges for which he has been found guilty.

Institute of Chartered Accountants of India v. P.K. Mukerji & another (1968)

Chartered Accountant was held guilty of professional misconduct under clause (O) of the Schedule to the Chartered Accountants Act, 1949.

Case : Anand Bazar Patrika Ltd. is a joint stock company and has got an Employees' Provident Fund Scheme which was being managed by the Board of Trustees. The respondent is a Chartered Accountant and was appointed by the Board of Directors of the company to audit the accounts of the Provident Fund for the year 1953 and audit the accounts of the Provident Fund for the years 1953 and 1954. It appears that in year 1954 the Trustees of the Fund had made certain advances amounting to about Rs. 6,21,864 to the company incontravention of the Rules of the Fund. The Directors of the company issued various cheques in repayment of advance, but at the request of the management of the company the cheques were kept with the trustees of the Fund uncashed and not credited in the account of the Fund. After receipt of the cheques the Trustees of the Fund made book entries showing the repayment of the loan so granted to the company, though in fact none of these cheques had been cashed when such entries were made. The auditor wrote about this to the company as follows :

"It appears that certain loans were granted by the Trustees of the Fund to the company in 1954 which although adjusted within the accounting year, do not appear to be in accordance with the Provident Fund Rules. We disapprove such transaction and believe it will not recur in future. Cheques issued by you to the Fund should also be cleared promptly."

The auditor signed the statement of accounts ending December, 31, 1953 on May 14, 1954 and the statement of accounts ending December 31, 1954 on June 30, 1955. But after signing the statement he gave the following certificate :

"Checked with the books and accounts produced and found correct."

Judgment : In the course of judgment, Ramaswami J., said : "It is not correct to say that Respondent No.1 owed a duty only to Company which had appointed him to perform the auditimg. The contributors to the Provident Fund had a beneficial interest in the Fund and the primary object of auditing the Fund was to appraise them of the true financial position of the accounts and investments made from time to time. Respondent No.1 therefore owed a duty to the contributors to the Provident Fund for making a true report to them of the financial position. In other words, the auditing was intended for protection to the beneficiaries and the auditor was expected to examine the accounts maintained by the trustees with a view to inform the beneficiaries the true financial position. The auditor is, in such a case, under a clear duty towards the beneficiaries 'to probe into the transactions' and to report on their true character. In our opinion, the legal position of the auditor in the present case is similar to that of the auditor under the Companies Act, 1956. In such a case the auditor is intended for the protection of the shareholder and the auditor is expected to examine the accounts maintained by the Directors with a view to inform the shareholders of the true financial position of the company.

Decision : The auditor was held guilty and was ordered to be severely reprimanded for professional misconduct.

QUESTIONS FOR EXERCISE

1. Describe the composition and membership of the Institute of Chartered Accountants.
2. When are the members of ICAI deemed to be in practice ?
3. Distinguish between associates and fellows of the Institute of Chartered Accountants.
4. When will a person be entitled to have his name entered in the Register of Members of the ICAI ? What are the disabilities for such registration ?
5. Define the term "professional misconduct" and briefly discuss the proce- dure of instituting an enquiry against an auditor under section 21 of the Chartered Accountants Act so as to suspend or terminate his membership.
6. How can the name of a Chartered Accountant be removed from the Register of Chartered Accountants or membership of the Institute of Chartered Accountants of India ?
7. Examine the provisions of the Chartered Accountants Act and Schedules thereto with regard to the professional misconduct.